The Old Protestantism and the New

The University of Chicago Press   B. A. Gerrish

The Old Protestantism and the New

Essays on the Reformation Heritage

B.A. GERRISH is professor of historical theology at the University
of Chicago.

Extracts from *Calvin: Institutes of the Christian Religion,* edited by
John T. McNeill, translated by Ford Lewis Battles (volumes 20 and 21 of
The Library of Christian Classics), copyright © 1960 W. L. Jenkins, are
used by permission of The Westminster Press.

The University of Chicago Press, Chicago 60637
T. and T. Clark Limited, Edinburgh

©1982 by The University of Chicago
All rights reserved. Published 1982
Printed in the United States of America
89 88 87 86 85 84 83 82   1 2 3 4 5

Library of Congress Cataloging in Publication Data

Gerrish, B.A. (Brian Albert), 1931–
    The old Protestantism and the new.

    Bibliography: p.
    Includes index.
    1. Reformation—Addresses, essays, lectures.
2. Theology, Doctrinal—History—Addresses, essays,
lectures. I. Title.
BR309.G39   230'.044'0903   82–2730
ISBN 0–226–28869–2   AACR2

Contents

To June   *With gratitude*

Preface

For some two decades, roughly the years between *Grace and Reason* and *Tradition and the Modern World,* most of my historical effort went into scattered papers and addresses on modestly defined themes. Friends and colleagues have urged me to put them together in a single, readily accessible volume; but I was reluctant to do so until confident that the result would be a book, not a mere assortment of individual pieces. This end has been the more easily reached because over the years I have worked, as far as I could, with a tacit agenda: although every chapter in this volume, without exception, was originally written by invitation, in choosing my subjects (or bending them to fit) I have tried to move toward an inclusive historical interpretation of Protestant thought. My intention is eventually to use the conclusions reached along this way in a more comprehensive study of the course of modern religious ideas—a task I believe to be, in turn, prerequisite to the constructive work of Christian theology. But the form of the present volume is well suited to a more limited review of just those ideas that mark Protestantism as a distinct variety of religious belief: that is, a review of the cardinal Reformation beliefs and their legacy.

The Protestant Reformation and its intellectual heritage have been the subjects of an immense body of scholarly literature. Inevitably the following chapters, though unified by the approach set out in the introduction, vary greatly in the degree to which they can claim to bring something new. Some represent a fresh venture into well-plowed fields; others are given to topics that have been neglected in English, but not in foreign works; and at least one (chapter 9) presents a line of interpretation known well enough to specialists but still without much corresponding impact on general works of history. On the other hand, anyone who is curious about the relationship of Schleiermacher, the presumed father of modern theology, to the Reformation heritage will find the literature deficient in any language: it is not only thin, but sometimes written out of party interests. Troeltsch has fared even worse than Schleiermacher, since he has hardly been taken seriously as a theologian at all, to say nothing of his place in a particular theological tradition. And I may add, finally, that in one of my Reformation topics (chapter 7) my question seems not to have been asked before, so that I found myself having to improvise the categories of interpretation.

I am painfully aware that some of the topics I discuss could be expanded endlessly. As a matter of fact, three of the chapters (5-7) were by-products of a larger research project, begun twenty years ago when I unwisely announced as "forthcoming" a comparative study of church, ministry, and sacraments in Luther and Calvin. Publication of excellent works in this area by others, some of them Roman Catholics, made my project seem less urgent, and I turned my attention elsewhere. But the design has never been quite abandoned, and the material has grown until it now fills a suitcase. (Chapter 6 is an indication of the particular approach I have in view.) No doubt, almost any of the other topics in this volume could also fill a suitcase. Even the more heavily trodden paths, however, may be worth a map; perhaps they need it all the more just because of the bewildering crisscross of many tracks. It depends on what travelers one has in mind.

My hope, at least, is that the book may be of use and of interest, not only to those whose special concern is with religion or theology, but also to students of history, for whom religious belief is only one strand in the complex web of the past. Unfortunately, as I have taken pains to show throughout the book, there is often a wide gap between the beliefs of Luther and Calvin and the stereotypes of them that make their way into history textbooks. With the nonspecialist reader in mind, then, I have resisted the temptation to clutter the text with too much detail. Each chapter, whether originally an address or not, is designed to be gone through fairly comfortably at one sitting; but in the notes, besides the documentation the specialists will look for, I have located translations (even when I have not myself used them), drawn attention to some important items in the secondary literature (especially in English), and indicated lines for pursuing the subject further. The bibliographical notes, in particular, should be of more practical value than an extensive, composite bibliography—arranged alphabetically by author—at the end of the book.

All of the chapters have been previously published in whole or part, and all have been revised—some extensively. Until I undertook to put them together, it had not occurred to me how various their original audiences had been. Most of the chapters began as addresses (the exceptions are chapters 3, 4, 10, and 12); the audiences have included a historical society and a theological society, students as well as teachers, church as well as academic groups, and members of an interdisciplinary seminar at the University of Chicago. I am grateful for the invitations that occasioned these addresses, for the encouragement and criticism they have evoked, and for the permission to bring them out again in their new format.

Publication details for the earlier versions are given in the notes to the Introduction. Chapters 8, 10, and 14 were originally brought out by the University of

Chicago Press. I would like to record my thanks to the appropriate publishers and editors for permission to reuse copyright material in the other chapters: to Cambridge University Press (chapter 13), Fortress Press (chapter 2), Kreuz Verlag (chapter 15), the Pickwick Press (chapter 12), Scottish Academic Press (chapter 3), Yale University Press (chapter 1); and to the respective editors of *Church History* (chapters 5 and 11), *Concordia Theological Quarterly* (chapter 9), *Lutheran Forum* (chapter 6), *McCormick Quarterly* (chapters 4, 6, and the Conclusion), and *Theology Today* (chapter 7). Acknowledgments are also due to Fortress Press for quotations from the American Edition of *Luther's Works* (jointly published by Fortress and Concordia Publishing House). My biblical citations, wherever possible, follow the Revised Standard Version.

Naturally, I have incurred many debts of other kinds over the years in which this volume was in the making. Some I would especially like to mention here. I owe much to the teaching and example of Wilhelm Pauck, whose own book *The Heritage of the Reformation* was a model of what a collection of essays can achieve. His death on 3 September 1981 was a great loss to the cause of historical theology. The two chapters on Ernst Troeltsch (13 and 14) would not have been written without a research leave funded by the John Simon Guggenheim Memorial Foundation. Patient work was done on my heavily corrected manuscripts by Rehova Arthur and Martha Morrow. ("It *is* a challenge," Mrs. Arthur admitted.) The laborious task of preparing the index was cheerfully undertaken by Christoph Stauder, who also helped me to correct the proofs. Finally, I have dedicated the book to my wife as a (slightly overdue) silver wedding present.

Introduction

*I mean the theology that searches out the
kernel in the nut, and the grain in the
wheat, and the marrow in the bones.*

Luther
Letter of 17 March 1509

The much-debated question whether the Reformation is best understood in religious, theological, political, social, or economic terms need not detain us. Our business here is with religious ideas that can be traced back to Martin Luther, not with claims about their influence in the sixteenth-century world. Luther's own place in the history of Christian thought is of course secure. But if our subject is Protestant ideas, not just Luther's, then the attempt must be made to place his thought in a wider setting, which is acknowledged as at once pluralistic and transient.

There are limits—practical rather than theoretical—on the extent to which a wider perspective can be attained. To mention only Erasmus, Zwingli, and Calvin is admittedly to do no more than scratch the surface of the sixteenth-century theological world in which Luther lived and thought. Why not Melanchthon, or Cajetan, or Cranmer? Why not some of the radicals, whose originally distinctive ideas were later, like those of Christian humanism, to flow into the mainstream of Protestant history? The limits we have imposed are in some measure arbitrary. But it will hardly be denied that a special significance belongs to the relationship between Luther and Calvin, the leaders of what are sometimes called "the two churches of the Reformation." Similarly, to speak (as we shall) of Schleiermacher and Troeltsch and their role in the subsequent history of Protestant thought scarcely begins to take account of liberal theology. Why not Baur or Ritschl? But to borrow the terms given currency by Troeltsch, Schleiermacher stands in relation to the "new Protestantism" *(Neuprotestantismus)* much as Luther stands in relation to the "old" *(Altprotestantismus);* and Troeltsch himself marks—more clearly perhaps than any other theologian—the point at which the new itself became old.

Many of the most eminent Luther scholars of our century have been theologians rather than historians, and this may account in part for the tendency to view Luther's theology as a self-contained subject of inquiry. Church historians

1

have criticized the tendency insofar as it neglects the fact that Luther's Reformation was, after all, an event of church history—or of European history. But the isolation of Luther's theology is objectionable also from the standpoint of the historical theologian. With one or two notable exceptions, the scholars have not concerned themselves equally with Luther and Calvin; and (again with exceptions) it is two different groups of scholars who work on classical and liberal Protestant thought, respectively. The demands of specialization are inescapable. But the significance of Protestant ideas cannot be appraised historically if Luther is treated as the sole point of reference, or if the Reformation is treated as something more than a critical moment in a larger historical development, to which liberal Protestantism also belongs. Of course, it is a development to which medieval thought belongs, too. Much of the best Reformation research in recent years has been done from this retrospective viewpoint, and it has proved astonishingly fruitful for ecumenical relations between the present Roman Catholic and Protestant churches. But the discovery that in the sixteenth century there was not so wide a gap as we imagined between Protestant and Roman Catholic views on justification or the Eucharist is of limited worth, if definitions made then cannot legislate for all time.

It is not so clear to me as it was to Schleiermacher that Christian experience has a constancy that persists through ever-changing conceptualizations of it. But if the object of inquiry is to be identified as "theology" or "religious thought," it is certainly required to state what that is; and Schleiermacher's answer comes as close as any I know to the position I myself wish to take. Christian theology is reflection on a specific, historically given way of believing *(Glaubensweise)*. I do not need to make the further claims that all doctrines are simply the result of reflection on experience, that the task of interpreting religious belief requires one first to have it, and that the task is not complete until past faith is grasped as a living option in the present. It is sufficient to insist only that faith and doctrine are not identical. Hence the historian's assignment, insofar as he makes the history of theology his field, is not just to give an accurate report of doctrines once held, but to grasp the faith which lay in them or behind them and which (if they were living doctrines) they had the power to evoke.

The approach of the following chapters, then, insofar as it is distinctive, has been shaped by three dominant interests: in the relation of Luther's thought to Calvin's (and in that of their respective spiritual progenies to each other); in the relation between classical and liberal Protestant thought; and in the religious experience behind theological formulas. The further explication of these interests belongs in the individual chapters themselves. But I cannot forbear from pointing out in advance that all three of my interests have an affinity with opinions expressed by Calvin, who not only adopted a pluralistic and progressive appreciation of Luther but also tirelessly insisted that the only knowledge of God worthy of the name is piety. Anyone who takes this view must venture a hermeneutic which, in Luther's metaphor, is willing to crack the nut to get at the kernel.

I

Two of Luther's most important contemporaries were Erasmus and Calvin himself, leaders respectively of Christian humanism and the Reformed church. The attitude of Erasmus to Luther has been the subject of extensive discussion and sometimes of sharp disagreement. He has been portrayed as weak and devious. In contrast to Luther's defiant stand at Worms, it has been said that Erasmus's motto, in effect, was: "Here I stand—but also here, and here." In my opinion, the position of Erasmus was not vacillating but firmly ambivalent. He approved of some of Luther's criticisms of abuses, but he was repelled by his vehemence and did not share Luther's lofty estimate of dogma and theology. Hence, when forced into debate, the issue of free will suited Erasmus's purposes well because to him, within limits, it was a mere school question: it sufficed to distance him from Luther without (so he supposed) requiring a total severance of relations with Wittenberg. The "friendly conversation" did enable Erasmus to state his own position on free will (a position that was neither Augustinian-Thomistic nor Semi-Pelagian), and to register his disapproval of Luther's, which he thought must logically entail a paralysis of moral effort. But more important, it enabled him to expose what he took to be Luther's fundamental flaw (*not* his heresy): the Reformer was wedded to a scholastic style of theologizing that could only inhibit the nurture of piety, even though it was in part an expression of Luther's piety.[1]

Unlike Erasmus, Calvin shared with Luther the dogmatic standpoint of Protestantism; and unlike Zwingli, he held the Lutheran view of sacraments as efficacious signs. He was deeply influenced by Erasmus, and he took up Erasmus's theme that the German Reformer was guilty of gross, if understandable and even necessary, exaggerations. But whereas the humanist *repudiated* Luther's theology, Calvin argued for the necessity of *developing* it. In claiming a continuity of development rather than of formal identity, he anticipated the historical and progressive view of Luther's Reformation that came into its own in the eighteenth and nineteenth centuries.[2]

II

It has become customary to sum up the faith of the Protestant Reformers in the three slogans "Scripture alone," "Faith alone," and "The priesthood of all believers." The appeal to scriptural authority, the so-called formal principle of the Reformation, is distinctively Protestant only if it is understood as an appeal to the message rather than the letter of the Bible and to a method of interpretation free from ecclesiastical control and allegorical fantasy. This is not to deny that Luther and Calvin continued to speak, in traditional terms, of the entire Bible as consisting in the oracles of God. But the modern conflict over biblical criticism arose partly because their followers emphasized what was medieval in their doctrine of Scripture (the notion of inspiration) more than what was distinctive in it (their notion that the Bible is authoritative as a witness to something else, the gospel concerning Christ). And Calvin, at least, affirmed the distinctively Protestant view of the Bible as a witness without losing the characteristically "catholic" insistence that the Bible is the *church's* book.[3]

It follows that, properly speaking, the religious authority for the Protestant Reformers was the gospel of grace itself, the so-called material principle. But their understanding of the gospel became so entangled in intricate—Erasmus would say "scholastic"—arguments over the manner of a man's justification by faith alone, that there can be few matters on which historians of theology are less agreed than the exact nature of Luther's supposed "rediscovery of the gospel." Still, the evident psychological power of Luther's gospel can be shown, without unwarranted reductionism, to be independent of the intricacies of dogmatic correctness. Given his conception of sin as self-will, it is understandable that he should have approved the spiritual strategy of the mystics rather than that of the Nominalists: the way of deliverance does not begin with the call to the sinful self to do its best, but with the invitation to see that the best life was lived by another.[4]

The priesthood of all believers is commonly identified as the third Protestant principle. It is often interpreted, however, in a sense largely foreign to Luther himself, as though it referred to an individual privilege as an end in itself ("private judgment," "immediate access to God") and not rather to the mutual responsibility of the faithful to minister to one another. Scholarly opinion differs on the question whether Luther derives the evangelical ministry from the common priesthood; but there can be no doubt that he held the "mutual conversation and consolation of the brethren" to be a real means of grace alongside the public ministry of Word and sacrament—a far cry from the stereotype of Luther's religion of solitude![5]

The three Reformation principles do not exhaust the points at issue between the Protestant Reformers and Rome: there were also the sacramental questions, and these divided the Reformers among themselves. At the heart of Calvin's theology lay the notion of a "secret communion" with the living Christ, mediated to faith through Word and Spirit. The sacraments, he held, are simply the Word made visible in an act of bodily cleansing (baptism) and an act of bodily nourishment (the Lord's Supper). His application of the old christological formula "distinction without division" to the relationship of sacramental signs with the reality they signify puts him in agreement with Luther's view: that the Eucharist is a vehicle of Christ's actual self-giving. The formula also establishes his disagree-ment with the medieval doctrine of transubstantiation, which he sees as a confusion of sign and reality, and the Zwinglian doctrine of merely didactic symbols, which separates the reality from the sign. It is undeniable that in some respects Calvin differed with Luther, and in some respects was simply obscure. But if the historian had to take account only of Luther and Calvin, it would surely be possible to identify the notion of an efficacious sign as a fourth princi-ple of Reformation theology.[6]

In actual fact, however, the Reformed confessions show that within the Re-formed church a Zwinglian theory of signs persisted alongside the Calvinistic theory. Indeed, if we distinguish between Zwingli's "symbolic memorialism" and Calvin's "symbolic instrumentalism," a closer look reveals yet a third doctrine of signs: the "symbolic parallelism" of Bullinger. The difference between the last two views may perhaps be considered just another school question, not unlike the medieval division between Thomists and Franciscans: at issue is only the question how, not whether, the grace of Christ is given in the sacraments. But in Zwingli's view the sacrament becomes a sign only of past grace, not of present grace; and the congregation, rather than its Lord, is the subject of the eucharistic action. What is at stake *here* is therefore nothing less than the gift-character of the Eucharist, which for Calvin and Bullinger, as well as for Luther, was neither a good work nor a devotional exercise.[7]

The Reformation principles, even if we add a fourth one, do not exhaust the distinctive ideas of Luther and Calvin. Their notion of the hidden God (in one of its two senses) remains as a striking reminder that the principles do not pretend to give the whole truth about God; or, to put it in experiential terms, a reminder that confidence in God through Christ occurs in a context of existential anxiety, which faith cannot wholly dissipate. The Reformers did not imagine that the ob-served course of nature or of human affairs makes faith obvious. Especially in the doctrine of predestination they encountered an inscrutable will of God that appeared to contradict the free offer of the gospel; for if only those whom God has chosen can respond in faith, how can it be proclaimed that he "desires not the death of a sinner"? Not Scripture alone, but observation, too, taught them that none of the good things in life are bestowed with an even hand; this belongs to the mystery of human existence. There is something here that is essential to Reformation faith (which is belief in spite of appearances) and to the Reforma-tion image of God (who is not only the heavenly Father but also the abyss).[8]

Still, faith's *object* is not the hidden but the revealed God. And the knowledge of man in Calvin's theology is the exact counterpart of the knowledge of the re-vealed God: that is to say, the paternal deity is defined as "the fountain of all good," and man is defined as the point of creation at which the sheer goodness of God is reflected or imaged in an act of filial piety or thankful love. This, for Calvin, is the meaning of man's bearing the image of God. In a universe not finally made for him, man, the mirror of God's goodness, has his place as spectator and even agent of the manifestation of God's glory, in which alone the cosmos has its final meaning. Sin is simply the inverse condition of man, in which thanklessness and self-love infect every human achievement, even the best and the noblest— this, correctly interpreted, being the much-maligned notion of "total depravity."[9]

III

No intellectual problem has more persistently confronted Protestantism in the modern world than the problem of science and religion. The relationship of religion to *natural* science takes on a special interest because the Copernican and the Protestant revolutions coincided closely in time. Whether Lutheranism and Calvinism were hostile or hospitable to the new science continues to be debated. But what can be shown with certainty is that Luther and Calvin worked with sophisticated theories of religious or theological language (the miscalled "theory of double truth" and the priniciple of accommodation) that made a conflict of theology and science unnecessary, or even logically impossible. The problem of religion and natural science would nevertheless have remained, even if their followers had been more faithful to them, because Christian theology had in fact become wedded to a world view that was out of harmony with newly acquired knowledge and new ways of thinking.[10] But that does not exhaust the problem of religion and science.

In another form, as the problem (or problems) of theology and history, the apparent conflict of religion and science was taken up by Friedrich Schleiermacher. We are accustomed to thinking of him as the initiator of a new movement in theology, and so he was. But he himself thought he belonged still to the period initiated by the Protestant Reformation, though he held this to be quite another thing than being bound to Reformation creeds. Hardly any attempt has been made in the secondary literature to explore his Protestant consciousness in this light; in fact, very little has been done to appraise his work in church history generally. Inquiry shows his historical thinking as a pioneering attempt to deal with the necessity of doctrinal change—that is, with the problem of religion and *historical* science. He set Christianity within the framework of a total interpretation of mankind's religions, taking as his cardinal categories the notions of "individuality" and "development" much loved by romantic-idealist philosophers of history; and it was chiefly by means of the category of development that he sought to relate modern Protestantism to the Reformation.[11]

Indeed, we can carry the relationship further: Schleiermacher's claim that he belonged to the Reformed or Calvinist school invites a particular comparison between his and Calvin's dogmatics. The question of his actual debt to Calvin is hard, perhaps impossible, to answer. But a systematic comparison reveals interesting parallels of structure between the *Institutes* and *The Christian Faith* and, what is more, a closely similar resolve to use the concept of "piety" as a hermeneutic rule. The rule excludes from the scope of dogmatics anything merely speculative or lacking in pertinence to Christian piety: that is, to the specific, historically given Christian way of being religious. Both the affinities and the remaining differences between the two masters of Protestant theology are clearly reflected in their doctrines of God, and especially of the divine Trinity. While Schleiermacher maintained that one cannot get from piety to an immanent doctrine of the Trinity, Calvin believed that without the doctrine of the Trinity Christian piety would not be possible.[12]

Besides the theological significance of his understanding of church history, there is Schleiermacher's revolutionary—and more frequently discussed—attempt to historicize the task of theology itself. The implications of historicizing for theological method were explored with keen insight by Ernst Troeltsch, who saw in Schleiermacher's work the basis for a new "dogmatics of the history of religions school." His own dogmatics, which (following Schleiermacher) he termed a *Glaubenslehre* (literally a "doctrine of faith"), has been almost totally neglected, overshadowed by the rise of neoorthodoxy. But it represents an interesting and important attempt to transform the Protestant heritage. In particular, the reappraisal that Troeltsch's theology deserves should consider his suggestive, but problematic thoughts on the meaning of historical existence for religious sensibility, on the uses of tradition, and on the primacy of the historical over rational proof.[13]

As far as the specific content of Reformation theology is concerned, as distinct from its style or method, Protestant sensibilities are never more aroused than when its very center appears to be be jeopardized by historical science. The debate stirred up by Arthur Drews's thesis that Jesus never existed affords an instructive case study of the impact of historical science on inherited beliefs. Troeltsch held, in opposition to various rival standpoints, that confidence in the historicity of Jesus is needed, if only to give historical anchorage to the central symbol of Christ around which the Christian community rallies. But it remains doubtful whether this "social-psychological" reaffirmation of faith in a historical redeemer is really demanded by Troeltsch's commitment to the historicizing of theology: his own historical principles seem to point the development of the Reformation heritage in another direction, indicated by some of his opponents. The saving historical events on which faith depends are facts of present experience, not remote facts recovered by historical science. Facts of experience make up the "history" with which theology is immediately concerned; this, essentially, was what Schleiermacher was after in his redefinition of the theological task, though he was not consistently loyal to his own insight.[14]

Finally, changing Reformed opinions of the Augsburg Confession, the pioneer statement of Protestant faith, furnishes an interesting mirror of doctrinal shifts and shifting ecumenical relations. John Calvin, the greatest Reformed theologian of the sixteenth century, subscribed to the confession and was actually appointed a Lutheran delegate to conferences with the Roman Catholics, and he strove to prevent his Lutheran sympathies from turning sour in the later eucharistic controversies. In the nineteenth century, Schleiermacher's famous sermons on the Augsburg Confession attest the fact that by then party divisions had taken their place alongside confessional divisions as occasions of Christian disunity. And in the twentieth century, Karl Barth's critique of the Lutheran two kingdoms doctrine marks a new point of controversy between Lutherans and Reformed.[15] The past, it seems, though always instructive, does not provide a secure haven from change but itself is an affair of change.[16]

Part One   Martin Luther

One   Piety, Theology, and the Lutheran Dogma: Erasmus's Book on Free Will

I had rather be a pious theologian with Jerome than an invincible one with Scotus.[1]

The papal bull *Exsurge Domine* reached Luther by 10 October 1520. His books containing certain specified errors were to be burned, and he himself had sixty days in which to recant.[2] On 10 December, as the days of grace ran out, the pope had his answer. In reprisal for the burning of Luther's books, a bonfire was ignited just outside Wittenberg, and the papal constitutions, the canon law, and books of scholastic theology were committed to the flames. Luther himself then threw in the papal bull. "As they did to me," he explained in the words of Samson, "so I have done to them."[3]

Forty-one propositions were condemned in the bull as "respectively heretical, or scandalous, or false, or offensive to pious ears, or seductive of simple minds, and opposed to catholic truth." Among them was Thesis 13 from Luther's Heidelberg Disputation (1518): "Freedom of choice, after the fall, is a reality in name only [*res est de solo titulo*]; and in 'doing what is in it', it sins mortally."[4] That the language of the thesis was none too happy—or, rather, deliberately provocative—appears from the accompanying "explanations."[5] But *Exsurge Domine* did not occupy itself with Luther's refinements; it merely cited, in Article 36, the thesis itself. For his part, Luther sharpened the offense. In his *Assertion of All the Articles of M. Luther Condemned by the Latest Bull of Leo X* (1520), he ironically "revoked" Article 36:

> I was wrong when I said that freedom of choice before grace is a reality in name only. I ought to have said simply: Freedom of choice is a fiction or a name with no reality [*figmentum in rebus seu titulus sine re*]. For to purpose

11

anything either evil or good is in no one's control, but (as Wycliffe's article condemned at Constance rightly teaches) everything happens by absolute necessity.[6]

The German version (or *vernacula assertio,* as Luther called it) concluded more modestly: "I wish that little word 'freewill' had never been invented. It is not found in scripture and should more aptly be called 'selfwill'."[7] Understandably, his adversaries preferred to deplore the more shocking Latin version, especially since Luther there embraced an earlier heretic. Moreover, they took due notice of his declaration that the article on freedom of choice was "the best of them all and the very essence of our case [*omnium optimus et rerum nostrarum summa*]";' beside it, the questions of the papacy, of councils, and of indulgences were mere trifles.[8]

The reason why Luther singled out Article 36 is clear from his defense of it in the *Assertion.* It was his bulwark against the new Pelagians who taught that a man could prepare himself for grace by morally good deeds, performed by his natural powers under the general impulse of divine providence. To be sure, the attempt had been made, as Luther noted, to mitigate the appearance of antici-pating God and wresting his grace from him. Not that the works were held to be strictly meritorious *(de condigno);* rather, merit of congruity *(de congruo)* was assigned them by God, who does not refuse anyone who does what is in him. Luther was unimpressed. "The same impious mentality persists, by which grace is believed to be given, not freely, but on account of our works....The same Pelagius has held the field triumphantly."[9] Indeed, the new Pelagianism was worse than the old; for whereas Pelagius denied the necessity for grace, the new theology put grace at the disposal of men. Such a scheme is contradicted by Scripture and experience alike. When the will of fallen man "does what is in it," it sins mortally. Why? Because what is in a man, since the fall, is more aptly called "selfwill" than "freewill": an aggressive, all-consuming, self-seeking will, which Luther considered to be the fundamental spring of human action (apart from grace).[10] Self-will seeks its own, not only in what is base but also in what is good and noble—even in religion and in God himself. The best works of such a man are not base; but insofar as they are infected with his self-will they remain radically defective. To appeal to the fallen will is therefore a fearful mistake; for the will can only arouse itself to further acts of self-seeking, or else fall into the misery of despair.

Whether Luther's driving concern for the grace of God was wisely defended with the dogma of absolute necessity, may well be doubted. But our interest is in Erasmus's response to Luther and whether it implies, as Luther believed, that the humanist had taken up the cause of the Pelagians. Luther concludes his dis-cussion of Article 36 with a challenge and a wish. He sees no sign that anyone is disposed to take up the real issue and join battle with him. He can only express the wish that some new Ezra would appear, equipped with the biblical languages, to recover the Scriptures.[11] Erasmus never fulfilled the wish—not, at least, as Luther intended it. But he did take up the challenge; and Luther was later to announce (with some exaggeration): "I heartily praise and commend you for this: that you alone, unlike all the rest, have attacked the real thing, that is, the essential issue...."[12]

I

On 8 October 1520, just two days before the bull reached Luther, his books had been ceremoniously burned in Louvain, where Erasmus then resided. The very next day, Nicholas Egmond, a Carmelite friar and a theologian at the university, was preaching in St. Peter's Church when he noticed Erasmus in the congregation, deserted his theme ("charity," so Erasmus recalled), and publicly denounced him as a Lutheran. At a meeting arranged, on Erasmus's request, by the rector of the university, Egmond could find no stronger argument to support his accusation than the fact that Erasmus had not written against Luther. "Why then," was the response, "by the same reckoning I shall take you for a Lutheran, too, for you do not write anything against him either!"[13]

In a series of important letters during the years 1519–20, Erasmus had taken up a cautious and balanced stance toward what he variously called "the Lutheran tragedy," "the Lutheran malady," or simply "the Lutheran affair."[14] He explained that he did not personally know Luther and could not be held responsible for Luther's books, which, since he had only leafed through them, he could neither defend nor condemn. But the enemies of learning had used the Lutheran affair to attack *him,* too, alleging a connection between scholarship and heresy. One source of the affair (not the only one) was thus *odium bonarum literarum.*[15] This is how Erasmus summed up his position in a letter to Luther himself: "As for me, I remain impartial, as far as I may, in order to be more useful to the renascence of learning."[16]

The Erasmian program was a different one from Luther's, and Erasmus preferred to be a spectator, rather than an actor, in the tragedy.[17] Still, he could not ignore the Lutheran movement, not only because of the attempt to discredit him by association with it but also because the revival of learning was, after all, harnessed to the cause of church reform. Erasmus had written against ecclesiastical abuses long before he learned of Luther's existence, and he more than once admitted that he had, in a sense, "precipitated a great part of it all."[18] Hence the programmatic letters of 1519–20 insist upon the crying need for reform, the irreproachable character of Luther, and the requirement of gentleness in dealing with him. But at the very beginning of the Lutheran affair, Erasmus suspected that the indiscretion was not all on the side of Luther's opponents, whom he urged to oppose Luther with the pen and not with slander and uproar. There was the further problem of the Reformer's own temperament, which, by its natural vehemence and impatience, could turn reform into disorder and division. Besides, he made a public issue out of matters which ought to be handled more discreetly. Luther, too, could be bad for the cause of learning, and Erasmus constantly recalls the advice he gave Froben not to print Luther's books. In short, the danger (for *bonae literae*) was that the Lutheran affair would become the Lutheran uproar *(tumultus)*.[19]

It was a policy of mediation, therefore, that Erasmus pursued, culminating in his activities at Cologne during the last few days of October and the early days of November 1520.[20] But already by the month of December, a note of bitterness and disillusionment obtruded. In a world that thirsted for the pure and living waters of the evangelists and apostles, Luther had appeared as perhaps the man of the hour. But the offensiveness of his writings did not reflect the gentleness of the apostolic spirit.[21] By spring the following year, there was little optimism left for the Cologne policy of mediation, though Erasmus did not abandon it. Luther's burning of the decretals, his *Babylonian Captivity,* and the extravagant *Assertions* had "rendered the malady, so it seems, incurable."[22] As Luther's enemies helped him, so he was helping them.[23] He put the sword into their hands.[24]

Erasmus's fears thus proved to have been prophetic: the Lutheran affair was a disruptive affair *(seditiosa res),* and Luther's medicine was worse than the disease.[25] And yet, as the action shifted from Cologne to Worms, Erasmus could not bring himself to oppose Luther totally. A certain "scrupulousness" *(religio quaedam)* held him back, and he played the part of Gamaliel (Acts 5:33–39), lest he be found opposing God.[26] Though he did deem it proper to muzzle both Luther and his opponents, he continued to warn against excessive severity.[27] Much the same advice was given by him to Adrian VI two years after Worms. Harsh measures had been tried before, against the Wycliffites, with no great success. While recommending censorship and the restraint of novelties, which promote disruption more than piety, Erasmus urged amnesty for past offences; for this is the way God deals with us every day, not remembering our trespasses. The sources of the malady should then be investigated and remedied. To this end, as at Cologne, he proposed a commission of cool-headed and highly respected men.[28]

The constant complaint of Erasmus was that no one seemed willing to oppose Luther with the pen, to refute him rather than to defame or to crush him.[29] His friends agreed, and they thought it should be Erasmus's pen. To begin with, he protested that he lacked time or talent to oblige them.[30] He did once decide to write, but on concord, not against Luther; and even this plan was set aside because tempers had waxed too hot.[31] Finally, as the pressure to write continued unremittingly,[32] Erasmus yielded. Now, it may seem natural enough that he chose as his theme the question of freedom and necessity. After all, Luther's adversaries had agreed with him, if in nothing else, at least in judging that his doctrine of necessity was the heart of the matter. Duke George singled it out as "the most fertile spring of the Lutheran errors."[33] The fact is, however, that the question of freedom and necessity had a quite different status in Erasmus's mind than it had either for Luther or for Duke George.

Erasmus was being summoned by friends and patrons to dispose of a heretic.[34] In his reply to von Hutten's *Expostulation,* however, he insisted that he made no mention of a "heresy" but spoke rather of "tragedy," "dissension," "uproar." The issue, he explains, does not concern the articles of faith but matters commonly debated in the schools. (His list includes the question whether freedom of choice contributes to salvation.) Such matters warrant neither the taking of another's life nor the sacrifice of one's own. For his part, Erasmus is not willing to be a martyr for Luther or his paradoxes; and he does not think that paradoxes are cause enough for throwing the whole world into an uproar.[35]

The same point was made in a letter written about the same time to Zwingli, to whom Erasmus dedicated his writing against von Hutten. The first Lutherans to die for their faith had recently been burned in Brussels (1 July 1523), and Erasmus had martyrdom on his mind. He marvels at the constancy of one who could lay down his life, not for an article of faith, but for the paradoxes of Luther. "For these," he admits, "I myself would not care to die, since I do not understand them." The enigmas propounded by Luther are then specified: that all the works of the saints are sins, that freedom of choice is an empty name, that a man is justified by faith alone. Erasmus comments: "I do not see what fruit it would yield to argue over what Luther may mean by these [enigmas]." And this is what he claims for himself: "I think I have taught nearly everything Luther teaches, only not so harshly, and I have refrained from certain enigmas and paradoxes."[36] Erasmus once wrote that the world had been lulled to sleep by endless talk about matters which, even if true, were not of much help for "evangelical vigor."[37] Now, it seemed, Luther had awoken the world only to vex it with some fruitless questions of his own.

Erasmus never did quite oblige his patrons, then, since he did not regard the issue as one of heresy.[38] But his estimate of the issue was poles apart from Luther's appraisal, too, since he thought it not worth an altercation, much less a martyrdom. What *was* it worth, then? A polite discussion. The theme so dear to Luther and so abhorrent to Duke George suited Erasmus's purposes very well; it sufficed to establish his distance from Luther, but by no means demanded a total severance of relations. It enabled Erasmus to be as he had always been toward Luther: not vacillating, but firmly ambivalent. While denying the allegation that he was a Lutheran, he wished to remain on speaking terms with Wittenberg.[39] Even before he had focused on freedom of choice as his theme, he had intended a work *On Settling the Lutheran Affair* which would take the actual literary form of a fictitious conversation, a *collatio* more than a *disputatio*. A series of three dialogues between Thrasymachus (Luther or a Lutheran), Eubulus (a papalist), and Philalethes (Erasmus or an Erasmian) was to deal, in order, with Luther's manner of proceeding, with some of his doctrines, and with Erasmus's counsel for assuaging the uproar.[40] Erasmus did not carry through his original design.[41] But perhaps there are echoes of it in a letter to Laurinus, which may be said to stand midway between the original design and the final product: it contains an imaginary dialogue with a Lutheran, and it moves toward preoccupation with the problem of free choice.[42]

II

Publication of the book continued to be delayed until long after Erasmus had finally agreed to write it.[43] But he did eventually bring himself to the point of squandering five precious days on the irksome task, and—most likely, in the winter of 1523—he was able to send a first draft to Louis Ber for his expert theological counsel. (Ber responded with a memorandum on the distinction between *necessitas consequentiae* and *necessitas consequentis*.)[44] Another copy of the first draft went to King Henry VIII. If a taste of the work met with His Majesty's approval (and that of other learned men), Erasmus would finish it and have it printed. But not in Basel! "For here, I suppose, there is no printer who would venture to print anything that reflects in the slightest upon Luther, though you may write whatever you please against the Pope."[45] Rankled by a well-intentioned but overbearing letter from Luther, which offered him a truce, Erasmus professed that he had still not written against Luther, but added that nothing would please him more than if Luther were to write against him.[46] In the end, he decided to make the first move. The word was out: it was known well enough that he had been preparing a book against Luther. And Erasmus judged that, in any case, he had treated his subject with such moderation that not even Luther could be displeased. Better to publish what he had written than to permit suspicions that it was something worse.[47] By the end of August 1524 the book was—at last!—in the press.[48] In September, Erasmus distributed copies to key personages in Rome, England, and Saxony.[49] The *Discourse on Free Choice* had been printed— and, to be sure, in Basel.[50] "The die is cast," Erasmus announced rather dramatically. "The little book on free choice has gone out into the light of day."[51]

The book gathers up many themes from the correspondence of 1518–24, often with verbal echoes. In particular, it is one of Luther's *doctrines* that is under discussion (I a 3). (No mention is made of any Lutheran *heresy*.) Nonetheless, this one "dogma" is a culpable exaggeration, a "paradox" in a derogatory sense[52] (I a 10, I b 6): namely, Wycliffe's claim that all things—both before and after grace, good things and bad alike, and even things indifferent—happen by pure necessity. Although it makes us mere instruments of God, like tools in a craftsman's hand, Luther expressly approves this opinion in his *Assertion* (II b 7-8; cf. I a 1). The issue, then, is whether the human will can be considered "free" in the sense of possessing ability to choose between alternatives.[53] More exactly, as Erasmus's definition of *liberum arbitrium* indicates, the issue is whether a man has freedom of choice in the matter of his salvation: "Now, by *liberum arbitrium* I mean, in this place, a capacity of the human will by which a man is able to apply himself to the things that lead to eternal salvation, or else to turn away from them" (I b 10).

The central structure of the treatise is given by the remark (I b 10) that there are many passages in Scripture which seem plainly to establish freedom of choice (discussed in sec. II), others which seem entirely to take it away (discussed in sec. III). Since the whole of Scripture is inspired by the selfsame Spirit and therefore cannot contradict itself, the problem is to arrive at a harmonizing interpretation, which can be shown to possess superior probability, first, because it is supported by weightier and more numerous texts and, second, because the alternatives have undesirable or even absurd consequences (I b 10, IV 1, IV 17). Plainly, the discussion is to be exegetical: if the labyrinth of free choice confronts us in the Scriptures (I a 1), then the method appropriate for dealing with it will be through the clash of texts and arguments (I a 3). This also suits the refusal of the partner in the discussion to listen to anything but the canonical Scriptures—as well as the readiness of Erasmus himself to economize his efforts (I b 1). And yet it should not be overlooked that no previous writer has totally abolished freedom of choice, except Mani, Wycliffe, and perhaps Laurentius Valla (I a 6, I b 2, IV 16). To point this out is not to surrender the unique authority of Scripture, but simply to give due weight to the overwhelming consensus among its interpreters (I b 3, IV 17). Of course, the majority is not necessarily right; but it is more likely to be right than the private judgment of an individual or two (I b 2), just as a philosopher has the advantage over a fool or a council over a conventicle (I b 5).

The pivotal argument of Erasmus can readily be picked out. Looking in the Bible for proofs of free choice, he remarks, is like looking for water in the ocean (II a 17). The Bible is filled with imperatives, exhortations, promises, accusations, threats, all of which make no sense on the supposition that everything happens by necessity (II b 1-2, III a 13, III b 6, etc.).[54] Indeed, Scripture hardly speaks of anything else but conversion, zeal, effort for improvement (II a 16). The metaphors of running a race, fighting the good fight, toiling for the harvest, cannot be reconciled with the notion that the will is not active but passive (II b 4). For two reasons, the Lutheran dogma must be overwhelmed with this ocean of texts. First, man's freedom of choice (together with his knowledge of the good) is the condition of human responsibility—of blame and praise, reward and merit (II b 1-2, III a 6, III a 10, IV 3, IV 11, IV 16). "Had the will not been free, sin could not have been imputed; for it ceases to be sin where it is not voluntary...." (II a 7). This holds good not only for Adam but for his entire progeny: in no man can freedom of choice be wholly extinguished, not even when habituation to sin makes it appear otherwise (II a 8). Second, man's freedom of choice is the condition of the divine justice and mercy (IV 7). For if the will were not endowed with freedom of choice, then God would be responsible for evil actions as well as for good (II b 5, IV 12). And what kind of justice or mercy would inflict anger upon any who had not done wrong of their own accord, but had no choice to be other than they were (II b 3, IV 4, IV 13, IV 16)?[55] Those whom God hates or loves he surely hates or loves for just reasons (III a 12).

From among the many questions that may occur to the reader of the *Discourse,* two may be taken as worthy of a closer look. Where, as he goes about refuting the Lutheran dogma, does Erasmus himself seem to stand on the old problem of divine grace and human freedom? And why, in the introductory and concluding reflections (sec. I and sec. IV), does he so carefully frame his subject between apparent admissions of its relative unimportance? Pursuit of these two questions will show that Erasmus was no Pelagian (as Luther thought) and not quite a Semi-Pelagian (as others have thought); further, that the message of the book concerns the relation of theology to piety at least as much as the relation of grace to freedom. In this second respect, in particular, the *Discourse* marks the culmination of those thoughts on the Lutheran affair that Erasmus recorded in his correspondence between 1518 and 1524.

III

In the course of the treatise, and especially in the first part of Section I and the Conclusion, Erasmus outlines the alternative views on grace and freedom. By the fall of man, the will was so depraved it could not recover by its own resources, but lost its liberty and was obliged to be the servant of sin. All Christians agree, as Erasmus sees it, that sin is forgiven by God's grace and the will in some measure made free. But he notes a difference, from this point on, between the Pelagians and the orthodox. In the Pelagian view, the will is then able to gain eternal life without the help of further grace, salvation being ascribed to God simply in the sense that it was he who created and restored the will. (Erasmus does not ask *how,* according to the Pelagians, God restores the will.) In the orthodox view, it is only with the help of further grace, continually sustaining man's effort, that the will is able to persevere in the right condition. And even then, in this view, the inclination to sin is not eradicated—not because grace could not do so, but because it would not be good for us (II a 3; cf. II a 9, III c 5, IV 10).

Among non-Pelagians, however, differences remain. They all insist on the need for continuous divine aid, but they entertain various opinions about the manner in which divine aid is given. Some hold that in his fallen state a man is able, without any divine action beyond God's providential concurrence with the creature (the *influxus naturalis*),[56] to perform deeds that prepare him for grace and move God to mercy (II a 11). This party is identified by Erasmus as the followers of Scotus, who, he says, are "rather favorably disposed" to freedom of choice.[57] "They believe its capacity is sufficient for a man, even before the reception of forgiving grace, to be able by his natural capacities to perform what they call 'morally good' works, through which they merit sanctifying grace—not strictly, but by congruity" (II a 9). Another party argues, by contrast, that there can be no preparation for sanctifying grace without special grace *(gratia peculiaris)* (II a 11). Their view is diametrically opposed to that of the Scotists since they contend that morally good works, if they do not proceed from faith and love to God, are as detestable to him as criminal acts like adultery and murder (II a 10). Here Erasmus must have in mind "St. Augustine and his followers," whom he goes on to name in the same paragraph.[58] Augustine denies that a man in sin can turn himself to amendment of life or do anything that would contribute to his salvation unless he is stimulated by the gratuitous gift of God (as *gratia operans*).[59]

Now Pelagius seems to attribute too much to freedom of choice, and even Scotus allows it a great deal (IV 16; cf. IV 7). For their part, the Augustinians attribute most to grace and almost nothing to freedom of choice—yet without quite abolishing it! Their opinion therefore differs from two final options, which it is Erasmus's intention to contest.[60] According to Carlstadt, the sinful will is "free" only to do evil, so that grace alone performs good works—not through or with, but *in* our "freedom of choice," the will remaining like wax in a modeler's hand. According to Luther, the will is free neither for good nor for evil, whether before or after grace, since everything happens by pure necessity and "freedom of choice" is an empty name.

There are, then, five opinions in all: those of Pelagius, Scotus, Augustine, Carlstadt, and Luther. The first is disqualified because unorthodox. The last two are the opinions Erasmus is writing against. They are distinguished as *durior* (Carlstadt's view) and *durissima* (Luther's):[61] that is, as "harsher" and "harshest" in comparison with the Augustinian view, which is the one Erasmus designates as "likely enough." The reason why the Augustinian view earns this cautious endorsement *(satis probabilis)* is because it leaves a man's zeal and effort, but leaves him nothing to ascribe to his own powers (II a 12). How, we must now ask, does Erasmus understand this "Augustinian" formula?

The fallen will, he assumes, is unable to restore itself *(sese revocare ad meliorem frugem)*, and in this sense its liberty is lost (II a 3). It is ineffectual with respect to eternal salvation, unless grace is added (II a 5). But it does not follow that man has no freedom to will the good at all. We do not wholly lack either the capacity or the use of free choice (III c 1; cf. II a 14). In particular, when the offer of assisting grace comes, a man retains the freedom to accept or reject it. Erasmus's central thought, then, seems to be that freedom of choice is inalienable; it includes the freedom to speak or be silent, to sit or to stand—and also to attend to the things, such as sacred books and sermons, by which God awakens the sinner and makes him a "candidate" for the final, sanctifying grace. The distinction between this view and the view of the Scotists, it appears, is that what to them was preparation for special grace is for Erasmus a free response to it (II a 11).[62] The greatest of all the commandments—to turn to the Lord—is not only possible but easy to fulfill (II a 17). Of course, unlike Adam's will (before the fall), our will is not poised in perfect equilibrium, so to say, but biased toward evil.[63] And yet our freedom of choice, though impaired, is never extinguished (II a 7-8). Hence, at that crucial moment when the assistance of grace is offered, it is possible for us freely to embrace it or to turn our hearts away and close our eyes to the light (II b 6, IV 8-10). Assistance and necessity are, indeed, mutually exclusive notions (II b 5), while grace understood as aid and sin as weakness are correlative and logically presuppose freedom. For we do not call "weak" someone who can do nothing, nor do we say someone is "helping" if in fact he does it all (III c 12).[64] Grace and freedom belong together (III a 16-17, III c 13); this is the guarantee that grace shall be grace, inviting without compelling (III c 3; cf. II a 11).[65]

Erasmus's "moderate" solution is therefore a both-and. The two seemingly contradictory sets of scriptural texts are easily reconciled if we simply join human effort and divine grace. The knotty problem of grace and freedom is then unravelled (III a 17; cf. II b 6). Man's effort and God's aid are united. Not, however, in equal proportions! That would be a quite false inference from the concept of grace as aid. "I like the opinion of those who attribute something to freedom of choice, but most to grace." Room is then left for good works and merits, but it is not enough to boast about (IV 16). In a sense, it can even be said that we owe the whole work to God, without whom we bring nothing to completion (IV 7). More exactly, we owe *wholly* to God the beginning and the end, while the middle—the continuance—depends *chiefly* on him.

> It is because of this proportion that a man should ascribe his salvation wholly to grace, since what the free choice does here is precious little [*perpusillum*] ; and the very fact that it can act at all is of God's grace, who first created the will with freedom to choose, then freed it, too, and healed it [IV 8].[66]

All is of grace, though stage 2 is not of grace in quite the same sense as stages 1 and 3. For there is, in the middle stage, a minimum that Erasmus apparently attributes to the grace of nature (III c 4), which many people do not understand to be grace at all (II a 11). If this sounds, in the end, dubiously Augustinian, it must at least be admitted that the intent to go as far as possible with Augustine is clear.[67] The initiative of God's grace is strongly affirmed *(qui nos aversos vocavit)* (III c 5), and the total scheme can be stated in language almost as paradoxical as Luther's:

> The mercy of God goes before our will, accompanies it in its endeavor, gives a happy issue. Yet all the while, it is we who will, who run, who reach the goal—but in such wise that even this which is ours we ascribe to God, for we are wholly his [III a 4].

And so, Erasmus can readily demand (III c 5), in the words of that favorite Augustinian text (1 Cor. 4:7): "What have you that you did not receive?"

Still, Erasmus did find *some* Augustinian notions extreme and distasteful, and he could make them sound even more extreme than they actually were (I a 10).[68] At times, he speaks as though it were more a matter of courtesy than of dogmatic accuracy to ascribe *everything* to God.[69] Similarly, on the other side, he puts in a good word for the *intention* of the rival, Scotist party: they did, at least, invite a man to exert himself, like Cornelius (Acts 10), in the hope of obtaining salvation (IV 7).[70] And he showed how their fundamental notion could be reconciled with the primacy of grace—by recalling that a man does not possess his natural powers *ex sese* (III c 4).

Small wonder that the scholars continue to differ about Erasmus's real sympathies! The problem becomes still more complex if his subsequent affirmations on the subject are added to those of the *Discourse.*[71] The options seem to be either to admit a certain oscillation in his thinking,[72] or to move him toward one or the other of two poles, the Augustinian-Thomistic[73] or the Semi-Pelagian.[74] A much fuller investigation is called for than is possible here. But I may at least risk a tentative statement on the direction in which, I believe, the evidence points. I cannot see that Erasmus fully appreciated the notion of operative grace.[75] But if this casts doubts upon his right to be classified with the Augustinians and Thomists, it does not follow that he must therefore belong with the Semi-Pelagians. If I have correctly located the point at which Erasmus, for all his wariness, does take a firm stand, then his kinsmen are not so much the medieval Semi-Pelagians, whom Luther attacked, as the Lutheran synergists, who were, of course, Erasmus's stepchildren. Not meritorious preparation for grace, but the natural freedom to consent to grace is the minimum of free choice that he will not surrender.[76] On occasion, he does suggest the possibility of uniting the two schemes: it would not be improper, he thinks, to subsume the free response to prevenient grace under the scholastic terminology of *merita de congruo.*[77]

Insofar as that is his proposal, he makes the terminology something not quite "Semi-Pelagian" in the customary sense.

Is this, then, all that needs to be said about Erasmus's *real* view? Surely not. His view on grace and freedom was also that there are *several* views on grace and freedom. He was later to complain, in his response to Luther's attack, that an *opinio probabilis* is not the *opinio sola, certa, et indubitata.*[78] And he would have registered no surprise had he been able to foreknow that, after his death, the Lutherans were to be divided over their synergist controversy, Dominicans and Jesuits were to debate efficacious grace, and Calvinist was to fall out with Calvinist over effectual calling. This would merely have confirmed his persuasion that the relationship of grace and freedom, within limits, is a matter of opinion.

IV

In the first paragraph of the *Discourse on Free Choice* Erasmus judged that his theme had marvelously occupied the talents of philosophers and theologians, both ancient and modern, but with more toil than fruit (I a 1). It remained, for him, a school question, and he could not concede that it had the importance assigned it by his adversaries (I b 4), who even contended it was the chief point *(caput)* of the entire teaching of the Gospel (I b 8). To him, it was a *quaestio disputata.* Hence, although the goal of the inquiry was of course to try whether the truth could be made more evident, he proposed nothing more conclusive than a civil conversation; and he wanted to avoid anything as unseemly as a contentious debate or gladiatorial combat (I a 1-3, I b 9). Any issue which carries one beyond the inviolable authority of Scripture or the pronouncements of the church calls for tentativeness and reserve rather than fanatical addiction to one's own opinion. Unlike Luther, then, whose *Assertion* had rekindled the old debate, Erasmus disowned any taste for "assertions" about such matters. He was willing to remain a skeptic (I a 4). In fact, he admitted that he had not entirely made up his mind about all the various options, except that he did think there was *some* capacity of free choice. On this, Luther's *Assertion* had not yet *(nondum!)* persuaded him otherwise (I a 5). He believed he had understood Luther but granted he could be wrong; and he therefore played the debater, not the judge, the inquirer, not the dogmatist (I a 6).

It is not true, however, as Luther and others after him have alleged,[79] that Erasmus considered the entire issue of free choice to be trivial—although he may have expressed himself incautiously. What he intended was to circumscribe the points that mattered and could be stated definitively, leaving in an outer circle, so to say, points open to debate. (Luther believed that the inner circle could only be secure if certain questions in the outer circle were first settled). For Erasmus, the practical criterion of what mattered was *pietas.* Hence the first of the summarizing conclusions (at the end of the *Discourse*) is this: "It is of no advantage to piety to investigate [the matter] more deeply than necessary, especially in the presence of laymen" (IV 17).[80]

Erasmus offers a list of affirmations concerning free choice that can be made on the basis of the Scriptures. In essence, they simply set out the obligation of human effort and the availability of divine mercy. This, he judges, is enough for Christian piety without intrusion upon such remote—not to say superfluous—questions as whether God knows anything contingently (that is, whether he can foreknow contingent events), whether our will is of any avail in what concerns salvation or whether it is only passive under the action of grace, whether the good or evil we do is done by us (or rather to us) by pure necessity. It is not piety, but *irreligiosa curiositas* that pries into such questions (I a 8). The paradox of Wycliffe and Luther—that "whatever is done by us happens, not by freedom of choice, but by pure necessity"—is classed among those matters which, even if we supposed them true, could not usefully be made public before the whole world.[81] To the same class belongs Augustine's assertion that God works in us both good and bad and rewards his own good works in us and punishes the bad.[82] To proclaim such an utterance among the masses would be to throw open the window to impiety: the fainthearted would weary of the struggle against the flesh, the wicked would not endeavor to mend his ways. And who could induce himself to love with his whole heart a God who prepares the flames to punish in his victims his own evil deeds (I a 10)?

Erasmus certainly found Luther's dogma a challenge to his credulity. Presumably, he included it among those new hyperparadoxes which had not yet been verified by so much as the curing of a lame horse (I b 6). But his fundamental concern was for the moral and religious consequences of the paradox—in short, for *pietas,* understood as a matter both of good conduct and of a proper attitude toward the Deity.[83] Luther's denial that confession is a binding obligation was, to Erasmus, a similar case in point: even had the denial been correct, he would have feared to make it public since compulsory confession restrained the impulse to scandalous sins *(flagitia).*

> There are some diseases of the body which it is a lesser evil to endure than to cure.... Paul knows the difference between what is "allowed" and what is "expedient" [1 Cor. 6:12]. It is allowed to speak the truth, but it is not expedient to do so in front of anyone, any time, or in any way [I a 9].

Luther's critique of the penitential praxis and his denial of free choice were thus subject to the same objection: they undermined religious endeavor. Indeed, when judged by the norm of *pietas,* the dualism of Mani was perhaps less injurious *(minus inutile ad pietatem);* it at least left grounds for imploring the Creator's help against the powers of darkness, whereas Wycliffe's pure necessity left room neither for prayer nor for effort (I b 2).

Did not Paul himself, however, lay claim to a wisdom that he uttered among the more mature (1 Cor. 2:6)? Matters noxious to the masses, like wine to the fevered, could perhaps have been discussed among the learned or in schools of theology, though even there only with sobriety (I a 11). Without some such allowance, Erasmus's exploration of free choice in the *Dialogue* would have lost its justification. But it can hardly be doubted that he was more interested in preserving the inner circle than in arguing about the outer, for there was always the risk that a discussion among scholars might become a public performance for the multitude. And that would be, not just useless, but pernicious. Erasmus accordingly ends his preface with the remark:

> For this reason, I should prefer it if, rather than either refuting or affirming Luther's dogma, we could be persuaded not to fritter away time and talents in labyrinths of this kind. It would justly be thought that I had been too wordy in this preface were it not almost more to the point than the disputation itself [I a 11].

If Erasmus had left out the little word "almost," we might well wonder, with Luther, why he went ahead and disputed anyway. Even with the "almost," we may still nurse a few lingering doubts, which the ending of the introduction only confirms:

> Half my book is already done. For if I carry my intended point—that it is better not to quarrel too fussily over matters of this sort, especially before the common people—then the argument for which I now gird myself is not needed. . . . [I b 10].

In the conclusion of the *Discourse,* Erasmus returns to the introductory theme of dogma and piety. But resumption of the theme is not mere repetition. The test of *pietas* is now employed, not simply to draw a firm line between fundamental affirmations and theological opinions, but to display the point of the opinions themselves. The reference to *pietas,* we may say, is not just a limit but a hermeneutic principle. The two extremes, between which Erasmus looks for a "moderate" position, have each been supported by one-sided appropriation of the Scriptures; but the inner reason for the divergence he thinks he can trace back, behind the proofs, to different religious concerns. Considering men's negligence in the pursuit of piety and the risk that they may be infected with despair of salvation, the one side has been betrayed into overemphasis on freedom of choice. The other side, noting what a plague upon genuine piety is man's confidence in human powers and merits (which he even presumes to offer for sale), has either diminished freedom of choice or wholly exterminated it. Either way, the attempted cure is another disease (IV 1; cf. II a 9–10). In the correction of morals, the saying holds good: "To straighten a bent stick, bend it in the opposite direction." But in dogmatics *(in dogmatibus)*, a balanced statement is desirable. "The Scylla of arrogance was not to be evaded by being carried into the Charybdis of despair or indolence.[84] The dislocated limb should not have been remedied by bending it back in the opposite direction, but by resetting it where it belongs" (IV 16).

The claim of Erasmus in the *Discourse on Free Choice* is that he has preserved Luther's religious concerns *(quae Lutherus pie quidem et Christiane disseruit)* without the troublesome paradoxes. It is hardly true, though often repeated,[85] that Erasmus failed to appreciate Luther's concerns, despite his own belief that he had understood him. At least, he knew it was Luther's wish to transfer confidence from human merits and capacities solely to God and his promises (IV 17; cf. IV 18).[86] And he could gladly exclaim: "Surely, it is a pious and winsome opinion that takes from us all conceit, transfers all our boasting and confidence to Christ, drives from us the fear of men and of demons, makes us mistrustful of our own resources, and gives us strength and courage in God." These are thoughts Erasmus applauds—short of exaggeration *(usque ad hyperbolas)* (IV 2).[87] And exaggeration is what it is if anyone asserts that there is no merit, that the works even of the pious are sins, that everything we do or will must be traced to absolute necessity (IV 3). In Erasmus's judgment, Luther was forced to such extremes by the demands of polemic. At one time, Luther did allow something to freedom of choice, but he was driven in the heat of argument to abolish it entirely (IV 7). Perhaps he also took a certain natural delight in hyperbole. In any case, he countered one extreme with another: the traffic in merits with the denial of merit, and so on with satisfactions, papal power, monastic vows, and the rest. There may be a place for an occasional use of hyperbolical language—for reassuring the timid that "God does everything" or admonishing the proud that "man can do nothing but sin." But "from the clash of such exaggerations the thunder and lightning are generated that now shake the world" (IV 15-16).

What Erasmus offers in his conclusion is a genetic account of the Lutheran dogma. He uncovers the root religious concern (and unambiguously approves it). The expression of this concern in harsh and exaggerated language is explained as an understandable by-product of controversy—though Erasmus hints that Luther did seem to *like* hyperbole, too. Even the exaggerations may be warranted if taken functionally as belonging more to exhortation than dogmatics. But the language remains defective insofar as it loses the (equally legitimate) interests of the rival party. Luther's view is rejected for the sake of piety. But it is also interpreted as an expression of authentic piety.

Erasmus may not have solved one of the knottiest problems in the history of theology. But he did, in the course of exploring it, offer some absorbing insights into the nature of theology itself, what to look for in it and how to improve it.

The Lutheran dogma thus became the occasion for a characteristic Erasmian reflection on theology and piety.[88] In the end, Erasmus's verdict upon Luther was that he did not overcome the "sophistic theology" but merely offered another version of it.[89] Yet it would be a mistake to conclude that while Luther stood for scholastic theology, the Erasmian renewal of theology was more closely linked with religion. The twofold irony of the debate on freedom of choice is that Luther began by sharing the Erasmian concern for a practical theology and Erasmus ended (in his *Hyperaspistes*) by trying to show himself better at scholastic theology than Luther.

If we overlook the dual gap between intention and execution, we may justly conclude that what divided them was less a difference over the need for anchoring *theologia* in *pietas* than a difference over the requirements of *pietas* itself. This is not to exclude the possibility of generous overlapping between the two conceptions of religion. Still, a difference remains. For Erasmus, the prime requirement was for strength to supply what was lacking in the will's best efforts. For Luther, the moment of the will's highest endeavor was the moment of greatest anguish because it marked the end of a tragic mistake. The issue over freedom of choice, whether or not it is the chief point of the gospel, is at least an index to two different modes of being religious. That there is freedom of choice was, to Erasmus, a point on which there could be no yielding. Luther admitted that he would not want free choice even if he could have it.[90]

Two The Pathfinder: Calvin's Image of Martin Luther

Martin Luther and John Calvin were, by common consent, the two most eminent figures of the Protestant Reformation. There were other distinguished leaders in both Germany and Switzerland—Melanchthon and Zwingli, for instance—to say nothing of national heroes in other lands. But they do not quite measure up to the stature of the two giants, who can justly be compared only with each other. One naturally expects, then, that the question will have been asked frequently, almost too frequently: What is the relationship between these two? How, in particular, did they think of each other? In actual fact, scholars in the English-speaking world seem to have been strangely uninterested in setting the two Continental Reformers side by side, even when confessional allegiance might have compensated for patriotic indifference. The theme "Luther and Calvin," with variations in approach and content, has been handled rather more regularly in German,[1] occasionally also in French and Dutch.[2] And, of course, the more general studies, such as the biographies of Calvin, always have something more or less weighty to say on the theme, even if only incidentally.[3] But the literature in English is thin.[4]

One reason for the delinquency of British and American scholarship in this respect is perhaps the tendency to concentrate mainly on the *Institutes* and (rather less) on Calvin's commentaries. The casual reader of the *Institutes,* who is not skilled in identifying unacknowledged debts or anonymous opponents, could be pardoned for concluding that the author had never heard of Luther. Although the pages of Calvin's systematic work bristle with citations from biblical, patristic, scholastic, and classical authors, no explicit reference is made to the great German Reformer. In the commentaries, to be sure, the veil of anonymity is lifted from time to time, and Luther is openly mentioned, often, though by no means always, to illustrate a piece of faulty exegesis.[5] But the most important sources for my theme are among the least read: namely, Calvin's correspondence[6] and the so-called "minor theological treatises."[7] For this reason, and also because some of the pertinent materials are not even available in English translations,[8] I devote a good deal of space, in what follows, to direct quotation of Calvin's most important judgments on Martin Luther.

I

A glance at the dates of some of the articles devoted immediately to my theme (1883, 1896, 1959, 1964) reveals that the sacred festivals of Protestantism—the birthdays or deathdays of the Reformers and the appearance of the definitive edition of the *Institutes*—have been the chief stimulus to publication. Approaches to the theme have been various. The personalities of Luther and Calvin have been contrasted, with inevitable assistance from ethnology and sociology: the impetuous Teuton is set beside the precise Frenchman, the peasant's son beside the boy who grew up among the gentry.[9] Likewise, the respective theologies of the two Reformers have been compared, and an attempt made to locate the points of difference.[10] Finally, their actual personal relationships and opinions of each other have been reviewed and evaluated.[11] I think it can be said, however, that a special underlying concern often binds essays together which seem, on the surface, quite different in approach. Indeed, *all* the essays which originate from the continent of Europe show traces, some more and some less, of this concern: to see what light the relationships between Luther and Calvin can shed on the division between the two communions that are descended from them. And here, perhaps, a word of caution may be called for.

We cannot help looking back on the Reformation in the light of four centuries of confessional mistrust. This is made particularly plain in the essay by the Dutch scholar A. Eekhof, written during the First World War. He concludes his theme "How did Calvin think about Luther?" with an extraordinary remark from Harnack, who professed to see in the war confirmation of the fact that Calvinism really does have another spirit than Lutheranism. Harnack had written:

> The war shows us that the Reformed territories of Western Europe and America stand over against us with a lack of understanding which makes them susceptible to every defamation. We German Protestants are still just as isolated as three hundred years ago.[12]

Eekhof was able to point to another, possibly wiser statement of Harnack's, published the very same year (1917), in which the German historian reaffirmed his belief in the power of Christianity to induce a sense of unity among the nations. But if, comments Eekhof, it is in fact true that the confessions stand against each other, then another German scholar, August Lang, has shown the way to future reconciliation: we are to learn from the example of Luther and Calvin that the Evangelical church, despite all its divisions, is called to brotherly unity. With this one would not wish to quarrel. But it does already remind us, at least implicitly, that Calvin's situation was not ours, since we are being invited to go back beyond the experience of confessional animosity.

It cannot be too strongly emphasized at the outset that Calvin did not think of himself as "Reformed" in the sense of inner-Protestant polemics. Calvin was not a Calvinist but an Evangelical, and what he thought about Luther can only be understood from this viewpoint. He identified himself wholly with the common Protestant cause and never faced the Wittenbergers as the sponsor of a rival movement. This was at no time made more plain than when Calvin learned of the struggle between the Saxon Lutherans and Heinz von Wolfenbüttel (1545). He immediately obtained permission from the Genevan authorities to hold a special service of intercession, and from his pulpit he exhorted the people of Geneva: "I am not speaking of Geneva alone, but of all towns and territories where the gospel is proclaimed.... May we set ourselves apart? May we say, 'They are far away from us'? No, they belong to the church, and we are their members."[13] Moreover, as is well known, Calvin testified to his solidarity with the Lutherans by accepting the Augsburg Confession.[14] Of course, the eucharistic debates repeatedly menaced the relations between Calvin and the Lutherans. But it is common knowledge that on the points at issue between Luther and Zwingli he recognized the validity of Luther's case.[15] And he did not permit even the bitterness of his debate with Joachim Westphal to shake his confidence in the German Reformer, whose memory he continued to cherish.

II

We may say, then, that Calvin's churchmanship and evangelicalism prevented him from being narrowly confessional. Nevertheless, the plain fact is that his affection for Luther was occasioned by the generosity of Luther himself. Calvin's earliest remarks on the Saxon Reformer were inclined to be censorious. But he was utterly disarmed by the news that he himself was more kindly judged in Wittenberg. Not that he ever recanted his early estimate of Luther's character and opinions. Rather, he was enabled to set the negative judgments within the context of a warm admiration for the person and insight of the older man. Further, he learned to view the beginnings of the Reformation from a historical perspective which did not demand of him a plain yes or a plain no to Martin Luther, but rather led him to adopt the stance of a critical disciple. And, as often happens with strong-willed disciples, he would leap vigorously to his master's defense, and yet claim for himself the right to criticize him freely.

Luther and Calvin never met, and it may be that Calvin's understanding of Luther was hampered by his ignorance of German. This, at any rate, was the accusation brought against him by the Reformers in German Switzerland, as we shall see. Similarly, when the Lutheran Heshusius began his polemics against Calvin, the Swiss Reformer was embarrassed by the fact that his opponent attacked him in German. A third party, Wolph, thoughtfully sent Calvin some selected passages translated into Latin, and explained: "You, most learned Calvin, who are a Frenchman by race and do not understand German, no more understand the insults he spews out against you than I would if insulted in Arabic."[16] We may take it, then, as an established fact that Calvin knew Luther directly only through such of his writings as had been written in Latin or else translated from German.

Further, if Luther and Calvin never encountered each other face to face, neither can one speak of a correspondence between them. We have but one letter from Calvin to Luther, and none from Luther to Calvin. It is true that when the editors of Calvin's works were assembling his correspondence, a certain Count Henri de Sarrau informed them that he had in his possession a letter addressed by the German Reformer to his Swiss counterpart.[17] It bore the improbable inscription *amico et patrono;* and though *patronus* could conceivably mean "advocate" rather than "patron," the letter remained suspect. From an exact copy it was then discovered (by Herminjard)[18] that the count's treasured letter was in fact not from Luther, but from Simon Sultzer, pastor and professor of theology at Berne.

Calvin's earliest sentiments about Luther were expressed in a letter he wrote to Martin Bucer (12 January 1538) during the negotiations which followed the adoption of the Wittenberg Concord (1536). The Concord had achieved reconciliation between the Wittenbergers and the South Germans. The next step was to attempt the inclusion of the Swiss. Calvin was less than enthusiastic. He shared the suspicion of the Swiss theologians that, under the veil of an ambiguous formula, Luther might dream about a transference of Christ's flesh into ours (or of our flesh into Christ's), or might attribute an infinite body to Christ, or, finally, might insist upon a local presence. A "concord" was to be desired such as all good men could accept in sincerity. Calvin then continues with some remarks on Martin Luther:

> If he is able to embrace us with our confession [Calvin means the First Helvetic Confession of 1536] there is nothing that I would more gladly desire. However, he is not the only one in the church of God whom we have to consider. We are thrice unfeeling and barbarous if we take no account of the thousands who are being fiercely reviled under the pretext of the Concord. I do not know what to think of Luther, although I am fully persuaded of his godliness [*pietate*]. I sincerely hope that what many are proclaiming, who otherwise have no desire to be unjust to him, is not true: that there is a bit of obstinacy mixed in with his firmness.[19]

Calvin suspects Luther of being too fond of winning theological victories, and this, he believes, will threaten the Concord. Moreover, he is severely critical of Luther's theological position. Luther is guilty, not just of contemptuousness and abuse, but also of ignorance and gross delusion *(crassissima halucinatione)*. This is pretty strong language and does not promise well, one would think, for future relations between the two Reformation giants.

On the other hand, a glance at the first edition of Calvin's *Institutes,* already published in 1536, is sufficient to prove that he was deeply indebted to Luther, and this, no doubt, promised better things. Quite apart from the fact, often pointed out, that Calvin modeled the structure of his first edition on Luther's catechisms, he borrowed freely from the fund of Lutheran ideas, not least on the Lord's Supper. His basic understanding of what a sacrament is unmistakably echoed the classic treatment in Luther's *Babylonian Captivity.* In short, unlike Zwingli, who proclaimed his theological independence, Calvin was a conscious debtor, who deliberately appropriated Lutheran insights. It is true that, on this point, Émile Doumergue challenged August Lang, who had argued for Calvin's dependence on Luther in the first edition of the *Institutes.* Doumergue maintained that, in actual fact, Calvin there rejected the three fundamental ideas of Luther's eucharistic teaching in the *Babylonian Captivity:* consubstantiation, the glorified body of Christ, and the identification of the bread and the body.[20] But, in my judgment, Lang quite rightly refused to recant,[21] since the differences pointed out by Doumergue are not incompatible with agreement on the nature of a sacrament. Calvin criticized Luther's teaching on the mode of Christ's presence in the Eucharist, but he accepted the idea of a sacrament as a sign that confirms the divine promise.[22] Hence we must conclude that, despite the wholly negative appearance of Calvin's remarks to Bucer, he was already under Luther's theological influence.

Then, in 1539, news came from Wittenberg that Dr. Martin held Calvin in high esteem. With almost childlike joy the young Reformer reported the good news to his friend Guillaume Farel, and the entire tone of his judgments upon Luther henceforth changed, even if they remained much the same in content. In a letter to Martin Bucer at Strasbourg, where Calvin was then residing, Luther had ended with these words: "Farewell. And will you pay my respects [*salutabis...reverenter*] to John Sturm and John Calvin. I have read their little books with singular enjoyment."[23] Calvin quoted this commendation of his writing when he addressed a letter to Farel (20 November 1539),[24] and he added: "Just think what I say there about the Eucharist! Consider Luther's generosity [*ingenuitatem*]! It will be easy to decide what reason they have who so obstinately disagree with him." Calvin was also able to add two further testimonies of Luther's goodwill. The first was a statement in a letter from Melanchthon (now lost), according to which "Calvin has found great favor." The second was an incident Melanchthon had instructed the messenger to deliver orally. Here is how Calvin repeats the communication to Farel:

Certain persons, to irritate Martin, pointed out to him the aversion with
which he and his followers were alluded to by me. So he examined the passage in question and felt that he was there, beyond doubt, under attack. After
a while, he said: "I certainly hope that he will one day think better of us. Still,
it is right for us to be a little tolerant toward such a gifted man."[25] We
are surely made of stone [Calvin continues] if we are not overcome by
such moderation! I, certainly, am overcome, and I have written an apology
[*satisfactionem*] for insertion into my preface to the Epistle to the Romans.

Generosity had evoked an answering generosity. Indeed, Calvin's eager testimony to Luther's magnanimous spirit was found embarrassing by later Calvinists.
Theodore Beza, who edited Calvin's writings, went through the letter with a cen-
sor's quill and crossed out the most compromising phrases.[26] As for Calvin's
"apology," Melanchthon persuaded him to leave it out of the preface to his
Commentary on Romans.[27] But he did write it, and sent a copy to Farel for his
approval.[28] The content of the apology has been thought to shed some light on
an interesting question posed by Luther's letter to Bucer: Which book (or
books)[29] of Calvin had he "read with singular enjoyment"? Since Luther immediately goes on to make a thrust at Cardinal Sadoleto—"As for Sadoleto, I wish
he would believe that God is the creator of men even outside of Italy"—it is
natural to suppose that he must have been thinking about Calvin's *Reply to
Sadoleto*, published earlier that same year (1539). In his apology, however,
Calvin refers to the new edition of the *Institutes*, which also appeared in 1539,
and denies that he there intended to attack the Germans.[30] This does not, I
think (*pace* Doumergue),[31] enable us to identify the *Institutes* of 1539 as the
"little book" which Luther "read with singular enjoyment." It seems to me
more likely that, in his letter to Bucer, Luther really did have the *Reply to
Sadoleto* in mind. But when confronted with the section on the Eucharist in the
new edition of the *Institutes*, he refused to retract his favorable opinion of the
author. And Calvin, on his side, was wholly captivated by Luther's magnanimity.
He hastened to explain that he had not really meant to attack the Lutherans at all.

III

In the years immediately following the Wittenberg Concord, Luther maintained
a friendliness toward the Swiss that contrasts strikingly with the bitterness of the
Marburg Colloquy (1529).[32] Indeed, even the common image of Luther as the
intransigent antagonist of Zwingli in the castle of Philip of Hesse has been much
overdone. At that time he was rather more conciliatory than Philip Melanchthon,
even though the conference did begin badly when Luther took his piece of chalk
and wrote his text on the table. Despite his tempestuous tirades, Luther was on

the verge of giving the Swiss the right hand of fellowship, but Melanchthon dissuaded him.[33] In the 1540s, however, the eucharistic debate flared up once more. Luther's wrath against the Swiss waxed steadily hotter, until even his friend Melanchthon no longer felt safe in Wittenberg. In August 1543, Luther dashed off an angry letter to the Swiss publisher Froschauer, warning him never again to send him anything written by the Swiss, against whom he intended to pray and teach until the end of his days.[34] In 1544 he published his *Short Confession on the Holy Sacrament*, in which his powers of invective carried him to new heights, as in the the famous description of his adversaries as possessing an *eingeteuffelt, durch teuffelt, uberteuffelt, lesterlich hertz und Luegenmaul.*[35] In January 1546, shortly before his death, Luther summed up his sentiments in a parody of the first Psalm: "Blessed is the man who walks not in the counsel of the sacramentarians, nor stands in the way of Zwinglians, nor sits in the seat of the Zurichers."[36]

How, we must now ask, did Calvin's affection for the German Reformer stand up in the face of these vigorous blasts from Wittenberg? The answer is that it remained steadfast as ever. More surprising, Luther, for his part, seems to have been at least half-willing to exempt Calvin from his tirades against the Swiss.

Luther's letter to Froschauer prompted Calvin to write to Melanchthon (21 April 1544), asking him to lay a restraining hand on his colleague and friend:

> Bullinger has recently complained to me that all the Zurichers have been savagely mangled [*atrociter laceratos*] by Dr. Luther. And he sent a copy of a letter in which I, too, feel a lack of humanity. I beseech you, do all you can to restrain, or rather prevent, Dr. Martin from giving way to his violence against that church. Maybe he has reason to flare up against them, but it is proper to deal more gently with godly and learned men.[37]

Indeed, had not Luther himself, in 1539, said the same? Later, when Luther's *Short Confession* had appeared, Calvin wrote to Bullinger (25 November 1544):

> I hear that Luther has at last broken out with savage invective, not so much against you as against us all. . . . Now I hardly dare ask you to remain silent. For it is certainly not just that the innocent should be molested and denied the chance to clear themselves; and it is hard to decide whether it is even good policy. But I desire you to bear in mind, first, Luther's greatness as a man and his outstanding gifts: the stoutheartedness and steadfastness, the skillfulness, and the effectiveness of teaching with which he has labored to destroy the kingdom of antichrist and spread abroad the doctrine of salvation. I often say that even if he should call me a devil, I should still pay him the honor of acknowledging him as an illustrious servant of God, who yet, as he is rich in virtues, so also labors under serious faults. . . . It is our task so to reprehend whatever is bad in him that we make some allowance for those splendid gifts.[38]

At the very moment when tempers were hottest over the renewed eucharistic debate, Calvin wrote a letter to Luther himself—the only letter ever addressed by one of the two Reformers to the other. The occasion for writing, however, was not furnished by the controversy over the Eucharist, but by persecution of the Protestants in France.[39] Fearing for their lives, some of them had outwardly conformed by attendance at the Roman mass, but remained, as they said, inwardly devoted to the true religion. They were named "Nicodemites," because, like Nicodemus, they came secretly to the Savior. Calvin challenged the weakness of his countrymen with characteristic vigor in his *Short Treatise Showing What a Faithful Man Should Do, Knowing the Truth of the Gospel, When He Is among the Papists* (1543).[40] The French Protestants found his imperatives too uncompromising, and even hinted that Geneva was scarcely the most convincing place from which to commend the cross of martyrdom. Calvin wrote a reply, *The Apology of John Calvin to the Nicodemite Gentlemen Concerning the Complaint They Have Made that He Is Too Rigorous* (1544).[41] But his countrymen were not convinced, and they felt that a milder verdict could be expected from the Reformers of Wittenberg. They requested Calvin to consult with the Germans by sending a messenger or, if possible, by traveling to Wittenberg himself.

Not surprisingly, Calvin felt unable to make the journey in person. To Wittenberg and back by horse was a two-month ride, and he had neither the leisure nor the constitution for such a rugged journey. Besides, he was handicapped by his ignorance of German and, he admitted, was also too deeply in financial debt to go traveling. Finally, the time for conferring with Luther was still remote, since the passion of controversy had not yet subsided.[42] Instead of a personal visit, then, Calvin translated his two treatises into Latin and sent them by messenger to Wittenberg, together with letters (dated 21 January 1545) to both Luther and Melanchthon.[43] He asked, not for agreement, but for a frank appraisal of what he had written.[44]

In his letter to Luther, Calvin makes profuse apologies for claiming the time of an already overburdened man, and requests Luther to read the two treatises, or have them read, and to give his verdict. Luther is addressed as "most respected father," and Calvin is highly deferential throughout, making plain that he shares with the French Protestants a high regard for Luther's authority.

> Both because I thought it of the most importance for them to be helped by your authority, so that they should not be forever wavering, and also because this was something to be desired by myself as well, I was unwilling to refuse them their request.... How I wish I could fly to you there, so that I might enjoy your company for but a few hours! For I should prefer, and it would be much better, to discuss with you in person, not this question only, but others too. But since it is not granted us here on earth, it will shortly be ours, as I hope, in the Kingdom of God.[45]

What, then, it will be asked, did Luther make of Calvin's letter? The answer is that he never received it, and probably never knew that it had been written. Melanchthon wrote back on 17 April that the struggle he had previously avoided was growing worse, and he expected banishment. "I have not shown your letter to Pericles [i.e., Luther]. For he is inclined to be suspicious, and does not want his replies on such questions as you raise to be passed around."[46]

It would be quite unfair to conclude that Calvin had made a gesture of conciliation to Luther, only to be frustrated by the high-handedness of his supposed friend, Melanchthon. Calvin trusted Melanchthon completely. Knowing the situation at Wittenberg, he had sent both letters to Melanchthon, leaving him to determine, at his own discretion, what to do with the letter addressed to his colleague.[47] It has indeed been suggested that Calvin, in a letter to Pierre Viret, "seems to play down the importance of the affair,"[48] as though he wrote to Luther somewhat reluctantly, and solely to pacify his obstinate countrymen. This may well be true.[49] But it is plain that Calvin had hoped to seize the opportunity to assure Luther directly of his deep respect, and one cannot help wondering how Luther might have responded to the younger man's homage. Perhaps Melanchthon knew best, after all. Certainly, Luther's growing intransigence terrified Melanchthon and severely strained Calvin's admiration.

Later in the year (28 June 1545), Calvin urged Melanchthon to greater openness about his eucharistic convictions and, while commending his prudence and moderation, warned him against the policy of appeasement—this time the appeasement, not of Rome, but of Luther. Not that Calvin intended to side with the men of Zurich. He told Melanchthon that he found their answer to Luther (the *Orthodox Confession* of 1545) feeble and childish, distinguished more by stubborness than by learning; they excused Zwingli and reproached Luther with equal injustice, and should either have written differently or else have kept quiet. But he could not overlook that they had been deeply provoked by the thundering Pericles of Wittenberg.

> I indeed, who revere him from my heart, am violently ashamed of him. . . .
> I admit we all owe him much. And I am not reluctant to let him be pre-
> eminent with the highest authority, provided he knows how to govern his
> own self. But in the church we must see that we do not go too far in our
> deference to men. It would be all over if any one man counted for more than
> all the rest.[50]

Throughout the renewed crisis, then, Calvin managed to maintain a balance and restraint that prevented him from simply taking the side of the Swiss against Luther. His attitude rested partly on the conviction that neither side had a monopoly on the truth, partly on his refusal to forget the debt that Protestantism owed to the "illustrious servant of God." Indeed, he suspected that Luther was permitting himself to be led by lesser men, especially Amsdorf.[51] And in this he was more than half right.[52] Further, there is evidence that Luther, for his part, did not permit the new phase of the eucharistic controversy to alter his estimate of Calvin. This, however, is another question, and it cannot be allowed to divert us from our theme.[53]

IV

Other features of Calvin's attitude toward Luther could be documented from his correspondence. He had, for instance, some interesting and discerning comments on Luther as an exegete, suggesting that he was a little too quick in drawing the "fruitful" conclusions from the Scripture text.[54] But we must now turn from the correspondence to certain of Calvin's theological treatises in which his picture of Luther takes on sharper contours and is set within the frame of something like a historical interpretation of the Reformation. Three treatises written during Luther's lifetime will be considered first: the *Short Treatise on the Lord's Supper* (1541), the treatise against Pighius (1543), and the *Humble Exhortation to Charles V* (1543).

The *Short Treatise on the Lord's Supper* contains an interesting survey of the eucharistic controversy among the Protestants.[55] There is good reason to believe that Luther himself examined this section of the treatise and gave it his approval.[56] It is characteristic of Calvin to insist at the outset on two points. First, one could hardly expect that a proper understanding of this intricate question would have been attained all at once. "We shall not be at all surprised that they [the disputants] did not grasp everything at the outset." But, second, beneath the outward scandal of disagreement he detects a genuine movement toward unity. With a glad expectancy, later to be disappointed, Calvin anticipates a final settlement of the debate. All are now agreed that "we are truly made partakers of the proper substance of the body and blood of Jesus Christ." It is just that some are better than others at explaining how this happens. Within this movement toward unity both parties erred and refused to hear each other. The case against Luther is that he employed ill-advised similitudes, appeared to teach a local presence, and spoke with too sharp a tongue. But Calvin does not doubt that Luther was right to resist the opposing tendency to reduce the sacrament to a matter of "bare signs." The view of the Zwinglians was entirely too negative and destructive. "For although they did not deny the truth, all the same they did not teach it as clearly as they ought." In any case, Calvin says, our part is not to censure either side, but to recall in thankfulness what we have received from both.

The subject of Calvin's controversy with Pighius is indicated in the full title of his treatise: *A Defense of the Sound and Orthodox Doctrine of the Bondage and Deliverance of the Human Will against the False Accusations of Albert Pighius.*

The first part of the treatise contained a remarkable defense of Luther against many of the charges that are still brought against him in our own day. Whether or not one judges it a merit, Calvin must be acknowledged as a vigorous and skillful polemicist, with a flair for the telling phrase. More important, no doubt, he displays a sensitive appreciation of Luther's thought and personality. He has grasped the meaning of the famous *Anfechtungen* (or "spiritual assaults"), and he recognizes in the admitted extravagance of Luther's style precisely the kind of hero for whom the times cried out.

Calvin refuses to be diverted into a detailed analysis of Luther's moral character.

> As for the denunciations with which he [Pighius] slashes Luther's character and morals, it is no part of my present design to rebut them. They do not contribute much of importance to the subject under debate, neither does Luther need any defense of mine. Pighius behaves just like some hungry, ravenous dog, which, finding nothing to get its teeth into, vents its spite by yapping.[57]

In any case, the worst that Pighius could find to say against Luther's character was that he must have been a very monster from hell, since he was often tormented with oppressive struggles of conscience that were like the anguish of the damned. Calvin retorts that if only the windbag Pighius had the least inkling of what those struggles meant, he would either have held his peace or become Luther's admirer. It is the common lot of the godly to undergo "fearful tortures of conscience," by which they are made familiar with true humility. A man may even say, in times of unusual testing, that he is not only surrounded and beset by the agonies of death, but swallowed up by hell itself. For among the saints there are certain exceptional men whom God has chosen to be the special objects of his strange judgments. The echoes of characteristically Lutheran language in this passage are unmistakable, and they testify to Calvin's insight into the religious struggles of the German Reformer. He would not, I think, have wished to include himself among the *ex sanctis praestantissimi,* the exceptional religious personalities in whom the marvelous judgments of God are displayed. But "spiritual assaults" were not foreign to him, and he knew how Luther understood them theologically.

On the problem of the enslaved will Calvin steps forward as Luther's champion, except that he thinks it necessary to tone down some unguarded and exaggerated language. And he insists that, understood within their historical context, even Luther's extravagant expressions were justified. Pighius deplored, for instance, the fact that Luther was obliged, as a corollary of his views on the bondage of the will, to regard all human works as sins, and that he pressed this theme with gross exaggeration. Calvin replies:

I grant it, but still say that there was good reason that drove him to such exaggeration. He saw the world stupefied by a false and pernicious confidence in works, as if by a fatal lethargy. What was needed to awaken it was not voice and words, but the trumpet blast, thunder, and lightning.[58]

On the matter of "necessity" in providence and predestination Calvin refuses to be embarrassed by the accusation that there were inconsistencies in Protestant theology, not only between one theologian and another, but even within the writings of a single theologian. There is no reason why all should be expected to use precisely the same mode of expression, nor any reason why an author should be forbidden to improve what he has once written. The expression of the truth is always perfectible. Melanchthon, for example, has adapted to a more popular style much that Luther wrote in the scholastic mode *(scholastico dicendi genere)*. And for himself, Calvin's claim is this:

That which is most important in this question, and for the sake of which everything else is said, we defend today just as it was declared by Luther and others at the beginning; and even in what I have declared less necessary to faith my own concern has been to avoid offense by softening the mode of expression.[59]

In his treatise against Pighius Calvin sums up his understanding of Luther in a single sentence: "We regard him as a remarkable apostle of Christ, through whose work and ministry, most of all, the purity of the Gospel has been restored in our time."[60] The same picture of Luther reappears in the appeal to Charles V, written in the same year and laid before the Diet of Speier in 1544. The appeal was published "in the name of all who desire Christ to reign," under the long-winded title, *A Humble Exhortation to the Invincible Emperor, Charles V, and the Most Illustrious Princes and Other Orders Now Assembled at the Diet of Speier that They Should Choose Seriously to Undertake the Task of Restoring the Church.* (From the object of the appeal the treatise is commonly and more manageably titled *The Necessity for Reforming the Church*.) Here Calvin speaks of Luther as the man whom God raised up at the beginning, along with others, to hold a torch over the path to salvation.[61] Before Luther became known, all the world was bewitched by irreligious opinions about the merit of works.[62] But when the truth of God had been choked by thick clouds of darkness, and when religion had been corrupted by godless superstitions, Luther appeared and others after him, who took counsel together to purge religion from a host of defilements. "In this course," Calvin adds, "we still continue today."[63] He is particularly anxious to present his man as the reluctant reformer driven, against his intention, from protest to revolt. Luther pleaded with the pope to heal the maladies of the church. The plea fell on deaf ears.[64]

When Luther first appeared, he pointed gently to but a few abuses that were too gross to be endured any longer. So unassuming was he that he did not venture to correct them himself, but rather made it known that he longed to see them corrected. It was the opposing party that promptly sounded the call to arms. As the contention flared up, our enemies judged it the best and shortest way to suppress the truth with force and brutality. . . . And now we have to listen to the same reproach that the godless Ahab once brought against Elijah, that he was a troubler of Israel (1 Kings 18:17). But the holy prophet absolved us with his reply: "It is not I," he says, "but you and your father's house [that trouble Israel], for you have forsaken the Lord and gone after Baalim."[65]

We have it on reliable authority that Luther read the *Humble Exhortation* and gave it his glowing recommendation.[66] And well he might! Seldom has a more sympathetic and loyal picture of the Reformer been given outside the limits of his own communion. But one thing stands out clearly in the three treatises of the years 1541 and 1543: for all his devotion to Luther, Calvin never appeals to his ideas as though they were final or definitive. Luther, for him, was not an oracle but a pathfinder—a pioneer, in whose footsteps we follow and whose trail has to be pushed on further. We hurry on, still today, in the path he opened up.[67] The Reformation (if we may so express Calvin's meaning) is open-ended: it had its beginning in the person of that "remarkable apostle of Christ," but it did not end with him. It is this conviction of Calvin's that was sharpened after Luther's death, when a further round of eucharistic debates was opened.

V

The eucharistic controversies of the 1550s were evoked, in part, by the adoption of the Zurich Consensus (1549) as the bond of union between the French- and German-speaking Protestants of Switzerland.[68] In the eyes of the strict Lutherans the consensus showed Calvin in his true colors: all along, he had been one of the "sacramentarians." During the bitter quarrels that followed, Calvin made no attempt to revise his estimate of Luther, but he had to defend it openly on two fronts: against the Swiss, who detested the memory of Luther, and against the ultra-Lutherans, who (in Calvin's opinion) idolized him. And it must be admitted that he did not have much success with either. For the one group, the name of Luther could only evoke bitter recollections of the past, while in the eyes of the other group a nimbus had settled over the deceased Reformer's shoulders.

Calvin's battle may be read in his correspondence during the period. Against Luther's detractors he insisted that Luther could not but give his blessing to the new agreement among the Swiss on the doctrine of the Lord's Supper. He hon-

estly believed that he had discovered the fundamental point of Luther's contention for the real presence, that between the two of them there had never been
any disagreement on this point, and that since the point was now unambiguously
affirmed by the Swiss theologians Luther, were he alive, could not withold his
approval.

> If Luther, that distinguished servant of God and faithful doctor of the church,
> were alive today, he would not be so harsh and unyielding as not willingly to
> allow this confession: that what the sacraments figure is truly offered to us
> [*vere praestari*], and that therefore in the sacred Supper we become partici-
> pants in the body and blood of Christ. For how often did he declare that he
> was contending for no other cause than to establish that the Lord does not
> mock us with empty signs but accomplishes inwardly what he sets before our
> eyes, and that the effect is therefore conjoined with the signs?[69]

Many of the Swiss theologians were not impressed with Calvin's thoughts on
what Luther would doubtless do, were he alive. They found it astonishing that
he should persist in making himself Luther's champion.[70] With all the tact they
could muster, the pastors of Zurich put it down to Calvin's ignorance of German.

> Possibly you do not know, dear brother, how crassly and barbarously Doctor
> Luther thought and wrote concerning this spiritual feast. You have not been
> able to read or understand his books, since he wrote the greater part of this
> sort in German. . . . So that you may not be ignorant, therefore, of what it had
> been especially useful to know in this affair, we will rehearse a few particular
> passages of his. We give the substance faithfully but specify the page, so that,
> if you like, you can invite an interpreter skilled in the German language to
> translate for you word for word. And if you do not possess the books, we
> have them and shall be happy to lend them to you.[71]

As for Calvin's view that Luther would gladly give his hand to those who conceded
the union of the sacramental sign with the thing signified, the men of Zurich
retort: "Dear Calvin, he would *not* offer us his hand—that right hand which,
when living, he did not wish to offer to Zwingli and Oecolampadius, when they
were living, though they made all these same concessions and professions."[72]

As far as the other party was concerned—those who refused to move beyond
the details of Luther's own eucharistic teaching—Calvin consistently asserted,
and not very politely, that there is a difference between a disciple and an ape.[73]
This, admittedly, was not a choice of language that was apt to commend his
point. Still, the point was worth making, and he could, on occasion, deliver it
more courteously, though no less forcefully. Hence to one correspondent he
wrote, in reply to the charge that he did not always subscribe to the interpretations of Luther:

But if now it will not be permitted to each exegete to make public what he thinks about a particular passage of Scripture, to what kind of servitude are we reduced? Indeed, if I was not permitted at any point to depart from the opinion of Luther, it was utterly ridiculous of me to undertake the work of exegesis [*munus interpretandi*].[74]

What Calvin feared was that some of Luther's adherents would make their master's opinions the touchstone of dogmatic truth, thereby repudiating, in effect, Luther's own fundamental principle that the Word of God stands always above the doctrines of men.[75]

Once again, the evidence of the correspondence may be filled out by examining certain of Calvin's theological treatises: in particular, the treatise *On Scandals* (1550), the *Second Defense against Westphal* (1556), and the ironical work against Gabriel (1561).

Calvin has occasion more than once to speak of Luther in his work *On the Scandals by Which Many Today Are Deterred, and Some Even Alienated, from the Pure Doctrine of the Gospel*. For, as he himself remarks, "How many fables have Luther's enemies repeated about him, both in addresses and in published books, for a full five and twenty years!"[76] Among other things, the adversaries of the Protestants alleged that the Reformation was a kind of Trojan war—fought, that is, for the sake of women. Luther, they explained, was spurred on by the lust of the flesh and procured for himself the liberty to marry. It must be admitted that Calvin replies very much in kind. "What could be more ridiculous," he inquires, "than for those who cannot maintain chastity of life to flee from the papacy?"[77] But this, of course, is merely skirmishing beyond the real battle lines.

Of chief interest in the work *On Scandals* is what Calvin has to say on the scandal of a divided church.[78] For even "the most prominent teachers of the reborn gospel [*primarios renascentis evangelii doctores*]" are divided on matters of doctrine. Especially unhappy is the contention over the sacraments. Calvin finds it odd that the Protestant differences should somehow appear more scandalous than the fierce theological quarrels among the Roman schools. Further, he reminds the scandalized that among the faithful servants of God there have always been sharp disagreements, such as set Paul against Barnabas and Peter against Paul. But the controversy of Luther and his Protestant opponents, so he argues, moved within the lines of fundamental agreement on the nature of the gospel. "There was a remarkable consensus among them on all that is essential to godliness [*in tota pietatis summa*]." They agreed, for instance, that the whole of salvation resides in the grace of Christ, and they overthrew all confidence in works. "They extolled magnificently the excellence of Christ [*Christi virtutem*], which had lain prostrate or hidden from sight." Only on the sacraments was there dissension. And even on this question Calvin's considered opinion is that only polemical passion and mistrust delayed reconciliation. The miracle is that

Luther and others who labored in his day for the restoration of sound doctrine were able slowly to emerge from the darkness of ignorance and error. True, there are those who profess themselves offended because Luther and his contemporaries did not see everything in a flash, and they refuse to continue in the course already begun. But Calvin says of them:

> They are behaving just like the man who blames us because at the first break of dawn [*primo aurorae exortu*] we do not yet discern the midday sun.... Surely, those who talk like this are unwilling to allow progress to the servants of God or are distressed that the Kingdom of Christ should move on to something better.[79]

If one may so put it, Calvin here represents Luther, not John Wycliffe, as the "Morning Star of the Reformation." And it is plainly a continuing reformation that he has in mind—reformation as defined by "progress" (*profectus*) and "movement" (*promoveri*). Yet it is still movement from a fixed point, at which stands the extraordinary figure of Martin Luther, God's chosen pioneer.

Luther's name was invoked frequently in the debate between Calvin and Westphal, especially in Calvin's *Second Defense of the Godly and Orthodox Faith Concerning the Sacraments against the False Accusations of Joachim Westphal*. That Westphal, the ultra-Lutheran, appealed to Luther's memory, was natural enough.[80] But it is precisely Westphal's right to claim Luther as spiritual father that Calvin contests, recalling the warmth of his own friendship with the first generation of Lutheran Reformers. From the very beginning, when he was just emerging from the darkness of the papacy, he had been turned from Zwingli and Oecolampadius by his reading of Luther. Later, he was kindly received by all Luther's keenest advocates. And Luther's own judgment of him, after examining his writings, can easily be shown through reliable witnesses, including Melanchthon.[81] Calvin's respect for Luther remains unchanged. It is true that the German Reformer was sometimes carried away by his violent disposition, but the flame was sparked by mischief-makers.[82] And it is surely pathetic that some of Luther's followers should choose to mimic only his personal shortcomings. "Ah, Luther! How few imitators of your excellence have you left behind you—and how many apes of your holy belligerence!"[83] As for himself, Calvin rejects the charge that his *Commentary on Genesis* was crammed with harsh judgments on Luther, though he leaves us in no doubt that he found more to disapprove in Luther's own commentary than he chose to mention. "More than a hundred times I refrain, out of respect, from mentioning his name." But wherever he does name Luther, the "illustrious servant of Christ" is treated with all due honor.[84]

The point is, then, that although Calvin both regretted Luther's disposition and frankly dissented from some of his expressions,[85] he considered this the legitimate right of an avowed disciple; for the disciple, unlike the epigone, is one who *continues* in the course begun by his master. Calvin insists, as usual, that the *terminus a quo* for a genuine "Lutheran," as far as the Eucharist is concerned, is the efficacious character of sacramental signs. It is here that we have to begin, and not with those unfortunate exaggerations by which Luther himself advanced beyond the essential matter (*ultra . . . progressum esse*).[86] Dogmatic development, so it appears, is not always for the better (*in melius,* as Calvin wrote in the work *On Scandals*). Indeed, Calvin elsewhere speaks of certain of Luther's opinions as reactionary—a failure to free himself from medievalism, or perhaps a temporary accommodation to the times.[87] Therefore, not progress, but regress! The disciple's duty is to move on. Westphal, however, is like "the man who enters upon the right path, but, as soon as the one who showed him the path turns back, obstinately digs his heels into the one spot and refuses to move on further [*ultra progredi*]."[88]

The last of our sources for Calvin's views on Luther is his *Congratulation to the Venerable Presbyter Gabriel of Saconay, Precentor of the Church of Lyons, on the Beautiful and Elegant Preface Which He Wrote to the Book by the English King*. Gabriel had reissued Henry VIII's famous polemic against Luther and had furnished it with a preface. For relaxation, Calvin wrote his ironical response and published it anonymously, referring to himself throughout in the third person. Here we find once more judgments that are already familiar from the earlier sources. First, Luther was lacking in moderation. It is no wonder that he was shocked by Carlstadt's foolish invention, but he should have listened calmly to men like Occolampadius. In fact, he overstepped the limits and spoke in anger.[89] Second, it is preposterous to identify as "the last Elijah" either Luther or anyone else. (Gabriel had hinted that Calvin begrudged Luther the title only because he fancied it for himself.)[90] Third, Calvin again presents the idea of a reformation-in-progress. Only now the main thought is, not that the appearance of Luther was one event among others in a continuing movement, but that Luther's own thought was only gradually unfolded. Indeed, we can assume that, were he alive today, he would continue to make progress in the truth.

A key factor in the shaping of Luther's mind was the negative role played by his critics—a thought Calvin had already expressed in his work against Pighius.[91] The positions occupied by his critics forced Luther to more radical offenses against Rome. If, then, Luther once said that the kernel of Christianity is in the papacy, Calvin assures Gabriel that, were the Reformer still alive, he would take that saying back. For what would prevent him from making good progress (*in melius proficere*) in the space of thirty-three years?[92] It is quite true that Luther shifted his position on such matters as the papacy, purgatory, invocation of the saints, the sacrifice of the mass, celibacy, and confession.

But what, I beg you, was Luther to do at a time when but a faint spark of light had shone upon him? He disclosed, with sincerity, what he knew—that is, little more than nothing. . . . The wonder is that you do not charge him with failure to speak even before he emerged from his mother's womb.[93]

The import of these three treatises from the years 1550, 1556, and 1561 is transparently clear: Calvin wishes to claim for his reformation a continuity with the reformation of Martin Luther. But the claim of continuity is a claim of legitimate development, not of formal identity. In his own estimate, he does not merely transmit the heritage of Luther, but neither does he set his own reformation in opposition to Luther's.[94] In this sense Calvin, in the words of Peter Meinhold, was "the greatest and indeed the only 'disciple' that Luther had."[95] For only he had both the depth of understanding and the creative talents to fashion out of Luther's heritage something that bore the imprint of his own genius. This, at least, was how Calvin himself thought of his relationship to Luther. But it seems less lacking in modesty to have it said by someone other than Calvin.

VI

That Calvin's attitude toward Luther, as I have now described it, raises a whole host of historical and theological problems, hardly needs to be asserted. I have sought only to carry out the first-stage historical task of marshaling such evidence as seems most relevant to my limited theme: What did Calvin actually say about Martin Luther? But the further question suggests itself: Was Calvin right? Was he right in the way he understood his relationship to Luther? Of course, this question, too, is in part historical. But only in part. It also touches on points where theological commitments are at stake.

Even the historical aspects of the question are too complex to be readily solved. What Calvin said about Luther, including what he said about Luther's theology, is a manageable historical problem, which has been adequately handled more than once. But the existing literature is far less satisfactory, in my judgment, where it seeks to compare Luther and Calvin from a neutral standpoint beyond their judgments upon each other. It does not seem to me that historical scholarship has yet sorted out the elements of continuity and discontinuity between the two major Reformers. The attempt to enumerate their theological differences, even though it has often been carried out with sensitivity and insight,[96] leaves much to be desired. Contrasts are too quickly drawn and made to rest upon an insufficiently comprehensive examination of the sources, which are admittedly formidable in bulk for either Reformer alone. Divergent lines of thought are taken to represent a difference between Luther and Calvin, when a more thorough investigation would show that the divergence lies on both sides—

that it exemplifies, in fact, the complexity of a theological outlook which the two Reformers had in common. For example, both speak of faith as at once knowledge and trust, and both regard Scripture as at once inspired words and witness to the living Word, Jesus Christ. And yet, by means of "diagonal" comparisons which link the Reformers' unlike utterances instead of pairing the resemblances, it can be alleged that Calvin's idea of faith was more intellectual than Luther's and his understanding of Scripture more inclined toward literalism. By an equally judicious selection of sources the exact opposite could be "proved."[97]

Much more historical research is needed to determine whether seeming differences are really matters of emphasis or even wholly illusory. Only then can we decide how far Calvin was in fact what he claimed to be, a genuine disciple of Luther. However, setting aside this problem for the moment, I content myself with stressing two conclusions of my present theme, which has been concerned only with Calvin's explicit judgments on Martin Luther. In each of these conclusions my interest is in the shape or form of Calvin's thinking rather than in its specific content. I do not ask whether his reading of Luther and the Reformation was correct in detail, but what kind of a reading it was.

In the first place, whether materially justified or not, Calvin's estimate of Luther was historical, not dogmatic, in form. He viewed Luther and the Reformation from a progressive, not an absolutist, perspective, reading Luther's story as a gradual unfolding of the gospel in its various historical relationships—a process in which Luther's opponents played a key role. Calvin rejected not only every effort to elevate Luther's teaching to the status of finished dogma but also any temptation to remove the person of Luther beyond the categories of history—to make him, so to say, an apocalyptic rather than a prophetic figure. Though divinely called, the Reformer was not himself a supernatural person. Calvin did not even object to Luther's being called by the name of Elijah. What he repudiated was the eschatological language which identified him as "the Last Elijah."[98]

It is hardly too much to claim, with Ernst Walter Zeeden,[99] that Calvin anticipated the pietistic-Enlightenment idea of the historical character (the *Geschichtlichkeit*) of Luther and of the Reformation. This is, I think, particularly clear in the treatise against Pighius, where we have found Calvin arguing that theological truth is not formulated once and for all. The *actus tradendi* is also *actus formandi:* "If Pighius does not know it," he wrote, "I want to make this plain to him: our constant effort, day and night, is also to *fashion,* in the manner we think will be best, whatever is faithfully *handed on* by us."[100] This, of course, was not intended by Calvin to allow for changing the content of the Faith. He meant precisely that in the theological task *formare* is always *fideliter tradere,* even though the handing on cannot leave the mode of expression unchanged. Hence he went on to state in these words Melanchthon's intention in preparing the Augsburg Confession: "He had no other wish than to abide by that doctrine which alone is proper to the Church and necessary for saving knowledge."[101]

No doubt, such an interpretation of the theological task is extremely hard to implement, precisely because it poses so acutely the problem of continuity. It does not really furnish exact norms but is rather an announcement of good intentions. Calvin was obliged to argue, for instance, that one could disentangle Luther's essential concern in the eucharistic debates from certain accidental crudities of expression. He never denied that Luther and he disagreed on the idea of an oral manducation *(de substantiali manducatione)*. Yet he believed that he had recognized—and, indeed, presented in Luther's own words—the reason why the German Reformer pressed his eucharistic doctrine with such passion:[102] he had kept inviolate Luther's sacramental principle, which stood above their theological differences and was therefore capable of furnishing the basis of unity-in-diversity. But how do we judge what is essential and what is accidental? This is the difficulty in all attempts to "continue the Reformation."

The modern liberal Protestant may turn on Luther and Calvin alike with the judgment that they both stood aside from the real line of progress, which was opened up by Servetus and Socinus. "In the name of progress in Biblical theology," it has been said, "modern Protestantism will proceed to a critical revision of dogma, which the Reformers did not undertake."[103] Here Calvin's own principle of development is, in effect, directed against Calvin himself. But in a sense this serves only to validate his own fundamental point that an earlier theological achievement, however magnificent, cannot relieve the church of the duties of exegesis and dogmatics. Moreover, one can also recognize from his arguments against Westphal that he would by no means concede the subjectivity of his quest for Luther's essential concern. For if he was wrong about Luther, and if, as Westphal argued, Luther condemned indifferently all who denied his understanding of the real presence, how could the unquestionable sympathy between the two Reformers be explained? This is the question that Calvin threw back at Westphal.[104]

In the second place, Calvin's estimate of Luther points to a pluralistic reading of Reformation history, according to which no one party or individual had full possession of the truth. This has to be added to the former conclusion for an obvious reason. It would be easy to assume that Calvin's sole purpose in viewing Luther's work as imperfect was to represent his own work as perfect—or, at least, as very much better. There is, I think, something in this. He does seem, on occasion, to fall into the common illusion of the "progressivist," who may picture the movement of history coming to a halt in his own system. And it cannot be denied that his self-estimate frequently stood in need of the same wisdom he displayed in his sentiments about Luther. Calvin, as we all know, could be dogmatic, overbearing, annoyingly self-confident, and acrimonious in criticism. He possessed a keen theological intellect and was ruthless in exposing the confusions of less gifted rivals. Moreover, he was stubbornly certain that he spoke as God's mouthpiece, although, as he engagingly assures us, he did not make up his mind on a certain matter until he had considered it more than three times.[105] From all of which it certainly seems as though Calvin did not really believe in an *ecclesia reformans,* but merely dated the finished reformation to coincide with his own life and work; so that a fixed norm appears, after all, to be the supposed outcome of the sixteenth-century struggle within the Western church. It must be replied, however, that this appearance is not the whole picture.

If Calvin thought of himself as God's mouthpiece, he thought of Luther in the same way, and this did not prevent him from regarding Luther as fallible.[106] Further, it could be demonstrated from a host of citations that he really did believe in that *gemeinsames Hören,* that hearing the Word along with others, which has been missed in the writings of Luther.[107] In the *Short Treatise on the Lord's Supper* his claim is that the truth lay in the dialogue, not on either side of it, and his conclusion is notably undogmatic.[108] In the negotiations that led to the Zurich Consensus he engaged in a remarkably frank correspondence with Heinrich Bullinger, in which each really listened to the criticisms of the other.[109] Further, it could be pointed out that Calvin disapproved on principle of the drafting of confessions of faith by a single hand, citing the legendary origin of the Apostles' Creed in his support.[110] Finally, he longed to see the assembling of an international congress of theologians which might produce a unified Evangelical witness.[111]

In all these ways, Calvin revealed his consciousness of standing under the Word of God along with others. But perhaps the most striking token of his "pluralistic" attitude toward the Reformation and its theology is the interesting phenomenon of the Genevan "congregations," at which the Reformed pastors from the surrounding territory, together with a handful of devout lay people, gathered together to discuss some prearranged passage of Scripture. Calvin believed firmly that this was the proper manner to carry out the interpretation of Scripture. "For as long as there is no mutual exchange, each can teach what he likes. Solitude provides too much liberty."[112] In the last year of his life, when he was too ill to teach or preach, Calvin still—against the counsel of his anxious friends—made his painful way to the Friday morning congregation, whenever he could, and there "added that which God had given him to say upon the text."[113] Practice here coincides perfectly with the principles which he prefaced to his *Commentary on Romans* and which have sometimes been identified with the "apology" he promised to the Lutherans in 1539:

God has never seen fit to bestow such favor on his servants that each individually should be endowed with full and perfect knowledge on every point. No doubt, his design was to keep us both humble and eager for brotherly communication. In this life, then, we should not hope for what otherwise would be most desirable, that there should be continual agreement among us in understanding passages of Scripture. We must therefore take care that, if we depart from the opinions of those who went before us, we do not do so because excited by the itch after novelty, nor driven by fondness for deriding others, nor goaded by animosity, nor tickled by ambition, but only because compelled by pure necessity and with no other aim than to be of service.[114]

In so writing Calvin was loyal to the intention of Luther himself, for whom the Word of God is not given up to the control of any man or any institution, but continually creates for itself a fellowship of hearers and doers.

Part Two   Reformation Principles

Three   The Word of God
and the Words of Scripture:
Luther and Calvin
on Biblical Authority

That the distinctively Protestant understanding of biblical authority can be grasped only by seeing it against its medieval background, may appear to be a truism. But the affirmation is necessary, if for no other reason, at least because the relationship of Protestantism to Roman Catholicism has too often been interpreted as one of simple opposition. In part, the Reformers' understanding of biblical authority arose directly out of Scholasticism not by conscious opposition, but by unquestioning acceptance. The differentia of Protestantism cannot be defined simply by appeal to the so-called formal and material principles, unless the twin principles are themselves carefully defined. There was nothing new in the mere fact that the Reformers resorted to the Bible for verification of their theological convictions, or even in their insistence on the necessity of grace for salvation: the medieval church had a rigorous doctrine of biblical inspiration, and it found grace as indispensable for justification as did the Reformers themselves.

I

No doubt the earliest disciples took their view of inspiration and authority from Judaism. To begin with, their Scriptures were the Jewish Scriptures, and they themselves were Jews. But it was natural enough that the Jewish belief in verbal inspiration should persist even after the church had become predominantly Gentile. The authority of Scripture was made to rest on a concept (or an image) of inspiration: the words of Scripture were binding because, in the last analysis, they were the words of God. The inspired writers were no more than the Spirit's pen, and the finished product was a sacred text inerrant in all its parts.[1]

The emphatic biblicism of the early church, which passed into the main stream of medieval thought, was qualified, however, by the growth of allegorization. According to Origen, the Scriptures admit of a threefold interpretation: as a man has a body, a soul, and a spirit, so the Scriptures have a bodily or literal sense, a psychical or moral sense, and a spiritual or symbolic sense. And it is the last that is regarded as the highest.[2] To be sure, the practice of allegorical exegesis never went unchallenged: the school of Alexandria was opposed by the school of Antioch, and both had their successors in the Middle Ages. St. Thomas himself expressed strong reservations about the use of allegory.[3] Nevertheless, the practice of fanciful "spiritual" interpretation was a limitation on the medieval church's avowed principles of biblical authority and inspiration: a sufficiently astute theologian could, without much difficulty, find any of the church's beliefs hidden or symbolized in the most unlikely corners of both the Old and the New Testaments.

A second limiting factor, which also tended to modify the effectiveness of the biblical norm, was the power of the ecclesiastical hierarchy. The only way to check heresy was by appeal to an authority apart from Scripture, for (notoriously) the heretic makes use of Scripture no less than the orthodox. The Bible remained the professed authority, but in fact there was a second authority that controlled it. Augustine repeatedly declares that his supreme norm and standard is the Scriptures; yet it is the church that decides what is and what is not Scripture, and it is the church that guarantees their authority and interprets their meaning.[4] Thomas attributes a certain necessity to biblical arguments, which in theory raises them above all merely probable arguments from secondary authorities;[5] yet, in practice, his premises are drawn impartially from the Bible, the fathers, and "the Philosopher." In Duns Scotus the either-or is stated explicitly: "Nothing is to be held as of the substance of the faith except that which can be expressly derived from Scripture or which is expressly declared by the church. . . ."[6] Equally unambiguous, it appears, are two pronouncements of the Council of Trent (1545-63): that the church's traditions are to be received with the same devotion as the Scriptures, and that the Scriptures themselves must be understood only according to the sense held by Holy Mother Church. The question: Who shall speak for the Holy Mother? was not finally determined until a century ago, when, by the promulgation of *Pastor Aeternus* (1870), the First Vatican Council made it clear that the authority of the Roman Church is virtually the unique authority of the pope.[7]

The attitude of the Nominalists to biblical authority is of particular importance for understanding Luther's standpoint, since Erfurt, where he learned his theology, was a stronghold of Occamism. It is significant that the advocates of the *via moderna* stressed the authority of Scripture even more forcefully than their predecessors. Occam, indeed, plays off the Bible against the pope. Yet fundamentally he is a "catholic," and his appeal is not from the church but only from the pope. Hence, in the preface to his *Compend of Papal Errors,* he writes as an obedient son of the Roman Church: "I submit myself and my words to the correction of the Catholic Church."[8] While, therefore, he can affirm both the sufficiency and the inerrancy of the Bible, Occam is still content to accept the admittedly nonbiblical dogma of transubstantiation simply on the church's authority.[9] The truth is that any idea of an actual *discrepancy* between the teaching of the Bible and the beliefs of the "Catholic Church" is far from the thoughts of any of the Nominalists.

What was new, then, about Luther's and Calvin's use of the biblical norm? Where did they depart from the principles and practice of the Schoolmen? The answer revolves around a cluster of three closely related problems, for which we may use the provisional rubrics "the authority, the character, and the interpretation of Scripture." The second and third are treated here as subordinate to the first—and, indeed, are discussed only insofar as they throw light upon it. The first and third speak for themselves. By "character" I intend to suggest the fundamental question: What does the Bible consist of? Two replies are of special importance for the problem of authority in Luther and Calvin: the one maintains that the Bible consists of sacred oracles, the other that it consists of testimony to God's revelation. The expression "content of Scripture" could perhaps be employed equally well.

II

As early as the *Marginal Notes on the Sentences of Peter Lombard,* Luther shows the utmost respect for biblical authority, in one place dismissing the opinion of several eminent doctors precisely on the grounds that they do not have Scripture on their side.[10] But this does not mean that he was already a Protestant in 1510, since there is nothing in this curt dismissal that could not equally well have been written by Occam, D'Ailli, or Biel. And we must say the same of similar assertions that are to be found in the *Lectures on the Psalms* (1513-15): it is not Moses, but God himself who speaks; God speaks through the prophets; the prophet desires only to be the Spirit's instrument. This is the way Luther likes to speak of the men to whom and through whom God revealed himself, and he clearly thinks of the Scriptures as a faithful record in writing of what God said— what was actually heard from his very mouth. Indeed, in the Gospel we virtually hear the Lord speaking now.[11]

By the time of his *Lectures on Romans* (1515-16), Luther had come to conceive of his mission as a protest against philosophy in the name of Scripture: "I for my part believe that I owe the Lord this duty of speaking out against philosophy and of persuading men to heed Holy Scripture."[12] In May 1517 he wrote to a friend that Aristotle was on the way out, that the Bible and Augustine (or some other doctor of real standing) would alone find an ear in his university.[13] Yet for all this, in September of the same year he could conclude his ninety-seven theses *Against Scholastic Theology* with a model expression of pious submission to the Church.[14]

The turning point seems to have been occasioned by the Leipzig debate of 1519, in which Eck revealed (to Luther himself as much as to anyone else) the true logic of the Reformer's protest. That Luther still revered the Roman Church on the very eve of the debate, appears from a letter written on 5 March 1519: "It was never my intention to secede from the Apostolic Roman See; I am content that it should be called, or even should be, the lord of all."[15] But in the course of the debate (held in July) Luther was finally driven to assert the principle *scriptura sola*—the Bible *alone* in all matters of faith. The immediate occasion for his outburst was the charge of "Bohemianism."

> As for the article of Hus that "it is not necessary for salvation to believe the Roman Church superior to all others," I do not care whether this comes from Wyclif or from Hus. I know that innumerable Greeks have been saved though they never heard this article. It is not in the power of the Roman pontiff or of the Inquisition to construct new articles of faith. No believing Christian can be coerced beyond holy writ. By divine law we are forbidden to believe anything which is not established by divine Scripture or manifest revelation.[16]

Luther summed up his position the next year (1520) in the oft-quoted words of the *Babylonian Captivity:* "Whatever is asserted without scriptural proofs [*sine scripturis*] or an accredited revelation may be held as an opinion, but need not be believed."[17] And the final, culminating affirmation must be reckoned to be Luther's famous reply at the Diet of Worms (18 April 1521) when asked to recant:

> Since then Your Majesty and your lordships desire a simple reply, I will answer without horns and without teeth. Unless I am convicted by Scripture and plain reason—I do not accept the authority of popes and councils, for they have contradicted each other—my conscience is captive to the Word of God. I cannot and I will not recant anything, for to go against conscience is neither right nor safe. [Here I stand, I cannot do otherwise.] God help me. Amen.[18]

The distinctive element in this affirmation is really what it denies rather than what it affirms. What marks Luther off from the Scholastics (and especially from the Nominalists) is not that he asserts the authority of the Bible but that he denies the authority of church and pope. There is an implicit *sola* in his declaration before the Diet of Worms, and it is this that makes his stand revolutionary.

To turn to the second problem—the content or character of the Scriptures—does not mean leaving the question of authority behind; the problem is to see how authority is related to content. Does Luther establish the authority of Scripture on a theory of inspiration, or does he regard Scripture as authoritative because it is a witness to revelation? The answer is, I think, that whereas the Schoolmen took the first alternative, Luther oscillates between the two.

On the one hand, Luther repeatedly declares that the content of Scripture is Christ, and from this fact he seems to derive its authority. Christ is the *punctus mathematicus sacrae scripturae:* all Scripture turns about him as its true center.[19] This holds for the Old Testament no less than for the New: "Here you will find the swaddling cloths and the manger in which Christ lies.... Simple and lowly are these swaddling cloths, but dear is the treasure, Christ, who lies in them."[20] It is this christocentric principle that explains, in part, Luther's high regard for St. Paul: "Paul always has Christ on his lips and cannot forget Him."[21] Indeed, this same principle affords him what is virtually a test of canonicity:

> All the genuine sacred books agree in this, that all of them preach and inculcate [*treiben*] Christ. And that is the true test by which to judge all books, when we see whether or not they inculcate Christ. For all the Scriptures show us Christ, Romans 3[:21]; and St. Paul will know nothing but Christ, 1 Corinthians 2[:2]. Whatever does not teach Christ is not yet apostolic, even though St. Peter or St. Paul does the teaching. Again, whatever preaches Christ would be apostolic even if Judas, Annas, Pilate, and Herod were doing it.[22]

This enables Luther to formulate an inner canon—a canon *within* the canon. "John's Gospel and St. Paul's epistles, especially that to the Romans, and St. Peter's first epistle are the true kernel and marrow of all the books."[23] And it also enables him to dismiss James as a letter of straw, of which he can exclaim: "One of these days I'll use Jimmy to light the fire!" The condemnation is simply that the writer names Christ several times but teaches nothing about him.[24] For it is not the mere *mention* of Christ that Luther applauds (though this is sometimes what he appears to be saying) but *preaching* Christ: that is, presenting him as Savior from sin.[25]

On the other hand—equally clearly—Luther repeatedly appeals to Scripture as authoritative on the grounds that it is the Word of God, verbally inspired by the activity of the Holy Spirit. That is to say, he takes the former of my two alternatives. "The Holy Scripture is God's Word written—spelled (so to say) and in the form of letters, as Christ is the eternal Word of God veiled in human nature."[26] "We refer all Scripture to the Holy Spirit." The Spirit "speaks through" the human agent. Hence we may say that, in effect, "Holy Scripture has been spoken by the Holy Spirit."[27] "Not only the words [*vocabula*] but also the expression [*phrasis*] that the Holy Spirit and the Scripture employ is divine."[28] Of Peter and Paul Luther writes that God would have us reverence, not their apostolate, but "the Christ who speaks in them and the Word of God itself that proceeds from their mouth."[29] Perhaps the most remarkable testimony to his strict view of verbal inspiration arises out of the sacramentarian controversy and the interpretation of the words: "This is my body." Luther maintains that "these words were spoken by the mouth of God." He is at pains to insist that every word in the sentence is divine; therefore, the *is* is inescapable. We must not trifle with God's words as they do who force the word *est* to mean "signifies."[30] Indeed, he seems himself to have desired to twist the words of institution in precisely this way. "I confess that if Dr. Karlstadt, or anyone else, could have convinced me five years ago that only bread and wine were in the sacrament he would have done me a great service.... But I am captive and cannot free myself. The text is too powerfully present, and will not allow itself to be torn from its meaning by mere verbiage."[31] There is no reason to doubt Luther's honesty in this piece of autobiography, and it certainly is a remarkable testimony to his attitude to biblical authority.

There are, then, so it appears, two distinct answers in Luther to the question: Wherein lies the authority of Scripture? He replies, on the one hand, that Scripture is authoritative because it bears witness to God; and, on the other hand, that Scripture is authoritative because it is the verbally inspired Word of God. Of course, there is not necessarily a contradiction between these two points of view; but the distinction is important because the first answer has seemed to many to provide a way of combining authority with biblical criticism. The attempt has accordingly been made to show that Luther himself was something of a higher critic.

An impressive list of instances is brought forward by Reinhold Seeberg, which is alleged to demonstrate that "Luther employed 'criticism' in the widest variety of forms. Almost all the criteria employed at the present day were applied by him in his own way." (1) The text of the prophets has often fallen into confusion. (2) The prophets were often in error. (3) The Books of the Kings are more trustworthy than Chronicles. (4) By whom Genesis was composed is a matter of indifference. (5) It would be better if the Book of Esther were not in the canon. (6) The composition of Ecclesiastes by Solomon is doubtful. (7) The reports in the Synoptic Gospels are not of uniform value. (8) The Letter of Jude is derived from the second Letter of Peter. (9) The Letter to the Hebrews errs in denying a second repentance. (10) James wrote a letter of straw. (11) The Apocalypse is not to be regarded as an apostolic book.[32]

The list of critical judgments is certainly very striking, and it could no doubt be extended. But one ought to ask what exactly it proves. In particular, is this kind of criticism necessarily inconsistent with a belief in verbal inerrancy? Of the examples given by Seeberg one (the first) relates to textual or lower criticism: three (nos. 4, 6, and 8) relate to authorship; and four (nos. 5, 9, 10, and 11) to canonicity.[33] Only three (nos. 2, 3, and 7) appear to relate to errors in the original text of canonical writings, and there are Luther scholars (M. Reu, for example) who find it possible to maintain that even these three are inconclusive. If Luther admits that the prophets err, he does not admit that there are errors in the prophecies transmitted to us in the canonical Scriptures. If 1 and 2 Kings are more trustworthy than Chronicles, that is not because the Chronicles contain errors but because the Books of the Kings include richer detail. If there are apparent discrepancies in the narratives of the four Gospels, this is not because the Evangelists made errors of chronology but because they never intended to present a strictly chronological narrative at all. Obviously, such explanations as these cannot be proved either true or false. The most one can say is that they are possible.[34] But it does seem clear that Luther never questioned the medieval theory of inspiration, although some would add that he provided a way of escape from it.

The third problem, Luther's interpretation of Scripture, can be dismissed more briefly, since I am concerned with interpretation only insofar as it bears on the problem of authority. The pertinent exegetical principles can be summed up under five major heads. First, the literal meaning is to be preferred to the allegorical when we are seeking to establish points of doctrine. To the principle "Scripture alone" Luther adds the further principle "the historical sense alone." Allegories may be used *afterwards*—as ornaments, not as proofs. Even then we must observe the analogy of faith: "that is, accommodate them to Christ, the church, faith, and the ministry of the Word."[35] Second, Luther insists that the understanding of Scripture is fundamentally simple. Partly, this is asserted in opposition to the Roman Church's claim that only the pope can interpret Scripture—a view against which Luther argues in the *Address to the German Nobility*.[36] Elsewhere he asserts that "the Holy Spirit is the simplest writer and adviser in heaven and on earth. That is why his words could have no more than the one simplest meaning, which we call . . . the literal meaning."[37] This does not mean that Luther neglects scholarship; on the contrary, with the utmost respect he calls the literary skills of humanism "forerunners of the Gospel," as John the Baptist was forerunner to Christ.[38] Third, Luther believes that many difficulties can be cleared up—and many errors evaded—by interpreting each passage in the light of the biblical message as a whole. Scripture is its own interpreter.[39] Fourth, however, his method is not purely technical; the Scriptures must always be understood in faith. We must feel the words of Scripture in the heart. Experience is necessary for understanding the Word, which must be lived and felt.[40] Fifth—and this is perhaps another way of saying the same thing—we must listen to the voice of the same Spirit who wrote the Scriptures.[41] In the light of affirmations such as these, we can understand Luther's characteristic dicta that "it is better to leave reason at home" and submit to Scripture; or that "even the humble miller's maid, nay, a child of nine if it has faith," can understand the Bible.[42]

To sum up, Luther affirmed the authority of Scripture as emphatically as any of the medieval Schoolmen; but what is far more significant, he insisted on the principle of *scriptura sola* and refused (in principle) to be led astray by allegorical exegesis. "It is the emphasis upon the *sole* rather than the *supplementary* character of the ultimate Scriptural norm that distinguishes the Reformers from their predecessors." Paul Lehmann's remark correctly points to one side of the cardinal issue.[43] The other side is well stated by Emil Brunner: "The struggle of the Reformers for the sole supremacy of Scripture as the doctrinal authority was ... only significant in the fact that at the same time they followed the line of the literal historical and philological exposition of the Scriptures."[44] But this is to speak only of what was fresh and distinctive in Luther's approach to biblical authority. As Lehmann and Brunner both contend, insofar as his thinking followed unquestioningly lines already laid down in the Middle Ages (and earlier), Luther bequeathed a problem to later Protestantism: how to reconcile verbal inspiration and the claims of biblical criticism. Along with the problem he may have bequeathed a partial solution, and both the problem and the solution will be reserved for further comment in the conclusion (sec. IV). But first, the question must be asked how far Luther's view of biblical authority was perpetuated by Calvin.

III

Calvin's view of Scripture is put together mainly, though by no means exclusively, in the first book of the 1559 *Institutes*. He introduces the Bible as a supplementary aid, in addition to God's disclosure of himself in mankind's innate awareness of him (chap. 3) and in the works of creation and providence (chap. 5). The Scriptures are like a pair of spectacles that clarify weak and defective vision.[45] So grave is mankind's religious myopia that, without the Word, there would be no sound perception of God in the world at all. "In order that true religion may shine upon us, we ought to hold that it must take its beginning from heavenly doctrine and that no one can get even the slightest taste of right and sound doctrine unless he be a pupil of Scripture."[46]

The natural awareness of God (the *sensus divinitatis*) serves, in practice, only to render man inexcusable, since he deliberately smothers it. Calvin denies that the inborn knowledge of God can ever be totally extinguished; it can be distorted (in the form of superstition and idolatry), or suppressed (by denial of God's providence if not of his existence), but never annihilated.[47] He is caught, in fact, between two necessities: on the one hand, the light of nature must be bright enough to render man's ignorance culpable; and, on the other hand, it must not be so bright as to render unnecessary the light of the Word. The problem is solved by his understanding of human sinfulness: there is no defect in the revelation of God in the workmanship of creation, but it is nullified by man's perverseness. Therefore, although Calvin apparently has two sources of knowing God—nature and Scripture—only one is of immediate normative significance. This is the position he has reached by the conclusion of book one, chapter 6. In chapter 10 he rounds off the argument by a comparison between the content of the revelation in God's works and the content of the revelation in Scripture.[48] The chapters in between (7-9) are a parenthesis on the authority of Scripture,[49] and it is with these that we have to do—primarily, but not of course exclusively— as we ask about Calvin's views on the authority, inspiration (or "character"), and interpretation of Scripture.

The formal principle, which in Luther was expressed by the characteristic formula *scriptura sola,* appears in Calvin as a more fully articulated doctrine of sufficiency. The sufficiency of Scripture is repeatedly affirmed both in its negative and in its positive form: we are not to look outside of Scripture for guidance on faith and morals, since Scripture contains everything we may require. Calvin insists on the impiety both of holding beliefs that cannot be demonstrated from Scripture and of failing to hold fast anything that can. The principle of sufficiency applies to faith, morals, rites, and even matters that fall outside any of these three categories.

The sufficiency of Scripture in matters of *belief* is nowhere more strictly adhered to than in Calvin's treatment of predestination: he believes in the double decree (of election and reprobation) only because he finds himself forced to do so by the Word of God. He accordingly addresses some severe remarks to two classes of men: the curious, who want to know more than God is pleased to reveal, and the reticent, who are willing to keep silent about what God has in fact revealed. To the first class he says:

> Let this, therefore, first of all be before our eyes: to seek any other knowledge of predestination than what the Word of God discloses is not less insane than if one should purpose to walk in a pathless waste [cf. Job 12:24], or to see in darkness.

And to the second:

> Scripture is the school of the Holy Spirit, in which, as nothing is omitted that is both necessary and useful to know, so nothing is taught but what is expedient to know.

And to both:

> I desire only to have them generally admit that we should not investigate what the Lord has left hidden in secret, that we should not neglect what he

has brought into the open, so that we may not be convicted of excessive curiosity on the one hand, or of excessive ingratitude on the other.[50]

Parallel admonitions are to be found in the discussion of providence, where the theological difficulties are much the same as in the doctrine of predestination. There Calvin concludes with an emphatic declaration of biblical authority: "Our wisdom ought to be nothing else than to embrace with humble teachableness ... whatever is taught in Sacred Scripture."[51]

Similar affirmations are made on matters of *morals,* in which the Church of Rome, in Calvin's eyes, had presumed to add to the explicit requirements of God's Word. In his discussion of the moral law he roundly condemns the "irreligious affectation of religion" that dares to usurp the place of God's law and to substitute an endless host of human inventions. He takes his stand on Moses' warning: "Everything that I command you, you shall be careful to do; you shall not add to it or take from it" (Deut. 12:32), and comments:

> The best remedy to cure that fault [of devising new duties] will be to fix
> this thought firmly in mind: the law has been divinely handed down to us to
> teach us perfect righteousness; there no other righteousness is taught than
> that which conforms to the requirements of God's will; in vain therefore do
> we attempt new forms of works to win the favor of God, whose lawful worship
> consists in obedience alone.[52]

In other words, Calvin's principle is: *Quod non iubet, vetat*—what God has not expressly enjoined, he means to prohibit. "In his law the Lord has included everything applicable to the perfect rule of the good life, so that nothing is left to men to add to that summary."[53]

Calvin's attitude to *rites* may be illustrated from his comments on the Eucharist:

> There is ... nothing safer than for us to lay aside all the presumption of
> human understanding, and to cleave solely to what Scripture teaches. And
> surely, if we ponder that the Supper is of the Lord and not of men, there is
> no reason why we should allow ourselves to be moved even a hairsbreadth
> from it by any human authority or time-hallowed prescription.[54]

Again, of the alleged necessity for episcopal confirmation he remarks ironically: "I thought that everything pertaining to Christianity was prescribed and included in the Scriptures."[55]

Surprisingly, however, Calvin's principle of biblical sufficiency does not seem to be limited to "everything pertaining to Christianity." There are passages in the *Institutes* where he seems to be saying that Scripture contains, not merely all that can be known concerning our salvation, but all that is worth knowing.[56] This does not mean, however, that he considered the Bible an exhaustive treatise on all conceivable subjects; it rather implies a severe limitation on what is to be thought worth knowing. We may say, quite simply, that worth knowing in Calvin's view is precisely whatever concerns our salvation: the knowledge of God and of ourselves. Indeed, he can speak not merely of what it is profitable, but even of what it is legitimate, to know: we must not try to go beyond the lawful boundary of wisdom. Almost all men are infected with the disease of wanting to acquire useless knowledge, but one thing alone is sufficient: the knowledge of the love of Christ.[57]

The important feature of Calvin's doctrine of authority, then, is his insistence on the Bible's absolute sufficiency as the Christian's guide to belief and conduct. And the doctrine is certainly maintained with extraordinary consistency throughout the *Institutes*, as Calvin proceeds in his endeavor to provide a systematic "sum of religion in all its parts."[58] He condescends at times to point out certain parallels between Christian truth and the opinions of the philosophers; but these parallels never really attain to the status of proofs, and pious readers do not need them.[59] Nor is he able to understand how anyone could bring himself to doubt what the Scriptures clearly teach. He deplores the arrogance—the blasphemy even—of those who, confronted with the plain meaning of Scripture, can still say: "To me it seems otherwise."[60]

On what grounds did Calvin base his confidence in the authority of Scripture? This brings us to our second problem once again: the character or content of the Bible. He can maintain as strongly as Luther that the unity of the Bible's content is to be sought in its revelation of Christ; and just because he severely circumscribes the domain of true wisdom, he can propose the Scripture's testimony to Christ as a kind of hermeneutic limit:

> This is what we should . . . seek in the whole of Scripture: truly to know Jesus Christ, and the infinite riches that are comprised in him and are offered to us by him from God the Father. If one were to sift thoroughly the Law and the Prophets, he would not find a single word which would not draw and bring us to him. And for a fact, since all the treasures of wisdom and understanding are hidden in him, there is not the least question of having, or turning toward, another goal. . . . Our minds ought to come to a halt at the point where we learn in Scriptue to know Jesus Christ and him alone, so that we may be directly led by him to the Father who contains in himself all perfection.[61]

Even the law is to be understood strictly from the christological point of view. It is nothing but a dead letter if cut off from the grace of Christ. "But if through the Spirit it is really branded upon hearts, if it shows forth Christ, it is the word of life."[62] This single sentence, though strictly it is about the letter of the law (as Paul speaks of it in 2 Cor. 3:6), might well be taken to summarize Calvin's view of the written Word in general: the words in which the Christian message is presented become the Word of life as, by the action of the Holy Spirit, they offer Christ.[63]

Calvin has his own favorite way of expressing the christological unity of Scripture by relating it to the idea of the "covenant." For him the theme of the whole Bible is the one convenant of grace, and the mediator of the convenant is Christ. Of course, he speaks of the "old" covenant and the "new"; but he admits no difference of substance between them, only a difference in the manner of their dispensation. The Old Testament and the New both set forth Christ, and in this lies their identity of substance: the patriarchs were saved by faith in Christ; the law prefigures Christ; the prophets foretell Christ; and so on. Hence the Incarnation was the full manifestation of the Christ seen dimly and distantly in the law and the prophets. The light had already dawned under the old dispensation, though in the first promise—made to Adam (Gen. 3:15)—it merely glowed like a feeble spark. It grew from day to day until, at last, Christ the Sun of Righteousness arose (cf. Mal. 4:2) and shed the fullness of his rays over the whole earth.[64]

Calvin's strong emphasis on the christological content of the Scriptures leads him, in an interesting argument, to propose a restrictive use of the expression "Word of God." The words that present Christ to us are, strictly speaking, the promises. Accordingly, when he turns to his discussion of faith (in book three, chapter two), Calvin first maintains that faith and the Word belong together, then argues that not every word of God is the proper object of faith, but only the promises: that is, those words that show him as merciful father. And since these words of promise are found in Jesus Christ, who is the pledge of God's love, the object of faith is precisely defined as "the freely given promise in Christ."[65] This remarkable line of argument plunged Calvin into controversy, since one of his Roman Catholic adversaries, Albert Pighius, pointed out that apparently the Protestants did not, after all, believe all the words of God. Calvin replied that of course faith believes every word of God, but it *rests* solely on the promises given in Christ. In short, the "word of *faith*," as the Apostle calls it (Rom. 10:8), is the gospel.[66]

These interesting reflections on the goal of Scripture study, the unity of the Testaments, and the word of faith are seldom given their due in the secondary literature. But it may still be argued, with Edward A. Dowey, that Calvin did not adequately relate his doctrine of faith and his doctrine of authority;[67] for while his faith was strongly christocentric, he continued to work with the Bible—in the medieval fashion—as an external and formal authority. He could not have approached the Bible with the remarkable freedom that Luther displayed (at one stage of his career); and while Luther could cheerfully offer to set his doctor's cap on any man's head who could reconcile Paul and James, Calvin gravely tried, in effect, to earn it.[68] Certain books of the Bible do seem to have given Calvin difficulty: notably, the Apocalypse and the Song of Songs, on neither of which did he write a commentary. But if the significance of the Revelation of John the Divine eluded him, this did not prevent him from occasionally citing it as Scripture. And if he never ventured to write a commentary on the Song of Songs, he judged Castellio unfit to be a minister on the grounds *(inter alia)* that he spoke of it as a lascivious love-poem.[69]

For Calvin, in practice, the whole Bible is the Word of God: the expressions "Scripture says" and "The Holy Spirit says" are used synonymously (passim). In the Scriptures God "opens his own most hallowed lips," and we are certain that they came to us "from the very mouth of God." Hence Calvin introduces his exposition of the Ten Commandments with the invitation: "Now let us hearken to God himself as he speaks in his own words."[70] As we would only expect, then, he tends to minimize the part played by the human agents in the production of the Holy Scriptures: they were the instruments or amanuenses of the Spirit, and they did not speak of their own accord.[71] The real author of Scripture is God himself: the writings of the apostles are to be regarded as the oracles of God. Calvin can even say that the Scripture comes from God alone and has no human admixture in it.[72] In a word, the Scriptures are produced by the dictation of the Holy Spirit, and this has the all-important corollary that they are thought of as a depository of heavenly doctrine.[73]

These citations, which could be multiplied indefinitely, would seem to demonstrate conclusively that Calvin held the Bible to be the faultless, verbally inspired Word of God, were it not for one very curious circumstance: in his commentaries he occasionally notes errors in the text he is interpreting. A favorite solution to this puzzle, particulary in the older Calvin literature, was to argue that he attributed the errors to a copyist, so that he could still presume the original document to have been free from error.[74] Others have held this solution to be—in at least *some* contexts—gratuitous, since errors that do not affect the teaching conveyed by a biblical text simply did not matter to Calvin. In this view, it is not the words but the doctrine that is divine.[75] A third solution does fuller justice to Calvin's talk of verbal inspiration by arguing that the words, for him, were indeed inspired—but only insofar as they are the form of the doctrinal matter. This appears to combine the evidence for both the other views in an ingenious synthesis, and it may well be very close to Calvin's intention.[76] In any case, it is clear that the Bible had objective authority in his eyes partly, at least, because he viewed it as a compendium of supernaturally imparted information.

The subjective perception of the Bible's authority is another matter. Calvin holds that one can never be fully and personally persuaded that Scripture is from God until convinced by the secret testimony of the Spirit. Although it is really something intrinsic, the authority is recognized for what it is only when the Holy Spirit illumines the mind. True, Calvin claims that the Bible is "self-authenticated," and that it bears on its face clear evidence of its truth, as black and white things do of their color, sweet and bitter things of their taste. But he believes that it authenticates itself *to this or that man* only through the testimony of the Spirit. For God alone can properly bear witness to himself in his

Word, which will not obtain full credit in the hearts of men until sealed by the inward testimony of the Spirit.[77]

It is important to make clear what exactly it is that the Holy Spirit testifies to. It cannot be maintained that in his notion of the Spirit's inward testimony Calvin holds Word and Spirit together in a kind of dynamic relationship—as though the authority were not vested in the Scriptures per se, but rather in the Spirit speaking through them.[78] He is concerned, rather, to parry the Roman Catholic claim that the authority of the Bible depends on the testimony of the church.[79] He retorts, in effect: No, it depends on the testimony of God himself, the Holy Spirit. He is concerned to establish the external authority of the Bible *as a whole,* and it is no accident that he alludes in this context to the question of canonicity.[80] His use of time-honored apologetic proofs of the Bible's divine origin points in the same direction: there is a parallel between them and the testimony of the Spirit inasmuch as they are invoked for the same purpose as he is, to authenticate the Scripture, though they differ in the effectiveness with which they achieve it.[81] They do not constitute another source of revelation, and they are not even coadjutors with the one source of revelation; not themselves the light, they bear witness to the light. And the same holds good for the secret testimony of the Holy Spirit. Warfield rightly describes the Spirit's witness as a "subjective operation . . . on the heart" of sinful man, a "repairing operation" prerequisite for the actual receiving of revelation.[82] As the final norm of Christian belief and practice, then, we end with an accredited book—whether of inspired words, or of heavenly doctrine, or both.

On our third problem, the interpretation of Scripture, little needs to be added to what has been said for Luther, since Calvin's exegetical principles were essentially the same. Indeed, the Reformers were fundamentally at one in all three divisions of our topic. With their common emphasis on the *sole* authority of Scripture and the *sole* regulative status of its literal interpretation, they fought to remove the two limiting factors imposed by the medieval church, so they believed, on the supremacy of the biblical norm. In their understanding of the character and content of the Bible, so far from opposing the medieval church, they accepted its viewpoint (in part) unquestioningly: the Bible contains revealed doctrine, the infallible oracles of God. But this was not the only answer they gave to the question of content: both of them could affirm on occasion that the Scriptures contain nothing but Christ. And if there is no necessary contradiction between the two answers, neither is there any necessary connection between them: they do not stand or fall together.[83]

IV

"The Bible, I say, the Bible only is the religion of protestants!"[84] Chillingworth's famous dictum has probably misled far more than it has enlightened. Luther's and Calvin's Protestantism, at any rate, can only very dubiously be identified as a religion of a book. They were agreed that the ultimate authority for Christian faith and practice lies in knowledge of Jesus Christ; that the Bible therefore has the character of a witness, pointing to something beyond the letter of the text; and that sound interpretation of Scripture, while faithful to the historical sense, must always understand particular passages by the character of the book as a whole. Important as these considerations are for their own sake, in defining the nature of original Protestantism, they have acquired a further, long-range significance for Protestant thinking insofar as they have proved hospitable to a modern understanding of the Bible. For one possible response to the theological problems raised by biblical criticism, so it has been argued, is to recover Luther's understanding of the Bible as a witness to the revelation in Christ and to discard the medieval remnants that still cling to his thinking.

Christ, for Luther, is the Lord of the Scriptures (as of all things else): if Scripture must reign as queen, yet Christ is king even over Scripture.[85] If necessary, Christ and Scripture can even be set over against each other. "Scripture is to be understood, not against, but for Christ: either it must be referred to Him, or else it must not be held to be true Scripture.... If my opponents have urged Scripture against Christ, we urge Christ against Scripture."[86] "You urge the slave, that is, Scripture—and that only in parts.... I urge the Lord, who is King of Scripture."[87] Such utterances as these show that Luther was emancipated—at least in principle—from the medieval understanding of the Bible's content: for him, Scripture is authoritative *insofar as it bears witness to Christ*. For this reason, Brunner is correct in saying that "Luther was the first to represent a biblical faith which could be combined with biblical criticism."[88]

We are confronted, then, with the strange historical circumstance that the immediate successors of the Reformers developed the less distinctive, more vulnerable side of their twofold answer to the question of the Bible's character and content. It is clear that an ambiguity is already present in Luther and Calvin; indeed, some have held that Calvin has already begun to stress the medieval element at the expense of the distinctively Lutheran insight. The medieval—or, as Brunner terms it, the "reactionary"[89]—element was from Calvin onwards more and more in the ascendancy. "So that," as Lehmann puts it, "what has unhappily occurred is that the ways in which the Reformers were children of their time have triumphed over the ways in which they were pioneers in the use of the Bible."[90] In Lehmann's terms, the Reformers' "interpretation" (that is, their consciously stated analysis of the Bible's content) was overcome by their "apperception" (that is, by "all those ways in which in their use of the Bible the Reformers were children of their time.")[91] It has required all the impact of modern scientific, literary, and historical criticism to drive Protestantism back to its original insight.

It is only putting the same thing another way to say that the Reformers "drew a distinction between the word of God and the Scripture which contains or presents that word."[92] In his *Treatise on Christian Liberty* (1520) Luther writes:

> Let us then consider it certain and firmly established that the soul can do without anything except the Word of God. . . . You may ask, "What then is the Word of God, and how shall it be used, since there are so many words of God?" I answer: The Apostle explains this in Romans 1. The Word is the gospel of God concerning his Son. . . . Faith alone is the saving and efficacious use of the Word of God.[93]

This Word Luther found, of course, in the Scriptures. But it was not just one of many items on which the written word instructed him. Quite the contrary, he calls the gospel "our guide and instructor in the Scriptures," and he holds that the gospel itself (as "good news") exists more properly in spoken than in written form.[94]

No doubt, the christological sense of "the Word" made it easier for the Reformers to distinguish the Word of God from the words of Scripture: God's Word or Wisdom—the *substantial* Word—is his Son, who, as Calvin puts it, is the actual "wellspring of all oracles."[95] But their conception of the *spoken* Word is equally important. It helps explain why, for Luther and Calvin, the Word belonged with the sacraments: because it has to do not simply with instruction but with the means of grace.[96] To be sure, it is contained in the Scriptures, but Calvin insisted, as Luther did, that for each to read privately at home is not enough;[97] as proclamation, the Word takes on a public, churchly character, and the Reformers speak of it as, with the sacraments, the "means" by which God acts toward us.[98] It is through the gospel that Christ is given.[99] In the proclaimed Word, we may say, we have the substantial Word, to whom the written words bear witness.

The notion of the Word as a means or instrument is present in the last chapter of Calvin's excursus on Scripture (chapter 9), although there the *proclaimed* Word receives no special emphasis. Previously (in chapter 7), he used the "witness of the Holy Spirit" only to buttress the external authority of the written Word: his final court of appeal was to the Scriptures as such, and the function of the Spirit was to attest the Scripture *en bloc.* But in the later chapter there is more than a hint of another way of thinking, set out in defense against the "enthusiasts" or "fanatics" who invoked the Spirit alone: the appeal to the Bible is now modified by the introduction of the Spirit as a second factor in the final authority. Calvin does not deny the leading of the Spirit, but he insists that the Spirit has bound himself to Scripture as the medium of revelation. Hence, just as the Word is not certain for us until confirmed by the Spirit, so we embrace the Spirit with confidence because we recognize him from his image in the Word.[100] Word and Spirit are united by an "inviolable bond," and the ultimate norm is

Scripture-plus-Spirit.[101] The Word has become the instrument by which the illumination of the Spirit is dispensed.[102]

Such a conception of authority, however, was not likely to sound persuasive to the Roman Catholics, who held that the Bible had been committed to the church and that to the church Christ had promised his Spirit. Luther's line of defense was to insist on the clarity of the Word of God: every baptized Christian could read and grasp the Bible's message for himself—without the need for the authoritative guidance of church or pope. The notion of the clarity or perspicuity of Scripture struck Luther's adversaries as problematic in theory, and it seemed to them to encourage, in practice, the rampant individualism of what came to be called "the right of private interpretation."[103] Luther's extraordinary self-assurance in voicing the gospel—*his* gospel—did not help but provoked the skeptical question, "Are you alone wise?"[104]

Calvin, on the other hand, was more careful to assert the collective, ecclesial nature of hearing the Word.[105] Although that may have a great deal to do with his special talents as a reformer, it also arose in part out of the "Lutheran" insight that the gospel is, above all, proclaimed Word, not so much words written in a book to be studied in solitude at home. But when he comes to speak of the power of the church,[106] Calvin takes the public character of the Word a step further: he argues for the doctrinal authority of the church, resting his case, as his Roman Catholic opponents did, on the abiding presence of Christ's Spirit in the church. But he reaffirms the principle that the Spirit wills to be joined by an "indissoluble bond" to God's Word. The church, therefore, cannot coin new doctrines; its doctrinal authority has to do only with expounding the sense of God's Word—even, when necessary, by adoption of terms that are not to be found in the Bible.[107]

When assembled in council under the presidency of Christ, the church has the specific power to issue doctrinal definitions. What, then, is the status of these definitions? Calvin expressly denies that his position gives every man the right to accept or reject the decisions of councils as he pleases; but he does hold that a conciliar decree must be measured against the Scriptures and appraised in terms of its historical circumstances. For one council has sometimes disagreed with another, and those present at a council are only human, capable of being stupid, irresponsible, contentious, and wrong.[108] Nonetheless, Calvin does not doubt that a definition derived from the Scriptures and agreed upon by a synod of pastors has more weight than whatever a man may conceive at home on his own. Hence he maintains that convening a synod is the best remedy for doctrinal dissension. And even though a council may err, the truth itself does not die in the church.[109]

In this way Calvin affirmed the characteristically Protestant view of the Bible as a book about Christ without losing the characteristically "catholic" insistence that the Bible is the church's book. Of course, a modern view of the Bible must recognize that the interpretation of Scripture is not just a question of who does the interpreting, but also of the hermeneutic principles according to which it is done; and here the Reformers were clearly pioneers. But without something like Calvin's strong ecclesial sense, Protestantism might find itself adapting to modern biblical scholarship only to fall victim to modern individualism, to which some think the Reformation itself gave birth.

Four

By Faith Alone:
Medium and Message in
Luther's Gospel

All the words and all the narratives of the Gospel are a kind of sacraments: that is, sacred signs by which God effects in believers what the narratives signify.[1]

Luther's authority was not, in the end, the written Word as such, but the gospel to which the Scriptures bear witness. The material principle, which is the message of salvation by faith alone, defines the formal principle of "Scripture alone"; the Bible borrows its authority from the message it contains. It would be natural to anticipate, then, that describing the content of Luther's gospel must be an easy matter. Curiously, this is not so; or, we might better say, it is so only up to a point. Few, if any, of Luther's readers would care to deny that his "chief article," as he called it, is embodied in his doctrine of justification by faith, which he did in fact employ as the critical norm for judging the beliefs and practices of the church.[2] But there is no consensus on how exactly the doctrine is to be understood: agreement on what *is* Luther's gospel is not matched by agreement on what, in detail, his gospel *means.* No Reformation theme, ironically enough, has been the subject of more intense debate than the central theme of justification by faith.

The problem is not occasioned by the fact that Luther sometimes identifies the chief article in other terms than "justification by faith." It is not difficult to see that whether he calls it "justification," or "forgiveness," or "faith in Christ," or even "the divinity of Christ," it is all the same thing.[3] Perhaps the fluidity of his language does not make for clarity, and the interpreter is handicapped by the necessity to assemble the pattern from widely scattered pieces that may not quite match. Indeed, one finds oneself confronted, on occasion, by shifts of vocabulary in a single work, or even in one and the same passage.[4] But the real difficulties lie elsewhere: in the substance, not in the form, of Luther's thinking. And it may be doubted whether he could have resolved them even if he had finished the treatise on justification that he once promised.[5]

The task of interpreting Luther's thoughts on justification has been complicated, but also enlivened, by the publication of manuscripts from his early, pre-Reformation period. Most important of the materials made available have been his notes for lectures he delivered (in 1515–16) on the Letter to the Romans. The story of the manuscript is one of the curiosities of church history. There seems to have been little interest in what became of it, until a sixteenth-century copy by Johann Aurifaber turned up in (of all places) the Vatican Library and was used by the Dominican scholar Denifle in his exposure of Luther's intellectual deficiencies.[6] Then it was discovered that Luther's own original had been accessible for years, but unnoticed, at the Royal Library in Berlin. A provisional edition of the lectures (or, more properly, the notes) was published in 1908, and in 1938 the definitve version appeared in the Weimar edition.[7] Largely on the basis of the *Lectures on Romans,* Karl Holl advanced the controversial thesis that for Luther justification meant an actual, if incomplete, *making* righteous,[8] whereas it had always been the shibboleth of correct Protestant doctrine to assert that justification is a forensic, declarative act by which God *imputes* righteousness to the sinner, leaving the sinner's actual condition unchanged.[9]

The debate over Luther's doctrine of justification has been closely intertwined with another much-mooted problem: the date and content of his theological reorientation, variously referred to as his "discovery," his "breakthrough," or (from the place in which it happened) his "tower experience." It is evident that not only biographical, but also theological and confessional interests have been at stake. When did Luther cross the line between Roman Catholicism and Protestantism? And does the codification of Reformation doctrine in Protestant orthodoxy faithfully represent Luther's own original ideas? It has seemed reasonable to suppose that these questions are most likely to find answers through investigation of the decisive turning point in his intellectual development. Indeed, the problem of interpretation has sometimes had less to do with understanding a particular Luther text than with the desire to locate each text within Luther's development and to view the development itself either as a movement out of the medieval tradition, or as a movement toward Protestant orthodoxy, or both.

The historical problems have been so intensively examined that it has become possible, even necessary, to compile an anthology of scholarly positions—a small fragment from the existing literature.[10] It is not my intention to propose yet another solution, but only to make some comments, in turn, on the sources (sec. I), on two of the most important contributions to the discussion (secs. II and III), and on the understanding of justification in one source from the mature Luther (sec. IV). In conclusion (sec. V), the nagging question is posed: If the nature of the sinner's justification is an unresolved problem of theological debate, some of it highly technical, how are we to account for the undoubted practical impact that Luther's gospel made on the German churches?

I

Luther's *Lectures on Romans* are not only the most important of the sources we now have for understanding his early theological development: they are among the most remarkable products of his entire career. But the question is asked, How far can they be viewed as documents of *Protestant* theology? No one will expect to find in them untarnished Evangelical doctrine a year or two before the outbreak of the indulgences controversy. They are, no doubt, a mixture. But should we see in them an occasional flash of later insights, overcast by a fundamentally medieval piety? Or may we view the vestiges of an outlook soon to be left behind as, in a phrase of Gordon Rupp's, "like unmelted blocks of ice drifting for a time upon the warmer waters"?[11] Posed in this form, the question is perhaps too vague, and we do better to try the more manageable question whether, by the time of the *Lectures on Romans,* Luther had already made the exegetical discovery that he himself spoke of as the occasion of his new birth.

Luther's own testimony, contained in the preface to the first volume of his Latin works (Wittenberg, 1545), has been central in nearly all discussions of his theological progress. The pertinent section may be translated as follows:

Meanwhile, that same year,[12] I had already returned to interpreting the Psalter once more, relying on the fact that I was more experienced after dealing in the classroom with Paul's letters to the Romans and Galatians and the Letter to the Hebrews. I had been seized with a quite extraordinary desire to understand Paul in the Letter to the Romans. What had stood in my way until then was not "chilly blood my heart around,"[13] but one single word in the first chapter [v. 17] : "The *righteousness* of God is revealed therein [sc. in the gospel] ." I hated that word, "the *righteousness* of God," because I had been taught by the use and custom of all the doctors to understand it philosophically of what they call the "formal" or "active" righteousness by which God is righteous and punishes sinners and the unrighteous.

I felt that, however irreproachably I lived as a monk, in the sight of God I was a sinner with a troubled conscience, and I could not be sure that I had appeased him with my satisfaction. I had no love for this righteous God who punishes sinners; indeed, I hated him, and I was resentful against God, if not with secret blasphemy, certainly with monstrous murmuring. I said to myself: "As though it were not enough that wretched sinners, eternally damned by original sin, should be overwhelmed with every kind of disaster by the law of the Ten Commandments, through the gospel God has to add sorrow upon sorrow and *through the gospel also* threaten us with his righteousness and wrath!" Thus I raved, my conscience wildly confused. But I continued knocking importunately at Paul's door in this place [Rom. 1:17], thirsting most ardently to know what St. Paul meant.

At last God had mercy on me. As I pondered day and night, I noticed the connection of the words: that is, "The righteousness of God is revealed therein—as it is written, 'The righteous man lives by faith.'"[14] Then I began to understand the "righteousness of God" as that by which the righteous man lives by the gift of God, that is, by faith, and that this is the meaning: the righteousness of God is revealed by the gospel—namely, the passive righteousness by which the merciful God justifies us through faith, as it is written, "The righteous man lives by faith." Hereupon, I felt that I had been altogether born again and that I had entered through open gates into paradise itself. From that moment the face of the entire Scripture appeared different. I then ran through the Scriptures, as far as memory allowed, and arrived at an analogous interpretation of other words: thus the "work" of God is that which God works in us; the "might" of God, that by which he makes us mighty; the "wisdom" of God, that by which he makes us wise; and so also the "strength" of God, the "salvation" of God, the "glory" of God.

I now lovingly extolled what had become for me the sweetest of words, "the *righteousness* of God," as ardently as I had hated it before—so truly was that Pauline text my gate into paradise. Afterwards, I read Augustine's *On the Spirit and the Letter,* where, quite unexpectedly, I discovered that he, too, interpreted the righteousness of God in a similar way as that with which God clothes us when he justifies us. Although this was still not perfectly expressed and does not clearly explain everything about imputation, I was nevertheless content that the righteousness of God by which we are justified should be taught.

Better armed with these reflections, I began to interpret the Psalter a second time, and the work would have developed into a large commentary had I not been compelled to abandon the work I had begun when, the following year,[15] the Emperor Charles V summoned me to Worms.[16]

From this autobiographical sketch, it *seems* that what Luther discovered was, quite simply, a sense of the expression "the righteousness of God" different from the sense he had learned as a student of theology: the righteousness of which the Apostle speaks in Romans 1:17 is not "active" (that by which God himself is righteous), but "passive" (that by which he justifies or makes *us* righteous). The reader of the *Lectures on Romans* finds, however, that Luther seems plainly to have made this discovery by the time he reached Romans 1:17 in the classroom. He says:

> The righteousness of God is the cause of salvation. And here again, by the righteousness of God we must not understand the righteousness by which He is righteous in Himself but the righteousness by which we are made righteous

by God. This happens through faith in the Gospel. Therefore blessed Augustine writes in chapter 11 of *On the Spirit and the Letter:* "It is called the righteousness of God because by imparting it He makes righteous people, just as 'Deliverance belongs to the Lord' [Ps. 3:8] refers to that by which He delivers." Augustine says the same thing in chapter 9 of the same book.[17]

So close is the parallel between the 1545 preface and the exegesis of Romans 1:17 in the lectures that the matter might seem to be settled, unless one wishes to see *how much* earlier the discovery was made.[18] But on closer inspection a number of second thoughts come to mind.

Four difficulties are particularly worrisome. (1) Since Luther is speaking of the time when he began his second course of lectures on the Psalter (1518), there is at least a prima facie case for arguing that his discovery was made immediately before the course began. But that was two years after the *Lectures on Romans.* (2) If his discovery consisted merely in interpreting the righteousness of God in Romans 1:17 as "that by which he makes us righteous," then we are forced to an odd conclusion: the seeds of the Reformation must have been sown by a piece of interpretation that was the common property of the medieval exegetes. (3) "Passive righteousness" does not appear in Luther's writings as a technical term before his treatise *On the Bondage of the Will* (1525) against Erasmus; and it can hardly be said that the concept is fully developed until the period of the ("Larger") *Commentary on Galatians* (published in 1535 on the basis of lectures delivered in 1531). Further, in the latter work it seems to mean something more, if not something other, than the righteousness of which Luther speaks in the *Lectures on Romans.* (4) Finally, it is sometimes said quite bluntly that we cannot date Luther's discovery earlier than 1518 because his writings till then were still "prereformatory."

Faced with the first of these difficulties, the great majority of scholars abandoned the prima facie date for Luther's discovery. Ernst Stracke showed how this might be done without concluding that Luther's own testimony is unreliable: Luther's account of his discovery may be seen as a kind of retrospective parenthesis, in which his memory went back to a period even before the *Lectures on Romans.* That, Stracke claimed, is why he introduced his reminiscence with the "double pluperfect" *captus fueram,* "I had been seized...."[19] Further, while Denifle found in Luther's allusion to the "doctors" proof that he was either an ignoramus or a liar, Holl and Hirsch were able to point out that Denifle overlooked the very sources Luther most likely had in mind.[20] By this route, too, the credibility of Luther's testimony was strengthened, and the last two difficulties could hardly be considered insuperable. The discovery could have been made long before Luther coined the technical term for its content ("passive righteousness"). And to say that his thinking was "prereformatory" at the time of the *Lectures on Romans* seems to be a case of begging the question.[21] Something like a scholarly consensus emerged, which was able to do justice to the striking parallel between Luther's reminiscence in 1545 and the actual content of his exegesis of Romans 1:17 thirty years earlier. It is significant that the one notable scholar who stood by what we have called the "prima facie" date of Luther's discovery, the Jesuit historian Grisar, could do so only at the cost of presuming that the Reformer had misrepresented his real point of difference from the medieval tradition; and that, Grisar maintained, was in fact his conception of faith as "trust" or "confidence."[22] This, however, was before the publications of Cranz and Bizer, which reopened the discussion in the 1960s.

II

The most important English-language study of Luther's theological development since Rupp's *Righteousness of God* was Cranz's *Essay on the Development of Luther's Thought on Justice, Law, and Society.*[23] Cranz's claim is that Luther's "reorientation" must be dated 1518-19, not only on the grounds of his own testimony, but also (and primarily) on the internal evidence of his writings; for "this is the point at which the material naturally divides" (p. xiv). The decisive turning point in Luther's thinking came "toward 1518-19," when he began to distinguish two realms of Christian existence (p. xvi). The Christian exists simultaneously "before God" and "in the world," or, as Luther put it, in a "heavenly" and an "earthly" realm. What, then, does this mean for the concept of righteousness (or "justice," as Cranz prefers to say)?

Cranz finds the fundamental point to be a distinction between "total" and "partial" righteousness. He writes: "In the total realm of existence before God, the Christian is totally just in Christ or totally sinful apart from Christ; in the partial realm of existence in the world, the Christian is partly just and partly sinful" (ibid.; cf. p. 57). That is to say (if I may unpack the distinction a little), as we stand before God we are either under grace or under wrath. There is no middle ground: either we are justified, or we are not. For righteousness before God is not a quantitative notion at all; it is a matter of the divine verdict upon us— a yes or a no—that admits of no degree. As we face our fellow men, on the other hand, righteousness is precisely a matter of degree, and some of us have more of it than others. We are all, in this realm, partly righteous, partly unrighteous.

This conception of righteousness Cranz does not find in the *Lectures on Romans* or any other of Luther's writings in the period 1513-18. At this stage of his development Luther simply teaches that God has begun to make the Christian righteous and will, in the future, justify him wholly (pp. xvi-xvii). The basis for Luther's understanding of justification in the *Lectures on Romans* is not the doctrine of the two realms but the "theology of the cross": that is, the paradox that all our blessings are hidden under their opposites, as the cross demonstrates—

life under death, glory under shame, salvation under damnation, righteousness under sin (p. 22). Hence Luther finds the beginning of righteousness in the confession of unrighteousness, and justification in the recognition of sin (p. 23). As Cranz comments: "The Christian must deny himself any justice and claim to God's favor, and yet this denial is itself in some way a justice and a claim." This is the meaning Luther discovers in Romans 3:4, where Paul cites the words of the Psalmist: "So that thou art justified in thy sentence and blameless in thy judgment." God has declared all men to be sinners. But when a sinner accepts this judgment upon him, he is reckoned righteous by God: the sinner justifies God by believing his Word, and God justifies him by reckoning this faith as righteousness (pp. 24-25). Of course, such righteousness is only a beginning, and sin remains in the Christian; but, provided he resists sin, God does not impute it to him (p. 26).

Two points in Cranz's presentation deserve a special mention: his interpretation of the formula *simul iustus et peccator* ("righteous and sinner at the same time") and his understanding of Luther's relationship to Augustine. In Luther's assertion that the Christian is both righteous and a sinner at the same time many have seen the heart of the Reformation gospel. Cranz does not, strictly speaking, challenge this opinion, but he insists that the formula is not unambiguous. Hence, whereas Pauck detects here a point of difference between Luther and Augustine, who "could only go so far as to say that the Christian is 'partly' *(partim)* righteous and 'partly' sinful,"[24] Cranz interprets the formula in the *Lectures on Romans* to mean precisely "that the Christian is partly just and partly a sinner now or that the Christain will be just in the future though a sinner now" (p. 27). That this is Luther's meaning seems clear to Cranz from the close association of the formula with the image of a sick man who is being healed: he "can be described as both ill and well." Only in Luther's mature period does the formula come to mean that the Christian is at once wholly righteous and wholly sinner from different points of view (pp. 51-52).

It is the often repeated simile of the sick man that shows, as Pauck concedes, how much Luther was under the influence of Augustine at the time of the *Lectures on Romans*. But Cranz is evidently more impressed than Pauck by the extent of Luther's early Augustinianism, at any rate in the matter of justification. Thus he argues that Luther's reorientation eventually led him to a conscious but reluctant critique of Augustine (pp. 58-61). By the early 1530s the Reformer had learned to distinguish two views of justification. The view that he rejects "may in general be identified with his own position from 1513-18," and he concedes (with qualifications) that it was also the view of Augustine.

Cranz is, I think, right in viewing the doctrine of justification in the *Lectures on Romans* as basically Augustinian.[25] That is to say, Luther does seem at this stage to regard justification as a healing process, which, as long as the cure is incomplete, requires God's willingness to overlook the remaining sin. More technically expressed: justification is a real making righteous plus the non-imputation of sins.[26] Further, I should agree that the doctrine of the two realms provided the mature Luther with a new and different framework for understanding Christian righteousness. And the substance, if not the terminology, of this doctrine does begin to determine his thinking on justification about 1518.[27] But is this new framework really what Luther understood to have been the content of his "tower experience"?

The difficulty with Cranz's view is that he does not seem able to do justice to the 1545 preface, but shifts the focus of Luther's discovery from "righteousness" to "the two realms." The contrast between active and passive righteousness is taken as a paradigm for the distinction between two realms of Christian existence, and the distinction between the two realms is then used to explain what Luther meant by active and passive righteousness (p. 43). Cranz is plainly uneasy about Luther's preface and warns us against being too closely bound by it in our efforts to understand Luther's theological development (p. 42). He mentions the fact that in the *Lectures on Romans* Luther speaks of God's righteousness as that by which we are justified by God (pp. 23–24), but he does not point out how closely this language corresponds to the language of the preface.[28] Reading Cranz's account of the *Operationes in Psalmos* of 1518–21 (Luther's second course of lectures on Psalms), one may even have the impression that the Reformer's reorientation led him *away from* the contrast between righteousness as God's attribute and righteousness as God's gift *to* a new contrast between the believer's righteousness in Christ and his righteousness in the world. In other words, the antithesis between two sorts of righteousness, active and passive, has become a description of the Christian rather than of God. "Active righteousness" no longer refers to God's punitive, retributive justice; it is the justice man achieves and expresses by his activity in the social order. It need not be denied that such a shift does take place in Luther's writings. But can it be doubted that the 1545 preface speaks of the first contrast, not the second?[29] Cranz says that "the 'justice of God' now [in the *Operationes*] begins to drop out of Luther's writings as a technical term" (p. 85). Surely, then, it is hard to believe that the tower experience occurred in 1518–19; for the consequence of this experience, Luther tells us, was that the "righteousness of God" became for him the sweetest of words.

A further question. Cranz is an extremely cautious worker, who recognizes that there are ambiguities in Luther's writings. But does he still perhaps try to make the Reformer's development too straightforward? Augustinian patterns of thought have an embarrassing habit of turning up again in the later writings, even when the tidy-minded scholar would have preferred their permanent retirement. (To this point we shall need to return.) Conversely, there are already in the *Lectures on Romans* elements that strain to the breaking point the conception of Christian righteousness as, so to say, a magnitude that admits of growth and increase. Cranz himself mentions one such element: the identification of Christian righteousness with Christ (p. 29). But there are others. (1) The doctrine of righteousness as "hidden" militates against any identificaiton of it with empirical piety.[30] (2) "Imputation" suggests a righteousness that is not an ethical possession but a divine verdict.[31] (3) The "not yet" that is so characteristic of Augustinian and scholastic ideas of righteousness[32] is occasionally overcome by the clear consciousness that the Christian *is* righteous—in hope![33] (4) The *simul iustus et peccator* does sometimes approach the view that Cranz regards as characteristic of the mature Luther.[34]

It seems, then, that to assign Luther's reorientation to the year 1518, though it solves some of the difficulties of an early date, runs into difficulties of its own if the content of the reorientation is taken in Cranz's sense. And I still find it more plausible to view the *Lectures on Romans* as the work of a man who, as we can see more clearly in retrospect, had already struck out along a fresh path. It need not follow that no more discoveries lay ahead of him. On the contrary, the restless, mobile character of Luther's theological reflection at this stage leads us to *expect* change and progress: like the doctrine of justification they contain, the lectures exhibit movement, not rest. But the evidence suggests that their author had already taken what he himself regarded as the first steps; in particular, he had learned to see God's righteousness not as a threat but as a gift.[35]

III

Bizer's *Fides ex auditu* ("faith by hearing"), which first appeared shortly before Cranz's study, arrived independently at a similar dating of the tower experience (1518).[36] But the content of the experience Bizer interpreted quite differently. According to him, the theological significance of Luther's discovery has to do with assurance of salvation, the Reformer's attitude to the papacy, the conception of the sacraments, and the distinction between law and gospel (p. 172); but the heart of the tower experience was Luther's discovery that the Word is the means of grace (pp. 7, 167, 175–78). And Bizer finds Luther's theology of the Word arising out of his new conception of the sacraments (that is, out of the third of the four enumerated themes). As Jetter showed, in his earliest writings Luther had remarkably little to say about the sacraments.[37] But as he came to see in them the point at which God makes his promise, he learned to value them more highly, to understand them as means of grace in the sense that they awaken or communicate faith. Hence, as Bizer puts it:

> The Lutheran doctrine of the sacrament has two characteristics. the sacrament is understood in terms of the Word, and the Word itself acquires sacra-

mental character. The point of departure for both is the new understanding of Romans 1:17, "In the gospel the righteousness of God is revealed," i.e., it is given through the Word (p. 178).[38]

Bizer's thesis is of great importance theologically as well as historically. In some respects it comes close to the interpretation of Luther's development put forward by Grisar. The crucial difference is that Bizer's Luther also discovered the *ground* of faith's confidence: the gospel that gives or communicates faith (cf. p. 172 n.). How, then, does Bizer's thesis require us to understand our two principal sources, the *Lectures on Romans* and the preface to the Latin works?

The roots of Luther's early theology Bizer finds already in the interpretation of God's "judgment" in the first course of lectures on the Psalms (1513-15). The judgment of God damns in us all that we have of ourselves, thereby working humility in us. "Tropologically" (that is, in its application to the individual Christian), God's judgment is to be interpreted precisely as humility (p. 15), and this humility is the Christian's righteousness (p. 16). "Faith" is simply another name for the same virtue (p. 20); it is not confidence in the Word of God but the "formed faith" of Scholasticism—faith formed, so to say, by humility (p. 21). Luther has not moved beyond the theology of John Staupitz, vicar-general of his monastic order (p. 22).

The same ideas are carried over into the *Lectures on Romans.* Hence Bizer finds himself taking up the thesis of Hartmann Grisar, which Holl had dismissed as a childish joke, that Luther is thinking of Christ's righteousness as "appropriated through humility" (p. 24). The theme of the entire letter Luther takes to be the humbling of man: it is humility that earns, or simply is, righteousness. True, as Holl insisted, humility is not a "work" or human achievement; it is passive submission to the divine judgment. But that is still not justification by faith in the evangelical sense. What part, for example, does Christ play in this scheme? The answer, according to Bizer, is that Christ is viewed mainly as the pattern of that humiliation and exaltation by which God deals with all the "saints" (p. 26) and in which the way to salvation essentially consists (p. 27). This is the picture of Christ that lies at the heart of the so-called theology of the cross (p. 25).

Sometimes Luther attributes to faith what he elsewhere attributes to humility, and it is this that has enabled the scholars to interpret the lectures as reformatory (p. 31). But Bizer explains this faith as no more than the belief that the way of Christ, which is the way of humility, is *our* way to salvation. Faith is the "root of humility," and it is not improper to say that justification "comes from faith." If we ask why it is faith we need in order to acknowledge the way of humility to righteousness, the answer is because this righteousness is never obvious; it is profoundly hidden. That our poverty is wealth can only be believed (p. 32). Faith, in this context, must be taken in the sense of Hebrews 11:1: it is *argumentum non apparentium,* being persuaded of things that are not apparent or evident.

The stage thus set, Bizer turns to the interpretation of Luther's comments on Romans 1:17. He writes:

> There the passive character of the divine righteousness is strongly emphasized: the righteousness of God is not his attribute, but that by which we are justified by him; and that happens through faith in the gospel. God is the "cause of righteousness" because he communicates it to man through faith. After what we have said so far, that can only mean: because he humbles him through faith. The humbling of man does not spring out of his own resolve but is the work of God, and the consequent righteousness is a "passive" righteousness. It happens through faith in the gospel (p. 33).

Consistently with this interpretation, Bizer then goes on to show at greater length that faith, as faith in the crucified and faith in the unseen, embraces the annihilating judgment of God, which the believer perceives as also a *saving* judgment. "The believer accepts the judgment of God upon him, and exactly by so doing he escapes from the tribunal" (p. 33). Here Bizer finds the clue to the "justification of God in his words," of which Luther speaks in his comments on Romans 3:4. Luther's idiom at this point has a reformatory ring to it, inasmuch as faith in the Word is what justifies. But he means only the faith that believes the accusation of God and suffers itself to be humbled by it; he shows hardly any concern for faith in forgiveness. It is the accusing, not the gracious Word of God that is the object of faith (p. 37), and therefore it cannot be supposed that what we have here is reformatory theology.

The greater part of Bizer's study traces in detail the emergence of the genuinely reformatory understanding (pp. 59-164). He sees the beginnings of the new conception of faith in the *Lectures on Hebrews* (1517-18),[39] but only in the report of Luther's meeting with Cardinal Cajetan (1518) does he detect the first evidence of a reformatory breakthrough.[40] There Luther infers from Romans 1:17 that "only he is righteous who believes in God"; for faith *is* righteousness, and faith is nothing other than belief in God's promise, which works or causes it (pp. 117-19). But we cannot follow Bizer's careful and absorbing analysis any further. While only a comparable feat of exegesis could hope to appraise his interpretation adequately, a few comments are in order, among them some comments on his interpretation of Luther's preface.[41]

The question must be raised, first, whether Bizer does justice to those elements in Luther's *Lectures on Romans* that seem to transcend a theology of humility. An undeviating "reformatory conception" of the lectures (as Bizer calls it) does not have to be maintained by those who see in them the beginnings of a distinctivley Protestant theology. Despite his patent honesty in dealing with passages that do not readily fit his interpretation, does Bizer, on the other side, hold on too firmly to a single *prereformatory* thread, albeit an obtrusive one? Even if one went so far as to grant that the theology of humility (in Bizer's sense) is the dominant theme of the lectures, they nevertheless contain judgments about faith, the work of Christ, and the distinction between law and gospel that seem to push beyond it. (1) Luther can speak of faith as the organ by which Christ dwells in the believer.[42] (2) In harmony with this conception of faith, he views salvation as given through the imputation of Christ's righteousness,[43] and he describes clearly and forcefully the thought of Christ's work as a happy exchange.[44] Bizer notes the occurrence of this notion but relegates it to a footnote (p. 27 n.). Is it not worthy of greater attention as a reformatory element in Luther's thinking that was bound eventually to demand revision of the theology of humility? (3) Again, it is true that in some passages one misses the sharpness of the later distinction between law and gospel. But if there is some vagueness in the comments on Romans 7:5-6 (cf. Bizer, p. 44), what Luther has to say on Romans 10:15 includes a striking analysis of the distinction. The gospel points to the Lamb of God, who takes away the sin of the world (John 1:29). Therefore, while the law exposes sin and makes one guilty and sick, the gospel offers grace, remits sin, and cures the sickness.[45]

If we can detect what appear to be reformatory elements already in the *Lectures on Romans,* we must ask, secondly, whether there is not a remainder from the theology of humility as late as the *Commentary on Galatians* (1535). This, after all, is what we should expect, for the notion of God's humbling the sinner does not simply disappear from Luther's theology; it remains as the "foreign work" that God executes by means of the law. Luther learns to distinguish more consistently and more sharply two movements that tend to coalesce in the early theology of humility. In the lectures on Psalms and Romans the Word of judgment often appears as itself redemptive, when the sinner bows before it; in the mature theology, on the other hand, judgment is redemptive only indirectly — by making the sinner hear the *other* Word, the Word of forgiveness that God speaks in Jesus Christ. It is not at all reactionary when, in the *Commentary on Galatians,* Luther names God the *Deus humilium* (the "God of the humble");[46] or when he concludes that just because the Christian is *simul iustus et peccator,* he "remains in pure humility."[47] Humility is the negative correlate of faith. And the positive side of faith is not exhausted by the idea of accepting the promise; for Luther, as for Calvin, faith culminates in the thought of union with Christ.[48]

This much needs to be said of Bizer's remarks on the theology of humility. How is it with the theology of the Word, which, he maintains, supplanted it? We may well grant that one has the full Lutheran doctrine of justification only when imputation is gratis and the Word of promise is the medium of God's dealing with men (Bizer, p. 50); further, that we do not find these elements in the *Lectures on Romans.* But if we do not find them in the 1545 preface either, it is still possible that Luther had already made the (to him) decisive discovery by 1515. We must ask, then, thirdly, whether Bizer's thesis can provide a convincing interpretation of Luther's own testimony.

Bizer's analysis of the preface (pp. 165-166) takes the sentence "The righ-teousness of God is revealed therein [sc. in the gospel]" to contain the heart of Luther's discovery. It does not, he says, express the mere commonplace that the gospel *talks about* God's righteousness; it means, rather, that the gospel itself *communicates* God's righteousness. Not some mysterious power in the sacra-ments, not some inner experience or penitence, but simply the Word or gospel! Luther made this discovery, according to Bizer, as he realized the connection between the word "faith" (in the Habakkuk citation) and the word "gospel" (in the first part of the text Romans 1:17). The faith by which righteousness is received is the faith that acknowledges the gospel, and passive righteousness is the righteousness of him who hears and believes.

In this way, no doubt, Bizer does show how the preface *could* be interpreted agreeably to his view of Luther's theological development. But does he convince us that it *should* be so interpreted? If we concede a prima facie case for dating Luther's discovery to the year 1518 (and since Stracke's essay it is by no means certain that we must), surely we must also acknowledge that the preface has a prima facie meaning: it appears to be about different sorts of righteousness. Bizer shifts the center of attention from the righteousness of God to the correla-tion of faith and the gospel. It seems to me, however, that what Luther means to affirm must be understood by what he denies: namely, that the righteousness of God in Romans 1.17 is that by which God himself is righteous and punishes sinners. The question really is: What sort of righteousness is revealed in the gospel? And it is significant that a passage in Luther's *Table Talk* unambiguously treats the Habakkuk citation as an "explanation" of the righteousness that the gospel reveals.[49] Bizer lends plausibility to his case only by taking the word "reveals" in the unnatural sense of "imparts": "'In the gospel the righteousness of God is revealed', that is," according to Bizer's gloss, "it is *given* through the Word" (p. 178).[50]

Although, then, Bizer may have traced successfully the genesis of Luther's theology of the Word, we may well end by posing his own question: "We still have to ask, however, whether this is the change Luther wants to describe in the preface of 1545" (p. 165). In short, we have the same reaction to Bizer as to Cranz: each has given an admirable discussion of certain aspects of the develop-ment of Luther's thought without quite persuading us that he is talking about the tower experience, or that the line of demarcation between the young and the mature Luther can be so sharply drawn. Hence, as interest in solving the puzzle of the tower experience waned during the 1970s, the value of these two contri-butions to the Luther literature proved more durable. By any reasonable standard, the doctrine of the two realms and the theology of the Word are among the most significant elements in Luther's mature theology, whereas the question of the tower experience was unduly inflated by the publication of Luther's early lectures. True, the fact that the problem of Luther's discovery no longer attracts as much interest as it did in the 1960s cannot be attributed to the emergence of some new consensus. But my own opinion, as will by now be clear, is that the *old* consensus has not been overthrown. It will not do to insist that Luther cannot have made his discovery by the time of his *Lectures on Romans* because his theology at that time was still prereformatory; one might better ask what significance it has for ecumenical theology that Luther could identify his decisive step with an insight that was essentially Augustinian—and therefore, I may add, can hardly be termed uncatholic. But his development did not end there; and the studies of Cranz and Bizer are indispensable contributions to the attempt to trace his further progress. It remains to be asked, next, if the subsequent developments supersede the notion of a righteousness by which God makes us righteous, as that righteousness is explicated in the *Lectures on Romans.*

IV

"The reason why some do not understand how faith alone justifies is because they do not know what faith is."[51] Promising though this judgment sounds as a clue to understanding Luther's doctrine of justification, it labors under the difficulty that his concept of faith, too, is complex. If we apply the judgment to a classic work of Luther's maturity, the 1535 *Commentary on Galatians,* we seem to find not one but several explanations of how faith justifies, and they correspond to the different elements in Luther's concept of faith.[52]

First, faith is hearing the Word of promise. No one attains to justification and life before God except the believer, who obtains them—without the law or love— by faith. Why? Because a promise, which is something other than a law, is grasped not by doing but by believing.[53] This seems plain enough. But if one presses further and asks why faith in the promise justifies, Luther's answer seems immediately to relocate the actual power to justify. His longest excursus on faith as hearing is occasioned by Galatians 3:2: "Let me ask you only this: Did you receive the Spirit by works of the law, or by hearing with faith?"[54] Luther maintains that the whole of the Book of Acts is about the gift of the Holy Spirit through the hearing of the gospel. Cornelius and his household, for instance, did nothing but sit and listen; and through the proclamation of Peter the Holy Spirit entered their hearts.[55] No doubt the Pauline text itself (Gal. 3:2), from which he starts out, then leads Luther, in summary, to assign the actual agency in justification to the Holy Spirit. It is not the voice of the law that justifies. What then does? Hearing the voice of the bridegroom, which is the Word of faith; it is this Word that, when heard, justifies. Why? Luther answers: "Because it brings the Holy Spirit who justifies."[56]

Second, faith is the bond that unites the believer with Christ. Hence Luther can say explicitly:

Faith justifies because it grasps and possesses this treasure, Christ present. But how he is present is beyond understanding. . . . And so it is Christ grasped by faith and dwelling in the heart who is the Christian righteousness on account of which God reckons us righteous and grants eternal life.[57]

Our question must be, however, not "How is Christ present?" (a difficulty of which Luther was evidently conscious, though he sets it aside as unanswerable), but: "How does Christ's presence, if we take it as a fact, bring about our justification?" And once again we do not find a single, consistent reply. Luther can say simply that Christ alone justifies me; or that we are justified by faith alone because faith alone grasps the victory of Christ; or that in some way Christ's righteousness is exchanged for our unrighteousness; or that his righteousness or satisfaction of the law covers us, protects us, bears our sins.[58] Whatever ambiguities there may be in these various expressions, Luther certainly does not seem to have in mind a merely external arrangement by which Christ's righteousness is "imputed" to the believer (or reckoned to his account); rather, it is the "inherence" of Christ within him that effects his deliverance.[59] Anything less than this would have to misrepresent Luther's concept of faith.[60] It follows that his view of justification resembles medieval notions—with the crucial exception that in the place of infused grace he puts Christ working effectually within.[61]

Third, faith is incipient righteousness. When Abraham's faith is said to have been reckoned to him as righteousness (Gen. 15:6, Rom. 4:3, Gal. 3:6), it is not said without reason, since faith really *is* a formal righteousness. From the "imputation" of righteousness to Abraham it can be properly inferred that righteousness begins by faith, by which we have the first fruits of the Spirit. But faith is only a tiny spark, and the notion of imputation implies, in Luther's estimate, a judgment that makes up what is lacking in faith or "perfects" it.[62] "Imputation" here does not mean a reckoning of Christ's righteousness to us in such wise that we are not really righteous at all. The man who has faith is righteous in truth, if only incipiently; and the divine imputation is an act that simply overlooks the deficiency. But we must, of course, ask why God counts as righteousness what is only the beginning of righteousness; and once again we do not have a simple answer. God's imputation is because of Christ, or because you have believed in God's Son, or because of your faith in the Son of God, and so on.[63] But the imputation is also made to rest on yet another element in Luther's concept of faith—an element he apparently finds in the biblical testimony that what Abraham believed was (from reason's viewpoint) unlikely. Abraham's faith did not waver when God promised him—an old man with a barren wife—that he would be the father of many nations. He honored God by taking him at his Word.[64]

Fourth, then, faith is the rendering of glory to God. And this leads Luther to make another explicit statement about the reason why faith justifies:

To attribute glory to God is to believe him—to reckon him truthful, wise, righteous, merciful, omnipotent; in short, to acknowledge him as the author and giver of every good. . . . From this it can be understood what a great righteousness faith is. . . . Faith justifies because it renders God his due. . . . Whoever believes God's word as Abraham did is righteous in the sight of God, because he has faith that gives glory to God, that is, renders to God his due."[65]

We seem to be left, then, with no fewer than five or even six answers to the question: Why does faith justify? Faith justifies because it believes the promises of God, because it brings the Holy Spirit, because it appropriates the righteousness of Christ, because it is the germ of righteousness, because it is imputed as righteousness, and because it glorifies God. But stated in this fashion, the appearances are misleading. True, Luther does not trouble to show expressly how the pieces fit together; but it is not difficult to reduce the data to order, his fundamental scheme in the *Commentary on Galatians* being in fact reasonably clear. The scheme is twofold, and it is already implicit in the conception of a real, but derivative and imperfect righteousness of faith.

Faith really *is* a kind of righteousness, though opposed to the spurious righteousness of works. The difference between faith-righteousness and works-righteousness is that the former has its source, not in the sinner's own activity, but in Christ's. Faith lays hold upon Christ, who is the Word of God, the content of the promise; it is only through its hold on this "precious gem" that faith, taking God at his Word, deserves the name of righteousness. Nonetheless, the righteousness of faith is only seminal: it is not yet perfect but holds out the hope of future perfection. The source of this imperfection is not in faith's object but in faith's poverty; for it is weakened by the remainder of sin in the flesh.

From these two basic attributes of faith-righteousness—its dual character as derivative and imperfect—Luther puts together his doctrine of justification. God accepts the believer's faith because it is in truth righteousness, though of such a kind that no one could attain it by his own native abilities. This is part one of justification; but it is not the whole. Since the righteousness of faith is only embryonic or rudimentary, the imputation is also necessary by which God "connives at" the believer's shortcomings, *counting* his faith as righteousness. This is justification part two. Thus Luther says expressly:

> Christian righteousness consists in two things: heartfelt faith [*fide cordis*] and the imputation of God. Faith is indeed a formal righteousness, but it is not enough because even after faith remnants of sin still cling to the flesh. . . . The second part of righteousness, which perfects it, must be added; and that is the divine imputation.[66]

Only a few lines further on Luther repeats the twofold scheme:

As I have said, these two things perfect Christian righteousness. One is heart-felt faith itself, which is a divinely given gift and formally believes in Christ. The other is God's reckoning this imperfect faith as perfect righteousness for the sake of Christ, his Son, who suffered for the sins of the world and in whom I have begun to believe. Because of this faith in Christ God does not see the sin that is still left in me.[67]

Yet a third formulation of the Christian's twofold righteousness follows shortly afterwards:

These are the two things in which Christian righteousness consists: first, faith that attributes glory to God; second, God's imputation. For faith is weak, as I have said. Hence the reckoning [reputationem] of God has to be added, because God does not choose to impute the remnant of sin: he does not choose to punish it or to damn us on its account, but rather to cover it and overlook it as though it were nothing—not for our sakes or for the sake of our worthiness or works, but for the sake of Christ himself, in whom we believe.
    So the Christian man is at once righteous and a sinner, saint and profane, God's enemy and his son.[68]

Luther arrives, then, at the neat formula: "Faith begins righteousness, imputation perfects it."[69] But how does this differ from the allegedly prereformatory doctrine of justification in the *Lectures on Romans?*

What we find in the *Commentary on Galatians* turns out to be remarkably like the Augustinian scheme that Luther is supposed to have surrendered. Righteousness is understood as inchoate: it moves from a modest start to eschatological perfection. This is why the Christian, all his life long, must remain in humility, and why we can only say that he *is* righteous by divine imputation.[70] And Luther, like Augustine, finds it natural to think of the Christian's progress as a course of healing.[71] Nor has this pattern of thought somehow found its way accidentally into the *Commentary on Galatians:* it appears in other sources of the same period.[72] Hence the kind of contrast between Augustine and the mature Luther that Saarnivaara, for instance, proposes does not seem to work for some of the most important of the later sources. Saarnivaara argues that while both Augustine and Luther taught salvation by way of two gifts of God, for Augustine justification was renewal supplemented by the nonimputation of sins, and for Luther it was the nonimputation of sins (or imputation of righteousness) with renewal as its "fruit" (or the second work of God).[73] In actual fact, the Augustinian scheme appears not only in Luther's *Lectures on Romans* but also in the *Commentary on Galatians.* This is hardly surprising, since in both works he had to interpret the Pauline use of Genesis 15:6, "And he [Abraham] believed the Lord; and he reckoned it to him as righteousness."[74]

V

Divided opinions on Luther's chief article plainly reflect both the diversity of his language and the vested interests of diverse theological parties. And one may well marvel that his message of faith alone has not merely survived in the theological schools but has somehow managed to capture the loyalty of Christian people who are innocent of the subtleties of sound doctrine. In actual fact, as I wish finally to show without intending to be reductive, the effectiveness of Luther's gospel is entirely comprehensible at the psychological level. This will be most apparent if we start from where the preceding section left off: from the thought, in the *Commentary on Galatians,* that God counts faith as righteousness.

Luther's God says: "If you want to appease me, do not offer me your works and merits, but believe in Jesus Christ. . . . Then I will accept you and pronounce you righteous."[75] As it stands, the admonition appears to mean that the one deed God really rewards is believing. But to interpret Luther in this sense is not to move one step beyond the supposition that, one way or another, the business of religion is a *quid pro quo;* and that goes against the whole tenor of his theology. What he intends is better expressed when he goes on to assert that Christian righteousness is properly defined as "confidence [*fiducia*] in the Son of God, or confidence of the heart in God through Christ."[76] Presumably, then, Luther means that anyone who has faith *in this sense* will be "right."[77] Not that it is prerequisite to justification, as merits were in some of the old scholastic schemes; rather, it is constitutive of the divine-human encounter on its human side. The believer does not earn the divine imputation with his faith, neither is there any legal fiction: God counts the confidence of the heart as "right" because that is what it is. Its rightness lies in the fact that faith, for its part, does not make God an idol but takes him for exactly what *he* is: the author and giver of every good, the precise counterpart of the believer's confidence. In a sense faith, by believing, is the "creator of deity" in us: it lets God be God.[78] In short, it is right thinking about God.[79]

Luther speaks of the "virtue" of faith, and he plays on the classical sense of "justice" as the virtue that gives the other his due.[80] But he does not mean virtue in a moral sense; that would be the very misconception that occasions so much of the debate whether the Christian is righteous by infusion, by imputation, or by prolepsis. Faith, for Luther, is nothing but the reflex of God's self-disclosure in Christ: it is confidence only because it perceives God as he is, that is, as he shows himself in his Word. A man thinks correctly about God when he believes God's Word,[81] and the Word of the gospel is this: "Take heart, my son, your sins are forgiven" (Matt. 9:2).[82] Because the confidence of the heart thus rests entirely on instruction by the Word, Luther can say that he is righteous by faith *or by knowledge.*[83]

Conversely, false religion rests on a false perception of God. Where faith is not present, God is robbed of his glory: he is not regarded as merciful, but is taken for an angry judge who must be satisfied by works. And this is to despise God and his Word, to deny Christ and all his benefits, and to set one's own fancies in the throne of God.[84] In Luther's view, the effect of false religion—the religion of law and reason—is to throw a sick man back on his own resources, as though he could be cured by adding to his afflictions. It is as if one beggar should come to another to make him rich; as the proverb says, the one is milking a billy goat, and the other helps him with a sieve. Those who seek justification in the works of the law become twice as unrighteous: that is, weaker and even less capable of any good work. "This," Luther adds, "I have experienced in myself and in many others."[85]

It was Luther's conviction, born of experience, that this false religion was nurtured by the teaching of the Nominalists on grace and merit. In the *Commentary on Galatians* he returns again and again to their pernicious scheme of salvation, outlining it no fewer than three times in his exposition of a single verse (Gal. 2:16).[86] Although he thinks of the Nominalists as the new Pelagians, they did not deny the necessity for an infusion of habitual grace before a man could attain blessedness. But in Luther's eyes they compromised the divine initiative, teaching that grace is given to those who have first done their best without it.[87] The Nominalist order of salvation began with the merits of the ungraced man, though it was recognized that these "congruous" merits fall short of the "condign" merits that a man can subsequently acquire with the help of grace. The rationale behind this scheme was embodied in the jingle:

> God will no more require of man
> Than of himself perform he can.[88]

Surprisingly, Luther and Zwingli arrived at quite different perceptions of the injunction "to do one's best" *(facere quod in se est)*. Zwingli thought that everyone always does his best, however trifling, so that anyone, if the Nominalist principle held good, could be justified by works.[89] Luther, too, recognized that the Nominalist path could lead to a false security; but in his own experience the way of merits led to a frenzy of activity, a frantic quest for certainty that he had in fact done his best.[90] By the time of the *Lectures on Romans,* he had already concluded that the Nominalists were fools and pig-theologians, crypto-Pelagians who had subverted nearly the entire church with their noxious formula. For while they strutted about in perfect security, those who truly do good works always wonder if their best is pleasing to God.[91]

If the Nominalists, as Luther saw them, displayed the symptoms of a spiritual malady, he found the diagnosis and the cure (or at least found them confirmed) in his reading of the mystics. His very first publication was an edition, with a preface, of a fourteenth-century manuscript that he titled *A Spiritually Noble Little Book on the Correct Distinction and Understanding of the Old and New Man* (1516). Shortly afterwards, he discovered a more complete manuscript of the book and published it with the title it has borne ever since: *A German Theology* (1518).[92] In the new preface Luther wrote that, next to the Bible and St. Augustine, no book had come to his attention from which he had learned more about God, Christ, man, and everything. He predicted that through its dissemination German theologians would come to be recognized as without a doubt the best theologians.

The anonymous author of the *German Theology* locates the human predicament in man's suspension between two possibilities: he can acknowledge that to God alone belong being and goodness (which is heaven), or he can claim something for himself (which is hell, seeing that hell consists of nothing but self-will). The malady of sin is turning away from God and turning in upon oneself: it is arrogating goodness, knowledge, wisdom, and power for oneself, and so robbing God of his glory. The mark of the sinner is that he is forever saying "I and me and mine." But in seeking himself in the things around him—in wanting to be something—he falls unwittingly into bondage to himself. And if being a sinner means being bent in upon oneself, the remedy or being saved can only mean to straighten up and be freed from self-tutelage.[93] How, then, does this come about?

Plainly, it cannot be brought about by the sinner's own effort. The argument of the treatise echoes the language of the Gospels: he who loves his soul will lose it (John 12:25). But the words of Jesus are taken for a shrewd psychological insight, that any injunction to the self-willed man to *do* something can only, in the nature of the case, be an invitation to further exercise of his self-will. As long as a man actively seeks his best, it is not his best that he is seeking, because his true best would be to seek or love himself no longer. And to offer aid to a man's self-will is to help him to his worst, throwing him back more heavily on the actual source of his problem. Consequently, the way of merits is rejected.[94] The spiritual strategy can only be to point the sinner elsewhere, to show him the best life as it was lived by another: in short, he must die to himself, and dying to self is the Christ-life. In the story of Jesus the "Friends of God" discovered a religious force powerful enough to break through the hard shell of self-love. "You must constantly and intently look to your Master, and see to it that you believe, obey, and follow Him."[95]

The young Luther came to acknowledge the diagnosis of sin in the *German Theology,* and he grasped the psychological importance of shifting the anguished soul's attention from itself. This, indeed, was a lesson he learned also from the pastoral wisdom of John Staupitz, who urged him, when tormented with doubt whether he was one of God's elect, to "contemplate the wounds of Jesus."[96] Whatever ambiguities may remain in the teaching of the *German Theology,*[97] in a sermon from the year 1519 Luther himself combined the message of turning to Christ with a striking affirmation of the Word as its effective medium: the words and narratives of the Gospels are invested with a sacramental efficacy by which God brings about in believers what the narratives signify.[98] As Luther had asserted in his *Lectures on Hebrews,* it is not a question of struggling to imitate a pattern disclosed in the words and works of Jesus; that would be one more way of rushing into works. Rather, one must begin first, in faith, with the story as sacrament.[99] In the later *Commentary on Galatians* some of the terms have changed, but Luther again declares the effective presence of Christ's saving deeds. Christ came once historically, and he comes spiritually to the Christian every day; he brought life and liberty to light then, and the same happens now. The advent of Christ, now as then, is the time of grace or the gospel, which puts an end to the time of the law. By faith in the Word of grace the Christian is to turn his attention to Christ, who comes every day; and through this Word of the gospel, faith, too, comes every day.[100]

Luther's message of faith alone has been perceived again and again first as subjective, secondly as inimical to moral conduct. But faith, for him, was exactly a turning away from the subjective self, brought about by the presentation of Christ in the gospel; and the liberation of a man from constant anxiety about the condition of his soul is what makes him, Luther believed, available to his neighbor. Hence it is precisely in a treatise on good works (1520) that Luther expresses some of his best insights on the faith that springs from the Word or from the wounds of Christ. For this faith is confidence toward God, without which bold action is inhibited by timidity; it has no thought of garnering merits, since it does not doubt that God is kind and overlooks the believer's shortcomings. Faith is the goodness in all good works, the health of the person, from which cheerful activity proceeds.[101] The same case is made the same year in the *Treatise on Christian Liberty:* the Christian does not need good works for his own righteousness or salvation, and he is therefore free to attend to the need and good of his neighbor.[102] Morality, in other words, no less than religion, requires emancipation from the self-centeredness that confuses a good deed with a merit.

The most apt definition of Luther's (and Calvin's) faith may be, in the final analysis, *Christi intuitus:* undivided attention to the Christ who is presented in the Word.[103] Here medium and message perfectly coincide. What is needed is that the sinner be liberated from the endless round of self-seeking; and the offer of freedom comes as a Word from beyond, a Word that grasped Luther (if one dare so put it) in its sheer spokenness. This was why he was so sure of his theology: because it tears us out of ourselves, so that we no longer rely on our own resources, but on something outside of us—the promise and truth of God, which cannot deceive.[104]

Five Priesthood and Ministry: Luther's Fifth Means of Grace

At the Diet of Augsburg in 1530 Philip Melanchthon advised against discussion of the priesthood of all believers, relegating it to the "odious and unessential articles that are commonly debated in the schools." In the Augsburg Confession, which had already been finished and read when he gave this judgment, the doctrine is passed over in silence. But Protestant tradition has not followed Melanchthon in this respect; the priesthood of all believers has come to be regarded, along with biblical authority and salvation by faith, as one of the three main points of Evangelical theology. Like the other two, however, it has not always been interpreted in the same way, nor taken as seriously in practice as in theory. Often, it has become a dead letter in a clergy-dominated institution; and where it has come alive again, it has been used to support a bewildering variety of practices, such as congregational polity, the Quaker meeting, pietistic *ecclesiolae,* and the Methodist commissioning of lay preachers. Sometimes, again, it has become associated with such slogans as "the right of private judgment" or "immediate access to God," and interpreted so individualistically that any institutional or corporate expression of it becomes unthinkable. Finally, it is perhaps not superfluous to point out that the "royal priesthood" is not a Protestant invention but a biblical category, which had an interesting history before Luther and has never been wholly neglected in the "Catholic" tradition. This fact, too, complicates the problems of interpretation.[1]

What is still perhaps the popular interpretation in the Anglo-Saxon world is well represented by the influential writings of T.M. Lindsay, the distinguished Scottish historian. Though he died in 1914, Lindsay's major, two-volume *History of the Reformation* has been reprinted many times; the last reissue, of 1948, is still widely read in Britain, possibly less so in America. Lindsay detected a kinship between Erasmus and Luther in their attitudes toward the externals of religion. The whole aim of Erasmus's *Enchiridion* (1503), as Lindsay says with good reason, was to "assert the individual responsibility of man to God apart from any intermediate human agency." So far, so good. But he continues: "Erasmus ignores *as completely as Luther would have done* [my italics] the whole mediaeval thought of the mediatorial function of the Church and its priestly order." This, according to Lindsay, makes the book "essentially Protestant." For him the priesthood of believers meant the privilege of direct access to God, viewed against the background of priestly tyranny in "Romanism." Our "fellow-men are not to be allowed to come between God and the human soul; and there is no need that they should." This religious principle "delivered men from the vague fear of the clergy." "It is the one great religious principle which lies at the basis of the whole Reformation movement."[2] What this implies is particularly clear in Lindsay's earlier, more popular work, *The Reformation*, in which he reduces the traditional "formal" and "material" principles to corollaries of the common priesthood. The priesthood of all believers means "the right of every believing man and woman, whether by lay or cleric, to go to God directly with confession seeking pardon, with ignorance seeking enlightenment, with solitary loneliness seeking fellowship, with frailty and weakness seeking strength for daily holy living." The Protestant appeal to the Scriptures means that anyone with the Bible in his hands can hear God speaking directly; and justification by faith means that God himself, without the need for a priestly mediator, speaks pardon directly.[3]

An obvious difficulty with such an interpretation is that it undermines, not only the medieval priesthood, but also the Evangelical ministry. Indeed, some historians do not hesitate to treat Luther's high opinion of church and ministry as a logical inconsistency. "A man alone in his room with God and God's Word, the Bible, like Luther in his tower room—this [according to E. Harris Harbison] would be the true picture of a Christian," had Luther been more logically inclined.[4] The historical question with which this chapter is concerned is whether Luther, correctly understood, may have held a less dissonant view of ministry and priesthood than Lindsay's interpretation allows.

I

The writings in which Luther speaks most directly of the relation between priesthood and ministry arise from very different situations, and partly for this reason different interpretations of Luther's position have been argued in the secondary literature. Questions concerning the ministry appear scattered throughout the Luther-corpus: for instance, in his sermons and letters. It is hardly possible to comment on the incidental and subsidiary allusions. In some of his treatises, however, the doctrine of the ministry plays a central role, and it is important to observe the various historical contexts in which the more extended discussions occur.

In one class of writings, the priesthood of all believers is used mainly as a polemical instrument against Rome. Of the familiar "Reformation Treatises" written in 1520, for example, the first two give the doctrine a largely polemical use. In the appeal *To the Christian Nobility of the German Nation*[5] the common priesthood is Luther's chief weapon against the papal obstruction of temporal interference. The clergy cannot retreat behind the wall of special privilege and so imagine themselves secure from the temporal powers, because the traditional division of Christendom into clergy and laity is a false one: all are priests, including those Christians who wield the temporal sword. The same polemic is carried over into the *Prelude on the Babylonian Captivity of the Church*,[6] in which the Roman sacrament of ordination to the priesthood is sharply criticized. "Unless I am mistaken, if this fictitious sacrament should ever fall, the papacy itself will hardly survive." And fall it must, since every baptized Christian is already a priest. In the third of the trio, the *Treatise on Christian Liberty*,[7] the common priesthood is introduced as one of the benefits of faith in Christ; and yet here, too, Luther cannot resist a little incidental polemic.

Two treatises of importance for our theme were directed in 1523 to a quite different problem: How can a congregation acquire ministers when there is no bishop available to ordain in the traditional manner? Luther answered this question, first, for the congregation at Leisnig, in Saxony, which had gone over to Lutheranism, dismissed the Roman incumbent, and elected two Evangelical pastors. The answer is contained in the treatise, *That a Christian Gathering or Congregation Has the Right and Power to Judge all Teaching, and to Call, Appoint, and Dismiss Teachers, Established and Proved from Scripture*.[8] Here the claim is that in being anointed to the common priesthood Christians have commited to them a duty to proclaim God's Word. If the bishops will not make the necessary provisions for a ministry of the Word, then the congregation both may and must. For Paul bids any Christian in case of emergency to stand up without a call (1 Cor. 14:30). How much more does the whole congregation have the right in necessity to call someone to the teaching office! The second of these treatises from the year 1523, *On Appointing Ministers of the Church*,[9] was addressed, not to a Lutheran congregation, but to the Hussite church in Bohemia. Luther again argues that each and every Christian, by reason of the common priesthood, has the right to minister in the Word and the duty to do so if there are no other teachers in the church or only heretical teachers. Again the inference is: How much more, in necessity, may the church as a whole appoint officebearers to minister for it!

Luther's severe letter, *On the Sneaks and Furtive Preachers*,[10] addressed in 1532 to a Saxon magistrate, deals with the opposite situation: the question here is not how to obtain a sufficient supply of preachers but how to check the growing band of eager, self-made preachers who were overrunning Saxony. Astonishingly, Luther revises his earlier interpretation of 1 Corinthians 14:30. Paul was not inviting just any Christian to speak, but only other authorized prophets, when he said: "If a revelation is made to another sitting by, let the first be silent." Otherwise any drunk from the tavern might chime in, or even the women. "Oh what a beautiful fair, revel, and carnival that would be!" Hence Luther takes his stand on the divinely instituted parish system and the necessity for official credentials. The congregation becomes the laity *(Leyen)*, and over against them stands the clergyman *(Pfarher)*. Use of the term "layman" is justified by reference to the *idiōtēs* of 1 Corinthians 14:16, who is supposed simply to say "Amen" to what the prophets utter. In contradistinction to the medieval view, Luther's antithesis is prophet and people rather than priest and people. But it is clear that the priesthood of all believers here plays no role; the official ministry seems to have suppressed it. Luther says in as many words that it is the duty of the prophet to speak, of the people to listen. Similar thoughts, provoked by the "sneaks," had already appeared in Luther's *Exposition of Psalm 82* (1530),[11] in which the use of the word "clergyman" is supported from 1 Peter 5:3: each pastor has a portion of the people "allotted" to him. In a somewhat less plausible piece of exegesis, the Lord's silencing of the demons is said to mean that not even a devil may be permitted to set the bad example of preaching without a call.

Aside from these major sources, parts of other writings by Luther are devoted to the ministry or priesthood. (1) The first part of the tract *On the Misuse of the Mass* (1521)[12] shows how a wrong view of the mass inevitably entails a wrong view of the priesthood. In actual fact, the priesthood belongs to all Christians, and its "offices" are the spiritual (or "reasonable") sacrifice and the proclamation of the gospel. (2) Similarly, in his later work *On Private Masses and the Consecration of Priests* (1533),[13] Luther asserts that Christians are born, not made, priests: they inherit their priesthood by right of baptism. From the number of these "born priests" some are called to exercise the office of preaching, not of offering private masses. (3) Luther's *Sermon on Keeping Children in School* (1530),[14] though it mentions the temporal gains of education, is largely concerned with the recruitment and training of ministers, and should be included in documents bearing on his view of the pastoral office. (4) Lastly may be mentioned the passage in the treatise *On the Councils and the Church* (1539)[15] in which the ministry is discussed as one of the distinctive "marks" of the church.

It is obvious that Luther's teaching on ministry and priesthood is presented in a variety of historical contexts: particularly, the polemic against Rome, the demand for evangelical pastors, and the threat of the radical reformers. It is undeniable that verbal inconsistencies appear between one writing and another, even within a single writing, and that Luther changed his exegesis of a crucial passage in Paul to meet the exigencies of a new situtation. The question is, however, whether, despite changes in wording, emphasis, and argumentation, the main lines of a generally coherent view of ministry and priesthood can be traced. Or does Luther have more than one way of relating the two categories?

II

Since the nineteenth century, the secondary literature has been focused on the question whether, for Luther, the special ministry rests on the common priesthood or on a direct divine institution. Each of these two possibilities has been found in the sources. Variations of emphasis and argumentation are open to the advocates of either interpretation, but the general contrast remains constant. Those who derive the ministry from the common priesthood assign the ministerial functions to the whole congregation of believers; the necessity for the special office is then based mainly on the need for "order," treated by some as little more than a matter of expediency, as in the political theory of the social contract. Hence the congregation has a certain priority over the ministry both in time and rank. Against this, those who refer the ministry to a special institution of Christ argue that the existence of a congregation itself depends on the ministerial proclamation, so that the ministry is prior to the common priesthood in time and rank.

On the answer to this question, whether the ministry has its origin "from below" or "from above," there seems to depend the understanding of ministerial authority, also of ordination. Does the minister receive his authority from the congregation by delegation or from previously ordained ministers by transmission? Each possibility has its obvious risks: the former may reduce the minister to a functionary of the people, the latter may reduce the people to passive spectators. The champions of the so-called delegation theory denied that they jeopardized the minister's authority; Höfling,[16] for example, derived the authority of the minister from the divinely instituted means of grace rather than from the will of men, even though he regarded the ministry as given, not to a special class within the church, but to the royal priesthood. Yet it was clearly the fear of the opposing group that ministerial authority might be made to rest on the good pleasure of the congregation. According to Stahl,[17] the clergy are ministers of the church, the divine institution, and not of the congregation, which comes into being through the will of men; for Luther, the exercise of the ministerial functions rests on divine authority, not on "the will, commission, or consent" of the people.

A steady flow of writings since the Second World War has kept these questions alive. Hans Storck's essay on the priesthood of all believers[18] and the study by Vilmos Vajta on Luther's theology of worship[19] both contained important discussions of ministry and priesthood. And there have been many articles in the journals. Klaus Tuchel, writing in the *Luther-Jahrbuch* for 1958,[20] rightly pointed to the absence of any substantial monograph that might serve as a reliable basis for further research. This, however, is no longer true: the literature has been greatly enriched by two important monographs, which gather up the work of previous authors, take a further look at the sources, and will certainly provide the starting point for future discussion. In view of the history of past Luther research, it is hardly surprising that these two studies fail to reach full accord. But it is arguable that, between them, they have given a decided encouragement to the trend, already apparent in the literature, toward the institution theory of the ministerial office. The difference is that, whereas Wilhelm Brunotte finds *only* the institution theory in Luther, Hellmut Lieberg admits the presence *also* of another, but subordinate line in Luther's thinking, according to which the ministry is in fact derived from the common priesthood.[21]

III

The notions of priesthood and ministry in Luther's theology are directly related to his fundamental understanding of the gospel of the forgiveness of sins or justification by faith. This is therefore the obvious point at which to begin a constructive statement of his position.

Justification is by faith. But faith comes through hearing the Word of God; forgiveness, strictly speaking, is placed in the Word, and the Word means not so much Scripture as the lively proclamation of the gospel. Faith is not to be understood as a human possession, nor as a permanent disposition, but as the correlate of the divine Word. Hence, although Luther does speak of the Word as "requiring" faith, he nonetheless treats the Word as efficacious or powerful, so that it evokes, awakens, or creates the faith that it demands. In a sense, Word and faith are mutually dependent; they belong together. But the Word, properly speaking, has priority, so that God and not man may be the author of salvation. Faith is the work of God, which he works in man through his Word.[22]

Faith, then, is not implanted in the soul once and for all, and then left to grow naturally of itself. Its continued existence depends on the repeated proclamation of the gospel. This proclamation therefore becomes the most urgent task of the Christian community, and is indeed the first "mark" of the church's presence in any given time or place. This does not mean that the church controls the Word; the church is constituted by the Word, not the Word by the church. The church is less than the Word: her life is "in the Word." "Since the church owes to the Word of God its birth, nourishment, protection and strength, it is obvious that it cannot be without the Word; if it is without the Word, it ceases to be the church." Again: "The church owes its birth to the Word of promise through faith, and by the same Word it is nourished and protected. That is, the church is constituted by the promises of God. ... For the Word of God is incomparably higher than the church."[23]

The proclamation of the Word, by which the church lives, belongs to the church as a whole and to each member individually. This is what Luther means, in part at least, by the repeated affirmation that all Christians, by right of baptism or faith, are priests. Strictly, there is but one priest of the new covenant.

> Neither does his priesthood consist in the outward splendor of robes and gestures, like the human priesthood of Aaron and of our church today, but in spiritual things, whereby he intercedes with God for us by virtue of his invisible office in heaven.... And within our spirit he teaches us with the lively teachings of his Spirit. These two are the proper offices of a priest, as is figured visibly in the prayers and preaching of those who are priests of flesh and blood.[24]

And yet all who are united with Christ by baptism and faith share in this one priesthood. As Christ's *consacerdotes* ("fellow priests") they participate in his double office of intercession and instruction. In other words, the commission to proclaim the gospel is given to every Christian because faith has made him one with the priest and mediator of the new covenant. "We are all equally priests, that is, we have the same power in the Word and any sacrament." "All have the right and power to preach," for "there is only one office of preaching God's Word, and this office is common to all Christians." "If it is true that they have the Word of God and are anointed by him, they are bound to confess, teach, and spread it abroad." Preaching is to "proclaim God's wonderful deeds," and Peter tells us that this belongs to the royal priesthood.[25]

From this it follows that the individualistic interpretation of the common priesthood, according to which each man is his own, self-sufficient priest, misses the main direction of Luther's thinking: the priest faces toward his neighbor and serves him in the things of God. To be sure, it is the privilege of the priest that he has free access to God. Luther can therefore state categorically that we need no other priest or mediator than Christ. Such a statement, viewed in isolation, might well seem to support the individualistic interpretation of the common priesthood. But it must be interpreted by Luther's repeated insistence that to be a priest is to be a priest *for others*. For the function of a priest is "to mediate between God and men—to make sacrifice to God on men's behalf, and to teach and instruct men concerning God." The notion that every Christian is a priest, and that no Christian needs a priest, comes perilously close to being nonsensical. Luther's view is rather that the members of the Christian community are mutually interdependent, not that each can subsist alone "like Luther in his tower room." The believer is a king for himself, but a priest for others; and for this reason the priesthood is higher. "We are not only the most free of kings, but are also priests forever. That is something far more excellent than ruling, since through the priesthood we are worthy to appear before God, to pray for others, and mutually to teach one another [*nos invicem*] the things of God. For these are the offices of priests...."[26]

IV

The Roman priesthood is therefore doubly wrong. First, the Roman Catholic church reserves the priestly functions for a particular class within the body of Christ. Against this Luther takes his stand on the spiritual equality of all Christians, despite the many inequalities (physical, intellectual, social) that exist in the eyes of men. Even the distinction between the official minister and the ordinary Christian must be understood as a distinction within the royal priesthood, within the one spiritual estate, and it says nothing about one's standing before God or about freedom of access to his presence. This is the repeated theme of the familiar treatises of 1520. "All Christians are truly of the spiritual estate [stands]...." "All of us together are one body...." "Baptism, the gospel, and faith—these alone make us spiritual and a Christian people." "Through baptism we are all of us consecrated priests." "We are all priests, as many of us as are Christians." "Injustice is done to the words 'priest,' 'cleric,' 'spiritual,' 'ecclesiastic,' when they are transferred from all other Christians to the few who are now (by a pernicious usage) called ecclesiastics."[27] And so on.

Secondly, in the Roman view, the priestly functions center on the offering of a propitiatory sacrifice, not on the proclamation of the gospel. The Roman priesthood and the Evangelical priesthood are therefore two totally different things. "He who does not preach the Word, although called by the church for this very thing, is certainly no priest.... They who are ordained only to read the canonical hours and offer masses are indeed papal, but not Christian, priests. For not only do they not preach, they are not even called to preach."[28] It was for this reason that Luther warned the Bohemians against seeking ordination from Italian bishops or accepting as a minister any one so ordained (unless he first renounced the Roman view of ordination). On the Roman interpretation, it was the power to consecrate the elements and to pronounce absolution, conferred in the sacrament of order, that made a priest.[29] For Luther, on the other hand, the priestly functions are chiefly intercession and the proclamation of the Word.

V

The proclamation of the Word, in Luther's thinking, assumes more than one form. Hence he can speak on occasion of several priestly functions. We must say, indeed, that he assigns to the royal priesthood all the functions that, in other places, are assigned to the church's official ministry. In the treatise *On Appointing Ministers of the Church* he lists seven priestly functions: teaching or preaching, baptism, consecration or the administration of the Lord's Supper, binding and loosing sins, intercession, sacrifice, and the judging of doctrines.[30] Most, perhaps all, of these functions are understood as concrete forms of the Word.

"The first and foremost of all, on which everything else depends, is the teaching of the Word of God. For we teach with the Word, we consecrate with the Word, we bind and loose with the Word, we baptize with the Word, we sacrifice with the Word, we judge all things by the Word." And again: the "foundation for all the other functions" is "the function of preaching the gospel."[31] Especially the sacraments and the keys are understood as, like the sermon, forms of the Word; for the Word sometimes means, not preaching as one form of the proclamation, but the actual content of preaching—the gospel itself.

Luther takes up each of these priestly functions in turn and shows seriatim that they all belong to the whole priesthood and to every member. The priestly functions are committed in the primary sense to the church, and to individuals consequentially as parts of the whole. Christ gave the keys, for example, not to Peter, nor to any other individual, but to the church. Each individual Christian may use the keys by virtue of his membership in the body;[32] and the Roman Catholic claim that, though the *power* of the keys is given to all, their *use* is reserved for the bishops cannot be supported.[33]

And yet Luther's own argument often seems to turn around a similar distinction between "power" and "use." He himself apparently reserves the exercise of the priestly functions for a special class within the church. Certain officials are to be appointed who shall use the powers given to all "in the place, and by the command, of the rest."[34] From some of Luther's writings—the appeal *To the Christian Nobility,* for example—one might fairly draw the conclusion that the common priesthood confers little more than a dormant privilege, which is awakened only in some special emergency. The Christian may baptize, grant absolution, judge doctrine, call a council—*in case of emergency.* His priesthood also includes the right to become a minister, but only if so charged by his fellow priests; this, too, is more a potential than an actual privilege. Even the right to share in the election of ministers can only, in the nature of the case, be exercised from time to time. The only regular function of the common priesthood in the "appeal" seems to be the judging of doctrine; and Luther is interested in this, too, only because of the breakdown of the clerical office. At this point a clarification of the relationship between priesthood and ministry becomes essential.

VI

Occasional hints in Luther's writings seem to imply that the church could exist without an official, public ministry of the Word. He thinks that the Hussites might well leave the ministry of the Word and the administration of baptism to the father in each family.[35] And he dreams of a "truly Evangelical church order," according to which real Christians would not meet publicly, but in private homes."[36] But the advice to the Hussites was made in an emergency, and perhaps the Evangelical house-church was not meant to exclude a special class of ministers—nor even, in addition, a public liturgy. In any case, Luther never built on these incidental hints. Rather he sees the church's need for the Word as demanding the setting aside of men specially fitted for the work of proclamation. The great commission is fulfilled in a succession of ministers going back to apostolic times. "If the apostles, evangelists, and prophets have ceased, others must have come in their place, and must continue to come until the end of the world, for the church shall not cease until the end of the world...."[37] It is the ministry in *this* sense—a special, set-apart class of men—that constitutes a mark of the church. In other words, the apostolic ministry belongs to the *esse* of the church; and it is something distinct from the royal priesthood.

As is known well enough, Luther's refusal to dissolve the ministry in the common priesthood rests on his view of the ministry as a public office exercised within an established congregation. All three words, "public," "office," and "congregation," are important. (1) The main point of distinction between the set-apart pastor or preacher and the rest of the royal priesthood is his "office," "work," or "ministry." This difference of job or function does set the minister apart from the rest, but only in the sense that one must also distinguish between princes, cobblers, smiths, and farmers. These are all differences within the spiritual estate, within the body; for each limb has its own function for the good of the whole.[38] (2) It belongs to the essence of this ministerial office that it is performed in public. "Although it is true that we are all equally priests, yet we are not all able to serve and teach *publicly* [my italics], nor should we if we could."[39] (3) Finally, the locus of the ministry is an established congregation, a parish. "It is true that all Christians are priests, but not all are pastors. For besides being a Christian and a priest, one must also have an office and a parish [*kirchspiel*] committed to him." In opposition to the "sneaks," Luther claims explicitly that the parish system was ordained of God, and this claim belongs inseparably with his idea of the ministerial office.[40]

But all this does not answer the question, Why do we need an official ministry in the church? It is not sufficient to answer that the ministry exists for the proclamation of the Word, for we have already seen that this proclamation is entrusted to the church as a whole. The apparent ambiguity of Luther's answer may perhaps be detected in a single sentence from his treatise *On the Councils and the Church.* He tells us there that we must have pastors and preachers to minister both publicly and individually "for the sake, and in the name of, the church, but still more because of the institution of Christ."[41] Here the delegation theory and the institution theory seem to lie together side by side, unreconciled, but with a definite bias toward the idea of divine institution. They are linked simply by *viel mehr aber* ("but still more"). And each line of thought can be further documented from the sources.

According to one line of answer, the ministry is in the church because, although all have the right to minister, not all should. So Luther continues in *On the Councils:* "The whole group cannot do this, but must commit it, or allow it to be committed, to just one. Otherwise, what would happen if everyone wanted to speak . . . ?" The ministry is there for the sake of good order: if all exercised their priesthood when the congregation came together, chaos would result; it would be like the chatter of housewives on their way to market, none wishing to listen but all wanting to talk; there would be a din like a chorus of frogs; the church would become a tower of Babel. Similarly, if all insisted on doing the baptism, the poor infant would be drowned. So, then, whereas Protestants sometimes object, Why do we need a professional ministry if all are priests? Luther (in one line of thought) infers the necessity for the ministry precisely from the universality of the priesthood: it is because all are priests that the exercise of the priestly functions in public must be delegated.[42]

This line of thought is particularly strong in the treatises of 1520. The appeal *To the Christian Nobility* gives the familiar illustrations of the ten princes and the captive Christians. The point to be illustrated is stated in these words: "Consecration by the bishop is just as though, in the place and person of the whole congregation, he were to take one from the multitude, all of whom have the like power, and charge him to exercise this same power for the others." This, Luther tells us, is as though ten brothers, all sons of a king and alike heirs, were to choose one of their number to rule the inheritance for them. Or again, he bids us suppose that a little group of Christian laymen, taken prisoner and confined in a deserted area, were to choose one of their number by common consent and charge him with the ministerial office. Then the man would truly be a priest—that is, presumably, a pastor or clergyman.[43] Luther adds the second illustration to make the first clearer. But one is bound to say that the point of the second illustration is, if anything, somewhat less clear. Perhaps all he is saying is that the act of choosing is what makes an Evangelical minister and this choosing belongs properly to the Christian congregation. But it seems that in following this line of thought he does use the idea of representation or even delegation. The minister performs his work *for* the rest and *on their authority*. "For" cannot mean simply "for their good" (W. Brunotte), at least not in every place where it occurs. It seems to mean that the public exercise of priestly rights—though not the rights themselves—is always subject to the will of the people, all of whom possess them. The minister is the mouthpiece of us all: he ministers "in the place and name of all." Hence, from the fact that the ministry is committed to someone only by common consent Luther infers that the papists "have just so much right to lord it over us as we of our own accord permit."[44] It does appear, then, that—sometimes, at least—he establishes the ministry from below, deriving it from the common priesthood. But this is certainly not his only line of thought.

In other places, Luther speaks of the ministry as a distinct, a divine institution: that is, the existence of a special ministry in the church is traced to an express command of Christ. It is perhaps surprising that this view is stated unambiguously in the appeal *To the Christian Nobility,* the same writing that also serves as the favorite source for the rival interpretation. In his fourteenth proposal for reform (on celibacy) Luther writes: "I say that according to the institution of Christ and the apostles each town ought to have a pastor [*pfarrer*] or bishop, as Paul clearly writes in Titus 1...." Again: "I am not here concerned with popes, bishops, canons, and monks, whom God has not instituted.... I want to talk of the pastoral estate [*pfarr stand*], which God has instituted and which must rule a congregation with preaching and the sacraments, dwell and set up house among them."[45] Christ did not merely give the Word and sacraments to the church; he also ordained that the public proclamation of the Word and administration of the sacraments should be assigned to certain specially designated officials. "As he has bound the Holy Spirit to the Word, so he has bound the proclamation of the Word to the institution of the ministry."[46]

Various attempts have been made to harmonize these two lines of thought. In particular, several scholars have pointed out that Luther's appeal to order is based on the words of Scripture (1 Cor. 14:40): that is, he is speaking precisely of a divinely instituted order, not of simple expediency.[47] My own judgment is that we cannot fully eliminate the tension in Luther's position. His language clearly indicates that social-political analogues are present, at least in the back of his mind, even though they play a strictly subordinate role. Indeed, given Luther's characteristic view of the church, they *can* only play a minor, uncertain role; for the church is not a democratic association of men with equal rights. If Luther occasionally speaks in this way, what he then says can only be regarded as marginal. This conclusion is in fundamental agreement with Hellmut Lieberg's, who maintains that the way in which Luther bases the concrete ministry on the common priesthood is certainly not free from the principles of political association *(genossenschaftsrechtliche Elemente).*[48] And yet, as Lieberg insists, Luther's view cannot be accounted for solely in terms of secular associations or democratic procedures: the notion of delegation is qualified by Luther's understanding of the church as the communion of saints, acting under Christ's commission, as well as by the other, more prominent notion of the ministry as a divine institution. Perhaps there is also something to be said for Lieberg's finding in the bipolarity of this position a safeguard against the opposite tendencies of Rome and congregationalism, each of which, he claims, isolates one of the two distinct lines of thought.

VII

One consequence of Luther's teaching on the ministry is that the idea of the common priesthood is strictly limited. And yet it would be an injustice to him to speak as though the priesthood of all believers had no permanent validity of its own. It is not merely a bridge over which one must pass to formulate an

Evangelical doctrine of ministry; it belongs as an irreducible factor in his teaching on the means of grace.

In general, every Christian is under the obligation to witness to God's Word in the private sphere. The word "private" perhaps suggests to us something different than it did to Luther. Nowadays, when a Protestant speaks of the "right to private interpretation," for example, he pictures the individual Christian alone with his Bible; and the meaning of the common priesthood has often been explained in this way. For Luther, on the other hand, the priesthood of all believers was being exercised privately when one brother mediated the Word of God to another in personal converse. In this context "private" means simply "nonofficial." Conversely, "public" means "official"; and absolution pronounced by an ordained minister in the course of his pastoral duties to an individual penitent would not be "private," in this usage, even if it were given behind closed doors. But when one Christian speaks to another a word of reproof or consolation, the priesthood of all believers is being exercised. For "among Christians each is the other's judge and, conversely, also subject to the other." And "Christ has given to every one of his believers the power to absolve even manifest sins."[49]

Beyond this normal and permanent exercise of the common priesthood, a Christian may on occasion be bound to exercise his priesthood even in public; for necessity knows no law. In an emergency—that is, a situation in which the official ministry is not available—any Christian may and must assume the responsibility of administering the Word. Such a situation would arise if the Christian found himself in an area where there was no congregation, or in a congregation in which the Word was not preached purely, or in a location that the ordained minister could not reach in time to perform urgent services. Hence the unordained Christian must proclaim the Word among the heathen; he must contradict a minister whose teaching is in error; and he must be ready to perform emergency baptism or grant deathbed absolution.[50] It seems that the only priestly function the unordained may not perform, either regularly or occasionally, is the administration of the Lord's Supper. Luther offers three reasons for this firm refusal: the Lord's Supper is by its very nature a public act of the church; it is not (as is the Word or gospel) absolutely necessary for salvation; and to administer the Supper outside of public worship would be schismatic.[51]

There is a further sense in which the exercise of the common priesthood is limited: although it is the sufficient spiritual *right* for receiving a call to the ministry, Luther added to it in practice certain general and special *qualifications*. In general, a call may not be issued to women, children, or idiots, though they belong to the royal priesthood; equality of spiritual rights and standing cannot be permitted to outweigh the inconveniences, much less the express prohibition of Scripture against women preachers.[52] The candidate who is not excluded on these general grounds must still undergo a detailed examination to determine special qualifications or aptitude: he must be sound in doctrine, apt to teach, and pure in life. In short: "Although everyone has the right to preach, one should not use anyone for it, nor should anyone undertake it, unless he is better qualified for it than the rest."[53]

VIII

The act by which one member of the common priesthood is set apart from the rest for the regular and public exercise of the priestly functions is ordination. For Luther, ordination is virtually synonymous with calling. Sometimes he makes the simple equation explicitly; at other times he has in mind the liturgical act which confirms and completes the call. In any case, Hans Storck rightly says that "calling, ordination, and installation are identical in theological content."[54] Formerly, God called at least some directly; nowadays, a call has to come through the church, or else to be supported by the performance of miracles. Luther was not impressed by claims to an inner call of the Spirit; on the contrary, he was inclined to see in such claims evidence of satanic working. In the outward call of the church, on the other hand, he found the most solid assurance against the temptation to vocational uncertainty.[55]

In Luther's remarks on ordination the ambiguity in his doctrine of the ministry again makes an appearance. Sometimes the human agency through which the call comes is the congregation, and their right to call rests (in part) on their common priesthood. And yet it must be granted that the idea of the ministry's transmission through a succession of ministers was not alien to Luther. We should make allowance for historical context when he speaks of the congregational call as sufficient: this is the procedure acceptable in an emergency. No doubt, the emergency situation demonstrates that he did not regard episcopal ordination as essential; indeed, he even recognized the legitimacy of calling by the secular authorities. But what he was prepared to accept in necessity does not tell us what he would have preferred under better circumstances. If he allowed that ordination by bishops was not essential in emergency, he could also conceive of an emergency in which the bishop should ordain without the people's consent. What Luther really wanted was a process of calling in which both people and superiors had their place. He hoped that in the second generation (so to speak) the episcopate would be restored and would resume its traditional responsibility in ordination, but always with the people's consent. His advice on emergencies shows that this hope could not have been founded on a view of the episcopate as the exclusive transmitter of the apostolic ministry.[56]

To the question whether ordination—in particular, the laying on of hands—confers some special charisma or divine grace, the answer should probably be, for Luther, No. In his way of thinking, everything centers on the idea of calling, and to speak of ordination as imparting a special gift is to shift the center elsewhere. "In Luther's view ordination is only a public confirmation of calling, and what is received in calling is not some special gift of grace or power but a commission."[57] Nor does ordination transmit any "indelible character." Luther does not think of the ministry as attached to the person in this manner; he defines it in such strictly functional terms that it cannot be considered inalienable. If the ordained pastor neglects his ministerial functions, he forfeits his office, and it is the duty of the common priesthood to remove him. The ideas of "ordination" and "succession" in Luther's thought do not guarantee the purity of the Word. The Word always stands over the minister, and he may be judged by it. Hence although Luther can speak of a "succession" in the church, this was not, in his judgment, guaranteed by the grace of ordination, but by the will of God who raises up ministers of the Word when and where he will.[58]

IX

How, then, does Luther relate priesthood and ministry? The most appropriate formula seems to be that he identifies their functions but makes a distinction between their normal spheres of exercise. The appointment of a professional minister, therefore, cannot mean that the priestly rights of the congregation are thereupon resigned to their elected representative. We may speak (with Hans Storck) of resigning in love the right to be a *public* servant of the Word.[59] The priestly functions themselves, however, are inalienable, and their exercise is not merely a privilege but an obligation. The public exercise of the ministry and the private exercise of the priesthood exist together in the church as complementary vehicles of the Word. Luther expressed this succinctly in his Smalcald Articles (1537):

> I want now to come back to the gospel, which gives us counsel and help against sin in more ways than one, for God is lavishly rich in his grace: first, through the spoken Word, in which the forgiveness of sins is preached in all the world, this being the proper office of the gospel; second, through baptism; third, through the holy sacrament of the altar; fourth, through the power of the keys; and, finally, *through the mutual conversation and consolation of the brethren.*[60]

What Luther elsewhere identifies as the inalienable duty and privilege of the entire priesthood is here elevated to the status of a fifth means of grace alongside preaching, the two sacraments, and absolution. It is one of the forms the gospel assumes in the richness and diversity of divine grace. In this context, then, ministry and priesthood are not confused; neither is derived from or reduced to the other, but they exist together as mutually enriching modes of God's working, different in form but identical in content.[61]

It is true that the clarity and simplicity of this position is clouded not only by the attempt (made elsewhere) to derive the ministry from the priesthood, but also by an inconsistent terminology. (1) Though Luther's characteristic use of the word "priest" makes it synonymous with "believer" or "Christian," he continues to use it also in the traditional sense (for a Roman Catholic clergyman) and, equally, to designate the Evangelical minister of the Word. But the meaning is usually obvious from the context, and he sometimes explicitly qualifies his usage.[62] (2) Similarly, in some of his writings Luther brings back the old terminology of the clerical estate. But, once again, there is no reason why this need prove embarrassing, for the terminology is clearly given a Lutheran interpretation: "estate" *(Stand)* is defined by "office" *(Amt)* and is parallel to the secular estate of worldly authority, in which also there are various offices. True, Luther considers the spiritual estate higher, but this is because of what God works through it: not just outward peace, but the salvation of souls.[63] (3) Finally, Luther does further violation to his own terminology by assigning to the common priesthood as such various "offices," though here, too, he notes that this is done out of deference to inherited usage. In English, we do better to speak of priestly "functions" rather than "offices." The important thing is that for Luther the priesthood of all believers is not *amtlich* in the sense of something official, though it certainly entails the performance of a brotherly service, and it may not be wholly inappropriate (though possibly it invites confusion) to speak of this service as "ministry."[64]

It is another question whether this fundamental standpoint, even when shown to be coherent, correctly interprets what the Scriptures mean by the royal priesthood; for Luther pictures a mutual priesthood within the church rather than a priestly mission of the church to the "nations." Certainly, his view is not individualistic, but neither is it corporate in quite the same sense as the biblical priesthood. It is rather societal, and treats the church as a community of mutually related individuals. This is not to say that the Bible knows of no such relation within the church, only that this does not seem to be the meaning of the royal priesthood; Luther's priesthood of all believers is not unbiblical, but it is not exegesis either.[65] One might well argue that the biblical view of the royal priesthood has been maintained, not in the Protestant churches, but in the "catholic" tradition, both Roman and Anglican. The question remains, of course, whether Roman Catholic theology succeeds in relating biblically the royal priesthood and the Christian ministry—or, as the Roman Catholic himself might put it, the two priesthoods. The same question must also, however, be asked of Luther, since the New Testament nowhere builds a doctrine of the ministry on the priesthood of believers. Perhaps Luther's successors saw this more clearly than did Luther himself, for Melanchthon and Calvin abandon the subordinate line in Luther's doctrine of the ministry: both refer the ministry solely to the institution of Christ, and remove discussion of the common priesthood to another context.[66]

Six

Gospel and Eucharist:
John Calvin on the Lord's Supper

In a widely used history of Christian thought the judgment is made that "Calvin can be studied, exhausted, and mastered." He is contrasted in this respect with Luther, who left behind him unpolished gold, so that successive generations of scholars have studied his writings "seemingly without exhausting them." The judgment and the contrast rest on the common image of Calvin as a logical, systematic thinker with a special talent for organization. In actual fact, the clarity and consistency of his teaching, not least on the Lord's Supper, can be exaggerated. In his own opinion, a merit of his position, over against the views of his rivals, was indeed its superior clarity. But whether or not a claim for Calvin's *relative* clarity could be sustained, it still remains true that his language is complex; it could lead in more than one direction, and it is not easy to harmonize all his different assertions. Further, some of the terms he uses—such as "substance"—are ambiguous, perhaps obscure. The task of "mastering" his eucharistic ideas is by no means simple.[1]

The present century has witnessed something of a "Calvin renaissance"—a little renaissance, let us say, since it was not able to match the enormous output of the Luther scholars. One result of the renewed interest in Calvin was the breaking of certain inherited stereotypes that had lent the illusion of simplicity to his theological thought. It is no longer possible, for example, to assume that predestination is the structural center of his entire system. Again, the old image of Calvin as a severely theocentric thinker has been modified by a fresh appreciation of the christological strand in his theology. Finally, to mention just one more point, recent literature on his doctrine of the Lord's Supper has drawn attention to the differences between Calvin and Zwingli. One reason for the new look in Calvin research has been the refusal to regard him as a man of a single book; the entire corpus of his writings, and not just the *Institutes,* has been subjected to careful study. Another reason has been the influence of the Barthian theology, which has made us aware of much in Calvin that the orthodox Calvinists neglected or overlooked. Whatever other explanations there may be for the breaking of the old stereotypes, all three of the shifts in interpretation that I have mentioned must play a significant role in any discussion of Calvin's eucharistic ideas.

If caution is needed because of the complexity of Calvin's thinking, a further note of warning has to be added by reason of the highly controversial nature of eucharistic questions. During the sixteenth century, each party's teaching on the Lord's Supper was developed dialectically, in conversation with rival interpretations; and conversation sometimes became bitter polemic. Hence it may be hard to approach the historical questions unmoved by confessional commitments. In the final analysis, theological decisions may have to be made. But only in the final analysis. The decisions should not be there at the beginning, where they control the course of the historical interpretation. Calvin's doctrine of the Lord's Supper is not adequately understood as, for example, a critique of medieval teachings; nor as a deviation from Lutheranism; nor as an attempt to formulate a compromise position among the various Protestant options. It would be easy to point to attempts at interpretations along these lines. But the only approach that does justice to Calvin himself must begin with his own chief theological concerns, and must ask how he saw the relationship between his gospel and his understanding of the Lord's Supper. Calvin's thought moves outwards from his apprehension of the gospel to his interpretation of the Eucharist. The inner coherence of his thinking is of far greater importance than its dialectical relationships, although no actual separation should or can be made between the inner and the outer concerns.

To take a concrete case in point, it makes no sense to begin from the Marburg Colloquy, at which Calvin was not present, and then to interpret the subsequent eucharistic debates on the Marburg model. It is surprising how often the debate of 1529 between Luther and Zwingli and their respective followers has been taken as the paradigm for the Lutheran-Reformed differences on the Eucharist. Not Zwingli's, but Calvin's mind was to be the decisive influence on the Reformed church; and in the judgment of Calvin, Luther was the clear victor in the first intra-Protestant debate on the Lord's Supper. So certain did he feel about his verdict that (as he himself admits) he did not at first even trouble to read Zwingli's eucharistic arguments; later he pronounced Zwingli's opinion on the use of the sacraments "false and pernicious."[2]

With these preliminary remarks in mind, I propose to approach Calvin's doctrine of the Lord's Supper from the perspective of his gospel. Only the main features of the theme "Gospel and Eucharist in Calvin" can be considered; I take them to be suitably gathered under four rubrics: the centrality of Christ's presence, the manner of Christ's presence, the eucharistic presence, and, finally, Calvin and the Reformed doctrine of the Lord's Supper.

I

What needs to be said under my first heading can be summarized in a single sentence from Calvin himself: "This," he asserts, "is the purpose of the gospel, that Christ should become ours, and that we should be ingrafted into his body."[3] The very structure of the *Institutes,* in its final edition, is designed to show the unconditional necessity for Christ as mediator. No doubt Calvin has, on occasion, been misread as furnishing a kind of natural theology, on which revealed theology is afterwards built up. In actual fact, he reverses this well-known order and holds that a knowledge of God in nature is attained only by those who have been reconciled to God through Christ. For Adam in paradise, the natural order would certainly have led from the school of nature to eternal life. But this route is no longer open to fallen man.[4] And in any case, Calvin points out, the fall of man was itself a turning away from Christ; for in him was man's life from the beginning, and man's salvation consists in returning to that source.[5] The entire history of salvation is presented as centering upon the person and work of the one mediator; even the patriarchs of the Old Testament were saved by Christ, though they lived before the manifestation of Christ in the gospel of the New Testament.[6]

We do not need to follow the details of Calvin's presentation in order to establish the obvious point that the content of the Christian faith is understood by him in strictly christocentric terms: Christ is the content of the gospel. In modern times no topic of Calvin research has been more hotly debated than the question, What is Calvin's central doctrine? Much of the older literature presumed that predestination was the center of his thinking; nowadays, there is general agreement that the older view was mistaken and can only be explained as a misreading of Calvin through the spectacles of later Calvinistic theology. But no other central doctrine has been found to take the place of predestination. The truth seems to be that Calvin did not teach the kind of theological system in which everything is inferred from some basic principle or principles. Nevertheless, the strongly christological character of his thinking has been more fully recognized; and if we cannot say that christology is the systematic center of his entire theology, still the christological reference does determine both the structure of the *Institutes* and the content of the major doctrines.

But in the quotation with which I began Calvin claims something more than this. Christ is not merely the content of the gospel; the purpose of the gospel is that he might become ours. In other words, when he speaks of the gospel, Calvin is not talking merely about Christ as the content of the saving history, but about the presence of Christ in the here and now. Though he seeks to show at length how Christ obtained our redemption by the whole course of his obedience,[7] his thinking culminates in the idea of a "secret communion" by which Christ-for-us becomes Christ-in-us. Calvin spoke frequently and emphatically about this "communion with Christ," and his friend Peter Martyr wrote him for further details. The reply deserves to be considered Calvin's most important discussion of the theme. He writes (in part):

> We become truly members of his body, and life flows into us from his as from the head. For in no other way does he reconcile us to God by the sacrifice of his death than because he is ours and we are one with him. . . . How this happens, I confess is something far above the measure of my intelligence. Hence I adore this mystery rather than labor to understand it. . . . He dwells in us, sustains us, gives us life, and fulfills all the functions of the head.[8]

The benefits of Christ, according to Calvin, are ours only as a result of this secret communion that we have with Christ himself.[9] In the *Institutes* he distinguishes two "graces" we receive from Christ: reconciliation (or justification) and sanctification.[10] Neither of the two is given precedence as the supposed center of Evangelical theology, since both look away to the christological point of reference above them. The dominant motif is the "real presence" of Christ with the Christian as the head of the body. This, of course, is to put the matter in our own words, not Calvin's, since he prefers to speak of the *arcana communicatio* or "secret communication" of Christ. But whichever term we use, we are already using eucharistic language before we come to speak directly about the Lord's Supper.[11]

II

If there lies at the heart of Calvin's gospel the thought of Christ's real presence or his real self-communication, the next question to be answered concerns the manner of that presence: *How* does Christ communicate himself? What is the vehicle of the real presence?

The question can be answered from three different viewpoints, and it is essential to hold the three together in giving a fair and adequate account of Calvin's teaching.[12] We may answer the question, first, from the standpoint of the human subject: Christ is present in the act of believing. Second, we may answer from the standpoint of the divine subject: Christ is present through the activity of the Holy Spirit. Third, we may speak of the external means: Christ is present through the Word. These three—faith, Spirit, and Word—must not be separated. To use an expression that is much in vogue at the present and that (in my opinion) represents Calvin's view very well, we must speak of an "event" in which Christ is redemptively present; and faith, Spirit, and Word are the essential factors in this event.[13]

Calvin's conception of faith is complex, built up out of several different moments, and yet remarkably consistent and well unified. Faith includes knowledge, and its proper object is Christ. But it is not mere historical knowledge; it does not look at Christ from the distance but embraces him.[14] Hence it is correct to say that by faith we "put on Christ" or are "engrafted into him."[15] But the mystery of faith is that we have it as a divine gift, not as a human accomplishment. Our thoughts must therefore be carried back to "the secret energy of the Spirit, by which we come to enjoy Christ and all his benefits": it is by the Spirit that Christ unites himself to us.[16] But we can press the argument further and ask *how* the Spirit confers the gift of faith upon us. And the answer is, through the Word or the gospel. Accordingly, Calvin can say that the proper object of faith is Christ "clothed with his gospel";[17] or he can state, without further qualification, that the Word is the instrument by which Jesus Christ is given to us.[18] Obviously, then, we have to hold these various factors together: faith, the Holy Spirit, and the Word or Gospel. And sometimes Calvin reminds us explicitly of their interconnection, since it was the error of the enthusiasts or fanatics to dissolve it. The Word is the Spirit's instrument, and the two are joined together by an indissoluble bond.[19]

Where, then, do the sacraments come in? As Calvin thinks of them, they are simply another form of the Word, so that what he says of the Word applies also, in general, to the sacraments.[20] The spoken form of the Word (in the church's proclamation) is in itself the sufficient vehicle of Christ's self-communication, but God has regard for the sensuous nature of his creatures and adds the Word in visible form.[21] From Augustine Calvin takes over the description of a sacrament as *verbum visibile* ("a visible word") in distinction from preaching as the Word spoken and heard.[22] The identity of content between sacrament and proclamation provides him with the clue to solving many of the old questions about how a sacrament works.

In general, the function of the sacramental signs is to represent the promises of God graphically: they picture the content of the Word, make the promises visible to the eye. In the final analysis, they are simply proclamation (or "seals" of the proclamation); and, like the Word preached, they are intended to support faith.[23] Hence it is a mistake to ascribe to the sacraments some kind of secret powers, endowed with quasi-magical effect.[24] "He is mistaken who thinks that something more is conferred on him by the sacraments than is offered by the Word of God and received by true faith."[25] Or again, we may say that since the sacraments are the Spirit's instruments, then without his working they are of no use, so that we may not view the signs in abstraction from the activity of the Spirit. The efficacy of the sacraments lies in that triple conjunction of Word, Spirit, and faith at which we have already looked. Any attempt to break the unity of this conjunction can only lead to misunderstanding.[26]

On the other hand, if the sacraments confer no more than the Word, it is equally clear to Calvin that they confer no less. The sacraments have the *same* function as the Word of God: to offer and present to us Jesus Christ.[27] In other words, the sacraments, like preaching, are the vehicle of Christ's self-communication, of the real presence. Only the most perverse misreading of the sources could conclude that the sacraments have for Calvin a purely symbolic and pedagogical function. Regrettably, one could point to such misunderstandings in the general literature, though not of course in the monographs; it should be plain, however, from our entire presentation that to treat the sacraments as, for him, merely didactic would undermine not only his view of the sacraments but also his conception of the Word of God. What we have in his teaching is not an either-or, but a both-and: Word and sacraments certainly have a pedagogic function, but this does not make them any the less vehicles of Christ's self-giving; the sacraments do instruct by means of graphic symbols, but they are also real means of grace by which the thing symbolized is communicated.

If this were not already clear enough from the entire progress of thought in the *Institutes*, it should be removed beyond all doubt by Calvin's careful and explicit statements about the nature of sacramental signs. To the relation of sign and thing signified he applies the language of the christological formula, "distinction without division": we must distinguish the sign from the thing signified, but we cannot separate them. Where the sign is, there is the reality also.[28] And since Christ himself is the reality—the "matter" or the "substance" of the sacraments[29]—the signs are nothing less than pledges of the real presence; indeed, they are the media through which Christ *effects* his presence to his people. The sign cannot be or become the reality, but it is not the symbol of an absent reality either. It is hardly too much to say that Calvin's entire sacramental theology lies implicit in his doctrine of sacramental signs (which, of course, he borrowed from St. Augustine).[30]

III

Once the idea of Christ's living presence, effected through the Word of God, has been presented as the heart of Calvin's gospel, his doctrine of the eucharistic presence is already half stated. The role he assigns to the Lord's Supper in the life of the church is traced to the fact that communion with Christ is not whole and perfect from the very first, but subject to growth, vicissitudes, impediments. He does not think of "receiving Christ" as a crisis decision, achieved once and for all, but rather as a magnitude subject to variation. In fact he is willing to say of receiving Christ what he refuses to admit concerning justification: it is partial *(ex parte)*.[31] An infinitesimal faith in Christ is enough for justification, but a fuller possession and enjoyment of Christ is always open to the believer.[32] And it is with this fuller possession that the Eucharist has to do.

The very nature of its symbolism suggests to Calvin that the Lord's Supper is a matter of nourishing, sustaining, and increasing a communion with Christ to which the Word and baptism have initiated us. To be sure, he makes no rigid, doctrinaire distinction between baptism and the Supper: he recognizes the possibility that ingrafting into Christ, normally the function of baptism, may be effected in the Eucharist.[33] Still, the eucharistic symbolism points in general to the deepening of a communion already begun: it is an aid by which, being already ingrafted into Christ, the Christian may be united with him more and more, until the union is made perfect in heaven.[34]

The special reverence Calvin felt for the sacrament of the Lord's Supper is too plain to be overlooked; nowhere is the man's piety more clearly disclosed. The person of the living Christ dominates his reflections on the sacrament; and yet the presence of the Lord remains in the end a mystery to be adored, not captured in theological explanations. What Calvin wrote to Peter Matyr about ineffable communion with Christ is echoed in his language about the Eucharist, in which the communion is nurtured: he is content to marvel at what he cannot comprehend.[35] Nevertheless, the main features in his interpretation of the central Christian rite can readily be identified. I put them in the form of seven propositions with brief elucidations. And at this stage it should not be misleading to note how he defines his own standpoint in opposition to the views he finds defective in others, since it can now be shown how his positive intent determines the polemic, not vice versa.

First, *the Lord's Supper is a gift*. This is fundamental to the whole orientation of Calvin's thinking on the sacrament. Nor is it by any means something obvious; it is precisely at this point that he parts company with Zwingli and stands in uncompromising opposition to Rome. (I leave aside the question how fair he was to either of the rival positions, since my interest, at the moment, is only in determining his own stand.) The Roman Catholic, so Calvin believed, thought of the Eucharist as a "good work," an offering presented by man to God. Against this notion he bluntly asserts: "There is as much difference between this sacrifice [of the mass] and the sacrament of the Supper as there is between giving and receiving."[36] It is God who gives; we do not give, we receive. The Eucharist is not a human offering but a divine gift.

Calvin found the Zwinglian position, in this respect, scarcely less defective than the Roman Catholic. To Zwingli, the Supper was an occasion for thankful recollection of Christ's death, and so for taking one's stand with the Christian community; the celebration moved at the level of the imagination and the understanding, and talk about "partaking of Christ's body" could only be a metaphor for believing in his sacrifice. Calvin, by contrast, disapproved of the Zwinglian tendency to make primary in the sacraments what is strictly secondary—the Christian's outward profession[37]—and he asserted that the body of Christ was once sacrificed so that we might partake of it now. Christ gave his body on the cross; he gives it daily.[38] True partaking of him as the bread of life is more than to believe, as eating is more than seeing; our mysterious communion with his life-giving flesh is not faith, but a consequence of faith.[39] Indeed, the concept of faith is itself at issue here: it does not see Christ in the distance but embraces him.[40] In short, the Supper is a gift; it does not merely remind us of a gift.[41]

Second, *the gift is Jesus Christ himself*. This Calvin never tires of saying. The gift is not to be identified with the benefits of Christ,[42] nor is our communion solely with the divinity of Christ. In the Eucharist we have to do with the whole Christ—indeed, in a special sense with his body and blood. For it was in his humanity that he won our redemption, in his flesh.

> It is not merely a question of being made partakers of his spirit; we must also participate in his humanity, in which he rendered all obedience to God his Father. . . . When he gives himself to us, it is in order that we may possess him entirely. . . . . Our souls must feed on his body and blood as their proper food.[43]

Third, *the gift is given through the signs*. Once again a criticism of both Zwingli and Rome is implied: against both, though for different reasons, Calvin levels the same accusation that both misrepresent the nature of a sign. In the Roman theory of transubstantiation the sign is in effect transformed into the thing signified: the substance of the bread becomes the substance of the body. The symbolic relationship is destroyed by a failure to maintain the distinction.[44] In the Zwinglian view, on the other hand, sign and reality are divorced, since the body of Christ is absent from the Supper. This, too, in its own way, destroys the symbolic relationship, in which the sign guarantees the presence of what is signified. When the elements are offered to us, Christ is offered to us with his body and blood. The signs "present" what they "represent": they are not bare or empty signs, but are joined with the reality they signify.[45]

Fourth, *the gift is given by the Holy Spirit*. This is all that can properly be meant if one ventures to talk of a "spiritual presence" (or a "spiritual eating") in the Calvinist Supper. It should not be taken to mean that Christ is present only in spirit, or only in the believer's imagination. (Both these views have been erroneously attributed to Calvin, although he takes pains to deny them in all his major writings on the Lord's Supper.) In Calvin's view, it is precisely the body and blood of Christ that are made present by the secret power of the Spirit; by assigning the presence of the body and blood to the work of the Spirit, he believed he could avoid any suggestion that Christ, if present, must somehow be enclosed in the elements of bread and wine.[46] He held that the Holy Spirit is the bond of union between the worshiper and the true, life-giving flesh of Christ; and he admitted that the mind could not be expected to comprehend what he thus proposed as an item of faith.[47] It follows that the sacraments are strictly *the Spirit's* means or instruments: where the Spirit is absent, the sacraments achieve no more than the sun shining on blind eyes or a voice sounding in deaf ears.[48]

Fifth, *the gift is given to all who communicate*, pious and impious, believers and unbelievers. This is not to say that it makes no difference whether we believe or not: if we receive the elements without believing, we receive them to our condemnation, not discerning the Lord's body.

> Christ proffers this spiritual food and gives this spiritual drink to all. Some feed upon them eagerly, others haughtily refuse them. Will the latters' rejection of them cause the food and drink to lose their nature? ... Nothing is taken away from the Sacrament; indeed, its truth and effectiveness remain undiminished. ... This is the wholeness of the Sacrament, which the whole world cannot violate: that the flesh and blood of Christ are no less truly given to the unworthy than to God's elect believers.[49]

Sixth, *the benefit of the gift is received by faith*. The sixth proposition rests on the intimate association of the sacraments with the Word of God, and it is directed, above all, against the impersonalization of sacramental efficacy in medieval Scholasticism. The Schoolmen taught that the sacraments of the new law confer grace provided only that no obstacle of mortal sin is in their way. Calvin detected in this "pestilential" notion a superstitious attachment to the sacramental sign as a mere physical thing—and, indeed, an implicit denial of the cardinal Reformation doctrine of justification by faith. A sacrament received without faith cannot be a sacrament correctly understood as an appendage to the divine Word or promise. The Word could in fact achieve its ends without the sacramental seal.[50] When the Word accompanies the sacrament, it must retain its essential character as proclamation; it is not a magical formula empowered to consecrate the elements even if mumbled in Latin. The sacramental Word is not an incantation but a promise; therefore, the eucharistic gift benefits only those who respond with the faith that the proclamation itself generates.[51] To revert to our previous language, the event in which the real presence occurs is not the consecrating of the elements, but the reception of the elements in faith under the action of the Holy Spirit.[52]

Seventh, *the gift evokes gratitude*. The sacrament, properly speaking, is an act of God; but in the broader liturgical sense—that is, as the service of worship in which the elements are given and taken—it is also an act of the church. As the name "Eucharist" implies, it is the church's thanksgiving for the gift given. According to Calvin, a eucharistic sacrifice, as opposed to a propitiatory sacrifice, is an indispensable part of the liturgy. It has nothing to do with the sacrifice of the mass, but is a liturgical act by which the communicants respond in grateful dedication to the Lord who surrendered his own life for their sake. And Calvin saw this liturgical act as something inseparable from the entire existence of the church and the individual Christian, since the life of faith is nothing but a eucharistic sacrifice: a thankful self-offering by the royal priesthood.[53]

IV

Perhaps there really is, at least on the pedagogical level, a surface simplicity about Calvin's eucharistic theology or, one might better say, his eucharistic faith. What he believed concerning the sacrament was summed up in this brief confession: "In his Sacred Supper [Christ] bids me take, eat, and drink his body and blood under the symbols of bread and wine. I do not doubt that he himself truly presents them, and that I receive them."[54] In his role as a teacher—notably in the Geneva Catechism—he skillfully exploited the symbolism of nourishment, convinced that the sacrament, so interpreted, was comprehensible even to the dullest of devout minds.[55] And he was able to link the symbolism with his favorite image of God as father: in the Supper God fulfills the offices of a solicitous parent, feeding the children he adopted in baptism.[56] In sum, the Lord's Supper for Calvin was an effective image of the central Christian mystery, which eludes intellectual comprehension: it was an image of the Christian's secret union with Christ.[57]

Why, then, did the Reformed doctrine of the Lord's Supper become the subject of bitter contention? With Zwingli, it is not difficult to see why Luther was angered. In the Zwinglian view the unity of sign and reality, taken for granted by every party in the medieval controversies, fell apart; and with it went the naive confidence that in handling signs one is in touch with reality. Wonderfully expressive of a new mentality were the words adapted by Cornelisz Hoen from the Gospel of Matthew (Matt. 24:23): "If anyone says to you, 'Here [in the bread] is Christ,' do not believe him."[58] It was Zwingli who published Hoen's famous letter; and well he might, so persuasive did he find its sacramental ideas. Eric Heller has pointed out that the Marburg Colloquy did not merely occasion some scholastic logic-chopping but signaled a revolution. "And ever since Zwingli the most common response to the reality of symbols has been a shrugging of the shoulders, or an edified raising of eyes and brows, or an apologia for poetry, or an aesthetic theory."[59]

But Calvin is not Zwingli. Not only do our seven Calvinist propositions come very close to Luther's doctrine of the Lord's Supper, but it could also be shown in detail that at many points the language used echoes Luther's. Unlike Zwingli, who found the eucharistic imagery as repulsive as to speak of eating one's own children out of love, and who therefore had to make of it a harmless metaphor for faith,[60] Calvin seems to have thrived on it, as Luther did. He was convinced that Luther's understanding of the Lord's Supper was essentially the same as his, and that the difference concerned only the "mode" of Christ's presence (or the "mode" of partaking of him).[61] But some of the Lutherans suspected him of deviousness: he was merely trying, they thought, to cloak a Zwinglian view of empty signs.

The Calvinists (or crypto-Calvinists) are the "subtle Sacramentarians" condemned in the *Formula of Concord* (1577) as even more dangerous than their forthright Zwinglian kin.[62] The Lutheran test question for exposing a Calvinist was whether he allowed that in the Supper an oral eating of the body of Christ takes place (the *manducatio oralis*), and whether the wicked therefore partake no less than the devout (the *manducatio impiorum*).[63] Calvin did not pass the test but deplored it as a symptom of crass wrongheadedness. In his view the oral eating of the elements was a symbol for the imparting of life from the body and blood of Christ—and a means (or "instrument") by which it is brought about. He did not profess to know how this communication occurred (beyond attributing it to the Holy Spirit); but he believed it possible to affirm its occurrence without conceiving of Christ's presence as spatial extension "in the bread," and without the (to him) fearful assumption that the impious as well as the devout receive the body of the Lord.[64] By eating, the believer receives the body of Christ, while the unbeliever—to whom also the body is *given*—receives only the empty signs.[65]

It is not difficult to see why many of the Lutherans were not persuaded that Calvin differed from them only on the mode of partaking: if he could not confess that he took the body and blood of the Lord with his mouth, then, as they saw it, he did not receive the same eucharistic gift as they did. Perhaps the Lutheran insistence that the reception, though oral, is not "Capernaitic" could reopen the possibility of rapprochement.[66] But, be that as it may, the Lutherans found their suspicions confirmed by the apparent slipperiness of Calvin's use of such words as "substance" and "substantial." He claimed that in the Supper our souls feed on the substance of Christ's flesh, yet he never retracted his early denial (in the 1536 *Institutes*) of a substantial presence.[67] Further, his tendency was to employ various circumlocutions for what he took "eating Christ's body" to mean: he speaks of "receiving life *from* the body," of "the *power* of the body," and so on.[68] And his Lutheran critics could not fail to notice that a very Zwinglian thought was the cornerstone of this linguistic edifice: that the body of Christ, having ascended into heaven, is still circumscribed by the limitations of its humanity and cannot be physically present here below.[69]

No doubt, Calvin was struggling to assert somehow that the body of the Lord can be effectively present *to* the believer (not *in* the elements!) without occupying adjacent space.[70] He thought this entirely plausible if he identified the Holy Spirit as the "channel" between our bodies (on earth) and the Lord's (in heaven),[71] and if he said that Christ does not descend into the elements but raises us up to himself.[72] It does not seem to have occurred to him that others might justly find this language as crass as he found Luther's. Perhaps the most charitable construction we can put on his strange imagery is suggested by some reflections of the philosopher Leibniz, whose irenic thoughts on Protestant divisions were of some influence on the older Calvin literature (probably through Ebrard). We might say that Calvin was moving toward a fresh conception of the substance of Christ's body precisely as its force or power, so that the substance is present, albeit in a nondimensional way, wherever its power is applied.[73] This certainly accords well with Calvin's favorite simile: the radiance of Christ's Spirit imparts to us the communion of his flesh and blood, as the sun, by shedding its rays, casts its substance on the earth to give life and growth.[74]

There was one other feature of Calvin's sacramental theology that made it an occasion for controversy: strong though his affirmation of the sacramental union undoubtedly was, it was qualified by the doctrine of election. He read in Augustine that the sacraments effect what they symbolize only in the elect, and he drew the inescapable inference: figure and truth are not, after all, so joined together that they cannot be separated. Interestingly, however, he then goes on to state that a sacrament is separated from its truth by the unworthiness of the recipient, which is not the same point; and he concludes by admonishing us to grasp the Word in faith, so that we may not have an empty sign.[75] Would it be fair to conclude that Calvin was not much interested in bringing his sacramental theology into direct and explicit relationship to his predestinarianism?

His controversy with Joachim Westphal certainly bears this out. Among his many charges, Westphal alleged that Calvin jeopardized the efficacy of baptism by making it contingent upon predestination. In reply, Calvin admits that he did mention election in passing; but he insists that his Lutheran adversary has put a wholly false construction on the offhand remark, which was not intended to divert the attention of pious minds from the promise or the signs. (He evidently generalizes the point to include the Eucharist as well as baptism.) Now Calvin does not hesitate to reaffirm his conviction that in fact the Holy Spirit enlightens only the elect and sees to it that they do not use the sacraments in vain. No doubt there is a theological—or at least a practical—difficulty here, if the communicant's confidence in the signs of Christ's body and blood is exposed to predestinarian anxieties. But if Calvin thought the relationship of the sacraments to predestination worth only a mention in passing, we probably should not give it more but should leave the question of election, as he did, for another time.[76] What he wants us to think about in the sacramental context is that crucial conjunction of Word, Spirit, and faith that is the heart of Calvinist sacramental theology.

Seven   Sign and Reality: The Lord's Supper in the Reformed Confessions

It would be no great surprise if the classical Reformed confessions of the sixteenth and seventeenth centuries were found to contain a variety of eucharistic theologies. The confessions are both numerous and in origin diverse,[1] and it is common knowledge that the Reformed theologians of Switzerland were at first divided among themselves on the meaning of the Lord's Supper. Two types of eucharistic theology developed among them, with Zwingli and Calvin furnishing the respective models. What one might expect, in view of the mixed parentage of the Reformed church, is the coexistence of two independent eucharistic traditions, or a merging of the two, or, it may be, the eventual triumph of one over the other. In actual fact, the evidence is not so simple: it seems to call for the distinguishing of yet a third eucharistic type, of which Bullinger's Second Helvetic Confession may serve as the model. It is not claimed that these three types need be mutually exclusive, nor that each coincides completely with the thought of the Reformer who provides the confessional model. A full historical inquiry, which would take into account the nonconfessional writings of the Reformers and the eucharistic controversy as a whole, is not here attempted. It is suggested only that careful analysis of the confessions themselves invites the triple distinction.

I

The assumption still lingers, in the minds of their friends and their foes alike, that the differences between Zwingli's and Calvin's views on the Lord's Supper are not fundamental. Certainly, Calvin did share a number of Zwingli's eucharistic ideas. Nevertheless, the fact is that they represent two different types of eucharistic theology.

A number of Zwingli's writings may be considered confessional or quasi-confessional in character.[2] Without attempting, for the moment, to define the

118

notion of a "confession," I shall simply take account of the documents from Zwingli's hand that are included in one or more of the major collections of Reformed confessions. The earliest of these documents, Zwingli's Sixty-Seven Articles of 1523,[3] is terse, vigorous, and in tone polemical—a kind of Swiss Ninety-Five Theses. It does not contain a full or careful presentation on the Lord's Supper. Nonetheless, two basic notions are already present in this, the earliest Reformed confession: the Lord's Supper is both a memorial and a pledge. Christ offered himself up once and for all as an abiding satisfaction for sins. It follows that the mass is not a sacrifice, but a commemoration (*widergedächtnüss*) of the sacrifice once offered on the cross and a pledge (*sicherung*) of the redemption made manifest by Christ (Art. 18).

In the *Short and Christian Introduction*[4] of the same year, Zwingli again assails the sacrifice of the Roman mass and insists that Christ's "ordinance" is rather a commemoration and preaching of his one sacrifice upon the cross: not the breaking of the bread, but his death, was his sacrifice. All a man can now offer to God is himself, not Christ. He cannot sacrifice Christ, but he can commemorate the sacrifice of Christ, who has left us "a certain visible sign of his flesh and blood." Hence Christ called the Supper, not a sacrifice or mass, but a testament and memorial. Nevertheless, Zwingli freely uses the traditional terms "sacrament" and "food of the soul";[5] and he even speaks of "feeding believers with the body and blood of Christ" and "eating and drinking [*niessen*] the body and blood."[6] Apparently, his motives are pedagogic: he is plainly anxious to avoid offense to tender consciences, and his argument seems to be that *the people* have always believed the right thing about the Lord's Supper—that it is the food of their souls—despite the efforts of *the priests* to deceive them with the doctrine of the sacrificial mass.

Any possibility of interpreting this language in a "Lutheran" sense is ruled out in the *Fidei Ratio*[7] of 1530, Zwingli's "Augsburg confession," addressed to the Emperor Charles V. Here Zwingli bluntly repudiates the entire notion of the means of grace. The grace or pardon of God is given solely by the Spirit, who needs no vehicle; the sacraments merely testify in public that grace has been received in private. Thus in baptism testimony is given to the church[8] that grace has been exercised on him to whom the sacrament is given. A sacrament, in short, is a sign of past grace, of pardon consummated: it is *factae gratiae signum*. More precisely, it is a kind of picture or image (*figura, exemplum*) of the invisible grace God has given, a similitude (*analogia*) of what has been done through the Holy Spirit. Hence the washing of baptism signifies that by God's goodness we have been gathered into the fellowship of the church, which worships its Lord by purity of life.[9] The sacraments visibly associate with the church those who have previously been received into it invisibly.

It is no surprise, then, that when Zwingli turns to the Lord's Supper (or "Eucharist," as he prefers to say), he uses realistic language in a consciously figurative sense; for by his definition of a sacrament he has already ruled out any possibility of treating the signs as a vehicle by which Christ's body might be communicated (Art. 8). That the true body of Chirst is present to faith *(fidei contemplatione)* means that, while the worshipers thank God for his benefits in his Son, everything Christ did in the flesh becomes *as if (velut)* present to them. A plain "No" is therefore addressed to the Papists and "certain who look back to the fleshpots of Egypt": the natural body of Christ is not present in the Supper essentially and really, nor masticated with the mouth and teeth.

Obviously, then, despite his liberal use of the high sacramental terminology, Zwingli has not moved beyond the position of the Sixty-Seven Articles. It is made plain that realistic-sounding language about Christ's body is to be considered figurative or metonymous. To "distribute the body and blood in the Supper," for example, means to distribute the elements, which are signs of the the body and blood.[10] The key notion remains that of a memorial; the idea of a "pledge," on the other hand, recedes into the background.[11] But a third idea is added, that of a public confession which identifies a man with the Christian community. Aside from this third factor, the main contribution of the *Fidei Ratio* is to make more explicit Zwingli's understanding of sacramental language, and he believes that he derives his understanding from the fathers. The teaching of the fathers was "not that sacramental eating could cleanse the soul, but faith in God through Jesus Christ, the spiritual eating, of which the external [eating] is a symbol and figure [*symbolum et adumbratio*]." Zwingli displays a tendency, which becomes universal in Reformed thinking, to elaborate the symbolism of the sacramental elements and actions. "Just as bread sustains the body and wine enlivens and exhilarates it, so the fact that God gave us his Son confirms the soul and makes it certain of his mercy; and it revives the mind that the sins which consumed it have been extinguished by Christ's blood." We may say, then, that this fondness for symbolism is a fourth aspect of Zwingli's confessional writing on the Lord's Supper. But it is not just an ingredient like the other three; it is the overarching theory of sacramental language. The three basic ingredients are thankful recollection, the reassurance of faith, and union with the church. And where in the world, asks Zwingli, can that be better found than in the celebration of the sacraments? This is what the elements "say" to Zwingli (his own expression): they proclaim that salvation is from God, they exercise our faith, and they draw us together in a common confession. In other words, they have to do with our threefold relationship to God, self, and neighbor.[12]

In general, the *Fidei Expositio* (1531)[13] moves along the same lines. Zwingli's symbolic interpretation of the sacrament is developed in the direction of a kind of parallelism. In the Lord's Supper the spiritual feeding upon Christ by faith is symbolized by an outward eating of the bread: "You do inwardly what you enact outwardly." An inward spiritual occurrence is symbolically represented by a parallel outward and physical occurrence. The relation between the two occurrences is not causal, as though the outward eating gave rise to the inward;

Zwingli has nothing more to say about it than simply that the outward represents the inward.[14]

The *Fidei Expositio* also heightens the emphasis on the corporate aspect of the sacrament by giving an ecclesiological interpretation to the "body of Christ":[15] in the Eucharist we have to do with the ecclesial, not only the natural, body of Christ. This is an aspect of Zwingli's eucharistic thinking that has been strongly emphasized of late (notably by Julius Schweizer and Jaques Courvoisier).[16] I have no doubt about its theological importance, but its role in Zwingli's confessional writings is not especially prominent. The discussions on the Lord's Supper are mainly interested—though possibly for polemical reasons—in Christ's natural body; and even where Zwingli interprets "not discerning the body" ecclesiologically, he interprets it christologically also in the self-same sentence.[17]

At neither of these points—"parallelism" and the "ecclesial body"—does the *Fidei Expositio* add anything substantially new to the *Fidei Ratio*. It develops and undergirds what we have already noted in the earlier work; to be precise, it develops our fourth aspect (Zwingli's symbolism) and undergirds the third (identification with the Christian community through a public testimony).

II

The editors of the *Corpus Reformatorum* included ten writings under the heading "confessions" in their edition of Calvin's works.[18] But the only one of the ten that has established a place among the Reformed confessions is the French Confession, of which Calvin was not strictly the author. Some of the astonishing omissions from the standard collections can perhaps be explained.[19] But the neglect of one of Calvin's confessions remains (to me) a mystery: the excellent Confession of Faith he wrote in his closing years (1562) for the Reformed Christians of France. I shall make occasional reference to this confession, but I shall use as my main Calvin source the Geneva Catechism. Though the Catechism does not appear among the ten confessions in the *Corpus Reformatorum*, it is selected as Calvin's chief contribution in three major editions of Reformed symbols.[20]

The resemblance of Calvin's sacramental ideas to those of Zwingli is striking, and it is not surprising that the two positions have been judged substantially the same. What I have disentangled as the three ingredients of Zwingli's position all reappear in Calvin. In general, Calvin views the sacraments as pledges of God's goodwill toward us, which represent his spiritual benefits (Q. 310). This is their primary function. They also serve, secondly, as "badges of our profession," by which we identify ourselves with the Christian church (Q. 362). Here, then, are two of the fundamental Zwinglian ideas. Least in evidence is the notion of the Supper as a commemoration; but this also is perhaps implicit in the affirmation that the Lord's Supper "sends us back to [Christ's] death" (Q. 349). Finally, like Zwingli, Calvin has a fondness for elaborating the details of sacramental symbolism. The pouring of water pictures both cleansing from sin and the drowning of the old Adam (Qq. 325–26). Eating and drinking picture the sustenance and exhilaration we receive from Christ's body and blood (Q. 341).

What, then, justifies us in speaking of two types of eucharistic theology? The answer lies in the fact that Zwingli and Calvin held two totally different views of religious symbolism. Because the nature of the symbolical is not simply a fourth ingredient but the total determinant of sacramental theology, it follows that even the verbal agreements of Zwingli and Calvin are totally qualified and may conceal actual disagreement. Hence, though both can detect the same "analogies" in baptism and the Lord's Supper, the disagreement between the two men is more fundamental than their agreements, and puts Calvin on Luther's side of the line, not Zwingli's. For in Calvin's view it is the nature of the sacraments to cause and communicate *(apporter et communiquer)* what they signify.[21] On baptism Calvin says: "It is a figure in such fashion that the truth is joined with [*simul annexa;* Fr. *conioincte avec*]. God does not deceive us when he promises us his gifts. It is certain, therefore, that forgiveness of sins and newness of life are offered us in baptism and received by us" (Q. 328). Similarly, in the Lord's Supper the benefits of Christ are not just signified but given (Fr. *données*), so that he makes us participate in his substance (Q. 353). The Confession of 1562 is just as strongly worded: "Through the signs of the bread and wine our Lord Jesus presents to us his body and blood." The Supper is addressed both to the wicked and to the good, "to offer Jesus Christ to all without discrimination." The Lord Jesus "vivifies us with the proper substance of his body." "He does not fail to make us partakers of the substance of his body and blood."[22] And so on.

Such passages make it obvious why Calvin, without dismissing it, cannot make much out of Zwingli's favorite notion of commemoration: the focal point of his sacramental theology lies elsewhere—in the notion of the means of grace, a notion Zwingli had rejected. The two Reformers were both careful to make a distinction between sign and thing signified, and for the same reason: to avoid the merging of sign and reality in Roman Catholicism and Lutheranism. But this cannot obscure their complete disagreement over the nature of religious symbols. For Zwingli, symbolism is what enables him to use realistic language without meaning it realistically. For Calvin, symbolism is what assures him that he receives the body of Christ without believing in a localized presence of the body in the elements. No one, Zwingli tells us, can speak so grandly of the sacraments as to give him offense, provided the symbolical is taken for what it is, and no more. Let signs be signs! "If [the sacraments] bestowed the thing or were the thing, they would be things and not a sacrament or sign."[23] Calvin agrees that the sacraments cannot be both signs and the things signified.

But his position is still, in effect, the exact opposite of Zwingli's: *because* a sacrament is a sign, *therefore* it bestows what it signifies. More correctly, because sacraments are divinely appointed signs, and God does not lie, therefore the Spirit uses them to confer what they symbolize.[24]

III

In the next three sections it is not my intention to subject the Reformed confessions to detailed examination, but to ask of the major confessions which eucharistic type they seem to follow. And the point of division is whether their central thought on the Lord's Supper is commemoration or communication.

Of the Swiss confessions the First Helvetic Confession of 1536, a team product of the Reformed theologians, deserves to be mentioned first.[25] It shows plainly that what I have labeled the "Calvinistic type" of eucharistic theology is older than Calvin himself. The sacraments are signs, but not "mere empty signs" (Art. 20). They consist in "signs and essential things." (Latin: "They consist of signs and things at the same time.") In other words, the thing signified is inseparably bound up with the sacramental sign. In the Lord's Supper the thing signified is the communion *(communicatio)* of the body and blood, the salvation won on the cross, and forgiveness of sins, which are received in faith as the signs are received corporeally. It is, indeed, *through* the signs that the Lord offers his body and blood—that is, himself—to his people (Art. 22). The signs convey and offer the spiritual things which they signify. As with Calvin, so in the first Helvetic Confession the echoes of Zwinglian ideas are unmistakable. But at the decisive point Zwingli is left behind. The sacrament of the Lord's Supper does not *only* symbolize, commemorate, move us to joyful thanksgiving, and bind us in loyalty to the head and members of the church: it is also the means by which God gives what he promises.

It comes, then, as something of a surprise to turn to the Geneva Confession of the same year (1536) and find an explanation of the Lord's Supper that does not move beyond Zwingli. No doubt, it *could* be interpreted Calvinistically, but its language does not *require* such an interpretation. The sacraments represent, but it is not said that they give. It is hard to believe that Calvin even approved the statement, let alone wrote it, and it is significant that the latest research is inclined to attribute the Geneva Confession to Farel. Nevertheless, Calvin did not disapprove of the confession, and it was his desire that the Genevan citizens should be herded into the Cathedral of St. Pierre, lined up by the police, and obliged to confess under oath that this was their faith (July 1537).[26]

Heinrich Bullinger demonstrated in 1545 that Zwinglianism was still very much alive. His Zurich Confession,[27] provoked by renewed Lutheran attacks on the Swiss, defiantly asserts that remembering is the "real chief part and purpose" of the Supper. He who believes *has* eaten Christ's body, for eating is believing. The believer therefore brings Christ *to* the Supper in his heart; he does not receive him *in* the Supper. Of course, it is possible that an unbeliever may be present at the Supper, and he may certainly receive Christ there: that is, may become a believer. But the saving events themselves are present only in the believing imagination *(Eynbildung)*.

By the time Bullinger wrote the Second Helvetic Confession (probably in 1561), the Zurich Consensus had already closed the gap between the two eucharistic theologies. Schaff's description of the Second Helvetic Confession as "the last and the best of the Zwinglian family" needs some qualification.[28] In the Zurich Consensus[29] the favorite Zwinglian terminology was liberally employed, and Calvin trod softly in the introduction of non-Zwinglian ideas.[30] The consensus did not say all Calvin liked to say about the sacraments, only what he was not prepared to omit. But enough was said to put it beyond all doubt that Bullinger had moved beyond his teacher. God truly offers *(praestat)* what the sacraments symbolize (Art. 8). The reality is not separated from the signs, but Christ is received with his spiritual gifts (Art. 9). And so on.

That Bullinger did not consent to such expressions merely for a political accommodation with Geneva, is proved by the use of similar language in the Second Helvetic Confession,[31] in which he taught a sacramental union of sign and reality (Art. 19). And yet in some passages (Art. 21) Bullinger seems to be thinking in terms of a symbolic parallelism: outwardly we eat the bread, inwardly *at the same time* we also feed upon Christ's body. (In Latin, the connection is denoted by the words *intus interim*: "Meanwhile, inside.")[32] This, of course, does take us beyond Zwingli, whose characteristic tense is the past, not the present. In Zwingli's view, the elements call to mind something that has happened: Christ's body *was* broken, we *have* turned to him in faith.[33] And yet Bullinger's parallelism is not Calvin's position either, for it lacks the use of instrumental expressions; the outward event does not convey or cause or give rise to the inward event, but merely indicates that it is going on.

Perhaps, then, the original distinction between a Zwinglian and a Calvinistic type of eucharistic theology is not adequate for classifying the Reformed confessions. Is there, in fact, also a third type of Reformed Eucharist, of which Bullinger's Second Helvetic Confession serves as the model? I advance this suggestion at this point as a hypothesis, to be tested by other Reformed confessions.

IV

My hypothesis seems to me to be confirmed by the three main Continental Reformed confessions that originated outside of Switzerland: the French and Belgic Confessions and the Heidelberg Catechism. The French Confession of

1559, though not from Calvin's own hand, is for the most part a faithful summary of his theology, especially his sacramental theology.[34] The two sacraments are not empty signs, nor yet do they possess any intrinsic power; they are instruments employed by God to strengthen faith (Art. 34) and to give us Jesus Christ (Art. 37). God signifies nothing to us in vain (Art. 34). In both sacraments he gives us really and efficaciously (Lat. *efficaciter*) what he there represents to us, and with the sign is joined the true possession of what is signified (Art. 37).

The Belgic Confession (1561) was closely modeled on the French Confession, which in some articles it simply amplifies. On the sacraments, however, I would classify it as only semi-Calvinist. The statement on the sacraments in general (Art. 33) seems to follow the French Confession; but the article on baptism looks rather to Zwingli and Bullinger, and the article on the Lord's Supper then reverts to Calvinism.[35] If this is a correct reading of the Belgic Confession, then we have to make a further observation on the sacramental theology of the Reformed confessions: not only are different theological types represented in the *corpus confessionum* as a whole, but there may also be strange combinations within a single confession. However, on the Lord's Supper itself the Belgic Confession does not seem to differ from the French model: "This feast is a spiritual meal in which Christ communicates himself to us ... nourishing our poor souls by the eating of his flesh" (Art. 35).

The Heidelberg Catechism (1563)[36] shows a subtle variation from Calvin's Geneva Catechism at the very beginning of its presentation on the sacraments: it asks, not how does Christ communicate himself to us (cf. Geneva Cat., Q. 309)? but how do we obtain faith (Heidelberg Cat., Q. 65)? This is not, I think, a trivial distinction, but a quite fundamental one; for the Heidelberg Catechism is apparently shy about the notion of sacramental means. Despite the contrary judgments of Schaff and Müller, it does not seem to me that the catechism teaches a full Calvinistic doctrine of the sacraments.[37] The treatment is highly didactic and intellectualistic: the sacraments confirm faith, seal the promise, help us to understand, point us to the cross, remind and assure us, testify to us, and so on. The characteristic formula is *"so gewiss ... so gewiss":* as certainly as I am washed with water and eat the bread, so certain can I be that Christ's blood cleanses me from sin and his body nourishes my soul. Of course, the sacraments do not merely inform us that forgiveness is like washing, believing like eating; they also assure us that we really are washed from our sins and united with Christ's body. The broken bread of the Lord's Supper does not only point back to the body broken on the cross, but means also that by the same broken body I am continually fed. The signs are also pledges. The catechism explicitly teaches a communion with the body of Christ and, like Calvin, makes the Holy Spirit the bond of union between Christ's body in heaven and ourselves on earth. But the elements do not convey this union; they remind us that we have it independently of the sacraments. Hence those who should come to the table are those who trust that their sins are (already!) forgiven and desire to strengthen their faith and improve their life. The overall verdict on the catechism must be, then, that its sacramental theology owes more to Zwingli and particularly to Bullinger than to Calvin.

V

Finally, I would wish to argue along the same lines in interpreting the British Reformed confessions: if my triple distinction is used as the measure, the results are again very mixed. Whether or not the Anglican Thirty-Nine Articles (1563/71)[38] belong among the Reformed confessions, I would classify their teaching on the Lord's Supper as cautiously Calvinistic. Zwinglianism is plainly ruled out, and the focal point is the *communicatio corporis*: the body of Christ is "given, taken, and eaten in the Supper, only after an heavenly and spiritual manner" (Art. 28). This could, of course, be read as parallelism; it is at least ambiguous, and neither on the sacraments in general nor on the other sacrament do the articles say unambiguously that through the signs God gives what they signify.[39] The definition of a sacrament in the Anglican Catechism (1662),[40] on the other hand, expresses Calvin's intention exactly: a sacrament is "an outward and visible sign of an inward and spiritual grace given to us, ordained by Christ himself, as a means whereby we receive the same, and a pledge to assure us thereof." Taken in conjunction with this definition of a sacrament, the statement on the Lord's Supper must also be judged faithfully Calvinistic.

Curiously enough, the Westminster Confession's[41] teaching on the sacraments (1647) is not so plainly Calvinistic as the teaching of the Anglican Catechism; and the confession comes as close to symbolic parallelism as do the Thirty-Nine Articles. Since the aim of the Westminster divines was to produce a more strictly Calvinist confession than the Thirty-Nine Articles, their lack of clarity in the area of sacramental theology is surprising. The Calvinistic intention of their teaching on the sacraments has to be gleaned from incidental phrases that presuppose the instrumental view.[42] In itself, the article on the Lord's Supper invites the parallelistic interpretation of the sacramental union: "Worthy receivers, outwardly partaking of the visible elements in this sacrament, do *then also* inwardly ... feed upon Christ crucified ..." (Art. 29, sec. 7). Indeed, the statement that Christ's body is present "to faith" could be understood in a purely Zwinglian sense.

If the hesitance of the Westminster Confession is surprising, even more surprising is the fact that the teaching of the two Westminster catechisms[43] does not fully coincide with that of the confession. Perhaps the difference may be traced to the catechetical structure, which treats Word and sacraments as answers to the question what the outward means are by which Christ communicates to us the benefits of his mediation (L. C., Q. 154). The sacraments are effectual means of salvation (Q. 161), which exhibit Christ's benefits (Q. 162) and by means of which the benefits are communicated to us (Q. 154). Hence when the catechisms speak of feeding upon the body of Christ, they must surely mean a spiritual feeding that is effected through the outward eating of the bread. Although much of what the confession says on the Lord's Supper is simply repeated in the catechisms, they set it in a clearer light by treating it explicitly under the rubric of the means whereby Christ communicates himself to his people.

That the idea of Christ's self-communication was the heart of the matter for the Westminster divines is demonstrated by comparing the two catechisms. The Larger Catechism lists five functions of a sacrament (Q. 162) and four or five functions of the Lord's Supper (Q. 168). In the interests of brevity, the Shorter Catechism restricts itself precisely to those functions that go beyond Zwingli's or Bullinger's eucharistic types, and particularly to the function of communicating Christ and his benefits (S. C., Qq. 92, 96). The notions of a testimony to our thankfulness, our engagement to God, and our mutual fellowship with one another are simply omitted. The point could hardly be more forcefully made that, although these notions belong to the full presentation of Reformed teaching on the Eucharist, they lie close to the perimeter and can, if necessary, be cut out. The essential part of the sacrament is the divine gift conveyed by it, not the church's profession of its faith or love, nor even the church's "affectionate meditation" upon Calvary (L. C., Q. 174). One is astonished at the effectiveness with which the Shorter Catechism puts to flight the oppressive, introspective spirit of the Puritan that broods over the Larger Catechism. In the Larger Catechism generous attention is given to the inward state of the Christian before (Qq. 171–73), during (Q. 174), and after (Q. 175) the sacrament. (Especially formidable is the exhortation to examine ourselves after, as well as before, the sacrament: "The duty of Christians after they have received the Sacrament of the Lord's Supper, is seriously to consider how they have behaved themselves in it, and with what success ..." [!].) In the Shorter Catechism, on the other hand, the objective gift of grace, not the subjective operations of grace, holds the center.[44]

I close this section by pointing out that the Scottish church was particularly emphatic in its adherence to the "high Calvinistic" view of the sacraments. In Scotland the Westminster Standards superseded the native Scots Confession (1560),[45] which affirmed the full Calvinistic doctrine of the Lord's Supper in strikingly realistic language. It has indeed been said that the sacramental affirmations of the Scots Confession can lay claim to a validity that is transconfessional: not just *reformiert* but *reformatorisch*. "Here in fact," writes Paul Jacobs, "the Reformed and the Lutheran concerns are woven together in a new affirmation."[46] I do not share that verdict, but find it significant that such a verdict has been given.[47]

VI

The conclusion to this survey of the Reformed confessions is plain. The judgment that Calvin's eucharistic teaching "must be regarded as the orthodox Reformed doctrine" oversimplifies the evidence.[48] In actual fact, Zwingli's view continued to find its way into the confessions even after Calvin's emergence as foremost leader of the Reformed church; and Bullinger's Second Helvetic Confession exhibits a third eucharistic type. There seem to be, then, three doctrines of the Eucharist in the Reformed confessions, which we may label "symbolic memorialism," "symbolic parallelism," and "symbolic instrumentalism."

Nevertheless, the major Reformed confessions do not display three equally vigorous and wholly exclusive eucharistic traditions. The characteristic Zwinglian view is represented only in the minor confessions. (Zwingli's own great confessional works, the *Fidei Ratio* and *Fidei Expositio*, never attained symbolic authority and ought strictly to be excluded from the *corpus confessionum*.) The view contained in Bullinger's Second Helvetic Confession, on the other hand, appears in several other important statements, including the most respected of the German-language confessions.[49] And yet it is not so much anti-Calvinistic as timidly Calvinistic: *all* the leading confessions place the emphasis on communication rather than commemoration, but *some* reflect a certain shyness toward the idea of the means of grace. Perhaps this hesitancy did owe something to Zwingli. Yet the real division in the Reformed confessions is not Zwingli versus Calvin, but (so to say) "Franciscan" Calvinists versus "Thomistic" Calvinists. For while the major confessions generally insist (against Zwingli) on a sacramental union between the sign and the thing signified, they are not agreed on the nature of the union. Communion with Christ actually takes place in the Lord's Supper and is the focal point of interest. But is the communion given *simultaneously with* the elements (a kind of "Franciscan" interpretation) or *through* the elements (a "Thomistic" interpretation)? The difference is perhaps just a "school" dispute.[50]

Why did the Calvinists—of both varieties—refuse to follow Zwingli's lead into symbolic memorialism? The answer to this question attests to a fundamental bond between Roman Catholics, Lutherans, and Reformed. The Roman Catholic controversialist John Eck may be given the credit for spotting the weakness in Zwingli's sacramental theology. He laughs at Zwingli's claim to be the hammer of the Anabaptists, since he was in fact the founder of the sect.[51] "How near is Zwingli now to the Anabaptists whom nevertheless ... he torments to death ...

and tortures limb by limb." This is not merely unfounded maneuvering to implicate Zwingli in the guilt of the Anabaptists. Zwingli's sacramental theology really does point the way to the denial of infant baptism and to the interpretation of a sacrament as an act of public confession. Against this, Eck makes the same fundamental claim as do Luther and Calvin: a sacrament is a sign, not of past grace only, but of present grace.

It would, I think, be unjust to Zwingli should we explain his theology as the product of a philosophical bias. That the Spirit needs no vehicle, least of all a material vehicle, is certainly one of his reasons for rejecting the old concept of the means of grace. But he was also motivated by what one may perhaps call anachronistically a "Barthian" dread of putting God at man's disposal. If grace were bound up with the sacraments, they would profit and renew whenever they were celebrated. The clergy would then have infallible power to grant or withhold salvation. Indeed, they would have the fearful power to sell God at a higher price than Judas asked. Zwingli is therefore speaking as reformer and pastor in his protest against abuses in sacramental theology and practice. Do not buy what you possess already! The sacrament is simply a public testimony that you do indeed possess what God has given freely. Zwingli's sacramental theology sounds persistently the joyful note of possession: the "image" of Christ in the Eucharist, like the ring the husband gives to his wife, is a perpetual reminder to the church that he is wholly ours in all that he is.[52]

Zwingli is by no means to be underestimated. He held the same gospel as Luther or Calvin, and he wanted the Evangelical Eucharist to give cultic expression to the Evangelical faith. Nevertheless, it does make a profound difference that for Zwingli the Lord's Supper was an act of thanksgiving for the gospel, whereas for Luther and Calvin it was a concrete offer of the gospel. The gift of Christ lies, for Zwingli, in the past, as does the gift of faith, and accordingly it is the Christian believer or the Christian community that is the subject of the present sacramental action: *we* give thanks, *we* make confession before men. Calvin, by contrast, held that the living Christ is the subject, not merely the author, of the Sacrament, and that he gives himself here and now.

Bullinger's position, as represented in the Second Helvetic Confession, avoids some of the pitfalls of Zwinglianism. For Bullinger, as for Calvin, Christ is the one who gives, not only gave; and we are to receive, not only to remember that he once gave. But critics have always found something arbitrary and irrational about what I have nicknamed the "Franciscan" way of speaking. Grace, on this view, bypasses the human understanding: by some mysterious divine arrangement, grace is given at the same time as the sacrament is administered *(concomitatur!)*. On the strictly Calvinistic ("Thomistic") view, God really works by means of symbols *(significando causant!)*.

It is probably clear enough already what I intend by putting Calvin and Luther together against Zwingli. I have tried to draw the line at a different place than the Lutherans have traditionally selected. The test questions concerning the *manducatio oralis* and the *manducatio indignorum* have simply been ignored in my presentation. If *they* are allowed to define the boundaries, then Calvin stands opposed to both Zwingli *and* Luther, since he teaches that the body of Christ is given to all but received only by faith. In drawing the line elsewhere I do not believe that I am simply exercising the theologian's right to draw lines anywhere he pleases. My line-drawing is historically conditioned. It is an attempt to answer the question *why* the Lutherans made the *manducatio indignorum* the test question. Obviously, I must be excused for not dealing with the historical problem at any length. But it seems to me that what Luther himself was fighting for—especially in his magnificent work *Against the Heavenly Prophets* (1525)—was precisely the gift character of the Lord's Supper. Luther was shocked at Carlstadt's view, which, he thought, turned the Blessed Sacrament into a devotional exercise. Instead of receiving the crucified and risen Lord, who offered himself with the broken bread and poured-out wine, Carlstadt strove to focus his thoughts upon Jesus of Nazareth suffering on the cross. As Luther saw it, nothing less than the gospel was at stake, as in his controversy over the Roman mass. Christ gives himself to us in the sacrament; but some presumed to offer him to God, and others turned to their devotions. Both made the gift of God into a work of man. Whether these accusations are well founded or not, the heart of Luther's own position seems clear: the sacrament is a gift, and the gift is Jesus Christ. If that is what was dearest to Luther in his reverence for the sacrament, then the Calvinist confessions are on Luther's side of the line.[53]

Eight

"To the Unknown God"
Luther and Calvin
on the Hiddenness of God

There are those who commend the reply of Simonides,
who, when asked by the tyrant Hiero what God was,
begged he be granted a day to consider. The next day the
tyrant repeated the question, and he requested two days
more. Finally, after he had frequently doubled the number
of days, he replied: "The longer I consider, the more
obscure the subject seems to me." It was indeed sensible to
suspend judgment on a subject he found obscure. But from
this it appears that, were men taught by nature alone,
they would hold nothing certain or solid or clear, but
would be so attached to confused principles as to worship
an unknown God.[1]

Calvin borrowed the anecdote from one of his favorite classical sources, Cicero's *On the Nature of the Gods*. The moral of the story he learned, not from his classics, but from the Acts of the Apostles (17:16–34).[2] When the Apostle Paul was at Athens, we are told, he disputed in the marketplace, his spirit aroused by the city of idols. Curious and eager to hear about Paul's strange gods, certain of the philosophers led him to the Areopagus ("Hill of Mars"), for at Athens one spent one's time hearing and telling about the latest thing. In his eloquent address, Paul declared to the Athenians the Unknown God, whose altar he had noticed as he passed by. Nobody can really be sure what the inscription "To an Unknown God" may have meant.[3] Possibly someone had received a good turn and did not know which god was to be thanked for it. Or perhaps a timid worshiper was afraid of missing out from his devotions some lesser deity, whose name he did not know (which would be like not inviting the thirteenth fairy to the birthday party). But whatever may have been meant by the inscription reportedly seen by the Apostle Paul, the expression "the unknown God" passed into Christian literature as a description for the total otherness of deity.[4] Paul's discourse, we learn, was not a very great success. When he announced that the Lord of heaven and earth, in whom we live and move and have our being, had appointed Jesus to be judge at the last day and had raised him from the dead, some laughed; others said, more politely, "We will hear you again" (that is, some other time, not today); but a few believed. And among the believers was Dionysius.

Luxuriant legends have grown up around the figure of Dionysius: they bring his story to a remarkable end at Paris, where he became bishop, was martyred, and made patron saint of France. His name has fittingly, if incorrectly, been given to a body of mystical writings which constitute a moving tribute to the unknown God. Through John Scotus Erigena, the theological vocabulary of Dionysius the Areopagite passed permanently into the Western tradition, especially in the form of the familiar "way of negation." Oddly perhaps, Dionysius is most often upbraided by his detractors for professing to know too much, rather than too little, about the deity. Calvin found *The Heavenly Hierarchy* subtle and keen in many respects, but "for the most part mere prattle." "If you were to read that book, you would think a man fallen from heaven related, not what he had learned, but what he had seen with his eyes." The Apostle Paul, on the other hand, though caught up to the third heaven, did not talk about it.[5] A comparison of this negative assessment with a passage from Luther's *Babylonian Captivity* (1520) indicates that Calvin probably had a judgment of the German Reformer's in mind.[6] But in his earliest writings, at least, Luther found the language of the pseudo-Areopagite very appealing. Indeed, the *language* of the mystical tradition remained always congenial to him in some respects.[7]

I

As early as the first *Lectures on the Psalms* (the *Dictata* of 1513-15), Luther speaks of the incomprehensibility of God, and, in so doing, he refers favorably to Dionysius. Commenting on Psalm 18:11 ("And he made the darkness his hiding-place"), he offers a fivefold application for the expression God's "hiding-place": God hides in the darkness of faith, in light inaccessible, in the mystery of the Incarnation, in the church or the Blessed Virgin, and in the Eucharist. But it is immediately noticeable that he speaks of God here, not as "unknown," but as "hidden" *(absconditus)*.[8] In tracing the development of his theology in and beyond the first *Lectures on the Psalms*, Luther scholarship has gathered under the general rubric of "the hidden God" several different theological ideas.[9]

After a long period of relative neglect, the hidden God was rediscovered in the pioneering work of Theodosius Harnack.[10] He found that the notion of hiddenness expresses a double relation of God to the world: outside of Christ he is the free, all-working, majestic God of the law; in Christ he is the gracious Redeemer who has bound himself to his Word and sacraments. Not absolutely unknown, but rather unknown in respect of his grace, the Creator-God is the God of wrath. A second milestone in the interpretation of the *deus absconditus* was set up by Ferdinand Kattenbusch, who pointed to a quite different strand in Luther's thinking: God hides himself *in* his revelation, so that revelation and hiddenness are not opposed, but coincide.[11] It goes without saying that each of these distinguished scholars based his case on careful analysis of the sources. The question naturally arises, then, whether the rubric *deus absconditus* covers two distinct strands in Luther's theology, which have nothing in common with each other except the notion of hiddenness itself.

It is not difficult to group Luther interpreters, despite differences within each group, according as they stress that the hidden and revealed Gods are antithetical (Theodosius Harnack, the two Ritschls, Reinhold Seeberg, Hirsch, Elert, Holl), or identical (Kattenbusch, Erich Seeberg), or both (Althaus, Heim, von Loewenich).[12] In his excellent monograph on the subject, Hellmut Bandt asserts that the existence of two very dissimilar lines of thought side by side "is the fundamental problem given to the interpreter of Luther's doctrine of the hidden God."[13] The problem is further complicated, we might add, by the fact that the elevation of the term *deus absconditus* to the status of a general rubric is in part a scholarly device. Luther's own language displays characteristic variety. To mention only the most important variation, he sometimes speaks—especially in his latest period—of the "naked God." His language clearly indicates that, at this point, the image of God fades into sheer negativity: the *deus nudus* is God in himself, a strange, terrifying, indeterminate presence.[14] This being so, it appears that one must take into account, not only a dual relationship of God to the world, but also a conception of God as *deus absolutus,* out of relation to the world. This God, too, stands in antithetical relation to the revealed God, for the *deus revelatus* is the *deus indutus*—the God who is not naked but clothed with his Word.

So different have the two main lines of thought been felt to be—God hidden *in* his revelation and *behind* his revelation—that the effort has been made to distinguish them by different terminologies, whether the intent is to expound Luther's vocabulary or to improve upon it. Emil Brunner argued that Luther's "revealed" God is simultaneously "veiled," but not strictly "hidden";[15] and in one of his systematic works Paul Althaus contrasts the "hiddenness" of God *apart from* Christ with the "mystery" of God *in* Christ.[16] The most fascinating attempt to distinguish the two strands and to give them different terminologies was made by Walther Koehler, who contrasts *der verborgene Gott* and *der sich verbergende Gott.*[17] The "hidden God" is the unknown God of the ancient world, God beyond the reach of human intelligence: he belongs to the domain of Logos, but marks its boundary or limit. The "God who hides himself" belongs to Mythos: he is the divinity who achieves his ends by disguising himself. It is the ancient myth of the hidden savior that reappears in Luther's notion of revelation, complete with the picture language about the deceiving of the devil. And yet the other line of thought remains "on the margin": it stands for the transcendence of the naked God, who cannot be seen even with the eye of faith, but remains the unknown.[18]

Now, one can safely hazard the generalization that whereas the hiddenness of God in his revelation (let us call it "hiddenness I") has been found theologically fruitful in recent years, the hiddenness of God outside his revelation ("hiddenness II") has been found something of an embarrassment. The extraordinary power of Luther's *theologia crucis*, in which the hidden form of revelation finds its sharpest expression, has been fully appreciated and appropriated. In Christ, God works in a paradoxical mode *sub contrariis*. His wisdom is hidden under folly, his strength under abject weakness. He gives life through death, righteousness to the unrighteous; he saves by judging and damning. The hidden God is God incarnate, crucified, hidden in suffering *(deus incarnatus, deus crucifixus, deus absconditus in passionibus)*. In contemplation of the cross, Luther's fertile mind filled with vivid expressions of God's hiddenness in his revelation, and they have been gratefully appropriated in Protestant dogmatics.[19] Less welcome have been Luther's thoughts on hiddenness II: first, because this is another line of thought, which seems to defy harmonization with hiddenness I; second, because it implies a knowledge of God outside of Christ; and, third, because it converges upon the problematic doctrine of double predestination.

It is not my intention to attempt a synthesis of the various lines of Luther's thought on God's hiddenness. I do not find myself driven by the kind of harmonizing impulse that motivates the excellent study by Hellmut Bandt. Neither have I the least wish to soften or explain away Luther's most extreme utterances on predestination. (I am, I trust, too good a Calvinist to want to do that.) I want, rather, to inquire about the ranges of religious experience that lie behind the notion of hiddenness II and to show how they shape the Reformation idea of faith.[20] I may add that no disrespect is intended to Luther and Calvin if I thus presume to inquire into the religious roots of their statements on the *deus absconditus*. Hellmut Bandt insists that Luther wished his remarks in his work *On the Bondage of the Will* (1525) to be taken as a presentation of his theological judgment, not as an "eruption of his volcanic experience of God."[21] I agree. But this does not alter the fact that the most critical passage does reflect the "depth and passion of the religious experience" of the Reformer (as von Loewenich rightly maintained). And our warrant for focusing our attention at this point could be taken from Luther himself, who once wrote that "it is by living—no, rather, by dying and being damned—that a theologian is made, not by understanding, reading, or speculating."[22] With this in mind, I shall not neglect the theological argument of *On the Bondage of the Will*, but I shall attempt to deal sympathetically with the experience of God that can be sensed behind the argument as Luther tells about the God who hides himself and wills to remain unknown.[23]

II

Both forms of divine hiddenness can be found in Luther's treatise *On the Bondage of the Will.*[24] In his review of Erasmus's preface, he writes:

> Faith is concerned with "things not seen" [Heb. 11:1]. So that there may be room for faith, all the things that are believed need therefore to be hidden. But they are not more remotely hidden than under the contrary object, perception, experience. So, when God makes alive, he does it by putting to death; when he justifies, he does it by making guilty; when he transports to heaven, he does it by bringing to hell. As the Scripture says in 1 Kings 2 [1 Sam. 2:6]: "The Lord slays and makes alive; he brings down to hell and raises up again." ... So, God hides his eternal mercy and kindness beneath eternal anger, righteousness beneath injustice.[25]

Luther excuses himself from giving any fuller account of this doctrine, since those who have read his books will be well acquainted with it. Plainly, these remarks fall under the heading of hiddenness I, the hidden form of God's revelation.[26] But the logic of Luther's main argument drives him to speak also about the God who is hidden outside of his revelation (hiddenness II). For, as he has already remarked earlier in his treatise, "nobody doubts that there is a great deal hid in God of which we do not know."[27]

Luther's central purpose throughout the treatise is to affirm the sole agency of God in bringing about man's salvation. In his judgment, those who, like Erasmus, wish to speak of free will are really seeking to find a place for merit. Indeed, Erasmus had asked explicitly: "If there is no freedom of the will, what room is there for merits?" The answer, Luther retorts, was given by the apostle Paul: "There is no such thing as merit, but as many as are justified are all justified freely, and this is ascribed to nothing but the grace of God."[28] Were it not so, the source of assurance would be snatched away from us: our confidence rests in the knowledge that God has taken salvation out of the control of *our* wills and has placed it under the control of *his*.[29] It is but a short step from here to a full-blown doctrine of divine determinism. Perhaps Luther did not need to take that short step. He could have rested content with the claim that only our salvation is taken out of our hands. He does indeed suggest that a man can enjoy a limited measure of freedom in other ranges of his daily existence. But, whatever that limited freedom may mean, it does not prevent him from asserting a general doctrine of divine determinism. "God foreknows nothing contingently: he foresees, purposes, and does all things by an immutable, eternal, and infallible will."[30] "All things happen by necessity."[31] And Luther does not shrink from confirming this doctrine by appeal to the pagan notion of fate: "We see that the knowledge of predestination and of God's foreknowledge has been left to mankind no less than the notion of divinity itself."[32]

With the mention of the word "predestination" the heart of the problem lies open before us. The uncompromising argument has been that if a man is saved at all, that can only be because God has irresistibly directed the impotent human will, which is utterly incapable of turning itself toward salvation. If it is asked, then—as has been asked in every generation of the church's history—why some accept the good news and not others, it cannot be answered: Because men are free to accept or reject as they please. It is *God* who accepts or rejects as *he* pleases. But is it not written that the Lord desires not the death of a sinner, but rather that he should turn from his wickedness and live (Ezek. 18:23)? The question can therefore only be: Why does he not choose to change *every* man's will from bad to good if he alone can? Naturally, Luther answers that we just do not know. The source of grace is the predestinating purpose of God. Beyond that point we cannot go. We run up against that "concealed [*occulta*] and dreadful will of God, who, by his own design, ordains whom he wills to receive and partake of the mercy preached and offered, and what sort of persons they shall be. This will is not to be enquired into, but reverently adored as far the most awesome secret of the divine majesty, reserved to himself alone and forbidden to us...."[33]

This is all very well, but what a monumental theological problem Luther now has on his hands! And can it be resolved simply by counseling us not to think about it? A fundamental distinction has been made within the conception of God: we are to recognize that there is "God hidden" and "God revealed."[34] Erasmus's error, in the final analysis, is that he did not make this distinction. And yet, says Luther, to deny the distinction is to make God an idol, depriving him of his freedom.[35] Admittedly, Luther does not consider the antithesis within his conception of God to be indicative of a contradiction in God himself, although he grants the appearance. The problem is noetic, not ontic—in our understanding, not in God's being. Luther is confident that there is a solution even if it lies beyond history. "By the light of grace it is inexplicable how God damns a man who is not able by any of his own resources to do anything but sin.... But the light of glory declares otherwise...."[36] In the meantime, we have to admit the antithesis between God as revealed and preached, on the one hand, and God as hidden and unknown, on the other—indeed, as Luther puts it still more sharply, between the Word of God and God himself.[37] The practical solution—and it is only temporary—is to leave alone the nature and majesty of God, to view him solely as he clothes himself in the Word. But how satisfying can this practical solution be?

The seriousness of the theological problem must not be glossed over. By a strange, circuitous route, Luther's argument ends up by jeopardizing his own theological starting point. He insisted at the outset that he proclaimed nothing but Christ crucified.[38] But one of the doctrines that "Christ crucified brings with him" finally forces us to acknowledge an inscrutable will of God behind and beyond the figure of Christ. We began from God's revelation in Christ as the only secure basis for a knowledge of God's gracious will; we end by discovering that, after all, God wills many things that he does not show us in his Word.[39] And the problem is not merely that there is a hidden will alongside of the revealed will of God, but that the two are found to be in apparent contradiction. Says Luther: "He does not will the death of a sinner—in his Word, that is. But he does will it by that inscrutable will."[40] And the incarnate God must weep as the hidden God consigns a portion of mankind to perdition.[41] It is not easy to respond, except with agreement, to those who proclaim the collapse of Luther's doctrine of God at this point: the two wills fall apart in a bifurcation that he does not profess himself able to overcome. And the question seems inescapable that he elsewhere rejects as misguided and wrong headed: Granted that *Christ* speaks nothing but comfort to the troubled conscience, who knows how it stands between me and *God in heaven*?[42] Luther's assurance that we have the Father's will in Christ, and his counsel that we should flee to God in the manger or contemplate the wounds of Jesus, do not resolve the theological problem, and he does not pretend that they do.

Even as a theological problem, Luther felt the difficulty of predestination deeply enough: "This is the highest degree of faith," he admits, "to believe that he is merciful who saves so few and damns so many...."[43] But it is impossible to read him and not to recognize that there was a terror in his encounter with the hidden, predestinating God and that the emotional, religious, or spiritual content of the experience burst the limits of the merely rational and conceptual. We can judge from his own testimony that the encounter was a shattering one, which brought him right up to the rim of the abyss, where the naked and unknown God waited and threatened. True, even common sense and reason are offended that the merciful God should behave as though he delighted in the torments of the lost. But, asks Luther, "who would *not* take offense? I have taken offense myself more than once, down to the depths and the abyss of despair, so that I wished I had never been made a man."[44]

It is noticeable that Luther recalls his struggle with predestination as something he has behind him, and therefore as the experiential basis for his counseling of others. The despair is assigned to the past tense, to a time before Luther had learned to think of it as "health-giving" and "close to grace." But if the crisis belonged to the past, it seems clear that the predestinating God remained in the shadows. This is, indeed, implicit in the recognition that only a practical solution is open to man *in via*. Only the constant renewal of faith through contemplation of Christ, the mirror of God's heart, can vanquish one's anxieties concerning one's own standing before God; and even then the hidden will stays to challenge faith's confidence in the goodness of a God who permits many others to be lost. The practical solution is not instantaneous and final. We do not simply turn from the hidden God, and then forget all about him. The forbidding figure waits on the edge of faith and, for this reason, determines (in some measure) the content of faith, which has the character of a turning from the hidden God. The luminous object of faith is set against a dark, threatening background. Awareness of the hidden God, therefore, qualifies faith in Christ. How, indeed, could it be otherwise if, as Luther tells us, we should adore the hidden God? If the *deus absconditus* is thus endowed with religious meaning as the object of our veneration, it cannot be strictly true that we have nothing to do with him.[45] He is always there as the *terminus a quo* of the movement of faith, even though he does not have comparable significance to the Word of God, which is the *terminus ad quem*. Faith returns constantly from the God on the perimeter of human experience to the incarnate God whom it makes its center.

III

The significance of the debate with Erasmus is not that it furnishes material for a favorite theological puzzle—how can grace be sovereign and man be free?—but that it points to reaches of religious experience which may be overlooked if faith is defined purely as personal trust in Christ. Or, to make the same point from the side of the doctrine of God, the celebrated free-will debate points to another moment in the Reformation concept of God, a moment antithetical to the attributes of mercy and love. The image of God does not, after all, fully coincide with the picture of Jesus. Now it is important to recognize that predestination was not the only problem that led Luther to acknowledge this "other" God. The "concealed and dreadful will of God," which freely disposes of grace or freely withholds it, is "the most awesome secret of the divine majesty," but it is not the only one. It is *one* way in which we are reminded of the God who hides himself beyond his revelation. But there are others. The hidden God stands for the "God" of everyday experience apart from Christ— the force behind the mysterious universe as we encounter it without the help of the Word. "'God preached' so acts that, sin and death being taken away, we may be saved.... But 'God hidden in majesty' neither deplores nor abolishes death, but works life, death, and all in all. Nor has he set bounds to himself by his Word, but has kept himself free over all things."[46] It is surely clear enough that "Father of our Lord Jesus Christ" does not exhaust Luther's conception of God. It is but one side of it.[47]

It is, no doubt, widely assumed that the Protestant notion of God leans heavily to anthropomorphism and transcendence: God is the Supreme Personal Being "up there." But one does not have to read far in Luther to realize that there is a remarkable tension at least in *his* idea of God. When he looked directly at nature, apart from the Word, he was aware of an awesome, creative power quite other than the God he encountered in Jesus Christ. It has often been noted how he appealed to this other aspect of deity in his controversial writings on the Eucharist. God is not to be pictured as a "great fat being" who fills the world like straw in a sack. His power cannot be contained or measured. He is "a supernatural, inscrutable being, who is at once wholly in every kernel of grain and yet in all, and above all, and outside all creatures."[48] This God creates and preserves all things by his immediate presence and power. And "his very divine being can be wholly in all creatures and in each individually, deeper, more inwardly, more presently than is the creature itself...."[49] It is *this* God who "works life and death and all in all." He is the creative, and at the same time the destructive, power that seems incredibly indifferent to the life of the creature.

Similarly, when Luther turned his thoughts from nature to history and contemplated it apart from the Word of God, he could not claim that the fatherly providence of God was evident.[50] The good cause is not always vindicated; the bad as often triumphs. "Just see! God so governs this physical world in outward affairs that, if you regard and follow the judgment of human reason, you are compelled to say either that there is no God or that God is unjust. As the poet said: 'Oft am I provoked to think there are no gods.'"[51] The God of history, like the God of nature, is hidden. An important element in Luther's doctrine of the hiddenness of God, this line of reflection nonetheless lacks the anguish and pathos of his experience of the God of predestination. The very images he employs in this context suggest that he was much more able to come to terms with the hiddenness of God in history. God "disguises" himself in the progress of world events. History is his "sport." And although it is certainly clear enough that Luther could not offer anything like a theistic "case" by reasoning from the course of the human story, nevertheless as a man of faith he can penetrate through God's disguise and see the actor behind the mask.[52] As *deus ludens*, so to say, God does put our faith to the test, but he hardly pushes the test to the limits of despair. Indeed, the "light of grace" has given away the secret of history: if the wicked sometimes flourish and the just suffer, the believer knows that there is a life hereafter in which the imbalance will be redressed. Where philosophers and even prophets have stumbled, the Christian treads firmly and confidently. "What looks overwhelmingly like the injustice of God and is traduced by such arguments as no reason or light of nature can withstand, is very easily disposed of by the light of the gospel and the knowledge of grace, by which we are taught that, though the ungodly do flourish in their bodies, yet they perish in their souls. And a short explanation of this whole inexplicable question is in one little word: namely, that there is a life after this life...."[53] It is easy to see why for Luther the problem of predestination was "far the most awesome secret of the divine majesty": because *there* faith cannot find the way out, but can only wait for the light of glory. And if it lingers too long, tries to penetrate the mystery of the hidden will, it can only lose itself in the abyss of the unknown God.

We must then, so it seems, construct a kind of scale for hiddenness II, which at one end approaches the horror of the unknown God and at the other the paradoxes of hiddenness I. Indeed, Luther seems to betray more intensity of feeling in speaking of hiddenness I than when he speaks of God's hiddenness in history. But, in any case, outside of Christ the hiddenness of God always means one thing: faith cannot rest in the God who is hidden beyond his revelation. For, as Luther states in his Large Catechism, God—for faith—is that to which I must look for all that is good.[54] The God who hides himself outside of Christ, whether in nature, history, or the eternal decree, does not move me to trust. What is perhaps most astonishing in Luther's thoughts of God is that he speaks of the hidden God as "God himself." But it was not, of course, his intention to admit that faith is fancy, inventing a God for its own comfort other than he is in himself. On the contrary, he insists that faith in Christ *is* knowledge of the hidden God. The resolution of the antagonism between God hidden and God revealed is admittedly practical—in that it consists in the counsel to flee from the one to the other—but it still points to the truth hidden in the one and only God. "Who can direct himself," Luther asks, "by a will that is utterly inscrutable and incomprehensible?"[55] Here is the practical motivation: we *must* be guided by the Word because there is no guidance to be had in the hidden will. And yet Luther also claims that, in his Word, the one God has lifted the corner of the veil, taken a step out of his hiddenness: "Begin from below, from the incarnate Son....Christ will bring you to the hidden God....If you take the revealed God, he will bring you the hidden God at the same time." The mystery of deity is not dissipated, but what we do see is a visible piece of the mystery. Like Moses, we are permitted to catch a glimpse of God's "back parts."[56]

It all sounds like an artful dodge, of course, and Madam Reason is scornful: "Here our smart, sarcastic Reason will surely say: 'This is a nicely devised way of escape—that, whenever we are pressed by force of arguments, we run back to that dreadful will of majesty and, when our adversary becomes annoying, reduce him to silence! Just like the astronomers who devised their "epicycles" to evade all questions about the movement of the heavens as a whole!'"[57] But there

Luther rests his case. To reason, it may well seem like desperation to invoke a sacred mystery. But that is the way things are.

IV

Luther's doctrine of the *deus absconditus* has been subjected to intense study in more than a dozen books and articles devoted directly to the theme, to say nothing of longer or shorter discussions in more general works on his theology; and incidental excursuses upon it, or allusions to it, abound even in books not mainly concerned with Luther. Not that the problems have all been resolved. Far from it! The debate continues. Surprisingly, however, there is no such body of literature on what Calvin thought about God's hiddenness.[58] Possibly, Calvin scholars have been skeptical about the genuine unity of the various motifs that have been clustered under the common rubric of "God's hiddenness." More likely, the problem has simply been neglected, at least in its full scope; and it would require a major monograph even to assemble the relevant sources and shape the "problematic" for an adequate, comprehensive analysis. The following remarks make no pretense at meeting that need. For the most part, they rest upon certain key sections of the *Institutes*, as the previous discussion grew mainly out of Luther's *On the Bondage of the Will*; and although no belittling of theological and exegetical arguments is intended, the focal interest, as before, is in the experiential roots of hiddenness II.[59] In point of fact, it could be shown that Calvin's thoughts on hiddenness parallel Luther's in their full range.[60] But for him, too, the profoundest depths of hiddenness are located in the problem of double predestination, in which the will of God appears divided against itself and the individual is threatened with the possibility of rejection and loss. Here Calvin, no less than Luther, finds himself on the brink of an "abyss of sightless darkness."

The revelation of God in Jesus Christ does not mean that God no longer has secrets he withholds from mankind. *Some* secrets are now open, insofar as this is good for us. Certainly, faith understands that the passage of events is nothing but the working out of a divine plan, which, though formerly hidden, has now been brought to light.[61] But this does not mean that we as yet fully understand the divine purposes. The plan is still partially concealed from us in the governance of the world and in the disposition of individual destinies. Indeed, "secret" *(arcanum)* remains Calvin's most characteristic description for God's "design" (his *consilium*), since we cannot always perceive *why* God moves events in just the way he does.[62] The secretness or hiddenness of God's design may be affirmed, on occasion, simply as an expression of pious surprise at an unexpected turn of events. So, for instance, Calvin speaks of the secret leading of

God's providence in his own spiritual pilgrimage, when he was turned aside from the study of law.[63] Or "secretness" may testify to the perplexity of the faithful at the fact, and even the triumph, of evil and disorder in the world. Good things and bad simply are not distributed in this life according to strict desert; in testifying of the man born blind that neither he nor his parents had sinned (John 9:3), Jesus indicated that there is more than that to the justice in God's secret design. Similarly, it is unthinkable that the afflictions of the epileptic boy in the Gospel (Mark 9:14–29) should be understood as punitive (even though he was not exempt from original sin!). Here the justice of God is hidden from us, and we can can only bow before it in humility.[64]

On a grander scale, the orderly progress of history itself sometimes dissolves, or so it appears, into utter confusion; and the thought insinuates itself that human affairs are whirled around under the blind impulse of fortune, or else the "flesh" is incited to complain that God plays games with men and throws them about like balls. True, God's wisdom becomes plain in the end to those who are patient. But Calvin cannot deny that the hand of God and the identity of God's people are alike hidden in the passage of events. God's secret design is worked out in history through opaque judgments *(occulta, obscura iudicia),* and the meaning of history is disclosed only to those who hear his Word in faith, at least until the Last Day, when his judgments will finally be vindicated and faith superseded by sight.[65] Small wonder, then, that Calvin could picture men in the world as stray sheep wandering in a maze before gathered to the flock of God![66] But beyond surprise and perplexity, the hiddenness of God's design in the world can also instill something like dread *(extrema anxietas et formido)* into the heart of the man who lives without the Word.

Perhaps Calvin is distinguished from Luther by a stronger sense of the visible orderliness of the world, through which the power of the Maker "shines forth." So deeply impressed was he with the tokens of design in the cosmos that he envied the natural scientists, whose observations enabled them to penetrate more deeply than most into the secrets of nature (which are *divinae sapientiae arcana*). It has even been claimed that the spirit of Calvinism may, in this respect, have contributed to the impressive growth of scientific research in the period immediately following upon the Reformation.[67] And yet in Calvin, too, there is a deep sense of awe before the cosmos, not merely because of its order and grandeur, but also because of its sheer enigma, which is impenetrable to the human mind. Nor can the shortcomings of the intellect be traced solely to the effects of the fall. True, the blindness of sin effectively negates God's self-disclosure in nature and prevents it from leading man to a saving knowledge of his Maker. But even for the redeemed, whose vision has been restored, the divine purpose in the world order cannot simply be read off from the face of nature and history. Calvin's doctrine of providence, so far from being inferred from the visible tokens of God's presence, is in fact developed despite God's hiddenness.

We do not invariably *see* that God's hand is at work; we *believe* it on the basis of the Word.[68] However things may be disposed in the design of God, to us, Calvin admits, they are fortuitous. "The order, reason, end, and necessity of events lie hidden, for the most part, in God's design." Calvin describes the First Cause of events as "hidden" *(procul abscondita)*, at any rate to the superficial view. (He does insist that a few sparks have always glowed in the darkness.) Similarly, providence is described generally as "concealed" *(occulta)*, and the movement of God's hand as "secret" *(secreta).*[69] Calvin expressly distinguishes the "mysteries" of revelation from the "abyss" of God's hidden will at work in the government of the universe: that is, he conveys the distinction between hiddenness I and II through distinct terminologies.

> It is certainly true that in the law and the gospel are comprehended mysteries that extend far above the bounds of our sense. But since God illumines the minds of his own with the spirit of understanding, so that they may grasp these mysteries which he has deigned to lay open by his Word, now no abyss is there, but a way in which we are to walk in safety and a lamp to guide our feet, the light of life and the school of certain and manifest truth. Yet his wonderful way of governing the world is justly called an "abyss" because, while hidden from us, it ought reverently to be adored.[70]

Perhaps the last phrase—"it ought reverently to be adored"—gives the impression that the Christian can make peace with the hidden will of God. But the point that must not be overlooked is that, for Calvin, the hiddenness of God in the world order is subjectively apprehended as a sense of terrifying contingency—apart from the Word of God. He could portray the threatening insecurity of human existence (its "ultimate anxiety and dread") with quite extraordinary power. Life itself is "enveloped with death." "Half alive in life, [man] hardly dares to draw an anxious, feeble breath, as though he had a sword perpetually dangling over his neck." Ignorance of providence is therefore the ultimate of all miseries.[71] The horror of this ignorance may even lead to voluntary self-destruction.[72] But the fact of providence is nonetheless anything but obvious. Calvin would surely agree with Luther that there is, in truth, no contingency *apud Deum simpliciter*, only *coram nobis.*[73] But he took that *coram nobis*—the subjective awareness of contingency—with utter seriousness. Only with the Word of God is it overcome, and even then problems remain. Moreover, we have yet to approach the point where God's design is most deeply hidden. Among those things he chooses to keep secret, even after his revelation, is the reason why some are destined for eternal life and others for eternal damnation.[74]

Like Luther, Calvin too finds the secrets of divine majesty illustrated, but not exhausted, in the "horrible decree" (as he himself calls it)[75] by which the hidden will of God foreordains a portion of mankind for final loss. The Pavlovian reflexes that the mention of this doctrine invariably lets loose may obscure some interesting features of Calvin's discussion. (As he himself remarks, it is as though the petulant human intellect had heard the bugle sound a charge.)[76] To comment on just one important point: although talk about eternal decrees has the sound of rampant speculation, the doctrine of election is in fact woven into the fabric of human experience. It is about experienced diversity, and Calvin finds this diversity inseparable from the notion of grace and its counterpart, gratitude.[77] Like Luther, he begins from the observed fact that some do, and some do not, believe the gospel. To trace this diversity back to a "horrible decree," whatever else it means, surely indicates that he finds it a source of anguish, yet ultimate (in the sense of being an inexplicable "given" of human existence).[78] Further, he observes that a principle of selection belongs to the strangeness of human existence as such, and is not limited to the matter of faith. Ingeniously, he finds this testified in the fact that, from the moment of birth, one infant discovers a full breast to suck, while another must endure a breast that is nearly dry. The mystery of predestination is continuous with a more universal mystery of human existence: life's goods, from birth onward, are bestowed or withheld with a discrimination that we ourselves do not control. *Experientia demonstrat!* It is a fact of experience.[79] Men are preferred above beasts, one nation is preferred above the rest, one brother above another.[80] Neither do the lesser inequalities determine the greater; for the preference of Jacob reversed the priorities of birth, and the calling of the Gentiles transcended the advantages of race.[81] Not all are privileged to hear the gospel; and yet of those who hear, not all receive it with joy. The seed may fall among thorns or on stony ground. Hardening and blessing alike are finally beyond our ability to explain; they are in the will and hands of God.[82] As Augustine exclaimed: "Peter denies, the thief believes. 'Oh, the depth!' Do you ask the reason? I shudder at the depth."[83]

Awe, humility, confidence, and thankful activity in the world are not, however, the only possible modes of response to this recognition of the facts of life. That many are called but few are chosen (Matt. 22:14), may, as Calvin well knew, give rise to an acute theological problem; and, as he also knew well, it could evoke anxiety and paralyzing despondency. Perhaps he went further than Luther toward a resolution of the theoretical problem of the "two wills," although at the fearful cost of reducing the universal benevolence of the revealed will to a mere appearance.[84] But the existential problem remained: Who knows how it stands between *me* and God in heaven? And here Calvin's counsel is no different from Luther's: to move beyond the Word (the revealed will) is to find oneself in terrifying darkness, a maze without exit, a pathless waste, a bottomless whirlpool, inextricable snares, an abyss of sightless darkness.[85] Assurance of our own election is to be found solely in Christ, the mirror of our adoption. Anxiety that what Christ tells us in the Word might, in the end, prove to be something other than the will of the Father is groundless, for Christ is the

Father's eternal wisdom.[86] And yet ... the anxiety is very persistent![87] The threat of the unknown God does not quite disappear; if it did, the exhortation to embrace Christ would surely be superfluous.

V

Reluctance to acknowledge the reality of the *deus absconditus* (in the sense of hiddenness II) goes back at least to Albrecht Ritschl, who charged Theodosius Harnack with unwarranted neglect of Luther's predestinating God, but proceeded himself to reject him as an unfortunate medieval figment. In giving a fresh direction to Luther research on the *deus absconditus*, Kattenbusch again tried to suppress the embarrassing sections of *On the Bondage of the Will*, but by interpreting them harmlessly rather than drastically rejecting them. His remarks can only be considered devious, even preposterous. Luther "had nothing else in mind," he explained, "than that God's love is not softness," and he denied that Luther "saw in God the *deus creator omnium* 'behind' the *deus salvator*."[88] God's majesty was reduced by Kattenbusch to a function of his love, whereas the problem is precisely that Luther speaks of a majesty beyond or beside his love. As Kattenbusch himself admits in a couple of coy footnotes, love, for Luther, has its limits.

More recently, Karl Barth's disapproval of the offending passages gave rise to a new flurry of interest. Even the hiddenness of God, according to Barth, is known only by revelation; it is not a general truth. It does not mean that there is a terrifying mystery behind God's revelation of himself as love. God really *is* what he has shown himself to be. The mystery is rather the freedom of his love: that is, the fact that he *decided* to reveal himself. Luther failed to affirm consistently the identity of the *deus absconditus* and the *deus revelatus*. This, however, does not alter the fact that he often did affirm this identity, and Barth freely avails himself of the acceptable passages in which Luther writes of the *deus absconditus in passionibus*. For Barth, as for Luther on one side of his thinking about God's hiddenness, the mystery of God is the revealed mystery of his grace.[89]

It was with Barth's questions in mind that Hellmut Bandt undertook his thorough study of the *deus absconditus*. In this respect, his work recalls the earlier book by John Dillenberger, of which he was apparently unaware. He tells the reader in his foreword that he disagrees with Barth. The disagreement is not elucidated, but the reader can readily infer that it must be directed against Barth's interpretation of Luther, not against Barth's own view of God's hiddenness. Bandt is in fact plainly motivated by a very Barthian concern to demonstrate the christocentrism of evangelical theology *(der christologische Ansatz)*. Only, he wants to argue that Luther, too, was a consistent practitioner of this method, not least in his doctrine of the *deus absconditus*. The thesis is presented on page 94, spaced out (in the original German) for emphasis: "In the final analysis, there is no other hiddenness of God for Luther than the hidden form of his revelation." A part of what this means for Bandt is that the *deus absconditus* must not be linked with any general sense for the enigmatic character of life, or with any merely philosophical doctrine of the unknowability of God; and he opposes, as energetically (almost) as Barth engaged the advocates of a natural theology, those scholars who make this erroneous link. The content of hiddenness, he insists, must be derived strictly from God's revelation in Christ.[90] In my judgment, Bandt's pursuit of the "inner unity" of Luther's doctrine, his attempt to demonstrate that all the various utterances are only extensions of the notion of the hidden form of revelation, leads to interpretations that are strained and unconvincing.[91] Hiddenness II is not the most prominent line in Luther's thoughts on the *deus absconditus,* but I think I have shown that it is not a mere extension of hiddenness I either.[92]

John Dillenberger had shown himself more ready to acknowledge the traces in Luther of belief in a knowledge of God apart from Christ; but he, too, wished to minimize them, and he accused Brunner of perversely isolating and elevating this belief, which was taken for granted in Luther's day, and making it normative for our own day. To speak of man's natural condition as existence under the wrath of God (the *deus absconditus*) makes no sense when belief in God has itself ceased to be "part of the fabric of the age." Brunner "elaborated a dated side of Luther as if it were a matter of permanent theological significance."[93]

If, for a moment, we can set aside the obligation to preserve the purity of a christocentric principle and simply ask whether the notion of hiddenness II in fact corresponds to something in the way we encounter hard reality (whether or not the insight came to us by revelation), then I think it is obvious what the answer must be. To be assured that it is raining, one need not depend on the weather man; it is enough to look out the window. Or, as Luther puts it, Reason herself can see the way the world goes, and she concludes that, if there is a God at all, he is not just. Belief in Christ is not needed for the attainment of *that* insight, but it does heighten the anguish. In 1955, the distinguished German historian Gerhard Ritter published a report on the last days of Karl Goerdeler, condemned to death as one of the conspirators against Hitler. The painful reflections of the condemned man express the anguish of the conflict between faith and experience, and Ritter claimed for them a more than individual significance because they pose the cardinal question of our time: the question of the reality of God. Goerdeler wrote:

> In sleepless nights I have asked myself whether a God exists who shares in
> the personal fate of men. It is becoming hard to believe it. For this God must
> for years now have allowed rivers of blood and suffering, mountains of horror

and despair for mankind. . . . He must have let millions of decent men die and suffer without moving a finger. Is this supposed to be a judgment?. . . Like the Psalmist, I have a controversy with God because I cannot understand him. . . . And yet through Christ I am still looking for the merciful God. I have not found him. . . .[94]

Ritter explains this as the collapse of the old liberal theology of the nineteenth century, which closed the door on Luther's *deus absconditus* and the Christ who was forsaken on the cross.

In a response to Ritter, Julius Richter challenged this use of the *deus absconditus*: it brings the despairing no comfort, he pointed out, but only the demand for submission to the mystery of God. No doubt, Richter was right to insist that, as far as Luther's own understanding of the *deus absconditus* is concerned, "it is certainly not very appropriate, if someone is despairing of God, to refer him to the 'hidden God.' That would be a burden that could only push the despairing still deeper into his despair."[95] There is no comfort in the hidden God: we flee *from* the hidden God, not *to* him. But there may, I suspect, be comfort in company—that is, in the recognition that we are not the first to have met him. Hiddenness belongs essentially to the conception of God that we inherit. The negative side of our religious experience has already been thematized. Further, I cannot agree when Richter asserts that if Luther could expect a demonstration of God's justice in the light of glory, "then strictly [*im Grunde*] the *deus absconditus* thereby loses his fearful character already; indeed, *for the believer* he loses even [*überhaupt*] the character of hiddenness. . . ."[96] It is not, I think, a "manifest inconsistency" if one continues to speak of the hidden God, precisely because the appeal to the *deus revelatus* must be understood within the concrete movement of experience and not as the final, logical resolution to an intellectual puzzle.

The thought of God's hiddenness arises where the sheer mystery of human existence becomes the object of reflection. Questions crowd in upon the believer—no less than the unbeliever—which evoke a sense of the strangeness or even the terror of being human. This strangeness, this terror, are the other side of God's hiddenness. Faith does not overcome them—not in the sense of superseding them. There is an unresolved dialectic in Reformation faith corresponding to a dialectic in the conception of God.[97] Luther's faith struggled constantly with strange assaults which he called his "attacks" *(Anfechtungen)*. At such moments, he discovered that the gracious God cannot be taken for granted. This experience undoubtedly shaped the form of his faith. Not, to be sure, in the sense that the object of faith became the hidden God. This could not be so, because faith's object is always the Word of God.[98] The hidden God is never the object of faith. But faith nonetheless takes on an urgency, perhaps even a passion, because of the hidden God, who prevents faith from becoming complacent.

Faith, in Luther's sense, was a dare, a risk, or—in one of his favorite words—a "flight." Under *Anfechtung*, a man must dare against God to flee to God *(ad deum contra deum)*.[99] Faith is not repose, but movement. Hence faith really does take into itself something of the meaning of God's hiddenness even though it is not directed toward that hiddenness; rather it is movement *away from* the hidden God.

The symbol of the hidden God, so far from being ready for the rubbish heap of discarded medieval superstitions, may even be said to have a peculiar strength, vitality, modernity about it. "Anyone," says Hans Grass, "who speaks of the hidden God can count on a greater understanding from the man of today than one who speaks of the revealed God."[100] Perhaps it is Luther's flight to the manger, where he found the cradle of the God made flesh, that will sooner strike the modern as most typically (or "charmingly") medieval. It is the strange, threatening *deus absconditus*—the God who takes upon himself the features of the devil—who strikes a chord of response. We could even, I think, add to the regions of experience that summon up the hidden God. Recall, for instance, the crushing, terrifying sense of God's naked majesty Pascal evokes by portraying man as "lost in this remote corner of nature." "What is a man in the Infinite?"[101] Here, in the anxiety of finitude and insiginificance, modern man experiences the hiddenness of God. And faith can only mean that in the revealed God he finds the possibility of affirming the meaning of life in spite of this anxiety—this other dark possibility that he really is lost in a boundless and senseless universe. In my judgment, it is precisely here that, despite admitted differences, modern faith will come closest to the faith of Luther and Calvin, because for them too, in their own way, faith was a flight from the hidden God.

A further step, however, can hardly be taken toward dealing with the religious problem of hiddenness unless much more is said about the revealed God, to whom Luther and Calvin turned in faith. For this God reveals himself precisely in the experience of forsakenness and despair, that is, in Christ as *der Angefochtene*, the archetype of man assailed by sin, death, and hell. It is remarkable that in the figure of Christ Calvin found the strangeness of human existence portrayed in respect of both its inequality (or "diversity") and its dread. In the very Head of the Church—conceived a mortal man, yet already chosen in the womb to be the salvation of the world—is, as Augustine discerned, the "brightest mirror of free election," and we may not ask: Why this man, and not another?[102] But God's chosen one was destined to take upon himself the agony of a man forsaken by God. "And surely no more terrifying abyss can be imagined than to feel yourself forsaken and estranged from God; and when you call upon him, not to be heard."[103] I do not see how it could be claimed that the experience of hiddenness II arises from the christological center. But that is where Luther and Calvin thought it must lead: to hiddenness I. If the enigma of human existence is to be identified as the hiddenness *of God*, for them, at least, that was because, like all things human, the experience of hiddenness was not alien to the Redeemer himself. In the passage from the abyss of the unknown God to the mystery of faith assailed by doubt they found the efficacy of the Christian story.

Nine   The Mirror of God's Goodness:
                    A Key Metaphor in
                    Calvin's View of Man

Where there is no zeal to glorify God, the chief part of uprightness is absent.[1]

Whatever the strange figure of the hidden God may have meant for Luther's faith, it is plain that his faith grasped the revealed God as "pure love" *(eitel liebe)*. In his Large Catechism (1529) he writes: "It is God alone, I have often enough repeated, from whom we receive all that is good.... He is an eternal fountain which overflows with sheer goodness and pours forth all that is good in name and in fact."[2] Calvin's understanding of man and his place in the world might almost be said to provide a theological exegesis of this matchless confession of Luther's faith.

In the opening paragraphs of his 1559 *Institutes*, Calvin announces that the knowledge of God and the knowledge of man—the two basic themes of theological wisdom—mutually condition each other. If, then, God is for him, as for Luther, *fons bonorum* (the Fountain of Good), we should expect the being of man to be somehow defined as the correlate of this regulative concept of God. It may be that the systematic coherence of Calvin's anthropology tends to get buried under the sheer mass of dogmatic material; and it has to be remembered that nothing less than the whole of the *Institutes* is required to set out his doctrine of man, just as the work *as a whole* presents his doctrine of God.[3] Nevertheless, it is fair enough to hold that two segments of the *Institutes* are of decisive importance for our theme.

There is, we are told, a twofold knowledge of man. God has made himself known to us as Creator and Redeemer; correspondingly, we are to know what man was like when first created, and what his condition is since the fall.[4] Human

150

nature as created is the particular theme of book 1, chapter 15; Calvin turns to human nature as fallen in book 2, chapters 1–5. That these two segments may not be taken to exhaust his doctrine of man is evident: he subsumes the fall and sin under the knowledge of God the Redeemer, and further discussion on man of course remains, particularly for the sections on christology and the life of the Christian man.[5] Indeed, there is plainly a sense in which, for Calvin, the restoration of man in Christ has dogmatic precedence even over the doctrine of the original estate, since, so he argues, we know of Adam's original blessedness only by viewing it in Christ, the Second Adam.[6]

If, however, with these reservations, we confine our attention to the two designated segments, we do in fact have enough to uncover a distinctive pattern in Calvin's anthropology. Admittedly, he has a lot of other important things to say even in these two segments, but I think we can fairly sum up the heart of the matter like this: The existence of man in the design of God is defined by thankfulness, the correlate of God's goodness; the existence of man in sin is defined by pride or self-love, the antithesis of God's goodness. To have said this much is, of course, already to recognize that in his understanding of man Calvin was working with ideas inherited from the Apostle Paul by way of Augustine.

As with Calvin's doctrine of God, one has to call at the outset for setting aside hoary misconceptions. It is not true that Calvin's was an authoritarian religion, in the sense that man's most fitting posture is one of cringing before the divine despot. (This is what students of psychology may think they have learned from Erich Fromm; but in truth it has more to do with Calvin's notion of idolatry than with his notion of piety.)[7] Neither did Calvin hold that fallen man is in no sense capable of achieving anything beyond his own self-degradation. Here, it must be admitted, his rhetoric sometimes obscures rather than reinforces a theological point. If his description of man as a "five-foot worm" was suggested to him by one of the Psalms (Ps. 22:6),[8] it is hard not to judge that he was carried away by his own sermonizing when he pronounced man unfit to be ranked with "worms, lice, fleas, and vermin."[9] But *how* does one judge that such language really is, in fact, the obfuscation of a strictly theological point? Only by taking due note of the sober theological distinctions made elsewhere; these enable us to see in the heavy rhetoric Calvin's horror that man in sin has surrendered his very humanity to a life of thanklessness.

I

Calvin has already introduced man at the end of his chapter on creation. Having fashioned the universe as a magnificent theater of his glory, God placed man in it last of all as the privileged spectator. Even in himself, adorned by God with exceptional gifts, man was the most excellent example of God's works. And he was endowed besides with the capacity to turn his eyes outwards and to admire the handiwork of God in others of his creatures.[10]

> How great ingratitude would it be now to doubt whether this most gracious Father has us in his care, who we see was concerned for us even before we were born! How impious would it be to tremble for fear that his kindness might at any time fail us in our need, when we see that it was shown, with the greatest abundance of every good thing, when we were yet unborn![11]

There, already, is the heart of Calvin's anthropology. But he turns to man in detail only in chapter 15 of the first book.

It is in this chapter (secs. 3–4) that Calvin writes of the image of God in man. He introduces the subject in a strangely offhanded way, apparently to clinch his argument for the immortality of the soul. But the notion of the divine image has far greater systematic importance than its modest entrance suggests. The way in which Calvin interprets it opens up, better than anything else, the heart of his understanding of man and his place in the world. Further, it constitutes an important link with other parts of the system. It is closely bound up, for instance, with Calvin's teaching on redemption, since Jesus Christ, as the Second Adam, is the one in whom the divine image is restored; being "saved" means being renewed after the image of God in Christ.[12] In addition, Calvin builds his social ethics partly on the endurance of the divine image even in fallen man. The sacredness and dignity of human life are guaranteed by the fact that man was made in the image and likeness of God, and that the remnants of the image persist. It is not only Genesis 1:26 that serves Calvin in this connection, but also Genesis 9:6: "Whoever sheds the blood of man, by man shall his blood be shed; for God made man in his own image." This meant, for him, that the image was not lost but remained regulative of man's social relationships.[13] (The christological connection of the divine image he found in, for example, 2 Corinthians 4:4, which speaks of the "light of the gospel of the glory of Christ, who is the likeness of God.")[14]

Perhaps Calvin's doctrine of the image of God in man did receive a somewhat external interest from the well-known debate between Barth and Brunner.[15] At least, it is largely to this debate that we owe the careful attention the scholars have paid to this theme in Calvin's theology.[16] But it does not follow that the image was marginal to his own thought. He made extensive use of it, perhaps more than the Scriptures warrant. At any rate, he pulled together under this rubric somewhat diverse biblical topics, linked accidentally by a single word, and gave them a distinctive interpretation. Whether or not the interpretation was strictly original, we do not, for now, need to inquire.[17]

What does he mean, then, by the "image of God"? His treatment of the term in the *Institutes* is highly characteristic of him. He liked formal definitions.

But, being trained in the rhetoric of the Renaissance, he thought it gauche to offer his definition first; it was more elegant to lead up to it. At the risk of appearing gauche, I will begin with it. Calvin writes:

> The integrity with which Adam was endowed is expressed by this word [*imago*], when he had full possession of right understanding, when he had his affections kept within the bounds of reason, all his senses tempered in right order, and he truly referred his excellence to exceptional gifts bestowed upon him by his Maker.[18]

It is apparent that what Calvin seeks in his definition is comprehensiveness. The image is anything and everything that sets man apart from the rest of God's creation;[19] or again, by argument back from the restoration of the image in Christ, it is anything and everything that we receive by redemption.[20] In detail, he seeks to divide the general concept by adopting common psychological categories, according to which, as he goes on to put it in a summary formula, Adam had light of *mind* and uprightness of *heart* (with "soundness of all the parts"). That is to say, Adam's intellect saw with clarity, and the affections were duly subordinated to it.[21]

Surveying the opinions of others (another of his favorite procedures), Calvin appropriates whatever he can, but does not hesitate to tell us where his predecessors went wrong. The distinction of Irenaeus between the "image" and the "likeness" of God he rejects: Irenaeus did not understand the nature of Hebrew parallelism.[22] Even Augustine went astray by suggesting that the image refers to the psychological "trinity" of man's intellect, will, and memory, which he held to be an image (or analogy) of the Blessed Trinity. This, Calvin decides, is mere speculation.[23] On the other hand, he apparently thinks Chrysostom had a point when he identified the image with man's dominion over nature. At least, this is part of it. But it is not the sole mark by which man resembles God, and the image is to be sought more correctly *within* man as an inner good of the soul.[24] Finally, Calvin does not want to reject out of hand even the exegesis of Osiander, although he was a man "perversely ingenious in futile inventions." Osiander thought the image pertained to the body as well as to the soul, in that Adam's body pointed forward to the incarnation of the Son of God. This, Calvin assures us, is unsound. But he has already admitted that the upright posture of the human body is at least an outward token of the divine image; for, as Ovid says in the *Metamorphoses*, while other living beings are bent over earthwards,

> Man looks aloft and with erected eyes
> Beholds his own hereditary skies.[25]

Perhaps, however, the desire to be comprehensive and to take the opinions of others into account may obscure the distinctive feature of Calvin's interpretation. And one has to look to his commentaries (as well as to other sections of the *Institutes*) to shed further light on his definition. The first point to notice is the exact metaphor Calvin had in mind when he spoke of an "image." He meant the image seen in a mirror—a reflection.[26] This was a metaphor he particularly liked, and he had used it already in earlier chapters of the *Institutes*; the whole of creation had been represented as a mirror in which the glory of God is to be viewed. We are, Calvin says, to "contemplate in all creatures, as in mirrors, those immense riches of his wisdom, justice, goodness, and power."[27] Similarly, in the chapter on man's nature as created Calvin states that "even in the several parts of the world some traces of God's glory shine."[28] If, then, the doctrine of the image of God in man is intended as a "tacit antithesis," to set man apart from the rest of creation, the question must be asked: How, or in what sense, is man peculiarly and particularly a mirror of deity? In what special manner is he the "reflection of God's glory"?

The answer is most clearly read in the last phrase of Calvin's definition: ". . . and he truly referred his excellence to exceptional gifts bestowed upon him by his Maker." While the entire created order reflects God's glory as in a mirror and in this sense "images" God, man is distinguished from the mute creation by his ability to reflect God's glory in a conscious response of thankfulness. It is this, above all, that sets him apart from the brute beasts: they likewise owe their existence to God, but they do not know it.[29] Man is endowed with a soul by which he can consciously acknowledge God as the Fountain of Good; the soul is not itself the image, but rather the mirror in which the image is reflected.[30] Properly, then, we can speak of man as bearing the image of God only when he attributes his excellence to the Maker.[31] Man is the apex of creation in the sense that the entire creation has its raison d'être in the praise that man alone, of all God's earthly creatures, can return to him.[32]

To sum up: In Calvin's view, the image of God in man denotes not an endowment only, but also a relationship. That is to say, he does not seek to define the image solely by what man possesses as his "nature," but also by the manner in which he orients himself to God. Man is not made in the image of God simply because he has reason, for instance, whereas the rest of God's earthly creatures do not. Even an individual endowed with a wealth of special "gifts" is not in the image of God, in the fully human sense, unless he *acknowledges* them as gifts of God. The relationship of man to God is thus made constitutive of his humanity; and, as we were led to expect, there is a correlation between the notion that is constitutive of deity and the notion constitutive of humanity. God as Fountain of Good has his counterpart in man as his *thankful* creature. And the disruption of this relationship is, for Calvin, nothing less than de-humanizing.

The distinction implicit here becomes crucial for understanding Calvin's view of sin and the fall. The scholars have found an ambiguity in Calvin's answer to the question: Is the image of God lost in fallen man? But if the image includes both man's rational nature and its proper use toward God, the answer is bound to be two-sided. Insofar as the image culminates in the thought of a "right spiritual attitude" (Niesel),[33] one can hardly speak of it as other than "lost" in fallen man, who (by definition) is man fallen out of the right spiritual relationship to God. Redemption, accordingly, is nothing less than restoration of the image. Later, in discussing the effects of the fall, Calvin will assert that faith and love for God, since they are restored to us by Christ, must be accounted lost by the fall—taken away. But the rational nature of man, by which he is *enabled* (in distinction from mere beasts) to love God, is not simply wiped out.[34] In short, the image of God in man embraces both a gift and its right use, both man's rational nature and its orientation to God in thankfulness. For: "We are no different from brutish beasts if we do not understand that the world was made by God. Why are men endowed with reason and intellect except for the purpose of recognizing their Creator?"[35]

II

With these remarks, the transition is already made from man in the design of God to man in the state of sin. Once again, the important point is to grasp the systematic coherence of Calvin's thoughts. Quite simply, if Adam's original state was one in which he acknowledged his endowments as the gifts of God, his fallen state was induced by the pride that claimed something for himself. Not content to be like God, he wanted to be God's equal; and in seeking his own glory, he lost the capacity to reflect the glory of God. If one can hold firmly to this cardinal thought, then much of the nonsense that is commonly retailed concerning "total depravity" can be quickly disposed of. Calvin had no interest in belittling the moral and intellectual achievements of man; he was too well schooled in the classics and in Renaissance scholarship to do that. But he had also gone to school with his master Augustine, and what he did wish to show was that all the works of man, even the very best, remain radically defective when the doer no longer receives his life as a gift. And precisely because he knew classical and Renaissance man so well, he could argue his case with penetrating insight.

Now there are several intricate questions in Calvin's discussion of sin that we must risk leaving out. In particular, he wrestled with two problems bequeathed to him by Augustine: the cause of Adam's sin and the mode of its transmission. These are important questions, and Calvin's reflections on them are intriguing.[36] But it is obvious that one could not, in any case, resolve the problems of sin's cause and transmission without determining what sin is. This, then, is the first matter on which I should comment; and the only other matter I wish to take up (because of its pertinence to my central theme) is the extent of the damage wreaked by sin on human nature.

We are not surprised to find that Calvin has his definition of original sin.[37] But what is the nature of the "depravity" and "corruption" to which the definition refers? His analysis of the concept of sin is in fact more clearly given in his interpretation of Genesis 3: it is the "history" of Adam's fall that shows us what sin is.[38] As usual, Calvin proceeds by telling us what others have said on the subject, especially Augustine.

We read that Adam ate a tempting fruit, "good for food ... a delight to the eyes" (Gen. 3:6). Was his sin, then, that he indulged his appetite? Calvin answers: "To regard Adam's sin as gluttonous intemperance (a common notion) is childish." The forbidden fruit was a test of obedience, an exercise of faith. In a paradise abounding with delights, abstinence from only one fruit would hardly have made him virtuous. Rather, "the sole purpose of the precept was to keep him content with his lot." So, Calvin moves on to Augustine's interpretation, which states that pride was the beginning of all evils. "For if ambition had not raised man higher than was meet and right, he could have remained in his original state." Is Augustine right? Well, the English translation says that he "speaks rightly." But what Calvin wrote was *non male*, and he seems to have meant it literally: Augustine's answer is not bad, but it is not quite right either.

Calvin wants, in fact, to get behind human pride to the root cause of it. And what is that? He has several words for it; perhaps "unfaithfulness" is the regulative one. But it is crucial to note that, for him, the essence of infidelity is *not listening to God*. That is the way he read the biblical narrative. The serpent's opening gambit, it will be recalled, is to ask the question, "Did God say ... ?" (v. 1). A little later, somewhat emboldened, he assures Eve: "You will not die" (v. 4). The serpent works by instilling contempt for the Word of God. Here is the theme Calvin wants to pick up, in order to show the root of pride and so to improve on Augustine. Adam, in short, was *verbo incredulus*: he questioned the Word. And this destroyed his reverence for God, whom he pictured as not only deceitful but envious and hostile to his own creature.

Finally, at the end, Calvin seems to return to the theme of carnal desire, and says: "As a result, men, having cast off the fear of God, threw themselves wherever lust carried them." Bondage to carnal desire, in other words, is not the beginning of sin but its final consequence. The heart of the matter, as Calvin saw it, is summed up like this:

> Unfaithfulness, then, was the root of the Fall. But thereafter ambition and pride, together with ungratefulness, arose, because Adam by seeking more than was granted him shamefully spurned God's great bounty, which had been lavished upon him. To have been made in the likeness of God seemed

a small matter to a son of earth unless he also attained equality with God—
a monstrous wickedness!

It will be noticed, in this passage, how Calvin can equally well make his point
with the word "ungratefulness'; or, from the perspective of God, he can state
that "Adam, carried away by the devil's blasphemies, as far as he was able
extinguished the whole glory of God." Plainly, here is the same complex of
ideas—with some shifts in terminology—that we have found already in Calvin's
thoughts on the image of God in man. But now everything is, so to say, inverted;
for whereas man was created to image God's glory in an act of thankful acknowledgment, he has fallen into thankless pride that spurns God's bounty.

Calvin rounds off his anatomy of sin with a remark that points forward to
redemption: "The door of salvation is opened to us when we receive the gospel
today with our ears, even as death was then admitted by those same windows
when they were opened to Satan." (As so often, he is quoting Bernard of Clair-
vaux.) But his immediate agenda requires him to address himself, next, to
original sin and the ravages of sin in the intellect and the will of man. Here we
find some of Calvin's gloomiest thoughts; yet it can hardly account for the
common opinion that there is a sharp difference between Roman Catholicism
and Protestantism on the extent of sin's damage to the soul.

Although he is sharply critical of the Schoolmen at many points, Calvin
thinks one cannot improve on their distinction between the natural and the
supernatural gifts of God: "The natural gifts in man were corrupted, but the
supernatural taken away."[39] The problem is that the Schoolmen did not agree
on a satisfactory *explanation* of the formula, and in this respect the earlier
Schoolmen are judged better than the "more recent Sophists."[40] Hence a great
part of the discussion requires Calvin, as usual, to sort out the sheep from the
goats among his predecessors and to arrive at satisfactory definitions of terms.
The sole point I want to stress, however, is that he seems explicitly to caution us
against "adjudging man's nature wholly corrupted."[41] At any rate, what he was
concerned to establish was, not that man is utterly bad, but that the taint of
sin vitiates even his best and leaves no corner of his life unblemished. And he
tried to demonstrate this thesis, in turn, with respect to both man's intellectual
and his moral achievements.

Writing of the human intellect, Calvin certainly will not allow that it can
attain to a sound knowledge of God; for it cannot reach the assurance of God's
benevolence (a point that Luther, too, liked to stress).[42] Nevertheless, it is
entirely consistent with Calvin's standpoint that he maintained a firmly positive
attitude toward the attainments of human culture, since failure to do so would
be denial of his fundamental notion of God as *fons bonorum.*

The mind of man, though fallen and perverted from its wholeness, is nevertheless clothed and ornamented with God's excellent gifts. If we regard the

Spirit of God as the sole fountain of truth, we shall neither reject the truth itself, nor despise it wherever it shall appear, unless we wish to dishonor the Spirit of God. For by holding the gifts of the Spirit in light esteem, we contemn and reproach the Spirit himself.[43]

Calvin then parades the cultural achievements of man in law, natural philosophy, logic, medicine, mathematics. And, as a good humanist, he concludes:

We cannot read the writings of the ancients on these subjects without great admiration. We marvel at them because we are compelled to recognize how preeminent they are. But shall we count anything praiseworthy or noble without recognizing at the same time that it comes from God? Let us be ashamed of such ingratitude, into which not even the pagan poets fell, for they confessed that the gods had invented philosophy, laws, and all useful arts.[44]

Similarly, when Calvin turns to his discussion of the fallen will, he insists that even in sin man cannot be wholly bad; otherwise, we could not say that one man is "better" than another.

In every age there have been persons who, guided by nature, have striven toward virtue throughout life. I have nothing to say against them even if many lapses can be noted in their moral conduct. . . . Either we must make Camillus equal to Catiline, or we shall have in Camillus an example proving that nature, if carefully cultivated, is not utterly devoid of goodness.[45]

Then, of course, comes the refrain: this "natural goodness," too, must be traced to the special bounty of God. "The endowments resplendent in Camillus were gifts of God." But now the question is this: Did the ancient heroes, such as the patriot Camillus, acknowledge gifts as gifts?

Calvin's answer is that "heroes" are driven by their own ambition. In other words, we may say, the glory they seek is their own. Hence Calvin grants that their virtues will have their praise in the political assembly and in common renown among men, but not that they make for righteousness before the heavenly judgment seat. For "where there is no zeal to glorify God, the chief part of uprightness is absent." While, therefore, in ordinary, day-to-day usage ("common parlance," as Calvin says) we do not hesitate to distinguish one man as "noble" and another as "depraved" in nature, we are still to include both under the theological verdict of human depravity. Plainly, Calvin is making the point that Luther conveyed by his distinction between "Christian" and "civil" righteousness. To say (theologically) that a man is "depraved" is not to say that, morally considered, he is a bad man. All turns on the motivation out of which a man acts: whether or not, that is, his deeds are done in thankfulness to the Fountain of Good. The doctrine of sin is not strictly about a person's moral condition, but about his relationship to God: it pronounces a religious, not an ethical, verdict. Pagan virtues, properly understood, are in truth tokens of grace; but insofar as they are the virtues of a man who claims them for himself, they differ from the virtues of the justified man because they issue from a quite different orientation of the total self.

While it cannot be claimed that Calvin's language is always perspicuously self-consistent, a consistent thread does run through his thoughts on human nature as created, fallen, and redeemed.[46] Man's being points beyond him to the source of his existence and of the existence of all that is. He was fashioned as the point of creation at which the overflowing goodness of the Creator was to be "mirrored" or reflected back again in thankful piety. This is the condition from which he fell, no longer heeding the voice of God; and it is the condition to which, through hearing the Word of God in Jesus Christ, he is restored. For all Calvin's persuasion that man has a privileged standing in the world, his cosmos is not man-centered: man has his place as spectator and even agent of the manifestation of God's glory, in which alone the cosmos has its final meaning. It may well be that, when demythologized, such an austere view of the dignity and finitude of man takes on a profounder relevance than Calvin ever dreamed of, as Western man moves out of the tight little world of the Middle Ages into the immense, mysterious cosmos of the modern astronomer.[47]

Part
Three

The Reformation Heritage

Ten   The Reformation and the
                       Rise of Modern Science:
                       Luther, Calvin, and Copernicus

The first half of the sixteenth century witnessed two revolutionary movements
in the intellectual history of the West. Twenty-six years after Luther's theses
on indulgences had shaken the Western church (1517), the strange theories of
Nicholas Copernicus were published at Nuremberg (1543) and called in question
the medieval picture of the cosmos. Neither event was a revolution in itself.
Copernicus was fully aware of his forerunners in the ancient world, and his
heliocentric theory required the criticisms and observations of his successors
before the scientific revolution was complete. Others, before Luther, had tried
to reform the Roman Church; and it could be argued that, viewed in the context
of European intellectual history as a whole, his religious "revolution" was not
much more than a minor disturbance within medieval thought. Not until the
Enlightenment were Christian ways of thinking about God and man radically
transformed. Still, the Protestant Reformation and Copernican astronomy were,
at the very least, parts of two incomplete revolutions, and their coincidence in
time invites inquiry into the relations between them. The later development of
Copernican astronomy and the wider question of Protestantism's place in the
modern world may be left outside the limits of this inquiry.

The relations of religion and science in the Reformation era were not confined to astronomical matters. Andreas von Carlstadt, for example, had his
doubts about medical science and suggested that the sick should turn to prayer,
not to the physician.[1] Again, the man who discovered the pulmonary circulation
of the blood, Michael Servetus, was burned in Protestant Geneva.[2] Of course,
he was not condemned for his physiological opinions. But one may still wish to
argue that Calvin's religious fanaticism delayed the physiological advances that
might have resulted from the discoveries of Servetus.[3] Moreover, if there was
nothing in the Christian revelation to contradict the pulmonary circulation of
the blood, one of the charges brought against Servetus was that he had cast
doubt on revealed geography: whereas the Old Testament called Palestine a land

flowing with milk and honey, Servetus reproduced a statement of Ptolemy's according to which Judaea was notoriously barren.[4] In his widely read work, *A History of the Warfare of Science with Theology in Christendom*,[5] Andrew Dickson White quite properly took note of such aspects of his subject. It is only for reasons of manageability that attention is focused, in the present essay, on Luther and Calvin and their attitudes toward astronomy. Other reformers and other sciences could have been chosen.

Even when the theme "the Reformation and the rise of modern science" has been so circumscribed, opinions about it are sharply divided. On the one side, it has been argued that the Continental Reformation, in each of its two major branches, proved itself hospitable to the new science. Lutheran men of learning played a prominent role in the publication of Copernicus's theories, and the principles of Reformed (or Calvinistic) theology were supposedly an important incentive to scientific research. On the other side, it is alleged that Protestant biblicism greeted the new astronomy with enraged opposition, and that by their obscurantism Luther and Calvin delayed acceptance of the helio-centric hypothesis. The Reformers, it is said, repudiated Copernicanism by quoting Scripture and initiated a campaign of suppression which was as vehe-ment, but not as effective, as the Roman Church's silencing of Galileo. Bias, perhaps, has played its part in the debate, and even among the defenders of Protestantism interest may sometimes be divided along confessional lines. Be that as it may, the question has to be faced whether, in actual fact, Luther and Calvin really were biblical literalists in their attitudes toward natural science. The answer is that Luther in his so-called "doctrine of twofold truth" and Calvin in his "principle of accommodation" were operating with theories of theological language which made a conflict of biblical and Copernican science unnecessary. The relation between Reformation and science thus appears to be many-sided, and it is still perhaps an open question.[6]

I

Copernicus boldly dedicated his major treatise to Pope Paul III. But the dedica-tory preface reveals the author's misgivings.[7] He is trying, in fact, to obtain the pope's protection against the expected slanderers; hence the judicious flattery of His Holiness as himself a learned mathematician. Diplomatically, Copernicus mentions the interest of Cardinal Nicholas Schönberg, of Capua, and Tiedeman Giese, bishop of Culm, together with "not a few other most eminent and learned men." Moreover, he represents his theory, not as an unprecedented novelty, but as a return to a neglected strand of antiquity, made necessary by difficulties in the accepted mathematics.[8] Copernicus anticipates that there will be those who oppose him on the basis of "some place of Scripture wickedly twisted to their purpose." But he hints, too, that his findings may be of practical utility to the church, since efforts under Leo X to reform the ecclesiastical calendar had failed for lack of accurate astronomical data. Copernicus did not live to witness either the religious controversy over his work or its ecclesiastical utility. The first copies of his *De revolutionibus orbium coelestium* (1543) reached him on his deathbed.

Among the "eminent and learned men" who showed interest in Copernicus's researches were certain Lutherans, whom he wisely neglected to name in his dedicatory letter. Although the *De revolutionibus* was not published until 1543, the manuscript was apparently completed much earlier (possibly by 1530), and the ideas it contained were not unknown in learned circles. A preliminary account had appeared in the *Commentariolus*, which Copernicus had written during the first decade of the century and distributed in manuscript among his friends.[9] In the spring of 1539, a young Wittenberg professor of mathematics, Georg Joachim Rheticus, was sufficiently intrigued by the rumors to pay a personal visit to Frauenburg in East Prussia (Ermland), where Copernicus was a prominent canon in the cathedral chapter. Rheticus became one of the keenest advocates of the new astronomy. The next year he published a preliminary report on Copernicus's findings;[10] and when he returned to Wittenberg (1541), he had been commissioned by Copernicus to publish the *De revolutionibus*.

The suggestion that Rheticus found himself persona non grata at Wittenberg has not been demonstrated from the sources.[11] The truth is that Copernicus's great work was published through the goodwill of the Lutherans, even—remarkably enough—the goodwill of those Lutherans who disapproved of Copernicus's thesis. Rheticus did not stand alone as the solitary Copernican among the associates of Luther. It was the Lutheran theologian Andreas Osiander who furnished *De revolutionibus* with an anonymous preface. One of Luther's closest friends and co-workers, Caspar Cruciger, professor of theology at Wittenberg, made no secret of his admiration for Copernicus. Erasmus Reinhold, a mathematician at the university, openly praised Copernicus and based a set of astronomical tables (the *Tabulae Prutenicae*) on his calculations. The evidence, then, seems perfectly plain: Copernicus won some of his keenest advocates among the Lutherans; and those Lutherans who remained unconvinced at least tolerated their more adventurous colleagues, even encouraged them.[12]

Reformed scholars were not so intimately involved in the early dissemination of Copernicanism. It is possible that at Geneva, as in Wittenberg, champions of the old and the new astronomy taught side by side during the sixteenth century.[13] But with regard to Calvinism the somewhat different claim is made that Reformed theology was in some degree a nursing mother to scientific research. Attention has been drawn to evidence that Protestants in general have predominated over Roman Catholics among the leading scientists of modern Europe, and that within Protestantism the Reformed churches (at least until the nineteenth century) played the larger role in nurturing men of science.[14] In this connection, the case of Calvinist Holland is particularly interesting. The telescope and the microscope are both claimed as Dutch inventions; the Reformed Christians of the Lowlands expressed their gratitude to God for deliverance from Roman Catholic powers by founding the University of Leyden; and many Dutch Calvinists distinguished themselves by their passion for the natural sciences.[15] Even when allowances are made for patriotic and confessional loyalties, the evidence may seem sufficient to catch the historian's attention, though not every historian is likely to be impressed.[16]

Various attempts have been made to explain the evidence by analysis of the Calvinist mentality. In fact, there is a parallel here to the attempts of Max Weber and others to establish a correlation between the Calvinist "ethic" and the "spirit" of modern capitalism.[17] It is noteworthy that S. F. Mason's attempt to explain the historical correlation of Protestantism and science echoes, in part, Weber's explanation of the connection between Protestantism and capitalism. The followers of Calvin, according to Mason, "experienced an imperative need to know whether they were predestined." They obtained this assurance through the performance of good works, including scientific activity, which was valued as beneficial to mankind. Hence the Calvinistic-Puritan mentality was not merely congruous with scientific activity but provided it with "a positive impulse," since it was able to use science for the attainment of religious ends.[18]

Other features of the Calvinist tradition have been highlighted as possible incentives to scientific activity: Mason finds a further "congruence between the early Protestant ethos and the scientific attitude" in Protestantism's antiauthoritarian appeal to religious experience and individual interpretation of the Scriptures.[19] W. F. Dankbaar maintains that the most significant feature of Calvin's Academy at Geneva was the way in which the entire pursuit of science was subsumed under the religious duties of glorifying God and christianizing society. Similarly, Prince William the Silent desired that at the University of Leyden science, in the service of God and for his glory, should dedicate its powers to the good of both church and society, religion and freedom. The scientific enterprise was given a certain religious dignity through its inclusion under the rubric of glorifying God.[20] Others have sought the clue in the Calvinistic doctrine of common grace, according to which truth in every domain comes from God, so that the quest for truth is an act of piety which honors him.[21] Finally, it is claimed that the doctrine of predestination, so boldly emphasized in the Reformed tradition, was "the strongest motive in those days for the cultivation of science." For God's decrees are the sure foundation of nature's laws, and scientific inquiry depends on confidence in the unity, stability, and order of nature.[22]

None of these attempts to explain the sympathy between Calvinism and the scientific temper amounts, I think, to a convincing demonstration, even if we grant the historical correlation which they seek to explain. Both the explanations and the correlation itself need further research. Mason's thesis concerning the Calvinistic use of science in the quest for assurance is not substantiated.[23] Dankbaar's argument, though more persuasive, is qualified by the admission that the University of Leyden was modeled on humanistic and medieval patterns, so that one cannot speak of a distinctively Calvinistic style of scientific activity.[24] Further, it may be asked, what makes even the "Calvinistic" concept of glorifying God anything more than a Christian commonplace, a vision shared by medieval educators as well? Nevertheless, the glory of God, common grace, and predestination—though none of them individually is without its counterparts in other Christian traditions—do seem to me, when taken together and given a special prominence, to be indicative of a distinctively Calvinistic view of the world and a corresponding Calvinistic "ethic." The vocation of the scientist receives a religious dignity,[25] and it may even be that the mechanics of providential working in Calvinist theology furnished a kind of midway point between the unpredictable angel- (and demon-) filled world of the Middle Ages and the deterministic order of seventeenth-century science. This much could be maintained without claiming that science everywhere had to cross over this particular bridge.

II

If, then, some of Copernicus's key advocates were enlisted from Lutheran circles, and if there seems to have been a certain affinity between Calvinism and the scientific temper, why has it been repeatedly maintained that Protestantism arrested the advance of modern science? The answer is that a kind of sacred tradition has been faithfully transmitted in the literature, both English and foreign,[26] according to which the first generation of Reformers initiated a campaign to suppress the new astronomy. The origins and foundation of this tradition are seldom examined by those who pass it on. And it has to be conceded that some who write as the avowed champions of science have been strangely reluctant to transfer the scientific temper and method into the domain of history.

The five main features of the tradition can be readily enumerated, though they do not always appear together. First, Luther, Melanchthon, and Calvin rejected the heliocentric hypothesis.[27] Second, they refuted Copernicus by quoting Scripture.[28] The first point is correct, and the second, as we shall see, two-thirds correct: Luther and Melanchthon did reject Copernicanism on biblical grounds. But from this evidence it is assumed, third, that the Reformers were in principle opposed to scientific investigation[29] and, fourth, that they sought to suppress the Copernican viewpoint.[30] This, as far as I can judge, is an unwarranted inference from the first point and is already refuted by our previous discussion.

Finally, it is suggested that, if Copernicanism nevertheless flourished in Protestant lands, this was only because the Protestants were less effective than the Roman curia in silencing scientific heretics.[31] This, too, is a suggestion which seems unnecessary in the light of our previous conclusions, since no campaign of repression was in fact undertaken during the Reformers' lifetime.[32] It remains, then, to examine the actual sources in which Luther, Melanchthon, and (allegedly) Calvin expressed opposition to Copernicus on biblical grounds.

By 1539, even before the publication of his major work, Copernicus had become a topic for conversation in Wittenberg. It was in the spring that Rheticus left for Frauenburg, to obtain firsthand information from Copernicus himself. The same year, on 4 June, Copernicus and his theories came up for discussion in Luther's household, and the Reformer's admiring disciples jotted down notes on the master's astronomical opinions. Here is Lauterbach's version of the discussion:

> Mention was made of some new astrologer [sic] who would prove that the earth moves and not the heaven, sun, and moon, just as if someone moving in a vehicle or a ship were to think that he himself was at rest and that the earth and the trees were moving. But [Luther's response] this is the way it goes nowadays: anyone who wants to be clever should not be satisfied with the opinions of others [der soll ihme nichts lassen gefallen, was andere achten]. He has to produce something of his own, as this man does, who wants to turn the whole of astrology upside down. But even though astrology has been thrown into confusion, I, for my part, believe the sacred Scripture; for Joshua commanded the sun to stand still, not the earth.[33]

The parallel passage in Aurifaber's version of the *Table Talk* includes the remark greatly beloved and faithfully reproduced in the secondary literature: "The fool wants to turn the whole art of astronomy upside down."[34] In general, Lauterbach is to be considered the more reliable reporter, so that there must be some doubt about the authenticity of the notorious "fool" clause.[35] Nevertheless, even without it the passage seems to be plainly anti-Copernican.

To be sure, Wilhelm Norlind has read Lauterbach's version as complimentary to Copernicus. "Now it is very curious," he remarks, "that, according to Aurifaber, Luther may *first* seem to praise the man ('er muss ihm etwas Eigens machen') and *then* blames him as a 'Narr'!" Since the disparaging expression *der Narr* was not in the corresponding passage of "the more trustworthy Lauterbach," we are bound, so Norlind maintains, to "regard the 'famous' expression given by Aurifaber as an interpolation not consistent with the text." It could be replied that Luther is not commending Copernicus for his inventiveness, but disparaging him for wanting to be thought clever.[36] In any case, the main point is sufficiently clear: Luther thought he could refute Copernicus by quoting

Scripture, though he did not therefore try to prevent the spread of Copernican astronomy.[37]

Melanchthon, too, like Luther, adduced scriptural arguments against Copernicanism.[38] But Melanchthon was not simply a theologian. He was also a philosopher of the humanistic type, and he held astronomical opinions on non-theological grounds. For him, the study of nature rested upon the authority of the approved ancients—that is, Aristotle and Ptolemy. Hence the greater part of his case against Copernicus consisted of arguments drawn from antiquity.[39] In other words, Melanchthon believed himself to be taking up the debate against a misguided effort to revive outmoded science. Nonetheless, he did not permit his disagreements to intrude upon his friendships nor even to detract from his respect for Copernicus.[40] So far from initiating a campaign of repression, he somewhat mitigated his criticisms after 1549.[41] Still, it must be admitted that Melanchthon, like Luther, thought it legitimate to refute a scientific theory with scriptural arguments. Moreover, he repaired the fateful alliance of theology and Aristotelianism that Luther had shattered; and thereby he created for later Protestantism a problem that did not exist for Luther and Calvin.[42]

As notorious as the "fool" passage in Luther's *Table Talk* is the rhetorical question commonly attributed to Calvin: "Who will venture to place the authority of Copernicus above that of the Holy Spirit?" But although the question is faithfully transmitted in the English literature, the exact reference does not accompany it, and it has so far proved impossible to locate it in any of Calvin's known writings. I have seldom come across it (or its equivalent) in the foreign literature;[43] and I suspect that its currency in English and American studies is the most striking proof of the influence of A. D. White. In White's own words:

> Calvin took the lead, in his *Commentary on Genesis*, by condemning all who asserted that the earth is not at the centre of the universe. He clinched the matter by the usual reference to the first verse of the ninety-third Psalm, and asked, "Who will venture to place the authority of Copernicus above that of the Holy Spirit?"[44]

Where, then, did White himself find Calvin's question, since it cannot be found either in the *Commentary on Genesis* or in the exposition of Psalm 93?

In a splendid piece of detective-work Edward Rosen has tracked the citation back to F. W. Farrar, who likewise offered only the "quotation," not the reference.[45] Rosen explains this omission by giving a rather mischievous turn to a eulogy of Farrar by his son, who wrote: "Quotation with him [F. W. Farrar] was entirely spontaneous, almost involuntary, because his marvellous memory was stored, nay saturated with passages." The famous Calvin quotation seems, in fact, to be a fiction due to Farrar's overconfidence in his marvelous memory. Rosen concludes: "What, then,...was Calvin's attitude toward Copernicus?

Never having heard of him, Calvin had no attitude toward Copernicus."[46] This, perhaps, says too much. It is hardly necessary to suppose that Calvin had never heard of Copernicus. What is plain, however, is that if he knew of Copernicus, he felt no compelling need to quarrel with him. It has not even been established that Calvin once mentioned Copernicus in all his voluminous writings.[47]

III

It remains true, however, that the Lutheran reformers, at any rate, did oppose Copernicanism with arguments drawn from Scripture. A. D. White and others were perfectly right in seeing here a phase in the warfare between science and theology, even though they constructed false inferences upon the evidence, some even magnifying rejection of the Copernican theory into an imaginary campaign of suppression. Luther and Melanchthon set the pattern for later Protestant biblicism, according to which the sacred Scriptures furnish inerrant information on scientific matters. The basis was already laid, by the first generation of Lutheran reformers, for what Draper called "the fatal maxim that the Bible contained the sum and substance of all knowledge useful or possible to man."[48] Luther and Melanchthon assumed that not only the meaning of the gospel, but also the scientific picture of nature could be read off from the pages of Scripture, literally interpreted. This much is clear enough in the sources used by White. It must now be pointed out, however, that gross injustice is done to Luther by the extraordinary procedure of isolating a solitary passage from the *Table Talk* and assuming that his entire attitude toward the natural sciences—and indeed the sacred Scriptures—is adequately presented in this stray, offhanded remark.

According to White, the Reformers "turned their faces away from scientific investigation."[49] Even in the narrow sense of modern English usage, which virtually identifies "science" with natural science, this statement is incorrect. Luther had a lively interest in scientific progress and explicitly raised the question of the relationship between science and theology.

It is true that a superficial reading of Luther could uncover further apparent evidence of hostility towards science. Part of the difficulty is resolved when one recalls that the natural sciences in the sixteenth century were entangled in sorcery, alchemy, and astrology. Some of Luther's judgments can only be understood as an attempt to disentangle science from quackery. What looks at first like an obscurantist assault on "natural philosophy" may turn out to be a protest against unwarranted procedures in science. "Those who lie about far-distant lands, lie with all their might, there being none with experience to contradict them." But science is tied to experience. For Luther, the two sources of knowledge were experience (*erfarung*) and revelation.[50] They correspond to philosophy and theology respectively, or to reason and faith (the two modes of cognition).[51] And by "philosophy" Luther understood the sum total of the human "sciences." Hence he admired astronomy as an empirical science, but had no respect for astrology:[52] and he contrasted the astrologer's predictions with the physician's prognosis, which has "symptoms and experience" as its guide.[53]

Luther was not ignorant of the fact that he lived in an age of scientific progress. He greeted the new science with enthusiasm and liked to contrast himself in this respect with the humanist Erasmus. In the advance of scientific knowledge he saw the gradual recovery of Adam's dominion over the world of nature.[54] Reason was understood by Luther as the divinely given organ by which man was to move out into the world and have mastery over it.[55] Hence he did not need to become defensive when science and Scripture ran into apparent conflict. He was willing, for example, to accept the astronomers' conclusion that the moon was the smallest and lowest of the "stars": perhaps the Scriptures, in calling the sun and the moon two great lights, were simply describing the moon as it looks to us.[56] Luther recognized that religious and scientific interest in nature are two different things. The light of the moon was for him, religiously, a token of divine care; but he acknowledged that the astronomer's concern was to show how the moon's light was in fact reflected from the sun.[57] In other words, even when theology and science are directed to a common object, like the heavenly bodies, they talk about it in different, but not necessarily exclusive, ways. Faith penetrates beyond the visible object to the unseen God, whose gracious care the object attests.[58]

It is the attempt to distinguish the proper spheres of theological and philosophical language that lies behind Luther's interest in the so-called medieval "theory of double truth."[59] As usually formulated, the theory maintains that a proposition may be true in theology but false in philosophy, and vice versa. It seems to have been not so much a consciously formulated doctrine as an accusation leveled against theological opponents,[60] and it is commonly assumed that the accused were guilty of a dishonesty which tokened the bankruptcy of scholastic theology.[61]

In his important *Disputation on the Proposition, "The Word was made flesh"* (1539),[62] Luther states explicitly, though without using the expression "double truth," that the same thing is not true in different disciplines. And yet his intention is not to allow, but to exclude, the possibility of contradiction between two disciplines. It remains axiomatic that one truth agrees with another.[63] Luther begins by affirming that the proposition "The Word was made flesh" is true in theology, but simply impossible and absurd in philosophy (thesis 2). In the course of the disputation the objection is made that if the same thing is true in theology and false in philosophy, then philosophy and theology contradict each other. Luther's reply, in effect, is that there can only be contradiction *within* a particular language system, not *between* one system and another.[64] "God is man" and "God is not man" would only be contradictory if both were asserted in the same discipline.[65] The fact is that the words "God is man" do not mean for the theologian what they mean for the philosopher. The philosophical sense of the word "man" is "self-subsistent person"; but when the theologian speaks of the Incarnation, he has in mind "a divine person bearing humanity."[66] Similarly, in the syllogism "Every man is a creature, Christ is a man, therefore Christ is a creature" there are really four terms, not the required three, since "man" has a different sense in the major premise than it has in the minor.[67]

In his distinction between the two uses of the word "man" Luther was borrowing from the Schoolmen. But he turns a scholastic distinction against the Paris Schoolmen themselves, and argues that if they find it necessary to invoke the notion of equivocalness, then they ought really to agree with him. That is, they should not attempt a reconciliation of theology and philosophy, but should concede his point that the same thing is not true in both theology and philosophy. A proposition could only be said to be true in both contexts if the terms of the proposition were used with the same significance.[68] In answer to a further objection, Luther insists that the propositions "God is man" and "Every man is a creature" are both "simple." He means, I take it, that they are unambiguous within *either* context, theology *or* philosophy.[69] But if you compare their meaning across disciplines, so to say, they are not strictly the same propositions, because (as Luther has already shown) the terms are differently used. We cannot admit ambiguity into our syllogisms *within* any discourse; we have to keep them unambiguous by distinguishing the disciplines.[70] When we observe the necessary distinction, then the fact that one discipline seems to affirm what another denies proves not to be a genuine contradiction.[71] The need to maintain the distinction of the diciplines is what Luther intends by thesis 14: Lady Reason must do as the Apostle says, and keep quiet in church.[72]

What Luther suggests, then, against the Sorbonne—that "mother of errors"— might properly be called a "theory of multiple discourse" rather than a "theory of double truth." Neither "double" nor "truth" expresses his position accurately. He is concerned with various disciplines, not just two (since "philosophy," in his parlance, is the sum of the departmental sciences); and with truth only indirectly, as a consequence of his theory of meaning. His thesis is that each of the various disciplines *(professiones)* operates with its own special discourse. Words and propositions do not have a fixed meaning in a universal language. Their meaning is relative to a particular discourse. A word transferred from one discourse to another may have a different meaning in its new context or even no meaning at all. Hence it is a mistake to ask how many lines there are in a pound, or how many feet there are in a pint; and in geometry you do not reckon up pounds and ounces.[73] If this principle holds true within philosophy—that is, among the various sciences *(artes)*—it is all the more true when we compare philosophy with theology, which works, from a wholly different kind of data.[74]

The conclusion is, then, that much more can be said about Luther and science than is contained in the notorious fool-passage. Not only did Luther take a lively interest in scientific progress, he also reflected about the relation of science and theology—that is, about the place of theology among the various university disciplines. And his overriding intent is plain: to give each discipline autonomy in its own "sphere." Admittedly, his reflections in the *Disputation* are not fully developed. But they are not out of harmony with his general theological position, in which theology and philosophy are related to the doctrine of the two realms. The thesis that the same word or proposition changes its meaning (and therefore its truth value) if transferred from one realm to the other is fundamental to Luther's thoughts on justification and ethics.[75] Words are like coins, which are acceptable currency only in the area where they are minted;[76] and the various disciplines are like the distinct spheres which God has placed in the heavens.[77] Clearly, it was Luther's intention to allow the various disciplines full autonomy within their own limits. But apparently he forgot at the dinner table on 4 June what he had argued in a public disputation on 11 January. Or, at least, he failed to draw the consequences. Even so, an obvious injustice is done to him if his dinner conversation is treated as the better source for his opinions on theology and science.

IV

The features of Calvinistic theology which may be viewed as inducements to a scientific interest in nature have already been noted. It hardly needs to be demonstrated that they have their source in Calvin's own thinking, even though later Calvinists may have developed the master's thoughts beyond the limits he himself imposed.[78] Calvin was intensely interested in the world of nature, on which he saw the manifest traces of God's handiwork. The world is a "mirror," in which God may be viewed.[79] It is the "theater" of God's glory, and men are placed in it as spectators.[80] True, since Adam's fall most people walk like blind men in this divine theater. But the Word of God is given to restore our eyesight— to furnish us, as Calvin puts it, with spectacles.[81] And although the evidences are open even to the unlearned, men of science are privileged to penetrate more deeply into the secrets of divine wisdom.[82] We should be guilty of base ingratitude if we failed to acknowledge the bountiful hand of God both in the works of nature[83] and in the human intelligence which comprehends them.[84] Of course, Calvin was not himself a "scientist" in our sense; that was not his special calling.[85] And only a faithful admirer could describe him as a *savant*, of prodigious erudition, who knew just about all there was to be known in his day.[86] But it is hardly true that Calvin "appears to have had no taste for the sciences."[87] On the contrary, he writes almost enviously of the astronomer, to whom the intricate workings of providence were more openly displayed than to other men.[88] And, like Luther, he felt a corresponding disdain for the astrologers, who abused the study of the heavens.[89]

It still has to be asked, however, whether Calvin left the scientists free from theological interference. Did he recognize the autonomy of science as well as its religious utility? It seems that, unlike the Lutheran reformers, he did not oppose the new astronomy on biblical grounds. But this is not necessarily to his credit; it may indicate only that he was less well informed than they. The real question is whether or not he believed that there are theological criteria for statements about the natural order. He ought, in principle, to have been freed from the practice of using Scripture as a source of scientific information, since he could present the christological content of the Bible as, so to say, an intellectual limit. That is, he affirmed that the function of the Bible was to furnish knowledge of Jesus Christ, so that our minds, as we read the Scripture, should come to a halt when this goal is attained.[90] From which one must justly infer that the Bible does not furnish, in addition, revealed information about astronomy. But in actual fact Calvin was no more consistent than Luther in maintaining a "christocentric" view of the Bible.[91]

It has been suggested by Albert-Marie Schmidt that Calvin bequeathed to his disciples as a criterion of scientific truth, not the letter of Holy Scripture, but "the test of God's glory as Scripture reveals it generally."[92] To which it must be replied that such a criterion would end the autonomy of science just as effectively as the biblical literalism of Luther's notorious *Table Talk*. But not one shred of evidence is advanced to demonstrate that this was in fact Calvin's approach to questions of secular learning. It is one thing to believe that the pursuit of science will give access to the glory of God, quite another to use God's glory as a test for scientific truth. Further, although Schmidt treats the opinions of Lambert Daneau (Danaeus) under the rubric *rédaction de la doctrine,* he is obliged to begin by drawing attention to the differences between the author and the redactor. Calvin considered as true all the scientific information contained in the Bible, but he set no limits on the scientific activity of the human spirit by which the information was to be elucidated. Daneau, on the other hand, spoke as though there were no need to look beyond the letter of Scripture, and he expressly opposed "those who deny that a knowledge of physics can truly and properly be learned from sacred Scripture."[93] If, then, Calvin's disciple performed the useful service of gathering what Calvin himself had sown throughout his various writings, it remains true, as Schmidt concedes, that he ruined the crop *(il dénature la récolte).*

More important is the fact, not mentioned by Schmidt, that Daneau explicitly rejected, or at least qualified, the hermeneutic principle by which Calvin was able to maintain simultaneously the truth of biblical science and the autonomy of natural science. True, Daneau admitted that there were some particulars concerning nature on which it is necessary to consult physicians and natural historians, "since that *Salomons* Bookes whiche were written copiously of the Nature of all thynges, are, through the negligence of men, perished." Cosmological questions, however, are not of this kind, but are chiefly to be settled by appeal to Scripture, inasmuch as the Author of Nature is best qualified to discourse about it. The contrary view, Daneau points out, rests on two arguments: that natural philosophy and divinity are two distinct disciplines, and that because Mosaic science is "fitted to our capacitie," an exact knowledge of nature is "other whence to bee drawne." In rejecting these contrary arguments, Daneau claims that Moses wrote "barely [i.e., in a plain style], but rightly." Calvin, on the other hand, went further, as did Luther, and made the language of Mosaic astronomy relative to the viewpoint of an untutored observer.[94]

According to Calvin, the forms of revelation are adapted in various ways to the nature of man as the recipient. His general term for the several types of adaptation is "accommodation."[95] It is axiomatic for Calvin that God cannot be comprehended by the human mind. What is known of God is known by revelation; and God reveals himself, not as he is in himself, but in forms adapted to man's capacity.[96] Hence in preaching he commuicates himself through a man speaking to men,[97] and in the sacraments he adds a mode of communication adapted to man's physical nature.[98] Now, in speaking of the Bible, Calvin extends the idea of accommodation beyond the mode to the actual content of revelation, and argues that the very diction of biblical language is often adapted to the finitude of man's mind. God does not merely condescend to human frailty by revealing himself in the prophetic and apostolic word and by causing the Word to be written down in sacred books; he also makes his witnesses employ accommodated expressions. For example, God is represented anthropomorphically as raising his hand, changing his mind, deliberating, being angry, and so on.[99] Calvin admits that accommodated language has a certain impropriety about it.[100] It bears the same relation to divine truth as does the baby talk of a nurse or a mother to the world of adult realities.[101]

Calvin allows for yet another form of accommodation, which is a concession, not to the finitude or sensuousness of human nature as such, but to the special limitations of the people to whom the scriptural revelation was originally given. For example, under the old dispensation spiritual benefits were depicted as earthly goods, and this is no longer necessary since the manifestation of the gospel in Jesus Christ.[102] Again, because of the uncultured state of the ancient Israelites, not only language about God and salvation but also language about the created order had to be "accommodated." Just as anthropomorphisms represent God, not as he is in himself, but as he seems to us,[103] so biblical statements about nature may represent the heavenly bodies as they appear to a simpleminded observer, and not as the astronomer would describe them scientifically.[104]

The principle of accommodation in this sense—that is, in the sense of conde-scension to the unlearned—underlies Calvin's entire exposition of the "history of creation." He expressly points to a number of statements in Genesis 1-3 as accommodated to the mentality or the received opinions of a simple folk.[105] And he repeatedly affirms that throughout the entire narrative Moses spoke in a popular, not a scientific, manner.[106] The story has, in fact, a strictly religious purpose: to make the believer aware by *revelation* of what he would see, were it not for the dullness of his vision, simply by *observation*, namely that he is placed in the world as a spectator of God's glory.[107] Biblical affirmations about the heavens and the planets are not scientific statements but inducements to thank-fulness, and they are therefore expressed in a homely style which even the simplest believer can understand. They are made from the standpoint of an unlettered man, who is simply using his eyes. For instance, the expression "great lights" in Genesis 1:16 does not refer to the actual size of the sun and the moon, but to the amount of light that an ordinary person observes coming from them. The expressions are relative to the observer. The moon simply *looks* bigger than the other planets, though in fact Saturn *is* bigger. Nor was it relevant to Moses' purpose to mention that the moon borrows light from the sun.[108]

If any are disdainful of this biblical simplicity, Calvin warns that they will "condemn the entire economy of God in ruling the church."[109] On the other hand, it would also be wrong to oppose the science of astronomy just because its conclusions are contrary to popular opinion. Astronomy is both enjoyable and useful, since it unfolds the marvelous wisdom of God. The astronomer is worthy of our praise, and those who have the leisure and the ability should not neglect "this sort of exercise."[110] The Bible, however, is the "book of the unlearned." Anyone who wants to learn about astronomy must therefore look elsewhere.[111]

Calvin's cosmology was, of course, geocentric. But it was geocentric because he accepted the established astronomical views of his day.[112] Had he been con-fronted—as nobody in fact was during Calvin's lifetime—with convincing evidence for the heliocentric hypothesis, there is no reason to assume that he would have found the evidence embarrassing. He considered it an act of accommodation when the Psalmist spoke of the sun as passing from one end of the sky to the other. The Psalmist's aim was to evoke thankfulness by pointing to what the eye sees; had he been talking among philosophers, he might have mentioned that the sun completes its revolution around the other hemisphere.[113] Would it have been so difficult, then, for Calvin to assimilate the new ideas and to admit that the Psalmist's language was rather differently accommodating than he had imagined? As Calvin remarks on another psalm, it was not the Holy Spirit's intention to teach astronomy; he preferred to use "baby talk" *(balbutire)* rather than close the door of learning against the uneducated.[114]

V

The relations between natural science and the Protestant Reformation prove to be much more complex and fascinating than the standard quotations (and pseudo-quotation) have allowed. A complete discussion would need to take account of the contrast between Reformation and later Protestant attitudes towards science.[115] Worthy of attention, too, are the opinions of other Reformers—of Andreas Osiander, for example, whose anonymous preface to the *De revolutionibus* presented the heliocentric theory as a method of calculation, not as a claim to objective truth. Osiander's account of an astronomical "hypothesis" was not just a piece of shrewd diplomacy, but deserves to be taken seriously as an interpretation of scientific language different from Copernicus's own.[116]

Further, the cosmologies of Luther and Calvin themselves are not fully considered until their use of such theological terms as "heaven" and "hell" has been examined. They recognized that the theological and the cosmological use of the terms are not to be confused. Hence Luther refused to think of Christ's Ascension as comparable to climbing up a ladder.[117] And Calvin could only understand the Descent into Hell as Christ's experiencing in his soul the torments of a man forsaken by God.[119] The theology of the Reformers was less closely tied to a particular cosmology than might be expected; "demythologization" had already set in. The doctine of twofold truth (to retain the usual designation) and the principle of accommodation by no means exhaust their reflections on the nature of religious language. It is true that neither of them had a comprehensive theory of religious language; Calvin's principle of accommodation, for instance, was used chiefly as a problem-solving device, to be rolled out only when needed. But it is also true that the problems of theological discourse had occurred to them, precisely in the context of scientific questions. Their tentative moves toward a solution are not without historical interest, whether or not they make a permanent contribution to the debate between religion and science.

But what impact, if any, did their theological ideas make upon the actual development of science? Our conclusions have been partly negative: Luther and Calvin did nothing to *hinder* scientific progress. And there was no theological reason why they should. The Reformers were not literalists in the sense that they took all biblical statements about nature as literal reports of the plain truth. They were literalists in the sense that they insisted on taking the Scriptures in the meaning intended by their authors (or Author). A. D. White himself gives a good example of the kind of nonliteral exegesis which the Reformers deplored. He tells us that a Dominican preacher countered the researches of Galileo and his disciples with a sermon on Acts 1:11: "Why do you Galileans stand gazing up into heaven?" A "wretched pun," as White justly remarks.[119] The "literalism" of Luther and Calvin was designed to rule out allegories and other forms of fancy exegesis, but it still left room for maintaining the autonomy of natural science. Where the reigning astronomical opinions seemed to conflict with Scripture, they knew how to make the necessary adjustments. But this meant that they had to make the adjustments to Ptolemaic, not Copernican, science, precisely because the scientific revolution remained incomplete during their lifetime.[120]

If Calvin himself did not apply the principle of accommodation to the problem posed by the new science, Kepler and Galileo did so apply it[121] —which raises intriguing historical questions about the origins and dissemination of the principle. Not only did scientific interest in nature find a congenial ally in Calvinistic theology, but the principle by which leaders of the new science sought to avert a conflict between science and religion was a key notion in Calvin's theology. The currency of this principle in some circles—in Puritan England, for example— may have owed something to John Calvin.[122] In any case, the principle of accommodation, whatever the means of its transmission, assumes a historical importance not shared by Luther's reflections on double truth.

But by the time the scientific revolution was complete—let us say by the time Newton's *Principia* was published (1687)—the problem of religion and science had moved to a deeper level. It was no longer a question of reconciling Scripture with the heliocentric hypothesis, but of finding a place for God in the cosmos. The Newtonian world was causally self-contained, needing God only to set the mechanism in motion and to solve (at least temporarily) one or two problems that continued to resist scientific explanation. Was it enough, then, to concede the methodological autonomy of science?[123] Or does the scientist also demand an actual autonomy of the physical universe?[124]

Eleven   Schleiermacher and the Reformation: A Question of Doctrinal Development

The month of December 1816 found Schleiermacher thinking about too many things at once and not at all in the best of health. To his friend Gass, who seemed to have no trouble combining scholarship with administration, he sent a plea for help:

> I have long been bent upon making just some superficial patristic and scholastic studies, in order to gather a few handy quotations for my dogmatics; and I never got around to it. I would be very much obliged if you would write me somewhat more exactly how you have gone about it and on what [passages] you have chiefly relied.[1]

This does not sound like the request of a man who, in Newman's phrase, is "deep in history"; and Newman, at least, would not have expected anything better from a Protestant theologian. ("To be deep in history," he said, "is to cease to be a Protestant.")[2] On closer inspection, however, Schleiermacher turns out to have been a strongly historical thinker, who even made some notable contributions to historical inquiry, not least in the field of church history. In fact he thought deeply about a problem we have come to associate with the name of John Henry Newman: the development of Christian doctrine.

We are accustomed to regarding Schleiermacher, not as a church historian, but as a phenomenon of church history; and that is no doubt how we should, and will, continue to regard him. Many, including Karl Barth, have applied to him his own description of the "great man," who founds not a school but an epoch.[3] This may be too generous. His claim to a niche in church history's hall of fame goes little further than his magisterial role in shaping modern theology. And we do not speak of the modern period as inaugurated by theological change; we speak of theology as painfully adapting itself to changes initiated elsewhere. A better nickname might be the one Barth cites from the title of a book:

179

Schleiermacher the Church Father of the Nineteenth Century.[4] In a divided church, not everyone will grant him this dignity either. But it is a remarkable testimony to his intellectual greatness that even an adversary like Barth could say no less of him than this: that he was a theological "hero," who has earned in the modern period the kind of deference we owe to the doctors of the ancient church.[5] Still, for the moment, our interest is in Schleiermacher as an interpreter, not a maker, of church history.

His direct contributions to historical learning are surprisingly varied and extensive, if we place together all his work on ancient Greek philosophy, the New Testament, and the history of the Christian church and its doctrines. Included must be two distinguished studies in historical theology, one of which, despite the unpromising letter to Gass, is on a patristic theme: the doctrine of the Trinity in Sabellius and Athanasius.[6] Indeed, it has been written of him that of all the periods of church history "only parts of patristics did Schleiermacher really master from the sources."[7] And yet even his work on the early Christian fathers hardly warrants, in my opinion, any claim that among his many talents Schleiermacher possessed in some special measure the skills of the professional historian. Rather, he was a profoundly historical *theologian*, who may perhaps induce other theologians to think historically, even at the cost of studying church history; and, equally, may coax church historians not to shirk the very kinds of question that may justify the separate existence of their discipline. What, in particular, he invites us to ask, is the specifically church-historical, indeed theological meaning of the Protestant Reformation? That is to say: When the data are in, the facts established, and the causal nexus laid out, however provisionally, what did and does it mean for the self-understanding of the Christian community that the Reformation happened?

Schleiermacher's thoughts on the Reformation are intriguing not least because they flatly contradict an opinion widely held in the middle third of our own century. Neoorthodox historiography persistently asserted that he stood outside the Reformation tradition. As Barth said of the line that runs back through Kierkegaard to Luther and Calvin, and so to Paul and Jermiah (!); "To leave nothing unsaid, I might explicitly point out that this ancestral line—which I commend to you—does *not include Schleiermacher.*"[8] Schleiermacher himself, by contrast, believed that the Protestant reform had established the church situation in which his own age still lived, and that Evangelical theology could still be pursued only as the Protestant theologian took his stand, with the Reformers, in opposition to Roman Catholicism. And yet, at the same time, he was fully conscious of the fact that much had changed since the Reformation, and that far more serious conflicts troubled the church of his own day than any that had divided Protestantism in its infancy. And this is one reason why he had recourse to the notion of development.

I

Schleiermacher's changing attitude to the study of history confirms one of his own maxims: the talent for history is withheld from youth and comes only with age.[9] In his autobiography he recalls his boyhood resistance to Latin and the natural sciences, and adds:

> In history also I could take no interest; I do not know whether it was that the lessons were not given with sufficient animation, but I know that they caused me deadly *ennui*, and that it cost me incredible trouble to retain the chronology of the four monarchies, and the order of succession of the Persian kings.[10]

A little later in his school days, another difficulty was added to the tedium of history: he came to suffer from "a peculiar thorn in the flesh," which he describes in these words:

> It consisted in a strange scepticism, the origin of which I can no longer recollect. I conceived the idea that all the ancient authors, and with them the whole of ancient history, were supposititious.[11]

But in due course both the boredom and the skepticism were overcome: by the time he attended university, he had seen the error of his ways. He writes:

> One thing ... I perceived that it was absolutely necessary to learn, and that was history, and more especially the history of human opinions, the need of which I keenly felt. In consequence I devoted myself to this science in both its branches, and soon began to search for the sources of those parts which particularly interested me.[12]

Schleiermacher never became a professional historian, despite his new appreciation for historical knowledge. Throughout his career, he remained essentially a theologian and a preacher. But besides his remarkable attempts to historicize the theological task itself, which do not concern us here, he did venture to lecture on church history soon after assuming his first academic post, at the University of Halle. The reason why he made so bold is transparently clear from the opening words of his course outline, which has survived in his own manuscript: he wanted to try out his own view of things in a branch of learning in which he could not hope to become an expert.[13] And he took the task up again after he had moved back to Berlin and had become professor of theology at the new university. His correspondence indicates that he had something of a struggle:

"How dogmatics and church history will get along together," he wrote, "God may know. Church history gives me agonies [*viel Pein*]." By now, however, it was the seduction of history that troubled him, and he found himself tempted to undertake major historical studies. He had to put such thoughts out of his mind, of course, taking only a fleeting glance at what might have been: "If I were ten years younger, it could very well be that I would throw myself exclusively into this discipline for several years."[14]

Schleiermacher lectured on church history three times: once in Halle (1806), twice in Berlin (1821–22 and 1825–26). He did not himself attempt to develop his notes for publication. But one of those who had heard him (in 1821–22) assembled something like a continuous church history out of Schleiermacher's own manuscripts and the notebooks of several students. In his editorial foreword he remarks that, although an acquaintance with the lectures on church history seems essential to a full understanding of Schleiermacher's theological system, they are among the least known of all his lectures.[15] The remark is as true today as it was in 1840, when it was written. During the first two decades of our own century the work of Ernst Troeltsch sparked an interest in Schleiermacher's philosophy of history.[16] But only one attempt, as far as I know, has ever been undertaken to subject the actual contents of his church history to a detailed analysis; and even this lonely attempt was apparently unfinished, remaining in effect one more formal inquiry into Schleiermacher's historical principles.[17]

Unfortunately, the lectures on church history afford very little direct insight into Schleiermacher's understanding of Protestantism. And yet, paradoxically, they say enough to make it clear that for him the Protestant Reformation was necessarily of the utmost historical importance. In part, but only in part, the paradox is to be explained by historical principles or, more exactly, by the tension between two principles. On the one hand, he attached special weight to the history that lay closest to his own day. He held that the utility of history lies in the understanding it gives us of the present, an understanding that enables us to affect the future.[18] It is the science of what is, not of what has been; and only by actually beginning from the present—not by recourse to such expedients as relating anecdotes, commending the usefulness of the subject, or requiring memory work—can teachers spark interest in younger minds.[19] In his university lectures, of course, Schleiermacher was dealing with a better informed, more mature audience, which did not need an inverted chronology. But understanding of the present was still the goal of the inquiry; the very last sentence of the lectures on church history says so explicitly.[20] For Schleiermacher, this meant that the Reformation took on the highest significance, because he believed that the situation of the churches in his own day had received its decisive stamp in the sixteenth century. He believed, in other words, that he himself lived still in the period inaugurated by Luther, that no "epoch" comparable to the Reformation separated him from the first generation of Protestants, and that his own period of church history was likely to endure for a good many more years.[21] This being so, readers of his church history may be surprised and disappointed to find that the later Berlin lectures end with the death of John Hus.

A wholly theoretical explanation for this failure even to reach the Reformation is not needed: Schleiermacher had so expanded some of the materials that he ran out of time. The earlier lectures, too, may have suffered from such mundane pressures. At any rate, while they, by contrast, had managed to reach the fourth or Reformation period, the treatment had been cursory and wholly unremarkable. Nevertheless, there *is* a matter of historical principle at work here, not just the shortness of a winter semester; and it runs into conflict with the determination to assign the highest importance to the most recent period. While historical knowledge of the present stands closest to the actual requirements of a theological education,[22] Schleiermacher doubted, on the other hand, whether a genuinely historical treatment of the most recent past is possible. Because the contemplation of history requires "distance," it is difficult to bring the story down to the present time without losing the historical "tone." The historian, as distinct from the mere chronicler of outward events, aims to present a genetic account of how things have developed; but the closer he approaches his own day, the easier it will be for him to speak critically and polemically out of his own circle and his own commitments. Consequently, even with plenty of time on his hands, Schleiermacher could not in principle have moved beyond what he calls the "consolidation" of Protestantism: that is, either the Peace of Augsburg (1555) or the Peace of Westphalia (1648). In his lectures on church history he would have had no occasion to address himself directly to the problem of the Reformation and the modern world, unless he were willing to step outside the historian's role.[23]

It may even be that present-day Reformation historians, who are finally disappointed by Schleiermacher's last lecture, will already have been alienated by the first. At the outset, he lays down principles of understanding that are likely to awaken methodological suspicion. He insists that, while church history is only a fragment of world history, from the Christian standpoint world history itself is understood to have its goal in Christianity. What distinguishes church history from history in general is simply the fact that, being also a theological discipline, church history must directly serve the ends of practical theology and dogmatics.[24] If it were objected that this is to make history captive to faith, Schleiermacher would have an answer ready, since he speaks of nonreligious or antireligious standpoints, too, as matters of "faith" or "belief." The point is not that there is an esoteric Christian history, but that if there is to be history at all, it must arise out of a definite point of view, although the adoption of a viewpoint should accompany rather than precede the acquisition of historical knowledge. Firm decisions, he insists, cannot be made without historical study, nor yet with historical study alone.[25]

Not worthy of the name "history," in Schleiermacher's opinion, is the *atomistic* approach, which leaves the myriad of events without connection and so can offer no more than a bare chronicle. It satisfies only a factual curiousity; and yet it may be less free from judgments of value than is supposed, since even the chronicler must select from the infinite number of past events. Only a little less defective, in Schleiermacher's eyes, is the *pragmatic* approach, which seeks a cause for every event but still fails to grasp the events in their interconnection. His own *organic* method does not treat history as a mechanical or chemical process, but as a living growth; and this requires an explanation that seeks the "inward" in the outward appearances.[26] So, the domain of church history is all that is given us in consequence of the new life that came into the human race through Christianity.[27]

> We start from Christ as the beginning of a new period in world history. But our concern [in church history] is not with the world-historical effect of Christianity: we want rather to see how this force has developed historically in the organism that it formed out of itself, the Christian church.[28]

The inward is the "spirit" or "principle" of Christianity; the outward is Christian life and doctrine.[29]

Not surprisingly, the secondary literature is sharply divided over the question whether or not Schleiermacher displayed any depth of historical understanding.[30] Of course, the question is often directed to his *theological* views. But even his more strictly *historical* endeavor, in the lectures on church history, places the story in a theological frame. From this it follows, or so it seems to me, that even if the lectures had dealt more fully with the Reformation, we would still be less interested in the narrative of events than in Schleiermacher's judgment about the meaning of the Reformation for the Christian community. And for what he says on *this* theme we cannot confine ourselves to the lectures on church history. But at least the lectures will have led us to expect that theoretical categories will be freely invoked.

To anticipate: What we find is that Schleiermacher's entire understanding of religion as a historical phenomenon is dominated by the interplay between two favorite categories of the romantic interpretation of history: individuality and development.[31] From this perspective one can readily sort out, in turn, his views on the relationship between Christianity and other religions, between Roman Catholicism and the Reformation, and, finally, between the Reformation and modern Protestantism. In other words, what is chiefly of interest in Schleiermacher's attitude to the Reformation is the way in which he tries to move beyond immediate description and narration and to interpret the Reformation within a total theory of religious development. In this, I suspect, lies the reason why church historians are apt to find themselves simultaneously repelled and attracted by him: repelled because they have come to assign to church history a more modest role, attracted because the nature of church history inevitably invites questions about the nature of religion in general.

II

From the very first, individuality and development dominated Schleiermacher's thoughts on the history of religion. In his earliest book, *On Religion: Speeches to Its Cultured Despisers* (first published in 1799), the two categories stand in unresolved tension. There he not only justifies religion as an essential and irreducible element in human nature but is constrained by the logic of his argument to justify, in addition, any and all of the concrete forms that religion historically assumes. It is the sheer variety and multiplicity of religious forms that we are to reverence, as they emerge from the teeming womb of the universe; and the meaning of nature's infinite production, so it seems, need not be sought anywhere else but in the abundance of the never-ending process itself. Not that the process leads somewhere; rather, multiplicity is necessary for the complete manifestation of religion—and for the availability of religion to persons of diverse makeup and circumstances.[32] The whole of religion cannot be historically given except in the sum of all its possible forms: "It can, therefore, be exhibited," Schleiermacher explains, "only in an endless series of shapes that are gradually developed in different points of time and space."[33] A total relativism appears unavoidable. But it is checked by an equally strong counter-tendency.

Already in the second speech there are traces of an attempt to order the religious manifestations in a graded sequence, to impose a teleology on the exuberant process of individualization. We are told that, while every religion is a feeling for the unity of things, not all religions represent the feeling of unity equally well; if this is the standard, then monotheism must clearly be ranked as a higher development than polytheism or the worship of idols.[34] But it is the task of urging the cultured despisers to take another look at Christianity that finally requires the apologist, in his fifth and last speech, to uncover a little more of the evolutionary thread in mankind's religious history: Christianity is now ranked above the parent religion of Judaism, although both occupy the highest, monotheistic stage.[35] Even so, Schleiermacher is a long way from representing Christianity as the absolute goal of the history of religions. He retains a respect for individuality, even while seeking to order some of the individual forms in a scale of value. Hence Judaism has (or had) its worth as a distinctive, if less mature, religion, and it is not to be viewed as merely a preparation for Christianity: "I hate that kind of historical reference," he says.[36] Further, even of Christianity he only ventures to claim that it is the best so far and can look forward to a long future.[37] The development of religion is by no means completed; and Schleiermacher pledges that, if a time should come when human affairs were unhindered by corruption, then he would gladly stand on the ruins of the religion he now honors.[38]

It is the question of Christianity and other religions that moves into the center of this first experiment with individuality and religious evolution. And we do not need to pursue it any further. It suffices to say that even in his great dogmatic work, *The Christian Faith* (1821–22; 2d ed., 1830–31), Schleiermacher does not permit as unambiguous a triumph of development over individuality as might at first appear. For if he can there affirm forthrightly enough that all other religions are destined to pass over into Christianity, he does so only as an affirmation of Christian faith; and he admits that adherents of other faiths may remain wholly unconvinced. To affirm the supremacy of one's own religious faith thus turns out to be "an affirmation of one's own religious individuality."[39] Intriguing though this paradoxical conclusion may be, we must leave it there and move on to our immediate concern: whether the language of the *Speeches* provides the frame of reference for the second relationship, too, that between Roman Catholicism and the Reformation.

At first glance, we seem to find ourselves in a totally different conceptual world. "Reformation" has to do neither with individuality, it seems, nor with development, but with the correction of errors and abuses. *Die Kirchen-verbesserung* is in fact one of the terms Schleiermacher uses for the Reformation, and it plainly connotes for him not just the *improvement* of the church, but its *correction* where it has gone wrong. It is exactly from this point of view that he explains the significance of the Protestant confessions. In his treatise "On the Proper Value and the Binding Authority of Symbolic Books" (1819) he even offers the blunt opinion that "the main thing in our symbolic books is every-where the setting up of a definite opposition to the [Roman] Catholic Church."[40] And in the same writing he goes on to propose a suitable formula of subscription, in which the Protestant minister is bound only to the negative content of the confessions: "I declare that I find wholly consonant with the Holy Scripture and the original teaching of the church everything that is taught in our symbolic books against the errors and abuses of the Roman Church."[41]

That this oddly negative variety of confessionalism was not a momentary aberration of Schleiermacher's but a firm conviction could be documented many times over. Perhaps the most striking confirmation comes from the series of sermons be preached in 1830 on the three-hundredth anniversary of the Augsburg Confession. He commends the confession, it is true, because it states the "one great main point of faith": that our merits cannot bring peace with God, but righteousness before God is attained by receiving him whom God has sent. But if this means that the true spirit of the confession is thus to hold fast to living faith in the Redeemer, Schleiermacher in effect turns the positive point into a negative one, making the confession essentially a *declaration against* teaching and practice that impair the main point.[42] And this, we may add, is wholly in harmony with what he says of the Reformation in the lectures on church history: there it is not Luther, nor Zwingli, nor Calvin that earns the highest praise, but the much-maligned Erasmus, who held the purest, most truly evangelical idea of reformation. Why? Because it was Erasmus who tried to show that, once a dam had been interposed against all that was harmful in practice, diversity of doctrine could be allowed to continue until better instruction made the basis for impure doctrines vanish of its own accord.[43]

Nevertheless, though integral to Schleiermacher's understanding of the Reformation, the correction of abuses and errors was not the whole of it. From the first, another equally important strand was there, in view of which many of the statements quoted so far, if taken in isolation, must appear one-sided. The other strand makes its earliest appearance in the second edition of the *Speeches* (1806), which in fact antedates all the sources I have quoted on the errors and abuses of Rome. In an epilogue Roman Catholicism and Protestantism are presented simply as distinctive expressions of the Christian idea, jointly necessary to the historical manifestation of Christianity; and the papacy is identified, not as the essence of the Roman Catholic Church, but as the corruption of it.[44]

The full, two-sided relationship between the two varieties of Christianity was later affirmed expressly in the first edition of Schleiermacher's *The Christian Faith*, where he writes in proposition 27: "In its opposition to Catholicism, Protestantism is to be viewed not only as a purification and return from abuses that had crept in, but also as a distinctive formation of Christianity."[45] The proposition was not carried over into the second edition with quite such explicit balance, but it was repeated in substance (in new proposition 24) and received an interesting commentary. What is at home in Catholicism, we are told, may be alien to "us" (that is, us Protestants) and still be entirely Christian; and even if the Catholic Church came around to "our" definitions on all the controverted points of doctrine, the result would not be a reunion.[46] A similar judgment found even more emphatic expression in Schleiermacher's lectures on Christian ethics, published posthumously, like the lectures on church history. In a section from the years 1826–27 he says:

It is true that many Protestants utterly deny the Catholic Church its distinctive character and hold that, if only it would lay aside its abuses and errors, it would necessarily coincide with our own church. But we think otherwise. We are convinced that the true, distinctive character of the Catholic Church must stand out clearly only when there are differences between it and us which all have, and will continue to have, their own just claims. For if the Catholic Church, too, were to accept the Scriptures as the sole foundation of Christian doctrine and Christian life, and were likewise to accept everything else of which we rightly believe that no Christian community may be without it; and if, on the other hand, she did away with the pope and everything else of which we rightly believe that it may not be permitted in any Christian community—nevertheless, as far as the cult, for instance, is concerned, in our church the Word would always have precedence, in the Catholic Church symbolic action. It can therefore never be right to contest, along with the errors of the Catholic Church, its distinctive character as well—not if the latter in no way belongs among its errors.[47]

Evidently, we have now been brought right back again into the orbit of individuality and development; only this time, unambiguously, the covering category is individuality. Although it cannot be denied that the first Reformers intended merely to purify, they were in fact driven to form a church of their own: to bring into existence a distinctive form—a new individualization—of the Christian community. For it is out of the question, in Schleiermacher's view, to represent the Reformation as simply the restitution of the apostolic age: what has once been can never be given back again at a later time.[48]

Curiously enough, however, having brought us to the point of viewing Protestantism and Roman Catholicism as equally Christian individual types, Schleiermacher seems at a loss to define the actual difference between the two. In the *Christian Ethics* the contrast is drawn between word and symbolic action. But the "provisional antithesis" suggested in *The Christian Faith* is quite different: namely, that while Protestantism makes the individual's relation to the church dependent on his relation to Christ, Catholicism makes the individual's relation to Christ dependent on his relation to the church. Whatever merits this contrast may claim, it surely suffers from one embarrassing defect: it seems, on the face of it, to put Schleiermacher himself among the Catholics, since he himself knows of no access to the Redeemer save throught the believing community.

There is no need to resolve the problem here.[49] I wish only to point out that the lectures on church history strongly confirm the presentation of the lectures on Christian ethics. In his church history Schleiermacher makes much of the Reformation's recovery of the Word. The medieval church, as he sees it, sacrificed understanding through the Word to the use of Latin as an outward token of unity. And so the clergy were divided from the laity, and the laity clung to understanding through symbolic usages. The turn to symbolic communication Schleiermacher judges to have been in conflict with original Christianity, and he sees the Reformation as in part a recovery of understanding through the Word. "This preponderance of symbolic actions over understanding through the living Word and the domination of political conditions by the papacy—this is what was understood," he says, "by the *reform* [*Verbesserung*] *of the church in head and members*."[50] And among the contributory factors that finally led to the achievement of reform (in the Protestant Reformation) he includes a heightened receptivity to the Word, brought about by the art of printing and the restoration of learning.[51]

One cannot fail to notice that in the lectures on church history, at least, the twofold relationship between Roman Catholicism and the Reformation is on the verge of collapsing: for the dominance of symbolic action is there identified as one of the abuses calling for correction, and not as an equally legitimate form of Christian expression. But Schleiermacher's intention in the dogmatic and ethical works is plain, despite the different ways in which the intention is carried out. In sum: Whereas the attempt to relate Christianity and other religions ends in unresolved tension between development and individuality, the opposition between the Roman Church and the Protestant Reformation falls unambiguously, if only in part, under the category of individuality.[52] How is it, then, if we turn finally in the other direction and relate the Reformation to modern Protestantism? In a sense, the question is already answered in Schleiermacher's claim, mentioned before, that the most recent epoch in the history of Christianity was the Reformation.

III

Naturally, the question can be raised whether Schleiermacher was not bound to carry the principle of individualization still further and to consider the Protestant churches themselves as distinct religious types, ever growing in number. In the aggressive confessionalism of Claus Harms, for instance, he encountered the claim that Lutheranism, as the only perfect embodiment of Christian truth, was equally far removed from the Reformed and the Roman Catholic communions. But this Schleiermacher found utterly incredible. He remained convinced that the Lutheran who plumbed the depths of his relation to the Savior would be bound to extend the hand of fellowship to his Reformed brother sooner than to the Roman Catholic. A narrower circle of thought and sensibility bound the Lutheran and the Reformed together than the circle that embraced them both together with the Catholics.[53] "To my mind," he wrote, "the Catholic Church stands on the one side and the Protestant on the other; and the difference between the two confessions of the Protestant church seems to me a little thing in comparison with the other difference." Or could it seriously be supposed that a Roman Catholic delegation to the Marburg Colloquy would have agreed as readily as the Zwinglians to the first fourteen of Luther's articles?[54]

That there *is* a difference between the Lutherans and the Reformed, Schleiermacher never doubted, and he did invoke his principle of individuality to account for it. What he wished to insist upon, however, was that the difference was only of theological "school." Without the slightest dissimulation, he announced his own allegiance to the Reformed school;[55] but he never saw in *this* difference grounds for the separate existence of the two Protestant communions. On the contrary, he perceived in it a parallel to the difference of sacramental theologies within the Reformed church, a doctrinal division that had never been permitted to interrupt "altar fellowship" between the Zwinglians and the Calvinists.[56] Schleiermacher's notion of inner-Protestant unity did not require negotiations leading to full doctrinal agreement; it presupposed only the resolution not to take confessional anathemas *(et improbamus secus sentientes!)* from the school to the table of the Lord.[57] He desired a union that would not deny but transcend individuality.[58]

If we shelve for the moment the question of other Protestant groups, which had their origin outside of Germany, we can say that for all practical purposes Schleiermacher viewed Protestantism as a single historical movement. But "movement" is precisely what, in his view, it was: there could be no possibility of simply identifying the Protestantism of the nineteenth century with the Protestantism of the Reformation. What he thought of modern Protestantism is plainly mirrored in his remarks on the Reformation confessions, on which he was obliged more than once to state his mind. The three-hundredth anniversary of Luther's Ninety-Five Theses was celebrated in 1817 by the formation of the Prussian Union. Schleiermacher himself approved the union; but it coincided with the rise of Lutheran confessionalism and even, by way of reaction, intensified it. Strict Lutherans feared possible infection from the sister communion, and for this reason they remained inflexibly opposed to association with the Reformed. Schleiermacher found it necessary to declare his own thoughts on the significance of the original Reformation creeds, to which the confessionalists demanded unswerving allegiance.

In the treatise "On the Proper Value and the Binding Authority of Symbolic Books" he professed astonishment that there were those who would have erased an entire period of church history and appropriated as their own a document from the sixteenth century. But if this set him against the confessionalists, it did not align him with the opposing rationalist party, who held that the Reformation confessions were written for their own time and could be seen only as historical documents with no special claims to present-day attention. This view, too, he thought, betrayed a lack of historical sense. There is a difference between the first decisive moments and the subsequent course of a historical phenomenon, and between a merely personal statement and one that represents a widespread conviction. It will not do, therefore, to cast the confessions in the same category to which belong the documents of other religious colloquies or the dogmatic productions of other individuals: that says too little, as the other view says too much. So Schleiermacher argued.[59] And the crucial point, of course, is the thought that a special importance is attached to beginnings. He was unwilling to admit that the confessions are related to Protestantism today exactly as the Scriptures to Christianity in general; for Protestantism is not an entirely new "spirit," but the Christian spirit become freer. Nevertheless, the Reformation did mark a relatively new beginning, and he therefore argued that the symbolic books have their unique worth as the first public expressions of the Protestant spirit.[60]

The commemoration of the Ninety-Five Theses was followed thirteen years later (in 1830) by the tercentennial celebration of the Augsburg Confession, and once again Schleiermacher took his stand squarely between the confessionalists and the rationalists. For the confessionalists, the festivities afforded a golden opportunity to extract from the Protestant clergy professions of loyalty to the original manifesto of Protestant belief. On the other side, the rationalists opposed the celebration on the grounds that to commemorate a confession which nobody confessed any more would betray a lack either of candor or of consistency.[61]

For his part, Schleiermacher gladly joined in the celebration; and yet what he commemorated was first of all a historical event, not a binding creed. Like his eminent rival, G. W. F. Hegel, he did not celebrate the document so much as its presentation to the imperial diet, not the "work" but the "deed." Still, he did believe that a sound historical understanding left room for a cautious honoring of the document itself. Once we have disabused our minds of the pernicious notion that a confession of faith has the power of excommunication, it should be entirely possible for everyone, he maintained, to extol the Augsburg Confession as a splendid work of its time.[62]

Because Schleiermacher's aim was to achieve a genuinely *historical* estimate of the confession—which meant an estimate that was neither confessionalist nor rationalist—the document acquired for him a human context and a human authorship. Hence we find him making the point that, three hundred years later, we have every right to judge with caution a document that did not for long enjoy the undivided approval even of its principal author. We may not treat the Augsburg Confession as though it were a perfect document whose author could simply be forgotten. No, Schleiermacher insists, the framers of our confessions were men like ourselves: they were theologians like us, and we, like them, are called to be reformers whenever necessary. Hence their works, whether exegetical or dogmatic, are to be treated no differently than ours, which we hand on to our own descendants for them to judge and use in freedom. We acknowledge no authoritative interpretation of the Scriptures and no final dogmatic formulas; we interpret the Scriptures for ourselves with a greater wealth of exegetical aids than was available at the time of the Reformation and with the support of the divine Spirit, who has not died out in the meantime.[63]

And so the argument rolls on, insisting that the formulas of one generation do not even *mean* the same to the next, and that it would be a dead work if, unlike the symbolic books themselves, we tried to present the Christian faith without any regard for what is being thought about it both on the inside and on the outside. A sense of the passage of time and of the relativities of history pervades the argument, which culminates in the interesting proposition: "We cannot be dependent on a symbolic book; quite the reverse, it has continued validity because and insofar as we confirm it anew by our doctrine and convince our youth of it." And it is no use binding a pastor to the letter if he lacks the spirit. Without in the least breaking his pledge, he will still preach moral platitudes and sentimental nature sermons.[64]

In these remarks on the Augsburg Confession and its role in the present-day church Schleiermacher has spoken his mind, it may be noticed, not only on the Reformation but also on the persons of the Reformers. Although he could speak freely of Luther as a heroic figure (our *Glaubensheld*), in his eyes no nimbus hovered over Luther's head or the heads of the other Reformers either.[65] We find, in fact, that his estimate of Luther was surprisingly reminiscent of Calvin's. Schleiermacher would not for one moment, any more than Calvin, allow that those who named themselves after Luther were the only ones who should or did honor his memory;[66] and yet at the same time, and again like Calvin, he refused to treat any reformer's teaching as strictly authoritative. Luther therefore emerges, for both Calvin and Schleiermacher, as the pathfinder: he opens up the way, but we have to press further along it than he did himself.

Schleiermacher's opinion of Luther is nowhere more forcefully expressed than in his stand during the liturgical dispute, which peaked between the two phases of the confessionalism debate. By 1819 Frederick William III and his advisers had abandoned plans for the presbyterian form of church government that Schleiermacher favored; and it was determined that a uniform liturgy would be introduced by royal command. Surprised when a majority of the clergy refused to accept the new order of worship voluntarily (1822), the king reversed his earlier, more indulgent policy and reminded his subjects of the royal prerogatives. But he did not hesitate, in addition, to justify the content of the liturgy by appeal to Martin Luther: in 1827 there appeared a document, attributed to the king himself, under the title *Luther in Relation to the Prussian Liturgy*. Schleiermacher's irreverent response took the form of an anonymous dialogue between two concerned Protestants.[67]

In the dialogue, a Luther is portrayed who did not become a Lutheran in a day but progressed slowly. No one, we are assured, can be more Lutheran than Luther, but the later Luther was more *Protestant* than the earlier. Hence it will not do to claim as Luther's work what he took over from a previous age or merely tolerated for a while. We can safely presume that a resurrected Luther, our hero in the faith, upon seeing our present, still more reduced order of worship, would be delighted that we have understood his own often-repeated maxim, that in time more would come of its own accord.[68] There is an unmistakable passion in Schleiermacher's protest against "our author [sc. the king!] and others of his ilk" who invoke the name of Luther.

Luther I know, but who are you [cf. Acts 19:15]? They cling to some letter
or other and chew on the husks, but they leave the kernel and do not grasp
the spirit. For this is the kernel and spirit of all Luther's orders of worship:
that everything must so proceed that the Word may prevail; that where God's
Word is not preached, it is better neither to sing, nor to read, nor to come
together; that order is an outward thing, and, be it as good as you please,
it can fall into abuse. And abuse is what it is if one makes of it, against the
freedom of faith, a necessary law.[69]

To preserve Luther's precious heritage of Christian freedom, Schleiermacher was
even ready to withdraw from the established church. He did see evidence of
inward progress in the church; if necessary, it would be continued outside, but
only if a sufficient number were bound in good conscience to affirm, "Here I
stand: I can do no other!" Come what may, then, *the Reformation still goes on.*[70]

Not individuality but development determined Schleiermacher's views on the
relationship between the Reformation and modern Protestantism. This, after
all, is what we would expect, since he held, as did many of his contemporaries,
that development was an essential mark of Protestantism, whereas the Roman
Church rested upon immutable norms. Because he understood the church as an
organism, not as a legislative body, he believed that both dogmatics and Christian ethics (*Glaubenslehre* and *Sittenlehre*), as functions of the church's growth,
were bound to exhibit a constant, restless movement. "The Protestant view of
the Christian church," he said, "includes this essential characteristic: that we
think of it as a totality in movement, as something capable of progress and
development." Consequently, he maintained that development was a purely
Protestant question. And he insisted on this fundamental difference in self-
understanding from the Roman Church, even though Protestantism, too, had its
unsurpassable standard in Christ. Progress, admittedly, could never be anything
other than a more correct understanding and more perfect appropriation of what
was given in Christ; yet it remained true progress when what had existed
personally in him passed over from him into the church.[71] In short, "Schleiermacher and the Reformation" is a question of doctrinal development.

To have determined the formal category under which Schleiermacher himself
placed the transition from classical to liberal Protestantism does not settle very
much; it presents an agenda of further questions. His interpretation of Protestantism is not self-evidently true but needs to be tested. Anyone who has learned
from Troeltsch will very likely discover *more* continuity than Schleiermacher did
between the medieval period and the Reformation, and *less* continuity between
Luther and the modern world. Is it really possible to hold, we must ask, that the
Reformation and what Troeltsch called "neo-Protestantism" are related as the
birth and the unfolding of a single historical development? Or can we finally
relate them, as in effect the dialectical theologians did, only by invoking the

other category, the category of individuality—so that liberal and classical Protestantism must in the end represent two religious types, as distinct from each other as mysticism and the Word?[72]

The next step would of course be for the historical theologians to search in Schleiermacher's writings for the elements of tradition and innovation, respectively, beginning with his own perception of them. In what did he perceive his solidarity with Luther and Calvin? In what did he avowedly dissent from them? And then, with that answered as best we can, the question will still remain: How far can the present-day historian view the total phenomenon of Protestantism as Schleiermacher did? These, admittedly, are big questions. But the historian ought not to resign them to his theological colleagues, who, in the recent past at least, stressed the elements of discontinuity with such one-sided zeal.

It will no longer do to measure Schleiermacher with the external norm of "christocentricity," it being presupposed in advance that to be christocentric is a very good thing.[73] Nor, I think, may it be presupposed that the question of Schleiermacher and the Reformation is equivalent to the question of Schleiermacher and Luther. At least one scholar expressly identifies the two questions,[74] and another refers to Schleiermacher's treatise on election—a treatise filled with Calvin quotations—only to retrieve a lonely Luther quotation that appears in a footnote.[75] A literature on Calvin and Schleiermacher hardly exists, and incidental remarks on the subject tend to be partisan or merely quaint. One scholar, for instance, warns us that Calvin took the first steps on the path that led to Schleiermacher because he permitted his own piety to determine what he heard in the Word of God. All will therefore be on their guard who, with Luther, intend to hold earnestly to the battle cry "The Word they must let stand!"[76] And yet, candidly partisan as this admonition is, it does, I believe, point in the direction most worthy of further exploration.

We must, of course, eventually ask about the way in which Schleiermacher understood the individual doctrines he inherited from the Protestant Reformers; and we will unquestionably find sharp differences, some of which cluster around his well-known rejection of the "wrath of God."[77] But somewhere between the formal category of development and the material content of individual doctrines comes a matter of theological style which, in my opinion, is where the inquiry might well begin. It has to do with the experiential roots of theological reflection; and while it may not be true to speak of Calvin and Schleiermacher as though their personal religiousness permitted them only a selective hearing of the Word, it unquestionably is true that, like Luther, they were interested only in a practical knowledge of God that has to do with piety.

It is here, first of all, that the continuity may be located: in a distinctive *style* of theologizing.[78] And from there it may be asked next whether the content of the experience exhibits a like continuity. I do not doubt that even here differences will be found. Luther's *Erfahrungstheologie* and Calvin's *practica notitia* have become in Schleiermacher something very close to what Troeltsch calls "the historical-psychological method":[79] that is, a strongly immanental reinterpretation of Evangelical faith which, while not intending to be reductive, nonetheless tries to understand faith as a natural phenomenon of historical existence, collective and individual. Schleiermacher himself was certainly aware of this line of continuity, and he thought it lent a certain freedom to Christian theology that it was in danger of surrendering to confessionalism. But this, as I say, belongs on an agenda of further inquiry, if we are to test Schleiermacher's claim from within. I end by simply quoting the claim in his own trenchant words: "Our lineage can no one take away from us. . . . We are legitimate sons of the Reformation and not bastards."[80]

| Twelve | Theology within the Limits of Piety Alone: Schleiermacher and Calvin's Notion of God |

We shall not say that, properly speaking, God is known where there is no religion or piety.

Calvin

A recent study of John Calvin gives a sensitive account, illustrated with apt citations, of what he meant by "piety."[1] Not the sole but the first aim of the anthology is to furnish a better grasp of the man than one is likely to obtain while plodding through his dogmatic masterpiece. But this implies no rift between Calvin the man of piety and Calvin the theologian. An anthology illustrative of the spirituality of the Reformer may in fact turn the reader back, with renewed understanding, to the formidable task of mastering the *Institutes*, the contents of which Calvin himself described as a *summa pietatis*.[2] Conversely, as I hope to show, failure to grasp the significance of "piety" in Calvin's dogmatics may account, in part, for some common misrepresentations of his God.

It may be thought odd, even perverse, if at each step of the way reference is made to certain dogmatic principles enunciated by Schleiermacher. Admittedly, the pioneer of liberal Protestant theology is hardly one of the acknowledged doctors of the Reformed church. We have been habituated by neoorthodox historiography to the view that he and Calvin were polar opposites. But no one who has attempted to master *The Christian Faith* (a still more formidable task than mastering the *Institutes*) will begrudge its author the highest praise for at least one thing: an unusually keen insight into the formal problems of Christian dogmatics—problems, that is, of structure and procedure. Possibly Calvin, had he lived four or five centuries later than he did, would have been as shocked as Brunner was at the content Schleiermacher gave to many of the traditional

Christian themes. He may, besides, have discovered only fitfully in *The Christian Faith* the elegance of style which, as a humanist, he had learned to admire and to cultivate. But he could not have failed to notice in Schleiermacher's dogmatics the presence of at least two formal characteristics that he regarded highly: conciseness and orderliness.[3] And he would have found Schleiermacher employing the contrast between piety and speculation—so fundamental to Calvin himself—as something like a procedural rule.

It is particularly the deliberate striving after order that invites comparison between these two masters of Protestant dogmatics. When Calvin at last, after many revisions, expressed his satisfaction with his *Institutes*, the final arrangement of the work was what he had in mind.[4] Surely he would have appreciated Schleiermacher's acute perception that the meaning of a doctrine is in part a function of its place in the total system.[5] It can further be shown that there is an affinity betwen the two systematicians, not only in the drive for order as such, but also in the actual shape of the order adopted. Indeed, once undertaken, a comparison of the two great systems of Protestant dogmatics, the classical and the liberal, suggests other formal parallels as well, not least with respect to the dogmatic procedure I wish chiefly to illustrate: that is, use of the concept of piety to monitor or police the dogmatic system. In both Calvin and Schleiermacher alike, "piety" functions to exclude inadmissible material and to control the treatment of what is admitted. Each of them in his own way was determined (if we dare adapt the famous title of one of Kant's works) to do theology within the limits of piety alone.

There need be no surprise to learn that Schleiermacher, for his part, commended the *Institutes* as an "invaluable book" precisely because it never loses contact with the religious affections, not even in the most intricate material.[6] More likely to evoke surprise is the fact that he vigorously defended what has sometimes been taken for the regulative theme of the *Institutes*, the doctrine of election.[7] But the extent to which he may have been actually dependent on Calvin's work, as he developed his own system, is a difficult and perhaps insoluble question; for now, it must be set aside. That there are in fact resemblances (as well as differences) between them, will become clear; so clear that it is tempting to wonder how far Schleiermacher may have been consciously or unconsciously appropriating, developing, and correcting insights acquired from his reading of Calvin.[8] But the temptation will be resisted. Bracketing the historical question of possible dependence, I ask only whether certain methodological principles that Schleiermacher keenly formulated can shed light on the order (sec. I) and the limits (sec. II) of Calvin's theology, and so can help rectify misapprehensions of his doctrine of God. Finally (sec. III), some thought will be given to the evident fact that a theology kept within the limits of piety alone poses an embarrassment for Calvin's doctrine of the Trinity, as it does, *mutatis mutandis*, for Schleiermacher's. But it is, of course, my intention to invite—

by a purely comparative approach—a reappraisal of the relationship between Calvin and Schleiermacher, and so between Reformation and modern theology.

I

"The doctrine of God, as set forth in the totality of the divine attributes, can only be completed simultaneously with the whole system."[9]

When Schleiermacher immediately adds that usually the doctrine of God is treated as a single unit and before any other points of doctrine, our historical curiosity is aroused. But he leaves it ungratified, foregoing any detailed comparison of his own scheme with the scheme prevalent in "our older and newer textbooks and systems." (Would he at this point, one wonders, have included the *Institutes* among the older systems?) "The method here adopted," he explains, "can only be justified by the finished argument itself." He will not be drawn aside into polemics or commend his own approach by subjecting the alternatives to detailed criticism. Still, his objections are plainly, if tersely, stated. One objection concerns us directly: that the "usual arrangement" is apt to conceal the relationship of the doctrine of God to the fundamental facts of the Christian religion, and so gives the impression of a quite independent, speculative theory about God. How, in other words, can you present a Christian view of God before you have specified the works of God in which he is made known? If there is a finished *locus de deo* that virtually introduces the system, must there not be a strong enticement to fill it out with "speculative" materials imported from elsewhere?

Schleiermacher's own arrangement is intended to rectify the defects of the more conventional dogmatic order. His system is divided into two parts, roughly corresponding (though he does not say so) to the double knowledge of God as creator and redeemer in the *Institutes*.[10] But the doctrine of God is not assigned exclusively to either part alone; it is given in the system as a whole. And since Part 2 is itself subdivided (according to the two aspects of the antithesis of sin and grace), propositions concerning the attributes and operations of God are distributed throughout the system in three clusters. *The Christian Faith* ends with the divine attributes which relate to redemption (secs. 164-69) and a conclusion on the Divine Trinity (secs. 170-72). In the strictest sense, the doctrine of God is only completed simultaneously with the system as a whole.

In an interesting and highly laudatory essay, Ebeling has discovered in Schleiermacher's treatment of God his "only complete departure from the traditional order of [dogmatic] articles."[11] The originality of Schleiermacher's procedure—his distribution of the divine attributes over the whole dogmatic system—is not to be denied. But it must be pointed out, in qualification of Ebeling's remarks, that the dogmatic tradition did contain at least a faint adumbration of Schleiermacher's approach: namely, in Calvin's final *Institutes*. And if Ebeling can affirm that "at the beginning of Schleiermacher's *Glaubens-lehre* there is—*cum grano salis*—no doctrine of God at all,"[12] must we not also affirm, even without the pinch of salt, that the *Institutes* nowhere *contain* a doctrine of God but *are* a doctrine of God? There is no *locus de deo* because the entire work presents the knowledge of God as creator and redeemer.

There is a difference of opinion among Calvin's interpreters on the extent to which the twofold knowledge of God, as creator and as redeemer, determines the structure of the 1559 *Institutes*. In his classic essay on the form and content of the *Institutes*, Köstlin argued that Book 1 deals with God's creation and government of the world in general, Books 2–4 (collectively) with the historical revelation and saving activity of God. The fourfold division into books, corresponding to the order of the Apostles' Creed, is thus embraced within another, twofold scheme, the second part of which is subdivided according to its three distinct aspects: the establishment of salvation through the incarnate Son (Book 2) and the Spirit's distribution of it to individuals (Book 3) through outward means (Book 4).[13] In the early 1950s, two studies on Calvin's doctrine of the knowledge of God appeared in English almost simultaneously: one agreed with Köstlin's analysis and the other did not. Arriving independently at Köstlin's conclusion, Dowey similarly maintained that after Book 1 the "whole remain-der" of the *Institutes* represents the revelation of God as redeemer.[14] Parker, on the other hand, concluded that it is Book 2 which presents the knowledge of God the redeemer, whereas Books 3 and 4 proceed to speak of the one God who has been shown as both creator and redeemer. The 1559 *Institutes* as a whole, Parker insisted, simply follows what Calvin held to be the four divisions of the Apostles' Creed: it is to be understood as an exposition of the Creed.[15]

My own persuasion is that Parker's criticisms did not invalidate Köstlin's interpretation. It was not quite just, in fact, for him to represent Köstlin as dividing the *Institutes* into two parts *instead of* four:[16] Köstlin spoke rather of the two parts of Calvin's system *in distinction from* the obvious division into four books. But the first of my three reflections on Calvin's doctrine of God—in the light of Schleiermacher's theological method—is relatively independent of the point at issue between Parker and Dowey (or Köstlin). What I wish chiefly to underscore is that, in any case, the doctrine of God in the *Institutes* remains incomplete in Book 1, and that only by a quite arbitrary selection could one presume to complete it from the chapters on predestination in Book 3 (chaps. 21–23). Yet that is exactly how Calvin's doctrine of God has commonly been presented.

Of the Calvin studies known to me Dowey's, as it happens, comes closest to the point I have in mind, because the complaint he registers in his preface is the exact epistemological counterpart of mine, which is made from the view-point of the doctrine of God. According to Dowey, the two major articles on the knowledge of God in Calvin's theology (one by Warfield, the other by Lobstein) both assume that the problem of knowledge is done with "when the doctrines of the revelation in creation and in Scripture have been formulated, in the first book of the *Institutes*"; hence in both there is a "lack of a study of Calvin's doctrine of faith."[17] This judgment, clearly, is the epistemological correlate of my own claim that Calvin's doctrine of God cannot be derived exclusively from Book 1 of the *Institutes*—or even from Book 1 supplemented with chapters 21-23 of the third book. And his concept of faith, crucial to his thoughts on how we come to know God, will provide us with an important clue to his teaching on what we know of God.

In Calvin's own words: "The whole knowledge of God the Creator that we have discussed would be useless unless faith also followed, setting forth for us God our Father in Christ."[18] His reason for so saying is, of course, rooted in his doctrine of sin: the fall of man makes the revelation of God in nature ineffectual, and apart from redemption through Christ there is no unalloyed knowledge of the Creator. But we can just as well make the same point from the perspective of the doctrine of God: methodologically, it is a mistake to treat Book 1 as though it were a sufficient source for Calvin's idea of God. We ought to anticipate that what he thinks of God will at least become plainer when he turns from creation to redemption. And yet it is a curious fact that many Calvin studies (to say nothing of obiter dicta by nonspecialists) fail to operate out of this expectation, except insofar as Calvin's statements on predestination are extracted from Book 3 to confirm the chosen statements in Book 1 that they most closely resemble.[19]

The question may certainly be asked whether the tendency to seek Calvin's doctrine of God in the first book of the *Institutes*—or in selected portions of it—is sufficiently explained by the perversity of his readers. Does it perhaps expose a weakness in Calvin's execution of his task? For if the dogmatic system as a whole is required for presenting the knowledge of God, then some concluding effort seems imperative to state the contents of the entire system, including its second part, in the actual form of a doctrine of God. Calvin seems committed by his arrangement of the material to asking in Part 2, on God the Redeemer, a question corresponding to the question of Part 1, "who that God is who founded and governs the universe."[20] A doctrine of God is surely something other than a presentation of his works, whether in nature or in the Incarnation,[21] although it may be only in his works that he is known.

Schleiermacher tried to solve the problem by drawing up separate clusters of divine attributes, some pertaining to creation and others to sin and redemption, so that he gives us in effect more than one *locus de deo*. The difficulty for readers of Calvin is that no such *locus*, which many look for in Book 1, is to be found anywhere at all in the *Institutes*.[22] As Warfield puts it, everything the Christian needs to know about the nature and attributes of God is present in the

Institutes "in solution, rather than in precipitate: distributed through the general discussion of the knowledge of God rather than gathered together into one place and apportioned to formal rubrics."[23] Nevertheless, Calvin's readers need not be totally at a loss about where to locate the center of gravity in all the scattered descriptions of God: Calvin's concept of piety makes it possible to determine at least *some* of his priorities.

II

"Dogmatic propositions never make their original appearance except in trains of thought which have received their impulse from religious moods of mind."[24]

Schleiermacher knows very well that this is a prescriptive rather than a descriptive judgment. As he puts it elsewhere: "We *wish* to have nothing to do with any conception of God reached by way of speculation."[25] In actual fact, the purely religious springs of an authentic dogmatics have often enough, throughout the church's history, been muddied by speculative intrusions. Or, to say it in Schleiermacher's own words, since the "conglomerate-philosophy" of the Middle Ages there has been an almost inevitable "confusion of the speculative with the dogmatic, and consequently a mingling of the two." And it has been the special concern of Protestantism, so he thinks, to separate out again the two types of proposition—the speculative and the dogmatic—that originally conveyed quite distinct contents.[26] He writes:

> Our method indeed would seem to be the one that will most easily get rid of all traces of the Scholastic mode of treatment, by which philosophy ... and real Christian Dogmatics were frequently mingled in one and the same work.[27]

On a first reading, these striking affirmations of the purely religious source of dogmatics, accompanied by a firm exclusion of speculation and scholasticism, sound very like authentic echoes of Calvin.[28] On closer inspection, however, it can readily be seen that the concept of piety functions as a dogmatic limit rather differently in Schleiermacher than in Calvin. In the first place, Schleiermacher's approach is rooted strictly in a theory of knowledge and is not, like Calvin's, simultaneously tied up with a doctrine of sin. Speculation is to be rigorously excluded, not because it is perverse, or presumptuous, or futile, but because it arrives at its talk about God by a quite different route than does dogmatics. And the concept of piety functions as a dogmatic limit simply because a specific modification of piety is what dogmatics is all about: it is "the study of religious affections."[29] The speculative philosopher, too, may—indeed must—arrive at the concept of God (if he does not start from it); but exactly because "God" does not for him denote the referent of piety, it can only lead to methodological confusion if he tries to combine speculation and dogmatics in a single system. In short, speculative philosophy is a different but equally legitimate enterprise of the human spirit: it is distinguished from, but not opposed to, dogmatics, which is determined to assert nothing that cannot be derived by reflection from the content of piety.[30] And there is therefore no reason why the theologian himself, when he is off-duty, may not try his hand at speculation and find the results entirely harmonious with his theology. Hence Schleiermacher's own confession on his deathbed: "I feel constrained to think the profoundest speculative thoughts, and they are to me identical with the deepest religious feelings."[31]

In the second place, Schleiermacher's approach to theological studies differentiates dogmatics, not only from philosophical speculation, but also from exegetical theology. The limit imposed by "piety" is established by the understanding of dogmatics as nothing but reflection on the immediate utterances of piety or, more specifically, of evangelical piety. Certainly, an injustice is done to Schleiermacher if one fails to verify (from secs. 128–35 of *The Christian Faith*) that he presents evangelical faith as a consciousness of being under the Word of God. And yet it remains true that he does not offer a biblical (or, as he puts it, "scriptural") theology. Given his essentially descriptive method, the most immediately pertinent texts are the Protestant confessions of faith— employed, of course, not as external authorities, but as indexes to the evangelical religious consciousness. Exegetical theology, in the sense of direct biblical interpretation, is for him not so much a moment in the dogmatic enterprise as a distinct, coordinate theological discipline *alongside* dogmatics.[32]

The contrast with Calvin's procedure is obvious. The piety of the sixteenth-century evangelical is not the datum of his dogmatic enterprise; rather, he has recourse directly to the Scriptures, even though the *Institutes* attempt something other than the commentaries. Indeed, "speculation" has a somewhat different connotation for him precisely because it suggests an arrogant refusal to be limited by what God has chosen to reveal in his Word. In order to test the moderation of faith, God purposely wills some things to remain hidden; speculation is therefore not merely out of place in dogmatics but wanton, wicked, and hurtful.[33] Writing of the angels, Calvin formulates a general dogmatic rule:

> Let us remember here, as in all religious doctrine, that we ought to hold to one rule of modesty and sobriety: not to speak, or guess, or even to seek to know, concerning obscure matters anything except what has been imparted to us by God's Word. Furthermore, in the reading of Scripture we ought ceaselessly to endeavor to seek out and meditate upon those things which make for edification. Let us not indulge in curiousity or in the investigation of unprofitable things.[34]

This, we may say, if we compare Calvin's warning here with his introductory remarks on the nature of the knowledge of God (Book 1, chap. 2), is the rule of piety; and it is clear that his main concern does not entirely coincide with Schleiermacher's. But there is an affinity of concerns, not least in what is deliberately excluded, and at times Calvin and Schleiermacher approximate each other's language surprisingly closely.[35] In particular, the veto on speculation—or the rule of piety—means for both of them that God is not to be known in himself but rather in the totality of his works as the devout man perceives them.[36]

True, this may at first seem to bring us not one bit further than the disconcerting result already reached: nothing less than the *Institutes* as a whole, it appears once more, can tell us how Calvin thought of God. In actual fact, however, we do now have a principle for ordering his priorities—not so much in our own selection of material as in the perspective of piety that he himself demands. Selective concentration on what Calvin says about the providential and electing will of God has fostered, perhaps even produced, the familiar caricature of his God as a distant and arbitrary despot, who bestows his favors on a chosen few. He does, to be sure, speak of God's hidden, inscrutable will, even though he expressly rejects the notion of *absolute* will with which his critics frequently confuse it.[37] But if we inquire about the significance of this unknown will for the man of faith, we find that it drives him—with a shiver of awe—all the more urgently to the Word, in which everything that is to be known of God's will is revealed.[38] Calvin's remarkable utterances on the terrifying abyss in the divine will do have their relevance for piety, but not so much in themselves as in the fact that they point the believer elsewhere—to the divine benevolence disclosed in the gospel. Schleiermacher seems to have understood this very well; at least he insisted, in response to a Lutheran opponent, that the so-called "unconditioned arbitrariness" of Calvin's deity could not be an occasion for confessional strife, since it lay in the province of the hidden, not the revealed, God.[39] In other words, it is with the revealed will of God that piety and therefore dogmatics have to do; to focus on the hidden will would be to confuse the center of piety with the circumference.

Indeed, we can surely take a further step and argue that for Calvin, as for Schleiermacher, the most basic concept of God is nothing other than the correlate of piety itself, so that to understand the meaning of piety is to have a definition of God.[40] Hence the heart, though not the whole, of Calvin's view of God really is, after all, to be found in Book 1 of the *Institutes*—in the introductory reflections on piety, even before the chapters in which his doctrine of God is commonly looked for. Admittedly, his notion of piety is more complex, less elemental than Schleiermacher's. Even here the affinity is unmistakable; and Seeberg, among others, held that "consciousness of absolute dependence on God" was the heart of Calvin's view of religion, transmitted through the Reformed tradition to Schleiermacher.[41] But for Calvin, it must be replied, the divine "Whence" is decisively qualified as source *of good (fons omnium bon-orum)* and pious dependence, correspondingly, as thankful and reverential love.[42] From the outset his language is specific and concrete, whereas, at the outset, Schleiermacher speaks abstractly of God as simply the Whence of ourselves and of the finite things on which our dependence is only relative. Calvin can therefore identify as the very first step to piety the recognition that "God is our Father to watch over us, govern and nourish us, until he gather us unto the eternal inheritance of his Kingdom." It follows, in a fallen world, that there is no saving knowledge of God apart from Christ, the Son in whom the infinite Father, as Irenaeus says, becomes finite. Already in Book 2, Calvin thus draws an explicit connection between piety and faith in Christ, although his actual discussion of faith is postponed until the third book.[43] The connection is crucial, because it removes any lingering doubts about what has precedence in his doctrine of God.

The fluidity of Calvin's language about true religion tends to crystallize in a twofold concept of piety as reverence and love, corresponding to a twofold concept of God as Lord and Father. It is remarkable that Warfield, who was by no means innocent of the tendency to equate Calvin's doctrine of God with chapters 10-18 of Book 1,[44] nonetheless—even within the framework of the first book—argued for the precedence of love both in true piety and in the character of God, as Calvin understood them: "His doctrine of God is preeminent among the doctrines of God given expression in the Reformation age in the commanding place it gives to the Divine Fatherhood."[45] If any misgivings remain about the sufficiency of Warfield's argument from the concept of piety (i.e., from Book 1, chap. 2), they must surely be resolved by Calvin's subsequent definition (in Book 3, chap. 2) of the closely related concept "faith," which denotes the specific form of piety in the context of redemption: *for faith*, God is above all the benevolent Father.[46]

Unquestionably, if we made a similar advance from "piety" to "faith" in Schleiermacher's theology, differences from Calvin would appear. But for Schleiermacher, too, the call of the Christian proclamation was to view the Father in the Son and to receive from the Son power to become children of God.[47] And, like Calvin, he was persuaded that recognition of the divine love "only comes with the efficacious working of redemption, and it comes from Christ."[48] We have the sense of divine love in the consciousness of redemption,[49] and this consciousness is essentially what Schleiermacher meant by "faith."[50]

But now, for both Schleiermacher and Calvin, the rule of piety raises a question about one of the traditional cornerstones of Christian belief. If the limits of piety enable us to assign preeminence to the fatherly goodwill of God (Calvin) or God's disposition of love (Schleiermacher), must they not at the same time rule out the apparently speculative assertion that in the divine essence there are, with the Father, the persons of the Son and the Holy Spirit? In a *summa pietatis* or *Glaubenslehre*, what room can there be for the dogma of the Trinity?

III

"The assumption of an eternal distinction in the Supreme Being is not an utterance concerning the religious consciousness, for there it could never emerge."[51]

The Christian experience of redemption enables us, according to Schleiermacher, to affirm a union of the divine essence (*Wesen*) and human nature in the personality of Christ. With this affirmation the church's doctrine stands or falls. What it affirms, moreover, is nothing other than the essential content of the doctrine of the Trinity, which arose precisely in its defense; significantly, the doctrine of the Trinity is lacking among sects that give deviant interpretations of redemption. Schleiermacher thus represents the notion of the Trinity as the capstone of Christian doctrine—but only insofar as it affirms, on the basis of Christian experience, the union of the divine essence with human nature.

The method of *The Christian Faith* affords Schleiermacher no means for tracing back the union of human and divine to distinctions that are in the Godhead antecedently to the union. Yet that is exactly what the dogma of the Trinity, as ordinarily understood, attempts to do. Now the exegesis by which this attempt is supported has never, Schleiermacher insists, been secured against constant attacks. But even if it had been, and if—on the authority of Christ and the apostles—we accepted the dogma as the assertion of a transcendent fact, it would make no difference to our living fellowship with Christ.[52] The doctrine of the Trinity is one of those points at which the temptation to "speculate" is particularly strong: having no formula for the being of God in himself, the theologian could only borrow one from the domain of speculation.[53] To head off the temptation, Schleiermacher takes at least one preliminary step toward reappraising the doctrine of the Trinity: he assigns it to its proper location at the end of the system, where its limits as a statement about the Christian consciousness can be more readily secured.[54]

The attitude of Calvin to the trinitarian dogma has been the subject of lively historical debate. In the last ten years of his life he conducted a vigorous literary campaign against the Italian Antitrinitarians, in whom he saw (somewhat undiscriminatingly) the spiritual kin of Servetus;[55] and yet, earlier in his career, his own trinitarian orthodoxy had been placed in doubt. The motives behind his refusal, when challenged by Caroli, to subscribe to the ancient creeds have been variously explained, partly because they were in fact complex.[56] But one thing is clear: throughout all the several exchanges, Calvin tried to hold fast to his rule of piety, contrasting (as he sometimes put it) "practical knowledge" and "otiose speculation."[57] And here again, as before, his approach was both like and unlike Schleiermacher's.

In his chapter on the Trinity (Book 1, chap. 13), the concern for piety is negatively expressed by Calvin in several ways: in his direct warning against idle speculations, in his refusal to follow his mentor Augustine in the quest for psychological analogies of the Trinity, and in his dismissal of the "silly" notion of an eternal generation of the Son.[58] Positively, he ends with the claim that his summary will have satisfied those who impose a limit on their curiousity, if not those who intemperately delight in speculation.[59] But no one will fail to notice that his professed zeal for the edification of the church permits him to say much more than Schleiermacher; for he has no doubt at all that, albeit God speaks sparingly of his essence, the Scriptures do inform us of three hypostases or persons in the divine essence—that is, of an eternal distinction.[60]

Indeed, it was Calvin's claim that pious experience itself *(ipsa pietatis experientia)* shows us in the divine unity God the Father, his Son, and the Spirit.[61] He even ventured the remarkable assertion: "No one will acknowledge from his heart that Christ is his God unless he first acknowledges a diversity of persons in the unity of essence."[62] Hence the reason why he preserved most of the old trinitarian vocabulary, which Schleiermacher found muddled and obsolete, was because he thought the hallowed terms still served their historical function of defending piety. The doctrine of the Trinity, in Calvin's view, did not transgress the limits of piety: it had its significance for piety chiefly as a *defensive* doctrine. He admitted he would have been happy to see the words "trinity," "person," and "consubstantial" buried—were they not needed for the sake of agreement in faith. And from the very first edition of the *Institutes*, long before he encountered the biblicism of Biandrata, he energetically justified the use of extrabiblical words if they do not add to Scripture but explain its meaning and, by unmasking the deceitfulness of the heretic, defend its truth. Arius said he believed that Christ was God, but he continued to speak of him as created; confronted with the word *homoousios* ("consubstantial"), his craftiness was exposed. Sabellius said he believed the Father was God, the Son was God, and the Spirit was God, but thought he had said no more than if he had described God as strong, just, or wise; with the notion of a *personarum trinitas* (a "trinity of persons") those who had piety at heart shattered his wickedness and fortified themselves against his cunning.[63] These sound like philosophical terms, to be sure. But within carefully defined limits we may, after all, philosophize in moderation, not speculating further than Scripture raises us but only giving its simple and genuine meaning.[64]

Calvin stood at the confluence of several streams of thought which, between them, moved Christian theology closer to the daily walk of the Christian. Disillusionment with the inherited scholastic style was one respect in which Erasmus, Luther, and Calvin were all at one, despite their differences: they agreed that the logic-chopping and idle speculations of the "sophists" had to yield to study of the earliest Christian documents, the springs of genuine piety. But if they could not follow Castellio in the radical verdict that even the dogma of the Trinity was an *adiaphoron*[65] —a thing of no practical consequence—their reasons for holding back were significantly different.

Even when he gave no indication of seeing much point in ecclesiastical dogmas, Erasmus bowed to the judgment of the church. The reason why he did so was because, for him, "piety" included such deference. "I am not so lacking in piety," he wrote, "as to dissent from the Catholic Church."[66] Luther, by contrast, maintained a sovereign freedom over against the judgments of the church and yet, as has been acutely observed, he managed inwardly to appropriate church doctrines in a manner Erasmus could not comprehend.[67] For his part, Calvin undertook to justify the dogma of the Trinity as a defensive doctrine, whose intent was not to reopen the door to as much speculation as one pleased but to philosophize no further than piety required.

Schleiermacher's methodological principles, though just as much (in their own way) a matter of piety, called for a more thoroughgoing critique of the dogmatic tradition. He held it to have been a defect in the theological program of the Reformers that they made no attempt to revise the trinitarian and christological dogmas, in whose original construction he detected an impassioned polemical zeal that invited error.[68] Others have argued since Schleiermacher that in actual fact a transformation or development of the dogmas was something the Reformation began.[69] Perhaps that says too much. But anyone who, like Schleiermacher, proposes a revision of dogma as part of the unfinished business of the Reformation has enough on his side to make a claim of continuity by no means implausible.

To say nothing here of the other Reformers, Calvin displayed a quite new attitude to the received dogmatic language. Where he felt bound to do so, he rejected hallowed terms (like "eternal generation"); where he accepted the inherited formulas in substance, he refused to be coerced into subscribing to their every letter, arguing that in any case the received language was not uniform.[70] It is hard to see how he could object *in principle*, though he might not approve the results, if another theologian undertook to conform dogmatic language more closely to the Reformation's own courts of appeal: the deliverances of Scripture and the experience of piety. But it must be admitted that *in practice* Calvin was inclined to be suspicious of nonconformists and to suppose that their reticence toward established formulas must cloak a defective faith. Schleiermacher, on the other hand, thought it possible that someone who could not reconcile himself to the difficulties in the trinitarian language might nonetheless have a piety by no means lacking in the specifically Christian stamp.[71] It was this openness, right or wrong, that more than anything else freed mainline Protestantism to think again about the descendants of Calvin's heretics.

Thirteen

The Possibility of
          a Historical Theology:
          An Appraisal of
          Troeltsch's Dogmatics

> *I know myself at one with these friends in the wish that the*
> *Heidelberg theologian not be quite forgotten in the Berlin*
> *philosopher of culture.*[1]

For the great generation of Protestant schoolmen, whose names today are scarcely remembered, dogmatics was a deductive, biblical science. Whatever initial aid they may have found in a natural theology, they derived the fundamental teachings of their church strictly from the written Word of God; and the indispensable prolegomenon to this enterprise was simply to establish the exclusive claims of Scripture. The oracles of God had been distributed to his people with a largesse that overflowed the bounds of mere order. It was the task of the theologian to bring them, with due humility, into a coherent system, which, precisely because it contained no more than the faith delivered once for all to the saints, had the character of an enduring and irrefutable body of divinity. Within the limits of such a scheme, historical study could scarcely be more than a branch of confessional apologetics, by which one's own party could be shown to have preserved the truth without adulteration or alteration.[2]

Friedrich Schleiermacher, by contrast, identified dogmatics as a part of historical theology. Protestant scholasticism did not, of course, constitute the entire background to his enterprise; but whatever may have been the contributory factors, past or contemporary, the move he made was nothing less than revolutionary. It meant that the heart of theology, its essential business, was now seen to be the explication of the life of the church (or of one aspect of it). Dogmatics has for its subject matter the same datum as church history: the Christian community as a phenomenon of change, growth, development. The difference between the two disciplines is that church history is directed toward the church in its past, whereas dogmatics deals with the church in the present. And since the past is pregnant with the future, and the present is the issue of the past, the dividing line is little more than a pragmatic convenience. So Schleiermacher presented the scope and task of dogmatics in his *Brief Outline* (1811 and 1830).[3]

His own dogmatic system, *The Christian Faith* (1821-22 and 1830-31), must be understood as the implementation of this same program. It is a contribution to historical theology, in that it offers historical knowledge of the (then) present condition of the Evangelical church. It is no longer a deductive, biblical theology in the old Protestant style.[4] Even what he calls "philosophical theology" is inextricably bound up with the historical task, since it is constantly to test the language of the church by reference to a distinctive "essence" of Christianity (or of Protestantism) that can be grasped only in its historical manifestations.[5] Plainly, in Schleiermacher's program the theological task is thoroughly "historicized"—made into a function of history. Not sufficiently, however, to satisfy some of his critics and successors!

The dogmatics of Schleiermacher was subjected to relentless criticism, from the side of historical thinking, by F. C. Baur, D. F. Strauss, Wilhelm Dilthey, and others.[6] It was pointed out that the *content* of his system—indeed, at its christological center—violated historical modes of thought. It appealed to an absolute moment of history, a fixed point to which theology had constantly to refer back as the unblemished norm and the unique center of mankind's history.[7] Further, the questionable content was traced to defective *method*. The method of the system, despite the explicit historical turn, remained incurably "dogmatic" (in a pejorative sense). And this was most notably the problem just at the place where the profession of historical-critical principles was most dutifully made: in his lectures on the life of Jesus.[8]

Schleiermacher was by no means unaware of the alleged inconsistencies his critics urged, and were later to urge, against him. But he did not believe it possible to surrender the absoluteness of Christ.[9] The desire of some of his successors, including Baur, was to make dogmatics more consistently historical by erasing vestigial blemishes in Schleiermacher's program. Others, like Franz Overbeck, were persuaded that historical method and dogmatic theology were, in the end, simply exclusive.[10] Here, then, is the question that was asked of Schleiermacher: Is a historical theology (in his sense) possible? And this is also the question addressed, in his own day and since, to Ernst Troeltsch.

I

Characterizing his own theological program in his *Glaubenslehre*, Troeltsch remarks: "No theologian of the present keeps so close to the method and intent of Schleiermacher, or feels himself in such inward agreement with him" (Gl., p. 130). As his very next words demonstrate, Troeltsch was by no means an uncritical disciple of the man he elsewhere calls "our great master."[11] In the course of his *Glaubenslehre*, he reproduces the more or less standard objections to Schleiermacher's system: that it is entangled in a monistic world-view, borrowed chiefly from Spinoza; that it obtrudes historical propositions about Jesus into the main body of dogmatics, where they do not belong; that it describes Jesus by means of predicates which cannot be derived from history (Gl., pp. 130, 79, 86).[12]

A similar stance of critical discipleship is adopted in others of Troeltsch's writings. One further example may suffice. In his essay on the dogmatics of the "history of religions" school, he judges that the program of Schleiermacher's *Brief Outline* "simply needs to be carried out consistently" and that "hardly any change is necessary." This, however, is to endorse only the program. For although Schleiermacher indicated the contours of a genuinely modern theology, the historical interpretation of Christianity has made enormous strides since his time, and his *Life of Jesus* is simply dated. So, too, in the light of progress in the history of religions, his theory of religious development appears as "a completely antiquated exercise of the imagination."[13]

What Troeltsch learned from Schleiermacher was a "theology of consciousness,"[14] which could appropriately be designated a "historical theology," although Troeltsch did not, in fact, adopt this feature of the master's peculiar terminology. Schleiermacher is singled out as the pioneer in modern dogmatics, first of all, because he built his theology on the double foundation of a comparative philosophy of religions and a historical-critical (therefore *religionsgeschichtlich*) investigation of Christianity itself. In other words, he made theology rest on a "philosophy of the history of religions," which, in turn, was rooted in what he called "ethics" (that is, the philosophy of history and of the human spirit). The design of such a philosophical approach is not, as in the old natural theologies, to prove the reality of the religious object, but to furnish an analysis of religion, its distinctive character, and its historical development.

Troeltsch identifies himself with Schleiermacher's general program, so understood. He differs, however, where revisions are required by advances, since Schleiermacher's time, in the historical-phenomenological foundations and in the analysis of the concept of development. Further, he judges that Schleiermacher's somewhat minimal philosophy of religion was cramped by an exclusive interest in laying the groundwork for dogmatics. What, for Schleiermacher, was merely the introduction to *Glaubenslehre* has since become a separate discipline. But the path opened up by him remains the right one.[15] It is easy to see why Troeltsch is willing to understand it as a program for a "dogmatics of the history of religions school."

Dogmatics, then, is intimately connected with philosophy and with the history of religions through a distinct discipline that Troeltsch calls "philosophy of religion" or "fundamental theology."[16] It is simply the grown-up child of Schleiermacher's introduction to his own *Glaubenslehre*, *The Christian Faith*. But dogmatics necessarily passes beyond the scope of its initial partners insofar as its proper business is to present a normative system of specifically Christian beliefs or (to follow Schleiermacher once again) a system of the essential Christian ideas that radiate out from the personality of Jesus. Troeltsch distinguishes three dogmatic tasks: first, by a comparison with other religions, to establish the supremacy of Christianity for our civilization; second, to trace the church's entire historical course and to draw out the essence of Christianity for the present; third, to explicate the content of the essence in appropriate concepts. It is clear that the first two tasks are closely related to Schleiermacher's two foundations of dogmatics, and that the third is its "real and specific business."[17]

There are several senses in which this dogmatic enterprise may be considered "historical." To begin with, the first and second tasks both proceed from historical data; and the third, more strictly dogmatic, task evolves out of the second. Hence Troeltsch can assert that the entire conception of dogmatics as the unfolding of Christianity's essence is conditioned by a history-of-religions viewpoint. Moreover, the actual ordering of the essence into its conceptual content, so Troeltsch claims, simply appropriates the common categories discovered by the history of religions in every higher religion. For every religious principle signifies a practical relationship of God, world, and man; and always associated with this fundamental relationship is a religious community and the hope for a final consummation. This yields the six concepts of Troeltsch's dogmatics, each of which presents the whole content of the Christian principle, but from a different perspective, and each of which receives a separate chapter in his *Glaubenslehre*: God, world, man, redemption, church, and consummation. The consequences of this history-of-religions orientation, Troeltsch adds, extend still further into the execution of the dogmatic task since they require that the critical standards of historiography should be brought to bear on the Christian story, which is not exempt from the relativity of all historical events nor from the uncertainties of all historical testimony. In this regard, the special standpoint of the history of religions only strengthens the earlier claims of historical criticism.[18]

There is at least one further respect in which dogmatics is a historical task: because it is itself a part of religious growth and becoming. Troeltsch's interpretation of Schleiermacher is at no point more fascinating than here, where the functional-ephemeral character of dogmatics comes into view. What does the theological student actually possess once he has mastered Schleiermacher's *Glaubenslehre*? Troeltsch replies that he will be equipped to nurture the religious sensibility of his future pastoral charges. *The Christian Faith* is a guide to preaching. It is a "technical-theological" book, and therefore unpalatable to laymen, not in the sense of being academically esoteric, but rather because its end is knowledge of the "technical" means by which religious feeling is represented and stimulated. Precisely as such, the *Glaubenslehre* of Schleiermacher takes on a strictly ephemeral character: it does not fix dogmas but only expresses, in forms suited to the moment, the religious strength that radiates from Christ. The means of expression have their source in Christ, but they are shaped by the situation of the present. Hence theology's task is essentially to mediate between old forms and new for the sake of practical ends.[19] Pursuit of this strand in Schleiermacher's dogmatics leads Troeltsch to his repeated insistence that *Glaubenslehre* is not a science, but rather "a confession of faith and a systematic exposition of this confession for the guidance of preaching and of religious instruction." It is, he argues, a part of practical theology. The most that can be claimed for the scientific status of dogmatics is that it retains contact with science through its relationship with the philosophy of religion and church history, both of which bear a purely scientific character.[20]

It is hard not to judge that Troeltsch here develops his master's thoughts one-sidedly. He claims that to classify dogmatics with practical theology is the intent of Schleiermacher's *Brief Outline*. And yet it is obvious that he has at least made a shift in Schleiermacher's language, since the *Brief Outline* in fact presents dogmatics as a part of historical theology, and practical theology as the crown or goal of theological studies in general.[21] Perhaps the verbal difference betrays a material shift as well. But it is not our purpose to assess the justice of Troeltsch's claim to be Schleiermacher's disciple at this point; only to comprehend Troeltsch's own theological program. And whereas others have sought to defend Schleiermacher against his apparent debasement of theology's scientific status,[22] Troeltsch develops the practical aspect fully and approvingly. He was convinced that dogmatics, because it deals with the confession of faith and from the standpoint of commitment to it, could not pretend to scientific status. Indeed, he speaks of it in language which invites comparison with the free, creative activity of the artist. Dogmatics is production out of the resources of Christian history; and its products, because they are values with an ineradicably personal stamp, resist incorporation with the uniform and universally valid objects of science.[23] We must surely ask, however, not only why Troeltsch classified dogmatics with practical theology, but also why, after all, he did *not* classify it as historical theology. Does this represent a substantive departure from Schleiermacher, one more germane—indeed, crucial—for our own theme?

Since no German theologian, with one exception, had adopted Schleiermacher's inclusion of dogmatics under historical theology, it is hardly surprising if Troeltsch did not do so either.[24] Schleiermacher's terminology was apparently felt to be eccentric, and even theologians who titled their systematic work *Glaubenslehre* omitted to take the further step of calling it *historische Theologie*. Still, the question remains whether something material was lost or gained by the omission. As far as Troeltsch is concerned, my own judgment is that the terminological departure from Schleiermacher really does signify a material point, but not such as to question Schleiermacher's design in calling dogmatics "historical theology."

Between Schleiermacher and Troeltsch, historical theology had become the secure fortress of those who wished to affirm the scientific character of their business, and the term frequently implied a clear repudiation of church dogmatics.[25] Besides, there really was (at that time) something eccentric in speaking of the present as "historical." Schleiermacher, of course, was moving towards the notion of man's "historicity" as a description of his temporal existence, and this was a notion whose time had not quite come. Troeltsch was not merely acquiescing in current usage, however, but himself acknowledging the need for differentiation when he declined to follow Schleiermacher's lead. This, admittedly, is an inference, since I am not aware of any place where he directly explains his own usage. It is clear, however, that he was impressed by the logical difference between strictly historical and strictly dogmatic functions. What historical inquiry discloses can never be more than a historical reality until it is changed by a judgment into a valid truth. The logical transition from the historical to the constructive theological task lies here—in an act by which a value is lifted out of mere fact.[26] But this could hardly be interpreted as a material criticism of Schleiermacher, since Troeltsch is not denying what Schleiermacher sought to affirm by his admittedly unfamiliar usage: namely, that dogmatics is directed to the present consciousness of the church, and that this can only be understood in continuity with its past.

Where Troeltsch does offer his most emphatic criticism, it concerns neither the raw material, nor the general method, nor the function of dogmatics, which we may fairly distinguish as the elements that warrant the appellation "historical theology." It concerns, rather, the end product, which Troeltsch understands as strictly conceptual in character. The concepts comprised in the essence of Christianity are to be presented "without any intermingling of historical elements," so that dogmatics, in the end, contains "purely present-day religious" or "purely metaphysical-religious" propositions. The criticism of Schleiermacher is that he mixed the historical and the metaphysical propositions. Troeltsch has chiefly in mind the way in which Schleiermacher mingled dogmatic propositions concerning the present experience of redemption with historical propositions about Jesus. In Schleiermacher's *Glaubenslehre*, the historical-religious propositions, he maintains, are the sorest point because they are forced dissonantly into the section where only present-day religious propositions belong (Gl., p. 79; cf. Gl., pp. 329, 348). Accordingly, Troeltsch thinks he improves on Schleiermacher by dividing his own *Glaubenslehre* into two parts. The first deals with Jesus Christ in the light both of his prophetic forerunners and of his subsequent interpreters. The second seeks to formulate the conceptual content of Christian faith understood as strictly a present experience.

Still, the logical segregation of historical and metaphysical propositions, Troeltsch points out, is but one side of the matter. Not only are the present-day formulations attained solely at the end of a historical inquiry, but present religious experience continues to receive its life and power from the vital world of history; this it is, and particularly the prophets and Jesus, that leads us to God.[27] And that was a particular insight of Schleiermacher's—indeed, from the early time of his *Speeches on Religion* (1799).[28] Even here, then, we come back again to the historical and to Schleiermacher as the great master of a historical theology. So decisive was the new direction he gave to Protestant theology that Troeltsch, while not adopting the term "historical theology" in Schleiermacher's sense, does hold that in principle Schleiermacher did away with the other term—"dogmatics." Henceforth *Dogmatik* was superseded by *Glaubenslehre* (Gl., p. 10), though in practice Troeltsch was no more able than Schleiermacher to dispense with the more traditional word. The new dogmatics is dogmatics no longer, since it knows no dogmas.[29]

It would, no doubt, be fruitful to turn next to some leading themes of Troeltsch's dogmatics and to compare them with some of Schleiermacher's. My purpose, however, is not to move from the methodological to the material concerns, but rather to raise some questions about the viability of the method. Such an exercise may well appear gratuitous in view of the scorn that a whole generation of theologians has heaped upon Troeltsch's theology. We have become accustomed to the verdict that Troeltsch led theology into a blind alley. No progress was possible, we are told, along the path he marked out. Hence his own departure from a theology chair at Heidelberg for a chair in philosophy at Berlin was a kind of symbolic or symptomatic act.[30] Either the theological task had to be taken up from another, fresh standpoint; or else it would dissolve into philosophy and the social sciences, and so cease to be theology.[31] In Germany, Bodenstein has given currency to the image of Troeltsch as a "tragic" figure, who represented in his own career the general tragedy of a whole era in German theology.[32] Similarly, in the English-speaking world, Reist has expressed the common sentiment that Troeltsch's theology simply "collapsed."[33] Bodenstein and Reist represent something close to a mainline consensus that stood, during the second and third quarters of our century, under the shade of neoorthodoxy (or perhaps one should better say "neoorthodoxies," in the plural). Although signs of a fresh interest in Troeltsch's theology have begun to accompany the decline of neoorthodoxy itself, reappraisal of the Heidelberg theologian has scarcely begun.[34]

Did Troeltsch bequeath to Christian theology anything more than a problem or a budget of problems? Did he perhaps offer, in addition, something like the ground plan for a historical theology? The obstacles to an affirmative answer are forbidding. It would not do simply to consider the neoorthodox chapter closed and to reopen the books at 1923. There can be no question of merely reproducing either the content or the idiom of Troeltsch's dogmatics; that would violate his own sense of the passage of time. Besides, formidable theological objections were raised against Troeltsch's enterprise: that he surrendered theology's own internal norms; that he placed at the center of his theology, as its cardinal motif, an outdated idealistic metaphysic of spirit; that, for all his emphasis on history, he had in the end no appreciation for truths of fact; that his entire enterprise founders on the problems of individuality and relativism.[35] (I say nothing of the further objection, which weighs less heavily in the Anglo-Saxon world than in Germany, that Troeltsch failed to appreciate the genius of Martin Luther.)[36] Small wonder, then, if Reist judges that it would be simply pointless to set out Troeltsch's theology in its full breadth and unpardonably stupid to reduplicate his errors.[37]

Obviously, one takes something of a risk if one proposes a serious reappraisal of the *Glaubenslehre*. But, at the least, I should like to move beyond the condescension with which the *Glaubenslehre* was addressed from the very first days of its publication. Erich Seeberg, for instance, treated it patronizingly in his review as a document of Troeltsch's personal piety and so of a religiousness from a bygone day.[38] I should like, by contrast, to take it seriously as a theological document. And, although Reist's call for caution is well-taken,[39] I cannot believe either that there is a very grave problem with the authenticity of the text or that there has been any great risk of too much dependence upon it as a source for Troeltsch's theology. On the second point, I need only remark that had there been *more* dependence on Troeltsch's *Glaubenslehre*, some of the objections alleged against his theology would be infinitely harder to sustain.[40] What we have really had too much of, if anything, is the endless summaries of *Der Historismus und seine Probleme*—or certain favorite portions of it.

On the first point: the transcript of the lectures, though admittedly not published by Troeltsch himself, was approved by him, incorporated his own dictation, and was the work of a highly competent assistant who aimed at fidelity to the spoken word.[41] No objection can be brought against the authenticity of the dictation (clearly distinguished in the text), and it would be over-fastidious not to use the freer portions of the lecture, which amplify the sense of the dictated paragraphs and are a remarkable testimony to the vividness of Troeltsch's speech. From Gertrud von le Fort's observations, we may conclude that the transcript is not so much a complete stenographic report as an accurate single-track abstraction from Troeltsch's multi-track discourse, in which he conveyed the same idea in a rich variety of formulations.

An adequate appraisal of the *Glaubenslehre* would certainly be obliged to meet in detail the various criticisms that have been advanced against Troeltsch's theology. (We should, indeed, not overlook criticisms from the left, so to say, any more than those from the right.)[42] For the moment, however, I do not wish to confront such favorite problems as historical relativism and historical knowledge of Jesus (though both are important, and I have addressed myself to them elsewhere).[43] Rather, I have selected three other themes from the *Glaubenslehre* that seem to have the merit of illustrating both the promise and the embarrassment of a historical theology. I need make no claims about their importance or unimportance in Troeltsch's total career. Even were it true (which I doubt) that the *Glaubenslehre* represents only a minor deviation in Troeltsch's own development, it would not necessarily follow that it had only a minor importance for the development of dogmatic theology.[44] On the contrary, particularly for those of us who still consider Schleiermacher the "great master" of modern dogmatics, the *Glaubenslehre* of Troeltsch is a fascinating and significant work, important both for the history of theology and for the construction of a viable theological method at the present time.

My three themes are all methodologically oriented; and, although they could be documented from others of Troeltsch's writings, I confine myself chiefly to his treatment of them in the *Glaubenslehre* and the closely related articles in *Die Religion in Geschichte und Gegenwart*. It will be clear that, for each theme, I have further confined myself to the preliminary historical task of entering sympathetically into Troeltsch's own world of thought, so that the questions I raise are presented as internal to his own system. (Naturally, the further, systematic or constructive task would call for the presentation of another standpoint in the vastly different idiom of the present day.) The themes have to do, respectively, with religious sensibility, the uses of the past, and the reality of history; or, we may say, with the materials, the method, and the premise of a historical theology.

II

The advantage of the new dogmatics, in Troeltsch's eyes, is that it enables the theologian to address himself to the feelings and instincts of his own age, appropriating the strength and the blessing of the past without making history a burden to be borne. The essence of Christianity for any age is always a "synthesis" that brings together the present situation and the historical resources. But what are the particular needs of the present that Troeltsch himself is anxious to address? He confesses that his dogmatics is not designed for missionary expansion, which can safely be left to the conservatives, but rather for the needs of the old Christianity, which finds itself in a severe internal crisis. How is religious clarity to be gained amid the perplexity of modern life? Every age has its peculiar problem. For ours, the problem is posed by the depersonalization of self and society. It arises from diverse changes that belong to the respective domains of historical thinking, natural science, and sociology. But it is, at bottom, one problem: how to regain possession of the soul. "We do not ask, How do I get a gracious God? We ask rather, How do I again find the soul and love?" A genuinely free dogmatics has the opportunity to articulate the question of the present, and not to discourse laboriously about dogmas inherited from an alien past. And yet it is free to appropriate the past in a manner the old dogmatics could never have allowed.[45]

Modernity thus enters into dogmatics as one of its major coefficients. And this is not merely a matter of dealing externally with modern ideas, but of consciously coming to terms with influences which have flowed in upon us quietly and unobtrusively (Gl., pp. 30-32) and which *must* materially affect a theology of consciousness.[46] The religious consciousness of the present is cumulatively conditioned by history (Gl., p. 20), even though it is the connection with the prophets, Jesus, and the Bible that remains determinative.[47] And it is not revelation itself that is the immediate object of theology, but the expression of it in forms shaped by the spirit of the time (Gl., pp. 42-43, 51).

Troeltsch's own profound grasp of the change in religious sensibility is nowhere more strikingly displayed than in his frequent meditations on the post-Copernican world-picture. This is not, by any means, to pass out of history into natural science, since it is the movement of history which demands an adjustment in the first place and the problem of the modern scientific world-picture is in part its meaning for man's historicity. The sun and the stars are no longer there just for us to set our watches by. The sense of intimacy with God has vanished, and we perceive ourselves as dayflies or as mere toys in the immensity of the universe (Gl., pp. 33, 177). We need only to pass through the prehistoric collection of a museum, with its endless rows of relics from time immemorial, and the question must force itself upon us whether our own civilization, too, will have its day, perhaps sinking back into a new ice-age. "A massive impression of the nothingness of all historical existence [*der Nichtigkeit alles geschichtlichen Seins*] comes over us at such possibilities..." (Gl., p. 94). "What will the end be? Presumably, a waning of solar energy and, with it, ever-increasing difficulties of nutriment, until finally the last man roasts the last potato on the last ember" (Gl., p. 292).

> We obviously cannot lock out the consequences of a Copernican system. We may not shrink from the immensity of the All, in which we, together with our whole solar system, are swept upon paths that defy thought. In view of the uniformity of the entire universe opened up by spectral analysis, the geocentric and anthropocentric view of things must vanish. Man has to adapt himself to no longer being able to establish a physical center of the universe. But from here there arise new, quite definite tinges of the religious feeling. The world of unspeakable grandeur that stands before us is another one than

that of the Bible's seven-day work. A current of immense majesty streams into our religious feeling from this world that has been extended into infinity. We know that the formation of our earth arose by detachment from another heavenly body, and our entire organic life on this earth seems, in comparison to the duration of the world, like breath on cold window panes, which disappears the next moment. But what the world is without organic life, we do not know. At some point we emerged from the development, at some point we will disappear again. More, science does not say. As the beginning was without us, so will the end also be without us. Transferred to religion, this insight means: the end is not that of the Apocalypse (Gl., p. 64).

A historical theology, we may say, is a theology of man's historicity—his confinement within the "nothingness of historical existence." Troeltsch found the new sensibility crushing but not paralyzing, since he grasped it (characteristically) as a task. It sets before *Glaubenslehre* the distinctive form of its present assignment. Negatively, it requires surrender of the churchly doctrine of redemption, because the old divine interventionism cannot be harmonized with the immensity of the world-process or the unbroken continuity of its working.[48] Positively, it opens up once more the duty of rethinking the Christian heritage. We do not become skeptics or materialists, but cling all the more firmly to the revelation of God which we possess in our hearts. We must transfer the old ivy-stock to the new wall (Gl., pp. 64–65).

A part of what this means—not the whole of it[49]—is that the distinctive Christian message for the day is shaped by the new question. And Troeltsch boldly—perhaps even defiantly—affirms that the God of the whole, whom none can name, is also the God who knows me in all my littleness and chooses to deal personally with me (Gl., pp. 274–75). Nothing falls from the hand of God. I am summoned to grow into his divine life, and so to overcome the threat of infinity. Troeltsch does not argue the point; he holds it out as an affirmation of faith against the sole alternative of being crushed (Gl., p. 250). He was deeply aware of the elements of immensity, mystery, terror in the idea of God (Gl., p. 161). Religious awe before the vastness of the cosmos does indeed belong to the religious sensibility, and Troeltsch can pronounce the somewhat melancholy aphorism, "The *whole* is our fate" (Gl., p. 259). But faith in the immediate activity of the living God is no less a datum of the religious sensibility. Though a distinctive trait of theistic faith, it obtrudes itself even into the less congenial worlds of Stoicism, Neoplatonism, and Buddhism. (Gl., p. 269).

It could well be argued that Troeltsch here reverses the movement of Pauline Christianity from transience to sin as the cardinal religious problem.[50] But his solution lay, not so much in a quantitative extension of human life, as in the affirmation of its worth despite transience; and he expressly distinguishes the modern problem, not only from the Reformation's concern with legalism, but also from antiquity's preoccupation with death. Our problem is broader: it concerns the worth of the soul (Gl., pp. 285ff.)—despite transience, yes, but also despite cosmic anxiety and the mechanization of modern life (Gl., pp. 177, 298). Here, however, there is a difficulty in Troeltsch's theology. It is not merely that the infinite value of the soul appears to be professed as a mere fideistic affirmation, nor that the value of the soul admittedly remains unrealized for the masses of mankind.[51] The difficulty, rather, is that the gospel of the soul's infinite worth is jeopardized by an ambiguity in Troeltsch's doctrine of God and a corresponding indecision in his eschatology.[52]

The initial line Troeltsch draws between theism and pantheism is, in the course of his presentation, virtually erased. The distinction is strongly affirmed in principle: the only live religious options are Christian theism and Buddhist monism, and the issue at stake is the value of personality. Only the theistic conception of God is capable of supporting personal worth and moral activity (Gl., pp. 73-76, 141-42, 169-70, 184-85, 196-97, 357-59). Schleiermacher is sharply criticized because, having rightly stated the choice in principle,[53] he was unable in practice to resist Spinozist monism (Gl., pp. 68-69, 130). For his part, Troeltsch is willing to pursue the supposed advantage of theism over monism even to the point of affirming that the development of finite persons has its meaning also for the life of God. The redemption of man is an enrichment of the divine being—indeed, it is God's redemption of himself (Gl., pp. 218-19, 236-38, 344). And yet one must ask: Was Troeltsch any more successful than Schleiermacher in affirming ethical theism in practice as well as in principle? Though he warns us that it is not possible to be a Spinozist with the head and a theist with the heart (Gl., p. 67), he apparently is tempted to try the impossible himself.

It is with respect to the ultimate destiny of the finite person that Troeltsch finds himself speaking an appreciative word for pantheism. He can both affirm the infinite worth of the soul and yet entertain the probability that the epic of human freedom will end in free surrender of selfhood to God. Certainly, the pantheistic notion of God provides the more natural counterpart to the dissolution of finite consciousness, whereas theistic hopes are for perfected communion of the finite spirit with the Spirit of God (Gl., p. 327). The relative freedom of man to make the world's purpose, which is the will of God, his own moral task is antipantheistic. It invites an eschatology of continued moral growth, in communion with God, beyond the grave (Gl., pp. 190-91, 298-300, 321, 362-63, 380).[54] But it cannot go on forever (Gl., p. 382)! The thought that it might, Troeltsch finds horrifying.[55] Hence, though declining to speculate overmuch on the content of the eschatological symbols, he finds himself bound to speak of a last stage, at which the finite self is "consumed," "returns to God," "sinks down into the divine life," "dies from the final perfection of blessedness."[56] Freedom thus attains its goal in the act of total surrender to God, even, it may be, to the point of dissolution of the separate consciousness (Gl., p. 297). And so we stand simultaneously before the elements of truth in theism and in pantheism, even if we cannot combine them in a unified conception of God; and a measure of right is to be granted to pantheistic feeling (Gl., p. 220). Troeltsch concludes: "For the practice of the present, we hold on to theism; and only in the sequel does the pantheistic notion emerge ..." (Gl., p. 239).

Plainly, there is a problem in this seemingly happy solution. Is it any safer to be a theist in your ethics and a pantheist in your eschatology than to be a Spinozist with your head and a theist with your heart? Is the affirmation of the person and its worth a kind of interim ethic (*zwischen Grundlage und Ziel* [cf. Gl., p. 297]), pending the return of the creation into the Creator?[57] And if, as Troeltsch suggests, the fate of the wicked is plausibly thought of as a dissolution of the self (Gl., p. 210), are "heaven" and "hell" diverse names for the same destination? Well, we should not chide Troeltsch if he could give no clear answer to the Buddha's question: Where does the flame go when it goes out? The point, rather, is that Troeltsch's theology was a theology of historicity, of human finitude and temporality. He affirmed this to the very end, to eschatology as the final chapter of *Glaubenslehre*, even though it could well be said to have threatened the heart of his gospel and not merely to have posed its central problem.

Adjustment to the modern world-view, of which natural science and historical thinking are the main arbiters, changes the religious sensibility that produces the materials of dogmatics. Against modern man's sense of his own temporality—his sense of the "nothingness of all historical existence"—Troeltsch sets his revisionist gospel of the infinite value of the soul. It is the methodological move that chiefly concerns us, for something like it must surely be risked by any modern theology whatever. Still, the intrinsic defiance of Troeltsch's own execution of the move is made even more problematic by the ambiguity in his eschatology, in which pantheistic piety, ruled out initially and in principle, reasserts itself. And whether or not Troeltsch's eschatology is correct, it obviously poses yet another methodological problem: the nature of dogmatic norms.

III

Naturally, Troeltsch's flirtation with monistic eschatology was pointed out disapprovingly as a betrayal of Christian thought. Normally sympathetic, R. S. Sleigh protested: "It is bad enough to lose God in man, as Hegel did, or tended to do [!], but it is worse to lose man in God."[58] Within the framework of Troeltsch's own attitude towards tradition, however, it is peculiarly difficult to hold him accountable. The method of dogmatics, like its material, is historicized; and this means a radical rethinking of the old problem of Scripture and tradition. The tradition acquires a new status which it could not have had for

Protestant orthodoxy. And yet the turn to Christian history cannot furnish conveniently fixed points of reference such as the old orthodoxy had (or thought it had) in Scripture. Once again, though in a quite different manner, the historical perspective is both liberating and disquieting.

A favorite canard during the heyday of neoorthodoxy was that Protestant liberalism lacked theological norms and therefore could do little more than underwrite existing social values. It might well be supposed that Troeltsch's insistence on adaptation to modernity formalizes just this error. In actual fact, however, he constantly reaffirms the theologian's duty to test the spirit of the times. A distinction has to be drawn between the latest novelty and "the total intellectual structure which shaped the last two centuries." Coming to terms with the spirit of the times cannot mean simply taking over everything that is modern. Polemic is one way of confronting the modern world. True, it would be futile to repudiate the settled habits of thought which constitute the modern, as distinct from the ancient and medieval, world-view and which do in actual fact shape the consciousness of us all (Gl., pp. 18–19, 22–23). But the attunement of religious sensibility to the new world-picture cannot mean endorsing the petty wishes of the bourgeoisie (Gl., pp. 145–146, 150).

Although, then, Troeltsch recommends adjustment as the only feasible way to affirm Christianity in the modern world,[59] he still insists on an inner discontinuity between cultural goals and the religion of redemption. The possibility of the higher life is opened to mankind as revelation and gift, which call for decision and a break with man's natural limits (Gl., pp. 332–33). Troeltsch has no doctrine of inevitable progress. "Development," he admits, is the magic word of the day, but by it untold mischief is done. Though in fact a quasi-religious belief, it is speciously clothed with the respectability of a natural law. The truth is that Nature knows no inevitable progress, but only a never-ending struggle; and it is just as easily possible that we should one day clamber up the trees again from which we came down (Gl., pp. 323-24).

But if the theologian has the means for judging, and not merely endorsing, the spirit of the times, whence does he derive them? Certainly not from his Bible alone. The sufficiency of Scripture, which had served as a fundamental principle of the old dogmatics, is firmly rejected. The New Testament, too, is a historical, time-bound entity, severely limited by its eschatological expectations, its demonology, and its anthropomorphic view of God. Not even Jesus can provide the sole religious norm. Rather, Bible and Jesus alike must be viewed in the light of their historical effects over two millennia of the church's history (Gl., pp. 11-13, 27-28).[60] The gospel of Jesus is not the exclusive norm, but the primitive and seminal form of Christian life. Subsequent church history is the development of this life, an its principal carriers have been outstanding personalities like Augustine and the Protestant Reformers.

If one seeks a common name for all this, what commends itself for this end is the name coined in Catholic dogmatics: "tradition." Only, this tradition is not a legal authority, but a body of material to be worked through in freedom [*ein frei durchzuarbeitender Stoff*]. Herein lies the difference between the Protestant conception of tradition and the Catholic; and the modern concept of development has pushed this version of tradition into the foreground, whereas it is a concept lacking in the Reformers, who thought to refer exclusively to the Bible ... [Gl., pp. 21-22]. Catholicism, thinking more practically and realistically than we, recognizes in the gospel only the germ out of which everything else has taken shape. The development of Christianity is not a matter of deviations [*Entfremdungen*], but of growth [*Gewordenes*] (Gl., p. 28).

It hardly needs to be stressed that this represents a remarkable break with the old Protestant dogmatics (though it is not exactly "Catholicizing," either). Dogmatics is shaped by the history of Christianity, no longer by the Bible alone. And history, so far from being an instrument of defense for a system which itself transcends history, now enters constitutively into the dogmatic task. Such a "constitutive historicism" (if we may venture the phrase) is alien both to the old orthodox dogmatics and to the newer dogmatics of neoorthodoxy, whose leader found merely historical questions "frightfully indifferent" (*schrecklich gleichgültig*).[61] It is also alien to any individualistic "theology of the present moment" that presumes itself liberated from the past. For Troeltsch, it is not individual autonomy but history—as the common work of entire generations—that has the first word. A strong and vital faith comes out of history as a revelation, which initially leaves little room for a man's own inventiveness (*Produktion*). Autonomy is not the starting point, but the high point of religious growth; and even from here there is need to turn back repeatedly to the historical resources that awaken and reassure faith. Autonomous insight is not so much productive of spiritual content as it is the mode of its appropriation.[62]

All of which may be very well said. But if one asks less for inspiration and strength than for dogmatic norms, it is obvious that the appeal to "tradition" has its difficulties. Hard enough if we confine ourselves to the complexities of the New Testament! What guidance can possibly be had from an additional two millennia of church history? The old, secure checkpoints of Pauline theology and ecclesiastical creeds dissolve into a forbidding torrent of historical data.[63] Troeltsch admits that the "body of material to be worked through in freedom" is indeed "an enormous one" (Gl., p. 29). So complex and diverse is it, that it is extraordinarily hard to trace the continuity through the centuries or even to be sure that it is ultimately one thing which is the subject of the endless mutations. Certainly, neither transformations nor reformations, even when they sacrifice much of the inherited symbolism, necessarily break the continuity.

They may even make it clearer.[64] But this cannot be asserted as a universal rule.

Troeltsch thinks that there is work here for church historians and historians of dogma, who must locate the continuity in Christian history (Gl., p. 48). Now he does affirm that we can "set our compass" by Jesus and Paul (ibid.); and although he dignifies the entire history of Christianity with the name "revelation," he does assign a certain priority to the primitive revelation.[65] But, when all is said and done, the attempt to extract dogmatic insight from the convolutions of tradition drives inexorably to the conclusion that pure historical science has its limits. Historiography is not dogmatics. The theologian is summoned, in the end, not just to write history, but to make history. Concern with the past thus acquires for Troeltsch what may appropriately be called a strongly "ethical" character: it achieves its finality in a deed to be done.

It is the problem of the "essence of Christianity" or the "Christian principle" that now confronts us. But I am concerned with it only so far as to make a methodological point. It is here that the limits of history (*qua* historical method) are most clearly seen and most frankly acknowledged—here that *Glaubenslehre* ceases to be a strictly demonstrative science and calls for personal impression, the taking of a stand, the risk of decision (Gl., p. 14).[66] In general, no doubt, progress of the Christian principle beyond the original biblical form admits of periodization, and Troeltsch's penetrating historical sketches of the several concepts implicit in the principle generally move from the primitive stage, through the Catholic and "old Protestant," to the "new Protestant" stage. And it is the "new Protestant" form of the Christian principle that is presupposed in present-day *Glaubenslehre* (Gl., pp. 2–3). Pattern in the story is by no means lacking.[67] Nonetheless, the adoption of the principle (in any form) and the determination of its content for the present are results of a decision. The synthesis of past and present occurs in personal religious experience, and it therefore remains ineradicably personal and individual. The selection and shading of the historical materials can never be strictly demonstrated. *Glaubenslehre* therefore remains a religious confession;[68] and the determination of what is essential in the changing religious forms is an ever-new task, in which each must determine the divine for himself, as it has attested itself to him.[69]

"Certainly," Troeltsch remarks in one place, "we feed on the tradition; but this tradition would be dead if the production of those who feed on it did not keep it alive" (Gl., pp. 38–39). The remark tersely conveys the strength of his idea of tradition. But no one will have any difficulty in pointing out its weaknesses. Initially invited to the grandiose historical task of establishing the essence of Christianity from its total development (Gl., p. 13), we are finally summoned to introspection of our own religious experience. The obvious perils of such a method are perhaps most painfully betrayed in Troeltsch's recommendation that we should seek in the Bible such texts as knock at the door of our own soul (Gl., p. 27). Naturally, one would not object to a devotional exercise of this sort did not one suspect that it is continuous with the theological method of Troeltsch. But, in fairness to him, his theology should be approached rather from the other side, on which it is continuous with *historical* method. The quest for essence, he insists, is simply a common enough exercise of modern historical thinking, which must reduce a complex of endlessly manifold phenomena to a central formula. The task can only be accomplished through utter surrender to the historical data. If a certain subjectivity is also requisite, Troeltsch characterizes it as *historical* intuition: that is, as something indispensable to the equipment of a historian. Hence the very method of history in dealing with the past already hovers on the margin of the axiological judgments by which the future is shaped. Nor can there be any question of bringing to the data a fixed and ready-made standard, for the standard must itself emerge in the course of the inquiry (Gl., p. 71).[70]

It would, I suppose, be possible to retort that even cultivated taste is still taste, nothing more. But I myself am inclined to locate the problems less in subjectivity as such, more in Troeltsch's apparent neglect (in this context, at least) of intersubjectivity. He is more eager to justify individual variety—by pointing out that variety has always been there in Christian history (Gl., pp. 331, 354)—than to recall that the theologian does his work along with others. It may be true that the historical task culminates in a judgment that transcends history, an act that is simultaneously the coronation and the abdication of historical theology.[71] But even when he moves beyond historical science, the theologian is not on his own.

We must grant Troeltsch's point that Schleiermacher's theology of consciousness is infinitely more difficult today, when the unified national or territorial communions have dissolved still further into pluralism (Gl., pp. 14-16). We may further agree that the problem of theological diversity is not to be resolved by doing away with professors of theology (Gl., p. 17). We may agree, finally, that dogmatics nowadays can only claim advisory, rather than coercive, status.[72] And yet when all of that is granted, we may still wish that Troeltsch had carried his profound sense of the social character of religion into a more explicit recognition of the corporate character of theology (as of any other academic discipline). His most characteristic sentiment on the subject is that the collective consciousness will take care of itself, automatically controlling the individual judgment and restraining the proliferation of divergent views.[73] His position would, I think, have been strengthened—and even made more consistent with its own principles—had he argued that dogmatics is a collective task. But in the lectures on *Glaubenslehre*, perhaps for autobiographical reasons, he appears to have spoken of it as essentially an individual task.

IV

"Nowhere does autonomy produce the contents of our modern thought and life. Everywhere they rest, for the most part, on tradition and authorities.... In religious thought, this is simply the case in greater degree...."[74] It would be hard to think of a sentiment that more perfectly summed up the major premise of Troeltsch's program. Indeed, it conveys a psychological trait as much as a logical premise—a pervasive attitude, a frame of mind, not just the beginning point of an argument. It embodies, we may say, the protest of the "romantic" against the spirit of enlightenment. In theology, it requires that we begin, not by pretending we know nothing, in order to see what we can prove on this unpromising supposition; but rather by receiving the heritage of faith in all its richness and asking what it all means. Faith goes before *Glaubenslehre*, whose task it is to order the luxuriant growth of faith—its images and ideas—into a systematic whole. Though not able to qualify as an exact science, *Glaubenslehre* is a "scientific treatment and regulation of faith." As such, it must be content to take faith for what it is, not trying to transform it into scientific and rational knowing. Even at the end of the theological task, faith retains a practical and symbolic character (Gl., p. 46). It is faith, we may say, *as a reality of history* that is the primary datum for a theology of consciousness.

"We come to the ever-repeated new birth," so Troeltsch maintains, "through the mediation of history" (Gl., p. 79). This, in large part, is the meaning of divine "grace." Knowledge of God is not simply the result of reflection on the contents of consciousness, but rather something acquired historically *(ein Erwerb der Geschichte)*. It comes to the individual only through history, and therefore it lays hold upon him as a gift of God, a power that grasps and transforms him. True, even as a "power of history" *(geschichtliche Macht)*, it is not the result of an immanent dialectic but always a new and creative revelation of God (Gl., pp. 338–39). Nonetheless, the divine activity is historically mediated, so that grace—the "gift-character" of redemption—is a thoroughly historical idea. Indeed, it coincides with the idea of the church.

> Christian redemption does not spring from religious autonomy. We have received it from history. This does not only mean looking to the person of Jesus as transmitted in history, the one in whose name we take heart toward God. It also means resorting to the Pauline-Johannine doctrine of spirit, by which the death of Jesus wins back its meaning for the idea of redemption. The death of Jesus is the overcoming of what was merely time-bound in his person. It is the great liberation of his spirit through suffering and death, and it makes possible a lively, continuous flow and an enduring contemporaneity from generation to generation. Hence redemption, in trust toward Jesus, is not turned backward. It acquires its connection with history only

because the community which is imbued with the spirit of Christ and which mediates redeeming faith to the individual soul has its origin in the historical figure of Jesus and inwardly regulates and strengthens itself from there (Gl., pp. 360–61).

To receive redemption from history means to receive it through the Christian community. It does not mean simply believing in a once-for-all saving deed, recalled by an effort of the memory. The significance of Jesus' death is that it transformed the individual historical manifestation into a continuing principle, which adapts itself to time and circumstance and is the actual driving force of the Christian community (Gl., pp. 346–47). It is precisely here that Troeltsch discovers the abiding truth of the idea of the "church" as distinct from that of the "sect." The resources of grace are prevenient, antecedent to the individual, in that they are embodied in a historical organism (a *Lebenszusammenhang*) that proceeds from Jesus.[75] The concept of the church, then—the community centered upon the figure of Christ—is one of the ways in which a connection is established between faith and history (Gl., pp. 81–82).

The primacy of history over personal insight, of collective over individual faith, is carried into theology as a methodological principle. A *Glaubenslehre* takes Christianity in its historical givenness. Just as the religious sense itself has precedence over rational argumentation, so the phenomenology of faith has precedence over any theology of proofs. The religious sense articulated by theology in its specifically Christian form is, of course, submitted to "scientific" scrutiny by Troeltsch's philosophy of religion. But this is a far cry from the old natural theologies which sought rational demonstrations for the existence of God. Troeltsch is a "romantic" theologian (my term, not his), who starts from the vitality of the individual forms of life; and he warns against the rationalistic theologies that put religious sensibility at the mercy of their own frigid, meager, and colorless spirit.[76] Dogmatics, Part I, deals, accordingly, with the realities of history. In other words, the primacy of the historical determines the very structure of dogmatics. Here is Troeltsch's version of a *christologischer Ansatz*. He begins his dogmatics with an appraisal of Christian history, centered upon the personality of Jesus, since this history is the vital power by which the Christian relationship to God is attained, strengthened, and anchored. The continuance of the peculiarly Christian organism (or *Lebenswelt*) depends on constantly bringing the historical into the present (Gl., pp. 72–73; cf. Gl., p. 85).

The historical point of view enters, further, into the treatment of particular dogmatic themes as well as into the structure of the whole. Here the two most obvious examples are Troeltsch's handling of the trinitarian and christological dogmas. The Trinity can only be interpreted, not immanently as describing internal relations in the being of God, but "economically" as claiming (more modestly) that the self-disclosure of God in history has its ground in the divine being. We have no need of the philosophical framework by which the Christian conception of God was once differentiated from Neoplatonic emanationism and made into an object of speculation (Gl., pp. 122–24). Similarly, Troeltsch detects in the ancient christology an understandable effort to determine the relationship of Jesus to God, and so to furnish a metaphysical grounding of his person. But he himself is content to keep close to the historical data and to inquire only after Jesus' meaning for faith. "Lord" he finds an acceptable title, but he shows a marked reserve about "Cosmic Redeemer" (Gl., pp. 116–17).

> Jesus was the possibility of redemption. The actual redeemer remains God.... For us personally, this is how things stand: we keep to what is within reach. We place ourselves under the spell of this personality and acknowledge in him our mystical head. Anyone who in good conscience is able to move beyond the psychological significance, should do so. He will then find it easier to make the connection with orthodoxy, since he will be able to speak (in a certain sense) of the "deity" of Christ. With respect to metaphysical interpretations, we owe one another nothing except toleration (Gl., p. 117).

Winsome though many of us may find such metaphysical reserve, it raises at least two problems. And as the historical-experiential starting point is close to the heart of Troeltsch's theology, so the problems touch the heart of the revolt against him. In the first place, does it not appear as though the reality of man's religiousness has become a surrogate for the reality of God? And, in the second place, what becomes of the historical standpoint when the reality of man's religiousness itself suffers attrition?

The former problem reflects the difficulty which many have detected in the entire design of a *Glaubenslehre* as inherited from the "great master." Recall, for instance, Schleiermacher's serious posing of the question whether dogmatics could dispense with propositions about the attributes and operations of God, since the primary dogmatic propositions have to do with the religious affections.[77] Following in Schleiermacher's footsteps, Troeltsch can bluntly assert that "in *Glaubenslehre* we only acquire information about ourselves" (Gl., p. 132). And he refers approvingly to Rothe's judgment that we analyze, not God, but our own idea of God (Gl., p. 131).

It is not difficult to see why Erich Seeberg detected in Troeltsch's theology a weakened interest in the question of truth. Amidst the display of ideas, Seeberg thought, reality and objectivity had fallen into the background; and he seems to have recognized that the alleged retreat from the question of truth had its roots, not only in Troeltsch's epistemology, but also in the historical mode of thought.[78] We could very well press the problem beyond the limits of the God-question and point out that, for Troeltsch, faith cannot give objective knowledge about history, nature, or the self either. Faith is a way of looking at the world, a stance toward the world, an interpretation of things (Gl., pp. 52, 241–42). With respect to history, it is interpretation of facts and cannot be supposed to establish facts

(Gl., p. 100).[79] With respect to the self, we are to understand, when faith speaks of the "soul," not an object of cognition, but an inward attitude of a man towards himself, a seeing of himself in a new light (Gl., pp. 282-83). Should it be pointed out that faith does not always seem to *know* that this is what it is doing, and that it *appears* to be making factual assertions, Troeltsch would presumably reply by referring to his striking, if problematic, notion that the language of faith is the product of the fantasy or imagination and therefore hardly to be confused with scientific judgments.[80] This, too, he believed himself to have learned from Schleiermacher.[81]

It requires a much more thorough investigation than I can attempt here if a just verdict is to be obtained on this apparent subjectivism run riot. It suffices to point out, for now, that Troeltsch no more than Schleiermacher *believed* himself merely to have exchanged the reality of God for the actuality of faith. "We have," he admits, "only the ray which falls upon our own soul" (Gl., p. 131). But the admission is not to be taken for skepticism about the existence of the sun. Even though the craving for proof cannot be gratified, this cannot of itself prevent the conviction that our idea of God comes from God (Gl., pp. 131, 133-34).[82] And although faith's language is supplied by the fantasy, faith is still "cognitive" in the sense that its referent is a "revelatory impulse" (Gl., pp. 42-44). A strong conviction of reality distinguishes faith from the free play of a merely artistic imagination. Against positivism, then, Troeltsch allows symbols a cognitive value, the measure of which is their adequacy to religious experience and not their conformity to the model of objective knowing (Gl., pp. 44-45).

In short, Troeltsch's essentially phenomenological method cannot get beyond the *conviction* of reality—plus a reasonable confidence in the normality of the religious consciousness. He grants the impossibility of taking a strictly scientific look "from the other side." But it simply is not the case that he surrenders the question of truth. Rather, as he expressly argues, the claim to religious truth calls for another apologetic, different in kind from the old natural theology (Gl., pp. 134-35).[83] Apologetics, however, does not properly belong to *Glaubenslehre*, whose business is with "positive, direct proclamation" (Gl., pp. 135-36).

Even if we take this as a satisfactory answer to the first problem, can Troeltsch turn aside the force of the second? Troeltsch was himself a pioneer in the exploration of modern secularism, the drift of Western culture away from its religious heritage. What, then, happens when the drive of our religious history seems to lose its force? One thinks of the remarkable letter the youthful Harnack wrote upon embarking on the study of theology. Even if Christianity were a mistake, would it not still be fascinating, he asks, to trace the history of this mistake, of the earthshaking events it has brought about, of the manner it has penetrated our entire civilization?[84] The invited reply may well be affirmative. But it would be only a call for what Schleiermacher distinguished as "historical theology in the narrower sense or church history."[85] And this was not for Troeltsch! For him, history always meant a task, not mere contemplation of the past. When Spengler's *Decline of the West* was published, it was greeted with a chorus of approval by the theological prophets of impending doom. Troeltsch remained as loftily indifferent to the author's thesis as he was contemptuous of his learning. It was, he announced, a matter of no importance whether our civilization was moving uphill or downhill. All that mattered was the ethical task that history sets before us.[86]

Troeltsch's *Glaubenslehre* is filled with a lively sense of the yet unexhausted possibilities of Christianity for meeting the summons of history. To describe this buoyant confidence was, after all, the very circumspect use to which the Heidelberg theologian put the old—and, surely, already inappropriate—expression "the absoluteness of Christianity."[87] But was the confidence not lost in the deepening gloom of Troeltsch's later years, the profound pessimism that has been documented by his biographers? Well, it is surely possible to attach too much weight to the moods of the moment, evoked (at least in part) by non-theological factors. The supposed nemesis that visits "historicism" has been far too freely seized upon as the theological explanation of his supposed *aporia*. Paradoxically, perhaps, the Heidelberg theologian had already offered historicism as an *antidote* to despondency over the future of Christianity. In one of his keenest observations on the passage of history and its wealth of individual formations, he had indicated how flux and relativity afford reasonable security against the loss of faith in our religious estate. The relativizing of all historical forms implies a relative truth in them all. And no conceivable new religious formation, even though it presupposed the decline of Christian-European culture, could make untrue what was once true, but would rather have to assimilate it.[88] This, too, is a principle of historical development. Perhaps it represents too modest a confidence to satisfy the critics. But is there sufficient reason to believe that nostalgia for something more was bound, in the end, to drive Troeltsch into despair?

Fourteen Jesus, Myth, and History: Troeltsch's Stand in the "Christ-Myth" Debate

On its first appearance (in 1909), *The Christ Myth*—to give the book its English title—evoked a swift, but very mixed response.[1] While dignified scholars showed themselves unimpressed, the contentious essay was greeted with dismay by great numbers of the ordinary faithful. Mass demonstrations confirmed the author's impression that, as he himself put it, he had scored a bull's eye and touched the sore point of Christianity. It gave him mischievous satisfaction when the minister for public worship presented himself at protest meetings, in which choirs sang, strengthened by musical instruments, and professions of loyalty to the old faith were duly executed.[2]

The man who moved the faithful to such heights of indignation and alarm was Arthur Drews, who explained the purpose of his book in these words: "This work seeks to prove that more or less all the features of the picture of the historical Jesus, at any rate all those of any important religious significance, bear a purely mythological character...." The gospel story of the "historical" Jesus, so Drews declared, was a pious fiction of the Christian community. There was no possibility for seeking any such historical figure behind the myth, and none was needed to account for the rise of Christianity. Should anyone assert that there *must* have been a historical figure behind the gospel, it could only be replied: "We know nothing of this Jesus."[3] This, however, was no genuine cause for dismay, since the "historical" Jesus had no religious interest at all, but at most concerned historians and philologists.[4]

The problem of the historical Jesus was scarcely a new one. It had been one of the persistent motifs of nineteenth-century German theology, thanks largely to D. F. Strauss and his critique of Schleiermacher's christology,[5] and in the work of Bruno Bauer it had already issued in doubt whether Jesus ever existed.[6] But it can hardly be claimed that Bauer had greatly shaken the world of German Protestantism. Towards the end of the century, shortly after the death of Albrecht Ritschl, a new phase of the discussion had begun, for which the year 1892 may stand as a convenient marker since it witnessed publication of the

230

notable studies by Kaehler[7] and Weiss.[8] However, renewed discussion had remained the relatively genteel preserve of professional historians and theologians. Arthur Drews's book, by contrast, became a cause célèbre because he enlisted historical skepticism into a vigorous public campaign on behalf of a post-Christian religious philosophy, which called for abandonment of faith in Jesus. To support the written word, a series of conferences and debates were organized, including the Berlin debate of 1910 between Drews and von Soden on the question: "Did Jesus live?"[9] Not all devout churchmen were moved by Drews's campaign. The Protestants in Bremen, for instance, politely declined the invitation to debate the burning issue on the grounds that the historicity of Jesus, though not really dubious, was of no religious interest (as Drews himself had pointed out).[10] But less sophisticated believers could not be quite so cavalier; as far as they could see, Drews and his friends had taken away the Lord, and they knew not where they had laid him.

I

While *The Christ Myth* alarmed many who were innocent of learning, it evoked only Olympian scorn from the historical establishment, who were confident that Jesus had existed; and there were theologians for whom it merely invited the intriguing hypothetical question: What if, in fact, he had not? To whatever effect, then, Arthur Drews's theory excited an astonishingly wide and intense debate. Some of Germany's most distinguished theological scholars addressed themselves to the issue, including Herrmann, Bousset, Weiss, Wobbermin, Loofs, and Troeltsch.[11] And the excitement passed over the Channel and the Atlantic Ocean into the English-speaking world, partly through the pages of *The Hibbert Journal*[12] and *The American Journal of Theology*[13] (precursor of *The Journal of Religion*). My interest is chiefly in Troeltsch's stand in the Christ-myth debate. But it can scarcely be understood except in the context of the wider historical dispute and of other theological options than the one he chose.

As for the professional historians, we may well permit Johannes Weiss to serve as spokesman. "I have been convinced anew," he announced caustically, "that it is the hardest task in the world to prove to nonsense that it is nonsense. I have often felt ashamed, ashamed for our German scholarship, which will need a long while before it has wiped out this stain; ashamed for myself, that I must busy myself with stuff like this. . . ."[14] Weiss could perhaps have taken some small comfort from the fact that Drews, though himself a German, appealed especially to two "foreigners": William Benjamin Smith, an American, and J. M. Robertson, who was British.[15] Indeed, Drews's presentation of his case contained little or nothing that was new. He characterized it as simply a compilation of arguments from the works of others.[16]

The cornerstone of Drews's thesis, on its historical side, was that a Jesus-cult existed among the Jews in pre-Christian times, going back in all likelihood to the Joshua of the Old Testament. It assimilated both Jewish apocalyptic ideas and the Hellenistic motif of a dying and rising redeemer. The Gospels do not record the history of an actual man but convey the Jesus-myth in quasi-historical form. There remains, therefore, no historical object on which faith could rest. The reason why Drews considered this theory no loss at all, on its religious or theological side, was because he found the real heart of Christian doctrine, not in a history, but in an idea or a metaphysical doctrine which must be reformulated in a manner suited to the thought of today. Naturally, Drews no more intended to give permanent validity to the mythological representation of the Incarnate Logos than to the pseudo-historical language of liberal Protestantism. What mattered, for him, was the *idea* of the God-Man: that is, the idea of the divine essence of mankind, an immanent deity which moves and struggles in every creature and overcomes finitude in the consciousness of man. The embodiment of the religious idea in an external divine personality, whether mythological or (supposedly) historical, would be a form of "alienation," a separation of God from man's essence. The old dualism of God and the world was to be overcome by monism. Only, it must not be the prevalent naturalistic monism (of Haeckel), but rather the idealistic monism (of von Hartmann), which counters the fatal superstition of the sole reality of matter.[17]

Drews sometimes cited the names of respectable historians of religion as though they could be numbered on his side. So, for instance, he refers to Sir James Frazer.[18] Naturally, Weiss could hardly have professed embarrassment at the work of such a reputable scholar. But in actual fact the "history of religions" approach to Christian origins had a quite different purpose than Drews (to say nothing of the quite different rigor of its method): namely, to determine *how far* Christian piety and theological reflection had overlaid the historical Jesus with motifs drawn from Hellenistic religions. And Frazer actually dismissed the denial of Jesus' historicity in a curt footnote,[19] even though he was concerned to indicate parallels between Christian and pagan mythology. In other words, for most historians of religions Jesus was an idealized person, not a personified ideal. Even the most skeptical treatments of the primitive documents generally assumed that behind the fanciful narratives of the Gospels lay a real human life. Drews, by contrast, held that the "real" Jesus was a deity—not a deified man, but a humanized god, a mythological divine being who was mistakenly entangled in history. The Gospels, accordingly, were not mythologized history, but historicized myth. So far from standing more or less where most historians of religion stood, Drews really turned their quest upside down. For their part, the liberal theologians did not doubt that Hellenistic accretions had clothed the historical figure of Jesus, as the historians of religions had argued. But they recognized it as quite another thesis when Drews and his associates denied that there ever was a body to clothe.

The Christ-myth theory, then, won little support from the historical specialists. In their judgment, it sought to demonstrate a perverse thesis, and it proceeded by drawing the most farfetched, even bizarre connections between mythologies of very diverse origin. The importance of the theory lay, not in its persuasiveness to the historians (since it had none), but in the fact that it invited theologians to renewed reflection on the questions of faith and history. Suppose the theory *were* persuasive: would it matter? To what extent is the historical Jesus a matter of relevance to faith? And even if the thesis of his nonexistence is an absurdity, does historical inquiry furnish as much information about the real Jesus as faith needs? An improbable historical claim, that there never was a Jesus of Nazareth, raised fundamental questions about the logic of faith. This, after all, was entirely fitting, since Drews never disguised his essentially religious design: to eradicate the romantic Jesus-cult which was supported by the practitioners of a "historical theology."[20] The various answers given to the theological (or religious) questions remain instructive today, long after the name of Arthur Drews has been almost forgotten. The most important difference of opinion lay between the liberal establishment, for whom the old house still stood firm, and the rationalist dissenters, who thought it was time for a move. I shall also make mention, in passing, of a third party: the conservatives, who surveyed the debate between liberals and rationalists from the detached security of their more ancient mansion.

By the "liberal" theologians is meant, at this time, the spiritual descendants of Schleiermacher and the mediating theology, most of whom were more or less closely linked with the so-called "Ritschlian school." Radical criticism of the Gospels was a more acute problem for liberalism than for orthodoxy, which remained relatively indifferent to the details of Jesus' ministry and was prepared to stake all on the saving efficacy of his death. Ritschlianism, on the other hand, to put it in the words of William Adams Brown, was nothing other than "the attempt to rethink the whole material of theology in the light of the life, teaching, and character of Jesus."[21] Such a program went well just as long as it could be claimed with confidence that historical criticism had given only a more human Jesus and therefore a more suitable object of religious apprehension.[22] The situation was radically changed, however, when the liberals, long accustomed to pointing out fictitious elements in the traditional christology, had to face the *tu quoque* argument that their Jesus, too, was fiction. The fundamental weakness in the christology of Schleiermacher was exposed, we may say, for the second time. It was Schleiermacher, above all, who had turned theology away from the rationalism of the Enlightenment and had sought the vitality of genuine religiousness in history rather than ideas. Hence it was the personal life of Jesus, not the dogma of the Incarnation, that he had identified as the moving force behind the Christian community. Strauss, certainly, had already raised the question whether the picture of the Christ operative in the Christian community could be so readily identified with the historical Jesus as Scheiermacher claimed. But by the turn of the century the dominant theology felt secure in its historical knowledge. The recourse to history (or supposed history) was even more emphatically affirmed than by Schleiermacher, and one of the meanings of *der Historismus* (or *der historisierende Standpunkt*) at this time was the attempt to establish the content and confidence of faith wholly upon the historical.[23]

Of course, the Ritschlians did not deny that much in the gospel tradition was of dubious historical worth. But their characteristic move was to turn from the "petty details" to the "essence of Jesus' message and the permanent significance of his personality and work."[24] This was by no means intended to imply that faith could be reduced to judgments of fact, supported by the authority of biblical scholarship. Rather, the historical data furnished materials, so it was held, for a judgment of worth—of the meaning of Jesus' person and work.[25] But such value-judgments could scarcely be disentangled from historical inquiry, which was presumed competent to determine what was in fact the fundamental thing in the Gospels. And it turned out that history could not be relied upon always to establish the desired theological result. Most notably, there seemed to be no way for a strictly historical method to justify the liberal notion of the ethical kingdom of God. As Bousset (and others) pointed out, another norm was operative here, not derived from the historical data themselves.[26] Less gentle was the verdict of Drews. No doubt, he went too far when he proclaimed that liberal Protestantism had been "pierced to the heart by the denial of the historical personality of Jesus" since it was not able, like the religion of Catholicism, to dispense with the fiction of his historicity.[27] The liberals never took the denial seriously enough to be mortally wounded. But Drews came closer to making a hit when he threw the charge of defective method, leveled against him, back to his theological critics: *they* imposed *their* Jesus-religion on the sources and "discovered" in the New Testament, as its moral-religious kernel, "the incarnation of the modern ideal of personality, or of some other fashionable theological view."[28]

While the liberals continued to insist that the sources really did yield a human Jesus, the conservatives, for their part, thought they yielded something much more. The German historian of dogma, Friedrich Loofs, for example, held that history is simply not competent to deal exhaustively with the sources insofar as it is bound to interpret the past on the analogy of present experience. Although none of the sayings attributed to Jesus is known, with certainty, to be free from the shaping influences of the community, the general impression of his words transcends purely human categories.[29] In America, a similar point was urged by the hyperorthodox Princeton theologian, Benjamin B. Warfield, who announced regally: "That the liberal theology has travailed and brought forth a monstrous birth [Drews's *The Christ Myth*] is not surprising; nor is it surprising that the fruit of its womb should turn and rend it."[30] For himself, Warfield found no occasion to panic over the historicity of Jesus, since he held that an unbiased historical criticism presents, not just an actual Jesus, but a supernatural Christ.[31]

But more interesting than his own rather conventional and wholly predictable standpoint are the views of a third party, whose members he distinguishes as "extreme radicals" and places as far beneath concern with the historicity of Jesus as the conservatives are above it. In agreement with the rationalism which finds Lessing's "ugly ditch" impassable, these radicals will not rest faith on the contingencies of history—whether out of genuine philosophical conviction or because of historical anxiety. ("They are not so much tempted to despise Jesus because he is historical as they are tempted to despair of him for fear he is not historical enough.") And so they turn for security to rational ideas that shine in their own light.[32]

Among his American representatives of this radicalism, Warfield names Douglas C. Macintosh,[33] and the cap may well seem to fit nicely. To the question, "Is belief in the historicity of Jesus indispensable to Christian faith?" Macintosh had replied cautiously: "Not indispensable, though very valuable." Essential Christianity, which is chiefly a filial relationship with a fatherly God, he explained, has generally found in Jesus its supreme historic exemplar. The loss of the exemplar would be serious, but not altogether irreparable.[34] In a rejoinder to a critical note by Shailer Mathews, Macintosh pointed out that a particular historic fact may be necessary to the well-being of Christian faith, but only its theological conceptions are essential to its very being.[35] It seems not to have occurred to Macintosh, in propounding his *bene esse* doctrine of historicity, to consider whether a purely mythical or symbolic Christ might serve the pedagogical needs of faith just as well. This, however, is exactly what Wilhelm Bousset did consider; and in so doing he displayed much more purely the rationalism of the radical type.

According to Bousset,[36] history cannot introduce anything strictly new. The religious ideas of the unity, purpose, and spirituality of the world shine with their own innate certainty. They are validated by reason's inability to do without them. Now this certainly looks like the reappearance of the old eighteenth-century rationalism which, just a few years earlier, Harnack was proclaiming outdated: the view that religion is a fixed endowment of nature and reason, so that a man can receive from history nothing he does not already possess.[37] But Bousset concedes to the nineteenth century at least this much: that the ideas of religion only emerge in history and only attain to clarity through laborious reflection. Still, so far from needing the authority of history, they become the measure by which history itself is judged and the transient distinguished from the eternal even in the person of Jesus. Against Schleiermacher, it must be maintained that for *cognition* ideas are the ultimate basis of religion, not mere feelings transmitted through the psychological influence of outstanding personalities. It does not follow, however, that the historical is merely a temporary crutch, as the older rationalism supposed. For practical *faith* cannot live directly upon ideas: it lives, rather, upon images and symbols in which the naked ideas are clothed. So, for instance, the meaning and value of the world are conveyed to faith through the image of the Father's care for the lilies of the field.

Bousset did not doubt that the bearers of the unfolding religious life of mankind are indeed the great religious personalities: first, because it is they who *create* the symbols of faith; second, because they themselves *become* symbols for the believing community. Nonetheless, he believed that his train of argumentation permitted him to lay to rest anxiety over the historicity of the Gospels. For if the picture of Jesus is correctly understood as symbol, there is no need to draw a line between truth and fiction, between what is historical in it and what may be the creation of the religious community. The reality, in any case, lies behind the symbol in the depths of reason. Faith could even survive the extreme, but unlikely, verdict of historical science that Jesus never existed at all.[38]

Troeltsch, for one, did not agree. He thought it would be all over with Christianity if the historicity of Jesus were ever disproved. His reasons for this drastic stand are very instructive, but, in my opinion, not necessarily entailed by his most basic historicist principles. The next step will be to locate Troeltsch's position in relation to the three options already described before testing it by the principles of his own *Theologie des Historismus.*[39]

II

Troeltsch's formulation of the problem is choicely phrased.[40] The primitive church made Jesus a suitable object for faith by taking him out of history and making him a divine being who appears in historical form. But historical criticism has given him back again to history. Is it, then, any longer possible to speak of an essential significance of Jesus for faith? To begin with, it had seemed as though criticism simply yielded a more human Jesus, but it soon became apparent how risky it is to burden faith with facts that are open to historical inquiry. To be sure, the question whether Jesus existed is silly, and the claim that he did not is monstrous. But the extremes of radical criticism do highlight a genuine problem: Is faith inseparably tied to Jesus—to a story which is at the mercy of historical science?[41]

Naturally, it is not a problem that can be taken seriously by orthodoxy, for which redemption is a saving deed wrought in the person of the God-Man. Since the old scheme of redemption stands or falls with the persuasion that Christ was a real historical person, even to raise the question of faith and history would be to issue the death certificate of Christianity. The orthodox will see it as their sole task to defend the superhuman nature of this Christ against those who are blinded by the arrogance of reason and to depose pastors who are unsound on this point.[42] The question has meaning only because a large number of present-day Christians no longer think in the old ways, including Troeltsch himself. For them, redemption is an ever-new work of God in the soul, effected through faith. It is practical knowledge of the innermost nature of God's will. Or, to put it in the current style, Christianity is a religious "idea" or "principle," and many have held that, once introduced into history, it stands by its own resources. A permanent, inner connection between Christianity and Jesus (its historical point of departure) is therefore not required.[43]

The liberal theologies are considered by Troeltsch under the rubric of "mixed forms" or the "mediating type," since they seek a compromise between orthodoxy and modernity, which seem at first to offer only an exclusive choice. Unlike the purely orthodox, the mediating theologians—Schleiermacher, Ritschl, Herrmann—accept the modern view of Christianity as *Glaubenserkenntnis Gottes* ("knowledge of God in faith"). But they still maintain a "relative inner necessity" for the historical person of Jesus on the grounds that there are impediments to the natural emergence of faith. Spiritual impotence must be overcome by the impact of Jesus' personality, mediated through the Scriptures and the church. A man is thereby enabled to receive the faith which otherwise lies beyond his grasp. It is not in question that Christianity is an idea of God, a faith-knowledge of what he is like. The historical personality of Jesus is needed, however, to evoke the faith and make the idea effective. Hence a compromise is brought about between the old idea of the historical Redeemer and the new idea of Christianity as essentially an understanding of God (a *Gottesgedanke*).[44]

The difficulty with such a compromise, Troeltsch argues, is first of all that it operates with the highly problematic notion of a personal relationship with Jesus, analogous to the impact of one man upon another. Historical criticism can only make such a notion still more problematic. If, on the other hand, the emphasis is shifted from direct encounter to the mediation of the community, then the argument for the connection with the historical person is undercut.[45] Further, Troeltsch finds in the hybrid varieties a lingering absolutism that continues to regard Jesus and the church as the sole redemptive spheres, outside of which the whole of mankind is shut up in total inability. And that is simply not historical thinking. Such christocentrism is the theological counterpart to geocentrism in cosmology—that is, an instance of outdated provincialism which elevates our own situation into a universal view. Modern thought will rather see the divine life breaking through at various nodal points of history, not exclusively in Jesus or the church.[46]

What, then, is the solution to our problem if the mediating theology can no more be sustained than orthodoxy? Must the knot be cut, and each man be left free to develop his own individual religious insight? Troeltsch does not think so. For the evidence does not bear out the assumption that individual religious faith *can* propagate itself by its own resources. It seems, rather, to live off the inherited resources of the churches. Religious individualism turns out to be mere utopianism, which overlooks the indispensable role of community and cult. Indeed, community and cult are deliberately excluded insofar as they savor of magic and mysteries; and any gathering of a community around a religious leader is ruled out as "historical." In their place are put solitary meditation or lectures on religion. "This lack of community and cult," Troeltsch observes, "is the actual sickness of modern Christianity and of modern religiousness in general." Lacking a single, dominant center, religiousness today has as many centers as individuals. Hence it has become chaotic and feeble. And yet it is one of the clearest findings of the history and psychology of religion that the essential thing in all religion is not dogma and idea, but cult and community.[47]

Troeltsch's own solution to the problem of faith and the person of Jesus is already implicit in these critical remarks against religious individualism. The place of Jesus in Christianity must be explained from the essentially social character of lively religion. In the ethical-spiritual religions cult and community are not established by magical rituals, as in the religions of nature, but rather by "the representation of a spiritual possession ... in a normative archetype."[48] From the first, Christianity took the form of a Christ-cult: it organized itself around reverence for Christ as the revelation of God.

> But what the original motive was for the rise of faith in Christ and for the attachment of the new faith in God to the cult of Christ, that it still is today (under other forms and conditions). . . . In the religions of spirit, it is the prophets and founding personalities who serve as archetypes [*Urbilder*], authorities, sources of power, rallying points. As images of personally concrete life, they are capable of that infinitely flexible and adaptable interpretation which no mere doctrine and no mere dogma have. At the same time, they possess a vividness and plasticity that appeal, not to theory and understanding, but to the imagination and feeling. . . . What is fundamental for community and cult is everywhere the representation [*Vergegenwärtigung*] of the prophets or, at the highest limit, the veneration of them as divine because they express the common divine truth, and not because they are additions to the pantheon. . . . Accordingly, a cult illuminated by the Christian idea will always have to have for its center the gathering of the community around its head, the nourishment and strengthening of the community by immersion in the revelation of God contained in the image of Christ [*Christusbild*], and propagation not through dogmas, doctrines, and philosophies, but by handing on [*Ueberlieferung*] and keeping alive the image of Christ— the adoration of God in Christ. As long as there will be a Christianity in any sense at all, it will be bound up with a cult that puts Christ in the center. Either that is how it will be, or else it will not be at all. This rests on social-psychological laws that have produced just the same phenomenon in the domains of other religions. . . .[49]

Granted the insight and even the eloquence of this argument, one may be surprised to recollect that it must, in Troeltsch's opinion, point toward an affirmation of Jesus' historicity. A solution to the problem of faith and the historicity of Jesus is, of course, the purpose of the entire discussion.[50] And yet the objection to Troeltsch's argument so far is obvious: If we allow that the Christian church requires a rallying point, and that only the image (or picture) of Christ can meet the requirement, why can we not be content with the image of Christ in the church's consciousness? Do we need to trace it back to the Jesus of history? Troeltsch does not hesitate to call Jesus the "symbol" of Christian faith.[51] Plainly, a further premise is required for execution of the argument if it is to demonstrate the need for connecting the symbol with the historicity of Jesus. And Troeltsch finally supplies the missing premise.[52] In so doing, he takes up his stand toward my third type, the "radical" or "rationalist" position that I illustrated from Wilhelm Bousset.[53] It is, he protests, mere aestheticism to expect the believer to satisfy his life-hunger with a purely mythical symbol when what he wants, rather, is to stand with his symbol on "the firm ground of real life." It is of genuine importance to him that a real man so lived, struggled, believed, and overcame, and that from this real life a stream of power and assurance flow down to himself. The symbol is a real symbol for the believer only because there stands behind it the stature of an exceptional and real religious prophet. The gathering of the community around Jesus must go back to a real life if it is to possess power and truthfulness.

The consequences of this final link in the argument are clearly seen and fully accepted: it is impossible to insulate faith against historical-critical inquiry. The "fact of Christ," like any other fact lying in the past, is given only in the form of evidence or "reports," and can accordingly be established only by historical investigation. This, however, is not to be understood as though Troeltsch were calling for a *Leben-Jesu-Forschung*, a quest for the historical Jesus in the sense of an attempt to do his biography. Rather, Troeltsch makes the characteristically "Ritschlian" move of dispensing with the details and concentrating upon the basic traits (*Grundzüge*) of Jesus' preaching and personality. "These it must be possible to establish as historical reality by historical-critical means if the 'symbol of Christ' is to have a firm and strong inner foundation in the 'fact' of Jesus."[54] Since not every little detail matters to faith, it is not at the mercy of the New Testament scholars as they pursue their endless arguments about the minutiae of interpretation. But at the very least the Christian community does require a general sense of historical reliability with respect to its foundations, and this only historical inquiry can give. In the end, then, there is a measure of dependence of faith upon scholars and professors.[55] And Troeltsch bluntly concludes: "The battle must be fought out. Should it be decided unfavorably to the historicity or even the knowability of Jesus, then that really would be the beginning of the end of the symbol of Christ...." For skepticism would inevitably percolate down from the scholars to the masses.[56]

III

As Troeltsch saw it, the Christ-myth debate posed once more the old Enlightenment question: Why should Jesus be considered anything more than the historical point of departure for a self-sufficient idea? He offered his response in two distinguishable steps, which are not, perhaps, of equal cogency. First, he maintained that the Christian community lives by constant recollection of the image of Christ. Second, he added that the image has efficacy only so long as the community trusts the basic correspondence of the image to a life actually lived. The difference of this standpoint from that of orthodoxy (or conservatism) is sufficiently obvious. It differs, further, from the mediating, liberal theology, not in holding firmly to the centrality of Christ (in Step 1), but in the nature of the reason advanced for so doing. It differs, finally, from the radical or rationalist view in the conviction (Step 2) that a purely mythical symbol would be insufficient.

No doubt, there are features in the first step of the argument which could be questioned. Troeltsch's notion of the community's "head" invites a somewhat one-sided interpretation of Christ as a religious leader, a prophet.[57] But this seems to be more or less accidental to the presentation, as could be proved from other places where Troeltsch develops more fully the content, as distinct from the status, of the Christian symbol.[58] Again, one could ask just how well founded is the alleged social-psychological law itself on which the status of Christ as leader of the community is made to rest.[59] But the sociological character of the argument is not really contingent upon establishing any such law. The claim is that the phenomenon of christocentrism expresses a social need, and this could well be so even though the phenomenon did not exemplify a universal sociological law. And it is a very persuasive claim, whether or not it provides a sufficient explanation for the phenomenon in question.

The achievement of Troeltsch was of the same order as Schleiermacher's achievement: he showed how the centrality of Christ could be grounded in a new way, when the old ways had broken down. He succeeded in explaining and justifying the heart of evangelical piety while surrendering the dogmatic foundations on which it had once been made to rest. Instead of the infallible Word of God, it was the Christian consciousness for Schleiermacher, and for Troeltsch a social need, which accounted for—and even warranted—the central place of Christ in Christian thought and worship. Indeed, I think one must go further and argue that Troeltsch did not so much achieve something analogous to Schleiermacher's achievement, but rather exploited Schleiermacher's own insights in ways that the real master of *Glaubenslehre* had perhaps not carried through consistently. As a matter of fact, Troeltsch himself concedes this toward the end of his essay. His solution, he admits, is not far removed from what he has called the "mixed" or "mediating" type. The results for the practical task of proclamation are similar. Only, he grounds his case differently, appealing to a general social phenomenon and not to the vestiges of an outdated dogma.[60]

> This social-psychological point of view is accordingly the one under which our problem must chiefly be seen.... In placing the personality of Jesus at the center, Christianity does not possess some special characteristic that sets it apart from all other religions and makes redemption a possibility for it alone. Rather, it is simply fulfilling, in its own characteristic manner, a law common to the life of the human spirit. Hence what is decisive for assessing the meaning of Jesus is not mankind's inability for redemption outside of Christianity, but the need of the religious community for a hold, a center, a symbol of its religious life.[61]

And it follows that we can show the centrality of Christ only for Christianity, not (as in the mediating theology) his centrality for all mankind.[62] But if this indicates an apparent departure from Schleiermacher, Troeltsch still recognizes that Schleiermacher was the pioneer in the sociologizing or (what comes to the same thing) the historicizing of theology.[63] Schleiermacher, and the Ritschlians after him, grasped the significance of Jesus' person as the formative factor in creating the Christian community. Only they failed to affirm this insight consistently and explicitly. Instead, they accommodated their christological claims to the accepted modes of dogmatic expression.[64] All Troeltsch finally asserts for himself, then, is that he has carried through more consistently the theological program of Schleiermacher,[65] applying a fundamentally historical and sociological approach to the problem posed by the Christ-myth debate. The question remains, however, whether the consistent historicizing of theology requires also the other step of the argument, by which Troeltsch tried to establish the need for the community's image of Christ to be demonstrably founded in an actual human life.

One may well agree with Troeltsch that the "Christianness" of the Christian principle is secured by constant reference to the personality of Jesus, and that this must be maintained against the rationalist tendency to fall back on highly abstract ideas.[66] One may further agree that the picture of Christ cannot be taken as "mythical" in Troeltsch's aesthetic sense—as a myth without an object, a myth which dispenses with any foundation in reality. Against the "aestheticizing game which is so often played with realities nowadays," Troeltsch protests that it is not the intent of the religious symbol just to gratify a playful desire of the imagination, even though it does appeal to the imagination. Neither will he allow that a myth is sufficient just because it is "ever so beautiful."[67] But *does it follow* that therefore the "symbol of Christ" cannot do its work unless the community which gathers around it is assured of its correspondence to the "fact of Jesus"? Of course, Troeltsch does not mean that every believer must do his own historical homework. As a matter of fact, he speaks of faith as reaching back to a historical foundation that is "present to the imagination."[68] Faith is not, as such, an exercise in historiography. Rather, the layman trusts his instinct for what is essential in the gospel tradition.[69] But it is just this instinct, Troeltsch believes, that could be inhibited by unwelcome news from the world of historical scholarship.

Here, it seems, Troeltsch makes an unwarranted move. He insists that a religious symbol must be rooted in history,[70] and from this he infers—invalidly, I think—that faith therefore needs assurance about the historical Jesus. In so doing, he identifies the historical anchorage of the symbol with its (putative) historical origins. But, surely, the very fact that the symbol is embedded in the life of a community gives it the concreteness and factual givenness which Troeltsch desires. And one must ask whether Troeltsch has followed through consistently enough his own insight that there is a world of difference between the pedagogical symbol, which an individual is free to use or not to use as he chooses, and the cultic symbol, by which a religious community is actually constituted. If the symbol belongs to the community, and maintains the community in being, it has an objectivity which places it over against the individual. Why may not this, of itself, constitute the required historical roots? What is crucial for the picture of Christ, if it is to qualify as a "historical" symbol, is not that it corresponds to the life once lived by a particular individual but that it exists, embodied in the corporate life of the Christian community, as the sacramental word by which the community is continually re-created. This is what makes it possible for faith to happen, to occur as an event of the present.[71]

Naturally, to sustain this line of criticism adequately would call for fuller development of the implied alternative. But I think it can at least be shown, without the need to step outside the framework of the Christ-myth debate, that the criticism points to a dissonance within Troeltsch's own thinking. More cautiously: Troeltsch's own most basic principles do not seem to demand the second step in his argument. On the contrary, his concepts of religious experience, tradition, and the believing community all contain features which tend in another direction, but which nonetheless lie close to the heart of his own historical thinking.

In the first place, assurance, for Troeltsch, grows out of the life and experience of the present. He identifies himself with the "modern" view that the knowledge of God is substantiated in the events of one's own experience, as the inherited religious knowledge is transformed into one's own awareness of divine disclosure.[72] Now it is significant that this sense of a revelation experienced in the present affords Troeltsch reassurance concerning the prospect for Christianity: the as yet indeterminate possibilities of the future do not devalue such experienced power and truth as are possessed in the present. Hence the haunting anxiety of relativism must be beaten out of one's head and the divine resolutely grasped as it offers itself now.[73] Granted the rule of laying hold upon present possessions, why need Troeltsch have been hesitant to assert of the past what he asserted of the future? Both sorts of anxiety—over the past origins as well as the future validity of the Christian symbol—could have been laid aside if neither past nor future can invalidate the truth and life which are mediated by the symbol in the present. Indeed, in the *Glaubenslehre* Troeltsch explicitly infers from the centrality of present experience that the reference of faith to Jesus is a secondary moment: it arises from reflection on the foundations of the community and its picture of Christ. "Faith in Christ is actually effected only through present experience of redemption: for the sake of this experience, we revere the starting point of this life as divine revelation."[74]

In the second place, even in Troeltsch's perspective on the past interest shifts from the point of origins to the total historical development, from the historical Jesus to the Spirit of Christ. The personality of Jesus does not come under consideration merely as a historical occurrence. As such, he was subject to the limitations of any historical person. We are not to view him within the confines of his appearance but in the full radiance of his effects, seeing in him what two millennia of church history have drawn from him.[75] In the *Glaubenslehre*, Troeltsch takes the position that it was death that released the Spirit of Christ from his historical limitations and made of him a continuing principle which changes with time and necessity. Hence it is the Spirit of Christ that is the actual driving force of the Christian community. Troeltsch does, to be sure, make the characteristic remark that the fundamental Christian ideas are taken from the original historical manifestation. Still, he insists that redemption as a present experience is connected with the Christ who is present in the Spirit, and that it takes place through the mediation of the Christian community.[76] Plainly, while he could not set aside the question of origins, as though it were of no significance for faith, he did judge its role to be strictly relative and limited. The initial event is only a part of a larger whole. It is the germ of a total growth, which Troeltsch names "tradition."[77] At the least, we may conclude that such a notion hardly calls for a drastic stand which stakes everything on knowledge of the historical Jesus.[78] And when Troeltsch admits that the fact of Jesus does not have to bear the whole burden alone,[79] we may well ask why it cannot *resign* the whole burden to the evidences of Christ's Spirit in the total story of the church. The answer cannot be that Jesus was a unique figure who stood, and stands, apart from common humanity. Such notions are entirely foreign to Troeltsch. He places Jesus in a series of strong religious personalities, who have drawn from him no differently than he drew from the prophets.[80]

The point can only be strengthened if we ask, further, what exactly it is, according to Troeltsch, that undergoes the total historical development. It is, of course, a symbol—the image or picture of Christ. He thinks it a special merit of Christ-centered piety that it functions with a flexible symbol, not an inflexible dogma, and he acknowledges that more goes into the symbol than was present at its inception.[81] Does it not follow that, for Troeltsch himself, the historical roots of the symbol are to be found in the life-history of the symbol itself? The historical referent of faith, from the very first, was not a biography but an impression, which is a historical magnitude with its own life-story. Troeltsch's entire dogmatics rests on the conviction that the church's proclamation must reinterpret the picture of Christ by using the full resources of Christian history, that is, of tradition.[82] Against this total context of his response to the Christ-myth theory, it is hard to see why, except as a momentary lapse, he could have risked assigning decisive significance to the question of origins—understood as the question of correspondence between the symbol and Jesus as he actually was.

In the third place, it follows (from our second point) that the actual historical resources of faith are gathered up as the present possession of the Christian community, in which, if anywhere, faith finds assurance. The power of the new life, according to Troeltsch, is mediated through the church.[83] It is not directly a matter of historical inquiry. To him, the meaning of "grace" is precisely that redemption is mediated to the individual through the community as an acquisition of history *(ein Erwerb der Geschichte)*, and so it lays hold upon him as a gift. Here "historical power" *(geschichtliche Macht)* coincides with the reality of the church.[84] The proximate source of assurance is the accumulated experience of the Christian community. And if we seek the source, in turn, of this corporate strength, it lies in an impression which lives on precisely in the corporate experience itself. "The impression of the personality of Jesus, *as it lives on interpreted by the life of faith of countless generations*, is, in the final analysis, what humbles us and raises us up and makes us sure of this knowledge of God."[85]

IV

There cannot, of course, be any presumption of having refuted Troeltsch from his own mouth, as though the second step in his argument betrayed actual contradictions. On the contrary, he is remarkably consistent in affirming the connection between the historicity of Jesus and the notions of religious experience, tradition, and the Christian community. The point, rather, is that the connection is not a necessary one, in the sense of being deducible from the notions themselves.[86] Neither did Troeltsch claim that it was. More, his principles at least *could* have led him in another direction, and one must ask of Troeltsch the kind of question *he* addressed to the mediating theologians: whether he had quite freed himself from certain dispensable presuppositions of orthodoxy. And if the critique is made along these lines, then the difficulties in Troeltsch's answer to

Drews need not herald the imminent demise of his entire theology.[87] Surgery may be called for, but not a funeral.

What exactly, then, is the nature of the connection Troeltsch sought to establish between faith and the historicity of Jesus? Troeltsch told us explicitly: it is purely psychological.[88] That is to say, the confidence of the believer, so Troeltsch feared, would be shaken if he were given reason to doubt the historicity of Jesus or even the possiblility of knowing about him. This may well be an accurate psychological observation. But the question remains whether the psychological need, in this instance, does not call for therapy rather than indulgence. The social-psychological need for cult and community may well be unavoidable if a sturdy religion is to survive. But the yearning for reliable information about the historical Jesus can be indulged only at the cost of taking at least two serious risks. First, there is the risk of not permitting historians a free hand in their examination of the New Testament sources. The mechanics of the psychological need for a historical Jesus were perhaps discerned correctly by Drews. He accused the liberals of projecting their ideal onto a supposedly historical figure, not because the evidence had compelled them, but in order to reassure themselves of the reality of their ideal.[89]

Second, there is the risk of undermining faith simply by allowing that so much—indeed, everything—hangs on a cheerful report from the New Testament scholars. The very posing of the historical question, when the stakes are so high, may be tantamount to issuing Christianity's death certificate, as Troeltsch put it in his own case against orthodoxy. The comforting word that the consensus of sound scholarship presently eschews radical extremes is not likely to achieve its end if one adds: But if at any time it did not, it would be all over with Christianity. This, it seems to me, is the inescapable psychological response to the psychological part of Troeltsch's argument. And it leaves him, practically speaking, no more secure than orthodoxy. The necessity for the God-Man survives in Troeltsch's thinking only as a psychological need—a need to know that the symbol is rooted in a life once lived. But on neither view could faith preserve its serenity as the historians go untrammelled about their business.[90] Or if it could, that would simply reveal the fact that faith's security lies, after all, elsewhere than in favorable results from historical research.[91] And that is exactly what was argued by another group of participants in the Christ-myth debate, whom we have not considered but who might be classified as a "left wing" of the liberal theology.

If we ask, in conclusion, about the direction Troeltsch could have taken to avoid the risks, then the answer lies, I suspect, somewhere along the path trodden by theologians of this fourth group, especially Troeltsch's distinguished adversaries, Herrmann and Wobbermin, and the lesser-known Wilhelm Fresenius.[92] Herrmann's argument was that facts which support the assurance of faith must be facts grasped in our own experience, not external narratives guaranteed by historical inquiry. Whatever the findings of historical scholarship, the personal life of Jesus can at least become a fact experienced by us *(ein von uns erlebte Tatsache)* if only we can gain a picture of this life through the New Testament.[93] It is but a short step from Herrmann's notion of an "experienced fact" to the claim that the saving event is itself a fact of our experience. And in Wobbermin we find the contention that this fact of experience has the character of a historical *(geschichtlich)* event. "No historical criticism can infringe upon its value to anyone who has had this experience of the picture [of Christ] and continues to have it anew."[94]

Fresenius's case, directed expressly to Troeltsch, was similar. Faith is essentially a "historical" experience in the sense that it is a matter of man's historical existence—his existence as an ethical agent in community. For "history" *(Geschichte) is* human life in community *(das menschliche Gemeinschaftsleben).*[95] Where a man of moral sincerity is found, the picture of Jesus can shine upon him from the pages of the Gospels with liberating force. It may remain a mystery just how such an influence "from person to person" is possible. "And yet," Fresenius affirms, "we stand before this fact, must acknowledge it in our life and know how to treasure it as the best thing in human life."[96]

Troeltsch remained sharply critical of Herrmann and Wobbermin. To say nothing of the arbitrary distinction between *Historie* and *Geschichte*, on which Wobbermin rested his case, Troeltsch could have no patience with Herrmann's talk about experiencing the personal life of Jesus. Further, he would brook no suggestion, as we have seen, that faith could make a judgment about what must have happened in the past.[97] Yet neither Herrmann nor Wobbermin, any more than Kaehler before them, could resist the temptation to move back from the confidence of faith to confidence in the historicity of the Synoptic Jesus.[98] Surely, Troeltsch had good reason to be skeptical of this move. For it is either a historical *(historisch!)* argument from effect back to cause; in which case, Strauss's critique of Schleiermacher ought at least to serve as a warning. Or else it is an inference of, and not merely from, faith; in which case, it cannot be anything more than a judgment of faith. One recalls, as a parallel case, Thomas Hobbes's sly observation that if any one says God spoke to him in a dream, this is no more than to say he dreamed that God spoke to him.[99] One cannot, by faith, acquire historical knowledge of Jesus' historicity; one can only believe it.

Nonetheless, it does seem to me that the essential shift proposed by Herrmann and Wobbermin—the relocation of the fact on which faith depends—was by no means incompatible with Troeltsch's own historical theology. And although I do not intend to argue anything more than this, it would be less than candid of me not to admit that I think it represents an improvement on Troeltsch's stand in the Christ-myth debate. The sole alternatives are not either to demonstrate the truth of religion by historical research or to show it by rational deduction. There is a third alternative, which Wobbermin called "discovering" or "reaching" the truth *(Auffindung, Erlangung)* as it presents itself in actual historical experience *(Geschichte)*.[100] As Wobbermin put it, what pertains to historical science cannot possibly be treated as fundamental, since it has a completely secondary character.[101] To this only one further word needs to be added: although the nature of faith is essentially *geschichtlich,* the language of theology can only be *historisch.* For as Wobbermin himself defines it, historical inquiry *(Historie)* is simply experienced history *(Geschichte)* that has been, or is to be, submitted to disciplined investigation.[102]

Theology, we may surely infer, must therefore be "historical theology"—if its essential business is simply to give a disciplined account of historical experience. And this is something that nobody has perceived more clearly than Troeltsch himself. Naturally, the relevance of *this* enterprise to faith, like the explication of the Christian symbol (with which it is closely connected), is another question, distinct from the question of Jesus' historicity. Whatever may be said about it, there surely cannot be any need for faith to await the latest results with anxiety. Explications of the life of faith and the Christian symbol will always vary. But the symbol survives them all, and it has the surprising power to speak for itself. It is not the task of the historical theologian to prove anything, but only to understand what is indubitably there. He can never be more, and should be no less, than a hearer of the Word.

Fifteen   Strasbourg Revisited: Reformed Perspectives on the Augsburg Confession

"The fact is, and it is useful to recognize this in the first place, that there is nothing in the Augsburg Confession which is not in agreement with our own teaching." So claimed John Calvin, the most eminent Reformed theologian of the sixteenth century, at a time when the Lutheran and Reformed communions were still in their youth.[1] But could one today reaffirm his amicable opinion? Or is the relationship between "the two Reformation churches"[2] better reflected in the truculent disdain of Karl Barth, the most eminent Reformed theologian of the twentieth century? To Otto Weber Barth confided (in a letter of 20 June 1949): "It really needs a wooden forehead and a brain to match to want to convince oneself and others that [the Augsburg Confession] is the rock on which today's church has to be built."[3]

I

With the wisdom acquired in recent years, the historian may initially be inclined to agree with Calvin. During the twentieth century, Barth's scathing remark notwithstanding, conversations between the two communions have repeatedly led to harmony, if not to uniformity, of confession. One thinks, for instance, of the Arnoldshain Theses (1957), agreed upon by representatives of the territorial churches in Germany—Lutheran, Reformed, and United—after the Second World War, albeit without the approval of one absent delegate. The ecumenical experience of "growing together" had been intensified by the German church struggle; and there was, besides, a confident expectancy that progress in the theological disciplines (notably, in biblical exegesis) had opened the possibility of transcending the old battle lines. Doctrinal differences were not swept under the carpets of indifference or of outward institutional and liturgical adjustment; and yet it was still found possible for old antagonists to frame a common eucharistic confession. Everyone, it was said, had been able to talk with his brothers without ceasing to talk with his fathers—truly a miracle of grace.[4]

Arnoldshain was not the first such consensus in our century. On the very eve of the war (1937), a synod of the Prussian Union had issued a declaration affirming the strictly dogmatic basis for table fellowship between Lutherans and Reformed: that is, the shared confession that Christ himself is the eucharistic gift.[5] But, of course, the seed sown on that occasion fell among thorns; and it was, in any case, a geographically more limited agreement than the postwar theses. What has happened since Arnoldshain is that the conversations have been still further extended; and we have witnessed the Schauenburg Theses (1967), which in turn made possible the "Leuenberg Agreement among the Reformation Churches in Europe" (1971). The agreement testified that there were no obstacles to pulpit and table fellowship between Lutherans and Reformed, or to mutual recognition of each other's ordination; a common understanding of the gospel made church fellowship possible.[6]

Across the Atlantic in the meantime, before the Europeans had concluded their conversations, leaders of their American sister-communions had anticipated their conclusions by half a decade. At the end of four years of dialogue (1962-66), representatives of the Lutheran and Reformed traditions in the United States and Canada testified that they had managed to shed some inherited caricatures and had discovered that varying doctrinal emphases may be complementary rather than contradictory. Of course, differences remained. However:

> We regard none of these remaining differences [it was said] to be of sufficient consequence to prevent fellowship. We have recognized in each other's teachings a common understanding of the Gospel and have concluded that the issues which divided the two major branches of the Reformation can no longer be regarded as constituting obstacles to mutual understanding and fellowship.[7]

Accordingly, the report recommended "discussions looking forward to intercommunion and the fuller recognition of one another's ministries."[8]

It seems to follow that Calvin's optimism has been vindicated—that there is, in truth, no doctrinal disharmony between the Reformed church and the church of the Augsburg Confession. But it is not really so simple. For, in the first place, the monuments of irenicism to which I have referred are situated along the path of a complex family history that has often degenerated into a bitter family squabble. As J. S. Whale has remarked, citing a Hindu proverb: "There is no hostility like that between first cousins."[9] Even the statement I have quoted from Calvin was made, not in the calm of an ecumenical conference, but in the heat and passion of his defense against Westphal, the strict Lutheran pastor in Hamburg. The fires of that sixteenth-century controversy have by no means gone out.

And the delegates to recent conferences have been more willing to make accords than their respective churches have been to implement them.[10] One reason for the foot-dragging has undoubtedly been the fear of antagonizing the conservative wing in each of the two churches; another has been the inevitable fact that only a handful of representatives (out of churches numbering millions) can directly experience the exhilaration of ecumenical dialogue. In short, even the most optimistic utterances, like Calvin's, are made in the context of de facto alienation.

In the second place, doctrinal developments since the Reformation have not invariably made it easier to endorse Reformation confessions. The Leuenberg Agreement rightly insisted that positions have changed in the course of four hundred years and that sixteenth-century anathemas do not always hit a twentieth-century mark. In this respect, change may be on the side of ecumenical rapprochement. But in relativizing the confessional differences, change may also relativize the confessions themselves, making it harder to regard sixteenth-century documents as still living. This, too, is at least implied by the Leuenberg Agreement, which states that while the questions of modern times have "led the churches to new similar forms of thought and life," they have led also to "new differences cutting right across those of confession."[11] Old divisions, then, may have undergone some welcome attrition; but new divisions have appeared on both sides of the confessional line, and it is widely held that they call for new confessions rather than for celebration of the ones the churches already have. There are historical reasons that make it more natural for the Reformed than for the Lutherans to regard the drafting of confessions as an unfinished, indeed never-ending obligation of the church. But the issues that seem to call for new confessions divide the Lutherans among themselves and the Reformed among themselves, greatly complicating the ecumenical round table. They are, in fact, not confessional but party divisions.[12]

Finally, in the third place, our own century has actually seen the rise of something like a new *confessional* division between the Lutherans and the Reformed—a division that would not have occurred to John Calvin or any of the older divines. It has to do with questions of civil government, secular vocation, and the social-political responsibility of the church. These are matters that have not historically been grounds for opposition between the two traditions.[13] But in our own century, mainly because of Barth's skepticism about the Lutheran doctrine of the two kingdoms, Lutherans and Reformed have come close to discovering here a fresh cause for contention. And the Augsburg Confession itself plainly exhibits the questionable consequences of a sharp distinction between the worldly and the spiritual realms.

For these three reasons, Calvin's remark about the confession, even if it was wholly true, is not the whole truth—certainly not for today. It has to be qualified by other truths. And I propose to make some historical comments on each of my three qualifications in turn.

II

Although we habitually speak of "*the* Augsburg Confession," the Lutheran charter read on 25 June 1530 was only one of the Protestant manifestoes presented to the imperial diet. Already in 1530 Protestantism was divided, and there were in fact three Augsburg confessions. The failure of the Marburg Colloquy the preceding year convinced the Lutherans that they should exclude Zwinglian sympathizers from their conferences, despite the fact that the Swiss had assented to fourteen of Luther's fifteen Marburg Articles (with which the first part of the Lutheran Augsburg Confession was closely related). The delegates of the four imperial cities of Strasbourg, Constance, Memmingen, and Lindau, who would have preferred a common evangelical statement, were obliged instead to prepare their own Tetrapolitan Confession. Mainly the work of Bucer, it was handed to the emperor, but not granted an official reading, on 11 July. By then, Zwingli's personal confession, the *Fidei Ratio,* had been delivered (8 July) by an emissary from Zurich. The spirits of Marburg thus haunted the diet; and they have repeatedly been conjured up again in Lutheran-Reformed relationships ever since.[14]

To gain admittance to the Smalcald League, the south Germans did subsequently sign the confession they had not been permitted to share in drafting. It might be supposed that the Wittenberg Concord (1536) would then have left the Reformed churches of Switzerland permanently and unambiguously Zwinglian. But this was not so. Two years later (1538), Martin Bucer was joined in Strasbourg by Calvin. To begin with, Calvin had been suspicious of the Wittenberg Concord, but only because he thought it might be used by Luther as a cover for promoting sacramental notions unacceptable to the Swiss; with its actual content he had no difficulties. Hence he could readily assume pastoral charge over the French congregation in Strasbourg. And by the following year (1539) his personal mistrust of Luther melted at the glad news that Luther, for his part, held his young French critic in high esteem. Calvin was overwhelmed by Luther's generosity. True, he remained entirely clear in his own mind about his continuing differences with Luther; but he was convinced that the notion of sacramental union established the essential bond between them.[15]

The Lutherans (or many of them) apparently agreed, and at the ecumenical conferences held under imperial auspices at Hagenau, Worms, and Regensburg (1540-41) Calvin was treated as a Lutheran representative. Any lingering doubts one may entertain about his status are removed by the fact that at Worms he was officially transferred from the Strasbourg delegation to the delegation of the Duke of Lüneburg.[16] Ernst Bizer's judgment certainly holds good for Calvin's Strasbourg period (1538-41): among the Lutherans Calvin "passed for one of themselves"—a fact all the more remarkable because his divergence from Luther's eucharistic theology was no secret.[17] There is no question here of dissembling or of misunderstanding. Calvin's opinion of Zwingli and his sacramental theory was frankly contemptuous. On the use of the sacraments, Zwingli's view, he wrote, was "false and pernicious";[18] and to Farel he confided: "You yourself know, if the two be compared [Luther and Zwingli], by what a distance Luther excels."[19]

Years afterwards, when Calvin professed his agreement with the Augsburg Confession, he sometimes expressly recalled the Regensburg Colloquy.[20] Understandably, it has been inferred by some historians that his agreement was only with the *versio variata,* drawn up by Melanchthon the previous year with an eye to the forthcoming negotiations. And when Calvin informs Martin Schalling that he actually "signed" *(subscripsi)* the Augsburg Confession, his words have been taken by the Dutch historian Nijenhuis in the metaphorical sense of "subscribed to" or "agreed with."[21] In other words, we should conclude that Calvin was simply recollecting his support of the *versio variata* at the time of the religious colloquies. Nevertheless, Nijenhuis still thinks it likely that Calvin did literally sign the confession, even if his words to Schalling do not linguistically have to be interpreted in that sense.[22] After his return to Geneva, he could therefore write to Jean Garnier, his successor in the French congregation at Strasbourg: "I do not see why you hesitate to sign the Augsburg Confession."[23] But, of course, the more intriguing question is: Which version of the confession did Calvin endorse, whether or not by literally signing it?

Nijenhuis finds no evidence that Calvin was under formal obligation to sign the Invariata upon his arrival in Strasbourg; he would have been required only to sign the Wittenberg Concord, although he must have acknowledged the Invariata as, with the Tetrapolitan Confession, the official standard of the Strasbourg church.[24] In an interesting rejoinder, Wilhelm H. Neuser points out that, as a precondition for agreement on the Lord's Supper, the text of the Wittenberg Concord actually includes an express profession of loyalty to Augsburg; *along with* the Concord, therefore, Calvin had in effect subscribed to the *Confessio Augustana Invariata* and its Apology. And this, Neuser thinks, is what Calvin meant in his remark to Martin Schalling.[25]

In any case, while the change of wording in Article 10 on the Lord's Supper (from "vere adsint et distribuantur" to "vere exhibeantur") may be closer to Calvin's usual manner of speaking, he need not have found the original wording unacceptable.[26] Had he lived long enough, he would have had no difficulty in saying, with the signatories of the Formula of Concord (1577):

> We therefore declare our adherence to the first, unaltered Augsburg Confession (in the form in which it was set down in writing in the year 1530 and submitted to Emperor Charles V at Augsburg by a number of Christian electors, princes, and estates of the Roman Empire as the common confession of the reformed churches) as our symbol in this epoch, not because this confession

was prepared by our theologians but because it is taken from the Word of God and solidly and well grounded therein.[27]

What Calvin would *not* have been able to say is that the Formula of Concord is the "correct and final explanation"[28] of the Augsburg Confession; he always insisted that the proper interpreter of the confession had to be its author, Philip Melanchthon.[29] But even among the Lutheran churches adoption of the Formula was not so prompt, universal, and unqualified as the adoption of the Augsburg Confession. Still today, endorsement of the *Book of Concord* is sometimes accompanied by careful differentiation of its component parts. The constitution of the Lutheran World Federation (1947) singled out for special mention, along-side the Augsburg Confession, only the Small Catechism.[30] And from Luther's catechisms, it will be recalled, Calvin took the ground plan of his first *Institutio* as well as some of its leading ideas.[31]

My first point, then, comes down to this: that, although situated in a complex history of alienation and misunderstanding, Calvin's allegiance to the Augsburg Confession does not forfeit its significance in the history of ecumencial dialogue. It may, in fact, have special significance precisely because it was reaffirmed during the second round of eucharistic debates, evoked by the furor over the Zurich Consensus (1549) and the subsequent realignment of the three Evangelical parties that had made their confession at Augsburg. It is ironical that the ecumenical triumph that brought the French and the German Swiss together—the center and the left, so to say—threatened the alliance of the center with the right wing.[32] But it remains an interesting fact that, amid all the asperity of his controversies with Westphal and Heshusius, Calvin constantly recalled the better times he had experienced at Strasbourg.

When the report of the recent Lutheran–Reformed conversations in America was published (1966), it appeared under the title *Marburg Revisited*. The historian may well ask: Why not Strasbourg revisited? The Calvinists will rightly insist that they were not present at Marburg and therefore cannot go back there—as if to undo something for which they ought to feel penitent. If historical inquiry generates regulative symbols as well as naked facts (or probabilities), then Calvin's example may serve as an enduring symbol of unitive intent in the midst of actual estrangement. For ecumenical theology, at any rate, the prince of Reformed divines representing Lutheranism from his headquarters in Strasbourg would be a much better symbol than Luther's opponent at Marburg compulsively chanting "The flesh profits nothing."

Indeed, it might not be improper to make my point more strongly and argue that, if we take Calvin's attitude seriously, the Augsburg Confession should have its place also among the *Reformed* confessions. This, it seems, was the opinion of Otto Weber, who at the time of his death (1966) was planning a critical edition of the Reformed *corpus confessionum*. Weber and his associates (among them the Lutheran Ernst Wolf) considered the inclusion of Augsburg in their volume.[33] As they were no doubt aware, there would have been good historical precedent—as well as the personal standpoint of Calvin—on their side, since more than one of the earliest collections of Reformed symbols had in fact found room for the Lutheran confession.[34] It does not follow, of course, that it could then have the same status among the Reformed as it has among the Lutherans, for whom it is the preeminent confession. As becomes clear from his energetic correspondence during the Colloquy of Poissy (1561), Calvin himself considered it inferior in construction, forthrightness, and clarity to the French *Confession de foi* of 1559.[35] To Beza he wrote:

> Its blandness has always displeased the judicious: the author himself regretted it. In several places it is adapted to peculiarly German use. I say nothing of the fact that, because several points of the utmost importance have been left out, its brevity is obscure and truncated. In short, it would be absurd to snatch it up and set the French Confession aside.[36]

Calvin was clearly piqued at the time, wounded both in his theological and in his national pride. As he wrote in another letter: "What! Shall the Germans lay down the law to us? Shall they dictate to us, as though we were children, what is to be believed?"[37] But actually he says no more than most would be prepared to grant, on whichever side of the confessional division they may be standing: that the Augsburg Confession does not present a comprehensive or exclusive system of Protestant theology. And that, for some purposes, is a merit.

III

To make my second point, I again venture into some church history, leaping three centuries to the year 1830 in Prussian Germany. By then, the Lutheran-Reformed union had been effected by royal decree (1817); and, to cement the union (as he said), Frederick William III sent a new directive (dated 4 April) to Minister Altenstein, commissioning him to arrange a tercentennial celebration. Special services of worship in all the Evangelical churches were to commemorate the presenting of the Augsburg Confession to Emperor Charles V. The confession, the king explained, was to be viewed as, "next to the Holy Scriptures, the principal foundation of the Evangelical church," and he professed his own sincere allegiance to its spirit. Interestingly, Altenstein's proclamation, although in part it echoed the royal directive, dropped the phrase "to its spirit" *(zu dessen Geist)* and spoke simply of allegiance "to the same" *(zu demselben).*[38] A slight enough alteration, but the times made it significant. The confessional question, raised earlier by the formation of the union, had been raised again; and the tercentennial was to be celebrated by a church officially united in confession but actually divided over the status of confessions.[39] From the consequent debates it becomes apparent that a striking change had appeared in ecclesiastical politics since Calvin. The change I have in mind has proved to be permanent; it is with us still.

The situation in the German Protestant churches lent the proposed festival a significance it might not otherwise have had. Earlier in the year, Hengstenberg's *Evangelische Kirchenzeitung* had stepped up its campaign against rationalism, urging that Protestant ministers should be held accountable to the Augsburg Confession. And it was widely feared that an Augsburg jubilee could only be taken for a victory of Hengstenberg's party. Liberal voices were raised in protest. Two Breslau professors, for instance, von Cölln and Schulz, announced in a forthright pamphlet that for the church to commemorate a confession which nobody confessed any more would be either contemptible hypocrisy or patent inconsistency. In their view, what the church needed was a new, modern confession. One preacher who did not agree with them was Friedrich Schleiermacher, who had determined to preach an entire series of Augustana sermons.[40] Both the sermons themselves and his justification of them aptly illustrate the change I wish to emphasize.

Against the two Breslau professors, Schleiermacher undertook to justify his participation in the festival. He admitted that, like them, he did not want compulsory subscription to the Augsburg Confession; but, unlike them, he did not want a new confession either. Still, he was not afraid that, if he appeared before his congregation on the day of the festival, he might be guilty of hypocrisy or inconsistency.

> I believe it was possible for a minister to say confidently on this festive occasion, even in the pulpit, that the document presented on that day should not be measured by the standard of our times, and that one must in many points judge it with caution.... And yet, even if ... we thankfully acknowledge that our church has not stood still for three hundred years in the purification of Christian doctrine by means of biblical scholarship, that could not detract one bit from our celebration.... For the celebration does not hold for the document anyway ... but for its presentation [*Uebergabe*] : it is not the work that is being celebrated but the deed.[41]

The Breslau professors registered surprise that Schleiermacher, being Reformed and therefore no true adherent of the Augsburg Confession, should have taken their remarks as meant for him.[42] But Schleiermacher's further exchange with them need not now detain us.

What we find full-grown in Schleiermacher is something present only embryonically in Calvin: the recognition—obvious enough to us these days—that confessions of faith are historical products, so that progress in understanding is always possible.[43] They are to be read with respect, but also critically. Indeed, what we chiefly celebrate in our forefathers, according to Schleiermacher, is *the fact that* they confessed their faith. Hence his very first sermon, preached on the Sunday before the festival, takes as its text 1 Corinthians 7:23 ("You were bought with a price; do not become slaves of men"), and it issues a solemn warning against self-incurred bondage. The act of presenting the Augsburg Confession to the emperor is lifted up as an act of evangelical freedom, so that it would be grotesque to require subscription to the confession as though it were a binding creed. Such a yoke of words would be an even worse betrayal of liberty than the slavery of outward works.[44] Similarly, the second sermon, Schleiermacher's offering on the actual day of the festival, speaks of the Augsburg Confession honorifically as the first and most widely accepted witness to evangelical truth, yet distinguishes sharply between the *work* as a composition and the *act* that brought it into being. We are to take care that the Roman Catholics will never be able to say that we Protestants too, in our own way, rest our confidence in God on outward things—not even on the good works of religious belief.[45]

Naturally, Schleiermacher does not ignore the actual contents of the confession; most of the ten sermons are in fact devoted to individual articles, and he tells his congregation that he thought it would be useful to take more time over the main points than the single day of the festival would allow.[46] But he considers himself entirely free, not just to expound the confession, but to appraise it in the light of his biblical texts. And so, when he turns in the third sermon to the first of the "main points," he indicates his intention to take things as they come—not cautiously selecting whatever can be expected to evoke general agreement, but taking what has become alien to us along with what remains true and valid.[47] In actual fact, though he speaks at one point of a "just balance,"[48] he devotes far more time (in sermons 3-7) to the greatness of the confession than to its defects. Perhaps the disparity was unplanned. At any rate, after the seventh sermon the series was broken off (from 29 August to 3 October) by a journey to Switzerland; and upon his return he had time for only two sermons of a more critical variety (nos. 8-9) before the requirements of the Christian year caught up with him.[49]

The eighth sermon takes issue generally with the anathemas that are sprinkled throughout the Augsburg Confession. The chosen text is Luke 6:37, "Judge not, and you will not be judged; condemn not, and you will not be condemned." And the conclusion is that we ought not to condemn those who believe differently from ourselves; otherwise, we risk condemning ourselves to isolation from that brotherly fellowship in which further enlightenment is made possible.[50] This then leaves us with the ninth sermon as the only one in the entire series that holds up for criticism a particular point of doctrine. Entitled "That we have nothing to teach about the wrath of God," it takes its stand upon 2 Corinthians 5:17-18 and relegates the notion of God's wrath to the old things that are passed away. We now have no need of anything else than the love of Christ, which casts out fear.[51] One is initially surprised to learn that Schleiermacher found "much too much talk" in the confession about the wrath of God, seeing that in fact the expression occurs there very seldom.[52] He must have considered the notion to be implicit in the entire theory of justification and reconciliation which pervades the document and according to which God is the object of reconciliation (that is, needs to be appeased). This he held to be incompatible with his text and alien to the spirit of Christianity. The time has come, he thinks, to call upon men, not to flee to the Son from the Father's wrath, but only to open their eyes and see the Father in the Son.[53]

It may well be said that the points at which Schleiermacher takes issue with the Augsburg Confession have nothing whatever to do with the traditional division between Lutherans and Reformed; they have to do, rather, with the difference between classical and liberal Protestantism, as (for the most part) does the question of confessional subscription.[54] But that, of course, is precisely my second point. Although the sixteenth-century divisions are still nursed by many, there may in fact be much deeper *party* divisions within Protestantism that cut across confessional lines. And time and again, in ecumenical gatherings, the kindred spirits have recognized one another across the confessional divide.

In sum, the present ecumenical situation is partially defined by the momentous changes that the individual traditions themselves have undergone. Perhaps none of them can speak with one voice any longer—if it ever could.[55] As Schleiermacher himself puts it:

In this respect we have something larger to achieve than had to be achieved back then [at the time of the Diet of Augsburg]. The [Evangelical] church was small then, and its spirit was fresh; and there was not so much inducement to look away from the main point to all kinds of details.[56]

Even to put the matter in this fashion conceals the radicalness of Schleiermacher's question to the Augsburg Confession. In the sermon on the wrath of God he is asking, in effect, whether the "main point" can any longer be formulated in Luther's way. The same question has been asked more directly by other modern theologians, many of them Lutherans like Troeltsch and Tillich.[57] And it was again the same question that ruffled the delegates of the Lutheran World Federation at Helsinki in 1963: whether the man of today still agonizes under the wrath of God.[58]

It is not my intention to claim that Schleiermacher was right, nor that he speaks for the Reformed churches in the post-Reformation world. As a matter of fact, for all that I have learned from him on both matters, I believe he was mistaken about the use of confessional documents and about the validity of the notion of God's wrath.[59] My purpose in referring to him is not, for now, to identify myself with any theological party, but simply to illustrate the fact that in the modern world there *are* theological parties. The controversies attending the tricentennial were symptomatic of far-reaching theological developments, in which the party took its place beside the confession as an occasion of division. This, too, qualifies the worth of Calvin's amicable verdict on the Augsburg Confession—but without wholly negating it. The churches of the Reformation can still go back to Strasbourg to mend some of their divisions, though they cannot presume that the only, or the most urgent, problems are still the old confessional ones.

IV

To add party differences to confessional divisions is still to move in the rarified atmosphere of dogmatic theology. These days, we are accustomed to search more widely for the social characteristics that mark off one group from another. This is not to deny that patterns of organization and behavior may have their roots in ideas. Most comparative inquiries into Lutheran and Reformed ethics and institutions have attempted to trace observed differences of behavior to different theological principles. And there seems to be a general consensus that while Lutheran faith is in principle a "living, busy, active, mighty thing,"[60] Calvinist faith has been, in practice, much busier. But it remains a delicate historical task to determine how far the contrast is rooted in divergent concepts of faith, and how far it has to do with differences of individual temperament and collective circumstances.

We may smile today at Ritschl's theory that in the opposition between Lutheranism and Calvinism is mirrored the temperamental antithesis between the unruly German's feeling for individual liberty and the ascetic Frenchman's readiness to accept regimentation.[61] (Ethnic folklore apparently varies from time to time.) And yet a contrast of sorts really can be traced back all the way to the persons of the Reformers themselves. For Luther, the meaning of "reformation" virtually coincided with the proclamation of the gospel. He preached the Word, slept, and drank his beer; and while he did nothing more, the Word did it all.[62] With Calvin things were quite different. As he lay on his deathbed, he fell to reminiscing about the course of his life and remarked: "When I first arrived in this church, there was almost nothing. They were preaching, and that is all. . . . There was no reformation."[63] We find in Calvin, at the very source of the Reformed tradition, a powerful sense of obligation to reform, not piety alone, but every department of public life. Still perhaps the classic expression of this Calvinistic trait is the famous series of Stone Lectures (1898) by the Dutch statesman-theologian Abraham Kuyper, in which Calvinism is presented as a total view of life self-consciously penetrating the domains of politics, science, and art as well as the domain of "religion" (more narrowly conceived).[64]

That there really is a difference here between Lutheranism and Calvinism has not, as far as I am aware, been seriously denied, though it has often been grossly overdrawn.[65] "Lutheran quietism" and "Calvinist activism" have become commonplaces of the secondary literature; and behind the inevitable caricatures serious historians have discovered firm evidence that calls for explanation. There is no consensus about the theological foundations of Calvinist activism, nor about the actual extent of its cultural impact, despite an ever-growing literature on Calvinism and capitalism, Calvinism and democracy, and even Calvinism and science.[66] But there seems to be a much more general agreement about the reason for Lutheranism's tendency to quietism. We may give it in the words of Troeltsch's *Social Teaching*:

> Lutheran Christian individualism has retired behind the line of battle of all external events and outward activity, into a purely personal spirituality.... This spirituality is based on nothing save the "Word," which is guaranteed by the Church; it therefore regards the Church simply as the Herald of the Word, endowed with a purely spiritual miraculous converting power; it has no conception of the Church as an ethical organization of Christendom as a whole.... As soon as the Christian believer turns from this spirituality to take his part in real life, he can only express his inner liberty through submission to the existing order....[67]

Troeltsch, admittedly, makes his point censoriously; but the same point has been made by more loyal Lutherans, whether with satisfaction or with pain. Ritschl, for instance, considered it a merit of Lutheranism that it remained faithful to the idea of the church as solely an organ of grace, whereas Calvinism admitted the exercise of discipline alongside the means of grace and so moved a step closer to Anabaptism.[68] William H. Lazareth, on the other hand, finds that the traditional concentration of Lutheranism on the gospel has led to a serious shortcoming: while it has energized a sound personal ethic of "faith active in love," it has lacked a corresponding social ethic of "love seeking justice" in the vast realm of institutional life. And, unlike many Lutherans, Lazareth plainly considers that the demands of God s law have to do with institutions, not just persons—with politics and economic life, not just with politicians and economists.[69]

The question of Lutheran social ethics seems to come to a particularly sharp focus in Article 16 of the Augsburg Confession, where Lutheranism's personal spirituality is anchored in the two kingdoms doctrine. Against the Anabaptists (and implicitly against monasticism),[70] it is asserted that the social-political realm *(weltliches Regiment)* belongs to the divine order: it is positively evaluated as the sphere in which the Christian exercises love by doing the works of his calling. By no means has the Christian to establish his perfection or righteousness by renouncing the activities of the worldly realm. And then comes the reason: "For the Gospel teaches, not an outward and temporal, but an inward and eternal being and righteousness of the heart; it does not conflict with the worldly realm...." Does this not imply that a both-and is possible—both personal spirituality and activity in the world—*because* Christian righteousness has nothing to do with the worldly realm? And although the intention is to appraise the state positively, does not the sixteenth article go on to present the Christian's relationship to the government as one of total submission and acquiescence—except when commanded to commit an actual sin? As Melanchthon puts it in his *Apology*, Christ directed his apostles to teach that the spiritual kingdom does not change the worldly realm.[71] It is not surprising that the Roman Catholic *Confutation* received Article 16 with complete satisfaction.[72]

Similarly in Article 28, on the power of the bishops, the doctrine of two governments is invoked to establish the difference between spiritual and temporal power rather than their connection. Whereas the power of the bishops has been confused with the temporal sword, the only authority they actually have lies in their commission to preach the gospel and administer the sacraments; their business is with that "eternal righteousness of the heart" of which Article 16 has already informed us. They must not interfere with the civil government, "because worldly government is concerned with very different matters than the Gospel."[73] Hence it can be asserted that the office of the gospel has nothing at all to do with worldly administration; worldly power has to do with the body, not the soul, as Christ himself indicated when he said, "My kingdom is not of this world" (John 18:36). What are we to say of this apparent dualism?

What most needs to be said of Article 16 (and, by implication, Article 28) from the Lutheran side was said already in 1930 by Paul Althaus: that the battle lines have changed, and that Protestantism today—if called upon to voice its confession concerning the worldly realm—could not be content merely to repeat the words of Article 16. The enemy today is no longer disdain for the secular orders or the attempt to subject them to a hierarchical bondage, but rather the assumption that they are a law unto themselves. There was a false ideal, at that time, of a Christian world-order; today it has become an anti-Christian order.[74] In one of his later essays (1957), Althaus points out that we ourselves have changed as well as the enemy, since we now face the secular powers not simply as subjects but as citizens whose civic responsibility goes far beyond obedience and prayer. Still, he thinks we need only to apply and adapt Luther's principles to a new situation, not to renounce them, even if they have been misused to justify political aggrandizement. And what is required by way of adjustment, he suggests, is to extend the notion of "office" *(Amt)* to include leaders who come forward from the people "outside the existing order" *(ausserordentlich)* and oppose the authorities simply out of civic responsibility.[75]

From the Reformed side, however, radical surgery has been proposed, and a few Lutheran theologians have agreed. Barth's utterances on the two kingdoms doctrine and the concepts it entails have been cited too often to need detailed quotation here. His claim, in brief, was that Luther's fatal mistake about the relationship of law and gospel, worldly and spiritual order, confirmed the natural paganism of the Germans; or, more plainly, that Lutheranism separated creation and law from the gospel and thereby allotted to German paganism something like a sanctuary of its own. Hence the Lutheran doctrine of the state could be, and had been, used as a "Christian" justification for National Socialism.[76] His intention, Barth insisted, was not to impeach the German people but to explain and excuse them.[77] But he excused the German church only by viewing it as in bondage to the "Babylonian captivity" of Luther's doctrine—his separation between Christ's kingdom and all worldly spheres.[78] It is not to be wondered at, then, if Barth's judgments were taken as a Reformed (and perhaps also a Swiss) critique of Lutheranism. He was in fact convinced that political quietism is endemic to German Lutheranism. When the attempt was made, during the war, to muzzle him even in Reformed Basel, he immediately perceived the threat in confessional terms. Because his outspoken addresses and letters were found prejudicial to Swiss neutrality, he was directed to speak theologically, not politically; and this he challenged as an attack on the Reformed confession, identical in content with the error of German Lutheranism.[79]

There are at least two difficulties in this diagnosis of Lutheranism's alleged moral failure: on the one hand, the doctrine of the two kingdoms, at least as Luther explained it, does not in fact separate the earthly realm from the heavenly; and, on the other hand, the doctrine was taken over from Lutheranism by Calvin, which surely qualifies it as also a Reformed doctrine. The scholarly debates over Luther's own utterances on the two kingdoms do not, I think, affect the particular question with which we are concerned. In opposition both to the temporal pretensions of the medieval church and to interference by the civil government in ecclesiastical affairs, he certainly insisted on *differentiating* the two realms; but, in opposition to sectarianism, he did not want them *separated*. One need go no further than the treatise *Temporal Authority* (1523) to recognize that he held up the ideal of a Christian ruler, insisted on the preacher's duty to see that rulers do in fact behave like Christians, and tried to specify the limits of civil obedience should the ruler err—three ways in which the two realms are held firmly together.[80] Nowadays, this may not be all we should wish to say; but it surely is enough to counter a political quietism that allows the state a "sanctuary" from moral and spiritual criticism.[81] The problems therefore seem to lie much less in the structures of obligation than in the lack of moral insight and courage. In that case, we should seek an explanation for quietism, not in Luther's doctrine of the two kingdoms, but in his doctrine of sin, according to which we may expect that the most elegant theological schemes will always be at the mercy of self-interest because sin (as *amor sui*) is spread evenhandedly over the whole of mankind.[82] It has been well said that "there is nothing so sick about Lutheran ethics that a strong dose of Luther can not cure."[83]

In comparison with the torrent of essays on Luther's two kingdoms doctrine, the same doctrine in Calvin has attracted precious little attention.[84] I cannot here do very much to redress the balance. Suffice it to say that if the problem with the doctrine lies in a tendency to separate the spiritual from the worldly realm, then Calvin's formulation of it is as risky as any of Luther's utterances.[85] Like Luther, he takes his stand on John 18:36, "My kingdom is not of this world." And, in a passage that carries us back beyond the Strasbourg period to the very first edition of his *Institutes*, he writes that the two kingdoms

> must always be examined separately; and while one is being considered, we must call away and turn aside the mind from thinking about the other. There are in man, so to speak, two worlds, over which different kings and different laws have authority.[86]

With characteristic self-assurance, Calvin tells us that the question is not a very difficult one. But it surely would be if we pressed his language about the "different kings" *(varii reges)* and "different laws" *(variae leges)*, and if Calvin had said no more on the subject.[87]

Admittedly, much of what he says elsewhere makes the question more, rather than less, problematic. When he entrusts the maintenance of true religion to the civil powers, this may well seem, from the Lutheran perspective, to be a confusion of the two kingdoms;[88] and some, no doubt, will detect here the theocratic or christocratic tendency in Reformed theology, which (it is said) dissolves the two kingdoms doctrine.[89] To which it must be replied that if Calvin tends to conflate the two kingdoms in principle, he does it in much the same way as the Lutherans conflated them in practice. For him the civil government becomes, not a mere "emergency bishop" acknowledged (for the time being) out of pure necessity, but rather a permanent and regular force in the ecclesiastical realm, entrusted with a specific religious task.[90] But, unless we are to charge him with downright self-contradiction, the role he assigns to the civil government cannot be identified with the "caesaropapism" he expressly rejects. The two kingdoms doctrine, far from being dissolved by him, is precisely what leads him to reject the use of worldly power in the church.[91] The most we would be inclined to admit is that Calvin perhaps gave a distinctive stamp to the doctrine he borrowed from Luther. As Joachim Staedtke puts it: "He took over Luther's two kingdoms doctrine but modified it by a theocratic accent, in order to counteract what he foresaw as the paganizing of the state."[92] Elsewhere, Staedtke suggests that since the lordship of Christ and the two kingdoms are both thought by both Reformers, we are justified in relating the two doctrines dialectically, each excluding the peculiar danger latent in the other.[93]

"There is nothing in the Augsburg Confession that is not in agreement with our teaching." Once again, we are brought to the conclusion that Calvin's affirmation of a harmony between the confession and his own teaching is not a self-evident truth but has, or has acquired over the years, the character of an affirmation *in spite of.* It is qualified, not only by confessional estrangement and party divisions, but also by differences of accent within a common language. How far differences of this sort may complement rather than negate one another is a question for the theologian to answer, not the historian. Not least of the contributions the historian can make, however, is to remind the churches that the question "What do the Reformed think of the Augsburg Confession?" is really not one question. The situation in which it is asked changes, and the question tacitly changes with it.

Conclusion

"The historical and the relative are identical."[1] Troeltsch's aphorism sums up a problem. Of course, one can always leave a historical study with a résumé of what has been said and a claim to have set the record straight wherever necessary. Some readers will not ask for anything more. But instead, I return to the three formative interests avowed in the introduction and offer some final thoughts on the historical and the relative. Of the third interest—in the piety behind the doctrines—enough has been said not only to exemplify it but also to show how widely it is present in the sources, not needing to be smuggled in by the historian's sleight of hand. It is the other two interests—in a pluralist and a progressive interpretation—that generate a problem.

All Christian theology is *sentire cum ecclesia,* "thinking with the church," if not in quite the sense Ignatius Loyola had in mind. The famous expression appears in a group of rules, at the end of the *Spiritual Exercises,* that were plainly anti-Protestant in intention. They invite us to put aside our own judgment and to hold fast to the even more famous principle, "What seems to me white I will believe black if the hierarchical Church so defines."[2] The theologian who is unwilling to adopt this principle as his own is by no means bound, as the sole alternative, to enter his study alone with his Bible "like Luther in his tower room."[3] His task has to do with that tradition (or "traditioning": *actus tradendi*) by which the church lives, the handing on of a sacred heritage from the past. And because this activity is not a mindless transmission of a static, fixed quantity but the active reshaping of it, the theological guild (as part of the church's leadership) may even be said to help *constitute* the tradition out of the apperceptive mass of the Christian heritage.

No theologian can participate responsibly in this task unless he keeps company with those who went before him as well as those who work with him in the present; indeed, his highest respect will be reserved not for the latest best-seller, but for the established classics that have done most to shape the tradition. (As

264

the Anglican divine Richard Hooker sagely remarked, "There are few things known to be good, till such time as they grow to be ancient.")[4] Here, in the classics, is the ecclesial context in which the theologian does his thinking, and it makes no demand for surrender of his own insight. John Oman said it well: "To be faithful to our own spiritual insight, it must be our constant endeavour to be faithful to our spiritual ancestry.... This ancestry and kinship form man's true Church. His debt to it is incalculable, and its authority in some form he must perpetually acknowledge."[5] But there is a difficulty in this eloquently stated position.

To enter into the study of history is to find oneself, unless protected by a sturdy dogmatic shield, in a pluralistic world of continual change. The Christian tradition makes its appearance only in the multitude of historical traditions: that is, in the individual forms the gospel has assumed, which are themselves in the midst of ceaseless transformation. Can historical inquiry, then, be anything but unsettling to the search for one's spiritual ancestry or "true church"? The problem of a theological norm—how to find the tradition in the traditions—is analogous at this point to the problem of historical knowledge. For the theologian, the question is whether he can talk of Christianity, or only of Christian sects and churches. For the historian, the question is whether there can be knowledge of a historical object that presents itself differently to different perspectives. Without some counter-tendency of the mind (such as Schleiermacher's attempted construct of a development), the perception of individuality, it may be said, can only lead to skepticism. But this, I think, is by no means to be granted as a logical necessity.

The solution to the theological problem, like the problem itself, has its analogue in reflections that have been made about historical knowledge. Karl Mannheim, for instance, held it to be Troeltsch's central thesis "that historical knowledge is only possible from an ascertainable intellectual location *(Standort),*" but he denies that skeptical consequences follow from it. By analogy with Husserl's discussion of "profiles" in the perception of an object in space, Mannheim argues: "The different historical pictures do not contradict each other in their interpretations, but encircle the same materially identical given historical content from different standpoints and at different depths of penetration."[6]

"Individuality," if incorporated in this way into a perspectivist theory of knowledge, need not be considered a sinister category. Neither need it be a theological principle always to move, as far as possible, away from particularity. While not everything particular is worth preserving, it may be through the particular that routes are opened up to Christian faith; and in that case it may be the duty of religious communities to defend rather than to surrender their individuality, to maintain their special identity, to keep intact their distinctive witness. The divergence in Christendom with respect to baptism, for instance— whether it should be administered to the children of believers or only upon the recipient's own profession of faith—appears to have opened two routes to Christian faith, one thematized in a theology of prevenient grace and the other in a theology of commitment. A relativistic confessionalism—that is, a standpoint that begins from a particular form of Christian faith without claiming that it alone is true—is an entirely possible foundation on which to build a theology. Individuality is, in short, a problem only to the absolutist persuasion that some fragmentary perspective is identical with Christian truth. And this is a persuasion commonly found in tandem with another: that the truth can be, and has been, stated for all times.

Once again, historical modes of thought are inescapably relativizing: if they incline us to locate truth in the dialogue rather than in the mouth of any one interlocutor, they incline us also to look for truth in a total historical career rather than in any transient moment of it. Such an approach is admittedly unwelcome to biblicism and creedalism. The problem with biblicism does not lie in the doctrine of verbal inerrancy, over which many a futile battle has been fought. The question that is pressed upon the theologian by the passage of time is: What shall he make of the Bible, infallible or not, in the twentieth century? In a characteristically brilliant essay, Benjamin B. Warfield undertook to answer the charge that the Scriptures are colored by the personality of their authors and cannot therefore be the pure Word of God. He asks:

> But what if this personality has itself been formed by God into precisely the personality it is, for the express purpose of communicating to the word given through it just the coloring which it gives it? What if the colors of the stained-glass window have been designed by the architect for the purpose of giving to the light that floods the cathedral precisely the tone and quality it receives from them?[7]

That is a point well made. But the more urgent question is of another order. Suppose the fashions of architecture and the style of ornamentation change. Suppose twentieth-century men and women find themselves to be mere tourists in an ancient Gothic shrine. What then? Can the architect still reproduce in them the impression his workmanship made on medieval man, who once prayed there?

The same question must be asked of the creeds and confessions of the churches. It is presumed to be a commonplace these days that ecclesiastical pronouncements are historically conditioned. But in practice creedalism is by no means dead. The 450th anniversary of the Augsburg Confession gave rise to avowals that the confession and its "chief article" were subject to historical limitations; yet the avowals were accompanied by a tendency to fall back on the Ecumenical Creeds instead, although the same historical principles must presumably apply to them, too.[8] And the debate in the Roman Catholic Church over the concepts of "transignification" and "transfinalization" evoked, in the encyclical *Mysterium Fidei* of Pope Paul VI (1965), an express statement that the church can formulate Christian truth in language that is valid for all men, in all places, and at all times. The dogmatic formulas of the church, it is said, express concepts

> which are not tied to one specific form of human civilization, nor definite period of scientific progress, nor one school of theological thought, but they present what the human mind by universal and necessary experience grasps of realities and expresses in suitable and accurate terminology taken either from the language commonly in use or from polished diction. For this reason, these formulae are adapted to men of all times and all places.[9]

Unhistorical modes of thought are far more tenacious in the churches, both Protestant and Roman Catholic, than is commonly admitted.

The history of Protestantism, on its theological side, is above all the history of two critical shifts in the Latin tradition: one split the Western church into churches, and the other split the churches into parties. The old confessional divisions at the time of the Reformation are still nursed by some, but they pale into relative insignificance beside the later party divisions, even though the parties have tended less to create new churches. Reconciliation in our century between Protestants and Roman Catholics has shown that the divisive questions of the sixteenth century can be resolved. With rapprochement has come, from the Protestant side, renunciation of the old supposition that the gospel of grace fled from the Roman Church on the eve of the Reformation; and from the Roman Catholic side has come a remarkable reassessment of Luther and his Reformation that acknowledges the continuing vitality of his ideas. But will it be possible for both Protestants and Roman Catholics to make a similar reappraisal of Protestant liberalism, the "new Protestantism"? The question is urgent insofar as liberal Protestantism has been the main bearer of a consistently historical approach to Christian theology.

The new Protestantism has admittedly become in turn the old; it was overshadowed for decades by a "new orthodoxy." It remains to be seen whether the emergence of neoorthodoxy marked the end of neo-Protestantism, or whether it was in some ways an interlude in the progress of modern theology. At least there has been a renewed interest in taking up Schleiermacher's and Troeltsch's questions, and there are good reasons for doubting that the case of neoorthodoxy against the liberals has been proved.[10]

Abbreviations

C.O. *Ioannis Calvini opera quae supersunt omnia*. Ed. Wilhelm
Baum, Edward Cunitz, and Edward Reuss. 59 vols. *Corpus
Reformatorum*, vols. 29–87. Brunswick: C. A. Schwetschke
and Son (M. Bruhn), 1863–1900. The exegetical and
homiletical works are identified as commentaries, homilies,
lectures (*praelectiones*), or sermons, respectively, and are
referred to by biblical texts as well as by volume and
column.

E.E. *Opus epistolarum Des. Erasmi Roterodami*. Ed. P. S. and
H. M. Allen and H. W. Garrod. 12 vols. Oxford: Clarendon
Press, 1906–58. Cited by number and line. The volume and
page, where given, are added in parentheses.

Gl. *Glaubenslehre*. Friedrich Schleiermacher, *Der christliche
Glaube nach den Grundsätzen der evangelischen Kirche
im Zusammenhange dargestellt* (1821–22; 2d ed., 1830–31).
Unless otherwise indicated, references are to the 7th ed.,
based on the 2d. Ed. Martin Redeker. 2 vols. Berlin: Walter
de Gruyter, 1960. Cited by section ("paragraph") and subsection. Page numbers in parentheses refer to the English
translation, which I have usually followed. *The Christian
Faith*. English translation of the 2d German ed. Ed. H. R.
Mackintosh and J. S. Stewart. Edinburgh: T. and T. Clark,
1928. Since 1976, published in America by Fortress Press.
The abbreviation Gl. is also used, where no confusion can
arise, for Ernst Troeltsch, *Glaubenslehre nach Heidelberger
Vorlesungen aus den Jahren 1911 und 1912* (Munich and
Leipzig: Duncker and Humblot, 1925). Cited by page.
To distinguish the *Diktat* from the *Vortrag*, the *Diktat* is
also cited by section and subsection; when the section in

the *Vortrag* is noted, it is followed (in parentheses) by page only.

G.S.   Ernst Troeltsch, *Gesammelte Schriften*, 4 vols. (1912–25). I have used the reprint edition (Aalen: Scientia Verlag, 1961–66).

Inst.   John Calvin, *Institutio Christianae religionis*. Cited, unless otherwise indicated, in the 1559 edition by book, chapter, and section. (I use the text in O.S. 3–5.) Volume and page numbers, where added in parentheses, refer to the standard English translation: *Calvin: Institutes of the Christian Religion*. Ed. John T. McNeill and trans. Ford Lewis Battles. 2 vols. Library of Christian Classics, vols. 20–21. Philadelphia: Westminster Press, 1960.

K.S.   Friedrich Schleiermacher, *Kleine Schriften und Predigten*. Ed. Hayo Gerdes and Emanuel Hirsch. 3 vols. Berlin: Walter de Gruyter, 1969–70.

L.B.   *Desiderii Erasmi Roterodami opera omnia*. Ed. Jean LeClerc. 10 vols. Leiden, 1703–6.

L.W.   *Luther's Works*. American edition. Ed. Jaroslav Pelikan and Helmut T. Lehmann. 55 vols. planned. St. Louis, Missouri: Concordia Publishing House; Philadelphia: Fortress Press, 1955–.

O.S.   *Ioannis Calvini opera selecta*. Ed. Peter Barth, Wilhelm Niesel, and Dora Scheuner. 5 vols. Munich: Chr. Kaiser, 1926–52.

R.G.G.   *Die Religion in Geschichte und Gegenwart*. Ed. Friedrich Michael Schliele and Leopold Zscharnack. 5 vols. Tübingen: J. C. B. Mohr (Paul Siebeck), 1909–13.

S.T.   Thomas Aquinas, *Summa theologiae*. Cited by part, question, and article. Volume and page numbers in parentheses, where given, refer to the American edition: St. Thomas Aquinas, *Summa Theologica*. Trans. Fathers of the English Dominican Province. 3 vols. New York: Benzinger Brothers, 1947–48.

S.W.   *Friedrich Schleiermachers sämmtliche Werke*. 31 vols. Berlin: Georg Reimer, 1834–64. Cited by division, volume, and page.

W.A.   *D. Martin Luthers Werke: Kritische Gesamtausgabe*. Weimar, 1883–.

W.A.Br.   Ibid. *Briefwechsel*.

W.A.D.B.   Ibid. *Deutsche Bibel*.

W.A.Tr.   Ibid. *Tischreden*.

Notes

Introduction

1. "*De Libero Arbitrio* (1524): Erasmus on Piety, Theology, and the Lutheran Dogma," in *Essays on the Works of Erasmus*, ed. Richard L. DeMolen (New Haven, Conn.: Yale University Press, 1978), pp. 187–209. This volume was compiled in honor of Craig R. Thompson. My contribution was read in draft form at a meeting of the University of Chicago's Renaissance Seminar.

2. "John Calvin on Luther," in *Interpreters of Luther: Essays in Honor of Wilhelm Pauck*, ed. Jaroslav Pelikan (Philadelphia: Fortress Press, 1968), pp. 67–96. A draft was presented in two lectures at what is now called Trinity Lutheran Seminary in Columbus, Ohio.

3. "Biblical Authority and the Continental Reformation," *Scottish Journal of Theology* 10 (1957):337–60. ©1957 by Scottish Academic Press.

4. "New Light on Luther's 'Rediscovery of the Gospel,'" *McCormick Quarterly* 16 (1963):12–25. A review article on the Luther books of Ernst Bizer and F. Edward Cranz, this essay was supplemented by conclusions reached many years ago in an S.T.M. thesis at Union Theological Seminary, New York: "Luther's Conception of Justifying Faith and Its Significance for Theology Today" (1956).

5. "Priesthood and Ministry in the Theology of Luther." Reprinted in revised form with permission from *Church History* 34 (1965):404–22. A paper read to a conference sponsored by the Department of Theological Cooperation of the National Lutheran Council.

6. "John Calvin and the Reformed Doctrine of the Lord's Supper," *Una Sancta* 25, no. 2 (1968):27–39; also in *McCormick Quarterly* 22 (1969):85–98. *Una Sancta* is now published as an occasional supplement to *Lutheran Forum*. Originally a set of theses prepared for a meeting of Lutherans and Presbyterians at the Lutheran School of Theology at Chicago (then in Maywood), this paper was developed into something closer to its first published form for a presentation at the Valparaiso Institute of Liturgical Studies.

7. "The Lord's Supper in the Reformed Confessions," *Theology Today* 23 (1966):224–43. A paper read before the American Theological Society (Midwest Division) under the title "Is There a Reformed Doctrine of the Lord's Supper?"

8. "'To the Unknown God': Luther and Calvin on the Hiddenness of God," *Journal of Religion* 53 (1973): 263–92. Paper read at a meeting of the University of Chicago's Renaissance Seminar and at Western Theological Seminary, Holland, Michigan.

9. "The Mirror of God's Goodness: Man in the Theology of Calvin," *Concordia Theological Quarterly* 45 (1981):211–22. A lecture at Concordia Theological Seminary, Fort Wayne, Indiana.

10. "The Reformation and the Rise of Modern Science," in *The Impact of the Church upon Its Culture: Reappraisals of the History of Christianity*, ed. Jerald C. Brauer, Essays in Divinity [commemorating the one hundredth anniversary of the University of Chicago's Divinity School] (Chicago: University of Chicago Press, 1968), pp. 231–65.

11. "Schleiermacher and the Reformation: A Question of Doctrinal Development." Reprinted in revised form with permission from *Church History* 49 (1980):147–59. Presidential address before the American Society of Church History.

12. "Theology within the Limits of Piety Alone: Schleiermacher and Calvin's Doctrine of God," in *Reformatio Perennis: Essays on Calvin and the Reformation in Honor of Ford Lewis Battles*, ed. B. A. Gerrish, Pittsburgh Theological Monograph Series, no. 32 (Pittsburgh: Pickwick Presss, 1981), pp. 67–87.

13. "Ernst Troeltsch and the Possibility of a Historical Theology," in *Ernst Troelstsch and the Future of Theology*, ed. John Powell Clayton (Cambridge: Cambridge University Press, 1976), pp. 100–135. This volume includes some of the papers, of which mine was one, from the University of Lancaster's Colloquium on Troeltsch.

14. "Jesus, Myth, and History: Troeltsch's Stand in the 'Christ-Myth' Debate," *Journal of Religion* 55 (1975):13–35. Presidential address before the American Theological Society (Midwest Division).

15. "Strasbourg Revisited: The Augsburg Confession in a Reformed Perspective," in *The Augsburg Confession in Ecumenical Perspective*, ed. Harding Meyer, LWF Report no. 6/7 (December 1979), pp. 129–58. The report is a collection of the papers read at a conference on "Rereading the Augsburg Confession in Ecumenical Perspective," sponsored by the Strasbourg Ecumenical Institute. The papers were also published in German: *Augsburgisches Bekenntnis im ökumenischen Kontext* (Stuttgart: Kreuz Verlag, 1980).

16. The reflections on theology and history in the Conclusion are drawn in part from an address, "Theology and the Historical Consciousness," delivered at McCormick Theological Seminary and published in *McCormick Quarterly* 21 (1968):198–213.

Chapter One

1. Desiderius Erasmus, *Methodus* (1516), in *Ausgewählte Werke*, ed. Hajo and Annemarie Holborn (Munich: C. H. Beck, 1933), p. 162. Later, in the 1519

edition of his *Ratio seu methodus compendio perveniendi ad veram theologiam*, Erasmus substituted "Chrysostom" for "Jerome" as the devout theologian with whom he identified himself (ibid., p. 304). In this chapter, and throughout the present book, translations for which no acknowledgment is made are mine. References to existing translations, where I have not adopted them in my quotations, are introduced by the abbreviation "cf."

2. The text of the bull is in Carl Mirbt and Kurt Aland, eds., *Quellen zur Geschichte des Papsttums und des römischen Katholizismus*, vol. 1, 6th ed. (Tübingen: J. C. B. Mohr [Paul Siebeck], 1967), pp. 504–13. On the arrival of the bull, see Martin Luther to George Spalatin, 11 October 1520, W.A.Br. 2.193–95 (no. 341); translation in Preserved Smith and Charles M. Jacobs, trans. and eds., *Luther's Correspondence and Other Contemporary Letters*, 2 vols. (Philadelphia: The Lutheran Publication Society, 1913–18), 1:365–66.

3. *Warum des Papstes und seiner Jünger Bücher ... verbrannt sind* (1520), W.A. 7.182.7, 12; cf. L.W. 31:395. The citation from Judges 15:11 concludes the work.

4. *Disputatio Heidelbergae habita* (1518), W.A. 1.354.5; cf. L.W. 31:40.

5. Ibid., W.A. 1.359–61 (*probationes* for Theses 13–18), 365–74 (*explicatio* of Thesis 6 [it is unclear what "Thesis 6" Luther had in mind]); L.W. 31:48–52, 58–70.

6. *Assertio omnium articulorum M. Lutheri per bullam Leonis X. novissimam damnatorum* (1520), W.A. 7.146.3–8.

7. *Grund und Ursach aller Artikel ...* (1521), W.A. 7.448.25/449.24; cf. L.W. 32:94.

8. *Assertio*, W.A. 7.148.14. The German has "chief article" (*hewbt artickell*), W.A. 7.448.7/449.7; L.W. 32:93.

9. *Assertio*, W.A. 7.142–49, esp. 146.20, 26.

10. In the remainder of this paragraph, I have used some themes from Luther's *Römerbriefvorlesung* (1515–16) to interpret the thirteenth Heidelberg thesis and the concept of *Eigenwille* in *Grund und Ursach*. See esp. W.A. 56.258.23–259.7, 304.25–305.20, 325.1–21, 355.28–357.26, 390.23–394.5. The translation in L.W. 25 is keyed to the pagination of W.A. 56.

11. *Assertio*, W.A. 7.148.35ff. Note the explicit statement that grace was the real issue.

12. *De servo arbitrio* (1525), W.A. 18.786.26; L.W. 33:294. In actual fact, others took up the *summa caussae* before Erasmus, who was himself partially dependent on John Fisher's *Confutatio assertionis Lutheranae* (1523). On Erasmus's relation to Fisher, see Bernhard Lohse, "Marginalien zum Streit zwischen Erasmus und Luther," *Luther: Zeitschrift der Luther-Gesellschaft* 46 (1975): 5–24, esp. pp. 13–15.

13. Erasmus to Godescalc Rosemondt (the rector), 18 October 1520, E. E. 1153.15 (4.362); to Thomas More, November (?) 1520, E. E. 1162.220–24 (4.389). The translation of Erasmus's letters for the *Collected Works of Erasmus*, published by the University of Toronto Press, has not yet progressed far enough to be of much service for my theme. Of the several volumes of selections from his letters in English, the most pertinent is Hans J. Hillerbrand, ed., Marcus A. Haworth, trans., *Erasmus and His Age: Selected Letters of Desiderius Erasmus*

(New York: Harper and Row, 1970), the fourth section of which is entitled "The Challenge of Luther and the Reformation: 1517–1529." Wherever this collection (hereafter cited as "Hillerbrand") includes, in whole or in part, the passage I am referring to, I have added a cross-reference. For the letters to Rosemondt and More, cf. Hillerbrand, pp. 152–53, 155–59.

14. See esp. E.E. 939 (to Frederick the Wise: Hillerbrand, pp. 134–36), 967 (to Thomas Cardinal Wolsey: Hillerbrand, pp. 138–39), 1033 (to Albert of Brandenburg: Hillerbrand, pp. 145–49), 1143 (to Pope Leo X), and 1167 (to Lorenzo Campeggio: Hillerbrand, pp. 159–62). Many of the themes of these programmatic (or apologetic) letters can be found scattered throughout Erasmus's correspondence in the period. It is not feasible to list the extensive secondary literature on the relation of Erasmus and Luther. I have probably learned most from Zickendraht, Augustijn, and (on Erasmus, but not on Luther!) Humbertclaude. Karl Zickendraht, *Der Streit zwischen Erasmus und Luther über die Willensfreiheit* (Leipzig: J. C. Hinrichs, 1909); C. Augustijn, *Erasmus en de Reformatie. Een onderzoek naar de houding die Erasmus ten opzichte van de Reformatie heeft aangenomen* (Amsterdam: H. J. Paris, 1962); H. Humbertclaude, *Erasme et Luther. Leur Polémique sur le libre arbitre*, Etudes de Théologie et d'Histoire (Paris: Bloud, 1909).

15. Used in the *Axiomata* (see n. 20 below), the phrase occurs also in the correspondence: e.g., to Gerard Geldenhauer, 9 September 1520, E.E. 1141.25 (4.340). The real target of the opposition was not Luther but the Muses: to Christopher Hegendorfer, 13 December 1520, E.E. 1168.30–31 (4.412–13).

16. To Luther, 30 May 1519, E.E. 980.37 (3.606); cf. Hillerbrand, p. 141.

17. To John Reuchlin, 8 November 1520, E.E. 1155.8 (4.371). With the words *Lutheri causam a tua bonarumque literarum causa seiungere* (p. 372, 1.18), cf. to Philip Melanchthon, 6 September 1524, E.E. 1496.50 (5.546); Hillerbrand, p. 174.

18. To Pope Adrian VI, 22 March 1523 (?), E.E. 1352.91 (5.259); cf. Hillerbrand, p. 171.

19. In addition to the letters already cited, see to John Lang, 17 October 1518 (?), E.E. 872 (3.408–10); 30 May 1519 (?), E.E. 983 (3.609). The Roman monarchy is the plague of Christendom (872.16–18), and Erasmus does not see who could attempt to abolish it without uproar (983.14). "Sed tamen haud scio an expediat hoc ulcus aperte tangere" (872.19). Cf. to Spalatin, 6 July 1520, E.E. 1119.27.41 (4.298); Hillerbrand, p. 149.

20. The monuments of these activities are Erasmus's "three Reformation tracts" (as Ferguson calls them): the *Acta academiae lovaniensis*, the *Axiomata*, and the *Consilium*. Wallace K. Ferguson, ed., *Erasmi Opuscula: A Supplement to the Opera Omnia* (The Hauge: Martinus Nijhoff, 1933), pp. 304–61.

21. To Campeggio, 6 December 1520, E.E. 1167.137–41, 155–58 (4.403–4); Hillerbrand, pp. 159–60. For Erasmus's sense of *kairos*, cf. *Axiomata*, 11. 37–38, and *Consilium*, 11. 114–16 (Ferguson, pp. 337, 359).

22. To Louis Ber, 14 May 1521, E.E. 1203.24 (4.494).

23. To Aloisius Marlian, 25 March 1521, E.E. 1195.33 (4.459).

24. To Richard Pace, 5 July 1521, E.E. 1218.2 (4.540).

25. To Jodocus Jonas, 10 May 1521, E.E. 1202.31–37, 48, 128–33 (4.487, 489). Luther is disruptive because of his manner (11.47–50), his radicalness (11.215–26), and his divulging to cobblers what should be kept to scholars (11.56–65). Note also the reference to his "paradoxes" (1.51).

26. To Marlian, 25 March 1521, E.E. 1195.128 (4.462). Despite the sentiments expressed to Jonas (n. 25 above), Erasmus could still wonder, even after publication of *De libero arbitrio*, whether perhaps God intended to heal the church by Luther's "bitter and drastic remedy" (E.E. 1495.7–11, 1497.1, 1523.137–41, 1526.132–39). In any case, he did not want the good in Luther to perish with him (e.g., E.E. 1313.12–17).

27. To Alexander Schweiss, 13 March 1521, E.E. 1192.55–78 (4.454–55).

28. To Adrian VI, 22 March 1523 (?), E.E. 1352.147–91 (5.260–61); Hillerbrand, pp. 173–74. The development of Erasmus's relations with Luther has been variously interpreted: it has been held that at the end of 1520 he was a committed advocate of Luther (Kalkoff); that a break had already been occasioned by the Leipzig Disputation of the previous year (Krodel); that his attitude had been two-sided from the first but a crisis occurred in 1520 (Augustijn). I cannot here discuss the problem, and I do not need to; it is sufficient to indicate certain Erasmian principles that remained constant as the circumstances changed. With the earlier letters already cited, cf. the retrospective apology to Duke George, 12 December 1524, E.E. 1526; Hillerbrand, pp. 178–82. That Erasmus was publicly understood to have turned against Luther after 1520 has been carefully documented by Heinz Holeczek, "Die Haltung des Erasmus zu Luther nach dem Scheitern seiner Vermittlungspolitik 1520/21," *Archiv für Reformationsgeschichte* 64 (1973): 85–112.

29. See, e.g., to Schweiss, 13 March 1521, E.E. 1192.19 (4.453).

30. E.E. 1217.138–46, 1225.239–41, 1263.43–50, 1313.50–54.

31. To Willibald Pirckheimer, 30 March 1522, E.E. 1268.79 (5.35); to Peter Barbirius, 17 April 1523, E.E. 1358.3 (5.276).

32. E.E. 1408.21–23, 1411.23–24, 1415.54–55, 1416.24. Duke George was particularly biting (E.E. 1340). Even after Erasmus had determined to write, George blamed him for writing too late (E.E. 1448.33–56).

33. Felician Gess, ed., *Akten und Briefe zur Kirchenpolitik Herzog Georgs von Sachsen,* 2 vols. (Leipzig: B. G. Teubner, 1905–17), 1.509 (no. 508). This was George's response to King Henry VIII's letter to the Saxon princes (20 January 1523), in which Zickendraht saw a key document for understanding Erasmus's choice of theme (*Der Streit zwischen Erasmus und Luther,* pp.16–17). Zickendraht's thesis, that the *Diatribe* "betrays its intellectual derivation from England" (p. 17), though a similar view was maintained by Freitag in his introduction to Luther's *De servo arbitrio* (in W.A. 18), has generally been judged an overstatement. See the critical remarks of Johannes von Walter in his edition of Erasmus's book, in *Quellenschriften zur Geschichte des Protestantismus,* no. 8 (Leipzig: A. Deichert, 1910), p. x. Henry does seem to have been especially influential on Erasmus's decision to write (E.E. 1408.21, 1415.54), but not necessarily on the theme chosen.

34. E.E. 1324.23, 1367.25ff., 1448.54.

35. *Spongia adversus aspergines Hutteri* (1523), L.B. 10:1654A, 1663A–B, 1672C. Erasmus means that he made no mention of heresy in his letter to Laurinus (see n. 42 below), which provoked Hutten's outburst; but the denial can be generalized, and elsewhere Erasmus states expressly that nowhere in his writings does he call Luther's doctrine a "heresy" (*Adversus calumniosissimam epistolam Martini Lutheri* [1534], L.B. 10:1537D).

36. To Ulrich Zwingli, 31 August [1523], E.E. 1384.2–14, 89 (5.327, 330).

37. To George, 3 September 1522, E.E. 1313.21–28 (5.126). The list of soporifics is revealing: "Mundus indormiebat opinionibus scholasticis, constitutiunculis humanis, nec aliud audiebat quam de indulgentiis, de compositionibus, de potestate Pontificis Romani" (11.22–24).

38. Not every error is a heresy: E.E. 939.81, 1033.234–43, 1202.253. See further nn. 41 and 88 below.

39. In his correspondence with Melanchthon after the printing of *De libero arbitrio*, Erasmus expresses the wish that he could visit Wittenberg in person (E.E. 1496.15), and he denies that the "salt" detected in his book by Melanchthon was intended for Luther (E.E. 1523.125). But he makes it plain that he does not want the gentle reply which Melanchthon assured him he could expect from Luther (E.E. 1523.120–24). In other words, he was counting on the vehemence he professed to deplore. It is possible to exaggerate Erasmus's virtue, which (in his own phrase) was not *sine certo consilio*. But this is not to doubt his sincerity in moving the issue onto the academic plane. On this strategy, see esp. Augustijn, *Erasmus en de Reformatie*, pp. 210, 296.

40. Mention is made of the plan to John Glapion, 21 April (?) 1522, E.E. 1275.20 (5.48); and the details of it are in the *Catalogus lucubrationum* contained in the letter to John Botzheim, 30 January 1523 (E.E. 1:34–36). The names of the participants in the planned dialogue (roughly, Mr. Contentious, Mr. Prudent, and Mr. Truthful) already tell us something about Erasmus's design. See also *Spongia*, L.B. 10:1651B. For a thorough study of the concept of *assertio*, Luther's literary form that stands in sharp antithesis to the *collatio* of Erasmus, see Dietrich Kerlen, *Assertio: Die Entwicklung von Luthers theologischem Anspruch und der Streit mit Erasmus von Rotterdam*, Veröffentlichungen des Instituts für europäische Geschichte Mainz, vol. 78 (Wiesbaden: Fritz Steiner Verlag, 1976).

41. Thompson offers the conjecture that the *Inquisitio* may be an abbreviated version of one of the planned dialogues: Craig R. Thompson, ed., *Inquisitio de Fide: A Colloquy by Desiderius Erasmus Roterodamus 1524*, Yale Studies in Religion, no. 15 (New Haven: Yale University Press, 1950), p. 37. Thompson's interpretation of the *Inquisitio* strongly supports the conclusion that, for Erasmus, the Lutheran affair was not a matter of heresy. See esp. pp. 2–3, 38–43.

42. To Marcus Laurinus, 1 February 1523, E.E. 1342.733–1021 (5.221–27). Echoes of this letter can be heard unmistakably in *De libero arbitrio*. One reason why Erasmus had become preoccupied with this theme is plain from 11.926–58: the Lutherans had attacked *his* views on freedom of choice. On Erasmus's alleged pelagianizing, see E.E. 1225.282, 1275.27.

43. To Henry, 4 September 1523, E.E. 1385.11 ("Molior aliquid adversus nova dogmata"); to John Faber, 21 November 1523, E.E. 1397.14 ("Si suppetent vires, addetur libellus De libero arbitrio"); to Paul Bombasius, 19 January 1524, E.E. 1411.24 ("Aggressus sum negotium"). As the letter to Bombasius indicates, the procrastination was partly out of fear that he might only add to the uproar. Cf. to Theodoric Hezius (?), 16 September 1523, E.E. 1386.22 (5.331).

44. To Ber, February 1524 (?), E.E. 1419 (5.399–400); from Ber, February 1524 (?), E.E. 1420 (5.400–402).

45. To Henry, March 1524 (?), E.E. 1430.12–20 (5.417).

46. From Luther, 15 April (?) 1524, E.E. 1443.67 (5.447); to Luther, 8 May 1524, E.E. 1445.16, 21–22 (5.451–52). For translations see Smith and Jacobs, 2:228–30, 232–35.

47. To Pirckheimer, 21 July 1524, E.E. 1466.58–60 (5.496); to Barbirius, 26 July 1524 (?), E.E. 1470.46 (5.506).

48. To Haio Hermann, 31 August 1524, E.E. 1479.182–85 (5.521). Note that Erasmus anticipated a sharp reaction from the extremists in the Lutheran camp, if not from Luther himself.

49. See the remarks of the editor on E.E. 1481–98 (5.525).

50. *De libero arbitrio* διατριβή *sive collatio per Desiderium Erasmum Roterodamum*. Although the book was published during September 1524 also in Antwerp and Cologne, the primacy of the Basel edition (by Froben) was maintained by Walter (pp. xiii–xvii). It was promptly translated into German—out of the recondite language of the scholars to which Erasmus's intent naturally assigned it! I use the text, edited by Winfried Lesowsky together with *Hyperaspistes I* in the *Ausgewählte Schriften*, vol. 4 (Darmstadt: Wissenschaftliche Buchgesellschaft, 1969), which follows the definitive edition of Walter. My references are to the divisions in Lesowsky (taken from Walter), which I give, as far as possible, in parentheses in the main body of the essay. I cite both books of *Hyperaspistes* (1526–27), Erasmus's reply to Luther's *De servo arbitrio*, from L.B. 10. Two English translations of *De libero arbitrio* are readily available (Winter and Rupp in collaboration with A. N. Marlow), but I have preferred to give my own versions and have not wished to clutter Lesowsky's already cumbersome system of citation with cross-references to others. Ernst F. Winter, trans. and ed., *Erasmus-Luther: Discourse on Free Will*, Milestones of Thought in the History of Ideas (New York: Frederick Ungar, 1961); E. Gordon Rupp and Philip S. Watson, eds., *Luther and Erasmus: Free Will and Salvation*, Library of Christian Classics, vol. 17 (Philadelphia: Westminster Press, 1969).

51. To Henry, 6 September 1524, E.E. 1493.4 (5.541).

52. Since even the apostles taught paradoxes, they are not excluded on principle (I b 6). But Luther's paradoxes are virtually "enigmas" (IV 16), and all Christendom is in uproar because of them (IV 17). One such paradox must generate a system of supportive paradoxes, such as an exaggerated doctrine of original sin (IV 13–14).

53. On the meaning of *liberum arbitrium*, which I have translated "free choice" or "freedom of choice," see esp. III b 4: "Porro voluntas huc aut illo

versatilis dicitur arbitrium." Cf. the phrases *voluntas, qua eligimus aut refugimus* (II a 3), *eligendi potestas* (II a 7), *utroque volubilis* (ibid.), and *voluntas huc et illuc flexilis* (II a 18).

54. Erasmus does not deny that God, in the Scriptures, does sometimes force a man's judgment, altering his volition or even depriving him of reason, as, for example, when he caused Balaam to bless those he meant to curse (Numbers 23:11). But this is not how God acts as a rule (III a 8, III b 7).

55. As often in Erasmus, the abstract argument is accomplished by lively analogies drawn from human relationships: the king and the commander, the lord and his servant (IV 5).

56. Since he speaks of this common grace as *insita*, Erasmus seems to collapse together what Thomas distinguishes as the form by which a created thing acts and the motion imparted by the Prime Mover (S.T. IaIIae, Q.109, Art. 1, etc.).

57. If *proniores in favorem liberi arbitrii* is intended as a comparison specifically with the Pelagians, then we would have to agree with Lesowsky (p. 49, n. 74) that this is an error on Erasmus's part. I have preferred to take the phrase as a more general comparison, a placing of the Scotists on the total spectrum. They are then in antithesis to the Augustinians, later to be described as *propensiores in favorem gratiae* (II a 10).

58. In *Hyperaspistes I* Erasmus includes Thomas in this group. It is, presumably, the same party that he subsequently describes in the *Discourse* as farthest removed from the Pelagians (II a 12). *Desiderii Erasmi Hyperaspistes Diatribae adversus Servum arbitrium Martini Lutheri*, Lib. I, L.B. 10:1327C.

59. Besides the *gratia naturalis*, Erasmus distinguishes three kinds of grace in II a 11: (1) *gratia peculiaris, exstimulans* or *operans* (granted, some think, to everyone at some time in his life); (2) *gratia gratum faciens, provehens,* or *cooperans* (presumably the same as *gratia, quae peccatum abolet:* II a 9); and (3) *gratia consummans*. But although he can speak of receiving the first without the third, he acknowledges the accepted view that, if we leave aside *gratia naturalis*, there is only one grace, divided in name according to the diversity of its operations in us. For *gratia naturalis* and *gratia exstimulans* (or *praeveniens*), see the interpretation (borrowed from Jerome) of the Parable of the Prodigal Son (III c 11).

60. The identity of the final two opinions is clear enough; it is made explicit in *Hyperaspistes I* (L.B. 10:1327C–D).

61. The difference between Carlstadt and Luther is restated in II a 15. Though not so bad as Luther's, even Carlstadt's view goes too far (*praeter casam*: II a 12), and Erasmus has a profound dislike for Carlstadt's impersonal metaphors (the potter's clay, the craftsman's axe: ibid., also IV 11 and IV 16).

62. Whether Erasmus fairly interpreted the Scotists, or whether he assimilated their view to that of Gabriel Biel, Luther's bête noire, depends on the status of *gratia gratis data* in the Scotist system; and this has been a matter of debate among the scholars. On the relations among the Thomist, "old Franciscan," and Scotist doctrines of grace, see Reinhold Seeberg, *Lehrbuch der Dogmengeschichte*, 5th ed., 4 vols. (Graz: Akademische Druck- und Verlagsanstalt, 1953–54), 3: 444–86 and 664–67, which takes account of the work of Minges. For

Biel, see Heiko A. Oberman, *The Harvest of Medieval Theology: Gabriel Biel and Late Medieval Nominalism* (Cambridge, Mass.: Harvard University Press, 1963), pp. 135–39.

63. At one point (III b 2), Erasmus finds the inclination to sin only "in most men." Cf. the qualifying *ferme* in the sentence: "Sunt enim ferme mortalium ingenia ... proclivia ad scelera ..." (I a 10). Elsewhere (II a 5), he recognizes the existence (along with the *lex naturae*) of a contrary bias towards virtue, though—without grace—it remains *inefficax ad salutem aeternam*. In general, Erasmus seems to think that, before grace, we are *more* inclined to evil than to good (II a 8). Cf. also III b 4.

64. On sin as weakness, see further II a 4 (where *ad honesta inefficax* presumably means "lethargic" rather than totally "impotent"), II a 5, II a 8 (sin is like an injury or disease), III b 1, and III b 4; on grace as help, see II a 6, III c 13. Luther's central thought on sin was rather that sin vitiates the motivation.

65. Once again the analogies are striking: the sheep and the branch (III c 3), the child and the apple (III c 3, IV 9–10). But the credit should go mainly to Augustine (*In Joann. evang. tract.*, xxvi.5, *Patrologia Latina*, 35:1609; *Nicene and Post-Nicene Fathers*, first series, 7:170). It should be noted that Erasmus must sometimes have in mind the continuing assent of the Christian to cooperative grace, not the reception of the first grace; but the *Discourse* does not make clear how he understood the relationship of justification to baptism.

66. See also III a 4, III c 4, III c 12, IV 7, IV 10. The *posse consentire et cooperari* is a *munus dei* (III c 4; cf. IV 7). God's unchangeable will does not work in us the *velle* itself (IV 3). Erasmus, accordingly, is glad to avail himself of Ambrose's interpretation of Phil. 2:13 (III c 6). But is the *munus* a gift of nature or of special grace? This, of course, is the crucial question. The answer to it, I think, is given in III c 11–12: the ability to apply oneself to prevenient grace is among the *dotes naturae*. Erasmus would thus endorse the notion, reported in II a 11, that repentance is possible to those who "apply the remnant of free choice, with all their might, to the assistance of the Deity, who invites, as it were, but does not compel them to betterment." Man's freedom to respond to prevenient grace, it appears, is a particular instance of the natural freedom of choice. Hence one must assume that when Erasmus speaks of the "freeing" or "healing" of the will (as in IV 8), he is implicitly denying, not the natural freedom of the will to say yes or no to grace, but its ability either (1) to control the offer of grace, without which a man does not perceive the right path, or (2) to achieve, without grace, the goal that grace presents.

67. The three stages correspond to the the three types of grace (see n. 59 above); and the distinction between *initium*, *progressus*, and *summa* (IV 8) indicates what Erasmus intends by the word *summa* in III c 1 and III c 4: the "completion" or "consummation" of the entire movement. Cf. also the distinction between *cogitare*, *velle*, and *perficere* (III c 4).

68. Cf. the remarks on pagan virtues (II a 10) and *peccatum alienum* (IV 13–14).

69. We attribute the whole to him because our contribution is minimal (III c 1; cf. III c 12). "God does not want a man to claim anything for himself, even though there were something he could claim deservedly" (III c 8).

70. The additional phrase *adiutus auxilio dei* in a similar passage in III b 3 perhaps moves the thought out of the Scotist orbit.

71. Besides *Hyperaspistes*, there is the important letter to Thomas More, 30 March 1527, E. E. 1804 (7.5–14). Naturally, these sources require an essay to themselves. There is now a useful article by Trinkaus on one section of *Hyperaspistes* (L.B. 10:1521B–1536F), which agrees at several points with my reading of *De libero arbitrio*. Charles Trinkaus, "Erasmus, Augustine, and the Nominalists," *Archiv für Reformationsgeschichte* 67 (1976):5–32. The letter to More, it seems to me, indicates that Erasmus would have liked to be more openly sympathetic to the Scotists than he was. "Mihi non displiceret opinio que putat nos ex meris nature viribus absque peculiari gratia posse de congruo, ut illi loquuntur, gratiam instituere, nisi refragaretur Paulus; quanquam ne scholastici quidem hanc recipiunt sententiam."

72. Walter concludes: "Über ein Schwanken zwischen Thomas, Alexander und Duns Scotus ist er nicht hinausgekommen" (p. xxx). McSorley places Erasmus "betwen Neo-Semipelagianism and Augustine'" Harry J. McSorley, *Luther: Right or Wrong? An Ecumenical-Theological Study of Luther's Major Work, "The Bondage of the Will"* (New York: Newman Press, and Minneapolis: Augsburg Publishing House, 1969), pp. 288–93.

73. Kohls argues that Erasmus's notion of a "will made free by grace" aligns him with Thomas. Ernst-Wilhelm Kohls, "Die theologische Position und der Traditionszusammenhang des Erasmus mit dem Mittelalter in 'De libero arbitrio'," in *Humanitas-Christianitas: Walther v. Loewenich zum 65. Geburtstag,* ed. Karlmann Beyschlag et al. (Witten: Luther-Verlag, 1968), pp. 32–46. Winsome though this line of interpretation may be, my remarks above (in n. 66) will betray the fact that I am not persuaded by it. When Kohls speaks of grace as simply the offer of grace and of freedom as simply the freedom to decide, it must be replied (1) that for Thomas the turning of the will is the effect of grace as *gratia gratum faciens* and *operans* (S.T. IaIIae, Q. 113, Art. 3) and (2) that for Erasmus freedom of choice is the gift of grace as *gratia naturalis*. Readers familiar with Kohls's other writings will be aware that his reading of Erasmus on grace is by no means intended to close the gap between Erasmus and Luther; on the contrary, Kohls thinks we must choose between them. See his *Luther oder Erasmus: Luthers Theologie in der Auseinandersetzung mit Erasmus*, 2 vols. to date, *Theologische Zeitschrift*, supplements 3 and 8 (Basel: Friedrich Reinhardt Verlag, 1972, 1978); cf. his brief statement in "Der Hl. Geist ist kein Skeptiker: Luther antwortet Erasmus," *Luther: Zeitschrift der Luther-Gesellschaft* 47 (1976); 142–44.

74. "Erasmus trat aus dem Bannkreis der von ihm bekämpften scholastischen Theologie mit ihrer Lehre vom meritum de congruo et de condigno nicht heraus." Max Richter, *Desiderius Erasmus und seine Stellung zu Luther auf Grund ihrer Schriften,* Quellen und Darstellungen aus der Geschichte des Reformationsjahrhunderts, vol. 3 (Leipzig: M. Heinsius Nachfolger, 1907), p. 61. Whatever the ambiguities of the *Discourse*, Humbertclaude—who thought that the Augustinian tendency of the work against Luther may have been merely prudential—detected an increasing sympathy for the Scotist view after 1524 (pp. 220ff.).

In this he is followed by John B. Payne, *Erasmus: His Theology of the Sacraments* (Richmond, Va.: John Knox Press, 1970), esp. p. 264, n. 18, and p. 265, n. 20. But I am not sure that Payne allows sufficient weight to the Pauline veto of merits *de congruo*, of which Erasmus writes to More (see n. 71 above).

75. Contrast, for instance, the remarks against Carlstadt in IV 11 with Thomas, S.T. IaIIae, Q. 111, Art. 2. Cf. also *Hyperaspistes I*, L.B. 10:1331E; *Hyperaspistes II*, L.B. 10:1528F, 1532A. Erasmus's position in fact resembles a view that Augustine retracted: "Ut autem praedicato nobis Evangelio consentiremus, nostrum esse proprium, et nobis ex nobis esse arbitrabar.... Nondum diligentius quaesiveram, nec adhuc inveneram, qualis sit electio gratiae" (*De praedest.*, iii.7, *Patrologia Latina*, 44:964–65; *Nicene and Post-Nicene Fathers*, first series, 5:500–501). Cf. the rhetorical question raised later: "Ut enim sit naturae, fidem posse habere; numquid et habere?" (ibid., v. 10, *Patrologia Latina*, 44:968; *Nicene and Post-Nicene Fathers*, first series, 5:503).

76. Erasmus employs the expressions συνεργὸς *gratiae* (III c 5) and *gratiae* συνcργcῖυ (IV 7), the Greek cognates from which the concept of "synergism" is derived (cf. 1 Cor. 3:9). The *Formula of Concord* (1577) expressly distinguishes the questions of preparation for, and acceptance of, grace in the preamble to the Epitome, Art. II. Cf. the corresponding distinction between the errors of Semi-Pelagianism and synergism (Epit., Art. II, secs. 10–11; Sol. Decl., Art. II, secs. 76–77). A clear summary of Erasmus's synergism appears in *Hyperaspistes II*, L.B. 10:1524 E, culminating in the proposition: "Ut igitur indignus gratia dicitur, qui vel oblatam negligit, vel possessam non servat, & abutitur, ita quoddammodo dignus est dono Dei, qui cum offertur alacritur accipit, & acceptam summa solicitudine cavet ne perdat."

77. This, I take it, is the intent of III c 12. Cf. *Hyperaspistes II*, L.B. 10: 1525D-E, 1533F-1534A.

78. *Hyperaspistes II*, L.B. 10:1340A. In *Hyperaspistes I*, Erasmus insisted that the Scotist view was a legitimate *opinio*, left open by the church (L.B. 10:1323D, 1327D). He makes no mention of the pronouncements of the Second Council of Orange (529), which in effect condemned both the errors that we have distinguished as "Semi-Pelagianism" (the Scotist-Nominalist doctrine of congruous merits before sanctifying grace) and "synergism" (the position of Erasmus himself). *Conc. Arausicanum* II (529), can. 7 and concl. I have used the text in Henricus Denzinger and Adolfus Schönmetzer, eds., *Enchiridion symbolorum ...*, 33d ed. (Barcelona: Herder, 1965), pp. 133 and 137.

79. W.A. 18.609.15ff.; L.W. 33:29.

80. "Das Problem der Willensfreiheit gehört auch und vor allem in das Gebiet der Frömmigkeit ...." Erasmus viewed it as *Seelsorger* and *Pädagog*. Karl Heinz Oelrich, *Der späte Erasmus und die Reformation*, Reformationsgeschichtliche Studien und Texte, no. 86 (Munster: Aschendorf, 1961), pp. 128, 133.

81. In I a 9, Erasmus distinguishes (1) matters God wants to remain wholly unknown to us (like the date for the Last Judgment), (2) matters we may explore only as far as reticence toward God permits (such as the distinction of persons in the Trinity), (3) matters God wants us to know thoroughly (namely, the precepts of the good life), and (4) matters which, even if true and knowable,

it would not be expedient to expose to common ears (e.g., that a council had erred). It will be noted that moral matters receive top priority. The belief that some matters ought not to be divulged to the laity is a constant theme in Erasmus's correspondence, sometimes accompanied by disavowal of Plato's "noble lie": E.E. 872.19, 1033.91, 1167.167–72, 1195.105–19; 1202.56–62, 123–28; 1523.84–87.

82. It is uncertain what passage from Augustine Erasmus has in mind (if any). See Lesowsky, ad loc.

83. The selfsame concern underlies Erasmus's reflections on trinitarian speculation (though this is an instance of class 2 matters: see n. 81): "At the high price of unity, we love less while wanting to know more than enough" (I a 9).

84. The same figure occurs in E.E. 1342.959–63 and (with the priorities reversed) 1804.96–99.

85. By Walter (p. xxxii) and McSorley (*Luther Right or Wrong?* p. 284), for example.

86. He also understood the doctrine of sin as radical defect (II a 10) and presumably could have answered the question he sets aside in IV 14: why the Lutherans taught the impossibility of keeping the commandments.

87. Cf. the honorific title bestowed on Luther in *Hyperaspistes II: doctor hyperbolicus* (L.B. 10:1345D).

88. Zickendraht's judgment that "the shell [of the *Discourse*] is more authentic than the kernel" (*Der Streit zwischen Erasmus und Luther*, p. 26) is of one piece with his claim that Erasmus was led to deal dogmatically with his theme (i.e., as a question of truth) only by external pressure (see n. 33 above). "It is plainly the main purpose of the *Diatribe* ... to permit validity to [*Glaubenslehren*] only as subservient aids for a pattern of ethical existence." Erasmus's case is not against *necessitas absoluta*, but against the overestimate of dogmatic formulations exhibited by the Lutheran movement (pp. 26–27). This is an intriguing interpretation of the *libellus*. But, surely, Erasmus *did* want to object to the Lutheran dogma; and he did so, in part, because he thought it was *false* (absurd as well as dangerous). Hence he argued against it with the norm of Scripture in the *Discourse* and, in *Hyperaspistes I*, with the authority of the church—finally asserting bluntly that to doubt free choice is considered by him to be heretical (L.B. 10:1259D).

89. "Neque tu sophisticam theologiam sustulisti, sed mutasti" (*Hyperaspistes I*, L.B. 10:1277B).

90. W.A. 18.783.17; L.W. 33:288.

Chapter Two

1. A. Zahn, "Calvins Urtheile über Luther: Ein Beitrag zur Lutherfeier aus der reformirten Kirche Deutschlands," *Theologische Studien aus Württemberg*, vol. 4, ed. Theodor Hermann and Paul Zeller (Ludwigsburg: Ad. Neubert'sche Buchhandlung, 1883), pp. 183–211; August Lang, "Luther und Calvin," *Deutschevangelische Blätter* 21 (1896): 319–32; Karl Holl, *Luther und Calvin*, Staat,

Recht und Volk: Wissenschaftliche Reden und Aufsätze, no. 2 (Berlin: Weidmannsche Buchhandlung, 1919); Hans Grass, *Die Abendmahlslehre bei Luther und Calvin: Eine kritische Untersuchung*, Beiträge zur Förderung christlicher Theologie, 2d ser., vol. 47, 2d ed. (Gütersloh: C. Bertelsmann, 1954); Ernst Walter Zeeden, "Das Bild Martin Luthers in den Briefen Calvins," *Archiv für Reformationsgeschichte* 49 (1958):177–95; Erwin Mülhaupt, "Luther und Calvin: Eine Jubiläumsbetrachtung," *Luther: Mitteilungen der Luthergesellschaft* 30 (1959): 97–113; Peter Meinhold, "Calvin und Luther," *Lutherische Monatshefte* 3 (1964): 264–69. Cf. also Bernhard Lohse, "Calvin als Reformator," *Luther: Zeitschrift der Luthergesellschaft* 35 (1964): 102–17. I have not been able to see the dissertation of Andrea Wiedeburg, "Calvins Verhältnis zu Luther, Melanchthon, und dem Luthertum" (Tübingen, 1961).

2. See, in particular: Auguste Lemaître, *Calvin et Luther*, Cahiers de 'foi et vérité', no. 38 [ser. 10, no. 2] (Geneva: Éditions Labor et fides, 1959), pp. 3–24; A. Eekhof, "Hoe heeft Calvijn over Luther gedacht?" Nederlandsch Archief voor Kerkgeschiedenis, n.s., 14 (1918): 273–96; A. D. R. Polman, "Calvijn en Luther," in *Vier Redevoeringen over Calvijn*, by D. Nauta et al. (Kampen: J. H. Kok, 1959), pp. 41–53; Charles Boyer, *Calvin et Luther: Accords et différences* (Rome: Gregorian University, 1973).

3. Of particular note is the full discussion in the magisterial work of Émile Doumergue, *Jean Calvin: Les hommes et les choses de son temps*, 7 vols. (Lausanne: Georges Bridel, 1899–1928), 2:562–87.

4. David S. Schaff, "Martin Luther and John Calvin: Church Reformers," *Princeton Theological Review* 15 (1917): 530–52, compares the careers, accomplishments, and characters of the two Reformers, but does not consider their actual relationships or opinions of each other. Allan L. Farris, "Calvin's Letter to Luther," *Canadian Journal of Theology* 10 (1964): 124–31, reproduces an old translation of Calvin's letter and adds some historical notes; he does not attempt a general discussion of Calvin's estimate of Luther. Alexander Barclay, in *The Protestant Doctrine of the Lord's Supper: A Study in the Eucharistic Teaching of Luther, Zwingli and Calvin* (Glasgow: Jackson, Wylie, 1927), compares the Reformers on this limited theme only. There are two comparative studies in English of the political opinions of Luther and Calvin: William A. Mueller, *Church and State in Luther and Calvin: A Comparative Study* (Nashville: Broadman Press, 1954), and Duncan B. Forrester, "Martin Luther and John Calvin," in *History of Political Philosophy*, ed. Leo Strauss and Joseph Cropsey (Chicago: Rand McNally, 1963), pp. 277–313. At the time when my own essay first appeared, I had not been able to find any previous study in English devoted directly to Calvin's opinions of Martin Luther; afterwards, I came across an article—by a Dutch scholar, but published in English—that does shed light on my theme: D. Nauta, "Calvin and Luther," *Free University Quarterly* 2 (1952–53): 1–17.

5. The index to C.O. 23–55 (in C.O. 58) lists ten references to Luther in Calvin's exegetical works, four of which occur in the *Commentary on Genesis*.

6. C.O. 10^2–20. Reference will also be made to A.-L. [Aimé-Louis] Herminjard, ed., *Correspondance des réformateurs dans les pays de langue française*,

9 vols., vols. 1–4 in 2d ed. (Geneva: H. Georg, 1878–97), whose editorial notes are invaluable.

7. C.O. 5–9. Some of the treatises will be found also in O.S. 1–2, but I give references only to C.O.

8. A number of Calvin's letters have been translated in *Letters of John Calvin Compiled and Edited by Jules Bonnet*, trans. David Constable and Marcus Robert Gilchrist, 4 vols. (Philadelphia: Presbyterian Board of Publication, n.d. [ca. 1858]). But this collection is by no means complete and does not contain all the letters that will be discussed in the present essay. A collection of the theological treatises in English has been reprinted: *Calvin's Tracts and Treatises*, trans. Henry Beveridge, 3 vols. (1844–51; reprint ed., Grand Rapids, Mich.: William B. Eerdmans, 1958). It includes only three of the six treatises that are important for our theme: *Short Treatise on the Supper of Our Lord, Necessity of Reforming the Church*, and *Second Defense against Westphal*. Mention may also be made of J. K. S. Reid, ed., *Calvin: Theological Treatises*, Library of Christian Classics, vol. 22 (Philadelphia: Westminster Press, 1954), which also contains in English translation the *Short Treatise on the Lord's Supper* and *Necessity of Reforming the Church*. There is now, in addition, a translation of Calvin's *Concerning Scandals* by John W. Fraser (Grand Rapids, Mich.: William B. Eerdmans, 1978). For simplicity of reference, I cite throughout only C.O., and even where older translations are in existence I have preferred to make my own.

9. Cf. Lemaître, *Calvin et Luther*, pp. 3–4; Mülhaupt, "Luther und Calvin," pp. 97–99. Mülhaupt also contrasts Luther the scholastic with Calvin the humanist and even describes Calvin as an industrious *Amateurtheologe*.

10. See the studies by Boyer, Lamaître, Lohse, and Meinhold, referred to above. On particular doctrines there are Barclay, Forrester, Grass, and Mueller. The interesting pamphlet by Karl Holl argues for the complementarity of the thought and activity of the two reformers. He concludes: "Wir sind im Weltkrieg mit calvinischen Mächten zusammengestossen und dabei unterlegen; wäre es nicht vielleicht richtiger, wenn wir einen Tropfen calvinisches Blut in uns aufnehmen?" (p. 19). Contrast Harnack's remark (see n. 12 below)!

11. So Eekhof, Lang, Nauta, Zahn, and Zeeden. Of course, some of the articles mentioned (e.g., the one by Mülhaupt) display an interest in all three divisions of the theme.

12. Quoted (in the German) by Eekhof, "Calvijn over Luther," pp. 295–96, from *Theologische Studien und Kritiken* 90 (1917): 225.

13. Serm. Ps. 115:1–3, C.O. 32:460–61.

14. C.O. 9:19, 91; 15:336; 16:263, 430; 17:139. But he considered it inferior to the French *Confession de foi*, as his correspondence with the Reformed participants in the Colloquy of Poissey (1561) demonstrates: C.O. 18:683–84 (to Beza), 733 (to Coligny). See chapter 15 below.

15. C.O. 5:458–60; 9:51; 10^2:346; 11:24, 438.

16. John Wolph (Wolf) to Calvin, 1 May 1560, C.O. 18:73 (no. 3189). Cf. Calvin to James André, C.O. 16:553 (no. 2674), where Calvin reports that he had passed on to a friend a book lent by André *quia linguae germanicae sum ignarus*.

17. C.O. 10^2 :xliv.

18. Herminjard, *Correspondance*, 7:284–86 (no. 1051).

19. Calvin to Bucer, 12 January 1538, C.O. 10^2 :138–39 (no. 87). Cf. Herminjard, *Correspondance*, 4:342, n. 11. See also Calvin to Farel, 24 October 1538, C.O. 10^2 :277 (no. 149); Calvin to Farel, April 1539, C.O. 10^2 : 340–41 (no. 169).

20. Doumergue, *Jean Calvin*, 2:569–70.

21. Lang's article, "Luther und Calvin," was reprinted in his *Reformation und Gegenwart: Gesammelte Aufsätze* (Detmold: Meyersche Hofbuchhandlung, 1918), pp. 72–87, after publication of Doumergue's second volume, to which a brief allusion is made.

22. "Principio animadvertere convenit, quid sit sacramentum. Est autem signum externum ... ut promissionem ipsam firmet atque obsignet ..." (*Christianae religionis institutio* [1536], C.O. 1:102).

23. The relevant part of his letter, dated 14 October 1539, is given in C.O. 10^2 :402 (no. 190). Cf. W.A.Br. 8.569.29 (no. 3349); L.W. 50:190–91.

24. C.O. 10^2 :432 (no. 197).

25. "Sed aequum est a bono ingenio nos aliquid ferre." Perhaps Luther meant "a man of good character," but in other judgments it was usually Calvin's intellectual ability that seems to have impressed him. The English translation of Calvin's letter by Constable gives a quite different rendering: "It is well that he should even now have a proof of our good feeling towards him" (*Letters* 1:143). This translation appears, without any explanation, in a footnote in C.O. 10^2 :432, n. 18.

26. Specifically the words translated "Just think ... disagree with him" and "We are surely ... to the Romans." See Herminjard, *Correspondance*, 6:131, nn. 49 and 53.

27. Calvin wrote to Farel on 10 January 1540: "Luther has very kindly inquired after me from Bucer. Philip judged that I should dispense with my apology [*excusatione illa mea ... supersedendum*]." Herminjard, *Correspondance*, 6:165 (no. 845). But why dispense with it? Because it was thought unnecessary, or because it might have the opposite effect to that intended?

28. Herminjard reproduces the text (*Correspondance*, 6:132–37). See also his important notes (pp. 131–32), which correct the editors of C.O. at certain points. Misled by an annotation of Farel's on the back of his copy of the *excusatio*, the editors supposed that there were two apologies, one intended for the *Commentary on Romans*, the other for the *Institutes*. The epistle dedicatory does in fact contain an interesting statement on the diversity of theological opinion (see n. 114 below), but this cannot be identified with the apology. A few fragments of the apology were incorporated into the *Institutio* of 1543.

29. Luther's wording (*quorum libellos*) leaves it open whether he read more than one book by Calvin. He *must* have read at least one each by Calvin and Sturm. He *may* have read more.

30. Herminjard, *Correspondance*, 6:132–37.

31. *Jean Calvin*, 2:571–72, n. 6. It should be added here that we have two further testimonies to Luther's approval of the *Reply to Sadoleto*: a letter from Marcus Crodel, a schoolmaster from Torgau, addressed to Calvin on 6 March 1545, C.O. 12:40 (no. 619); and an incident reported by Christoph Pezel in his

Ausführliche, wahrhafte und beständige Erzählung and cited by Doumergue (*Jean Calvin*, 2:572). According to Pezel, Luther was rereading the *Reply* as he traveled to visit the sick Melanchthon at Weimar (1540). To his travel-companion, Cruciger, he expressed his admiration for the work and predicted that Calvin would complete what he himself had begun against the antichrist. In his *Reply to Sadoleto* Calvin expressly rejects (1) a local presence of Christ's body in the eucharistic bread and (2) the ubiquity of Christ's human nature (*Responsio ad Sadoleti epistolam*, C.O. 5:399–400). Translations of the *Reply* will be found in both *Tracts and Treatises*, vol. 1, and Reid (see n. 8 above).

32. See, for instance, Luther to the Swiss Reformed Cities, 1 December 1537, W.A.Br. 8.149–53 (no. 3191) and 241–42 (no. 3240).

33. For Luther's conduct at Marburg, see Bucer to Ambrose Blarer, 18 October 1529, quoted by Walther Köhler, *Das Marburger Religionsgespräch 1529: Versuch einer Rekonstruktion*, Schriften des Vereins für Reformations-geschichte, no. 148 (Leipzig: M. Heinsius [Eger and Sievers], 1929), pp. 139–40.

34. Luther to Christoph Froschauer, 31 August 1543, W.A.Br. 10.387 (no. 3908).

35. *Kurzes Bekenntnis vom heiligen Sakrament*, W.A. 54.147.33; L.W. 38:296.

36. Luther to Jacob Probst, 17 January 1546, W.A.Br. 11.264.14 (no. 4188).

37. C.O. 11:698 (no. 544).

38. C.O. 11:774–75 (no. 586).

39. Cf. the brief account in Beza's life of Calvin (*Vita Calvini*, C.O. 21:138). The circumstances are more fully described in Calvin to Melanchthon, 21 January 1545, C.O. 12:9–12 (no. 606).

40. *Petit traicté monstrant que c'est que doit faire un homme fidele, cognois-sant la verité de l'Evangile, quand il est entre les papistes*, C.O. 6:537–88.

41. *Excuse de Iehan Calvin a Messieurs les Nicodemites, sur la complaincte qu'ilz font de sa trop grand'rigueur*, C.O. 6:589–614.

42. Calvin's excuses will be found in a letter, written in January 1545, to an unnamed friend, possibly one of his countrymen (C.O. 12:25–26 [no. 610]).

43. The two together, in their Latin version, were subsequently published together under the title *De vitandis superstitionibus*, with added comments from Calvin and other leading Reformers (see C.O. 6:617–44).

44. Calvin to Melanchthon, 21 January 1545, C.O. 12:10 (no. 606).

45. Calvin to Luther, 21 January 1545, C.O. 12:8 (no. 605).

46. C.O. 12:61 (no. 632). Luther was being nicknamed "Pericles" at this time because the ancient Athenian had been likened to Zeus the thrower of thunder-bolts.

47. C.O. 12:10 (no. 606).

48. See Farris, "Calvin's Letter to Luther," p. 128, n. 23.

49. See Calvin to Viret, 2 February 1545, C.O. 12:26–27 (no. 611).

50. C.O. 12:99 (no. 657).

51. See, e.g., Calvin to Bullinger, 25 November 1544, C.O. 11:774 (no. 586).

52. Cf. Melanchthon to Bucer, 28 August 1544, Herminjard, *Correspondance*, 9:373, n. 16.

53. "Tu unus semper probatus fueris Luthero," Farel wrote to Calvin on 17 October 1555 (C.O. 15:823). The most interesting testimony to Luther's con-

tinuing goodwill is an anecdote related by both Christoph Pezel and Rudolph Hospinian. Moritz Goltsch, a Wittenberg bookseller, brought back the Latin translation of Calvin's *Short Treatise on the Lord's Supper* from the Frankfurt Fair (1545) and presented a copy to Luther, who read the closing section with particular care and announced that, had Zwingli and Oecolampadius spoken like Calvin, there would have been no need for a long dispute. I do not currently have access to either of the two sources, but Pezel's account (the longer of the two) is given in full by Doumergue in French translation (*Jean Calvin*, 2:572–73). Mülhaupt ("Luther und Calvin," p. 103) suspects this story of being a mere embellishment of the incident Calvin reported to Farel in his letter of 20 November 1539, where, as we have seen, the writing in question is not identified. But this is mere guess-work, and the story may well be authentic; Pezel relates it with attention to details and also names the witness (one of Luther's table companions) from whom the incident is derived. On the other hand, it is quite plain from two passages in the *Table Talk* that Luther's attitude toward Calvin in the closing years of his life was a mixture of respect and suspicion: W.A.Tr. 5.51.19 (no. 5303) and 461.18 (no. 6050).

54. Calvin to Viret, 19 May 1540, C.O. 11:36 (no. 217).

55. *Petit traicté de la saincte cene de nostre Seigneur Iesus Christ*, C.O. 5:457–60.

56. See n. 53 above.

57. *Defensio sanae et orthodoxae doctrinae de servitute et liberatione humani arbitrii adversus calumnias Alberti Pighii Campensis*, C.O. 6:245.

58. Ibid., 249.

59. Ibid., 251. Taken in isolation, this passage might seem to imply that differences of expression affect only nonessentials, but I think that subsequent quotations will show that Calvin intended more: he meant that the apprehension of all truth is progressive.

60. Ibid., 250.

61. *Supplex exhortatio ad invictissimum Caesarem Carolum Quintum et illustrissimos Principes aliosque ordines Spirae nunc imperii conventum agentes, ut restituendae ecclesiae curam serio velint suscipere*, C.O. 6:459.

62. Ibid., 466.

63. Ibid., 472–73.

64. Ibid., 524–25.

65. Ibid., 499–500.

66. ". . . vehementer esse collaudatum." So the Spanish Protestant Dryander (Francisco d'Enzinas) wrote to Calvin (3 August 1545, C.O. 12:127 [no. 673]). Dryander lived at Wittenberg, 1544–46.

67. "In hoc cursu adhuc hodie pergimus" (C.O. 6:473).

68. *Consensio mutua in re sacramentaria ministrorum Tigurinae ecclesiae et D. Ioannis Calvini ministri Genevensis ecclesiae*, C.O. 7:689–748.

69. Calvin to John Marbach, 24 August 1554, C.O. 15:212–13 (no. 1998). For want of a better term to contrast with "*naked* signs," one could perhaps speak of the bond that Calvin discovers between Luther and himself as the notion of "*efficacious* signs"; and this may be suggested by the last sentence in my quotation from the letter to Marbach. But, for reasons that will become

clear in chapters 6 and 7 below, it was in some ways more natural for Calvin to speak of a "sacramental union" between sign and reality. Cf. *Defensio sanae et orthodoxae doctrinae de sacramentis, eorumque natura, vi, fine, usu, et fructu,* etc. (1555), where Calvin outlined what he believed was at stake for Luther in the eucharistic controversy (C.O. 9:18). But this did not mean, as we shall see, that Calvin revised his earlier judgment of Luther's opinions as in other respects idolatrous. "Ego tamen sepulta esse haec omnia cuperem," he wrote to Bucer in October 1549 (C.O. 13:439 [no. 1297]).

70. Cf. John Haller's remark to Bullinger, in a letter of 28 December 1554, that Calvin always seemed to defend Luther and Bucer too much (C.O. 15:362 [no. 2072]).

71. The pastors of Zurich to Calvin, 24 October 1554, C.O. 15:274 (no. 2034). The communication contains *iudicia* on the Zurich Consensus; the original is in Bullinger's hand.

72. Ibid., col. 276 (my emphasis).

73. See, e.g., Calvin to Martin Seidemann, 14 March 1555, C.O. 15:501–2 (no. 2148).

74. Calvin to Francis Burkhart, 27 February 1555, C.O. 15:454 (no. 2123).

75. "Nam quum Lutherus principium hoc semper tenuerit, nec sibi, nec cuiquam mortalium fas est, nisi ex verbo Dei sapere, mirandum ac dolendum est, tam imperiose eius placitis ecclesiam Dei astringi." *Ultima admonitio Ioannis Calvini ad Ioachimum Westphalum* (1557), C.O. 9:238; *Tracts and Treatises,* 2:477.

76. *De scandalis quibus hodie plerique absterrentur, nonnulli etiam alienantur a pura evangelii doctrina,* C.O. 8:64.

77. Ibid., 73.

78. Ibid., 56–59.

79. Ibid., 59.

80. See, for example, *Secunda defensio piae et orthodoxae de sacramentis fidei contra Ioachimi Westphali calumnias,* C.O. 9:61, 69, 80, 109, and 111.

81. Ibid., 51–52.

82. Ibid., 52. If Luther failed to make the needed distinctions among the opinions of those who dissented from him, this was because he was provoked by misinformation (col. 69). On Luther's vehemence, cf. cols. 56 and 109.

83. Ibid., 105. Cf. *Ultima admonitio ad Westphalum:* the faults should be buried, not embraced as virtues (C.O. 9:238). See also Calvin's letter to the pastors of Mömpelgard, 8 May 1544, C.O. 11:704–8 (no. 547). Even at that time Calvin was confident that Luther himself disapproved the *simiae* and *Thrasones.* From Wittenberg, as from Jerusalem, had sprung both the Gospel and also mischief-makers.

84. *Secunda defensio contra Westphalum,* C.O. 9:54. Here it is relevant to note that on 17 March 1546 Calvin urged Vitus Theodorus to complete the publication of Luther's *Commentary on Genesis* (C.O. 12:317 [no. 781]).

85. *Secunda defensio contra Westphalum,* C.O. 9:70.

86. Ibid., 91.

87. Ibid., 100.

88. Ibid., 104. Other references to Luther in the *Secunda defensio*, not discussed here, are C.O. 9:93, 94, 101, and 107.

89. *Gratulatio ad venerabilem presbyterum Dominum Gabrielem de Saconay, praecentorem ecclesiae Lugdunensis, de pulchra et eleganti praefatione quam libro Regis Angliae inscripsit* (1561), C.O. 9:438. Carlstadt's *commentum* no doubt refers to his odd theory that when Jesus uttered the words "This is my body," he pointed not to the bread but to himself. On Luther's *inconsideratus fervor*, see also col. 442.

90. Ibid., 438.

91. *Defensio contra Pighium*, C.O. 6:241. To Pighius (loc. cit.), as to Gabriel (C.O. 9:454), Calvin quotes Luther's famous utterance: "Whether I like it or not, my adversaries oblige me to become wiser every day." He does not give Luther's words exactly. See *De captivitate Babylonica ecclesiae praeludium* (1520), W.A. 6.497.7; cf. L.W. 36:11.

92. *Gratulatio ad Gabrielem*, C.O. 9:442.

93. Ibid., 453. For other references to Luther in the work against Gabriel, see cols. 428, 435, 437, 441, 443f., 448 (an important reminder that certain of Luther's works were translated and published at Geneva), and 454 (Gabriel hounded Luther even to the grave by claiming that he drank himself to death).

94. Cf. Eekhof: "Calvijn ziet dus zijne reformatie niet als aan die van Luther tegenovergesteldt, doch als voortzetting en in denzelfden lijn gelegen" ("Calvijn over Luther," p. 283).

95. "Calvin ist der grösste und wohl auch einzige 'Schüler', den Luther wirklich gehabt hat, d.h. der ihn zutiefst verstanden und, von ihm ausgehend, das Werk der Reformation mit einer eigenen Durchdringung der Botschaft des Evangeliums fortgesetzt und zu einer eigenen kirchlichen Gestalt gebracht hat" (Meinhold, "Calvin und Luther," p. 264).

96. See n. 10 above.

97. For instance, Luther says that faith is *notitia*, that it is *in intellectu*, that its object is *veritas* (W.A. 40^2.25.27ff.; L.W. 27:20–25); Calvin, that even assent is more a matter of the heart than of the mind (*Inst.*, 3.2.8, 33). Again, it was Luther who took his stand upon the letter of Scripture in the eucharistic debate; Calvin, on the other hand, states expressly that the sole function of Scripture is to draw us to Jesus Christ (C.O. 9:815).

98. *Ultima admonitio ad Westphalum*, C.O. 9:238. Cf. the "Lutherolatry" that angered Bartholomaeus Bertlinus: to Bullinger, 18 July 1554, C.O. 15:191 (no. 1987).

99. "... ich denke an den Gedanken der Geschichtlichkeit des Reformators; an die Idee der Weiterentwicklung der Reformation und an die beherzte Kritik an Luther vom Evangelium her." Hence Calvin could think of certain elements in Luther's teaching as vestigial blemishes. Zeeden, "Das Bild Luthers in den Briefen Calvins," p. 191.

100. "Nos huc dies noctesque incumbere, ut quae fideliter a nobis *tradita* sunt, in modum etiam, quem putamus optimum fore, *formemus*" (*Defensio contra Pighium*, C.O. 6:250; my emphasis).

101. Ibid., 251.

102. *Secunda defensio contra Westphalum,* C.O. 9:91. See also n. 69 above.

103. Lemaître, *Calvin et Luther,* p. 12.

104. *Secunda defensio contra Westphalum,* C.O. 9:69, 92.

105. *Excuse a Messieurs les Nicodemites,* C.O. 6:602.

106. Cf. *Defensio contra Pighium,* C.O. 6:239–40.

107. See Karl Gerhard Steck, *Lehre und Kirche bei Luther,* Forschungen zur Geschichte und Lehre des Protestantismus, ser. 10, vol. 27 (Munich: Chr. Kaiser Verlag, 1963), pp. 206–7.

108. C.O. 5:457–60.

109. See, for example, Alexander Barclay, *Protestant Doctrine of the Lord's Supper,* chap. 12.

110. See Jacques Pannier, *Les Origines de la confession de foi et la discipline des églises réformées de France: Étude historique* (Paris: Librairie Felix Alcan, 1936), pp. 90ff.

111. Calvin to Archbishop Thomas Cranmer, April (or early May) 1552, C.O. 14:312–14 (no. 1619).

112. Hence the custom of holding congregations is not merely useful but virtually necessary. See Calvin to Wolfgang Musculus, 22 October 1549, C.O. 13:433 (no. 1294).

113. From Nicolas Colladon, *Vie de Calvin* (1565), C.O. 21:96. I owe this and the preceding reference to the admirable discussion in Rodolphe Peter, ed., *Jean Calvin: Deux congrégations et exposition du catéchisme,* Cahiers de la Revue d'Histoire et de Philosophie Religieuses, no. 38 (Paris: Presses Universitaires de France, 1964), pp. xiii–xiv.

114. C.O. 10^2:405 (no. 191). The remarks were made in a dedicatory epistle to Simon Grynaeus, dated 18 October 1539.

Chapter Three

1. See Robert M. Grant, *The Bible in the Church: A Short History of Interpretation* (New York: Macmillan, 1948), chap. 2; J. N. D. Kelly, *Early Christian Doctrines,* 2d ed. (New York: Harper and Row, 1960), pp. 62–63. As Kelly points out, there were two strikingly different views of inspiration in the early church: in one the human consciousness was suspended by divine possession, in the other it was heightened so as to reach beyond its normal limits. The presumed infallibility of the sacred text led Augustine to account for apparent error in one of three ways: either the manuscript is faulty, or the translater is mistaken, or the reader has failed to understand. Augustine to Jerome, *Epist.,* lxxxii. 3, *Patrologia Latina,* 33:277; *Nicene and Post-Nicene Fathers,* first series, 1:350.

2. *De princ.,* IV, i, 8 ff.; *Patrologia Graeca,* 11:355ff.; *Ante-Nicene Fathers,* American edition, 4:355ff.

3. "All the senses are founded on one—the literal—from which alone can any argument be drawn, and not from those intended in allegory" (S.T. I, Q.1, art. 10, ad 1 [1:7]).

4. A representative discussion of Augustine's views on the sources of authority will be found in Eugène Portalié's article "Saint Augustin" in the *Dictionnaire de théologie catholique*, trans. by Ralph J. Bastian as *A Guide to the Thought of Saint Augustine* (Chicago: Henry Regnery, 1960), pp. 119-24, 239-41.

5. S.T. I, Q. 1, a.8, ad 2 (1:5).

6. Quoted from Scotus's commentary on the *Sentences* (the *Ordinatio* or *Opus Oxoniense*) by Reinhold Seeberg, *Text-Book of the History of Doctrines*, trans. Charles E. Hay, 2 vols, in 1 (Grand Rapids, Mich.: Baker Book House, 1954), 2:149 (emphasis mine).

7. The intention of the Tridentine decree on Scripture (sess. 4) has been the subject of debate ever since it was argued, notably by Joseph Geiselmann, that Trent did not define tradition as a supplementary body of revealed truth alongside the Bible. Hubert Jedin, the historian of Trent, thinks it beyond doubt that the majority at the council did in fact regard Scripture and tradition as complementary sources, and Heiko A. Oberman agrees. Oberman argues that the issue of the Reformation was not "Scripture *or* tradition" but "the clash between two concepts of tradition." In the one concept (he calls it "Tradition I"), which goes back to the anti-Gnostic fathers Irenaeus and Tertullian, the Scriptures are always to be interpreted in the context of the church's living proclamation from the time of the apostles to the present. In the other ("Tradition II"), which has its patristic roots in Basil the Great and Augustine, the Christian owes equal devotion to the written Word and the chain of unwritten traditions understood as complementary authorities. The Protestants, according to Oberman, were advocates of Tradition I, whereas Trent endorsed Tradition II; and yet a third concept, Tradition III, emerges with the First Vatican Council. The debate is not yet closed, although there seems to be little doubt about the position of the majority at Trent; at most, it might be possible to hold that, intentionally or unintentionally, the wording of the decree on Scripture leaves a crack in the doorway for those in the Roman Church who wish to maintain the material sufficiency of the Bible. More to the present point: In the concluding section of this chapter (sec. IV) I indicate evidence for something like Oberman's Tradition I in Protestantism, especially in Calvin. The pronouncements of Trent will be found in H. J. Schroeder, *Canons and Decrees of the Council of Trent: Original Text With English Translation* (St. Louis, Mo.: B. Herder, 1941). Philip Schaff includes the Vatican decree on infallibility in the third volume of his *Bibliotheca Symbolica Ecclesiae Universalis: The Creeds of Christendom, with a History and Critical Notes*, 3 vols., 6th ed., ed. David S. Schaff (New York: Harper and Brothers, [1931]). A representative statement by Geiselmann is available in *Christianity Divided: Protestant and Roman Catholic Theological Issues*, ed. Daniel J. Callahan et al. (New York: Sheed and Ward, 1961); and Oberman's standpoint is presented in his article, "Quo Vadis? Tradition from Irenaeus to Humani Generis," *Scottish Journal of Theology* 16 (1963):225-55.

8. "Si quid autem scripsero in praesenti opusculo quod scripturae vel doctrinae sanctorum seu sacrosanctae ecclesiae assertioni repugnet et adversetur, correctioni praefatae ecclesiae catholicae...me et dicta mea subiicio et expono." I owe this and the following two quotations (n. 9) to the excellent

assemblage of sources in M. [Johann Michael] Reu, *Luther and the Scriptures* (Columbus, Ohio: Wartburg Press, 1944).

9. "Christianus de necessitate salutis non tenetur ad credendum nec credere quod nec in biblia continetur nec ex solis contentis in biblia potest consequentia necessaria et manifesta inferri" (*Dialogus*, p. 411). "Qui dicit aliquam partem novi vel veteris testamenti aliquod falsum asserere aut non esse recipiendum a Catholicis est haereticus et pertinax reputandus" (ibid., 449). For Occam's acceptance of transubstantiation, see T. Bruce Birch, ed., *The De Sacramento Altaris of William of Ockham* (Burlington, Iowa: Lutheran Library Board, 1930), pp. 172–75; cf. Seeberg, *History of Doctrines*, 2:192–93.

10. *Randbemerkungen zu den Sentenzen des Petrus Lombardus* (1510/11), W.A. 9.46.16. Recent Luther scholarship has taken a social interest in the beginnings of his hermeneutics, prior to the conflict with Rome. But the principle *scriptura sola* is better viewed in the actual course of his revolt against Rome (1517–21). Some of the pertinent sources from these years are translated in L.W. 31–32 (on the "career of the Reformer"). Equally important are the prefaces Luther furnished for his German translation of the Bible (from 1522 until the year of his death); and these will be found in L.W. 35, which also includes Luther's *On Translating: An Open Letter* (1530) and *A Brief Instruction on What to Look for and Expect in the Gospels* (1521). Secondary literature on Luther and the Bible is endless, even if studies of his work on individual books of the Bible (particularly in the early years) are left out. General works on the Bible and the Reformation in English, dealing partly with Luther, include C[harles] Sydney Carter, *The Reformers and Holy Scripture: A Historical Investigation* (London: C. J. Thynne and Jarvis, 1928); Rupert E. Davies, *The Problem of Authority in the Continental Reformers: A Study of Luther, Zwingli, and Calvin* (London: Epworth Press, 1946); W[erner] Schwarz, *Principles and Problems of Biblical Translation: Some Reformation Controversies and Their Background* (Cambridge: Cambridge University Press, 1955); E. Harris Harbison, *The Christian Scholar in the Age of Reformation* (New York: Charles Scribner's Sons, 1956); J. K. S. Reid, *The Authority of Scripture: A study of the Reformation and Post-Reformation Understanding of the Bible* (London: Methuen, 1957); Robert Clyde Johnson, *Authority in Protestant Theology* (Philadelphia: Westminster Press, 1959). Among the studies (in English) devoted specifically to Luther are M. Reu (1944; see n. 8 above); Heinrich Bornkamm, *Luther and the Old Testament* [1948], trans. Eric W. and Ruth C. Gritsch, ed. Victor I. Gruhn (Philadelphia: Fortress Press, 1969); Jaroslav Pelikan, *Luther the Expositor: Introduction to the Reformer's Exegetical Writings* [companion volume to *Luther's Works*, American edition] (St. Louis, Mo.: Concordia Publishing House, 1959); Willem Jan Kooiman, *Luther and the Bible* [Dutch original n.d.], trans. John Schmidt (Philadelphia: Muhlenberg Press, 1961); A Skevington Wood, *Captive to the Word: Martin Luther, Doctor of Sacred Scripture* (Grand Rapids, Mich.: William B. Eerdmans, 1969). A selection from the German literature would certainly need to include H. Østergaard-Nielsen, *Scriptura sacra et viva vox: Eine Lutherstudie* (Munich: Chr. Kaiser Verlag, 1957), and two studies on the problem of the "clarity" of Scripture in Luther's theology: Rudolf Hermann, *Von der Klarheit der heiligen Schrift:*

Untersuchungen und Erörterungen über Luthers Lehre von der Schrift in De servo arbitrio, Gotteswort und Menschenwort in der Bibel, no. 2 (Berlin: Evangelische Verlagsanstalt, 1958), and Friedrich Beisser, *Claritas scripturae bei Martin Luther* (Göttingen: Vandenhoeck and Ruprecht, 1966). There is a section on Luther and the Bible in Gerhard Ebeling's *Luther-studien,* vol. 1 (Tübingen: J. C. B. Mohr [Paul Siebeck], 1971), pp. 286–301.

11. *Dictata super psalterium,* W.A. 3.347.11; 3.15.6; 3.262.30 (L.W. 10:293, 10, 221). "Evangelium audiendum est, quasi dominum praesentem, quasi Christum loquentem audiamus ..." (*Praelectio in librum Iudicium* [1516ff.], W.A. 4.535.1).

12. *Vorlesung über den Romerbrief,* W.A. 56.371.17; L.W. 25:361.

13. Luther to John Lang, 18 May 1517, W.A. Br. 1.99.8 (no. 41); L.W. 48:42.

14. "In his nihil dicere volumus nec dixisse nos credimus, quod non sit catholicae ecclesiae et ecclesiasticis doctoribus consentaneum" (*Disputatio contra scholasticam theologiam,* W.A. 1.228.34; L.W. 31.16.

15. Luther to George Spalatin, W.A. Br. 1.356.7 (no. 159).

16. Trans. Roland H. Bainton, *Here I Stand: A Life of Martin Luther* (Nashville, Tennessee: Abingdon Press, 1950), p. 116; cf. L.W. 31:321–22.

17. "Quod sine scripturis asseritur aut revelatione probata, opinari licet, credi non est necesse" (*De captivitate Babylonica praeludium,* W.A. 6.508.19; cf. L.W. 36:29).

18. Trans. Bainton, *Here I Stand,* p. 185; cf. L.W. 32:112–13.

19. W.A.Tr. 2.439.25 (no. 2383). In the christocentric understanding of the Bible Luther was partially anticipated by John Wycliffe: see Carter, *Reformers and Scripture,* p. 37. Cf. John T. McNeill's remarks on Rupert of Deutz in his "History of the Interpretation of the Bible, II: Medieval and Reformation Period," in *The Interpreter's Bible,* ed. George Arthur Buttrick et al., 12 vols. (Nashville, Tenn.: Abingdon-Cokesbury Press, 1952–57), 1:119. See further n. 61 below.

20. *Vorrede auff das alte Testament* (1545 [1523]), W.A.D.B. 8.12.5; L.W. 35:236. Although the quotation is from the Old Testament preface, the "here" seems to refer to the Scriptures in general.

21. *In epistolam S. Pauli ad Galatas commentarius* (1531/35), W.A. 40[1].600. 13; L.W. 26:394. Cf. W.A. 40[1].82.31; L.W. 26:32.

22. *Vorrede auff die Epistel S. Jacobi und Jüde* (1546 [1522]), W.A.D.B. 7.385.25ff.; L.W. 35:396.

23. *Vorrede auff das newe Testament* (1546 [1522]), W.A.D.B. 6.10.10; L.W. 35:361–62.

24. "Eyn rechte stroern Epistel" (*Vorrede auff das newe Testament,* W.A.D.B. 6.10.33; L.W. 35:362). "Ich werde ein mal mit dem Jekel den offen hitzen" (W.A.Tr. 5.382.17 [no. 5854]). "Er nennet Christum etlich mal, Aber er leret nichts von im" (*Vorrede auff die Epistel S. Jacobi und Jüde,* W.A.D.B. 7.385.20; L.W. 35:396).

25. *Vorrede auff das newe Testament* (1522 only), W.A.D.B. 6.10.20ff.; L.W. 35:362. Luther even rests his preference for the Fourth Gospel on the fact that John has more of Jesus' own preaching than the other Gospels.

26. *Bibel- und Bucheinzeichnungen Luthers,* W.A. 48.31.4.

27. *Von den Letzten Worten Dauids* (1543), W.A. 54.35.2, 48.19ff.; L.W. 15:275, 291.

28. *Commentarii in XV Psalmos graduum* (1532–33/1540), W.A. 40³.254.23.

29. *In epistolam S. Pauli ad Galatas commentarius,* W.A. 40¹.173.21; L.W. 26:94.

30. *Von abendmal Christi, Bekendnis* (1528), W.A. 26.448.18; L.W. 37:307. *Von anbeten des Sacraměts des heyligen leychnams Christi* (1523), W.A. 11.434. 17; L.W. 36:279.

31. *Eyn brieff an die Christen zu Straspurg widder den schwermer geyst* (1524), W.A. 15.394.12ff.; L.W. 40:68.

32. Seeberg, *History of Doctrines,* 2:300–301; quotation on p. 301, n. 1.

33. The manner in which Luther lists the New Testament books clearly indicates that he doubted the canonicity of Hebrews, James and Jude, and the Apocalypse: these four are separated from the genuine books by a blank space and, unlike them, are left unnumbered—exactly the way he distinguishes the apocryphal from the canonical books of the Old Testament (W.A.D.B. 6.12, 8.34–35). The individual prefaces to the four downgraded books explain and justify his treatment of them by a fascinating mixture of arguments. But the arguments cannot detain us; it suffices to point out that none of them can properly be regarded as a critical judgment about Scripture, although some of them testify to Luther's astuteness as a literary critic.

34. Reu's *Luther and the Scriptures* remains one of the best attempts to give a "conservative" interpretation of Luther. At two points Reu is surely right in arguing that Luther has been misunderstood. (1) Luther did not say in his preface to the *Annotations of Wenceslaus Link* that the writings of the prophets, as contained in the Old Testament, included hay, straw, wood as well as silver and gold. He was not referring to Scripture at all, but to annotations which he *presumes* the prophets to have made in reading Moses. (2) Luther does not accuse Paul of using an invalid allegory in Gal. 4:21–31 (W.A. 40¹.652ff.; L.W. 26:432ff.). What he says is that allegory does not serve for *proof* (here or anywhere else), but only for *illustration* of what has already been proved. See Reu, *Luther and the Scriptures,* pp. 68ff. Sometimes, however, Reu shows himself to be far more of a fundamentalist than Luther found it necessary to be. On Matthew 27:9 Luther says: "What does it matter if he does not give the name exactly?" Reu jumps on the "if" as proof that even here Luther was not persuaded that he was faced with an error (pp. 88–89). Again, in Stephen's speech (Acts 7) Luther admits discrepancies with "Moses"; but, Reu assures us, this is not to admit a fault in the sacred text, since the author is accurately recording Stephen's errors (p. 97). Whether Luther himself would have approved such artifice, may be at least doubted. He does, however, occasionally deny that the Scriptures could contradict one another (e.g. W.A. 40¹.420.27).

35. "Videbam Allegorias esse inanes speculationes.... Sola enim historica sententia est, quae vere et solide docet. Postquam haec tractata et recte cognita est, tunc licet etiam Allegoriis ceu ornamento et floribus quibusdam uti, quibus illustretur Historia seu pingatur" (*In primum librum Mose enarrationes* [1535–45/ 1544–54], W.A. 42.173.31; L.W. 1:233). "Sicubi autem Allegoriis vultis uti, hoc facite, ut sequamini analogiam fidei, hoc est, ut accomodetis eas ad Chris-

tum, Ecclesiam, fidem, ministerium verbi" (ibid., W.A. 42.377.20; L.W. 2:164). Luther believed that he found the "analogy of faith" in Romans 12:6, "Having gifts that differ according to the grace given to us, let us use them: if prophecy, *in proportion to our faith*" [my emphasis; the Greek is κατὰ τὴν ἀναλογίαν τῆς πίστεως]. This he took to mean "according to the norm or measure of the doctrine of faith," so that in practice Luther's gospel of faith in Christ became his hermeneutical key for interpreting the Bible. As Mackinnon points out, there is a risk that the analogy of faith, so understood, will become the "Lutheran equivalent of the allegorical method": that is, like the very exegetical method it is intended to control, a device for conforming interpretation to theological presuppositions. See James Mackinnon, *Luther and the Reformation*, 4 vols. (London: Longmans, Green, 1925–30), 4:298. On Luther's actual use of allegorical exegesis—often quite other than his principles would have required—see Hans Wernle, *Allegorie und Erlebnis bei Luther*, Basler Studien zur deutschen Sprache und Literatur, no. 24 (Bern: Francke Verlag, 1960).

36. *An den Christlichen Adel deutscher Nation von des Christlichen standes besserung* (1520), W.A. 6.411.8ff; L.W. 44:133ff.

37. *Auff das ubirchristlich, ubirgeystlich und ubirkunstlich Buch Bocks Emsers zu Leypczick Antwortt* (1521), W.A. 7.650.21; L.W. 39:178. It will be noticed that the "simplicity" of Scripture goes with the "literal sense." Already in the *Dictata super psalterium* (1513–15) Luther affirmed the primacy of the "historical sense," but his exegesis at that time was anything but simple (W.A. 3.11.33; L.W. 10:4). The emphasis on the *single* sense of Scripture emerges in the course of Luther's theological debates: against Eck's interpretation of the words "Tu es Petrus," for instance, he insists on the *unum, primum, principalem et proprium sensum*, and against Carstadt he asserts that natural speech is sovereign. See *Contra malignum Johannis Ecii iudicium ... defensio* (1519), W.A. 2.628.22; *Widder die hymelischen propheten, von den bildern und Sacrament* (1525), W.A. 18.180.17 (L.W. 40:190). Luther also stresses the letter of the text in *Ein sendbrieff von Dolmetzschen und Fürbit der heiligenn* (1530), W.A. 30².640.19; L.W. 35:194. And one of his reasons for doubting the canoncity of Revelation was that genuine apostles "prophesy in clear and plain words" (*Vorrhede auff die offinbarung Sanct Johannis* (1522 version), W.A.D.B. 7.404.7; L.W. 35:398).

38. Luther to Eoban Hess, 29 March 1523, W.A.Br. 3.50.24 (no. 596); L.W. 49:34. Luther's interest in education arose partly from his persuasion that you cannot have the gospel without a knowledge of languages, which are the sheath of the Spirit's sword, the case in which the jewel is carried: *An die Ratherren aller Städte deutschen Lands, dass sie christliche Schulen aufrichten und halten sollen* (1524), W.A. 15.38.7ff.; L.W. 45:360.

39. See, e.g., Luther's *Assertio omnium articulorum per bullam Leonis X. novissimam damnatorum* (1520), W.A. 7.97.23, 98.40, 99.18. The principle *scriptura sui ipsius interpres* is a necessary adjunct to *scriptura sola*: if the Scriptures are to stand without any external authority, it must be possible to arrive at their meaning by comparing Scripture with Scripture and interpreting the part in the light of the whole. Hence Luther challenged Eck's tendency to tear his proof-texts out of their setting: it is the *whole* of Scripture that has to

be kept in mind (*Disputatio Johannis Ecii et Martini Lutheri Lipsiae habita* [1519], W.A. 2.361.16ff.). Cf. *Von Dolmetzschen,* W.A. 30².640.33–642.25; L.W. 35:195–97. What Luther perceived to be the subject matter of the Bible as a whole was no doubt the product, in part, of his own religious experience, with which the fourth principle is concerned.

40. "Denn es mag niemant got noch gottes wort recht vorstehen, er habs denn on mittel von dem heyligen geyst. Niemant kansz aber von dem heiligenn geist habenn, er erfaresz, vorsuchs und empfinds denn" (*Das Magnificat Vorteutschet und auszgelegt* [1521], W.A. 7.546.25ff.; L.W. 21:299). The same holds good for the attempt to translate the sacred text: "Es gehöret dazu ein recht, frum, trew, vleissig, forchtsam, Christlich, geleret, erfarn, geübet hertz, Darumb halt ich, das kein falscher Christ noch rottengeist trewlich dolmetzschen könne" (*Von Dolmetzschen,* W.A. 30².640.25ff.; L.W. 35:194). To some extent the appeal to experience is a commonsense rule for interpreting any texts whatever: "Non satis est nosse grammaticam [the reading *grammatica* is presumably an error], sed observare sensum, nam cognitio rerum affert cognitionem verborum" (W.A.Tr. 4.608.6 [no. 5002]; L.W. 54:375). While languages are a help, one has to be familiar with *die Sache* (W.A.Tr. 1.524.38 [no. 1040]); so that no one can understand Vergil's *Eclogues* or *Georgics,* for instance, unless he has been a shepherd or a farmer for five years (W.A.Tr. 5.168.27 [no. 5468]). But in practice, of course, the experience Luther brought to the Scriptures was his own specific religious experience. In a sense, it may even be said that he introduced another principle alongside the *sola scriptura.* As he puts it: "Non solum scriptura ... sed etiam experientia.... Habeo rem et experientiam cum Scriptura" (W.A.Tr. 1.340.30 [no. 701]).

41. "Scripturas non nisi eo spiritu intellegendas esse, quo scriptae sunt, qui spiritus nusquam praesentius et vivacius quam in ipsis sacris suis, quas scripsit, literis inveniri potest" (*Assertio omnium articulorum,* W.A. 7.97.1).

42. See Carter, *Reformers and Scripture,* pp. 29, 66. The interlocking character of the five exegetical principles is clear. Perhaps one could even reduce them to a fundamental dialectic of text and experience. Schwarz, at any rate, finds in Luther, by contrast to Erasmus, a distinctive polarity of philology and inspiration that regulated his interpretation of the Bible (*Biblical Translation,* chap. 5, esp. p. 200). It should be added that according to Luther himself there are no fixed rules for interpreting the Word of God, since the Word of God must not be bound (*Epistola Lutheriana ad Leonam X. summum pontificem* [1520], W.A. 7.47.28; L.W. 31:341).

43. Paul L. Lehmann, "The Reformers' Use of the Bible," *Theology Today* 3 (1946–47):328–44; quotation on p. 333.

44. Emil Brunner, *Dogmatics,* vol. 1: *The Christian Doctrine of God,* trans. Olive Wyon (Philadelphia: Westminster Press, 1950), p. 108.

45. *Inst.,* 1.6.1 (1:70). In English, the most substantial treatment of Calvin's views on Biblical authority is H. Jackson Forstman, *Word and Spirit: Calvin's Doctrine of Biblical Authority* (Stanford, Calif.: Stanford University Press, 1962), which includes discussions of the previous literature. See also Ronald S. Wallace, *Calvin's Doctrine of the Word and Sacrament* (Edinburgh: Oliver and Boyd, 1953). A comparative study of the two Reformers will be found in

Hermann Noltensmeier, *Reformatorische Einheit: Das Schriftverständnis bei Luther und Calvin* (Graz-Cologne: Herman Böhlaus Nachf., 1935).

46. *Inst.*, 1.6.2 (1:72). "No real piety remains in the world" (1.4.1 [1:47]).

47. The words of the title to chapter 4 are carefully chosen: the innate knowledge of God is either "smothered" *(suffocari)* or "corrupted" *(corrumpi)*.

48. The ambiguities in Calvin's notion of a natural knowledge of God are particularly marked in this chapter (chap. 10). He adduces Psalm 145 as an illustration of the knowledge of God in Scripture, and adds: "And yet nothing is set down there that cannot be beheld in his creatures. Indeed, with experience as our teacher we find God just as he declares himself in his Word" (sec. 2 [1:98]). Here the two "knowledges" are presented as though they were each independent of the other, though identical in content. But Calvin has already shown that experience teaches us little or nothing of God unless it is experience guided by the Word. The contemplation of nature, for Calvin, is not so much a source of information about God as a devout exercise of faith.

49. Calvin begins: "Antequam longius progrediar, quaedam *inserere* operae-pretium est de Scripturae authoritate" (my emphasis).

50. *Inst.*, 3.21.2, 3, 4 (2:923, 924, 925).

51. *Inst.*, 1.18.4 (1:237).

52. *Inst.*, 2.8.5 (1:372).

53. *Inst.*, 4.10.7 (2:1185). The principle *Quod non iubet, vetat* is sometimes taken for the distinctively Reformed rule (in contrast to the Lutheran *Quod non vetat, permittit*). But it should be pointed out, in qualification of my remark here, that Calvin certainly did not apply the rule to everything indiscriminately in the life of the church; and that Zwingli, who is commonly supposed to have been still more of a biblicist than Calvin, included in his Reformation manifesto the affirmation, "Dz alles so Gott erlaubt oder nit verbotten hatt, recht ist." Zwingli, *Artickel und meynungen* (Sixty-seven Articles, 1523), art. 28, in *Die Bekenntnisschriften der reformierten Kirche*, ed. E. F. Karl Müller (Leipzig: A. Deichert [Georg Böhme], 1903), p. 4.

54. *Inst.*, 4.18.12 (2:1440).

55. *Inst.*, 4.19.9 (2:1457).

56. "There are passages in the *Institutes* which taken out of their context might almost seem to suggest that the Reformer was willing to confine men to Scripture entirely, as though nothing profitable could be found in any other place. But a consideration of his own educational system at Geneva alone is enough to refute such an idea." A. Dakin, *Calvinism* (London: Duckworth, 1940), p. 191.

57. Quoted by A. Mitchell Hunter, *The Teaching of Calvin: A Modern Interpretation*, 2d ed. (London: James Clarke, 1950), p. 82. But Hunter adds that Calvin "did not burn his classics; nor did he cease to peruse them" (pp. 82-83). Hunter's quotation is from Comm. Eph. 3:19 (C.O. 51:188).

58. "John Calvin to the Reader" (preface to the 1559 *Institutes*), trans. Battles (1:4).

59. See, e.g., *Inst.*, 1.15.2 (1:185). Charles Partee has examined Calvin's use of the ancient philosophers in his *Calvin and Classical Philosophy*, Studies in the History of Christian Thought, no. 14 (Leiden: E. J. Brill, 1977). For an

appraisal of Partee's argument, see my review in the *Journal of Modern History* 51 (1979):140–42.

60. *Inst.*, 1.16.4 (1:203), 18.3 (1:233).

61. Preface to Olivétan's New Testament (1535/43), trans. in *Calvin's Commentaries*, ed. Joseph Haroutunian, Library of Christian Classics, vol. 23 (Philadelphia: Westminster Press, 1958), p. 70. Calvin added this passage in the 1543 edition (French original in C.O. 9:815); his subsequent commentary on John 5:39, published in 1553, reads like a condensed version of it (see C.O. 47:125; trans. by T. H. L. Parker in *The Gospel According to St. John 1–10*, Calvin's Commentaries [Grand Rapids, Mich.: William B. Eerdmans, 1959], pp. 138–139). In the commentary, as the text itself suggested, Calvin opposes this understanding of Scripture to the false biblicism of the Jews, who mistakenly believed that the Scriptures are life-giving in themselves. See also the preface to the Geneva Bible given in C.O. 9:823–26, esp. col. 125. It is not necessary to suppose that Calvin's christocentric view of the Bible was entirely a debt owed to Luther. Erasmus's *Paraclesis*—the preface to his Greek and Latin edition of the New Testament (1516)—similarly regarded the Scriptures of the New Testament as the place where Christ lives for us almost more effectively than when he dwelt among men: "These writings bring you the living image of His holy mind and the speaking, healing, dying, rising Christ himself, and thus they render Him so fully present that you would see less if you gazed upon Him with your very eyes." Translated in John C. Olin, ed., *Christian Humanism and the Reformation: Selected Writings of Erasmus With the Life of Erasmus by Beatus Rhenanus*, rev. ed. (New York: Fordham Unversity Press, 1975), p. 106; cf. p. 102. The Latin original is in the *Ausgewählte Werke*, ed. Hajo and Annemarie Holborn (Munich: C. H. Beck, 1933).

62. *Inst.*, 1.9.3 (1:95).

63. The editorial note in the English translation (1:95, n. 3) states that "Calvin here comes close to the well-known dictum of Luther regarding Scripture books in his Preface to James and Jude, where the test of genuineness is whether they lay emphasis on Christ or not *('ob sie Christum treiben, oder nicht')*." But Calvin's language in fact goes beyond Luther's, even if we follow the L.W. rendering of *treiben* as "inculcate" (rather than the more customary "deal with"). It is not merely a matter of emphasizing Christ, but of "presenting" or "offering" him: *exhibere* is a key term in Calvin's sacramental vocabulary (see chap. 6 below).

64. The locus classicus for Calvin's understanding of the one covenant and the two testaments is *Inst.*, 2.9–11; but he has broached the subject already in 2.6, and he returns to it in 4.8. For the metaphor of the "Sun of Righteousness" see 2.9.1, 10.20, 11.5 (1:423, 446, 455); 4.8.7 (2:1154).

65. *Inst.*, 3.2.6–7 (1:548–51). Calvin has already stated in book two that the promises of the Old and New Testaments are the same: their common foundation is Christ (2.11.1 [1:450]).

66. *Inst.*, 3.2.29–30 (1:575–76).

67. Edward A. Dowey, Jr., *The Knowledge of God in Calvin's Theology* (New York: Columbia University Press, 1952; reprinted with a new introduction and updated bibliography, 1966), esp. pp. 160 ff.

68. Luther, W.A.Tr. 3.253.27 (no. 3292a); Calvin, *Inst.*, 3.17.11–12 (2:814–17).

69. See Benjamin B. Warfield, "Calvin's Doctrine of the Knowledge of God," *Princeton Theological Review* 7 (1909):219–325, esp. pp. 239–51. This essay has been reprinted, but my references are to the original publication.

70. *Inst.*, 1.6.1 (1:70), 7.5 (1:80); 2.8.12 (1:379).

71. *Inst.*, 4.8.9 (2:1157); Comm. 2 Tim. 3:16 (C.O. 52:383); Comm. 2 Pet. 1:21 (C.O. 55:458).

72. *Inst.*, 1.7.4 (1:78); 4.8.9 (2.1157); Comm. 2 Tim. 3:16, C.O. 52:383.

73. *Inst.*, 4.8.6 (2:1154); 1.6.3 (1:72). Cf. Comm. Gen. 17:4, C.O. 23:236.

74. See Warfield, "Knowledge of God," pp. 250, 257. Cf. n. 1 above. It ought perhaps to be added that the term *dictare* scarcely supplies Calvin with a fully articulated theory of inspiration. Neither Luther nor Calvin devotes much space to the manner of inspiration; they are more interested in the results. The real problem of the Reformers' teaching on this theme lies in their apparent assumption of an inerrant text; it is less just to attribute to them a mechanical view of inspiration. Several scholars have maintained that Calvin did not intend "dictation" to be understood literally at all. This may be true; in any case, Warfield is surely right in saying that "what Calvin has in mind is not to insist that the mode of inspiration was dictation, but that the result of inspiration is as if it were by dictation, viz., the production of a pure word of God free from all human admixtures" (p. 255). As for Luther, it is interesting that Reu, who attributes to him belief in an errorless Bible, denies that he held the dictation theory: "If only this would be recognized," he writes, "that one can maintain 'verbal inspiration' and at the same time reject the theory of dictation, not a little would be accomplished, because the assumption that these two are identical seems to be nearly ineradicable. Luther maintained the first and rejected the second" (*Luther and the Scriptures*, p. 3; see also pp. 109–16). Seeberg held that, by resting the authority of the Scriptures partly on their divine dictation and partly on the testimony of the Spirit working through them, Calvin was the actual author of the inspiration theory found in the older Protestant dogmaticians: it is, he says, precisely the combination of the later medieval conception of inspiration with the "theory of Luther" that constitutes the understanding of the Bible in Protestant orthodoxy (*Text-Book of the History of Doctrines*, 2:395–96).

75. This view was argued by John T. McNeill in his article "The Significance of the Word of God for Calvin," *Church History* 28 (1959): 131–46.

76. Werner Krusche, *Das Wirken des heiligen Geistes nach Calvin* (Göttingen: Vandenhoeck and Ruprecht, 1957), pp. 161–84, esp. the summary statement on pp. 182–84. Krusche maintains that Calvin does not have a doctrine of the inspiration of Holy Scripture at all: inspiration is not a static attribute of the Bible but refers to the action of the Spirit on the speaking and writing of the biblical witnesses. But the view that Calvin did in fact hold the plenary inspiration and strict inerrancy of the so-called original autographs continues to find advocates: see, for instance, Kenneth S. Kantzer, "Calvin and the Holy Scripture," in *Inspiration and Interpretation*, ed. John F. Walvoord, Evangelical Theological Society Publications (Grand Rapids, Mich.: William B. Eerdmans, 1957), pp. 115–55; A. D. R. Polman, "Calvin and the Inspiration of Scripture,"

in *John Calvin: Contemporary Prophet: A Symposium*, ed. Jacob T. Hoogstra (Grand Rapids, Mich.: Baker Book House, 1959), pp. 97–112. Less attention has been attracted to interesting places where Calvin speaks not of the fallibility of the text, but of its historical relativity: where, that is, he finds biblical injunctions or practices that are not binding in another day, such as primitive Christian communism, the regulation of usury, and Paul's directives on masculine hairstyle. There are, of course, incidental allusions in the secondary literature to Calvin's observations on these matters. (See, e.g., W. Fred Graham, *The Constructive Revolutionary: John Calvin and His Socio-Economic Impact* [Richmond, Virginia: John Knox Press, 1971], pp. 72, 91, and R. Hooykaas, *Religion and the Rise of Modern Science* [Grand Rapids, Mich.: William B. Eerdmans, 1972], p. 120.) But they seldom play a significant part in discussions on Calvin's understanding of biblical authority.

77. *Inst.*, 1.7.2, 4–5 (1:76, 78–80).

78. The Word-Spirit correlation takes on further significance, however, in the argument against the fanatics in book 1, chapter 9; and to this we shall need to return (sec. IV below).

79. *Inst.*, 1.7.1–3 (1:74–78).

80. *Inst.*, 1.7.1 (1:75). Cf. Dowey's remark: "If we should dare the Barthian expression that the Bible 'becomes' the word of God in faith, we must confess that it becomes it for Calvin by book-size units" (*Knowledge of God*, p. 120, n. 355).

81. *Inst.*, 1.7.4 (1:78), 1.8.1–13 passim (1:81–92).

82. Warfield, "Knowledge of God," pp. 221–22. "It is no revelation in [the] strict sense" (ibid., p. 223); the question concerns "the accrediting of Scripture" (p. 263). On the other hand, Warfield's estimate of the *probationes* (or *indicia*, as he likes to call them) is surely wrong: he exalts them to a status Calvin did not accord them and even tries to argue that Spirit and *indicia* work together as though inseparable (pp. 276–83). Similarly wide of the mark is Dakin's assertion that Calvin uses the proofs to "establish the Word of God against gainsayers" (*Calvinism*, p. 199). Calvin makes it entirely clear that they are secondary aids to *our* feebleness who already possess the inner persuasion of the Spirit (*Inst.*, 1.8.13 [1:92]). The difficulty is to see why he bothers to mention them at all, for he says that it is improper to subject Scripture to argument (1.7.5 [1:80]).

83. No less a person than J. Gresham Machen clearly recognized that a properly Christian understanding of the biblical message could be maintained without the strict doctrine of verbal inspiration that he himself defended. See Machen, *Christianity and Liberalism* (Grand Rapids, Mich.: William B. Eerdmans, 1923), p. 75. A good general introduction to Calvin's principles of exegesis is given in the introduction to *Calvin: Commentaries*, ed. Joseph Haroutunian. See also Hans-Joachim Kraus, "Calvins exegetische Prinzipien," *Zeitschrift für Kirchengeschichte* 79 (1968):329–41. One respect in which I believe there is at least a difference of emphasis between Luther and Calvin is taken up in the next section. It was touched on already in the conclusion to chapter 2.

84. William Chillingworth, *The Religion of Protestants: A Safe Way to Salvation* (1638), vi. 56, in *The Works of W. Chillingworth*, 12th ed. in one vol.

(London: B. Blake, 1806), p. 465.

85. "Haec Regina [sacra scriptura] debet dominari, huic omnes obedire et subiacere debent" (*In epistolam S. Pauli ad Galatas commentarius* [1531/35], W.A. 40[1].120.20; L.W. 26:58). "Tu urges servum, hoc est, scripturam, et eam non totam.... Ego urgeo dominum, qui rex est scripturae" (ibid. [1538 ed. only], W.A. 40[1].420).

86. "Scriptura est, non contra, sed pro Christo intelligenda, ideo vel ad eum referenda, vel pro vera Scriptura non habenda.... Si adversarii scripturam urserint contra Christum, urgemus Christum contra scripturam" (*Die Thesen für die Promotionsdisputation von Hieronymus Weller und Nikolaus Medler* [1535], *De fide*, theses 41 and 49, W.A. 39[1].47.3, 19; cf. L.W. 34:112).

87. See n. 85 above.

88. *Dogmatics*, 1:111. Cf. Brunner's remarks in his *Revelation and Reason: The Christian Doctrine of Faith and Knowledge*, trans. Olive Wyon (Philadelphia: Westminster Press, 1946), p. 276: "If we hold firmly to the Reformation principle of the Scriptures—*Christus dominus et rex scripturae*—then, in principle, the problem of Bible faith and Bible criticism is solved. The Bible is the human, and therefore not the infallible, witness to the divine revelation in the Old Covenant and in the history of the incarnate Son of God." It does not follow, of course, that *every* problem is thereby solved; as a matter of fact, one problem is exacerbated: the tendency of Christian exegetes to discover references to Christ in the unlikeliest corners of the Old Testament. But a problem that at least *could* have been solved is considered at length in chapter 10 below.

89. *Revelation and Reason*, p. 275. But the advocates of verbal inspiration usually argue that the notion simply accepts the Bible's witness to itself: in other words, it is biblical (not medieval!).

90. "Reformers' Use of the Bible," p. 342.

91. Ibid.

92. Thomas M. Lindsay, *A History of the Reformation*, 2 vols., 2d ed. (Edinburgh: T. and T. Clark, 1907–8), 1:461.

93. *Tractatus de libertate christiana* (1520), W.A. 7.50.38, 51.12, 51.17; L.W. 31:345–46.

94. *Eyn kleyn unterricht, was man ynn den Evangelijs suchen und gewartten soll* (1521), W.A. 10[1,1].17.1, 7; L.W. 35:123.

95. *Inst.*, 1.13.7 (1:129–30), 2.11.5 (1:455), 4.8.7 (2:1154–55).

96. This is perhaps more evident in Calvin's catechism than in the 1559 *Institutes*: see *Catechismus ecclesiae Genevensis* (1545), O.S. 2:127ff. (where cross-references are given to C.O. 6); translated in Calvin, *Tracts and Treatises*, trans. Henry Beveridge, 3 vols. (1844–51; reprint ed., Grand Rapids, Mich: William B. Eerdmans, 1958), 2:83ff., and in J. K. S. Reid, trans. and ed., *Calvin: Theological Treatises*, Library of Christian Classics, vol. 22 (Philadelphia: Westminster Press, 1954), pp. 129ff. Cf. *Inst.*, 4.14 (2:1276–1303). Luther's understanding of the Word as outward means is forcefully asserted against Carlstadt in *Widder die hymelischen propheten, von den bildern und Sacrament* (1525), W.A. 18.136.9ff.; L.W. 40:146–47. The Reformers do not seem to have detected any antagonism between what we may call the "pedagogical" and the "sacramental" functions of the Word. Calvin speaks of the Word in his catechism as the

spiritualis doctrina contained in the Bible (Qq. 300–301, O.S. 2:128); he must mean, therefore, that the Word is a means of grace precisely as doctrine. (Note that in Q. 301 the Word is expressly said to be "contained in" the Scriptures.) It is a particular merit of Steck's work on doctrine and church in Luther to have shown that for him, too, there was none of the disharmony present-day theology tends to feel between proclamation and doctrine. Karl Gerhard Steck, *Lehre und Kirche bei Luther,* Forschungen zur Geschichte und Lehre des Protestantismus, series 10, vol. 27 (Munich: Chr. Kaiser Verlag, 1963).

97. Luther,*Predigten des Jahres 1532,* W.A. 36.220.23ff; Calvin, *Catechismus,* Q. 305, O.S. 2:129.

98. "Non est aliud a verbo medium, ut loquuntur, quo se nobiscum Deus communicet? Verbi praedicationi adiunxit sacramenta" (Calvin, *Catechismus,* Q. 309, O.S. 2:130).

99. Ibid., Q. 345 (O.S. 2:138). In the following question it is affirmed that "tum in baptismo, tum in evangelio nobis *exhibetur* Christus" (O.S. 2:139; my emphasis). Cf. n. 63 above. Luther similarly asserts that the gospel brings and gives Christ with all his benefits (*Kirchenpostille* [1522], Epiphany sermon on Is. 60:1–6, W.A. $10^{1,1}$.520.21; *Luther's Epistle Sermons: Advent and Christmas Season,* trans. John Nicholas Lenker, 3 vols., *Luther's Complete Works,* vols. 7–9 [Minneapolis, Minn.: Luther Press, 1908–9]), 1:312.

100. *Inst.,* 1.9.3 (1:95).

101. *Inst.,* 1.9.1 (1:93); cf. 9.3 (1:95). Calvin here approaches the notion of the Westminster Confession that the supreme judge in matters of doctrine can be "no other but the Holy Spirit speaking in the scripture" (chap. I, sec. x).

102. *Inst.,* 1.9.3 (1:96). Calvin can speak of the "authority" of the Spirit (1.9.2 [1:94]), but this must inevitably be something different from the authority of a book.

103. See chapter 5 below.

104. See, e.g., *In primum librum Mose enarrationes,* W.A. 42.300–1; L.W. 2:54–56. Calvin, too, was not lacking in doctrinal self-assurance: "We have been amply equipped by the Word of the Lord for the full proof of our teaching and for the overthrow of all popery" (*Inst.,* 4.9.1 [2:1166]).

105. See chapter 2, n. 107, above.

106. *Inst.,* 4.8ff. (2:1149ff.). The power of the church in doctrine occupies Calvin in chapters 8–9 (2:1149–79). It is, unfortunately, often overlooked that without these two chapters and the chapter on faith (book 3, chap. 2) the discussion of Scripture in book 1 (chaps. 7–9) remains incomplete.

107. *Inst.,* 4.8.13, 15–16 (2:1162–63, 1164–66). Calvin's example of an extrabiblical term authorized by the church is "consubstantial" (*homoousios*: 2:1165). See further chapter 12 below.

108. *Inst.,* 4.9.8 (2:1171), 9.9 (2:1172), 9–12 (2:1173–75). Christ "presides" only when the assembly is "governed by his Word and Spirit" (4.9.1 [2:1166]).

109. *Inst.,* 4.9.13 (2:1176–77). It is clear from this passage that Calvin thinks of the indefectibility of the truth rather than of the infallibility of the church. But he is not wholly averse to saying that the church, if taught by the Spirit through the Word, cannot err in matters necessary to salvation (4.8.13 [2:1162]).

Chapter Four

1. "Omnia verba, omnes historie Euangelice sunt sacramenta quedam, hoc est sacra signa, per que in credentibus deus efficit, quicquid ille historie designant." Luther, *Predigten gesammelt von Joh. Poliander* (1519-21), no. 23: *In diem natalem Domini*, 25 December 1519, W.A. 9.440.3.

2. See, e.g., his Smalcald Articles (1536/38), W.A. 50.192-254; trans. in *The Book of Concord: The Confessions of the Evangelical Lutheran Church*, ed. Theodore G. Tappert (Philadelphia: Fortress Press, 1959), pp. 288-316, esp. p. 292. Cf. *Die Promotionsdisputation von Palladius und Tilemann* (1537): "Articulus iustificationis est magister et princeps, dominus, rector, et iudex super omnia genera doctrinarum, qui conservat et gubernat omnem doctrinam ecclesiasticam et erigit conscientiam nostram coram Deo" (W.A. 39^1.205.2).

3. "There may be found in Luther a very great variety of propositions, each of which is declared to be the 'chief article,' or 'the sum of the gospel.' In reality, they all amount in the end to the same thing." Reinhold Seeberg, *Text-Book of the History of Doctrines*, trans. Charles E. Hay, 2 vols, in one (reprint ed., Grand Rapids, Mich.: Baker Book House, 1954), 2:297, n. 3. Seeberg mentions more alternatives than my short list contains ("repentance," "grace," "liberty," etc.), and he gives specific references. See also the following note below.

4. In a single page in the "large" *Commentary on Galatians* (on Gal. 3:13), for example, he identifies the *praecipuus locus* as the *articulus de Divinitate Christi* and immediately continues: "Locus igitur Iustificationis, ut saepe moneo, diligenter discendum est. In eo enim comprehenduntur omnes alii fidei nostrae articuli eoque salvo salvi sunt et reliqui" (*In epistolam S. Pauli ad Galatas Commentarius* [1531/35], W.A. 40^1.441.13, 29ff.; L.W. 26:282-83). And in his preface to the same work Luther identifies the one doctrine that occupies his thinking day and night as *Fides Christi* (W.A. 40^1.33.7: L.W. 27:145). But he plainly indicates how these three concepts belong together. Only God can overcome sin. "Quare cum docemus homines per Christum iustificari, Christum esse victorem peccati, mortis et aeternae maledictionis, testificamur simul eum esse natura Deum" (W.A. 40^1.441.32; L.W. 26:283).

5. *Ein sendbrieff von Dolmetzschen und Fürbit der heiligenn* (1530), W.A. 30^2.643.12; L.W. 35:198.

6. Heinrich Denifle, *Luther und Luthertum in der ersten Entwickelung quellenmässig dargestellt*, 2 vols. (Mainz: F. Kirchheim, 1904-9). Denifle, who died in 1905, saw only the first part of the first volume through the press (in two editions); vol. 1, pt. 2, was edited and enlarged by Albert Maria Weiss, and vol. 2 appeared jointly under the names of Denifle and Weiss. A translation of vol. 1, pt. 1 (2d ed.), was published under the title, *Luther and Lutherdom, From Original Sources*, trans. Raymund Volz (Somerset, Ohio: Torch Press, 1917). *Ergänzungen zu Denifle's Luther und Luthertum*, 2 vols. (Mainz: F. Kirchheim, 1905-6), were also published: the first was the important *Quellenbelege* (see n. 20 below), and the second was a study of Luther's psychology by Weiss that was intended to confirm Denifle's interpretation of him.

7. *Luthers Vorlesung über den Römerbrief 1515/16*, ed. Johannes Ficker, 2 vols. (Leipzig: Dieterich, 1908); W.A. 56. Pertinent materials from the notebooks of students who attended the lectures are reproduced in the first part of W.A. 57. Besides the translation in L.W. 27, there was an earlier English version (with a valuable introduction) by Wilhelm Pauck, *Luther: Lectures on Romans*, Library of Christian Classics, vol. 15 (Philadelphia: Westminster Press, 1961).

8. Holl, "Die Rechtfertigungslehre in Luthers Vorlesung über den Römerbrief mit besonderer Rücksicht auf die Frage der Heilsgewissheit" (1910), revised and reprinted in his *Gesammelte Aufsätze zur Kirchengeschichte*, vol. 1: *Luther* (Tübingen: J. C. B. Mohr [Paul Siebeck], 1921). My own copy of Holl's collected essays, vol. 1, is the 6th ed. (1932); the study of Luther's doctrine of justification is on pp. 111–54.

9. In English there is a defense of the forensic interpretation of Luther's doctrine, partly in opposition to Holl's sanative interpretation, in Uuras Saarnivaara, *Luther Discovers the Gospel: New Light Upon Luther's Way From Medieval Catholicism to Evangelical Faith* (St. Louis, Mo.: Concordia Publishing House, 1951). Saarnivaara grants that the *Lectures on Romans* present a sanative doctrine of justification, but he argues that for just this reason they must be regarded as the work of a Luther who was not yet Protestant.

10. Bernhard Lohse, ed., *Der Durchbruch der reformatorischen Erkenntnis bei Luther*, Wege der Forschung, vol. 123 (Darmstadt: Wissenschaftliche Buchgesellschaft, 1968). The volume contains a preface by the editor and contributions or selections from contributions, all previously published, by Heinrich Denifle, Hartmann Grisar, Emanuel Hirsch, Ernst Stracke, Ernst Bizer, Gerhard Pfeiffer, Regin Prenter, Albrecht Peters, Heinrich Bornkamm, Kurt Aland, Heiko A. Oberman, and Otto H. Pesch. The last contribution (by Pesch) is an extensive review of the secondary literature. In English there is a briefer survey by Kenneth G. Hagen, "Changes in the Understanding of Luther: The Development of the Young Luther," *Theological Studies* 29 (1968):472–96.

11. Rupp used this phrase of the scholastic vocabulary in Luther's earlier lectures on the Psalms, the *Dictata super Psalterium* (1513–15). Gordon Rupp, *The Righteousness of God: Luther Studies* (London: Hodder and Stoughton, 1953), p. 139.

12. The context shows that Luther means 1519. In actual fact, he probably began his second course of lectures on the Psalms, the *Operationes in Psalmos*, in 1518, as the use of the pluperfect allows.

13. An allusion to Vergil, *Georgics*, II, 484.

14. Luther evidently means the connection between the two parts of the text. To make this clearer, I have taken the liberty of separating them by a dash.

15. Luther actually received the summons at the end of March 1521.

16. Text in W.A. 54.185.12–186.24; translation and emphasis mine. Another English version of the preface (in full) is given in L.W. 34:327–28.

17. Scholium on Rom. 1:17, W.A. 56.172.3ff.; L.W. 25:151–52, trans. Walter G. Tillmanns. The words "we are made righteous" in the second sentence do duty for the one Latin word *Iustificamur*.

18. A great deal of attention has been given to comparing the 1545 preface with Luther's exegesis in the *Dictata super Psalterium*. Vogelsang attempted to show, in an influential study, *which* Psalms Luther was expounding when the truth about God's righteousness dawned upon him, and he found the most important clue in Luther's tropological interpretation of Psalm 71. Erich Vogelsang, *Die Anfänge von Luthers Christologie nach der ersten Psalmenvorlesung: Insbesondere in ihren exegetischen und systematischen Zusammenhängen mit Augustin und der Scholastik dargestellt*, Arbeiten zur Kirchengeschichte, vol. 15 (Berlin and Leipzig: Walter de Gruyter, 1929), esp. pp. 40-61.

19. The simple pluperfect would be *captus eram*, but it is not possible to indicate the difference in English translation. Part of Stracke's essay, *Luthers grosses Selbstzeugnis 1545 über seine Entwicklung zum Reformator: Historisch-kritisch untersucht* (1926), is reproduced in Lohse, ed., *Durchbruch der reformatorischen Erkenntnis*, pp. 107-14. Lohse's extracts from Kurt Aland, *Der Weg zur Reformation: Zeitpunkt und Charakter des reformatorischen Erlebnisses Martin Luthers* (1965), include Aland's critique of Stracke's "double pluperfect" (pp. 384-412, esp. pp. 401-2).

20. Denifle, *Quellenbelege: Die abendländischen Schriftausleger bis Luther über Justitia Dei (Rom. 1:17) und Justificatio* (see n. 6 above); Holl, "Die *iustitia dei* in der vorlutherischen Bibelauslegung des Abendlandes" (1921), reprinted in *Gesammelte Aufsätze*, vol. 3: *Der Westen* (Tübingen: J. C. B. Mohr [Paul Siebeck], 1928), pp. 171-88; Emanuel Hirsch, "Initium theologiae Lutheri" (1920), reprinted in his *Lutherstudien*, 2 vols. (Gütersloh: C. Bertelsmann, 1954), 2:9-35.

21. "Prereformatory" serves for the German *vorreformatorisch*; but, like other terms current in the discussion (such as "tower experience"!), it is not a happy one. It would be improper to translate it "pre-Reformation," since it is used to denote a theological position rather than a historical event. Perhaps "pre-Protestant" would make the best of a poor expression, but I have settled for "prereformatory" and its opposite "reformatory" and will use them hereafter without further apology.

22. Hartmann Grisar, *Luther*, 3 vols. (Freiburg im Breisgau: Herder, 1911-12); trans. E. M. Lamond, ed. Luigi Cappadelta, 6 vols. (St. Louis, Mo.: B. Herder, 1913-17). In the English version see esp. 1:374-404. The emergence of a scholarly consensus comes somewhat later than Grisar. Cf. Hagen: "Perhaps the largest group of scholars ... , perpetuating something of a consensus in the thirties and forties, dated the *Turmerlebnis* during the period of the *Dictata*" ("Development of the Young Luther," pp. 490-91).

23. F. Edward Cranz, *An Essay on the Development of Luther's Thought on Justice, Law, and Society*, Harvard Theological Studies, vol. 19 (Cambridge, Mass.: Harvard University Press, 1959), cited in parentheses in the text of this section. Cranz's essay is a more independent study than Rupp's, and more sharply focused on Luther's breakthrough than the subsequent volume by Wicks, who expects to deal with Luther's reorientation in a sequel. Jared Wicks, *Man Yearning for Grace: Luther's Early Spiritual Teaching* (Washington and Cleve-

land: Corpus Books, 1968); see my review in *McCormick Quarterly* 23 (1970): 283-86.

24. *Luther: Lectures on Romans*, p. xliv.

25. Cf. Saarnivaara, *Luther Discovers the Gospel*, p. 121. But it must be admitted that even here there is no consensus among the Luther scholars: Prenter, for example, gives a very different picture of Luther's theology in the *Lectures on Romans*. Regin Prenter, *Spiritus Creator*, trans. John M. Jensen (Philadelphia: Muhlenberg Press, 1953).

26. "Ipsa quoque nostra justitia, quamvis vera sit propter veri boni finem, ad quem refertur, tamen tanta est in hac vita, ut potius peccatorum remissione constet, quam perfectione virtutum" (Augustine, *De civ. Dei*, xix.27, *Patrologia Latina*, 41:657; trans. in *Nicene and Post-Nicene Fathers*, first series, 2:419). "Ad haec respondetur, dimitti concupiscentiam carnis in Baptismo, non ut non sit, sed ut in peccatum non imputetur. Quamvis autem reatu suo jam soluto, manet tamen, donec sanetur omnis infirmitas nostra" (Augustine, *De nupt. et concup.*, I.xxv [28], *Patrologia Latina*, 44:430; *Nicene and Post-Nicene Fathers*, first series, 5:275).

27. Cranz's main sources are *Sermo de triplici iusticia* (1518; W.A. 2.43-47), *Sermo de duplici iustitia* (1519; W.A. 2.145-52), *In epistolam Pauli ad Galatas commentarius* (1519; W.A. 2.443-618), *Rationis Latomianae ... confutatio* (1521; W.A. 8.43-128), and the *Kirchenpostille* (1522; W.A. $10^{1,1}$.1-739). For translations, see L.W. 27, 31, 32, and 52. More extensive coverage of the postils will be found in the older version of J. N. Lenker.

28. See also Cranz's remarks (pp. 9-10, 81) on tropological justice in the *Dictata super Psalterium*.

29. It must be conceded, no doubt, that Luther himself is partly responsible for the difficulty here, since his distinction between active and passive righteousness in the preface seems to conceal a change of viewpoint. Why else would he term "passive" the righteousness by which God justifies us, even though "to justify" is no less active than "to punish"? The righteousness that justifies is passive from our point of view, not God's; and yet is is contrasted with the active righteousness not of man but of God.

30. The hiddenness of the Christian's righteousness is entailed by its identification with the righteousness of Christ; see Luther's use of Col. 3:3 ("Your life is hid with Christ in God") in W.A. 56.393.5; L.W. 25:383. On the righteousness of Christ see further W.A. 56.204.14ff.; L.W. 25:188.

31. See, e.g., W.A. 56.268.27ff.; L.W. 25:257. We are not righteous by a quality, but only by imputation (W.A. 56.287.19; L.W. 25:274). Luther also speaks of the *non*imputation of sin (e.g., in W.A. 56.274.9, 283.7, 291.9; L.W. 25:261, 270, 278), but the positive and negative forms (imputation and nonimputation) amount, in his view, to the same thing (W.A. 56.284.20; L.W. 25:272). More important: he uses the formula, sometimes considered the mark of his distinctive reformatory insight, that Christ's righteousness is imputed to the saints (W.A. 56.347.8; L.W. 25:336). Indeed, when he states that the Christian is a sinner in fact (*re vera*) but righteous by reason of the divine reckoning and

promise, he comes close to the "legal fiction" that was to become a bone of contention in later Protestant theology (W.A. 56.272.17; L.W. 25:260). Holl's well-known thesis, which put the emphasis on the phrase "righteous in promise," was that in Luther's thinking God could pronounce sinners righteous without compromising his holiness because he *intended* to make them whole (*Luther*, pp. 125, 128). See further n. 68 below.

32. The "not yet" perspective appears throughout the lectures, most strikingly in W.A. 56.441.14–443.8 (L.W. 25:433–35); see also W.A. 56.280.17 (L.W. 25:268). It is entailed by the Augustinian metaphor of healing; see, for instance, W.A. 56. 258.21, 275.25ff., 347.11; L.W. 25:245, 262–63, 336. Christ alone *is* righteous; we are *being made* righteous, i.e., being justified (W.A. 56.49.22; L.W. 25:43).

33. W.A. 56.269.30, 272.19, 347.12; L.W. 25:258, 260, 336. Note that in the second of these passages (272.3) faith is unambiguously belief in the doctor's promise of healing (see n. 38 below).

34. See, for example, Luther's comments on Rom. 4:7 and 7:25 (W.A. 56. 268.27–273.2, 347.8; L.W. 25:257–60, 336). In the second thesis that he advances in the first of these two passages he speaks of the formula *simul iustus et peccator* as descriptive of two ways in which God views his saints. In the second passage he clearly foreshadows his later formulation of the basis for this double judgment: namely, the fact that God may view the sinner either in Christ or through the law. But one is bound to grant that this is not all he has to say about the *simul iustus et peccator*; indeed, in the second passage the notion of inchoate righteousness is plainly expressed.

35. The preface to the complete Latin works itself implies that, although what Luther discovered was in substance nothing other than Augustine's interpretation of the *iustitia dei*, Augustine's view of justification still left something to be desired: "Et quanquam imperfecte hoc adhuc sit dictum, ac de imputatione non clare omnia explicet ...."

36. Ernst Bizer, *Fides ex auditu: Eine Untersuchung über die Entdeckung der Gerechtigkeit Gottes durch Martin Luther* (Neukirchen Kreis Moers: Verlag der Buchhandlung des Erziehungsvereins, 1958). My references, in parentheses in the text, are to the second edition (ibid., 1961). The third edition (ibid., 1966) has the same pagination as the second except in the new epilogue (pp. 179–204), in which Bizer responds to his critics and adopts the more exact date for the Reformation breakthrough proposed by Aland (see n. 19 above): between 15 February and 28 March 1518.

37. Werner Jetter, *Die Taufe beim jungen Luther: Eine Untersuchung über das Werden der reformatorischen Sakraments- und Taufanschauung*, Beiträge zur historischen Theologie, vol. 18 (Tübingen: J. C. B. Mohr [Paul Siebeck], 1954); see the summary on p. 337.

38. Since the preceding sentence mentions the mass, "the sacrament" may mean here the sacrament of the altar; but Bizer certainly thinks that Luther held a distinctive view of the Word and the sacraments in general. It should be emphasized that Bizer's interpretation of the Word in Luther's theology is itself

twofold: his thesis is that the Word *as promise* is the means of grace. Only part of the thesis is stated in the words "Meine These ist nun, dass Luther in der Vorrede davon berichte, wie er 'das Wort als Gnadenmittle' entdeckt habe" (3d ed., p. 180). The other part is that "ich . . . zu dem Ergebnis kam, die entscheidende Entdeckung sei die Entdeckung des Wortes als promissio, als Zusage und Gabe" (ibid., pp. 190–91). For a passage in the *Lectures on Romans* that already treats the Word as promise, though in the framework of a sanative theory of justification, see n. 33 above.

39. *Vorlesung über den Hebräerbrief*, W.A. 57(III).3–91 (glosses), 97–238 (scholia); L.W. 29:107–241.

40. *Acta F. Martini Luther Augustiniani apud legatum apostolicum Augustae*, W.A. 2.6–26; L.W. 31:259–92.

41. These comments were originally written for a review article on Bizer's and Cranz's books, before I could profit from the extensive discussion of Bizer's thesis in Germany. But I have left them unchanged and have not entered into the discussion, which is outlined in Pesch's article mentioned (in n.10) above. Cranz's study, it may be added, did not receive as much attention as it deserved.

42. W.A. 56.279.24ff., 280.3; L.W. 25:267.

43. W.A. 56.347.8; L.W. 25:336. Bizer argues that the nonreckoning of sin to those who have begun to be righteous is conditional on humility (pp. 50–51), but that does not seem to be the sense of this passage. And the express occurrence here of a locution (*Iustitia* [*Christi*] *eis imputatur*) that is often regarded as the shibboleth of orthodox Protestantism is striking, all the more so because the idea of imputation characteristic of the mature Luther does *not* employ this expression. See section IV below.

44. W.A. 56.204.15ff.; L.W. 25:188. See Gerrish, "Atonement and 'Saving Faith,'" *Theology Today* 17 (1960):181–91, esp. pp. 181–82.

45. W.A. 56.424.1–426.9; L.W. 25:415–18.

46. The expression *Deus humilium* appears at W.A. 40^1.488.15 (L.W. 26:314), but in the above paragraph I have drawn on the entire section: W.A. 40^1.487.15–490.35; L.W. 26:313–16. The distinction between law and gospel—the two words of God—could also be documented from the *Commentary on Galatians*: see, e.g., W.A. 40^1.232.16, 489.27, 556.20ff.; L.W. 26:131, 315, 364.

47. "Ista ex diametro pugnant, Christianum esse iustum . . . et tamen simul esse peccatorem. . . . Sic Christianus manet in pura humilitate" (W.A. 40^1.371.33, 372.19; L.W. 26:235). "Sic manemus in humilitate non ficta aut monastica, sed vera, propter sordes et vitia, quae haerent in carne nostra" (W.A. 40^2.107.33; L.W. 27:86). For further discussion of faith and humility, especially in the *Commentary on Galatians*, see my *Grace and Reason: A Study in the Theology of Luther* (1962; reprint ed., Chicago: University of Chicago Press, 1979), esp. pp. 110ff.

48. Gerrish, "Atonement and 'Saving Faith,'" pp. 183–84.

49. "Quae sententia est expositio illius iustitiae Dei" (W.A.Tr. 5.235.5 [no. 5553]).

50. Emphasis mine. In the epilogue to his third edition Bizer writes: "Und weiter muss dann das revelari als Beschreibung von Gottes Geben verstanden

werden; es ist als donari zu verstehen" (p. 180). The textual basis for this equation is Luther's phrase (in the 1545 preface) *qua [iustitia] iustus dono Dei vivit, nempe ex fide.*

51. "Quod autem aliqui non intelligunt, quomodo sola fides iustificat, in causa est, quod quid fides sit non cognoverint nec gustaverint unquam, somniantes eam esse qualitatem latentem in anima" (*Resolutio disputationis de fide infusa et acquisita* [1520], W.A. 6.94.7).

52. With the paragraphs that follow compare the discussion of faith's three "powers" in the *Tractatus de libertate christiana* (1520), W.A. 7.52.20–57.2; L.W. 31:348–54. There Luther explains that faith alone justifies because it believes the promises and is "absorbed by them," because it honors him whom it trusts and takes him at his word, and because it unites the soul with Christ and so is endowed with his righteousness.

53. *In epistolam S. Pauli ad Galatas commentarius* (1531/35), W.A. 40^1.424. 20–26; L.W. 26:271. Cf. W.A. 40^1 557.21; L.W. 26:365.

54. The excursus is in W.A. 40^1.328.22–346.22 (L.W. 26:202–16). I quote the text in the R.S.V. Luther's Latin has *ex auditu fidei* for the Greek ἐξ ἀκοῆς πίστεως. Cf. W.A. 40^1.387.16; L.W. 26:245.

55. W.A. 40^1.331.19, 333.27ff.; L.W. 26:204–6. The allusion is to Acts 10, especially verse 44: "The Holy Spirit fell on all who heard the word." Later, Luther appeals also to Luke 10:38–42, which tells of Mary's sitting at Jesus' feet while her sister was very busy (W.A. 40^1.344.31ff.; L.W. 26:214).

56. W.A. 40^1.336.27–31; L.W. 26:208.

57. W.A. 40^1.229.22, 28; cf. L.W. 26:130. It is by Christ's righteousness only that we are justified, i.e., the righteousness of faith or Christian righteousness (W.A. 40^1.64.16, 64.28, 204.16; L.W. 26:21, 113).

58. W.A. 40^2.20.12; 40^1.444.13, 567.21; 40^1.443.23; 40^1.232.29ff. (faith that takes hold of the Christ who bears the sin of the world is alone counted for righteousness), 40^1.503.23, 40^2.80.19: L.W. 27:17; 26:284, 372; 26:284; 26:132, 26:325, 27:64. It is, of course, the question of atonement that lies behind these various thoughts and images.

59. W.A. 40^1.284.16; cf. L.W. 25:167. Luther goes on: "*Quantum attinet ad iustificationem,* oportet Christum et me esse coniunctissimos, ut ipse in me vivat et ego in illo" (my emphasis).

60. "Fides enim apprehendit Christum et habet eum praesentem includitque eum ut annulus gemmam, Et qui fuerit inventus cum tali fide apprehensi Christi in corde, illum reputat Deus iustum" (W.A. 40^1.233.17; L.W. 25:132). We are members of Christ's body, and he is not present in us spiritually, as the sectarians imagine, but really and efficaciously (W.A. 40^1.546.21; L.W. 26:357). In an interesting phrase, Luther remarks that "in ipsa fide Christus adest" (W.A. 40^1.229.15; L.W. 25:129). Cf. W.A. 40^1.235.23, 297.30, 379.16; L.W. 26:134, 177, 240.

61. This is Seeberg's formulation (*History of Doctrines*, 2:263). It could certainly be supported from the *Commentary on Galatians*, where Luther suggests, for instance, that whereas the Schoolmen talked of faith formed by love, it is in fact Christ who in-forms faith (W.A. 40^1.228.26; L.W. 26:129). We are

justified by the faith that takes hold of Christ: "Quare nos quoque facimus qualitatem et formalem iustitiam in corde" (W.A. 40^1.232.23; L.W. 26:132). In this way Luther modifies his rejection of the view that Christian righteousness is a quality or an inherent form induced by the infusion of charity (W.A. 40^1.225.25ff.; L.W. 26:127). And yet in another place where the notion of an infused quality is rejected Luther concludes that our righteousness is not in us formally but outside of us—in the grace and imputation of God (W.A. 40^1.370.28; L.W. 26:234). I return to the subject of imputation below.

62. W.A. 40^1.363.28-364.28; L.W. 26:229-30. As will be indicated shortly, the notion of imputation in this passage is linked with the fourth description of faith (the attribution of glory to God). See also W.A. 40^2.25.23, 31.30, 33.19; L.W. 27:22, 26, 27.

63. W.A. 40^1.235.18, 366.25, 366.29, 367.18, 370.19, 370.24, 371.18ff., 372.26, 429.14; L.W. 26:133, 231-35, 274. Cf. W.A. 40^1.365.31ff. (L.W. 26:231): "Crede Iesum Christum, filium unigenitum meum, natum ... , tum acceptabo et pronuntiabo te iustum. Et quod reliquum est in te peccati, non imputabo tibi." For the negative formula "nonimputation," see further n. 69 above.

64. W.A. 40^1.359.25ff.; L.W. 26:226. Cf. Romans 4:18-22.

65. W.A. 40^1.360.21, 360.34, 361.12 (1535 and 1538); cf. L.W. 26:227. "Deus est qui sua dona gratis largitur omnibus, Eaque est laus divinitatis ipsius" (W.A. 40^1.224.28; L.W. 26:127). "Qui igitur crediderit filium Dei esse Mediatorem et Salvatorem nostrum, is honorificat patrem, Et Deus vicissim glorificat, id est, ornat eum suis donis, Remissione peccatorum, iustitia, Spiritusancto, vita aeterna" (W.A. 40^1.246.15; L.W. 26:141).

66. W.A. 40^1.364.11, 14; cf. L.W. 26:229.

67. W.A. 40^1.366.27ff.; cf. L.W. 26:231.

68. W.A. 40^1.368.20ff.; cf. L.W. 26:232. As in the *Lectures on Romans* (see n. 31 above), Luther sometimes states the idea of imputation in the negative form: the remnants of sin are *not* reckoned to us (W.A. $40^1$235.15, 364.22, 367.11, 367.27, 369.23, 408.14, 428.28; 40^2.108.11, etc.: L.W. 26:133, 230, 232 [twice], 233, 260, 274; 27:86). But he apparently regards the negative formula as equivalent to the positive (faith is imputed as righteousness). It is interesting that in the entire passage on Galatians 3:6 Luther says nothing about the imputation of Christ's righteousness to us, any more than Paul does in Galatians 3 or Romans 4.

69. "Quare fides iustitiam incipit, imputatio perficit usque ad diem Christi" (W.A. 40^1.364.27; cf. L.W. 26:230).

70. In addition to the passages already cited, see W.A. 40^1.233.25 (L.W. 26:132-33): "Et valde necessaria est Acceptatio seu reputatio, Primum, quia nondum sumus pure iusti, sed in hac vita haeret adhuc peccatum in carne." Complete and perfect righteousness is found in Christ alone, which is why we "abide in humility" (W.A. 40^2.107.33; L.W. 27:86).

71. W.A. 40^1.369.18, 408.12-21, 613.28-614.30, etc.; L.W. 26:233, 260, 403. Note that in the first of these passages the initial step toward health is the

admission that one is sick; in the second Christ is the Good Samaritan; in the third the woman with the hemorrhage illustrates the problem of false cures.

72. That the justified man is not yet righteous but in progress toward righteousness, or righteous by imputation, is clearly asserted in, for instance, two disputations from the 1530s. "Iustificari enim hominem sentimus, hominem nondum esse iustum, sed esse in ipso motu seu cursu ad iustitiam. Ideo et peccator est adhuc, quisquis iustificatur, et tamen velut plene et perfecte iustus reputatur, ignoscente et miserente Deo. Ignoscit autem et miseretur nostri Deus, intercedente et sanctificante nostrum initium iustitiae Christo advocato et sacerdote nostro" (Disputatio de iustificatione [1536], theses 23–25, W.A. 39^1.83.16ff.; L.W. 34:152–53). "Iustificatio ergo nostra nondum est completa. Est in agendo et fieri" (Die Promotionsdisputation von Palladius und Tilemann [1537], W.A. 39^1.252.8).

73. Luther Discovers the Gospel, p. 14. Saarnivaara regards the imputation of Christ's righteousness as the heart of the Lutheran (and Calvinist) doctrine of justification, and he points out that the doctrine was condemned by the Council of Trent (session 6, canon 11) in precisely this form (p. 17, n. 41).

74. It does not follow that there are no differences between Luther and Augustine (see n. 35 above), or between the young and the mature Luther; only that it is difficult to draw the dividing lines where they have so often been drawn. It would be easy to point to still more echoes of the Lectures on Romans in the later Commentary on Galatians: e.g., the notion of possession in hope (W.A. 40^1.236.29, 40^2.24.21; L.W. 26:134, 27:21). Even the theme of justifying God in his word of judgment is to be found in Luther's comments on Galatians 2:16, although it is expressly said to be only the first step (W.A. 40^1.224.15 [but not in George Rörer's transcript] ; L.W. 26:126).

75. W.A. 40^1.365.30; cf. L.W. 26:231.

76. W.A. 40^1.366.23; L.W. 26:231.

77. "Qui vult me placare, credat meum filium natum, passum; qui hoc credit, erit iustus" (W.A. 40^{1}365.12 [Rörer]). Cf. W.A. 40^1.246.15; L.W. 26:141.

78. W.A. 40^1.360.21ff.; L.W. 26:227. At some points, my analysis keeps closer to Rörer's transcript than to either of the published versions (1535, 1538). See further W.A. 40^1.224.28, 363.11, 365.26, 369.20; L.W. 26:127, 229, 231, 233.

79. W.A. 40^1.376.23; L.W. 26:238.

80. W.A. 40^1.360.18 (cf. 360.3), 361.12; L.W. 26:227. The virtus (i.e., "power") of faith is precisely that it gives God his due.

81. W.A. 40^1.376.25; L.W. 26:238. Although my remarks on fiducia cordis were not originally indebted to John McLeod Campbell, I became convinced, when rereading him for the third chapter of my Tradition and the Modern World, that he came as close as anyone to Luther's meaning. His remarks are not those of a Lutherforscher, but of a first-rate theological mind seeking to appropriate Luther's ideas. Campbell writes: "Faith is the right attitude of the human spirit towards God—the due response to His revelation of Himself to us, in rendering which our hearts are right towards God" (The Nature of the Atonement and

Its Relation to Remission of Sins and Eternal Life, 3d ed. [London: Macmillan, 1869], p. 390. For further discussion see *Tradition and the Modern World: Reformed Theology in the Nineteenth Century* (Chicago: University of Chicago Press, 1978), chap. 3.

82. W.A. 40^1.232.16; L.W. 26:131-32.

83. W.A. 40^2.27.14; L.W. 27:23. Faith is knowledge: it looks to the Word. The first requisite for a devout man is a right understanding, an intelligence formed by faith. Faith is conceived by instruction; hence we must consult the Word (W.A. 40^2.26.14, 26.21, 28.9, 28.25, 32.25; L.W. 27:22, 22-23, 23, 24, 27).

84. W.A. 40^1.224.29-32, 360.25, 363.16-27, 376.26; L.W. 26:127, 227, 229, 238.

85. W.A. 40^1.613.28-615.13; L.W. 26:403-4. For a more detailed treatment of the religion of law and reason, see my *Grace and Reason*, chap. 6.

86. W.A. 40^1.220.4ff., 225.26ff., 230.17ff.; L.W. 26:124-25, 127-29, 130-31. As his text indicates, Luther identifies the Nominalist scheme with justification by works or by the law (cf. his exegesis of Gal. 2:21, W.A. 40^1.300-308; L.W. 26:179-84). He also takes the *theologia sophistica* (as the heading in the 1538 edition calls it) to be, quite simply, the *opinio Papistarum*. For representative selections (in English) from the Nominalists Robert Holcot and Gabriel Biel, see Heiko A. Oberman, ed., *Forerunners of the Reformation: The Shape of Late Medieval Thought* (New York: Holt, Rinehart and Winston, 1966), chap. 3.

87. "Hi antevortunt dilectionem Dei et Christi, quia faciunt quod in se est, Item fiunt Monachi," etc. (W.A. 40^1.291.18; L.W. 26:172).

88. W.A. 40^1.291.29ff., esp. 292.19; cf. L.W. 26:173. This section is headed in the 1538 edition, *Facere quod in se est*. I have borrowed the translation of the verse (a hexameter in the Latin) from the old "Middleton" version. On the text and translations of the commentary see *Grace and Reason*, p. ix and chap. 4.

89. Huldrych Zwingli, *De vera et falsa religione commentarius* (1525), in Zwingli's *Sämtliche Werke (Corpus Reformatorum)*, 3:678-79; trans. in *The Latin Works of Huldrych Zwingli Together with Selections from His German Works*, vol. 3, ed. C.N. Heller "for the late S.M. Jackson" (Philadelphia: Heidelberg Press, 1929), p. 103.

90. W.A. 40^1.615.20ff., 40^2.15.15ff.; L.W. 26:404-7, 27.13. On the one hand, Luther asks: "Quis enim non potest virtute humana sine gratia facere opus bonum quo mereatur gratiam?" (W.A 40^1.230.24; L.W. 26:130). But on the other hand: "Quid enim homines conclusi sub peccatum, obnoxii maledicto legis et rei aeternae mortis, mererentur?" (W.A. 40^1.571.16; L.W. 26:374).

91. W.A. 56.274.14, 502.14-503.12; L.W. 25:261, 496-97.

92. *Ein deutsch Theologia, das ist ein edles Büchlein von rechtem Verstand, was Adam und Christus sei*. The text of the treatise, as Luther knew it, will be found in *Theologia deutsch*, ed. Hermann Mandel, Quellenschriften zur Geschichte des Protestantismus, vol. 7 (Leipzig: A. Deichert [Georg Boehme], 1908), which I cite by chapter. (Only Luther's preface was included in W.A. 1 and L.W. 31.) There is a fresh English translation of the treatise, based on the second printing of Luther's original Wittenberg edition (1518) and therefore titled

The Theologia Germanica of Martin Luther, trans. Bengt Hoffman, Classics of Western Spirituality (New York: Paulist Press, 1980). Hoffman is also the author of *Luther and the Mystics: A Re-Examination of Luther's Spiritual Experience and His Relationship to the Mystics* (Minneapolis, Minn.: Augsburg Publishing House, 1976), which introduces the reader to the problems but is less successful, I think, in sorting them out. The Pantheon edition of the old translation by Susanna Winkworth (New York: Pantheon, 1949) includes in English an introduction by Joseph Bernhart, editor of a modern German version of the treatise based on the Würzburg edition (with different chapter divisions).

93. The presentation of the *German Theology*, which may well be a compilation of edifying discourses, is not tightly ordered. I have put the picture of sin together from several passages, especially chapters 47 and 51. The theme of self-will appears passim; sinners are described as bent in upon themselves in chapters 24 and 38. The extent to which the young Luther echoes the language of the treatise is remarkable (see chap. 1, n. 10, above). For striking parallels to his notion of *Anfechtung*, his emphasis on humility, and his view of what makes a theologian (*not* reading or studying!), see respectively chapters 11, 33 (cf. 24), and 17. Luther's *Lectures on Romans* further agree that nature seeks self (W.A. 56.356.27; L.W. 25:346); and in the sixteenth of his Ninety-Five Theses he, too, "demythologizes" heaven and hell.

94. *Theologia deutsch*, chaps. 32, 42.

95. Ibid., chap. 20; trans. Hoffman, p. 87. The Christ-life is a pervasive theme in the treatise; see also chapters 16, 21, 24, 27, 41, 43, and 51.

96. See the texts translated in Saarnivaara, *Luther Discovers the Gospel*, chap. 2. Steinmetz has now added a sequel to his earlier work on Staupitz: David C. Steinmetz, *Luther and Staupitz: An Essay on the Intellectual Origins of the Protestant Reformation*, Duke Monographs in Medieval and Renaissance Studies, no. 4 (Durham, N.C.: Duke University Press, 1980).

97. Mandel thought that the *German Theology* presented Christ as merely the ideal or the model for imitation, and the treatise does in fact seem, at points, to teach a naively exemplary concept of Christ's work and person: we are told, for instance, that as Christ's soul had to visit hell, this is the path also for the souls of men (chap. 11; cf. chap. 52). But the constant emphasis on the work of God *within* the soul transcends the category of example (see esp. chap. 9); and even if it is not a very prominent feature, the treatise does speak of sacramental participation in Christ (chap. 43) and warns against the folly of imagining that one can outgrow the need for Christ, Scripture, sacraments, or symbols (chaps. 38, 23, and 12). Commenting on the relative neglect of the sacraments in the *German Theology*, Hoffman makes the interesting observation—rightly, I believe—that "it seemed to consider preaching on the basic religious attitude as a means of grace in itself" (p. 25). A somewhat different point is made by Ozment, who finds a connection with the semi-Pelagian *facere quod in se est* "even in the subtle mystical form of passive resignation—a 'doing' which is a 'doing nothing.'" Steven E. Ozment, *Mysticism and Dissent: Religious Ideology and Social Protest in the Sixteenth Century* (New Haven, Conn.: Yale University Press, 1973), p. 24, with reference to the end of chapter 20 of the treatise. Less

inclined to see any tendency to synergism in the *German Theology* or in Tauler is Bengt Hägglund, *The Background of Luther's Doctrine of Justification in Late Medieval Theology*, Facet Books, Historical Series, no. 18 (Philadelphia: Fortress Press, 1971), a useful, succinct review of both mysticism and nominalism in relation to Luther's doctrine, reprinted from *Lutheran World* 8 (1961):24-46.

98. See above, n. 1.

99. *Vorlesung über den Hebräerbrief* (1517-18), W.A. 57(III).114.7ff.; L.W. 29:123-24. Cf. W.A. 57(III).143.5; L.W. 29:148. On the important *sacramentum-exemplum* theme in Luther, see Erwin Iserloh, "Luther's Christ-Mysticism," in *Catholic Scholars Dialogue With Luther*, ed. Jared Wicks (Chicago: Loyola University Press, 1970), pp. 37-58, esp. pp. 51-57, which at some points corrects Bizer and Jetter. But Iserloh's own interpretation is suspect when he states that union with Christ, for Luther, takes place in the *Seelengrund*. (Here the writings of Ozment may serve as an important corrective.) See also Norman Nagel, *"Sacramentum et exemplum* in Luther's Understanding of Christ," in *Luther for an Ecumenical Age: Essays in Commemoration of the 450th Anniversary of the Reformation*, ed. Carl S. Meyer (St. Louis, Mo.: Concordia Publishing House, 1967), pp. 172-99. Nagel finds even the notion of *sacramentum* problematic insofar as it treats Christ's death as paradigmatic, not as unique and vicarious (p. 182).

100. W.A. 40^1.523.31-524.16, 526.21-32, 527.15, 538.30; L.W. 26:340, 342, 343, 351.

101. *Von den guten Werken* (1520), W.A. 6.204-76; translated in L.W. 44.

102. *Tractatus de libertate christiana* (1520), W.A. 7.49-73; translated in L.W. 31. Cf. Calvin, *Inst.*, 3.19.5 (1:837).

103. "Fides est pertinacissimus intutus qui nihil aspicit praeter Christum victorem peccati et mortis et largitorem iustitiae, salutis et vitae aeternae. Hinc Paulus in Epistolis suis fere in singulis versibus proponit et inculcat Iesum Christum. Proponit autem per verbum, cum aliter proponi non possit quam per verbum neque aliter apprehendi quam per fidem" (W.A. 40^1.545.30-35; L.W. 26:356). Both the 1535 text and Rörer's transcript read *intutus,* which is obviously a slip for *intuitus.* For some of Calvin's utterances on *Christi intuitus,* see Gerrish, ed., *Reformers in Profile* (Philadelphia: Fortress Press, 1967), p. 162.

104. "Haec est ratio, cur nostra Theologia certa sit: Quia rapit nos a nobis et ponit nos extra nos, ut non nitamur viribus, conscientia, sensu, persona, operibus nostris, sed eo nitamur, quod est extra nos, Hoc est, promissione et veritate Dei, quae fallere non potest" (W.A. 40^1.589.25; L.W. 26:387). Just before, the commentary has stated: "Hocque fundamentum est nostrum: Evangelium iubet intueri nos non benefacta et perfectionem nostram, sed ipsum deum promittentem, Ipsum Christum Mediatorem" (W.A. 40^1.589.17; L.W. 26:387).

Chapter Five

1. Melanchthon's advice was given in reply to the emperor's query whether the Lutherans wished to add further articles to those in the Augsburg Confession

(*iudicium*, dated 10 July 1530, C.R. 2:183). The outstanding attempt to trace the history of the notion of a "royal priesthood" will be found in the two learned studies by Paul Dabin, *Le Sacerdoce royal des fidèles dans les livres saints* (Paris: Bloud and Gay, 1941) and *Le sacerdoce royal des fidèles dans la tradition ancienne et moderne* (Paris: Desclée, 1950). In English there are two useful works by Cyril Eastwood: *The Priesthood of All Believers: An Examination of the Doctrine from the Reformation to the Present Day* and *The Royal Priesthood of the Faithful: An Investigation of the Doctrine from Biblical Times to the Reformation* (Minneapolis, Minn.: Augsburg Publishing House, 1962 and 1963). For an evaluation of Eastwood's two volumes, see my critical review in *McCormick Quarterly* 18 (1964): 43-48.

2. Thomas M. Lindsay, *A History of the Reformation*, 2d ed., International Theological Library, 2 vols. (Edinburgh: T. and T. Clark, 1907-8), 1:180, 443, 444.

3. T. M. Lindsay, *The Reformation*, 2d ed., (Edinburgh: T. and T. Clark, 1883), pp. 185-86, 187. A more recent individualistic interpretation of the common priesthood, as mordantly hostile as Lindsay's was enthusiastic, pervades the introductory remarks of Raymond Himelick, trans. and ed., *Erasmus and the Seamless Coat of Jesus: De Sarcienda Ecclesiae Concordia* (Lafayette, Ind.: Purdue University Studies, 1971). Himelick's translation may serve as a salutary reminder that there was more to Erasmus than Lindsay found in the *Enchiridion*. But our concern here is with his assumption that the Reformation moved from "Every man his own priest" to "Every man his own church," and that the schismatics not only disagreed among themselves but "scarcely agreed with themselves from one day to the next" (pp. 1, 10).

4. E. Harris Harbison, *The Age of Reformation* (Ithaca, N.Y.: Cornell University Press, 1955), p. 50.

5. *An den Christlichen Adel deutscher Nation von des Christlichen standes besserung*, W.A. 6.404-69, esp. 407.9ff.; L.W. 44:123-217, esp. pp. 127ff. Although I give my own translations, I have located in L.W. the major sources referred to in nn. 5-15.

6. *De captivitate Babylonica ecclesiae praeludium*, W.A. 6.497-573, esp. 560.19ff.; L.W. 36:11-126, esp. pp. 106ff.

7. *Tractatus de libertate christiana*, W.A. 7.49-73, esp. 56.35ff.; L.W. 31:343-77, esp. pp. 345ff.

8. *Das eyn Christliche versamlung odder gemeyne recht und macht habe, alle lere zu urteylen und lerer zu beruffen, eyn- und abzusetzen, Grund und ursach aus der schrifft*, W.A. 11.408-16; L.W. 39:305-14.

9. *De instituendis ministris ecclesiae ad senatum Pragensem Bohemiae*, W.A. 12.169-96; L.W. 40:7-44.

10. *Ein Brieff D. Mart. Luthers, Von den Schleichern und Winckelpredigern*, W.A. 30^3.518-27; L.W. 40:383-94.

11. *Der LXXXII. Psalm, Ausgelegt*, W.A. 31^1.189-218, esp. 210.9ff.; L.W. 13.42-72, esp. pp. 63ff.

12. *Vom missbrauch der Messen*, W.A. 8.485.28ff.; L.W. 36:137ff.

13. *Von der Winckelmesse und Pfaffen Weyhe*, W.A. 38.195-256, esp. 229.29ff.; L.W. 38:147-214, esp. pp. 187ff.

14. *Eine Predigt, das man kinder zur Schulen halten solle*, W.A. 30².517–88; L.W. 46:213–58.

15. *Von den Konziliis und Kirchen*, W.A. 50.632.35ff.; L.W. 41:154ff.

16. J. W. F. Höfling, *Grundsätze evangelisch-lutherischer Kirchenverfassung*, 3d ed. (Erlangen: T. Bläsing, 1853), p. 77.

17. F. J. Stahl, *Die Kirchenverfassung nach Lehre und Recht der Protestanten*, 2d ed. (Erlangen: T. Bläsing, 1862), pp. 67, 101, 111.

18. *Das allgemeine Priestertum bei Luther*, Theologische Existenz heute, n.s. no. 37 (Munich: Chr. Kaiser Verlag, 1953).

19. *Die Theologie des Gottesdienstes bei Luther* (1952); Eng. trans., *Luther on Worship* (Philadelphia: Muhlenberg Press, 1958).

20. "Luthers Auffassung vom geistlichen Amt," *Luther-Jahrbuch* 25 (1958): 61–98.

21. Wilhelm Brunotte, *Das geistliche Amt bei Luther* (Berlin: Lutherisches Verlagshaus, 1959); Hellmut Lieberg, *Amt und Ordination bei Luther und Melanchthon* (Göttingen: Vandenhoeck and Ruprecht, 1962). A third substantial work, though limited in its chronological scope, appeared during the 1970s: Jan Aarts, *Die Lehre Martin Luthers über das Amt in der Kirche: Eine genetisch-systematische Untersuchung seiner Schriften von 1512 bis 1525*, Schriften der Luther-Agricola-Gesellschaft, series A, no. 15 (Helsinki: Hämeenlinna, 1972). Aarts recognizes the presence in Luther of the notion that certain priestly tasks are "delegated" to the ministers of the church; but, in partial dependence on Regin Prenter (see n. 47 below), he denies that the act of delegation *constitutes* the ministerial office, which Luther understands solely as a divine institution. Aarts refers to one other major study, which I have not seen: Francisco Bravo, *El sacerdocio común de los creyentes en la teología de Lutero*, Publicaciones del seminario de Vitoria, no. 16 (Vitoria, 1963).

22. W.A. 30².455.37; 6.514.11, 517.8, 530.11 (cf. 520.26), 533.29, 538.7, 543.17; 30¹.215.34.

23. W.A. 11.408.8; 50.629.16; 8.491.34; 17¹.99.26; 7.721.9; 12.191.16; 6.560.33. As Hans Storck puts it: "[The Word] has taken over for Luther the place and function of Jesus Christ. The Word is *Christus praesens et vivens*, the present and living Christ" (*Das allgemeine Priestertum*, p. 7). The Word "assumes for us the place of the historical Jesus" (ibid., p. 9).

24. W.A. 7.56.26.

25. W.A. 7.57.28; 12.307.22 (where the priestly office is threefold: sacrifice, prayer, and proclamation; cf. 41.210.25); 6.566.26; 8.495.31, 498.15; 11.412.5; 12.180.17.

26. W.A. 8.486.29, 495.1; 16.407.33; 7.57.24. Sometimes faith itself is identified as the priestly office (e.g., W.A. 6.370.24). There are several distinct moments in the idea of the common priesthood. Storck lists three: immediate relationship to God, sacrifice for the neighbor, power to perform the acts of the spiritual office (*Das allgemeine Priestertum*, p. 53). W. Brunotte finds four basic elements: equality before God (including equal power in God's Word), free access to God and his Word, the obligation to make spiritual sacrifice, responsibility for proclaiming the Gospel (*Das geistliche Amt*, pp. 138ff.). A recent essay by Heinz Brunotte, *Das Amt der Verkündigung und das Priestertum aller Gläub-*

igen, Luthertum, vol. 26 (Berlin: Lutherisches Verlagshaus, 1962), distinguishes five elements in the common priesthood: spiritual equality, immediate access, independence of early mediators, the spiritual sacrifice of praise, and the duty to witness (pp. 19–20). The notion of immediate access to God, which appears (with minor variations of wording) in all three of these lists, no doubt provided the foothold for the individualistic interpretation of Luther's "priesthood of all believers"; and it is not to be denied that, in the context of his polemic against Rome, some of the remarks he let slip invited a one-sided preoccupation with this facet of his teaching. He states expressly, for instance, that in matters of faith every Christian is his own pope and church (*Operationes in Psalmos* [1518–21], W.A. 5.407.35). Aarts stresses the fact, which he finds neglected in the existing literature, that Luther based the common priesthood on the inward instruction of the Christian by God (*Die Lehre Luthers über das Amt*, pp. 188–89n., 305, 320). This is an important point, I think, as one tries to grasp the connection between Luther's own notion of priesthood and what subsequent Protestantism made of it. To put it in terms of biblical sources, it is John 6:45 at least as much as 1 Peter 2:9 and Revelation 1:6 that shaped the self-understanding of Protestants: Schleiermacher, for instance, finds in the Johannine text the eschatological goal of the history of the church (see chap. 11, n. 24). But as far as Luther's thinking is concerned, the crucial question is: Immediate access for what purpose? And the question can only be answered in the light of his notion that the Christian is a priest for others.

27. W.A. 6.407.13, 15, 18, 22; 6.564.11; 7.58.14.

28. W.A. 6.564.15, 24.

29. W.A. 12.173.9.

30. W.A. 12.180.1. "Binding or loosing sins" refers to the power of the keys (see Matt. 16:19). The key that binds is ultimately the power of excommunication, while the key that looses is the power of absolution. Luther devoted a special treatise to the subject: *Von den Schlüsseln* (1530), W.A. 30^2.465–507, 30^3.548–88; L.W. 40:325–77.

31. W.A. 12.180.5, 191.6.

32. W.A. 12.184.21 (cf. 2.191.16).

33. W.A. 12.183.38.

34. W.A. 11.412.32.

35. W.A. 12.171.17.

36. W.A. 19.75.3.

37. W.A. 11.411.22; 50.634.11.

38. W.A. 6.407.13, 409.1, 567.17; 30^3.521.7.

39. W.A. 7.58.19; cf. 12.189.21; 31^1.211.20.

40. W.A. 31^1.211.17; 30^3.519.25.

41. W.A. 50.632.36.

42. W.A. 50.633.5; 10^3.397.17; $10^{1,2}$.239.24; 12.189.21; 10^3.216.3; 8.495.31 (cf. 423.6).

43. W.A. 6.407.29, 32. 34.

44. W.A. 12.189.21; 6.564.6. For the ideas of "consent" and "representation" see, besides the passages already cited, W.A. 6.408.13, 566.26; 8.253.29; 10^3.396.7, 398.8.

45. W.A. 6.440.21, 441.22. This passage seems to rule out a developmental resolution of the ambiguity in Luther's teaching on ministry and priesthood. Cf. also the passage referred to in n. 41: in the later years, too, both lines of thought seem to lie together. Hence I am not persuaded by the thesis in Lowell C. Green's article. "Change in Luther's Doctrine of the Ministry," *Lutheran Quarterly* 18 (1966): 173-83.

46. Heinz Brunotte, *Das Amt der Verkündigung*, p. 26.

47. This suggestion was taken up by W. Brunotte (*Das geistliche Amt*, pp. 131-32), who gives full references to the earlier literature. Regin Prenter adopted a similar line of argument: see "Die göttliche Einsetzung des Predigtamtes und das allgemeine Priestertum bei Luther," *Theologische Literaturzeitung* 86 (1961): 321-32, esp. col. 325. True though it no doubt is, it will not suffice to say that the common priesthood does not establish the ministerial office but only appoints one of its number to fill it; for the question would still be why the one who fills it is said to function in the place of all. But, as Prenter points out, the affirmation that the office is exercised in the name of all in itself says nothing about the origin of the office: it cannot strictly be inferred that the office is derived from the common priesthood, since the "order" by which the minister acts for all could be identical with the divine institution (col. 326). Cf. Aarts, *Die Lehre Luthers über das Amt*, pp. 279-83, and n. 59 below.

48. *Amt und Ordination*, p. 102. Lieberg gives more complete references to the sources and literature than could be presented here. Aarts, too, finds it necessary to speak of *eine doppelte Gedankenreihe* in Luther's thoughts on the ministry, but he sees no contradiction between the idea of delegation and the divine origin of the ministry (*Die Lehre Luthers über das Amt*, p. 282).

49. W.A. 11.410.29; 6.547.17. Cf. the reference to the *Tractatus de libertate christiana* in n. 26 above.

50. W.A. 11.412.14, 33; 16.35.31; 17^1.509.24; 12.190.36; 41.456.19, 543.17, 546.11. Aarts maintains that in the emergency situations the Christian's witness takes on an *amtlich* character, whereas his *Verkündigungsaufgabe* in the private sphere is more properly *Glaubenszeugnis* than *Predigt des äusseren Wortes* (*Die Lehre Luthers über das Amt*, pp. 286-87).

51. Luther to Wolfgang Brauer, 30 December 1535, W.A.Br. 7.338-39 (no. 2281).

52. W.A. 50.633.12. Luther does concede, however, that many women could do as well as the preacher (W.A. 12.389.10).

53. W.A. 8.497.25.

54. *Das allgemeine Priestertum*, p. 37. For documentation see W.A. 6.564.15, 566.30; 38.228.27.

55. W.A. 40^1.56.21, 59.16, 60.22, 27.

56. W.A. 6.407.29; 11.414-16 (where the congregational election is defended on the grounds that the people will know their man better than the bishop could); 12.189.21. For the notion of a succession linking the apostles and the present-day ministry see, in particular, W.A. 40^1.59.18. Lieberg rightly comments that this passage does not speak of a *Weihesukzession* (a notion that Luther expressly rejects), but of a *Kette von Vokationen durch geistliche Amtsträger* (*Amt und Ordination*, p. 154). The kind of ordination service Luther

desired can best be judged from his advice to the Bohemians (W.A. 12.191.18, 193–94; L.W. 40:37, 40–41) and the various recensions of his Form for Ordination (W.A. 38.423–33; L.W. 53:124–26).

57. Gösta Hök, "Luther's Doctrine of the Ministry," trans. from the Swedish by Ross Mackenzie, *Scottish Journal of Theology* 7 (1954):18. The laying on of hands is likened by Luther to a notary's official attestation (W.A. 53.257.6). Lieberg may be correct in arguing that "effectual blessing" or "a real spiritual gift" is one element in Luther's view of ordination (*Amt und Ordination*, pp. 201, 214ff.). But that is a rather vague notion, and it certainly cannot be set alongside Luther's strong emphasis on confirming the call and commissioning for the work of the ministry as though all three ideas had equal prominence. This, of course, Lieberg does not deny: rather he wishes Luther had given a *firmer* foothold for the idea of an ordination charisma (ibid., p. 223, n. 296). W. Brunotte seems to preserve Luther's emphasis more adequately (*Das geistliche Amt*, p. 189), though I doubt if Luther would have approved the proposal to abolish the laying on of hands merely because it is liable to be misinterpreted (ibid., p. 202). Cf. Luther's retort to Carlstadt on the elevation of the Sacrament: "Das thun schad nicht, die lere aber ist der teuffel" (W.A. 18.113.14).

58. Not the commission of anyone to minister but the ministry itself is "perpetual" (W.A. 15.721.13). Cf. W.A. 53.74 for a succession grounded in the will of God who calls, not in the act of consecration as such. Luther's repeated insistence that a minister may be deposed (e.g., W.A. 6.408.18; 12.190.24) is not a pseudo-democratic idea, as though the minister were answerable to his congregation for what he says. He means that both are answerable to the Word: the minister by virtue of his office, the people by virtue of the common priesthood.

59. *Das allgemeine Priestertum*, pp. 40–41 (my emphasis). Similarly, Aarts says that what is "transferred" *(übertragen)* is the obligation of every believer, by reason of the common priesthood, *wenn nötig, die Predigtfunktion auszuüben:* "Wenn nach Gottes Anordnung einzelne mit dieser Aufgabe betraut werden, ist die Notwendigkeit für die übrigen nicht mehr gegeben" (*Die Lehre Luthers über das Amt*, p. 282).

60. *Die Bekenntnisschriften der evangelisch-lutherischen Kirche*, 4th ed. (Göttingen: Vandenhoeck and Ruprecht, 1959), p. 449. My translation is from the German text, which gives the last phrase in Latin *(per mutuum colloquium et consolationem fratrum)*.

61. In an article critical, in part, of the first version of this chapter, Robert H. Fischer pointed out that the church *is* a priesthood, and he therefore took me to task for saying that "ministry and priesthood exist together in the Church as complementary vehicles of the Word." Fischer, "Another Look at Luther's Doctrine of the Ministry," *Lutheran Quarterly* 18 (1966):260–71; see p. 270. He is, of course, entirely right in his insistence that the church, for Luther, *is* a priesthood; and I have gladly made some slight changes in wording to make it more clear, if it was not clear enough already, that in this paragraph I am describing as complementary the *public exercise* of the ministry and the *private exercise* of the priesthood. Since I repeated the common assertion that the technical terms "priesthood of all believers" and "common priesthood" are not Luther's own, I am also grateful to Fischer for drawing attention to the phrase

spirituali et communi illi sacerdocio in W.A. 12.180.27 (L.W. 40:22), although it seems to have been borrowed by Luther here from adversaries like Jerome Emser. Fischer's other criticisms have not moved me to make any changes. In particular, I do not believe he has shown that the entire question of the delegation theory versus the institution theory is bogus. ("You cannot get right answers to wrong questions," he says.) A subsequent contribution to the same journal took my side: Thomas G. Wilkens, "Ministry, Vocation and Ordination," *Lutheran Quarterly* 29 (1977):66–81; see p. 71. See also n. 65 below.

62. *Priester* may mean "minister" and "Christian" even in two consecutive sentences (W.A. 6.407.39, 408.2). Similarly, *sacerdotium* may refer to the (official) *ministerium verbi* (W.A. 6.564.13, 566.32). A characteristic qualification is *sacerdotes quos vocamus* (W.A. 6.564.11). And yet Luther can insist that it is improper to call a minister a "priest" (W.A. 12.190.11).

63. W.A. 6.441.24; 30^2.526–30; 30^3.525.20. In W.A. 6.408.18 belonging to the *priester stand* is interpreted as being an *amptman*.

64. W.A. 12.179.38: "... ex officiis sacerdotalibus (quae vocant)." Luther's general intention is clear from W.A. $10^{1,2}$.122.8, where it is said that not all *Dienst* is *Amt*. The terminological problems are reflected in the secondary literature. See especially Hök ("Luther's Doctrine of Ministry," pp. 21–22), Storck (*Das allgemeine Priestertum*, pp. 42–43, n. 183), and H. Brunotte (*Das Amt der Verkündigung*, pp. 16–17, 23).

65. Confirmation of my remarks on the biblical basis of Luther's notion of the common priesthood was sent to me (in a personal communication) by John H. Elliott, whose dissertation was published shortly afterwards: *The Elect and the Holy: An Exegetical Examination of 1 Peter 2:4–10 and the Phrase* βασίλειον ἱεράτευμα, Supplements to Novum Testamentum, vol. 12 (Leiden: E. J. Brill, 1966).

66. For Melanchthon's view I can refer to Lieberg. Of Calvin's conception of church order Niesel correctly remarks that "the thought of the priesthood of all believers ... plays no part in his doctrine." Wilhelm Niesel, *The Theology of Calvin*, trans. Harold Knight (Philadelphia: Westminster Press, 1956), pp. 202–3. It is interesting that Calvin, like Melanchthon, found in ordination to the evangelical ministry all the marks of a sacrament except one: it is not given to everyone in the church. See Leopold Schummer, *Le Ministère pastoral dans l'Institution Chrétienne de Calvin à la lumière du troisième sacrement*, Veröffentlichungen des Instituts für Europäische Geschichte Mainz, vol. 39 (Wiesbaden: Franz Steiner Verlag, 1965). Removed from the discussion of the church's ministry, the priesthood of all believers plays another role in Calvin's theology. It surfaces in fact in more places than one. See, for instance, the discussion of the Eucharist in the next chapter.

Chapter Six

1. See Otto W. Heick, *A History of Christian Thought*, 2 vols. (Philadelphia: Fortress Press, 1965–66), 1:420. The specialized literature on Calvin's doctrine

of the Lord's Supper is particularly rich. In English the older study by Nevin is still worth reading; along with the work of Ebrard (in German), it was a major resource for the comparative study by Barclay. Broader in scope, but still indispensable for Calvin's eucharistic ideas are the more recent volumes by Wallace and McDonnell. See John W. Nevin, *The Mystical Presence: A Vindication of the Reformed or Calvinistic Doctrine of the Holy Eucharist* (1846), reissued with another of Nevin's studies on the same subject in *The Mystical Presence and Other Writings on the Eucharist*, ed. Bard Thompson and George H. Bricker, Lancaster Series on the Mercersburg Theology, vol. 4 (Philadelphia and Boston: United Church Press, 1966); Alexander Barclay, *The Protestant Doctrine of the Lord's Supper: A Study in the Eucharistic Teaching of Luther, Zwingli and Calvin* (Glasgow: Jackson, Wylie, 1927); Ronald S. Wallace, *Calvin's Doctrine of the Word and Sacrament* (Edinburgh: Oliver and Boyd, 1953); Kilian McDonnell, *John Calvin, the Church, and the Eucharist* (Princeton: Princeton University Press, 1967). Pertinent foreign literature includes the following: August [J. H. A.] Ebrard, *Das Dogma vom heiligen Abendmahl und seine Geschichte*, 2 vols. (Frankfurt a. M.: Heinrich Zimmer, 1845–46); Joachim Beckmann, *Vom Sakrament bei Calvin: Die Sakramentslehre Calvins in ihren Beziehungen zu Augustin* (Tübingen: J. C. B. Mohr [Paul Siebeck], 1926); Wilhelm Niesel, *Calvins Lehre vom heiligen Abendmahl im Lichte seiner letzten Antwort an Westphal* [first published in 1930], Forschungen zur Geschichte und Lehre des Protestantismus, 3d series, vol. 3, 2d ed. [unaltered except for a new preface] (Munich: Chr. Kaiser Verlag, 1935); Helmut Gollwitzer, *Coena Domini: Die altlutherische Abendmahlslehre in ihrer Auseinandersetzung mit dem Calvinismus dargestellt an der lutherischen Frühorthodoxie* (Munich: Chr. Kaiser Verlag [1937]); Hans Grass, *Die Abendmahlslehre bei Luther und Calvin: Eine kritische Untersuchung* [first published in 1940], Beiträge zur Förderung christlicher Theologie, 2d series, vol. 47, 2d ed. (Gütersloh: C. Bertelsmann, 1954); Willem Frederik Dankbaar, *De Sakramentsleer van Calvijn* (Amsterdam: H. J. Paris, 1941); Jean Cadier, *La Doctrine calviniste de la sainte cène*, Études théologiques et religieuses, vol. 26 (Montpellier: Faculté de théologie protestante, 1951); G. P. Hartvelt, *Verum Corpus: Een studie over een centraal hoofdstuk uit de avondmaalsleer van Calvijn* (Delft: W. D. Meinema N. V., 1960); Joachim Rogge, *Virtus und Res: Um die Abendmahlswirklichkeit bei Calvin*, Arbeiten zur Theologie, series 1, no. 18 (Stuttgart: Calwer Verlag, 1965). I have commented on the work of Nevin in relation to the studies by Ebrard, Barclay, McDonnell, and Hartvelt in my *Tradition and the Modern World: Reformed Theology in the Nineteenth Century* (Chicago: University of Chicago Press, 1978), chap. 2; for further discussion of McDonnell's book, the most useful study of the subject in English, I may perhaps refer to my review in *Church History* (vol. 38, 1969). For Calvin's own claims concerning the merits of his eucharistic teaching, including the merit of clarity, see *Inst.* 4.17.19 (2:1382). Translations from the *Institutes* in this chapter are taken from the English version by Ford Lewis Battles (referred to by volume and page in parentheses).

2. Calvin, *Secunda defensio piae et orthodoxae de sacramentis fidei, contra Ioachimi Westphali calumnias* (1556), C.O. 9:51; Calvin to Andrew Zebedee,

19 May 1539, C.O. 10^2:346. There is a translation of the *Secunda defensio* in John Calvin, *Tracts and Treatises*, trans. Henry Beveridge, 3 vols. (1844; reprint ed., Grand Rapids, Mich.: William B. Eerdmans, 1958), 2:245-345; see pp. 252-53.

3. Comm. Rom. 1:9, C.O. 49:313.

4. *Inst.*, 2.6.1 (1:341).

5. *Inst.*, 2.6.1 (1:342).

6. This is a constant theme in the *Institutes*, book 2, chapters 6-7.

7. *Inst.*, 2.16.5 (1:507). The presentation of this theme (the course of Christ's obedience) takes Calvin through the second article of the Apostles Creed (ibid., secs. 5-19).

8. Calvin to Peter Martyr, 8 August 1555, C.O. 15:722-25. On the "wonderful communion" or "mystical union" with Christ see also *Inst.*, 3.2.24 (1:570), 11.10 (1:737). There is an excellent guide to Calvin's notion of communion with Christ in W[ilhelm] Kolfhaus, *Christusgemeinschaft bei Johannes Calvin*, Beiträge zur Geschichte und Lehre der reformierten Kirche, vol. 3 (Neukirchen: Buchhandlung des Erziehungsvereins, 1939).

9. *Inst.*, 3.1.1 (1:537). Cf. *Petit traicté de la saincte cene de nostre Seigneur Iesus Christ* (1541), C.O. 5:437; trans. in *Tracts and Treatises*, 2:169. The treatise will also be found O.S. 1:503-530 (French) and translated into English in J. K. S. Reid, trans., *Calvin: Theological Treatises*, Library of Christian Classics, vol. 22 (Philadelphia: Westminster Press, 1954), pp. 142-66.

10. *Inst.*, 3.11.1 (1:725).

11. Calvin was suspicious of the term "real," which suggested to him a crassly physical communication of Christ's body, but he indicated his willingness to accept it in the sense of "true" as opposed to "imaginary." See his *Defensio sanae et orthodoxae doctrinae de sacramentis, eorumque natura, vi, fine, usu, & fructu*, etc. (1555), C.O. 9:32 (O.S. 2:283); *Tracts and Treatises*, 2:239-40. As for the terms "Lord's Supper" and "Eucharist," in the first edition of the *Institutes* Calvin judged them interchangeable: "Vocamus autem [sc. the second sacrament] vel coenam Domini, vel eucharistiam, quod in ipso et spiritualiter benignitate Domini paschimur et nos illi suae beneficentiae gratias agimus" (O.S. 1:136; trans. Ford Lewis Battles as John Calvin, *Institution of the Christian Religion* [Atlanta: John Knox Press, 1975], p. 139). But his distinctive interpretation of the sacrament favored the term "Lord's Supper." See also *Inst.*, 4.18.12 (2:1440).

12. My analysis here rests mainly on *Institutes*, book 3, chapters 1-2.

13. For the Zwinglians, to claim that faith comes through the sacraments is to detract from the work of the Spirit, who alone bestows faith. Calvin replies that for the one blessing they proclaim (i.e., the Holy Spirit) he recognizes three: the Word, the sacraments (which confirm the Word), and illumination by the Spirit (*Inst.*, 4.14.8 [2.1283-84]). These three together (or these two, if we combine Word and sacrament) give rise to faith. Ebrard, in particular, stressed the event-character of Calvin's eucharistic thinking: the Lord's Supper has to do with an *actus in actu*, that is, a divine act in the liturgical act, not a divine substance in an earthly substance or *extensum in extenso* (*Das Dogma vom heiligen Abendmahl*, 2:459).

14. Comm. John 6:35, C.O. 47:145.

15. *Inst.*, 3.1.1 (1:537).

16. Ibid.

17. *Inst.*, 3.2.6 (1:548); cf. 2.9.3 (1:426).

18. *De la saincte cene*, C.O. 5:435; *Tracts and Treatises*, 2:166.

19. *Inst.*, 1.9.1 (1:93). See also n. 13 above.

20. The common characteristics of Word and sacraments underlie Calvin's statement about the sacraments in general (*Inst.*, book 4, chap. 14). In *De la saincte cene* he asserts explicitly: "Ce qui est dict de la parolle il appartient aussi bien au Sacrement de la Cene" (C.O. 5:435; *Tracts and Treatises*, 2:166).

21. *Inst.*, 4.14.3 (2:1278).

22. *Inst.*, 4.14.6 (2:1281).

23. *Inst.*, 4.14.5 (2:1280).

24. *Inst.*, 4.14.14, 17 (2:1289, 1292).

25. *Inst.*, 4.14.14 (cf. 2:1290).

26. The sacraments are of no benefit unless received in faith and accompanied by the Spirit (*Inst.*, 4.14.17 [2:1292–93]).

27. *Inst.*, 4.14.17 (2:1292).

28. See, e.g., *De la saincte cene*, C.O. 5:439; *Tracts and Treatises*, 2:172. Cf. Comm. 1 Cor. 10:3, C.O. 49:454: "Nam si man spiritualis erat cibus, sequitur non figuras nudas ostentari nobis in sacramentis: sed rem figuratam simul vere dari. Neque enim fallax est Deus qui figmentis inanibus nos lactat. Signum quidem est signum substantiamque suam retinet: sed quemadmodum ridiculi sunt papistae, qui nescio quas metamorphoses somniant: ita veritatem et figuram, quas Deus coniunxit, separare non est nostrum. Confundunt papistae rem et signum: divellunt signa a rebus profani homines, ut Svenckfeldius et similes: nos mediocritatem servemus, hoc est, teneamus coniunctionem a Domino positam, sed distinctam, ne quod unius est proprium, in alterum perperam transferamus." Niesel has been particularly emphatic about Calvin's use of the christological formula, though not so much in his monograph (see n. 1 above) as in his book *The Theology of Calvin*, trans. Harold Knight (Philadelphia: Westminster Press, 1956); see especially the summary on pp. 247–49.

29. *Inst.*, 4.14.16 (2:1291).

30. I return to Calvin's theory of sacramental signs in the following section (sec. III, proposition 3), and in chapter 7 I differentiate it more fully from alternative views. It ought perhaps to be expressly pointed out that Calvin does not start from a general theory of signs; he grounds the sacramental union of *signum* and *res* strictly in the divine Word, so that to doubt the presence of the reality is to question the fidelity of God. In addition to the passage quoted at length in n. 28 above, see, for instance, *Inst.*, 4.17.10 (2:1371). Calvin believes, of course, that he is simply following the Augustinian formula: it is the addition of the Word to the element that makes a sacrament (*Inst.*, 4.14.4 [2:1279]).

31. *Catechismus ecclesiae Genevensis* (1545), C.O. 6:126; *Tracts and Treatises*, 2:90.

32. The faith through which we are justified is simply an empty vessel (*Inst.*, 3.11.7 [1:733]). See also *Inst.*, 3.2.19 (1:565).

33. The dignity of the sacrament of the Lord's Supper is commended wonder-

fully enough "ubi tenemus, adminiculum esse quo inseramur in corpus Christi, vel insiti magis ac magis coalescamus, donec solide nos secum uniat in caelesti vita" (*Inst.*, 4.17.33 [2:1407–08]).

34. Ibid.

35. *Inst.*, 4.17.7, 10, 32 (2:1367, 1370, 1403).

36. *Inst.*, 4.18.7 (2:1435); trans. Battles.

37. *Inst.*, 4.14.13 (2:1289). As this judgment implies, Calvin's own definition of a sacrament was two-sided (4.14.1 [2:1277]): he included the Zwinglian definition, but he rejected the argument from the etymology of the word *sacramentum*, by which Zwingli would have reduced a sacrament to a profession (or "oath") of loyalty (4.14.13 [2:1288]). Here, as elsewhere, Calvin avoids express mention of Zwingli by name; but the object of his criticism is unmistakable (see the editor's note in the English translation).

38. *Inst.*, 4.17.1, 5 (2:1361, 1364). Of course, it is also true that partaking of Christ's body would have no saving significance had it not once been sacrificed (4.17.3 [2:1362], 17.5 [2:1364]).

39. *Inst.*, 4.17.5 (2:1365). Calvin insists, accordingly, that we do not receive Christ by mere knowledge (ibid.) nor by imagination (4.17.11 [2:1372]).

40. *Inst.*, 4.17.6 (2:1366).

41. "Eos vero qui Coenam volunt externae solum professionis notam esse, nunc praetereo .... Nisi in Deum respicimus, et amplectimur quod offert, nos sacra Coena recte non uti" (*Inst.*, 4.17.6 [2:1366]).

42. Comm. 1 Cor. 11:24, C.O. 49:487. See also the references in n. 9 above.

43. *De la saincte cene*, C.O. 5:438; cf. *Tracts and Treatises*, 2:170. See also *Inst.*, 4.17.7, 33 (2:1367, 1405). Nevin and Hartvelt, in particular (see n. 1 above), emphasized Calvin's notion of Christ's life-giving flesh, for which the most striking reference in the *Institutes* is 4.17.9 (2:1369). Calvin's appeal to Cyril of Alexandria is all the more remarkable in view of the alleged affinity of Calvinist christology with the heresy of Nestorius!

44. *Inst.*, 4.17.14 (2:1376); Comm. 1 Cor. 11:24, C.O. 49:487. See also *De la saincte cene*, C.O. 5:451; *Tracts and Treatises*, 2:185–86. Calvin was not opposed to the idea of a "conversion" by which the elements, though unchanged in substance, are set apart for sacramental use and in this sense are no longer common food (*Inst.*, 4.17.14–15 [2:1375–77])]). In later Reformed theology (and service books) the idea of a changed use was developed into a kind of prototype of modern Roman Catholic theories of transignification or transfinalization, as I suggested in a review in *The Christian Century* (84[1967]:274). The ecumenical possibilities of this affinity were explored in the University of Chicago dissertation of Jill Raitt; see her article, "Roman Catholic New Wine in Reformed Old Bottles? The Conversion of the Elements in the Eucharistic Doctrines of Theodore Beza and Edward Schillebeeckx," *Journal of Ecumenical Studies* 8 (1971): 581–604, and her book, *The Eucharistic Theology of Theodore Beza: Development of the Reformed Doctrine*, AAR Studies in Religion, no. 4 (Chambersburg, Pa.: American Academy of Religion, 1972).

45. *De la saincte cene*, C.O. 5:438–40, 458–59; *Tracts and Treatises*, 2:171–72, 195–96; *Inst.*, 4.17.10 (2:1371). It will be noted from these passages that Calvin

thinks of the signs and symbols as "instruments" by or through which God works (see also *Inst.*, 4.14.11-12 [2:1286-87], etc.). Properly speaking, therefore, the "efficacy" is God's (or the Spirit's) and must not be transferred to his instruments. Of the sacraments the Reformed confess: "Organa esse quibus efficaciter agit Deus in suis electis, ideoque licet a rebus signatis distincta sint signa, non tamen disiungi nec separari" (*Defensio doctrinae de sacramentis*, C.O. 9:18 [O.S. 2:271]; *Tracts and Treatises*, 2:224). Calvin disliked Lombard's talk of the sacraments as "causes" (see, e.g., *Secunda defensio contra Westphalum*, C.O. 9:116-17; *Tracts and Treatises*, 2:340-41; cf. *Inst.*, 4.14.16 [2:1291]); but it is clear that his conception of the sacraments does assign them a secondary causality or efficacy precisely as God's instruments, and he does not hesitate to speak of the *sacramentorum efficacia* (e.g., immediately after the citation just given from his *Defensio doctrinae de sacramentis*).

46. Inst., 4.17.33 (2:1405). Calvin does speak of the *presence* of the body, e.g., in *Inst.*, 4.17.32 (2:1404); but this same passage exemplifies his preference for the notion of a spiritual *partaking*.

47. *Inst.*, 4.17.10 (2:1370).

48. *Inst.*, 4.14.9 (2:1284), 14.12 (2:1287).

49. *Inst.*, 4.17.33 (2:1406-7).

50. *Inst.*, 4.14.14 (2:1289-90). On the sacrament as appendage or seal see 4.14.3, 5 (2:1278, 1280); on justification as *cardo* ("hinge") see 3.11.1 (1:726).

51. *Inst.*, 4.14.4 (2:1279-80), 4.17.15 (2:1377). The Word is not addressed to the elements, but to the communicants (4.17.39 [2:1416]).

52. *Inst.*, 4.14.17 (2:1292-93).

53. *Inst.*, 4.18.12-18 (2:1440-46). On Calvin's use of the word "Eucharist" see n. 11 above. On his notion of a eucharistic sacrifice see Gerrish, "Do We 'Offer Christ' in the Lord's Supper?" *McCormick Speaking* 13 (1959):14-20; Pierre-Yves Emery, "The Teaching of Calvin on the Sacrificial Element in the Eucharist," *Reformed and Presbyterian World* 26 (1960):109-14; Joseph N. Tylenda, "A Eucharistic Sacrifice in Calvin's Theology?" *Theological Studies* 37 (1976):456-66.

54. *Inst.*, 4.17.32 (2:1404).

55. *Inst.*, 4.17.1 (2:1361).

56. *Inst.*, 4.17.1 (2:1359-60).

57. *Inst.*, 4.17.1 (2:1361).

58. Cornelisz Hoen [Honius], *A Most Christian Letter* (1525), translated in *Forerunners of the Reformation: The Shape of Late Medieval Thought, Illustrated by Key Documents*, ed. Heiko A. Oberman and trans. Paul L. Nyhus (New York: Holt, Rinehart and Winston, 1966), pp. 268-76; see pp. 269, 270, 276.

59. Heller, "The Hazard of Modern Poetry," added to the American edition of *The Disinherited Mind: Essays in Modern German Literature and Thought* (New York: Farrar, Straus and Cudahy, [1957?]), p. 263.

60. Zwingli, *Christianae fidei brevis et clara expositio* (1531), secs. 72, 161, in H.A. [Hermann] Niemeyer, ed., *Collectio confessionum in ecclesiis reformatis publicatarum* (Leipzig: Julius Klinkhardt, 1840), pp. 50, 71.

61. *Inst.*, 4.17.16, 31 (2:1379, 1403). Cf. *Secunda defensio contra Westphalum*, C.O. 9:74; *Tracts and Treatises*, 2:282.

62. *Konkordienformel*, Epitome, art. 7, secs. 4–5; trans. Arthur C. Piepkorn, in *The Book of Concord: The Confessions of the Evangelical Lutheran Church*, ed. Theodore G. Tappert (Philadelphia: Fortress Press, 1959), p. 482.

63. Ibid., Solid Declaration, art. 7, secs. 63–64; Tappert, p. 581. This same passage insists that the oral eating is not "in a coarse, carnal, Capernaitic [see John 6:52–65] manner, but in a supernatural, incomprehensible manner"; and elsewhere it is said that "although such eating occurs in the mouth, the mode is spiritual" (ibid., sec. 105, p. 588).

64. *Inst.*, 4.17.31–32 (2:1403); 4.17.33 (2:1405). Cf. secs. 29–30 of the same chapter (2:1398–1403), where Calvin argues against the corollary of the *manducatio impiorum:* the notion of the ubiquity of Christ's body. A summary statement appears in sec. 16: "Si ita [sc. the Lutherans] sensum suum explicarent, dum panis in mysterio porrigitur, annexam esse exhibitionem corporis, quia inseparabilis est a signo suo veritas: non valde pugnarem. Sed quia in pane corpus ipsum locantes, ubiquitatem illi affingunt naturae suae contrariam, addendo autem Sub pane, illic occultum latere volunt: tales astutias e suis latebris paulisper extrahere necesse est."

65. This is Calvin's clearest point of divergence from the Lutheran position. I could have said in proposition 6, more simply, that the "the *gift* [not the benefit of the gift] is received by faith." Calvin's view is that where faith is absent, the recipient takes only an empty figure, a sign devoid of truth (*Inst.*, 4.14.15 [2:1291]): the rain falls on all, but runs off the hard rock (*Inst.*, 4.17.33 [2:1407]); or, to put it another way, the bread is only a sacrament to those who are addressed by the Word (*Inst.*, 4.17.15 [2:1377]). He still comes close to the Lutheran *manducatio impiorum* when he speaks of good food that only aggravates a sick stomach (*Inst.*, 4.17.40 [2.1417]).

66. See n. 63 above.

67. *Secunda defensio contra Westphalum*, C.O. 9:70; *Tracts and Treatises*, 2:277. In the 1536 *Institutes* Calvin wrote: "Docendi causa, dicimus [sc. corpus Christi] vere et efficaciter exhiberi, non autem naturaliter. Quo scilicet significamus, non substantiam ipsam corporis, seu verum et naturale Christi corpus illic dari: sed omnia, quae in suo corpore nobis beneficia Christus praestitit. Ea est corporis praesentia, quam sacramenti ratio postulat" (O.S. 1:142–43; *Institution*, p. 145). The "presence of the body" is even reduced here to a figure of speech (*non secus ac si corpore adesset!*) that stands for the distribution of the benefits won by Christ. Ought Calvin to have admitted to Westphal that he did have some second thoughts about the Eucharist? Perhaps so. But it is interesting to see how much of this language was carried over into the 1559 edition (*Inst.*, 4.17.18, 32 [2:1381, 1404]).

68. Emphasis mine. Extensive documentation and analysis of Calvin's eucharistic vocabulary is not possible here. By way of illustration only, we can refer to a single section in the *Institutes* in which he speaks of "the presence of the body," "[a presence] manifested in power and effectiveness," "partaking of the body," and "life from the substance of his flesh" (*Inst.*, 4.17.32 [cf. 2:1404]).

Elsewhere he speaks approvingly of a "true and substantial partaking" (*Inst.,* 4.17.19 [2:1382]) and of Christ's giving us the "proper substance of his body and blood" (*De la saincte cene,* C.O. 5:440; *Tracts and Treatises,* 2:172–73).

69. See in particular the discussion in *Inst.,* 4.17.26–30 (2:1393–1403), ending with the famous claim, borrowed from the Schoolmen, that "the whole Christ is present, but not in his wholeness" [*totus, non totum*].

70. Being *present to* is a manner of speaking found already in the 1536 *Institutio*: though Christ has ascended to heaven, he sits at the Father's right hand and therefore, since the reign of God cannot be circumscribed, he can be "present to his own" (O.S. 1:142; *Institution,* p. 145). Cf. *Inst.,* 4.17.18 (2.1381).

71. *Inst.,* 4.17.12 (2:1373).

72. A representative statement of this notion appears in the *Defensio doctrinae de sacramentis,* C.O. 9:33 (O.S. 2:284); *Tracts and Treatises,* 2:240. It will be noticed here that Calvin regards our "ascent to heaven" as synonymous with Christ's "descent by his *virtus.*" See also *Inst.,* 4.17.18, 31, 36 (2:1381, 1403, 1412–13); the last of these passages links the "ascent" with the liturgical *sursum corda.*

73. Ebrard's thesis was that Calvin represented a eucharistic theology, shared in part by Melanchthon and others, that mediated the dialectical opposition between Luther and Zwingli by showing the compatibility of a real union with the body of Christ (Luther) and the body's "circumscription" or physical limitation (Zwingli). He concludes: "Der grösste der christlichen Philosophen, Leibniz, hat es schon ausgesprochen, dass der eigentliche Vereinigungspunkt der beiden Confessionen darin liege, 'que la *substance* du corps consiste dans la *puissance primitive,* active et passive, et que c'est dans l'application immédiate de cette *puissance* que consiste la *présence* de la substance, même sans dimensions'; er hat auch anerkannt, dass Calvin (wo er nicht sicht selbst untreu werde), den Begriff der Leiblichkeit so gefasst, und daher die reale Vereinigung mit der Lehre von der Umschriebenheit zu vereinigen gewusst habe" (Ebrard, *Das Dogma vom heiligen Abendmahl,* pp. 413–14). But this interesting thesis is still not quite able to set aside the problem of the physical location of Christ's glorified body. I suspect that if Zwingli had not worked with a manifestly impoverished theory of sacramental signs, Protestant theology might have been able to take more seriously his shift of interest from the natural to the ecclesial body of Christ (see next chapter).

74. *Inst.,* 4.17.12 (2:1373); cf. 17.18 (2:1381).

75. *Inst.,* 4.14.15 (2:1290–91). The Augustinian dictum is alluded to again in *Inst.,* 4.17.34 (2:1410).

76. *Secunda defensio contra Westphalum,* C.O. 9:118–19; *Tracts and Treatises,* 2:343–44. In this passage Calvin challenges Westphal to produce one syllable "in which I teach that we ought to *begin* with predestination in seeking assurance of salvation" (my emphasis). It is precisely to the Word and sacraments that Calvin points the troubled conscience (see chapter 8 below). But the critics of the Reformed made the relationship of predestination and sacraments a polemical issue: the anti-Calvinist Saxon Visitation Articles of 1592, for example, raised the problem of sacrament and election in Calvinist theology with reference to

both baptism and the Supper. See the text and translation in Philip Schaff, *Bibliotheca Symbolica Ecclesiae Universalis: The Creeds of Christendom, with a History and Critical Notes*. 6th ed., ed. David S. Schaff, 3 vols. (New York: Harper and Brothers, [1931]), 3:181–89, especially the concluding paragraph. That Calvin's predestinarianism and his sacramental theology could fall apart and even be set over against each other as two distinct varieties of Calvinism is clear from the debate between Charles Hodge and John W. Nevin (see Gerrish, *Tradition and the Modern World*, pp. 60–65, 70).

Chapter Seven

1. The most comprehensive collection of Reformed confessions is E. F. Karl Müller, ed., *Die Bekenntnisschriften der reformierten Kirche: In authentischen Texten mit geschichtlicher Einleitung und Register* (Leipzig: A. Deichert [Georg Böhme], 1903). Other important collections are H. A. [Hermann] Niemeyer, ed., *Collectio confessionum in ecclesiis reformatis publicatarum* (Leipzig: Julius Klinkhardt, 1840); Philip Schaff, *Bibliotheca Symbolica Ecclesiae Universalis: The Creeds of Christendom, with a History and Critical Notes*, 6th ed., ed. David S. Schaff, 3 vols. (New York: Harper and Brothers [1931]); Wilhelm Niesel, ed., *Bekenntnisschriften und Kirchenordnungen der nach Gottes Wort reformierten Kirche*, 2d printing (Zollikon-Zurich: Evangelischer Verlag, 1938). I abbreviate these four works, respectively, as M, N, S, and Ns. Where a satisfactory text is available in M, I do not give duplicate references to the other editions, though I have checked them for variants. I give my own translations of the continental European confessions; but the most important ones will also be found in Arthur C. Cochrane, ed., *Reformed Confessions of the 16th Century* (Philadelphia: Westminster Press, 1966), and, wherever possible, I mention English versions of sources *not* found in this useful collection. As far as I have been able to ascertain, it is not possible to assemble a specific bibliography on exactly the theme of the present chapter, and I refer to the more general literature only as occasion arises. For a discussion of confessional sources and secondary literature in general, I may refer to Gerrish, ed., *The Faith of Christendom: A Source Book of Creeds and Confessions* (Cleveland, Ohio: World Publishing Company, 1963); further remarks on the Reformed confessions are made in my article, "The Confessional Heritage of the Reformed Church," *McCormick Quarterly* 19 (1966): 120–34.

2. They are as follows: *Syben und sechzig Artickel unnd meynungen*, 1523 (given by M, N, and S); *Ein kurtze Christenliche inleitung*, 1523 (M only); *Fidei ratio*, 1530 (M, N); *Christianae fidei brevis et clara expositio*, 1531/36 (N only). Of these four, only the second was ever published with official—i.e., "symbolic"—authority. Zwingli also had a hand in revising *Die zehen* [Berner] *Schlussreden* of 1528 (M, N, and S), but the draft was by Berthold Haller and Francis Kolb. Throughout this chapter, I give shortened titles for documents that often carried very long-winded ones; it is by short titles that most of the confessions are generally known. Both the *Fidei ratio* ("account of the faith") and the *Fidei*

expositio were translated in the second volume of S. M. Jackson, W. J. Hinke, and C. N. Heller, eds., *The Latin Works and the Correspondence of Huldreich Zwingli* [*Together with Selections from His German Works*], 3 vols. (New York: G. P. Putnam's Sons, 1912; Philadelphia: Heidelberg Press, 1922, 1929). A fresh translation of the *Fidei expositio* appeared in G. W. Bromiley, trans. and ed., *Zwingli and Bullinger*, Library of Christian Classics, vol. 24, (Philadelphia: Westminster Press, 1953). I know of no English version of the *Kurtze inleitung*.

3. M 1–6 (German; cited by page).

4. M 7–29 (German).

5. M 29, 7; 26, 25; 28, 15. (References to Müller in this form are to page and line.)

6. M 29, 10; 29, 14. Presumably the statement that the mass has another purpose than eating and drinking the body and blood of Christ (M 26, 19) refers to the Roman mass.

7. M 79–94 (Latin).

8. The English translation in the *Latin Works* has "... the Church certifies that grace has been given...." (2:47). But the Latin text (M 87, 12) reads *Ecclesiae testatur*.

9. This does not really fit too well with Zwingli's point of view, since holy living in the church strictly lies in the future for the baptismal candidate.

10. Art. 10 (M 92, 19).

11. What confirms and certifies is rather God's gift of his Son (M 91, 25). Sacramental eating is but a symbol of faith in Christ. Nevertheless, in his Letter to the Princes (1530), in which he defends himself against Eck, Zwingli comes surprisingly close to Luther and Calvin, arguing that the sacraments do in fact arouse, support, and restore faith (*Latin Works*, 2:113, 116).

12. The most important passage for Zwingli's idea of symbolism (from which the quotation is taken) occurs in his discussion of the Fathers (M 91, 18ff.). The three ingredients within this symbolic framework are explicitly brought together in Zwingli's Letter to the Princes (*Latin Works*, 2:116–17). He adds that strictly it is the Spirit who works all these things in us; and, if he so chooses, he can do so without the external instruments.

13. N 36–77 (Latin; cited by page).

14. See the entire section entitled "Praesentia corporis Christi in Coena" (N 44–50). Zwingli distinguished three ways of eating the body of Christ: naturally (which he rejects), spiritually (which he identifies with faith), and sacramentally (which is spiritual eating *adiuncto sacramento*). He denies, of course, that the sacraments can give faith, save in the sub-Christian sense of *fides historica*, but he admits that they may—and especially the Eucharist— help faith by engaging the attention of all five senses. See the section entitled "Quae sacramentorum virtus" (N 50–53).

15. This appears in two separate contexts: on the condemnation of the unworthy (the unbeliever dishonors the church because his participation in the sacrament is a false testimony to faith), and on the sacramental symbolism (which has a secondary "analogy," besides the idea of nourishment, in the fact that the one loaf is made up of many grains). See N 48, 67; 73, 171 (from the

Zurich order of service); 51, 78; 52-53, 82. (The second figure in each reference
to Niemeyer denotes the section, not the line.) In the last of these passages the
thought of dishonoring (failing to "discern"!) the body is linked with the interpretation of a *sacramentum* as an oath of allegiance: the unbeliever who partici-
pates in the sacrament is a traitor (*perfidus*).

16. Julius Schweizer, *Reformierte Abendmahlsgestaltung in der Schau Zwinglis*
(Basel: F. Reinhardt, 1954); Jaques Courvoisier, *Zwingli: A Reformed Theologian*
(Richmond, Va.: John Knox Press, 1963), pp. 74 ff.

17. N 53, 82.

18. C.O. 9:693-778. The list could be extended. It omits the Brief Confession
translated in John Calvin, *Tracts and Treatises*, trans. Henry Beveridge, 3 vols.
(1844-51; reprint ed., Grand Rapids, Mich.: William B. Eerdmans, 1958),
2:130 ff., and the Geneva Consensus of 1552 (on predestination), which is
included in Niemeyer's collection, pp. 218-310.

19. Of the ten confessions in C.O., all four major collections give the French
Confession (1559), and Müller adds the Geneva Confession and Lausanne Articles
(both 1536). Of the remainder, four are restricted to a particular doctrine
(the Trinity [1537], the Eucharist [1537], predestination [undated], and
the ministry [undated]), and two form a family group with the French Confession (namely, the Paris Confession [1557] and the Scholars' Confession [1559]).

20. I refer to the *Catechismus ecclesiae Genevensis* (1545) by the question
number (in parenthesis). My translations are from the Latin text (M 117-53),
but I have compared the Latin with the French text (Ns 3-41), from which I
have derived the numbering of the questions. The Latin catechism is translated
in *Tracts and Treatises*, 2:33-94, and J. K. S. Reid, trans. and ed., *Calvin:
Theological Treatises*, Library of Christian Classics, vol. 22 (Philadelphia: Westminster Press, 1954), pp. 88-139. An English version of the French catechism
(1541) will be found in Thomas F. Torrance, ed., *The School of Faith: The
Catechisms of the Reformed Church* (London: James Clarke, 1959), pp. 5-65.

21. *Confession à presenter à l'Empereur* (1562), C.O. 9:764 (I know of no
English translation). Cf. the scholastic formula *efficiunt quod figurant* (see chap.
2, n. 69, and chap. 6, n. 45, above).

22. C.O. 9:768, 769, 770-71.

23. This interpretation of Zwingli gathers together his arguments against
Eck (*Latin Works*, 2:117, 118, 122, 124).

24. See especially the Geneva Catechism, Qq. 312, 328, and 353.

25. *Confessio helvetica prior*, M 101-9 (German); S 3:211-31 (German
and Latin). With the First Helvetic Confession may be compared the Tetrapolitan
Confession (1530) and the Basel Confession (1534). All three think of the
Eucharist as an actual giving of the body and blood, not simply a representation
of the body once given. See M 72, 20 and 97, 22.

26. *Confession de foy de Genève*, C.O. 9:693-700. And yet the very next
year the three Genevan ministers (Farel, Calvin, and Viret) prepared a forthright
affirmation of eucharistic feeding on the substance of the Lord's body and blood:
Confessio de eucharistia (1537), C.O. 9:711-12. Interestingly enough, the
Strasbourg ministers Martin Bucer and Wolfgang Capito subscribed to this

brief confession—one year *after* the Wittenberg Concord. There is a translation in Reid, *Calvin: Theological Treatises*, pp. 168–69.

27. *Warhaffte Bekanntnuss der dieneren der kirchen zu Zürych*, M 153–59 (German, extracts only; untranslated). It was Luther's *Kurzes Bekenntnis vom heiligen Sakrament* (1544) that provoked Bullinger into this truculent response. Later, he gave his approval to the *Confessio rhaetica* (1552), which likewise does not seem to move beyond Zwinglian ideas (M 163–70, Latin; untranslated).

28. *Creeds of Christendom*, 1:390.

29. *Consensus Tigurinus*, M 159–163 (Latin); trans. in *Tracts and Treatises*, 2:212–20.

30. For example, it is made abundantly clear that the sacraments have no sacral efficacy in themselves, and for this reason the medieval *sacramenta conferunt gratiam* is denied (Arts. 12, 13, 17). But this is said, not to denude the sacraments, but to reserve the *agendi facultas* for God, who uses them in freedom (*ubi visum est*) as his instruments (Art. 13). The phrase *ubi visum est* says no more than the Lutheran *ubi et quando visum est Deo* (Augsburg Confession, Art. 5); and even the criticism of Scholasticism is a little specious, seeing that for Thomas, too, the instrumental causality of the sacraments does not alter the fact that the principal cause of grace is God alone (S.T. III, Q. 62, art. 1). See further the Geneva Catechism, Q. 312.

31. *Confessio helvetica posterior* (1566), M 170–221 (Latin).

32. M 210, 28. A similar passage occurs at M 211, 10, but it uses everyday eating as a general analogy to spiritual eating and has no specific reference to the Lord's Supper (cf. John 6).

33. In characterizing parallelism as Bullinger's typical contribution, I do not, of course, overlook the fact that Zwingli in some passages seems to anticipate him, apparently transcending his customary retrospective direction. Moreover, my concern here is only with the confessional sources.

34. *Confessio gallicana*, M 221–32 (French); N 329–39 (Latin). The French Confession needs to be read as a whole. Certain passages, if taken in isolation, could be given a parallelistic interpretation. A particular difficulty appears in Article 27, which seems to say that the thing signified in the Lord's Supper is not the body or communion with the body, but the *fact* that the body nourishes the soul. How, then, does God give us really and efficaciously what he signifies?

35. I have used the French version of the *Confessio belgica* in S 3:383–436, in preference to the later Latin version (M 233–49). Even the general article on the sacraments (33) does not say unambiguously that God gives what he represents; it could be read to mean that by the sacraments God works faith. This would go further than Zwingli, but stops short of Calvin. One can only speculate why baptism is interpreted in terms of enlistment and parallelistic representation (Art. 34). Perhaps the hint is to be sought in the statement (Art. 35) that the Word of the gospel is the instrument of regeneration—therefore (may one add?) baptism cannot be. It may also be pointed out that one section of the article on the Lord's Supper could, if taken out of context, be interpreted parallelistically: the phrase *aussi véritablement . . . aussi vraiment* is echoed by the Heidelberg Catechism's *so gewiss . . . so gewiss*.

36. *Der Heidelberger Katechismus*, M 682–719 (German). My exposition uses the entire section on the sacraments (Qq. 65–85).

37. S 1:543; M iii.

38. M 505–22 (Latin); S 3:487–516 (Latin and English).

39. Article 25 does not make clear *what* God works through the sacraments, but the answer seems to be that he strengthens faith. Article 26 speaks of four effects brought about through the instrumentality of baptism, but regeneration (of which baptism is the sign) is not among them, unless regeneration is taken ecclesiologically as engrafting into the church.

40. The Catechism dates from 1549, but underwent several changes before its definitive form of 1662. The section on the sacraments was added by Bishop Overall in response to a request made by the Puritans at the Hampton Court Conference (1604). At the Savoy Conference (1661) the Puritans objected in vain to the first three questions, which touch on baptism. The idea that sponsors can make vicarious vows and promises reappears in the questions devoted directly to baptism (M 522–25).

41. M 542–612 (English and Latin). The connecting link between the Thirty-Nine Articles and Westminster was the Irish Articles (1615) of Archbishop Ussher, which incorporate the predestinarian Lambeth Articles (1595) and yet move away from Calvin on the sacraments. Irish Article 89, on baptism, excludes the instrumental language of the Thirty-Nine Articles, and Article 94, on the Lord's Supper, develops the sacramental symbolism into a parallelism of two "parts," one outward and the other inward. Texts in M 525–26 (the Lambeth Articles in Latin) and 526–39 (the Irish Articles in English).

42. The expression "Grace which is exhibited [*exhibetur*] in or by the Sacraments" (Art. 27, sec. 3; cf. sec. 5) means more than "displayed"; the word "conferred" seems to be used as a synonym. The Latin commonly means "to hold forth" or "to present." Note also the expressions "Efficacy of Baptism" (Art. 28, sec. 5) and "the Grace promised is not only offered, but really exhibited and conferred" (sec. 6).

43. Larger Catechism (abbreviated L.C.) in M 612–43 (Latin); Torrance, *School of Faith*, pp. 185–234 (English). Shorter Catechism (abbreviated S.C.) in M 643–52 (English).

44. On the other hand, the Shorter Catechism persists in ranking *prayer* with the Word and sacraments as a means of grace, as did the Larger Catechism—a rather questionable arrangement. And perhaps both catechisms say too much about Christ's "benefits," although this is not intended to distract attention from his person (cf. L.C. Qq. 165, 170, 176).

45. I have used the texts in Ns 82–117 (Scots and Latin; cited by page). M 249–63 gives the Latin only.

46. *Das Schottische Bekenntnis: Reife Frucht reformierten Glaubens* (Witten/Ruhr: Luther-Verlag, 1960), p. 36. The fact that Danish Lutherans and Scottish Presbyterians practice intercommunion lends support to his thesis. But why speak of "conscious appropriation of Lutheran confessions" to account for Scottish emphasis on eating the body? Why not seek the model in the French, or other Calvinistic, confessions?

47. There is no space to discuss the interesting Scottish catechisms, which were virtually superseded by the Westminster catechisms. I should judge that they cover the entire spectrum of eucharistic types: from pure Zwinglian (e.g., *The Little Catechism*, 1556) to high Calvinist (e.g., John Craig's Catechism, 1581). Documents in Torrance, *School of Faith*.

48. S 1:456. Parallelism does not seem to have been a problem for Schaff, as it is in contemporary German discussions. That the distinction between parallelism and instrumentalism was not made a point of controversy within the confessions themselves, is apparent from the Declaration of Thorn (1645), which uses both types of language (N, pp. 681–682).

49. Walter Kreck's claim, that the eucharistic teaching of the Heidelberg Catechism cannot be adequately characterized as a "parallelism of two processes divorced from each other," may of course be granted if the qualifying phrase (*voneinander getrennten*) means simply "unrelated." See Kreck, "Das Ergebnis des Abendmahlsgesprächs in reformierter Sicht," in *Zur Lehre vom heiligen Abendmahl: Bericht über das Abendmahlsgespräch der evangelischen Kirche in Deutschland 1947–1957 und Erläuterungen seines Ergebnisses*, ed. G. Niemeier (Munich: Chr. Kaiser Verlag, 1961), p. 43. Cf. Paul Jacobs, *Theologie reformierter Bekenntnisschriften in Grundzügen* (Neukirchen: Neukirchener Verlag, 1959), p. 112. In a fascinating debate of mid-nineteenth-century America, John W. Nevin dismissed as absurd Charles Hodge's view that the Heidelberg Catechism was not purely Calvinistic in its doctrine of the sacraments. But the dividing lines were drawn differently by Hodge than by my own presentation in this chapter. See Gerrish, *Tradition and the Modern World: Reformed Theology in the Nineteenth Century* (Chicago: University of Chicago Press, 1978), pp. 60–65. The same holds good for the Dutch discussions of the Heidelberg Catechism reported by G. P. Hartvelt, *Verum Corpus: Een studie over een centraal hoofdstuk uit de avondmaalsleer van Calvijn* (Delft: W. D. Meinema N. V., 1960), pp. 195–201. Here, as in the debate between Nevin and Hodge, the focal question is whether Calvin's distinctive idea of sacramental nourishment with the substance of Christ's body and blood—the "life-giving flesh"—is maintained in the Reformed creeds. My own question is about the nature of sacramental signs. But the questions are not unrelated. And the fact that others, starting from a different point of inquiry, have seen the Heidelberg Catechism as the work of Bullinger's spirit more than Calvin's, lends some added weight to my argument.

50. On the contrast in sacramental theory between Thomas, on the one side, and Bonaventure and Scotus, on the other, see for instance Reinhold Seeberg, *Text-Book of the History of Doctrines*, trans. Charles E. Hay, 2 vols. in 1 (Grand Rapids, Mich.: Baker Book House, 1954), 2:126–27. It is, of course, not my intention to deny that there are instructive differences between Calvin and Thomas: in sacramental theology, as in other dogmatic themes, Thomas invites the image of a causal sequence, in which the effect of the divine activity is imparted to, and resides in, its object, whereas Calvin thinks in terms of the ever-present activity of God. But Calvin's retention of instrumental language seems to me to be of some theological importance just because of these differences. The

interesting question is whether such language is open to revision along what I take to be distinctively Reformation lines: that is, whether one can speak of an instrumentality of signs or symbols that are understood strictly as conveyers of meaning (of "the Word"). Naturally, this line of reflection has pre-Reformation roots that run all the way back to Augustine. It would be out of place to discuss them here. I should make clear, however, that there are scholars who in effect change the partnership I have proposed, and who hold that Calvin's sacramental theology not only resembles, but was influenced by, the Scotist tradition. A clear and succinct statement of this alleged Scotist affinity in Calvin will be found, for instance, in François Wendel, *Calvin: The Origins and Development of His Religious Thought*, trans. Philip Mairet (London: Collins, 1963), pp. 344–45. It is not to be denied that if we move beyond the confessional documents, traces of parallelism can be found in Calvin (e.g., in *Inst.*, 4.14.17, 17.5 [2:1293, 1364]). But I believe that I have sufficiently documented his instrumental language, in this chapter and the previous one, to warrant the conclusion that it would be mistaken to sum up his eucharistic theology in parallelistic terms, as Niesel, for instance, has done. Wilhelm Niesel, *Calvins Lehre vom heiligen Abendmahl im Lichte seiner letzten Antwort an Westphal*, Forschungen zur Geschichte und Lehre des Pretestantismus, vol. 3, 2d ed. (Munich: Chr. Kaiser Verlag, 1935), pp. 67–68.

51. See *Latin Works*, 2:82–83.

52. Ibid., 113, 118.

53. Luther's *Wider die himmlischen Propheten, von den Bildern und Sakrament* (1525) will be found in W.A. 18 and (translated) in L.W. 40; see esp. W.A. 18.136–67, 196–98, 202–4; L.W. 40:146–47, 207–8, 212–14. It must be admitted that the theological insight of these passages is not matched by a charitable spirit, and the same holds only a little less for Luther's earlier critique of the Roman sacrifice of the mass: *De captivitate Babylonica ecclesiae praeludium* (1520), W.A. 6.519–21; L.W.36:46–48. With the first of the citations from the work against Carlstadt compare (and contrast!) Calvin, *Inst.*, 2.5.5 (1:322).

Chapter Eight

1. John Calvin, *Inst.*, 1.5.12.

2. Although Calvin uses the expression *deus incognitus* in the passage cited, rather than the more customary Latin rendering *deus ignotus*, an allusion to Acts 17:23 is supported by the frequent echoes of the Areopagus address throughout chapter 5 of the *Institutes* (see secs. 3, 9, 13, and 14).

3. Besides the commentaries on Acts, see Martin Dibelius, *Studies in the Acts of the Apostles*, ed. Heinrich Greeven and trans. Mary Ling (New York: Charles Scribner's Sons, 1956), pp. 38ff., and Rudolf Bultmann's article on *agnostos* in *Theological Dictionary of the New Testament*, ed. Gerhard Kittel and Gerhard Friedrich, trans. Geoffrey W. Bromiley, 10 vols. (Grand Rapids, Mich.: William B. Eerdmans, 1964–76), 1:119–21, for the extensive literature on the problem.

4. In their strictly philosophical doctrine of the unknowability of God's essence, by which the sense of mystery was conceptualized, the Christian fathers were dependent upon Philo Judaeus. See Harry Austryn Wolfson, *Philo: Foundations of Religious Philosophy in Judaism, Christianity, and Islam*, 3d ed. rev., 2 vols. (Cambridge, Mass.: Harvard University Press, 1962), vol. 2, chap. 11.

5. *Inst.*, 1.14.4.

6. So McNeill suggests in *Calvin: Institutes of the Christian Religion*, ed. John T. McNeill and trans. Ford Lewis Battles, 2 vols., Library of Christian Classics, vols. 20–21 (Philadelphia: Westminster Press, 1960), 1:164, n. 14. The phrase "that Dionysius, whoever he was" does seem to echo Luther. It may be added that, in his commentary on Acts 17:34, Calvin expressly denies the identity of Dionysius the Areopagite with the author of the pseudo-Dionysian writings (C.O. 26:423).

7. A complex problem in itself, Luther's relations with mysticism were discussed at the Third International Congress on Luther Research (Järvenpää, Finland, 1966): see the proceedings in Ivar Asheim, ed., *The Church, Mysticism, Sanctification and the Natural in Luther's Thought* (Philadelphia: Fortress Press, 1967).

8. Martin Luther, *Dictata super Psalterium*, W.A. 3.124.29ff; L.W. 10:119–20. The reference to Dionysius is under the second application of the text. Besides *absconditus*, Luther also uses the adjective *occultus* ("Quinto Sacramentum Eucharistie, ubi est occultissimus") and the verb *latere* in this same passage. In his commentary ad loc., Calvin shows himself aware of the use made of Psalm 18:11 by previous exegetes, but judges that it refers, in fact, to God's anger (his retirement behind the clouds as his tent), not to the impenetrability of his glory (C.O. 31:176). A similar cautiousness marks his comments on Isaiah 45:15 (C.O. 37:141–42): although the interpretation is close to the general motif of the *theologia crucis*, Calvin will not permit the text to be referred to Christ as the *deus absconditus*.

9. There are two major studies of Luther's doctrine of the *deus absconditus*: John Dillenberger, *God Hidden and Revealed: The Interpretation of Luther's Deus Absconditus and Its Significance for Religious Thought* (Philadelphia: Muhlenberg Press, 1953); Hellmut Bandt, *Luthers Lehre vom verborgenen Gott: Eine Untersuchung zu dem offenbarungsgeschichtlichen Ansatz seiner Theologie*, Theologische Arbeiten, vol. 8 (Berlin: Evangelische Verlagsanstalt, 1958). Dillenberger's book is mainly a review of Luther's interpreters, including theologians as well as historical scholars. Bandt offers a very thorough treatment of the concept in Luther's own writings, which he discusses in chronological sequence. Reference should also be made to the following essays, all of which are devoted directly to the theme of the *deus absconditus* in Luther: Alfred Adam, "Der Begriff 'Deus absconditus' bei Luther nach Herkunft und Bedeutung," *Luther-Jahrbuch* 30 (1963): 97–106; Fritz Blanke, *Der verborgene Gott bei Luther* (Berlin: Furche Verlag, 1928); Heinrich Bornkamm, "Der verborgene und der offenbare Gott," *Theologische Rundschau*, n.s. 16 (1944): 38–52; Hans Grass, "Der verborgene und der offenbare Gott bei Luther," *Reformation und Gegen-*

wart: Vorträge und Vorlesungen von Mitgliedern der Theologischen Fakultät Marburg zum 450. Jubiläum der Reformation, Marburger Theologische Studien, vol. 6 (Marburg: N. G. Elwert Verlag, 1968), pp. 57-69; Egil Grislis, "Martin Luther's View of the Hidden God: The Problem of the *Deus Absconditus* in Luther's Treatise *De Servo Arbitrio*," *McCormick Quarterly* 21 (1967): 81-94; Rudolf Hermann, "Beobachtungen zu Luthers Lehre vom Deus revelatus—nach seiner Unterschiedenheit vom Deus absconditus—in 'De servo arbitrio,'" *Vom Herrengeheimnis der Wahrheit: Festschrift für Heinrich Vogel*, ed. Kurt Scharf (Berlin and Stuttgart: Lettner-Verlag, 1962), pp. 196-213; Ferdinand Kattenbusch, "Deus absconditus bei Luther," *Festgabe für D. Dr. Julius Kaftan zu seinem 70. Geburtstag* (Tübingen: J. C. B. Mohr [Paul Siebeck], 1920), pp. 170-214; Rudolf Koehler, "Der *Deus absconditus* in Philosophie und Theologie," *Zeitschrift für Religions- und Geistesgeschichte* 7 (1955): 46-58; Walther Koehler, *Der verborgene Gott*, Sitzungsberichte der Heidelberger Akademie der Wissenschaften, philosophisch-historische Klasse, vol. 33, no. 4, 1942/43 (Heidelberg: Carl Winter, Universitätsverlag, 1946); Julius Richter, "Luthers 'Deus absconditus'—Zuflucht oder Ausflucht?" *Zeitschrift für Religions- und Geistesgeschichte* 7 (1955): 289-303. In addition, there are numerous discussions of the theme in more general studies, some of which will be mentioned below.

10. *Luthers Theologie mit besonderer Beziehung auf seine Versöhnungs- und Erlösungslehre*, pt.1: *Luthers theologische Grundanschauungen* (Erlangen: Verlag von Theodor Blaesing, 1862), chap. 2, esp. sec. 7, pp. 111ff.

11. "Deus absconditus bei Luther," p. 204: the two ideas of *deus revelatus* and *deus absconditus* are *sachlich identisch*.

12. All of these interpreters, except the younger Ritschl, are discussed by Dillenberger, *God Hidden and Revealed*, chaps. 1-3 and chap. 5 (von Loewenich). See especially Dillenberger s summary statement on pp. 56ff. I return to Otto Ritschl below, n. 91.

13. *Luthers Lehre vom verborgenen Gott*, p. 19.

14. See, e.g., *Vorlesung über Jesaja* (1527/1530), W.A. 31^2.38.19 (L.W. 16:54-55); *In epistolam S. Pauli ad Galatas commentarius* (1531/35), W.A. 40^1.75.27ff., 174.2 (L.W. 26:28ff., cf. 26:95); *In primum librum Mose enarrationes* (1535-45/1544-54), W.A. 42.9.32ff., 294.3ff. (L.W. 1:11ff., 2:45ff.); *Disputatio [prima] contra quosdam Antinomos* (1537), W.A. 39^1.389-91; *Enarratio Psalmi LI* (1532/38), W.A. 40^2.386.14 (cf. L.W. 12:352).

15. *Dogmatics*, vol. 1: *The Christian Doctrine of God*, trans. Olive Wyon (Philadelphia: Westminster Press, 1949), pp. 168ff. Brunner acknowledges his primary indebtedness to Theodosius Harnack.

16. I owe this reference to Dillenberger (*God Hidden and Revealed*, pp. 58-59).

17. *Der verborgene Gott*, pp. 4-5.

18. Ibid., pp. 22 and 25ff.

19. The classic study of this theme is Walther von Loewenich, *Luther's Theology of the Cross*, trans. from the 5th German ed. [1967] by Herbert J. A. Bouman (Minneapolis, Minn.: Augsburg Publishing House, 1976). Rudolf Koehler, in his essay "Der *Deus absconditus* in Philosophie und Theologie,"

was even prepared to argue for the *philosophical* fruitfulness of the notion that God works *sub contrariis*, since it marks the overcoming of dualism.

20. In this respect I find myself in general sympathy with Rudolf Otto's sensitive approach to Luther in his celebrated study, *The Idea of the Holy: An Inquiry into the Non-rational Factor in the Idea of the Divine and Its Relation to the Rational*, trans. John W. Harvey, 2d ed. (Oxford: Oxford University Press, 1950), chap. 12, as also with his treatment of predestination in the preceding chapter (pp. 86–91). But it may be noted that, unlike Otto (p. 135), I regard *deus ignotus* as a fitting equivalent for *deus absconditus* (in one of its senses).

21. *Luthers Lehre vom verborgenen Gott*, p. 18. The phrase is from von Loewenich, whom Bandt is here criticizing.

22. *Operationes in Psalmos* (1519–21), W.A. 5.163.28. On the role of *Anfechtung* and *Erfahrung* in the making of a theology, see W.A.Tr. 1.146.12 (no. 352).

23. *De servo arbitrio*, W.A. 18.685.5. The English version in L.W. 33 is keyed to W.A. 18, so that there is no need to duplicate references; I have, in any case, made my own translations. In the passage cited, the phrase *ignorari a nobis vult* justifies the use of "Unknown God" as a description for the God of hiddenness II (as distinct from hiddenness I), and the inherited associations of the title do not render it inappropriate in a Reformation context. Bandt's effort to ground the limits of theological knowledge christologically seem one-sided and even doctrinaire (see section V, below). Luther presents the incomprehensibility of God as a limit that reason itself recognizes (W.A. 18.784.27), and from the earliest statement on the hidden God in the *Dictata* to the later utterances on speculation and the naked God in the *Commentary on Galatians* (W.A. 40^1.75. 27ff.; L.W. 26:28ff.) and the *Lectures on Genesis* (e.g., W.A. 42.10.3ff.; L.W. 1:11ff.) he did not hesitate to appropriate the inherited language concerning God's incomprehensibility—the hiddenness of God in himself. The contrast between the unknown God of the apophatic theology and Luther's revealed *deus crucifixus* is undeniable. See Fritz Hahn, "Faber Stapulensis und Luther," *Zeitschrift für Kirchengeschichte 57* (1938): 356–432, esp. p. 358. But the two lines of thought are not wholly exclusive: rather Luther differs from pseudo-Dionysius chiefly in his *attitude* toward the *deus nudus* (cf. the first of the *Antinomian Disputations* [1537], W.A. 39^1.389.13ff.) and, what amounts to the same thing, in his emphasis upon the *deus revelatus*. It may further be questioned whether even the *revelatio sub contrariis* (i.e., hiddenness I) is as peculiarly Luther's doctrine as Albert Brandenburg, for instance, maintains (following Hahn): *Gericht und Evangelium: Zur Worttheologie in Luthers erster Psalmenvorlesung*, Konfessionskundliche und Kontroverstheologische Studien, vol. 4 (Paderborn: Bonifacius-Druckerei, 1960), pp. 32–33, 114–15. Some of the parallels drawn in Weier's study of Luther, Faber, and Nicholas of Cusa are, I think, strained and unconvincing (e.g., between Faber and Luther on the *opus alienum dei*): Reinhold Weier, *Das Thema vom verborgenen Gott von Nikolaus von Kues zu Martin Luther*, Buchreihe der Cusanus-Gesellschaft, vol. 2 (Münster: Verlag Aschendorff, 1967), pp. 200 ff. But see the citations from Faber Stapulensis on the *arcana et abscondita filii Dei incarnatio* (p. 185, n. 71) and from

Nicholas of Cusa on the formula *ex contrario contrarium* (p. 179, n. 46); further, the reference to Nicholas's thoughts on the coincidence of humiliation and exaltation in the life, passion, and cross of Christ (p. 193). Although he argues that Faber served as the bridge between Nicholas and Luther, Weier does not, of course, limit the medieval influences to a single route. Indeed, it needs to be remembered that biblical and patristic thought patterns already lie behind the medieval heritage. Calvin found much of his material on the hidden will of God in Augustine. For some of the biblical material see Hellmut Bandt, "Verborgenheit Gottes," in *Die Religion in Geschichte und Gegenwart*, 3d ed., ed., Kurt Galling, 7 vols. (Tübingen: J. C. B. Mohr [Paul Siebeck], 1957–65), 6:1256–59.

24. On the major themes of the treatise and the extensive literature about them see the excellent study by Harry J. McSorley: *Luther: Right or Wrong?* (Minneapolis, Minn.: Augsburg Publishing House, 1969 [published jointly with the Newman Press]). See further Klaus Schwarzwäller, *Theologia crucis: Luthers Lehre von Prädestination nach De servo arbitrio, 1525*, Forschungen zur Geschichte und Lehre des Protestantismus, vol. 39 (Munich: Chr. Kaiser Verlag, 1970); Fredrik Brosché, *Luther on Predestination: The Antinomy and the Unity between Love and Wrath in Luther's Concept of God*, Acta Universitatis Upsaliensis: Studia Doctrinae Christianae Upsaliensia, no. 18 (Stockholm: Almqvist and Wiksell, 1978). Schwarzwäller has also written a useful review of modern secondary literature on Luther's book against Erasmus: *Sibboleth—Die Interpretation von Luthers Schrift De servo arbitrio seit Theodosius Harnack: Ein systematisch-kritischer Überblick*, Theologische Existenz heute, no. 153 (Munich: Chr. Kaiser Verlag, 1969). A critical appraisal of some attempts to exonerate Luther from the charge of determinism will be found in Linwood Urban, "Was Luther a Thoroughgoing Determinist?" *Journal of Theological Studies*, n.s., 22 (1971): 113–39.

25. W.A. 18.633.7.

26. Cf. W.A. 18.689.22: in the incarnate God, Jesus crucified, are all the treasures of wisdom and knowledge, only hidden (Col. 2:3).

27. W.A. 18.606.12.

28. Ibid., 769.30.

29. Ibid., 783.17.

30. Ibid., 615.12. Too much weight, it seems to me, will be attached to Luther's talk of freedom *in inferioribus* if it is not noticed that the concept of freedom in this context undergoes a change: "freedom" here is not from divine foreordination, but from specific divine precepts.

31. W.A. 18.617.19.

32. Ibid., 617.23, 618.13. Calvin was not so eager as Luther to claim a point of contact between predestination and fate. See *Inst.*, 1.16.8.

33. W.A. 18.684.32. The *fact* that God hardens many and chooses few is not itself hidden, but revealed. What is hidden—i.e., outside the scriptural revelation—is the reason *why* God so works (630.19–632.2). He reserves to himself the freedom to determine *quos et quales*. The hidden will is the divine counterpart of the very human question: Why some and not others? (See also 686.8, 689.25,

712.24, 724.30.) But to persist in the question is to be guilty of the arrogant "Why?" of the objector in Romans 9:19 (729.11). This, admittedly, does not hinder Luther from suggesting at least some partial answers (632.21ff., 730.10, etc.). Erasmus also spoke of impenetrable mysteries in God ("Corycian caves"), but he wrongly located them in the scriptural revelation itself (607.1ff.; cf. 653.31ff.). So, at least, Luther judged. But there is surely a counterpart here to Luther's experience of hiddenness II; and it could further be maintained that in his fascinating reflections on the *Sileni Alcibiadis* (see Margaret Mann Phillips, *The "Adages": A Study with Translations* [Cambridge: Cambridge University Press, 1964], pp. 269ff.) Erasmus presents a counterpart of hiddenness I.

    34. W.A. 18.685.3ff.

    35. Ibid., 706.15.

    36. Ibid., 785.29. It should be noted from this passage (pp. 784–85) that for Luther the problem is focused more on the justice than the mercy of God, though he mentions both. More precisely, the problem is whether it is just for God to have mercy only on some (cf. Rom. 9:14–15).

    37. W.A. 18.685.26.

    38. Ibid., 638.24.

    39. Ibid., 685.27.

    40. Ibid., 685.28. The problem had already taken much this form in Luther's earlier *Lectures on Romans* of 1515–16 (see W.A. 56.182.14; L.W. 25:163). Especially in the older literature, it has been suggested that Luther inherited the late scholastic distinctions between *potentia absoluta* and *potentia ordinata* and between *voluntas beneplaciti* and *voluntas signi*. See Dillenberger, *God Hidden and Revealed*, pp. 6ff. (on Albrecht Ritschl) and pp. 43–44 (on Reinhold Seeberg).

    41. W.A. 18.689.32; cf. 686.5. The debate at this point centers upon Jesus' weeping over Jerusalem (Matt. 23:37).

    42. *Kasper Crucigers Sommerpostille* (1544), W.A. 21.467.16 (on John 14:23–31); *Wochenpredigten über Joh. 16–20* (1528/29), W.A. 28.116.14; *Das XIV. und XV. Kapitel S. Johannis gepredigt und ausgelegt* (1538), W.A. 45.520.3 (L.W. 24:64–65). A translation of the first of these three expositions will be found in the standard edition of Luther's works: *The Precious and Sacred Writings of Martin Luther*, ed. John Nicholas Lenker, vol. 12 [= *Luther's Church Postil: Gospels*, vol. 3] (Minneapolis, Minn.: Lutherans in All Lands Company, 1907), pp. 297–340; see pp. 327–28. On the basic intent of Luther's christology, the old presentation of Wilhelm Herrmann still makes rewarding study: *The Communion of the Christian with God*, trans. J. Standys Stanyon, 2d ed. (London: Williams & Norgate, 1906), pp. 152–57. More recent is Ian D. Kingston Siggins, *Martin Luther's Doctrine of Christ*, Yale Publications in Religion, vol. 14 (New Haven, Conn.: Yale University Press, 1970); see esp. chap. 3. That "God *can* be other then the One revealed in Jesus Christ" is the implication, according to Brunner, of the hiddenness of God and is grounded in the doctrine of the Trinity (*Dogmatics*, 1:232).

    43. W.A. 18.633.15.

44. Ibid., 719.9.

45. Luther cites the "Socratic" principle: "Quae supra nos, nihil ad nos" (ibid., 685.6). But this is an implicit imperative, not a statement of fact. On the other hand, if the hidden God is *adorandus,* he is still not *deus cultus* (cf. 685.3). Heiko A. Oberman puts Luther's use of the dictum "Quae supra nos, nihil ad nos" in historical perspective in his essay *Contra vanam curiositatem: Ein Kapitel der Theologie zwischen Seelenwinkel und Weltall,* Theologische Studien, no. 113 (Zurich: Theologischer Verlag, 1974).

46. W.A. 18.685.19.

47. The two-sidedness of Luther's conception of God has been eloquently maintained by Heinrich Bornkamm, who speaks of "power" and "person," held together in tension, as the mystery of the real God: "Der verborgene und der offenbare Gott," p. 48. (This essay also appears in *Luther's World of Thought,* trans. Martin H. Bertram [St. Louis: Concordia Publishing House, 1958], along with other essays pertinent to my theme.) See also Bornkamm's *The Heart of Reformation Faith: The Fundamental Axioms of Evangelical Belief,* trans. John W. Doberstein (New York: Harper and Row, 1965), chap. 6. A study that deals with the hiddenness of God in creation is David Löfgren, *Die Theologie der Schöpfung bei Luther,* Forschungen zur Kirchen- und Dogmengeschichte, vol. 10 (Göttingen: Vandenhoeck & Ruprecht, 1960), esp. chaps. 5 and 6.

48. *Von abendmal Christi, Bekendnis* (1528), W.A. 26.339.25; cf. L.W. 37:227–28.

49. *Das diese wort ... noch fest stehen* (1527), W.A. 23.132.30, 136.31; cf. L.W. 37:57–58, 60.

50. For a brief, general presentation of Luther's views on history, with a useful bibliography, see Martin Schmidt, "Luthers Schau der Geschichte," *Luther-Jahrbuch* 30 (1963):17–69. The first section of John M. Headley, *Luther's View of Church History,* Yale Publications in Religion, vol. 6 (New Haven, Conn.: Yale University Press, 1963), pp. 2–19, is also pertinent.

51. W.A. 18.784.36. The quotation is from Ovid's *Amores.* Cf. *Über das erste Buch Mose: Predigten* (1527), W.A. 24.569.31: everything God does in the world goes *widdersynnisch.*

52. See *Der 127. Psalm ausgelegt an die Christen zu Riga in Liefland* (1524), W.A. 15.373.5; *In epistolam S. Pauli ad Galatas commentarius,* W.A. 40[1]. 173.24ff. (L.W. 26:94ff.);*In primum librum Mose enarrationes,* W.A. 43.229.36, 44.266.31, etc. (L.W. 4:131, 6:356).

53. W.A. 18.785.12.

54. *Deudsch [Grosser] Catechismus* (1529), W.A. 30[1].133.1; trans. Robert H. Fischer, in *The Book of Concord: The Confessions of the Evangelical Lutheran Church,* ed. Theodore G. Tappert (Philadelphia: Fortress Press, 1959), p. 365; cf. Bornkamm, "Der verborgene und der offenbare Gott," pp. 45–46, 48.

55. W.A. 18.685.31.

56. W.A. TR. 5.294.24, 34; 295.5; 294.4 (no. 5658a). Similar thoughts appear in the *Lectures on Genesis* (e.g., W.A. 43.403.8, 43.460.26, 44.376.15, 44.603.9; L.W. 4:371, 5:46, 7:104, 8:32).

57. W.A. 18.690.9.

58. T. H. L. Parker, in his *Calvin's Doctrine of the Knowledge of God*, 2d ed. (Edinburgh: Oliver & Boyd, 1969), p. 27, remarks that "the concept of *Deus absconditus* is as native to Calvin's theology as it is to Luther's," but he does not relate this remark to the various types and contexts of hiddenness distinguished by the Luther scholars. I am not aware of any discussion that does.

59. McNeill (2:932, n. 4) rightly draws attention to the pervasiveness of Calvin's appeal to experience in the discussion of election. As I shall indicate, Calvin makes a similar appeal in discussing providence.

60. On hiddenness I, which I cannot discuss here, it should at least be noted that for Calvin, as for Luther, revelation is a veiling of the "naked majesty" of God (*Inst.*, 2.6.4; cf. 1.11.3); and God's presence in Christ, through whom he emerges (in a measure) from his hiddenness (3.2.1), is accordingly at the same time a form of hiddenness (2.13.2). The interesting question with regard to hiddenness I is whether Calvin could follow Luther into the sharpest paradoxes of the *theologia crucis*, which culminate in the thought of the *deus crucifixus*. But the pertinent sources and literature are too scattered even to list here.

61. *Inst.*, 1.14.1; 3.21.1 (last sentence); 1.16.8; 3.24.3.

62. On the hidden "Why" see *De aeterna dei praedestinatione* (1552), C.O. 8:311–13; *Brevis responsio ... de aeterna dei praedestinatione* (1557), C.O. 9:257. I regularly translate *arcanus* by "secret," *absconditus* by "hidden," and *occultus* by "concealed." All three terms, and others of similar import, are found together in Calvin, as in Luther, and tend to be used interchangeably. There is a translation of the 1552 treatise in Henry Cole, *Calvin's Calvinism*, pt. 1: *A Treatise on the Eternal Predestination of God* (1856; reprint ed., Grand Rapids, Mich.: William B. Eerdmans, 1956). A more recent version is *Concerning the Eternal Predestination of God*, trans. J. K. S. Reid (London: James Clarke and Company, 1961).

63. Comm. Ps., preface, C.O. 31:21/22. English versions of Calvin's commentaries will be found in the volumes of the Calvin Translation Society (the commentaries were reprinted by William B. Eerdmans, 1948–50); the New Testament commentaries are also available in the more recent series edited by David W. and Thomas F. Torrance, 12 vols. (Grand Rapids, Mich.: William B. Eerdmans, 1960–72).

64. *Inst.*, 1.17.1; Comm. Mark 9:21, C.O. 45:494–95.

65. *Inst.*, 1.17.1, 11. Cf. 3.2.41, where Calvin paraphrases Hebrews 11:1 by defining faith as *demonstratio rerum occultarum*. For citations from Calvin's exegetical works see Heinrich Berger, *Calvins Geschichtsauffassung*, Studien zur Dogmengeschichte und systematischen Theologie, vol. 6 (Zürich: Zwingli-Verlag, 1955), pp. 51–55, 222, 224–26, 237–40. The *ecclesia abscondita* theme also belongs within Luther's range of thoughts on hiddenness: see, e.g., W.A. 18.651. 24ff., 652.23.

66. "Per mundi labyrinthum dissipati" (*Inst.*, 3.6.2).

67. *Inst.*, 1.5.2, possibly echoing a statement of Seneca's.

68. *Inst.*, 1.16.1, 2, 4, 9. In other words, Calvin asserts of providence what he has asserted already of creation (1.5.14): it is known only to faith. Calvin himself draws the reader's attention to this connection, repeating his scriptural proof

(Heb. 11:3), in 1.16.1. One would think that the hiddenness of God in his providence is a matter much more germane to the question of natural theology than is commonly recognized; but some careful distinctions need to be made which cannot detain us here. From Calvin's sermons Richard Stauffer assembles material pertinent to the doctrine of providence in his study, *Dieu, la création et la providence dans la prédication de Calvin,* Basler und Berner Studien zur historischen und systematischen Theologie, vol. 33 (Berne: Peter Lang, 1978).

69. *Inst.,* 1.16.9. With the expression *nobis fortuita* compare *fortuitum natura, ut est,* used in the same section. Calvin wants to insist that fortuitousness is not just an *illusory* appearance of things (an *imago*), but a proper attribute of things as they are. Hence his approval of the scholastic distinctions between relative and absolute necessity and between necessity of consequence and the thing consequent. But he finds it hard to make up his mind just how obscure the hand of providence is! With the *ut plurimum* used in the present section with respect to the hiddenness of providence contrast the more optimistic *interdum* in 1.17.1.

70. *Inst.,* 1.17.2. The favorite proof-texts for hiddenness II are faithfully cited in this section: Deut. 29:29, Ps. 36:6, and Rom. 11:33–34.

71. *Inst.,* 1.17.10–11. Cf. *De praedest.,* C.O. 8:351.

72. As an example of the plight of pagan man under the sway of fortune Calvin refers to the youth in Plautus's *Bacchides* who contemplated suicide (*Inst.,* 1.17.3).

73. *Römerbriefvorlesung,* W.A. 56.383.19; L.W. 25:373.

74. Predestination and reprobation are both described as "concealed" or "hidden" (*Inst.,* 1.15.8, 3.23.4). The *fact* of double predestination, however, is not hidden, but revealed; and in some measure it is attested by certain tokens, such as the call of Israel and the preservation of the remnant (3.21.5, 7) and the call and justification of the elect (3.21.7, 24.1). What remains hidden is the reason *why*, particularly why this one and not another (3.21.5; 3.23.5, 8; 3.24.1). Naturally, Calvin—like Luther—nonetheless goes a long way toward showing the wisdom of God's general design in making a distinction among men (e.g., 3.21.1). Also hidden, of course, is the identity of the elect, who are known only to God: see 4.1.2. and 8 (on the church and the *iudicium caritatis*) and 4.12.9 (on church discipline).

75. *Inst.,* 3.23.7. For Calvin's doctrine of predestination see, in general, Paul Jacobs, *Prädestination und Verantwortlichkeit bei Calvin,* Beiträge zur Geschichte und Lehre der reformierten Kirche, vol. 1 (Neukirchen: Buchhandlung des Erziehungsvereins, 1937). For the particular problem of God's hidden will, however, Jacobs has little help; and the same holds good for another generally excellent study that appeared one year later than Jacobs's book: Heinz Otten, *Prädestination in Calvins theologischer Lehre* (1938; reprint ed., Neukirchen: Verlag des Erziehungsvereins, 1968).

76. *Inst.,* 3.23.1.

77. *Inst.,* 3.21.1, 21.6, 23.10. In his interesting study *Der Prädestinationsgedanke in der Theologie Martin Luthers* (Berlin: Evangelische Verlagsanstalt, 1966), Gerhard Rost argues that Luther's idea of predestination has a "funda-

mental-*a priori* character," being grounded in his doctrine of God, and is not simply derived a posteriori from the experience of justification. This, I think, is true, and it holds good also for Calvin. But it needs to be pointed out further that the a posteriori element (at any rate in Calvin) is attached to the experience of diversity and not only of grace. On Calvin's hostility to speculation see E. P. Meijering's study of the term "curiosity": *Calvin wider die Neugierde: Ein Beitrag zum Vergleich zwischen reformatorischen und patristischem Denken*, Bibliotheca Humanistica & Reformatorica, vol. 29 (Nieuwkoop: B. De Graaf, 1980). Meijering perhaps overdoes the "biblicistic" roots of Calvin's antispeculative stand, which has to do also with how the Bible itself is interpreted and related to human experience, not simply with what it contains. See further chapter 12 below.

78. The will of God is ultimate; to seek a cause for it is, therefore (oddly), to picture something outside of the ultimate reality—or to want the world to be other than it is (see *Inst.* 3.22.4, 11; 3.23.2, 4). But although God's will is ultimate and hidden, we are certain it cannot be either capricious or unjust as the scholastic doctrines of *voluntas* (or *potentia*) *absoluta* and *deus exlex* wrongly implied (1.17.2; 3.23.2, 5, 9). Cf. *De praedest.*, C.O. 8:310, 361; *Calumniae nebulonis . . . de occulta dei providentia* (1558), C.O. 9:288.

79. *Inst.*, 1.16.3. Cf. 1.5.5 (on intellectual gifts), 2.3.4 (on moral gifts).

80. *Inst.*, 3.22.1; 3.21.5, 24.17; 3.22.5. Cf. 3.21.5-7, on the "stages" or "degrees" of election. It is sound Calvinism in principle, if not in tone, when J. S. Whale writes: "The modern mind which is revolted by this doctrine of Election cheerfully accepts the modern doctrine of Selection, and is not appalled by the thought: 'The warm-blooded mammals have I loved, but the Ichthyosauri have I hated " (*The Protestant Tradition: An Essay in Interpretation* [Cambridge: Cambridge University Press, 1955], p. 143).

81. *Inst.*, 3.22.5; 3.23.10.

82. *Inst.*, 3.24.12, 16 (cf. 3.21.1); 3.24.12-14, 22.10, 23.13; 3.23.1. Cf. 3.22.2 (that not all are members of Christ is open to observation); 3.24.15 (experience teaches that God does not touch every heart).

83. Quoted in *Inst.*, 3.23.5. The sense of the ambiguity of human existence— the two-handedness with which our lot is dealt out—seems to be at least as firmly rooted in the religious experience behind predestination as the "creature-consciousness" to which Otto tries to reduce it (*Idea of the Holy*, pp. 88-90). Not the "futility of one's own choice" (p. 89), but the diversity of human choice—and of human destiny in general—is brought to expression in the doctrine. But I think it is fair, borrowing a term from Otto (p. 102), to describe Calvin's doctrine of election as (from one point of view) a "caricature" of authentic encounter with the divine, and this might prove more fruitful than faulting it for lack of christocentricity (i.e., for being a tacit *theologia naturalis*).

84. The "hidden will" is mentioned by Calvin in three main contexts: the origin of evil (*Inst.*, 1.15.8; 3.23.4, 7, 8), God's providential use of the wicked (1.17.2, 18.3; 3.20.43), and the double decree by which God withholds from some what he seems to offer to all (3.3.21, 22.10, 24.1-2, 24.8, 24.15-17). The problem is further discussed in certain of the treatises (*De praedest.* [C.O.

8:300–301, 364ff.], *Brevis responsio* [9:262ff.], *Calumniae nebulonis* [9:302ff])
and commentaries (on Ezek. 18:23 [C.O. 40:445–46], Rom. 11:33–34 [49:230–
31], 2 Pet. 3:9 [55:475–76]). In his insistence that there is no division in God's
will itself, but only as it appears to us, Calvin cannot take such passages as
Ezekiel 18:23 or Matthew 23:37 to convey a genuine universal will to mercy:
the former simply states the condition (namely, conversion) upon which God
grants life but which he alone can fulfill; the latter uses accommodated language—namely, a very human expression of complaint and disappointment—to
display the wickedness of God's people. On the attempt of Amyraut (unsuccess-
ful, in my opinion) to discover in Calvin's theology a *bona fide* offer of salvation
to all, see Brian G. Armstrong, *Calvinism and the Amyraut Heresy: Protestant
Scholasticism and Humanism in Seventeenth-Century France* (Madison, Wis.:
University of Wisconsin Press, 1969).

85. *Inst.*, 3.21.1, 2; 3.24.4.

86. *Inst.*, 3.24.3–6; *De praedest.*, C.O. 8:306–307, 318.

87. "At subit futuri status anxietas ... ista sollicitudine liberavit nos Christus
..." (*Inst.*, 3.24.6). That Calvin has a perennial oscillation in mind is supported
from his sensitive treatment of anxiety and doubt (3.2.16–28)—not to mention
his demonology (1.14.13–19).

88. "Deus absconditus bei Luther," p. 205, n. 31.

89. Among the passages in *Church Dogmatics* critical of Luther see vol. 2,
pt. 1, Eng. trans. (New York: Charles Scribner's Sons, 1957), pp. 541–42; vol. 2,
pt. 2 (ibid.), pp. 65–66. Barth's own presentation of the hiddenness of God is in
pt. 1, pp. 179ff.

90. *Luthers Lehre vom verborgenen Gott*, pp. 40ff. (against Erich Seeberg),
and pp. 71–72 (against Fritz Frey).

91. So, for instance, the argument that the hiddenness of God in creation is
a hiddenness which is "not yet" the hiddenness of revelation and in just this
sense belongs to Luther's fundamental notion of revelation (ibid., pp. 127–28).
A further, more basic problem is whether Bandt takes seriously enough the
sharpness of the antithesis between the two wills in the much discussed passage
from the *De servo arbitrio*. He is eager to show how even this passage can be
brought under the single rubric of the hidden form of revelation. But he makes
his task too easy by setting up Otto Ritschl's interpretation as the alternative
(pp. 157–58). Ritschl accused Luther of a Marcionitic dualism of two gods,
which was inferior to Marcion's view, however, in that Luther assigned omnipotence to the *hidden* God. This is manifestly a piece of bull-headed literalism.
But I cannot see that Bandt himself takes the passage sufficiently earnestly
when he explains it as indicating "two aspects of the Christian knowledge of
God" (p. 159). The problem is that they are *contradictory* aspects! It is, moreover, surprising that Bandt only turns directly to W.A. 18.685.28 after (as he
says) his interpretation of hiddenness and predestination in *De servo arbitrio*
is already in essence completed (p. 155). If this is the most difficult passage for
Bandt to assimilate, the most congenial to his line of interpretation is undoubtedly 633.7ff. It can certainly be granted that there is a formal harmony or
functional parallel here between the two types of hiddenness insofar as each

exercises faith. But there are also large differences. It is a single act by which God slays and makes alive in the justification of the sinner, whereas the antithesis between eternal wrath and eternal mercy refers to two different divine acts or series of acts directed to two different objects. More importantly, Luther plainly implies in this very passage that the one series is hidden, not in the sense of being a revealed paradox, but because it lies outside of revelation. Of course, it must be added that the *fact* of reprobation, according to Luther, is *not* hidden in this sense, only the way in which this fact is to be reconciled with another revealed fact, God's will to mercy.

92. Bandt's case is strongest, I think, when he argues, not from *der christologische Ansatz* (*a tergo*, so to say), but from the movement toward faith *(a fronte)*. As will be clear, I, too, acknowledge that there at least *may be* a functional subordination of hiddenness II to hiddenness I.

93. Dillenberger, *God Hidden and Revealed*, p. 157.

94. Quoted by Richter, "Luthers 'Deus absconditus,'" pp. 289–90.

95. Ibid., p. 297.

96. Ibid., p. 293.

97. Klaus Schwarzwäller rejects the terms "dialectic" and "dualism" as inappropriate to the distinction between *deus absconditus* and *revelatus* on the grounds of the "identity of God" (*Theologia crucis*, pp. 197–98). I do, of course, agree that there can be no talk of an objective dualism, as far as the reformers are concerned; but a subjective dialectic seems to me inescapably present: that is, a perennial exchange between two images of God. The art of faith is to move the mind in *one* direction; but it cannot *halt* the reverse movement, only *counter* it.

98. Cf. W.A. TR. 5.294.6 (no. 5658a).

99. *Operationes in Psalmos* (1519–21), W.A. 5.204.26.

100. Grass, "Der verborgene und der offenbare Gott bei Luther," p. 57.

101. Blaise Pascal, *Pensées*, trans. W. F. Trotter (New York: Random House, 1941), no. 72, pp. 21ff.

102. *Inst.*, 3.22.1. Cf. *Inst.*, 2.17.1, and *De praedest.*, C.O. 8:266–67. Following Augustine, Calvin does not hesitate to use the word *exemplum* in this context and to stress Christ's humanity.

103. *Inst.*, 2.16.11. The "typical" character of Christ's experience is again conveyed, this time by the subtle change of pronouns from "he" to "you."

Chapter Nine

1. John Calvin, *Inst.*, 2.3.4 (1:294); trans. F. L. Battles. Throughout this chapter, which is intended as a short commentary on two passages from the 1559 *Institutes,* I have adopted Battles's translation (referred to by volume and page in parentheses).

2. Martin Luther, *Deudsch [Grosser] Catechismus* (1529): W. A. 30^1.135. 33ff.; trans. Robert H. Fischer, in *The Book of Concord: The Confessions of the Evangelical Lutheran Church,* ed. Theodore G. Tappert (Philadelphia: Fortress Press, 1959), p. 368.

3. Calvin's doctrine of God is taken up in chapter 12 below. What I there term the "rule of piety" could be applied also to man's knowledge of himself. See *Inst.*, 1.15.6 (1:193).

4. *Inst.* 1.2.1 (1:40), 6.1 (1:70-71), 15.1 (1:183); 2.6.1 (1:341).

5. *Inst.*, 2.6-17 (1:340-534); 3.6-10 (1:684-725).

6. *Inst.*, 1.15.4 (1:178).

7. In his widely read Terry Lectures, Fromm takes Calvin as a representative of "authoritarian" (as distinguished from "humanistic") religion, in which a man submits himself in obedience to a transcendent power not because of its moral qualities, but simply because it has control over him and the right to force him to worship it. Armed with one quotation from Calvin (*Inst.*, 3.12.6), he thinks it possible to characterize Calvin's religious experience as "that of despising everything in oneself," God being a "symbol of power and force" and "man in juxtaposition... utterly powerless" (Erich Fromm, *Psychoanalysis and Religion* [New Haven: Yale University Press, 1950], pp. 34-36). Similarly, in an earlier work Fromm ascribes to Calvin's God "all the features of a tyrant without any quality of love or even justice" (*Escape From Freedom* [New York: Rinehart and Company, 1941], pp. 87-88). He follows this description with a passage in which Calvin denies the priority of love over faith and hope (*Inst.*, 3.2.41), but he substitutes a row of ellipsis points for Calvin's explanation: that it is faith that engenders love. One can only guess how Fromm gathered his scraps from Calvin; had he reached book 3, chapter 2, section 41, by way of sections 1-40, he must have noticed that faith, for Calvin, is directed to the paternal benevolence of God. What he mistakenly identifies as Calvin's religion is closer to the idolatry, hypocrisy, and pagan superstition that Calvin deplores (see e.g., *Inst.*, 1.5.4. [1:50]). Unfortunately, however, such misunderstandings of Calvin are common, otherwise there would be no point in mentioning them.

8. *Inst.*, 1.5.4 (1:56).

9. I owe this citation from Calvin's Sermons on Job to Cairns (see n. 16 below), p. 139. It is important to recognize that it is a judgment on man "considered in himself," but for all that it still smacks of hyperbole.

10. *Inst.*, 1.14.20-22 (1:179-82).

11. *Inst.*, 1.14.22 (1:182).

12. *Inst.*, 1.15.4 (1:189), 2.12.6-7 (1:471-72), 3.3.9 (1:601).

13. See, e.g., *Inst.*, 3.7.6 (1:696-97); Comm. Gen. 9:6, C. O. 23:147 (there remains *aliquid residuum*). Translations of all Calvin's commentaries are available in the old edition of the Calvin Translation Society, more than once reprinted; the New Testament commentaries have been revised in the Torrance edition (see n. 35 below).

14. *Inst.*, 3.3.9 (1:601).

15. The debate was precipitated by Emil Brunner's *Natur und Gnade* and Karl Barth's response *Nein!* Originally published in 1934, both books were translated into English by Peter Fraenkel under the title *Natural Theology* (London: Geoffrey Bles, The Centenary Press, 1946). The exchange continued, especially in Brunner's *Mensch im Widerspruch* (1937) and in the third volume of Barth's *Kirchliche Dogmatik* (pts. 1-2, 1945); and it was Brunner's conviction that over

the years the gap between him and Barth narrowed (Brunner, "The New Barth: Observations on Karl Barth's *Doctrine of Man,*" *Scottish Journal of Theology* 4 [1951]: 123–35). The points at issue between Brunner and Barth are perhaps less important for our present theme than one point of fundamental agreement: their common effort to think of the *imago Dei* (and therefore of man's humanity) less in terms of natural endowments and more in terms of personal existence, i.e., of man's dual relationship to God and his fellowmen.

16. See especially Wilhelm Niesel, *The Theology of Calvin* [1938], trans. Harold Knight (Philadelphia: Westminister Press, 1956); T. F. Torrance, *Calvin's Doctrine of Man* (London: Lutterworth Press, 1949); David Cairns, *The Image of God in Man* (London: S.C.M. Press, 1953). Torrance's brilliant work is the most detailed and important study of the *imago Dei* in Calvin's theology; it is rich in citations from outside the *Institutes,* especially from the commentaries and the sermons on Job (to which his sixth chapter is almost entirely devoted). But the reader may find its argument more tendentious in the use of primary sources than the innocent methodological remarks in the preface appear willing to acknowledge (pp. 7–8). The author deliberately eschews all reference to the secondary literature on Calvin; but when he notes the relevance of his findings to "the modern theological debate," one cannot help inferring that there has been some "relevance" also in the opposite direction. At points, Torrance admits that he is pressing beyond Calvin's explicit utterances (see, e.g., pp. 44–45); at other points, the mosaic of quotations gives a misleading impression that Calvin says something he is not explicitly saying at all (for an example, taken at random, see the first sentence on p. 70). It should be pointed out that the method of culling citations from all over Calvin's exegetical and homiletical works, important and fruitful though it has proved to be, needs to be used with caution: while it is true that his treatises and the *Institutes* are often determined by polemical considerations, his expositions are even more determined (as one would hope) by his text. There is not much to be gained by quoting Calvin when he offers little more than a paraphrase of his text.

17. Brunner gave a historical excursus on the interpretation of the image in an appendix to his *Man in Revolt: A Christian Anthropology* [*Mensch im Widerspruch,* 1937], trans. Olive Wyon (London: Lutterworth Press, 1939), pp. 449–515, and much more briefly in his *Dogmatics,* vol. 2: *The Christian Doctrine of Creation and Redemption* [1950], trans. Olive Wyon (London: Lutterworth Press, 1952), pp. 75–78. More detailed are the historical chapters in Cairns's *Image of God.* Briefly, we may conclude on the basis of these three studies that there were in fact antecedents for Calvin's distinctive conception of the divine image and likeness. In contrast to the "image," which he thought of as man's rationality, Irenaeus understood the "likeness" to refer to man's proper relation to God and as such to the goal of redemption. Augustine held that the Trinitarian structure of man's psychological faculties is an image of God because it can remember, understand, and love God; and Thomas Aquinas likewise did not identify the image with man's intellectual nature as such, but with the aptitude of his intellectual nature for knowing and loving God. Luther, too, could assert that the image and likeness lie in knowledge and love of God. In short, there was

a strong tradition affirming (with variations of detail) that the image or likeness
lies in a relationship and not only in man's nature or endowments; and this is
the direction that Calvin's thoughts also take.

18. *Inst.*, 1.15.3 (1:188).

19. "... a tacit antithesis... raises man above all other creatures and, as it
were, separates him from the common mass" (*Inst.*, 1.15.3 [1:188]). See also
2.12.6 (1:471).

20. *Inst.* 1.15.4 (1:189).

21. Ibid. (and the definition quoted above). On the distinction between intellect and will, see *Inst.*, 1.15.7 (1:194-95).

22. *Inst.* 1.15.3 (1:187-88). Calvin does not mention Irenaeus by name, but
Cairns shows that the distinction Calvin rejects can in fact be traced back to
Irenaeus (*Image of God,* pp. 74-75).

23. *Inst.*, 1.15.4 (1:190).

24. Ibid. That it is Chrysostom whom Calvin has in mind, though he does not
name him, is clear from Comm. Gen. 1:26, where he admits that Chrysostom has
pointed at least to a very small part of the image (C.O. 23:26).

25. *Inst.*, 1.15.3 (1:186-87; cf. p. 188). I have borrowed Dryden's version of
Ovid's lines from the older translation of the *Institutes* by Henry Beveridge, 2
vols. (1845; reprint ed., London: James Clarke and Company, 1949), 1:162.

26. "Nondum tamen data esse videtur plena imaginis definitio nisi clarius
pateat quibus facultatibus praecellat homo, et quibus speculum censeri debeat
gloriae Dei" (*Inst.*, 1.15.4; Battles translates *speculum* here as "reflection,"
1:189). "Ad imaginem ergo Dei conditus est homo, in quo suam gloriam creator
ipse conspici quasi in speculo voluit" (*Inst.*, 2.12.6 [1:471]).

27. *Inst.*, 1.14.21 (1:180).

28. *Inst.*, 1.15.3 (1:188).

29. Comm. Heb. 11:3, C.O. 55:144 (on man's difference from brute beasts),
145 (on the image of God in the world). In *Inst.*, 1.6.3 (1:72), Calvin speaks of
the divine likeness imprinted on the form of the universe; but there the word
used is not *imago* but *effigies.*

30. The "seat" *(sedes)* of the divine image is in the soul (*Inst.*, 1.15.3 [1:186]).
Wilhelm Niesel writes: "Thus man's similitude to God implies something more
than his psycho-physical constitution, it signifies his right attitude towards his
Creator and thus his right attitude towards all other creatures.... The divine similitude consists not in the fact that man is endowed with reason and will, but in
the fact that these faculties in original man were directed wholly towards knowledge of and obedience to God" (*Theology of Calvin,* pp. 67-68). This is well
said, but it seems to me that the heart of the "right attitude" can be more exactly specified as thankfulness: that is, the attitude that acknowledges man's
endowments as gifts. In addition to the last phrase in Calvin's definition of the
image, see *Inst.*, 2.2.1 (1.256): "... Scriptura nihil aliud ei tribuit quam quod
creatus esset ad imaginem Dei: quo scilicet insinuat, non propriis bonis sed Dei
participatione fuisse beatum."

31. As Torrance rightly puts it: "There is no doubt that Calvin always thinks
of the *imago* in terms of a *mirror.* Only while the mirror actually reflects an object does it have the image of that object. There is no such thing in Calvin's

thought as an *imago* dissociated from the act of reflecting" (*Calvin's Doctrine of Man*, p. 36). Calvin occasionally uses the metaphor of an engraved image, but, so Torrance claims, "never dissociated from the idea of the mirror" (ibid.). I have noted the metaphor of an engraved image in, for example, *Inst.*, 1.15.3 (1:188) and 2.12.6 (1:471). Torrance produces a wealth of citations from the commentaries to document his interpretation of Calvin's anthropology; but he provides no specific reference for his statement that in the 1536 *Institutes* "Calvin practically equates the *imago* with the *actio* of gratitude" (p. 71, n. 6).

32. This is a theme suggested to Calvin by, for instance, his exposition of the Psalms. The earth was given to men that they might glorify the Creator; out of sinful humanity the Creator preserves a people for himself, so that the end (or "final cause") of creation will not be frustrated. "Hic nobis vivendi finis est ut simus in terra praecones gloriae Dei.... Nam quum ad pecudes et feras perveniant terrae opes, praecipue tamen in usum hominum creata esse omnia spiritus pronuntiat, ut Deum inde patrem agnoscant.... Nisi Deus ecclesiam conservet, inversum iri totum naturae ordinem: quia irrita erit mundi creatio, nisi sit aliquis populus qui Deum invocet" (Comm. Ps. 115:17, C.O. 32:192). Cf. Comm. Ps. 105:44–45, C.O. 32:114–15, where the "glorifying" of God includes keeping his commandments. In his *Commentary on Hebrews* Calvin links the end of creation with the metaphor of the "mirror": "Quare eleganter mundus divinitatis speculum nominatur.... Fideles autem, quibus oculos dedit in singulis creaturis, velut emicantes gloriae eius scintillas cernunt. Certe in hunc finem conditus est mundus, ut esset divinae gloriae theatrum" (Comm. Heb. 11:3, C.O. 55:146).

33. *Theology of Calvin*, p. 67.

34. *Inst.*, 2.2.12 (1:270). In this section (1:270–71) Calvin endorses the scholastic distinction between the corruption of man's natural gifts and the loss of the supernatural gifts. Perhaps the terminology suits his standpoint less well than he assumes; for if man was created to glorify God with thankful homage, how can it be said that faith and love for God are "adventitious and beyond nature" *(adventitia... et praeter naturam)?* However, by calling understanding and will "natural gifts" he intends to stress that, though corrupted, they remain distinguishing characteristics of man in contrast to brute beasts. Man is, in particular, a "rational being"; this Calvin infers from the prologue to the Fourth Gospel. But his view of man is incomplete unless one adds the reason *why* man was created a rational being (see the following note). For some representative statements in the *Institutes* on the question whether the image is lost, see *Inst.*, 1.15.4 (1:189–90), 2.2.17 (1:277), 3.3.9 (1:601), and the passage cited in n. 13 above. Calvin seems bent on stressing the fearful deformity of the image in fallen man as far as he can *without* asserting that it is totally annihilated. But he can also say that the image in Adam was "obliterated" (*obliterata: Inst.*, 2.1.5 [1:246]) or "destroyed" (*deleta:* Comm. Gen. 1:26, C.O. 23:26). Even the statement that the image was "destroyed," however, is immediately qualified: it means that the traces of the image are vitiated and that no part is free from the infection of sin (C.O. 23:27).

35. Comm. Heb. 11:3, C.O. 55:144; English quoted from Calvin, *The Epistle of Paul the Apostle to the Hebrews and the First and Second Epistles of St.*

Peter. trans. William B. Johnston, Calvin's Commentaries, ed. David W. Torrance and Thomas F. Torrance, vol. 12 (Grand Rapids, Mich.: William B. Eerdmans, 1963), pp. 158-59.

36. On the former question, despite his insistence that Adam was responsible for his fall (*Inst.*, 1.15.8 [1:195]), Calvin cannot but argue that Adam fell by divine decree (*Inst.*, 3.23.7 [2:955]). He leaves it to the devout reader to affirm two things that carnal reason cannot harmonize: God's decree and Adam's responsibility. See Calvin, *De aeterna Dei praedestinatione*, etc. (1552), C.O. 8:294-95; English in *Calvin's Calvinism*, pt. 1: *A Treatise on the Eternal Predestination of God*, trans. Henry Cole (1856; reprint ed., Grand Rapids, Mich.: William B. Eerdmans, 1956), pp. 87-88. There is a more recent English version of the treatise on predestination: Calvin, *Concerning the Eternal Predestination of God*, trans. J.K.S. Reid (London: James Clarke, 1961); see pp. 98-99. It is interesting that, despite the fall, Calvin thought Adam belonged to the number of the saved (*Inst.*, 2.10.7 [1:434]). On the second question, although Calvin freely uses the traditional language of "hereditary corruption," he expressly denies that the corruption of the whole human race in the person of Adam is to be attributed to procreation; it was the result of "the appointment of God" (Comm. John 3:6, C.O. 47:57). One reason for Calvin's conception of sin's transmission was undoubtedly the fact that he did not make the direct connections the Schoolmen made between sin and sensuality.

37. *Inst.*, 2.1.8 (1:251).

38. *Inst.* 2.1.4 (1:244-46). All Calvin's quotations in the following three paragraphs are from this section of the *Institutes.* It is instructive to compare Calvin's analysis of the fall with Luther's, who likewise traces the primal sin back to unbelief or doubting the Word. See Luther, In *primum librum Mose enarrationes* (1535-45), W. A. 42.112.20; L. W. 1:149.

39. *Inst.*, 2.2.4 (1:260); cf. n. 34 above.

40. *Inst.*, 2.2.6 (1:263).

41. "Exempla igitur ista monere nos videntur ne hominis naturam in totum vitiosum putemus" (*Inst.*, 2.3.3 [1:292]). See T. H. L. Parker, *Calvin's Doctrine of the Knowledge of God*, 2d. ed. (Edinburgh: Oliver and Boyd, 1969), p. 49, n. 2. As Parker's note indicates, there has been some difference of scholarly opinion on the interpretation of this sentence, which he takes to mean: These examples *seem* to warn us against judging man's nature wholly corrupt, but in fact they do not. In other places Calvin does speak expressly of fallen man's powers as "wholly depraved." See, for instance, his *Supplex exhortatio ad Caesarem de restituenda ecclesia* (1543), where he accuses his opponents of denying that man's powers are *prorsus depravatas* (C.O. 6:483); trans. in *Calvin: Theological Treatises*, trans. J. K. S. Reid, Library of Christian Classics, vol. 22 (Philadelphia: Westminster Press, 1954), p. 198. But against the interpretation Parker represents it has been pointed out that the word emphasized—"seem" *(videntur)*—does not appear in the Latin editions between 1539 and 1550, nor in the French translation. In any case, it will hardly be denied that if we attribute a doctrine of "total depravity" to Calvin, then we must take it to mean a depravity that

extends over the whole man: the totality is extensive rather than intensive. His argument is with theologians who, under the influence of philosophy, tended to equate man's problem with the downward pull of his sensuality, assuming his intellect and even his will to be unimpaired (*Inst.*, 2.2.4 [1:258-60]; cf. 2.2.2 [1:257]). In a vivid image, Calvin asserts that the gifts remaining to us since the fall are spoiled like good wine turned sour in a bad vessel (Comm. John 3:6; C.O. 47:57). It was also a concern of Calvin, as of Luther, to deny that sin is merely weakness; in fact, they held, the sinful will is vigorous but vitiated in its motivation (see. p. 12 above). This is Calvin's point in the passage just cited from the *Supplex Exhortatio,* and he remembers to add the qualification that of himself man possesses no ability whatever to act aright as far as spiritual righteousness is concerned.

42. *Inst.*, 2.2.18 (1:277).

43. *Inst.*, 2.2.15 (1:273-74).

44. *Inst.*, 2.2.15 (1:274). Calvin's estimate of the capabilities of man's fallen intellect closely parallels Luther's and includes a distinction between "heavenly things" and "earthly things" (*Inst.*, 2.2.13 [1:272]).

45. *Inst.*, 2.3.3, 4 (1:292, 293). All quotations in this and the following paragraph are from *Inst.*, 2.3.3-4 (1:292-94).

46. Calvin is so anxious to make his point about the radical defect of human good apart from grace (i.e., that such good is vitiated, from the religious point of view, by the absence of thankfulness to God), that he sometimes speaks of it as though it were a mere "show of good" (*Inst.*, 2.5.19 [1:340]). But one must surely infer from the passages already cited that fallen man is capable of real good—only in another order than the realm of righteousness before God. Niesel is undoubtedly right in affirming that for Calvin "sin is something other than moral failure" (*Theology of Calvin*, p. 89). But Torrance, with equal justice, concedes that Calvin does not consistently differentiate the moral and the theological points of view (*Calvin's Doctrine of Man*, pp. 19-20); and Cairns thinks that Calvin slips into inconsistency when he "interprets man's perversity in such a sense that the dignity and sacredness of human nature appear to have perished with the Fall" (*Image of God*, p. 138).

47. Calvin frequently speaks of the earth and even the universe as made and furnished for man (see, e.g., *Inst.*, 1.14.2 [1:161-62], 14.22 [1:181-82]; 1.16.6 [1:204]). But this must be understood in relation to his other line of thought according to which man himself was made for God, a thought that receives classic expression in the opening sentences of the Geneva Catechism (1545): "...he created us and placed us in this world to be glorified in us" (C.O. 6:10; trans. in *Calvin's Tracts and Treatises*, trans. Henry Beveridge, 3 vols. [1844-51; reprint ed., Grand Rapids, Mich.: William B. Eerdmans, 1958], 2:37). See also n. 32 above. This vision of God's glory requires "demythologization," I should think, because the anthropomorphic image of God's glorifying himself, if taken too literally, presents a narcissistic deity bent on contemplating his own image. But since Calvin does not seem to have felt the problem, there is no need to pursue it here any further.

Chapter Ten

1. Luther, W. A. Tr. 1.152.14 (no. 360; Johannes Aurifaber); cf. L. W. 54:54 (Veit Dietrich).

2. "...and after all Calvin did burn one of the few scientists of the age." Quirinus Breen, *John Calvin: A Study in French Humanism* (Grand Rapids, Mich.: William B. Eerdmans, 1931), p. 155.

3. So, at least, A. Wolf, *A History of Science, Technology and Philosophy in the 16th and 17th Centuries* (New York: Macmillan, 1935), p. 411. The English translation of Taton's history of science makes P. Delaunay say that "Calvin banished the physician Jerome Bolsec, with whose medical doctrines he disagreed." René Taton, ed., *History of Science*, vol. 2: *The Beginnings of Modern Science, from 1450 to 1800*, trans. A. J. Pomerans (New York: Basic Books, 1964), p. 170. This, however, is a misleading translation of the French original, which does not state that Calvin's disagreement was with Bolsec's medical doctrines. Taton, ed., *Histoire générale des sciences*, vol. 2: *La Science moderne de 1450 à 1800* (Paris: Presses Universitaires de France, 1958), p. 178.

4. See Roland H. Bainton, *Hunted Heretic: The Life and Death of Michael Servetus, 1511–1553* (Boston: Beacon Press, 1953), pp. 118ff. (on Servetus's discovery of the "circulation" of the blood) and pp. 94–95 and 184–85 (on the charge of impugning biblical geography). As Bainton points out, nothing was said about Ptolemy in the actual sentence on Servetus (ibid., p. 207).

5. Originally published in two volumes (London: Macmillan, 1896), White's fascinating study has been reissued as two volumes in one (London: Arco Publishers, 1955). He discusses Servetus's geographical heresy in 1:113. In the sixteenth century itself "science" would have included the "humanities" (the *Geisteswissenschaften*). Indeed, Choisy suggests that science for the man of the sixteenth century meant above all firsthand acquaintance with ancient literature, and that scientific method was the direct appeal to the sources instead of citing "authorities." Eugène Choisy, *Calvin et la science*, Université de Genève: Recueil de la faculté de théologie protestante, no. 1 (Geneva, 1931), p. 10.

6. As far as I can ascertain, there is no treatment in the literature which brings together all the various aspects of the theme as outlined above. Several of the problems are briefly discussed by John Dillenberger in his useful and discerning study, *Protestant Thought and Natural Science: A Historical Interpretation* (Garden City, N.Y.: Doubleday, 1960). The subject was also sketched in two articles of mine, "Luther" and "Reformation," in *The Encyclopedia of Philosophy*, ed. Paul Edwards, 8 vols. (New York: Macmillan and the Free Press, 1967), 5:109–113, 7:99–101. Although he has little to say about Luther and the Lutherans, there is now a good review of other aspects of our subject by R. Hooykaas, *Religion and the Rise of Modern Science* (Grand Rapids, Mich.: William B. Eerdmans, 1972).

7. The author's preface to *De revolutionibus* is reproduced in Leopold Prowe, *Nicolaus Coppernicus*, 2 vols. (Berlin: Weidmannsche Buchhandlung, 1883–84), 2:3–8.

8. The ancient authorities are Nicetas (whom Copernicus found mentioned in

Cicero) and Philolaus, Heraclides, and Ecphantus (all named by Plutarch). A reference to Aristarchus of Samos appears in Copernicus's manuscript, but it was stuck out before publication. See Dorothy Stimson, *The Gradual Acceptance of the Copernican Theory of the Universe* (New York: Baker and Taylor, 1917), p. 27. n. 7.

9. Stimson says of the *Commentareolus:* "probably written soon after 1530" (*Copernican Theory,* p. 30). But Norlind dates the work "probably between 1504 and 1509." Wilhelm Norlind, "Copernicus and Luther: A Critical Study," *Isis* 44 (1953): 273–276; see p. 273. The *Commentareolus* is given by Prowe (*Coppernicus,* 2:184–202). Rosen notes that the heliocentric system of the *Commentareolus* does not fully agree with the system taught in *De revolutionibus.* Edward Rosen, *Three Copernican Treatises,* Records of Civilization, no. 30 (New York: Columbia University Press, 1939), p. 7.

10. *De libris revolutionum Nicolai Copernici narratio prima.* Rheticus's report, in the form of an extended letter (dated 23 September 1539) to John Schöner of Nuremberg, is reproduced in Prowe (*Coppernicus,* 2:293–377). The first volume of Prowe's monumental work is a biography of the astromer (in two parts) and constitutes the leading authority for information concerning Copernicus's life and writings. The second volume is a collection of major documents. For Rheticus's journey to Frauenburg, see 1, 2:387–405; for the publication of *De revolutionibus,* see 1, 2:490–542.

11. Rheticus's alleged troubles at the University of Wittenberg are suggested, e.g., by Stimson (*Copernican Theory,* p. 31) and Kuhn. Thomas S. Kuhn, *The Copernican Revolution: Planetary Astronomy in the Development of Western Thought* (Cambridge, Mass.: Harvard University Press, 1957), p. 196. The salient facts, however, are these. (1) Rheticus resumed his professorship at Wittenberg after his return from Frauenburg and after publication of his *Narratio prima.* Almost immediately, he was made dean of the arts faculty. (2) To supervise the printing of *De revolutionibus* in Nuremberg, he was granted leave of absence, with salary, from his duties at the university. For this privilege he had the approval both of the Lutheran Elector of Saxony and of Philip Melanchthon, who gave him letters of commendation to friends in Nuremberg. (3) Nothing sinister can be inferred from the fact that publication was undertaken in Nuremberg, since Rheticus had a shorter work of Copernicus published in Wittenberg itself by the printer of Luther's German Bible (Hans Lufft). (4) Though Rheticus eventually left Wittenberg, he did so in order to assume a post at the University of Leipzig, which had also become Lutheran. In addition to the literature already cited, see Werner Elert, *Morphologie des Luthertums,* 2 vols. (Munich: C. H. Beck'sche Verlagsbuchhandlung, 1931–32), 1:369–75; Heinrich Bornkamm, "Kopernikus im Urteil der Reformatoren," *Archiv für Reformationsgeschichte* 40 (1943): 171–83, esp. p. 181. There is a translation of volume 1 of Elert's work by Walter A. Hanson: *The Structure of Lutheranism* (St. Louis: Concordia Publishing House, 1962). Prowe intended a third volume, in which he would furnish evidence that Rheticus and Reinhold were obliged, in the course of their teaching duties at Wittenberg, to abide by the Ptolemaic astronomy; further, that Rheticus moved from the university to escape the conflict between

duty and conviction, and that Reinhold continued to edit work based on the older system so as not to deprive himself of a source of income (*Coppernicus*, 1,2:280; cf. 1,2:232 n. and 2:395 n.). Unfortunately, this third volume seems never to have been completed.

12. The relationships between Lutheranism and Copernicanism are discussed by Elert (*Morphologie des Luthertums*, 1:370–74) and Bornkamm ("Kopernikus im Urteil der Reformatoren," pp. 180–81). A substantial new study was occasioned in 1973 by the Copernicus celebrations: Robert S. Westman, "The Wittenberg Interpretation of the Copernican Theory," in *The Nature of Scientific Discovery: A Symposium Commemorating the 500th Anniversary of the Birth of Nicholaus Copernicus*, ed. Owen Gingerich (Washington, D.C.: Smithsonian Institution Press, 1975), pp. 393–429; see also the report of the subsequent discussion, ibid., pp. 430–57. Other additions to the literature include Hans Blumenberg, *Die kopernikanische Wende* (Frankfurt am Main: Suhrkamp Verlag, 1965), pp. 100–121; John Warwick Montgomery, "Luther and Science," in Montgomery, *In Defense of Martin Luther: Essays* (Milwaukee, Wis.: Northwestern Publishing House, 1970), pp. 87–113; J. R. Christianson, "Copernicus and the Lutherans," *Sixteenth Century Journal* 4, no. 2 (1973): 1–10; William John Hausmann, *Science and the Bible in Lutheran Theology: From Luther to the Missouri Synod* (Washington, D.C.: University Press of America, 1978).

13. It has been suggested that Michel Varro, a pupil of Jean Tagaut at Geneva, anticipated the discoveries of Galileo, Kepler, and Newton. This seems to indicate at least a certain openness to astronomical novelties at Calvin's Academy. See Charles Bourgeaud, *L'Académie de Calvin 1559–1798: Histoire de l'Université de Genève*, vol. 1 (Geneva: Georg and Company, Libraires de l'Université, 1900), p. 67.

14. See, for example, S[tephen] F. Mason, *Main Currents of Scientific Thought: A History of the Sciences*, Life of Science Library, no. 32 (New York: Henry Schuman, 1953), chap. 16. Mason's book was published the same year in England, with the title and subtitle in the reverse order, by Routledge and Kegan Paul. His guides include the seminal studies of Candolle and Merton, who believed it possible to show, on the basis of the membership lists of scientific societies, that a disproportionately large number of leading scientists in France and England were Protestant by religious persuasion. See Alphonse de Candolle, *Histoire des sciences et des savants depuis deux siècles*, 2d ed. (Geneva: H. Georg, 1885); Robert K. Merton, "Science, Technology and Society in Seventeenth Century England," *Osiris* 4 (1938): 360–632. Mason refers to the first edition of Candolle (1873). The special role of the Calvinists is corroborated, so Mason argues (p. 141), by the fact that in Lutheran Germany no scientist of the caliber of Johannes Kepler appeared again until the nineteenth century.

15. W. F. Dankbaar, "De verhouding van Calvinisme en wetenschap in de 16de eeuw, bepaaldelijk aan de Leidsche Universiteit," *Vox Theologica* 15 (1944): 121–28; Abraham Kuyper, *Calvinism* (Edinburgh: T. and T. Clark [1899]), pp. 143–88.

16. "Voor de opkomst der wetenschap ... heeft het Calvinisme geen specifieke beteekenis gehad." So Johan Huizinga concluded; quoted by Dankbaar, "Calvin-

isme en wetenschap," pp. 121–22. Westfall thinks there really was an affinity between Calvinism and the scientific world view, yet finds the alleged influence of
Protestantism on natural science "nebulous." Richard S. Westfall, *Science and
Religion in Seventeenth-Century England* (New Haven, Conn.: Yale University
Press, 1958), pp. 5–7. Others have sought the religious condition for the rise of
modern science not in specifically Calvinist but still in distinctively Christian,
rather than Hellenic, ways of thinking about nature. See, for instance, the pioneer
essays of M. B. Foster, "The Christian doctrine of Creation and the Rise of Modern Natural Science," *Mind,* n.s., 43 (1934): 446–68; "Christian Theology and
Modern Science of Nature," ibid., 44 (1935): 439–66, 45 (1936): 1–27. A refinement of the creation argument is to be found in Eugene M. Klaaren, *Religious Origins of Modern Science: Belief in Creation in Seventeenth-Century
Thought* (Grand Rapids, Mich.: William B. Eerdmans, 1977), who distinguishes
three doctrines of creation and in so doing takes up another strand in the recent
literature: interest in the voluntaristic patterns of late medieval (nominalist)
thought. Heiko A. Oberman relates nominalism and scientific method in an
interesting essay, "Reformation and Revolution: Copernicus' Discovery in an
Era of Change," in *The Nature of Scientific Discovery,* ed. Gingerich, pp. 134–
69; see pp. 147–53. The creation argument is modified in Jaki's view that natural
theology and the scientific enterprise have a common presupposition in "moderate realism." Stanley L. Jaki, *The Road of Science and the Ways to God* (Chicago: University of Chicago Press, 1978). Without pretending that this exhausts
the possibilities (or the roster of their respective champions), we may mention,
finally, that there are of course those who prefer a frankly "secular" sociology
of natural science: Feuer's thesis, for example, is that the scientific intellectual
was born from the "hedonist-libertarian spirit." Lewis S. Feuer, *The Scientific
Intellectual: The Psychological and Sociological Origins of Modern Science* (New
York: Basic Books, 1963). In short, the significance of Calvinism for the emergence of modern science continues to awaken historical curiosity, and it is worth
exploring the alleged nature of the link between them; but alternative accounts
of the birth of science are plentiful.

17. An outline of Weber's thesis and the subsequent debate is offered in my
essay, "Capitalism and the Decline of Religion," *McCormick Quarterly* 18
(1965): 12–19. The titles of both this and the present essay are deliberately suggestive of R. H. Tawney's *Religion and the Rise of Capitalism* (New York: Har-
court, Brace, 1926).

18. See Mason, *Scientific Thought,* pp. 138–40. Mason himself does not
allude here to Weber's researches on the relation between Protestantism and capitalism. But Weber's influence on sociological interpretations of the rise of
modern science is plain, and it extends to the literature on technology as well:
see, for instance, Friedrich Klemm, *A History of Western Technology,* trans.
Dorothea Waley Singer (London: Allen and Unwin, 1959), pp. 171, 191–97.

19. *Scientific Thought,* pp. 138–39. This is a point that Mason makes of Protestantism generally, not of Calvinism alone. Whether the original Protestantism
of the sixteenth century was really so nonauthoritarian and individualist, is at
least debatable. See further chapter 5 above.

20. Dankbaar "Calvinisme en wetenschap," pp. 123, 125, 128.

21. Choisy, *Calvin et la science,* p. 12. The significance of *gratia universalis* for the relations of Calvinism and science is also noted by Dankbaar ("Calvinisme en wetenschap," pp. 126–27) and Kuyper (*Calvinism,* pp. 159ff.), though both put the accent elsewhere.

22. Kuyper, *Calvinism,* pp. 146, 150–51. Mason attaches a similar significance to the doctrine of predestination, and he notes the agreement of Calvinist theology with natural science in their common rejection of the medieval celestial hierarchy of angelic beings (*Scientific Thought,* pp. 141–43). In a sense, the Reformed view of the relation between Creator and creature means a "disenchantment" of nature, as Torrance has argued, though without appealing to the doctrine of predestination. T. F. Torrance, "The Influence of Reformed Theology on the Development of Scientific Method," in *Theology in Reconstruction* (London: S.C.M. Press, 1965), pp. 62ff. But it seems to me an oddity in Torrance's argument that he refers to Francis Bacon as evidence for Reformed theology. The tenuousness of Kuyper's appeal to predestination may be illustrated from the curious fact, noticed by Hooykaas, that the argument appears to be reversible: according to C. E. Raven, Calvinistic predestinarianism militated *against* scientific studies. Raven thus "attributed the opposite effect to the same cause" (Hooykaas, *Religion and the Rise of Modern Science,* pp. 102–3).

23. Mason's quotation from the Puritan John Cotton (*Scientific Thought,* p. 140) hardly proves his main thesis. If anything, it would confirm Dankbaar's argument, since the reasons Cotton advances for interest in nature are (1) because the glory of God may be viewed in the created order and (2) because the understanding of nature (e.g., in medicine and economics) has utilitarian value for society.

24. "Calvinisme en wetenschap," p. 128.

25. Cf. the remarks of Auguste Lecerf on science as a Christian calling: "De l'Impulsion donnée par le calvinisme à l'étude des sciences physiques et naturelles," *Bulletin de la société de l'histoire du protestantisme français* 84 (1935): 192–205, esp. pp. 194–95. (The article appears, with the same pagination, also in *Études sur Calvin et le calvinisme* [Paris, 1935]). Lecerf rightly views Calvinism as more than a theological school; it became a *principe universal* (p. 193), a kind of *Weltanschauung,* and Lecerf himself was a leading exponent of a "Reformed philosophy." See also William Young, *Toward a Reformed Philosophy* (Grand Rapids, Mich.: Piet Hein Publishers, 1952), which discusses the philosophy of the Dutch Calvinists, particularly Dooyeweerd. What Calvin himself might have made of these attempts at a "Calvinist philosophy" is another question.

26. In what follows I have concentrated on the literature in English. A similar tradition in the German literature is traced by Elert (*Morphologie des Luthertums,* 1:367, n. 1), who mentions Franz Beckmann, Franz Hipler, Adolf Müller, J. H. von Mädler, R. Wolff, L. Lohmeyer. He finds that even Prowe has not entirely escaped the influence of Beckmann and Hipler. Bornkamm, "Kopernikus im Urteil der Reformatoren," is mainly concerned with the more recent work of Ernst Zinner.

27. See, e.g., Wolf, *History of Science,* p. 25, and the references cited in n. 28 below. In providing these references, I am only concerned to support the claim that a particular "tradition" has been disseminated in the secondary literature—in works ranging from rationalist propaganda to important monographs in the history of science. Frequently, allusions to the Reformers are only incidental; some historians of science display little or no interest in the relations of the Reformers and Copernicanism. See, e.g., A. R. Hall, *The Scientific Revolution, 1500–1800: The Formation of the Modern Scientific Attitude* (London: Longmans, Green, 1954).

28. John William Draper, *History of the Conflict between Religion and Science* (1874; new ed., issued by the Secular Society, London: Pioneer Press, 1923), pp. 214–15; White, *Warfare of Science with Theology,* 1:26, 97, 126–27, 212–14, 2:176–77; Bertrand Russell, *Religion and Science,* The Home University Library (London: Thornton Butterworth, 1935), pp. 22–23; Kuhn, *Copernican Revolution,* pp. 191ff.; Stimson, *Copernican Theology,* pp. 39–41, 48, 99ff.; Marie Boas Hall, *The Scientific Renaissance, 1450–1630,* The Rise of Modern Science, vol. 2 (New York: Harper and Brothers, 1962), p. 126; Herbert Butterfield, *The Origins of Modern Science, 1300–1800* (London: G. Bell and Sons, 1958), pp. 55–56; Mason, *Scientific Thought,* p. 141. Mason (pp. 147–48) shows how the Puritan John Wilkins evaded the clash of science and Scripture, but he does not seem to be aware that Wilkins's exegesis was anticipated by the Reformers themselves.

29. See, e.g., White's remark that the Reformers "turned their faces away from scientific investigation" (*Warfare of Science with Theology,* 1:213–14). The drastic statement attributed to Delaunay in the English version of Taton's *History of Science,* that "Calvin denounced science as nothing but 'impudent curiosity and impertinence'" (2:170), turns out to be an over-enthusiastic translation of the original (see p. 178 of the French). Delaunay actually said that Calvin denounced the impudence and audacity of it (sc., science)—a sufficiently prejudiced selection of evidence, which needed no further embellishment. Even Merton supposed that "Calvin himself deprecated science" and "frowned upon the acceptance of numerous scientific discoveries of his day," and he found it paradoxical that the religious ethic stemming from Calvin should have inspired the pursuit of natural science ("Science, Technology and Society," p. 417, n. 6, p. 459).

30. According to Kuhn, "Protestant leaders like Luther, Calvin and Melanchthon led in citing Scripture against Copernicus and in urging the repression of Copernicans." The Protestants "provided the first effective institutionalized opposition" (*Copernican Revolution,* p. 196).

31. Ibid. The Protestants, according to Kuhn, lacked the "police apparatus" available to Rome. Cf. White, *Warfare of Science with Theology,* 1:126; Russell, *Religion and Science,* pp. 42–43; Stimson, *Copernican Theory,* pp. 99 and 104; William Cecil Dampier, *A Shorter History of Science* (Cambridge: At the University Press, 1944), p. 49 (Calvin was as bad as any Roman inquisitor, but he lacked comparable power).

32. Since it is sometimes supposed that Kepler was persecuted by the Lutherans as Galileo was by Rome, it is worth noting that he was held unacceptable as a teacher in his native Württemberg, not because of his astronomical views, but because he doubted the ubiquity of Christ's body. See Elert (*Morphologie des Luthertums*, 1:375-78), who also alludes to Kepler's efforts at reconciling his astronomy and his faith. As Elert mentions, the thought of invoking the power of the authorities against the upstart astronomer seems at least to have occurred to Melanchthon (ibid., pp. 368-69, n. 1). But the thought, expressed in an item of private correspondence, was not implemented. See Melanchthon to Burkard Mithobius, 16 October 1541, C.R. 4:679 (no. 2391).

33. W. A. Tr. 4.412.32ff. (no. 4638); translation mine (cf. L. W. 54:358-59).

34. W. A. Tr. 1.419.16ff. (no. 855): "Der Narr will die ganze Kunst Astronomiae umkehren." It is this version which is quoted by White, Stimson, Kuhn, Russell, and Boas Hall. See also A. C. Crombie, *Medieval and Early Modern Science*, vol. 2: *Science in the Later Middle Ages and Early Modern Times, XIII-XVII Centuries* (New York: Doubleday, 1959), p. 168; this volume is a revision of Crombie's *Augustine to Galileo: The History of Science A.D. 400-1650* (London, 1952), chaps. 5-6.

35. Anton Lauterbach's version represents the original transcript, Aurifaber's a later revision, though it was an edited version of Aurifaber that was printed first (1566). So Bornkamm, "Kopernikus im Urteil der Reformatoren," p. 173. Cf. also Elert, *Morphologie des Luthertums*, 1:372; John Dillenberger, *Protestant Thought and Natural Science*, pp. 37-38.

36. Norlind, "Copernicus and Luther," pp. 275-76. Heinrich Meyer rightly responded that "Er muss ihm etwas Eigens machen" is nothing more than a "sneer." Meyer, "More on Copernicus and Luther," *Isis* 45 (1954):99.

37. Cf. Bornkamm, "Kopernikus im Urteil der Reformatoren," p. 173.

38. See his *Initia doctrinae physicae* (1549), C. R. 13:216-17. Cf. Elert, *Morphologie des Luthertums* 1:367-68; Dillenberger, *Protestant Thought and Natural Science*, pp. 39-41.

39. *Initia doctrinae physicae*, C. R. 13:217-19. "Es sind die alten ptolemäischen Argumente, aber vor allem auch weithin dieselben Gründe, mit denen die alexandrinischen Jünger des Aristoteles den antiken Vorgänger des Kopernikus Aristarch von Samos, widerlegt hatten" (Bornkamm, "Kopernikus im Urteil der Reformatoren," p. 179).

40. Melanchthon's support of Rheticus has already been noted. It should be added that he was equally generous in his friendship for Reinhold. He commended the *Tabulae Prutenicae*, and he composed an address for Reinhold to read in honor of Caspar Cruciger. The address speaks of Copernicus with frank admiration. See Elert, *Morphologie des Luthertums*, 1:370-71, 372-74. Bornkamm notes other passages in which Melanchthon gave expression to his respect for Copernicus ("Kopernikus im Urteil der Reformatoren," p. 180).

41. Bornkamm ("Kopernikus im Urteil der Reformatoren," p. 180), in dependence upon Emil Wohlwill.

42. I have discussed elsewhere Luther's relationship to Aristotle and to philosophy in general. Gerrish, *Grace and Reason: A Study in the Theology of*

Luther (1962; reprint ed., Chicago: University of Chicago Press, 1979). Though Calvin may be said to have shared Luther's reservations about Aristotelian philosophy, it has often been pointed out that the Platonic tradition influenced him more positively. See Roy W. Battenhouse, "The Doctrine of Man in Calvin and in Renaissance Platonism," *Journal of the History of Ideas* 9 (1948): 447-71; Joseph C. McLelland, "Calvin and Philosophy," *Canadian Journal of Theology* 11 (1965): 42-53; Albert-Marie Schmidt, "La Doctrine de la science et la théologie calviniste au XVIe siècle," *Foi et vie* 36 (1935): 270-85, esp. p. 279.

43. Lecerf, for instance, apparently presumed that Calvin had no knowledge of Copernicus ("De l'Impulsion donnée par le calvinisme," pp. 193-94). But the notorious question attributed to Calvin does occasionally appear in Continental discussions, as is attested by Pierre Marcel's note, "Calvin et la science: Comment on fait l'histoire," *Revue réformée* 17, no. 4 (1966): 50-51. Having had no success in his request for the location of the saying in Calvin, Marcel insisted that Copernicus is in fact nowhere cited in the *Calvini opera* or *Supplementa Calviniana*, although, unlike Lecerf, he presumed that Calvin had read Copernicus and was familiar with his system.

44. *Warfare of Science With Theology*, 1:127. Psalm 93:1 reads: "The world is established; it shall never be moved" (RSV). Calvin's alleged question is repeated by Stimson (*Copernican Theory*, p. 41, n. 1); Kuhn, with express acknowledgment to A. D. White (*Copernican Revolution*, p. 192); Russell (*Religion and Science*, p. 23; also in his *History of Western Philosophy* [London: George Allen and Unwin, 1946], p. 550).

45. Frederic William Farrar, *History of Interpretation* (London: Macmillan, 1886), p. xviii. See Edward Rosen, "Calvin's Attitude toward Copernicus," *Journal of the History of Ideas* 21 (1960): 431-41.

46. Rosen, "Calvin's Attitude toward Copernicus," p. 441. Dillenberger had already written of the alleged Calvin quotation, as given by White: "I have been unable to find the passage in Calvin and doubt that it exists" (*Protestant Thought and Natural Science*, p. 38, n. 33). More recently, Hooykaas has claimed, without reference to Rosen: "For fifteen years, I have pointed out in several periodicals concerned with the history of science that the 'quotation' from Calvin is imaginary and that Calvin never mentioned Copernicus; but the legend dies hard" (*Religion and the Rise of Modern Science*, p. 121). The reference to Rosen's article by Marie Boas Hall (*Scientific Renaissance*, p. 357, n. 31) gives cause to hope that his conclusions will gradually be appropriated in the textbooks. That White's influence nonetheless persists is suggested by the fact that Hall still attributes biblical literalism to Calvin and refers to White for the usual Melanchthon quotation (p. 126).

47. Long before Rosen's article appeared, Breen had written that Calvin's "only possible reference to Copernicus" occurs in his commentary on Psalm 46, "where he appears to criticize the new astronomy" (*John Calvin*, p. 155); and subsequent discussions of the article have confirmed Rosen's conclusion that White's alleged Calvin saying was spurious and that Calvin in fact never mentioned Copernicus by name. But it has been argued (Ratner) that Calvin's silence about Copernicus does not prove he had never heard of him; and one Calvin pas-

sage unmistakably hostile to Copernican upstarts has been pointed out (Stauffer), although it neither names Copernicus nor refutes him by citing Scripture (Serm. 1 Cor. 10:19-24, C.O. 49:677). See Joseph Ratner, "Some Comments on Rosen's 'Calvin's Attitude Toward Copernicus,'" *Journal of the History of Ideas 22* (1961):382-85; Edward Rosen, "A Reply to Dr. Ratner," ibid., 386-88; Richard Stauffer, "Calvin et Copernic," *Revue de l'histoire des religions* 179 (1971): 31-40; Edward Rosen, "Calvin n'a pas lu Copernic," ibid., 182 (1972): 183-85. See also n. 43 above.

48. *Conflict between Religion and Science,* p. 215. Cf. White: "At the Reformation the vast authority of Luther was thrown in favor of the literal acceptance of Scripture as the main source of natural science" (*Warfare of Science with Theology,* 1:26). On occasion, White notes a more critical attitude to Scripture on Luther's part, whom he considers (despite everything!) to have been characterized by "strong good sense" (ibid., 2:305). The remarks of White and Draper on the Reformation use of the Bible are so plainly out of date that one would ignore them, were they not so widely disseminated in nonspecialist literature. See further chapter 3 above.

49. *Warfare of Science with Theology,* p. 214.

50. See Luther's postil on the Gospel for Epiphany (Matt. 2:1-12): *Kirchenpostille* (1522), W. A. $10^{1,1}$. 555-728, esp. pp. 565-74; L. W. 52:159-286, esp. pp. 164-70. The quotation (a proverbial saying) appears at W.A. $10^{1,1}$. 566.13; L. W. 52:164-65. "Experience," in Luther's parlance, has other meanings besides sense experience. Sometimes it refers to the inward appropriation of spiritual truth (e.g., W. A. Tr. 1.340.29f. [no. 701]; W. A. Tr. 3.363.4 [no. 3503]). But in the postil for Epiphany he clearly has in mind an exercise of the intelligence which is tied to observation.

51. "Philosophia versatur circa cognoscibilia ratione humana. Theologia versatur circa credibilia, id est, quae fide apprehenduntur." Luther, *Disputatio de sententia: "Verbum caro facta est* [John 1:14]" (1539), W. A. $39^{2}.6.26$f.; L. W. 38:262.

52. W. A. Tr. 2.457.28ff. (no. 2413). That the actual terms "astronomy" and "astrology" were not always so sharply distinguished by Luther is clear in the passage from the *Tischreden* cited on p. 168 above. In another "table talk" Luther suggested that the benefits Melanchthon derived from astrology he himself found in a strong draught of beer (W. A. Tr. 1.7.9 [no. 17]).

53. W. A. Tr. 4.668.22 (no. 5113).

54. W. A. Tr. 1.573.31 ff. (no. 1160).

55. See esp. the *Disputatio de homine* (1536), W. A. 39^{1}. 175-80; L. W. 34:137-44. As the organ of man's dominion, reason is inventress and mistress of all the sciences (theses 4-8). She remains queen of the earth even after the fall (thesis 9).

56. "Quare credo Mosen locutum esse ad captum nostrum, quia nobis ita videatur" (W. A. Tr. 5.34.15 f. [no. 5259]). This is the thought that Calvin developed in his theory of accommodation (see section IV below). Hence I do not find the difference between them that Oberman suggests ("Reformation and Revolution," pp. 139, 141).

57. *In primum librum Mose enarrationes* (1535–45), W. A. 42.31. 8ff.; L. W. 1:41 (on Gen. 1:14).

58. Sometimes, according to Luther, the visible sign is in contradiction to the grace of God, whose Yes is hidden in a No. But this opens up the question of Luther's *theologia crucis*, which cannot be discussed here even though it is of some importance for his understanding of nature. See, for example, Walther von Loewenich, *Luthers theologia crucis*, 4th ed. (Munich: Chr. Kaiser Verlag, 1954). For further discussion on Luther's picture of nature, see Heinrich Bornkamm, *Luther's World of Thought*, trans. Martin H. Bertram (St. Louis, Mo.: Concordia Publishing House, 1958). Cf. Bornkamm's essay, "Faith and Reason in the Thought of Erasmus and Luther," in *Religion and Culture: Essays in Honor of Paul Tillich*, ed. Walter Leibrecht (New York: Harper and Brothers, 1959), pp. 133–39.

59. See Karl Heim, "Zur Geschichte des Satzes von der doppelten Wahrheit," *Studien zur systematischen Theologie: Theodor von Haering zum 70. Geburtstag von Fachgenossen dargebracht*, ed. Friedrich Traub (Tübingen: J. C. B. Mohr [Paul Siebeck], 1918), pp. 1–16; Bengt Hägglund, *Theologie und Philosophie bei Luther und in der occamistischen Tradition: Luthers Stellung zur Theorie von der doppelten Wahrheit*, Lunds Unversitets Årsskrift, n.s., division 1, vol. 51, no. 4 (Lund: G. W. K. Gleerup, 1955), pp. 87–102; Gerrish, *Grace and Reason*, pp. 49ff.

60. Cf. Étienne Gilson, *Reason and Revelation in the Middle Ages* (New York: Charles Scribner's Sons, 1954), p. 58.

61. Cf. Clement C. J. Webb on the Renaissance philosopher Pietro Pomponazzi (1464–1525), in his *Studies in the History of Natural Theology* (Oxford: The Clarendon Press, 1915), pp. 319ff. Apart from Pomponazzi, the theologian Robert Holcot (d. 1349) is most often singled out as an adherent of the double-truth theory.

62. W. A. 39^2. 3–5 (the forty-two theses), 6–30 (three different transcripts of the disputation), 30–33 (notes prepared against the theses by an unknown hand). For an English translation see L. W. 38:239–77. In my discussion I have not discriminated among the three transcripts.

63. "Etsi tenendum est, quod dicitur: Omne verum vero consonat, tamen idem non est verum in diversis professionibus" (thesis 1, W. A. 39^2.3.1). "Sapientia non pugnat sibi ipsi, hoc nos quoque dicimus" (ibid., 13.5).

64. "Contrarietas debet fieri et esse in eodem genere et in eadem propositione. Deus est homo. In philosophia est falsa, quod sit Deus et homo" (ibid., 16.11).

65. "Deus homo et Deus non homo sunt contraria non in eodem ordine" (ibid., 16.23). "Deus et homo sunt 2 propositiones, in philosophia falsum, in theologia verum. Si essent ambae in theologia, tum consisteret argumentum" (16.33). The second of the two quotations is not entirely clear, but the general drift of the argument is plain enough.

66. "Hic enim fit novum vocabulum significans personam divinam sustentantem nostram humanam, ut albus significat hominem sustentantem albedinem" (ibid., 10.30). The illustration seems to require the insertion after *humanam*, not of *personam*, but of some such word as *naturam*. One of the parallel transcripts

has the phrase *Deum sustentantem humanam creaturam* (10.10). Luther goes on to say that God is man by *communicatio idiomatum* (11.25, 12.4). Later, he adds: "Ego capio hominem dupliciter, uno modo pro substantia corporali per se subsistente, alio modo pro persona divina *sustentante humanitatem"* (17.4; italics mine).

67. Ibid., 10.3, 11.8.

68. "... sic ipsi Parisienses distinguunt, et tamen dicunt, idem esse verum in philosophia et theologia. Cur ergo distinguunt? Si esset idem, deberet etiam esse univocatio, idem verbum, eadem significatio. Nescientes ergo, quid dicant, tamen distinguunt a philosophia theologiam" (ibid., 11.30).

69. Ibid., 17.28.

70. Ibid., 17.32; cf. 11.15.

71. "Sunt diversa, non contraria" (ibid., 26.31).

72. "Sed ubiubi impingit vel forma syllogistica vel ratio philosophica, dicendum est ei illud Pauli: Mulier in Ecclesia taceat" (ibid., 4.19). In the course of the disputation Luther asserts and illustrates the point that the procedural rules of philosophy do not apply in theology. But his interest, I think, is really in what we should call "informal," rather than "formal," logic. He does not deny that dialectic is needed as the handmaid of theology (24.24). And yet syllogisms which would be valid in philosophy break down in theology because *proprietas verborum* is relative to a particular discourse. See 19.7 (on *proprietas),* 19.24 (not everything that follows in philosophy follows also in theology), and the various particular arguments on pp. 20ff. Even the threeness of Father, Son, and Spirit is not a simple arithemetical three: "Longe alia trinitas est in theologia, quam in mathematica accipitur" (22.23). Hence: "Mathematica est inimicissima omnino theologiae" (22.1). And the disputation comes back, in the end, to the starting point: "... hominem, carnem etc. fieri nova vocabula, quando referuntur ad Christum" (30.18).

73. See theses 30–32 (ibid., 5.15–20). Luther uses these examples to illustrate the principle that the same thing is not true in all the sciences (theses 29, 36, 38). But it is clear that the principle is really a matter of meaning.

74. "Quanto minus potest idem esse verum in philosophia et theologia, quarum distinctio in infinitum maior est, quam artium et operum" (thesis 39). Cf. also theses 40 and 41.

75. For further discussion see my *Grace and Reason,* p. 21 (on the proposition "Fallen man can do no good"), pp. 72ff. (on the scholastic formula *facere quod in se est),* p. 96 (on the term *habitus),* and p. 112 (on *iustitia).* In a valuable article on Robert Holcot, Oberman has discussed Luther's rejection of the Nominalist doctrine *facere quod in se est.* Heiko A. Oberman, "Facientibus quod in se est Deus non denegat gratiam: Robert Holcot, O. P., and the Beginnings of Luther's Theology," *Harvard Theological Review* 55 (1962): 317–42. Strictly speaking, however, Luther never rejected the formula itself but transferred it to the *regnum mundi.* See, for instance, W. A. 44.87.23; L. W. 6:117 (on Gen. 32:13–15).

76. *Promotionsdisputation von Palladius und Tilemann* (1537), W. A. 39[1]. 232.13. This disputation is concerned, in part, with the same problem of "double truth."

77. "Fides non est regulis seu verbis philosophiae adstricta aut subiecta, sed est inde libera. Et sicut Deus multas sphaeras in coelo creavit, ita etiam in his facultatibus distinctae sunt" (W. A. 39^2.7.36). "Nam ut Deus condidit sphaeras distinctas in coelo, sic et in terra regna, ut unaquaeque res et ars suum locum et speciem retineat necque versetur extra suum centrum, in quo positum est" (ibid., 8.5). Elsewhere, Luther makes it a general "principle" that the sciences are both independent in their terminologies and yet interdependent in their utility (W. A. 42.36.11; L. W. 1:48, [on Gen. 1:14]).

78. I do not see, for instance, in what sense Calvin could have valued philosophy as the "natural foundation of supernatural knowledge" (Dankbaar, "Calvinisme en wetenschap," p. 127).

79. *Inst.*, 1.5.1 (1.52–53). Cf. *Catechismus ecclesiae Genevensis* (1545), C. O. 6:15–16; O. S. 2:77. An English translation of the catechism is most readily accessible in J. K. S. Reid, trans. and ed., *Calvin: Theological Treatises*, Library of Christian Classics, vol. 22 (Philadelphia: Westminster Press, 1954), pp. 91–139; see p. 93.

80. *Inst.*, 1.6.2 (1:72), 14.20 (1:179).

81. *Inst.*, 1.5.8 (1:61); 2.6.1 (1:341); 1.6.1 (1:70).

82. *Inst.*, 1.5.2 (1:53). Presumably the scientist needs the light of the Word to make him aware of what he is doing.

83. *Inst.*, 1:14.21 (1:181).

84. *Inst.*, 2.2.14–16 (1:273–74), where all the arts and sciences are traced to what later Calvinism called *gratia universalis;* cf. *Inst.*, 1.5.5 (1:57). See further chapter 9 above.

85. Cf. Lecerf, "De l'Impulsion donnée par le Calvinisme," pp. 194–95.

86. Choisy, *Calvin et la science*, p. 18.

87. Breen, *John Calvin*, p. 155.

88. As Kuyper says, "Thus vanished every dread possibility, that he who occupied himself with nature, were wasting his capacities in pursuit of vain and idle things" (*Calvinism*, p. 158).

89. Cf. his *Avertissement contre l'astrologie qu'on appelle judiciaire* (1549), C. O. 7:509–44.

90. The most remarkable affirmation of this principle appears in Calvin's preface to Olivétan's New Testament: "Voila ce qu'il nous fault en somme cercher en toute l'Escriture. C'est de bien congnoistre Iesus Christ ... Mais fault que nostre entendement soit du tout arresté à ce poinct, d'apprendre en l'Escriture à congnoistre Iesus Christ tant seulement" (C. O. 9:815). For an English translation, see Joseph Haroutunian, trans. and ed., *Calvin: Commentaries*, Library of Christian Classics, vol. 23 (Philadelphia: Westminster Press, 1958), pp. 58–73, esp. p. 70.

91. See chapter 3 above.

92. "La Doctrine de la science," p. 271.

93. Quoted by Schmidt (ibid., p. 276). Daneau's major work, *Physica christiana*, was published at Geneva in 1576.

94. My quotations are from the sixteenth-century translation of *Physica christiana:* Lambertus Danaeus, *The Wonderfull Workmanship of the World, wherein is conteined an excellent discourse of Christian naturall Philosophie ... specially*

gathered out of the Fountaines of holy Scripture, trans. T[homas] T[wyne] (London: A Maunsell, 1578), pp. 2, 6, 8f.

95. For a general discussion of Calvin's views on revelation, see Ronald S. Wallace, *Calvin's Doctrine of the Word and Sacrament* (Edinburgh: Oliver and Boyd, 1953). There is a discussion of accommodation in Edward A. Dowey, Jr., *The Knowledge of God in Calvin's Theology* (New York: Columbia University Press, 1952), pp. 3-17. See also Ford Lewis Battles, "God Was Accommodating Himself to Human Capacity," *Interpretation* 31 (1977): 19-38, an article that goes a long way toward closing the lacuna to which I drew attention in the earlier version of this chapter. Battles also notes other recent work on accommodation in Calvin's writings.

96. Comm. Ps. 78:60, C. O. 31:741. Revelation is therefore indirect: Comm. Exod. 33:21, C. O. 25:111. For English translations, see *The Commentaries of John Calvin,* Eng. trans., 46 vols. (Edinburgh: Calvin Translation Society, 1843-55; reprint ed., Grand Rapids, Mich.: William B. Eerdmans, 1948-56).

97. Serm. Eph. 4:11-14, C. O. 51:565. Cf. *Inst.,* 4.1.5 (2:1018).

98. *Inst.,* 4.1.1 (2:1012), 14.3 (2:1278); Serm. Deut. 33:18-19, C. O. 29:168; Comm. Acts 7:40, C. O. 48:153.

99. Serm. Deut. 32:40, C. O. 29:70; Hom. 1 Sam. 2:27-30, C. O. 29:356; Comm. Is. 6:8, C. O. 36:134. In the last of these passages, *attemperat* is used rather than *accommodat.* In Prael. Amos 9:4, C. O. 43:161, it is said that Scripture speaks *humano more* of God as seeing or not seeing. See further *Inst.,* 1.17. 13 (1:227), 2.16.2 (1:504).

100. Comm. Heb. 1:3, C. O. 55:11-12. Cf. Calvin's view of the *communicatio idiomatum* as a figure of speech which uses language improperly but not without reason: *Inst.,* 2.14.2 (1:484).

101. Calvin frequently speaks of Scripture as (so to say) God's "prattle." "Dieu s'est fait quasi semblable à une nourrice, qui ne parlera point à un petit enfant selon qu'elle feroit à un homme... nostre Seigneur s'est ainsi familierement accommodé à nous" (Serm. Deut. 5:22, C. O. 26: 387-88). See also Hom. 1 Sam. 2:27-30, C. O. 29:356, and *Inst.,* 1.13.1 (1:121), where the Latin word used by Calvin for God's accommodated speech is *balbutire.*

102. Prael. Amos 9:13-15, C. O. 43:161 and 172; Prael. Jer. 31:12, C. O. 38:660, where the same notion is expressed without use of the term "accommodation."

103. "Haec est porro submittendi [ad captum nostrum] ratio, ut se talem nobis figuret, non qualis in se est, sed qualis a nobis sentitur" (*Inst.,* 1.17.13 [1:227]).

104. Rosen notes Calvin's view that the biblical writers sometimes adopted a popular style, but he does not relate this to the principle of accommodation ("Calvin's Attitude toward Copernicus," p. 441). Dillenberger makes much the same point (*Protestant Thought and Natural Science,* p. 32), and he does mention the relevance of accommodation (ibid., p. 38).

105. Comm. Gen. 1:5, C. O. 23:17; Gen. 2:8, C. O. 23:36; Gen. 2:10, C. O. 23:40, where Moses' topography is said to be accommodated. Not merely the language of the narrative, but even God's decision to create over a period of six

days is traced to his consideration for man's limited comprehension (Comm. Gen. 1:5, C. O. 23:18).

106. Comm. Gen. 1:14–16, C. O. 23:20–23, passim. Cf. Comm. Gen. 2:10, C. O. 23:40; Gen. 3:1, C. O. 23:53.

107. Comm. Gen., argument, C. O. 23:9–10. This religious purpose requires us to regard the heavenly bodies as signs, but not in the astrological sense (Comm. Gen. 1:14, C. O. 23:21).

108. Comm. Gen. 1:15–16, C. O. 23:21–23. Note especially the remark: "Nos enim potius respexit [Moses] quam sidera, ut theologum decebat" (col. 22). Cf. Comm. Gen. 2:10, C. O. 23:40. Luther, too, recognized that biblical language about the natural order may be *secundum visionem oculorum.* See his *Auslegung der 25 ersten Psalmen* (1530), W. A. 31^1.370.16 (on Ps. 24:2).

109. Comm. Gen 3:1, C. O. 23:53.

110. Comm. Gen. 1:16, C. O. 23:22.

111. Comm. Gen. 1:6, C. O. 23:18.

112. See, e.g., Comm. Gen., argument, C. O. 23:9–10: "Nos certe non ignoramus finitum esse caeli circuitum, et terram instar globuli in medio locatam esse." Calvin was non-Copernican because he was well informed! Occasionally, he qualifies the accepted views for nonbiblical reasons: see Comm. Gen. 1:15, C. O. 23:22.

113. Comm. Ps. 19:4–6, C. O. 31:198.

114. Comm. Ps. 136:7, C. O. 32:364–65.

115. Dillenberger's study is particularly valuable on this question (see *Protestant Thought and Natural Science,* chap. 2).

116. On Osiander's understanding of a scientific hypothesis, see Prowe, *Coppernicus,* 1,2:519–39; Rosen, *Three Copernican Treatises,* pp. 22–23. The text will be found in Prowe's second volume, pp. 13–14. Osiander is discussed also by Bornkamm, "Kopernikus im Urteil der Reformatoren," pp. 174–78; Dillenberger, *Protestant Thought and Natural Science,* pp. 41–47; Elert *Morphologie des Luthertums,* 1:369–70; Oberman, "Reformation and Revolution," pp. 143–47.

117. *Sermon von dem Sakrament des leibs und bluts Christi, widder die Schwarmgeister* (1526), W. A. 19.491.7, 26; L. W. 36:342. Cf. the Reformed *Consensus Tigurinus* (1549), art. 25; C. O. 7:743.

118. *Inst.,* 2.16.10 (1:516). Cf. Luther's remarks on the Christus Victor theme in *Von Jesu Christo: Eine Predigt* (1533), W. A. 37.63.23ff.

119. *Warfare of Science with Theology,* 1:133.

120. Dorothy Stimson notes this fact but does not do justice to its importance (*Copernican Theory,* p. 41). Lecerf, on the other hand, rightly insists that primitive Calvinism was geocentric for the same reason that modern Calvinism has been Newtonian or Einsteinian: because Reformed theologians have accepted current astronomical doctrines ("De l'Impulsion donnée par le calvinisme," p. 198). See also Dillenberger, *Protestant Thought and Natural Science,* p. 29; Edwin Arthur Burtt, *The Metaphysical Foundations of Modern Physical Science,* rev. ed. (Garden City, N.Y.: Doubleday, 1955), pp. 36ff.

121. Dillenberger, *Protestant Thought and Natural Science,* pp. 84, 88–89. For others who used the same solution to the conflict of Bible and science, see

ibid., 72, 101, 107-8, 129. Cf. Hooykaas, *Religion and the Rise of Modern Science,* pp. 122-123.

122. But not necessarily, of course, since the principle was so widely used outside of Reformed circles. Paul H. Kocher, in his study *Science and Religion in Elizabethan England* (San Marino, Calif.: Huntington Library, 1953), rightly points out that it had patristic antecedents and was common among Renaissance interpreters (pp. 38-39). An interesting comparison could be made between Calvin and Origen of Alexandria, who likewise thought that God uses baby talk and acts angry as we do to keep our children in order. With *Inst.,* 2.16.2 (1:504-5), for instance, compare the passages from Origen's homilies quoted by Jean Daniélou, *Origen,* trans. Walter Mitchell (New York: Sheed and Ward, 1955), pp. 280-82. In the article referred to above ("God Was Accommodating Himself"), Battles traces back the use of accommodation—beyond the church fathers—to classical rhetoric.

123. Cf. Pelikan's use of the expression "technical autonomy." Jaroslav Pelikan, *The Christian Intellectual,* Religious Perspectives, vol. 14 (New York: Harper and Row, 1965), p. 58.

124. See Bertrand Russell, *The Impact of Science on Society* (London: George Allen and Unwin, 1952), pp. 18ff. Newton himself, no doubt, would not have formulated the problem of science and religion in this way; for an account of the religious impulse behind his scientific quest, see Frank E. Manuel, *The Religion of Isaac Newton* (Oxford: The Clarendon Press, 1974). The implications of the new picture of nature as a closed causal system are explored in my *Tradition and the Modern World: Reformed Theology in the Nineteenth Century* (Chicago: University of Chicago Press, 1978), chap. 4.

Chapter Eleven

1. Friedrich Schleiermacher to Joachim Christian Gass, 29 December 1816, *Fr. Schleiermacher's Briefwechsel mit J. Chr. Gass,* ed. Wilhelm Gass (Berlin: Georg Reimer, 1852), p. 128. Gass had recently undertaken a course of lectures on scholastic theology. In an earlier letter to him, written from Halle 6 September 1805, Schleiermacher confessed that he had not read much theology at all (ibid., p. 29). When he finally wrote a theology of his own, his *Glaubenslehre* assigned to patristic citations only a polemical use against Roman Catholicism: see Gl. 27, postscript.

2. John Henry Newman, *An Essay on the Development of Christian Doctrine,* Image Books reprint of the 1878 edition (Garden City, New York: Doubleday, 1960), p. 35.

3. See Karl Barth, *Protestant Theology in the Nineteenth Century: Its Background and History,* Eng. trans. (Valley Forge: Judson Press, 1973), p. 425.

4. Ibid. The book referred to is Christian Lülmann, *Schleiermacher der Kirchenvater des 19. Jahrhunderts,* Sammlung gemeinverständlicher Vorträge und Schriften, no. 48 (Tübingen, 1907).

5. Barth, *Protestant Theology,* pp. 425-27.

6. Pertinent titles and their location in the *Sämmtliche Werke* can readily be identified in Terrence N. Tice, *Schleiermacher Bibliography with Brief Introductions, Annotations, and Index*, Princeton Pamphlets, no. 12 (Princeton, N.J.: Princeton Theological Seminary, 1966), pp. 9-10. The other doctrine to which Schleiermacher devoted special historical study, besides the Trinity, was election.

7. Hanna Jursch, *Schleiermacher als Kirchenhistoriker*, vol. 1: *Die Problemlage und die geschichtstheoretischen Grundlagen der Schleiermacherschen Kirchengeschichte* (Jena: Frommann [Walter Biedermann], 1933), p. 53.

8. "The Word of God and the Task of the Ministry" (1922), in Barth, *The Word of God and the Word of Man*, trans. Douglas Horton (1928; reprint ed., New York: Harper and Brothers, 1957), p. 195. The emphasis is Barth's.

9. *Geschichte der christlichen Kirche* (1840), ed. E. Bonnell, S. W. 1,11:14. Cf. Schleiermacher's *Kurze Darstellung des theologischen Studiums zum Behuf einleitender Vorlesungen*, 3d, critical ed., ed. Heinrich Scholz (1910; reprint ed., Darmstadt: Wissenschaftliche Buchgesellschaft, 1961), sec. 155; trans. Terrence N. Tice as *Brief Outline on the Study of Theology* (Richmond, Va.: John Knox Press, 1966).

10. *The Life of Schleiermacher as Unfolded in His Autobiography and Letters*, trans. Frederica Rowan, 2 vols. (London: Smith, Elder, 1860), 1:3.

11. Ibid., p. 4.

12. Ibid., p. 14.

13. "Einleitung in das Studium der Kirchengeschichte" (1806), S. W. 1,11: 623.

14. Schleiermacher to L. G. Blanc [1821], *Aus Schleiermacher's Leben: In Briefen*, ed. Ludwig Jonas and Wilhelm Dilthey, 4 vols. (Berlin: Georg Reimer, 1858-63), 4:280.

15. Bonnell, in S. W. 1,11:vii. Bonnell took a student notebook from the 1825-26 lectures as his initial basis and worked into it (1) a second notebook from the same years, (2) five student notebooks (including his own) from the earlier Berlin lectures of 1821-22, and (3) Schleiermacher's manuscripts, which consisted of loosely organized sheets and slips of paper that could not all have been actually used in the lecture room. In addition, Bonnell gave as Appendix A (pp. 623-31) the introduction to the Halle lectures (see n. 13 above) and as Appendix B (pp. 632-37) the "Aphorismen zur Kirchengeschichte" that Schleiermacher prepared in connection with the 1821-22 lectures.

16. Among the most important studies of Schleiermacher's philosophy of history are: Hermann Mulert, *Schleiermacher-Studien*, vol. 1: *Schleiermachers geschichtsphilosophische Ansichten in ihrer Bedeutung für seine Theologie*, Studien zur Geschichte des neueren Protestantismus, no. 3 (Giessen: Alfred Töpelmann [J. Ricker], 1907); Hermann Süskind, *Christentum und Geschichte bei Schleiermacher: Die geschichtsphilosophischen Grundlagen der Schleiermacherschen Theologie*, pt. 1: *Die Absolutheit des Christentums und die Religionsphilosophie* (Tübingen: J. C. B. Mohr [Paul Siebeck], 1911). In his preface (p. v) Süskind draws attention to the influence of Troeltsch on both his and Mulert's studies as well as on a third book, which I have not seen: the Strasbourg dissertation of Georg Wehrung (1907). Jursch (see n. 7 above) mentions, in addition, two unpublished dissertations that have not been available to me, by E. Bock and E.

Meister. Mulert, it should be noted, is reluctant to speak of a "philosophy of history" in Schleiermacher after his romantic period; but Mulert's usage reflects his inclination to take Hegelian speculation as the definitive form of a philosophy of history.

17. I am referring here to the study by Hanna Jursch, already cited (n. 7 above).

18. S. W. 1,11:622.

19. See the second excursus in Jursch, *Schleiermacher als Kirchenhistoriker,* 1:98–101, for Schleiermacher's reflections on the teaching of history.

20. S. W. 1,11:622. In the *Kurze Darstellung* Schleiermacher insists that the divisions of historical theology should be studied in chronological sequence (sec. 85). But this, naturally, does not contradict his procedure for determining the periods partly by reference to th present-day divisions of the church: see *Geschichte der christlichen Kirche,* S. W. 1,11:32.

21. S. W. 1,11:36, 612. Schleiermacher held that while any moment of historical significance can be regarded either as a new beginning or as a gradual development, the entire career of every historical totality will be viewed as the alternate dominance of one or other of these two aspects; and this gave him his distinction between "epochs" and "periods." In his parlance, epochs are those revolutionary passages of time which divide history into periods. He detected three such markers in the history of the church: ca. 300, ca. 800, and ca. 1500. From the wider perspective of the history of religion, of course, Christianity may itself be thought of as constituting a period. But *within* church history the three epochs yield four periods. Properly speaking, the Reformation was an epoch that inaugurated a new period: it was a relatively short time of revolutionary change, and as such it included a veritable *Karton* of issues. No further epoch, so defined, has occurred since, so that the period ushered in by the Reformation is still with us. See *Geschichte der christlichen Kirche,* S. W. 1,11: 31–36, 47, 612; *Kurze Darstellung,* secs. 71–93, 186, 212.

22. *Kurze Darstellung,* sec. 81. Schleiermacher did not draw what looks like the obvious inference: that knowledge of the remoter past must therefore be merely auxiliary to knowledge of the present. As far as the needs of church leadership are concerned, the two bodies of knowledge are "coordinate" to each other (ibid., sec. 82).

23. S. W. 1,11:37, 47. Naturally, he did not consider himself totally bound to silence once he had reached the year 1648. He alludes, for instance, to Neology (ibid., p. 612), Pietism (p. 617), and Methodism (p. 618). But for purposes of formal periodization the Peace of Westphalia is his *terminus ad quem,* and the fact that he did not reach it in the 1825–26 lectures is purely accidental.

24. S. W. 1,11:2; cf. *Kurze Darstellung,* secs. 69–70. Schleiermacher pictures the goal of history as the fulfillment of John 6:45 (cf. Isa. 54:13, Jer. 31:34, 1 Thess. 4:9, Heb. 8:11, 1 John 2:27): that is, as a diminution of the influence of outstanding leaders until "the religious autonomy of the individual" is attained (S.W. 1,11:25). It should be noted that, for Schleiermacher, the progress of the Kingdom of God is made strictly according to immanent laws of history; rigorously excluded is any of the traditional interventionism ("supernaturalism,"

as Troeltsch would say) that makes some theological interpretations of history unacceptable to the modern historian. Schleiermacher rules out supernaturalistic explanations on principle—for dogmatic, not merely historical, reasons. See B. A. Gerrish, *Tradition and the Modern World: Reformed Theology in the Nineteenth Century* (Chicago: University of Chicago Press, 1978), chap. 4.

25. S. W. 1,11:5–9. The theological character of Schleiermacher's own standpoint is clear from the fact that he refers to his dogmatics (ibid., p. 10).

26. Ibid., pp. 2–6; cf. pp. 623–24 (from the "Einleitung" of 1806). See also Mulert, *Schleiermachers geschichtsphilosophische Ansichten*, pp. 26–29.

27. S. W. 1,11:11; cf. ibid., pp. 13–14, 24.

28. Ibid., p. 15; cf. p. 37. The presupposition that through the appearance of Christ a new principle has come into humanity is what justifies a separate history of Christianity (p. 17; cf. pp. 633–34 ["Aphorismen"] and *Kurze Darstellung*, secs. 78–80). Strictly speaking, however, *church* history begins only after the departure of Christ (S. W. 1,11:17; cf. Gl. 122).

29. S. W. 1,11:15–16. The organic language is here qualified by a distinction between natural production, in which the spirit forms the body, and historical production, in which the spirit penetrates an already existent body. At this point the introduction to Schleiermacher's church history should be compared with his remarks on "a biography that wishes to be a history" in his life of Jesus: *Das Leben Jesu: Vorlesungen an der Universität zu Berlin im Jahr 1832 gehalten*, ed. K. A. Rütenik, S. W. 1,6:3. In the *Kurze Darstellung*, too, Schleiermacher resorts to an expressly vitalistic analogy: he speaks of the underlying unity of a historical development *(das Innere)* as the "spirit" or "soul," and the congeries of events (das *Äussere*) as its changing "body." Historical understanding, as distinct from mere chronicle, is precisely the apprehension of the individual moments as the changing of something that nonetheless remains identical (*Kurze Darstellung*, secs. 150–53). Further on in the same work he describes Christianity as a "new effective principle," whose vital force is conveyed in the two basic "functions" of doctrine and life (secs. 161–62, 166), life being then subdivided into worship and morality (secs. 168–71).

30. See Jursch, *Schleiermacher als Kirchenhistoriker*, 1:4–8, 53–54 n., 92–97; Wilhelm Pauck, "Schleiermacher's Conception of History and Church History," in Robert W. Funk, ed., *Schleiermacher as Contemporary*, Journal for Theology and Church, vol. 7 (New York: Herder and Herder, 1970), pp. 41–56, esp. pp. 41–43.

31. I do not, of course, wish to imply either that these two are his *only* categories of historical interpretation or that they are *uniquely* romantic. The literature already cited (nn. 7 and 16 above) explores his conceptual apparatus more extensively, and at least one recent study cautions against regarding individuality and development as discoveries of the romantics: Peter Hanns Reill, *The German Enlightenment and the Rise of Historicism* (Berkeley and Los Angeles: University of California Press, 1975); see esp. pp. 214–15.

32. *Friedrich Schleiermacher's Reden über die Religion*, critical ed. by G. Ch. Bernhard Pünjer (Brunswick: C. A. Schwetschke and Son [M. Bruhn], 1879), pp. 241–43, 247–49, 257–59. For an English version see *On Religion: Speeches*

to Its Cultured Despisers, trans. from the 3d ed. by John Oman (1894; reprint ed., New York: Harper and Row, 1958), pp. 213–14, 217–18, 224. Hereafter, page references to Oman's translation are given in parentheses.

33. *Reden,* pp. 256–57 (p. 223); translation Oman's.

34. Ibid., pp. 60 (2d ed.), 125–30 (pp. 49–50, 96–98). Value judgments on religious types are present also when Schleiermacher discusses the ways in which the religious sense is awakened: ibid., pp. 79–114, 169–72 (pp. 63–87, 137–39).

35. Ibid., pp. 275–78 (pp. 238–41).

36. Ibid., p. 275 (p. 238); translation Oman's.

37. Ibid., pp. 283–89 (pp. 246–51). In this section of the fifth speech Jesus is designated "author of the noblest that there has yet been in religion." But it is denied that he ever claimed to be the only mediator, although (as Schleiermacher added in the second edition) he "has become historically the centre of all mediation." Further, it is predicted that Christianity "will yet have a long history." Schleiermacher's point seems to be that Christianity's end will come when no mediator is needed any more, and this is an event that lies beyond history (cf. 1 Cor. 15:28).

38. *Reden,* p. 289 (p. 251). Hermann Süskind, who was eager to find in Schleiermacher the prototype of Troeltsch's philosophical argument for the supremacy of Christianity, made the interesting suggestion that the Christianity of the *Speeches* could be considered at least formally unsurpassable: it possesses, for instance, a double universality, since it pervades all of history and every moment of a person's existence. Süskind, *Christentum und Geschichte,* p. 25; cf. the remarks on Christianity's capacity for self-criticism (ibid., pp. 25–26). Other scholars have been intrigued by Schleiermacher's unexplicated claim that "religion is nowhere so fully idealized *[idealisirt]* as in Christianity": *Reden,* p. 280 (p. 243).

39. The phrase is Süskind's: *Christentum und Geschichte,* p. 101. His discussion of the problem of Christianity and other religions in Schleiermacher is still the best, albeit his interpretation is complicated by over-eagerness to show what Schleiermacher *should* and (given his philosophy of history) *could* have offered: a rational proof for ranking Christianity highest on the scale of mankind's religions. For Schleiermacher's own reflections in the second edition of the *Glaubenslehre,* see Gl. 7–11.

40. "Über den eigenthümlichen Wert und das bindende Ansehen symbolischer Bücher," K. S. 2:162. Similar remarks are made elsewhere by Schleiermacher on the Augsburg Confession in particular: "An die Herren D. D. D. von Cölln und D. Schulz: Ein Sendschreiben" (1831), K. S. 2:230; *Gespräch zweier selbst überlegender evangelischer Christen über die Schrift LUTHER IN BEZUG AUF DIE NEUE PREUSSISCHE AGENDE: Ein letztes Wort oder ein erstes* (1827), S. W. 1,5:616–17 (where the issue concerns the attitude of the Reformed toward the Augsburg Confession).

41. K. S. 2:164.

42. *Predigten in Bezug auf die Feier der Übergabe der Augsburgischen Konfession 1830* (1831), K. S. 3:28. This is not to question Schleiermacher's ability to elucidate the main point—faith in Christ—with remarkable insight and eloquence, falling readily, as Calvin did, into eucharistic imagery (see, e.g., ibid.,

p. 56). Holding fast to living faith in the Redeemer is what he understood as the true spirit of the confession (pp. 28–29), the life in the letter (pp. 36–37), and the actual bond of unity even though a bond that admitted a variety of expressions (pp. 20, 23–24, 31, 33–34).

43. S. W. 1,11:582. For the treatment of the Augsburg Confession in the lectures on church history, see ibid., pp. 588–91.

44. *Reden*, pp. 301, 302 (pp. 268, 269).

45. The "propositions" *(Leitsätze)* of the first and second versions are given parallel to each other in Redeker's critical edition, 2:497–563; see esp. p. 506.

46. Ibid., 1:137 (=Gl. 24.1).

47. *Die christliche Sitte nach den Grundsätzen der evangelischen Kirche im Zusammenhange dargestellt* (1884), ed. L. Jonas, S. W. 1,12:212.

48. Gl. 24.1 (pp. 103–4); cf. 24.3 (p. 105).

49. One brief comment is in order: Schleiermacher's elucidation of proposition 24 of the *Glaubenslehre* (2d ed.) seems to indicate that what, for him, was actually at stake was two different concepts of the church. In the one concept the church is the instrument of Christ's efficacy; in the other his efficacy is transferred to the church (Gl. 24.3–4 [pp. 106–7]).

50. S. W. 1,11:45. The grammatical inconsequence is in the original. It does not conceal Schleiermacher's meaning, but it does attest to the rough character of the text.

51. Ibid., pp. 45–46; cf. pp. 575–76.

52. For further discussion of Schleiermacher's thoughts on the division of the Western church, see: Klaus Penzel, "A Chapter in the History of the Ecumenical Quest: Schelling and Schleiermacher," *Church History* 33 (1964):322–37; Hans-Joachim Birkner, "Deutung und Kritik des Katholizismus bei Schleiermacher und Hegel," in Hans-Joachim Birkner, Heinz Liebing, and Klaus Scholder, *Das konfessionelle Problem in der evangelischen Theologie des 19. Jahrhunderts,* Sammlung gemeinverständlicher Vorträge und Schriften aus dem Gebiet der Theologie und Religionsgeschichte, no. 245–46 (Tübingen: J. C. B. Mohr [Paul Siebeck], 1966), pp. 7–20. Both of these studies point out that Schleiermacher saw the opposition between Roman Catholic and Protestant also in ethnic terms: that is, as a contrast between the Romance and the Germanic peoples.

53. *An Herrn Oberhofprediger Dr. Ammon über seine Prüfung der Harmsischen Sätze* (1818), S.W. 1,5:340. It should be noted that Ammon softened the harshness of Harms's claim by suggesting that the better elements in all three communions were united in spirit.

54. Ibid., pp. 343–44; quotation on p. 343.

55. Ibid., p. 341. A school difference is a difference in doctrine that is not traceable to a divergence in the religious affections themselves, but only in the way they are represented; consequently, it leads to no corresponding practical divergence either in morals or in polity (the two branches of Christian life). See Gl. 24, postscript (pp. 107–8), where the English "an academic matter" translates the German *Sache der Schule.*

56. *An Ammon,* S. W. 1,5:369; cf. pp. 381–82 and p. 402. In the last of these three passages Schleiermacher maintains that within each church there are greater differences than those which divide the churches from each other. He liked

to hold up the eucharistic policy of the *Brüdergemeine* as a pattern to be followed (ibid., pp. 369–70), since there altar fellowship among Lutherans and Reformed had already been established. He found it significant, too, that divergent views of election had appeared in both branches of the evangelical church without disturbing eucharistic fellowship (pp. 379–80). See further Martin Stiewe, *Das Unionsverständnis Friedrich Schleiermachers: Der Protestantismus als Konfession in der Glaubenslehre* (Witten: Luther-Verlag, 1969).

57. *An Ammon*, S. W. 1,5:384–85.

58. Ibid., pp. 388–89. Cf. *Zugabe zu meinem Schreiben an Herrn Ammon*, S. W. 1,5:415.

59. K. S. 2:143–44, 159–60.

60. Ibid., pp. 160–62. This estimate of the confession does in fact closely resemble Schleiermacher's notion of the New Testament canon: see *Kurze Darstellung*, secs. 83, 103. In his church history he warns against the delusion that the essence of the religious impulse can be adequately and authentically displayed in the letter of doctrine, but he does not there make it so clear as elsewhere that he also rejected the opposite view of the rationalists (S. W. 1,11:615).

61. See further chap. 15, pp. 254–58, below.

62. "An von Cölln und Schulz," K. S. 2:230, 253.

63. Ibid., pp. 229, 237–38.

64. Ibid., pp. 238, 245–46; quotation on p. 238. My interest here is only in the significance attributed by Schleiermacher to the Reformation symbols, especially the Augsburg Confession. It is not part of my design to consider his views on confessions in general, to which he assigned little more than the function of marking a religious community's legal and political boundaries. This was one reason why, in opposition to von Cölln and Schulz, he denied the need for a new confession of faith—unless a split in the evangelical church made one necessary for purposes of identification. See ibid., pp. 249–50.

65. Luther is called *der Glaubensheld* in, for instance, the passage cited in n. 68 below (S. W. 1,5:547). Perhaps one would expect Schleiermacher to be at least as deferential to the initiator of the Swiss Reformation. In the opening sentence of his Reformation address, delivered at the University of Berlin in 1817, he does appear to align himself with Ulrich Zwingli: he expresses the hope that no one will be surprised to hear him, of all people, speak on that occasion, "qui Zuinglii magis quam Lutheri . . . doctrinae sim addictus." *Oratio in sollemnibus ecclesiae per Lutherum emendatae saecularibus tertiis in universitate litterarum Berolinensi d. iii. Novembr. A. MDCCCXVII. habita*, S. W. 1,5:311. I doubt if the remark is to be taken too seriously. In his writing against Ammon Schleiermacher did counter a Luther quotation with a quotation from Zwingli (S. W. 1,5:346). But it is clear that he had little sympathy for Zwingli's sacramental theology, which he describes as "rather meagre and dry" (ibid., p. 381); and this may have led him to his tendency to downplay the eucharistic differences between the Lutherans and the Reformed as, in the final analysis, merely a disagreement over *how* the believer partakes of the body and blood of the Lord. Hence he asks: "Do you believe that any devout Christian could be disturbed in the midst of this sacred action by the belief that, whereas he himself is

persuaded he partakes of the body and blood of Christ with the bread and wine, his neighbor believes he comes to share in that partaking only through the heavenly elevation of his soul?" (ibid., p. 386). Plainly, this is Calvin's viewpoint, not Zwingli's. In the addition subsequently made to the pamphlet against Ammon, Schleiermacher bluntly asserts: "Zwingli is not the Reformed church" (ibid., p. 413). But, of course, Schleiermacher's point is exactly that this does not warrant any excommunication of the Zwinglians: Ammon, he admits, may be right in arguing that Calvin was more Lutheran than Zwinglian up to the time of the Zurich Consensus (1549), but, he adds, this never led Calvin to break communion with the disciples of Zwingli (ibid., pp. 369-70; cf. pp. 381-82). In sum, it appears that Schleiermacher was not in fact *Zuinglii doctrinae addictus;* and he was further restrained from undue adulation of Zwingli by the recognition that the Swiss Reformation was a collective accomplishment. See *Geschichte der christlichen Kirche,* S. W. 1,11:577-78.

66. The Reformed, too, Schleiermacher remarks to Ammon, acknowledge Luther as a singular and chosen instrument of God, and they do not hesitate to join in glorifying his memory, not even at the price of leaving their Zwingli and Calvin more in the shade than they deserve. Hence, when the distinguishing names "Reformed" and "Lutheran" disappear in the united evangelical church, it will no longer seem as though the Reformed are any less respectful of the great man after whom the Lutherans formerly called themselves, while the Lutherans will no longer seem any less concerned than the Reformed not to glorify any man too much (S. W. 1,5:396-97).

67. A brief sketch of the liturgical dispute will be found in Martin Redeker, *Schleiermacher: Life and Thought,* trans. John Wallhausser (Philadelphia: Fortress Press, 1973), pp. 193-99.

68. *Gespräch* (see n. 40 above), S. W. 1,5:542-43, 545, 547-48.

69. Ibid., p. 552; cf. pp. 560, 570, 595.

70. Ibid., p. 625.

71. *Christliche Sitte,* S. W. 1,12:72-73; quotation on p. 72. Here Schleiermacher is thinking of development in the sphere of Christian *action* (cf. ibid., p. 69). In the development of *doctrine* he elsewhere discovers two processes at work: an inward reflection on the Christian self-consciousness and an outward adjustment to the prevailing state of knowledge. Similarly life, the second function of the Christian principle, is partially determined from the outside by the prevailing social and political conditions. See *Kurze Darstellung,* secs. 166-67, 177-83. Since great numbers of converts were made at the time of the apostolic church, the Christian principle had to struggle with error from the very first (ibid., sec. 103; cf. *Geschichte der christlichen Kirche,* S. W. 1,11:19-20). But adjustment to science contains further grounds for the possibility of error (*Kurze Darstellung,* sec. 167). Schleiermacher tries to refine his notion of the development of the Christian principle by distinguishing further between two "directions," intensive and extensive, and two "members," progress and regress (*Geschichte der christlichen Kirche,* S. W. 1,11:17). But it seems that overall he envisioned a steady progress, even if he allowed for temporary setbacks. See, for instance, the remarks on the Kingdom of God in *Das Leben Jesu,* S. W. 1,6:10.

In the church history he speaks in almost Hegelian terms of "the universal law of development through oscillation and relative antitheses" (S. W. 1,11:39).

72. I am here echoing, of course, the title of Brunner's well-known attack on Schleiermacher: Emil Brunner, *Die Mystik und das Wort: Der Gegensatz zwischen moderner Religionsauffassung und christlichem Glauben dargestellt an der Theologie Schleiermachers* (Tübingen: J. C. B. Mohr [Paul Siebeck], 1924).

73. Karl Barth's celebrated christological approach has been so imposed on the secondary literature that the distinctiveness of Schleiermacher's standpoint is readily lost. Schleiermacher found two elements *inseparably* present together in Christian experience, a general consciousness of God and a specific relation to Christ; hence his theology was not in the strict sense "christocentric," nor yet did it undertake an independent natural theology—if that means attempting to "ground" Christian dogmatics in a knowledge of God apart from Christ. He sought, rather, to describe the Christian consciousness in its twosidedness (see Gl. 62.3 [p. 261]; cf. proposition 39 in the first edition: Redeker, 2:510). But we find Brunner (see the preceding note) offering a Kierkegaardian critique of Schleiermacher that loses his concern for the particular, while Paul Seifert offers a Barthian defense of him that loses his concern for the universal. See Paul Seifert, "Schleiermacher und Luther," *Luther: Zeitschrift der Luther-Gesellschaft* 40 (1969):51–68; esp. pp. 58–59. A more satisfactory interpretation will be found in Richard R. Niebuhr, *Schleiermacher on Christ and Religion: A New Introduction* (New York: Charles Scribner's Sons, 1964), pp. 161–62, 211–12.

74. Georg Wobbermin, "Gibt es eine Linie Luther-Schleiermacher?" *Zeitschrift für Theologie und Kirche* 39 [n.s., 12] (1931):250–60, esp. p. 251.

75. Emanuel Hirsch, *Fichtes, Schleiermachers und Hegels Verhältnis zur Reformation* (1930), reprinted in Hirsch, *Lutherstudien*, vol. 2 (Gütersloh: C. Bertelsmann, 1954), pp. 121–68, esp. p. 140. In the passage referred to (S. W. 1,2:402 n.) Schleiermacher quotes Luther's affirmation concerning the one article that rules in his heart, *fides Christi:* Luther, *In epistolam S. Pauli ad Galatas commentarius* (1535), W. A. 40^1.33.7; L. W. 27:145.

76. Karl Friedrich Nösgen, "Calvins Lehre von Gott und ihr Verhältnis zur Gotteslehre anderer Reformatoren," *Neue kirchliche Zeitschrift* 23 (1912): 690–747; quotation on p. 747.

77. Hirsch's essay (see n. 75 above) has some discerning remarks on this rejection and its implications. See also Redeker, *Schleiermacher*, pp. 130 and 145.

78. Hints at such a line of continuity are present in some of Wobbermin's writings, of which I only became aware, however, after my own thoughts on the subject had already taken shape. In addition to the essay cited in n. 74 above, see Wobbermin, "Luther, Kant, Schleiermacher und die Aufgabe der heutigen Theologie," *Zeitschrift für Theologie und Kirche*, 2d series, 5 (1924):104–20; "Schleiermacher, Friedrich Ernst Daniel," in *Die Religion in Geschichte und Gegenwart: Handwörterbuch für Theologie und Religionswissenschaft*, 2d ed., ed. Hermann Gunkel and Leopold Zscharnack, vol. 5 (Tübingen: J. C. B. Mohr [Paul Siebeck], 1931), pp. 170–79; "Methodenfragen der heutigen Schleiermacherforschung," *Nachrichten von der Gesellschaft der Wissenschaften zu*

Göttingen aus dem Jahre 1933, philologisch-historische Klasse (Berlin: Weid-mannsche Buchhandlung, 1933), pp. 30-52.

79. I return to the historicizing of the theological task by Schleiermacher and Troeltsch in chapter 13. See also chapter 14, n. 63.

80. *An Ammon,* S. W. 1,5:400.

Chapter Twelve

1. Ford Lewis Battles, trans. and ed., *The Piety of John Calvin: An Anthology Illustrative of the Spirituality of the Reformer,* with music edited by Stanley Tagg (Grand Rapids: Baker Book House, 1978).

2. See the long title of the 1536 edition, O. S. 1:19. Battles has translated the 1536 *Institutes* into English as *John Calvin: Institution of the Christian Religion* (Atlanta: John Knox Press, 1975).

3. On Calvin's stylistic ideals, see the editorial comments in the McNeill-Battles translation of the 1559 *Institutes: Inst.,* 1:lxviii-lxxi.

4. "John Calvin to the Reader," ibid., 1:3.

5. Schleiermacher, Gl. 28.2 (p. 120).

6. *An Herrn Oberhofprediger Dr. Ammon über seine Prüfung der Harmisischen Säze* (1818), S. W. 1,5:345. Schleiermacher comments on the *Institutes* also in his *Geschichte der christlichen Kirche.* He ranks the work very highly for keenness of method, systematic range, and its *strenge Verbindung des wissenschaftlich kritischen und eigentlich religiösen*—as well as for its aggreeable Latin style (S. W. 1,11:602). And yet he points out that even in the *Institutes* the systematic impulse was attenuated by polemical interests (ibid., p. 616). In Schleiermacher's view, a purely systematic work could arise only out of evangelical principles, whereas a polemical interest leads to the scholastic method of questions, theses, and antitheses (ibid.).

7. Schleiermacher, "Ueber die Lehre von der Erwählung, besonders in Beziehung auf Herrn Dr. Bretschneiders Aphorismen" (1819), S. W. 1,2:393-484.

8. The difficulty with supposing a conscious dependence on Calvin's dogmatic *order* is that Schleiermacher apparently wished to claim originality for little else except his arrangement of the material. In the preface to the second edition of his *Glaubenslehre (The Christian Faith)* he writes: "I have invented nothing, so far as I remember, except my order of topics and here or there a descriptive phrase" (Eng. trans., p. viii). Less problematic than it might at first appear to be is his admission in one place that his knowledge of Calvin was only "slight" (*Zugabe zu meinem Schreiben an Herrn Ammon,* S. W. 1, 5:410). His words must be understood in context. The admission was addressed to an ecclesiastical opponent, C. F. von Ammon, who had attributed to Calvin a statement Schleiermacher found dubious, and it must be balanced against the confident denial that Calvin could possibly have made the statement at all. There is more than a little irony in Schleiermacher's disclaimer of being a Calvin scholar. He had expected, as he says, that Ammon's proof would come from "who knows

what seldom read commentary of Calvin's." But the troublesome statement turned out to be a misquotation of a passage on election in the *Institutes,* and Schleiermacher tartly informs von Ammon he is perfectly familiar with it. Particularly in his various discussions of the points at issue between Lutherans and Reformed—that is, election and the Lord's Supper—Schleiermacher displays a knowledge of the *Institutes* that is anything but slight, and in *The Christian Faith* he makes allusions to all four books of Calvin's work.

9. Schleiermacher, Gl. 31.2 (p. 128).

10. The logical relationship between the two parts seems, in addition, to be similarly understood, since Schleiermacher insists that Christians bear their entire consciousness of God as something brought about in them by Christ: *Schleiermachers Sendschreiben über seine Glaubenslehre an Lücke* (1829), ed. Hermann Mulert, Studien zur Geschichte des neueren Protestantismus, Quellenheft 2 (Giessen: Alfred Töpelmann [J. Ricker], 1908), p. 31. The doctrines of creation and preservation do not rest on an autonomous natural theology (cf. *Christian Faith,* Gl. 29.2 [p. 124]), although they do presuppose the "original revelation" of God set out in the introduction to *The Christian Faith* (Gl. 4.4 [pp. 17–18]). Schleiermacher's explanation that Part 1 considers the feeling of absolute dependence abstractly in itself, apart from the antithesis of sin and grace (Gl. 50.4 [p. 200], 64.2 [pp. 266–68]), corresponds with Calvin's announced intention to ask hypothetically about the primal knowledge of God to which nature would have led *si integer stetisset Adam (Inst.,* 1.2.1 [1:40]).

11. Gerhard Ebeling, "Schleiermacher's Doctrine of the Divine Attributes," *Schleiermacher as Contemporary,* ed. Robert W. Funk, *Journal for Theology and the Church,* vol. 7 (New York: Herder and Herder, 1970), pp. 125–62; esp. p. 149; cf. p. 152.

12. Ibid., p. 149.

13. J[ulius] Köstlin, "Calvin's *Institutio* nach Form und Inhalt, in ihrer geschichtlichen Entwicklung," *Theologische Studien und Kritiken* 41 (1868): 7–62, 410–86; see pp. 57–58.

14. Edward A. Dowey, Jr., *The Knowledge of God in Calvin's Theology* (New York: Columbia University Press, 1952), p. 41. The pagination of the second printing (New York: Columbia University Press, 1965) remained the same, except in the new preface and the supplementary bibliography.

15. T. H. L. Parker, *Calvin's Doctrine of the Knowledge of God,* 2d ed. (Edinburgh: Oliver and Boyd, 1969), pp. 5–11. Parker's book first appeared in the same year as Dowey's and was titled *The Doctrine of the Knowledge of God: A Study in the Theology of Calvin* (Edinburgh: Oliver and Boyd, 1952). The American printing, *Calvin's Doctrine of the Knowledge of God* (Grand Rapids, Mich.: William B. Eerdmans, 1959), though identified as "revised edition," was unchanged except for the insertion of an appendix on Dowey's book (pp. 117–25). Parker's criticisms of Dowey were carried over into the second edition, to which my references are made. By then, Dowey had responded in the preface to his own second edition.

16. Parker, *Knowledge of God,* 2d ed., p. 5.

17. Dowey, *Knowledge of God*, 1st ed., p. vii. Dowey intended his book to be "a critical exposition of Calvin's theological epistemology" (p. viii).

18. *Inst.*, 2.6.1 (1:341).

19. Even if it were possible, it would be tedious to attempt a catalogue of pertinent secondary literature. True, major studies of Calvin's doctrine of God are not so plentiful as one might expect. But hardly a book or an article has been written about Calvin and his work that does not touch on his notion of God, even if only indirectly or implicitly. Readers familiar with the secondary literature will recognize a dominant line of interpretation that runs somewhat as follows. I shall offer only a few among the many possible references. (1) The supposed heart of Calvin's conception of God is discovered in the chapters on providence in the final edition of the *Institutes* (Book 1, chaps. 16-18). Wendel, indeed, speaks of the doctrine of providence expressly as "completing" Calvin's doctrine of God. François Wendel, *Calvin: The Origins and Development of His Religious Thought*, trans. Philip Mairet (London: Collins, 1963), p. 268. (2) The three chapters from Book 1 are supplemented by reference to the chapters on predestination in Book 3 (chaps. 21-23). Sometimes, as justification for joining together what Calvin put asunder, it is claimed that the separation of providence and predestination, which had been combined in the 1539 edition of the *Institutes,* concealed his real manner of thinking. Otto Ritschl, *Dogmengeschichte des Protestantismus*, vol. 3: *Die reformierte Theologie des 16. und 17. Jahrhunderts in ihrer Entstehung und Entwicklung* (Göttingen: Vandenhoeck und Ruprecht, 1926), p. 163. (3) The dominant motif in Calvin's notion of God is then readily identified as the idea of omnipotent will, formed in part under Scotist influence and representing a metaphysical or speculative strand in his theology. So, for instance, the first edition of Reinhold Seeberg's *Dogmengeschichte*, which could well be taken as a handy compendium of all three items of interpretation listed so far; one notices in particular that his discussion on Calvin's doctrine of God seldom moves outside Book 1, except to give cross-references to the chapters on predestination in Book 3. In the "English edition," *Text-Book of the History of Doctrines*, trans. Charles E. Hay, reprinted as 2 vols. in one (Grand Rapids, Mich.: Baker Book House, 1954), see 2:396-98; cf. 2:405-8. A similar emphasis will be found in the French study by Maurice Neeser, *Le Dieu de Calvin d'après "l'Institution de la religion chrétienne,"* Memoires de l'Université de Neuchâtel, vol. 24 (Neuchâtel: Secrétariat de l'Université, 1956); see esp. pp. 10-12, 75-76. Because he finds both parts of the twofold knowledge of God to be dominated by the notion of absolute omnipotence or absolute sovereignty, Neeser thinks that Calvin obscured the distinction between nature and grace. (4) Even where the pertinence of Books 2-4 (or of faith, or of redemption) is more fully acknowledged, this is not permitted to change the priorities: Calvin, it is said, did not assign to God's love the preeminence it had in the theology of Luther. See Otto Ritschl, *Dogmengeschichte des Protestantismus*, 3:162-63, 174; Köstlin, "Calvin's *Institutio*," pp. 426, 475; Seeberg, *History of Doctrines*, pp. 397, 398 n., 407, 416-17. The later German editions of Seeberg, never translated into English, are richer and more

nuanced in their treatment of Calvin; but Seeberg continued to hold that the specifically Christian view of God was incorporated by the Reformers into a general, metaphysical notion, which in Calvin was filled out from the Old Testament. The fundamental elements of Calvin's doctrine of God are still said to be the divine omnipotence *(Allwirksamkeit)* and a consistent determinism, even though the specifically Christian knowledge of God ought rather to be sought in redemption and grace. Seeberg, *Lehrbuch der Dogmengeschichte*, vol. 4, pt. 2: *Die Fortbildung der reformatorischen Lehre und die gegenreformatorische Lehre*, rev. ed. (1920; reprint ed., Darmstadt: Wissenschaftliche Buchgesellschaft, 1975), pp. 570-81, esp. p. 578.

20. *Inst.*, 1.6.1 (1:70). Calvin does make a modest attempt to answer the question of Part 1 in the form of a cluster of divine attributes: see *Inst.*, 1.10.2 (1:97-98). The first edition of the *Institutes* virtually opened with a list of God's attributes: O. S. 1:37; *Institution*, p. 20.

21. For this reason, I am not persuaded when Niesel claims that no concluding summary is required of him once he has shown Calvin's pervasive concern with "the God revealed in flesh." Wilhelm Niesel, *The Theology of Calvin*, trans. Harold Knight (Philadelphia: Westminster Press, 1956), p. 246.

22. This point, already made by Köstlin ("Calvins *Institutio*," pp. 61-62, 423), was emphasized also by Muller. P. J. Muller, *De godsleer van Calvijn uit religieus oogpunt beschouwd en gewaardeerd* (Groningen: J. B. Wolters, 1881), pp. 10-11, 26, 38, 46.

23. Benjamin B. Warfield, "Calvin's Doctrine of God," *Princeton Theological Review* 7 (1909):381-436; quotation on p. 391. Against Muller, Warfield argues that the omission of a systematic doctrine of God in Calvin is not to be attributed to his a posteriori theological method, but to the practical religious purpose or literary form of the *Institutes* (ibid., pp. 382-83, 390, 412-13, 421-22). In other words, it is precisely Calvin's concern for piety that excludes a formal doctrine of God. Warfield's essay, together with its two companion pieces on the knowledge of God and the Trinity, was reprinted in the posthumous *Calvin and Calvinism* (New York: Oxford University Press, 1931) and *Calvin and Augustine* (Philadelphia: Presbyterian and Reformed Publishing Company, 1956). My references are to the original publication in the *Princeton Theological Review*.

24. Schleiermacher, Gl. 16, postscript (p. 82).

25. Ibid., 167.1 (p. 730); my emphasis.

26. Ibid., 16, postscript (pp. 82-83).

27. Ibid., 28.3 (p. 122).

28. I have in mind, of course, the introductory segment of the *Institutes* (Book 1, chaps. 1-2), from which my initial epigraph was taken (*Inst.*, 1.2.1 [1:39]).

29. Schleiermacher, Gl. 16, postscript (p. 83). Cf. the more specific definition of Christian doctrines in Proposition 15: "Christian doctrines are accounts of the Christian religious affections set forth in speech" (p. 76). It is this methodological principle that led Schleiermacher to prefer the term *Glaubenslehre* ("doctrine of faith") to *Dogmatik:* his aim was to unfold the contents of Christian faith. Interestingly, the German translation of Calvin's *summa pietatis* (the

first edition of the *Institutes)* titled it *Christliche Glaubenslehre* (see *Institution,* p. i).

30. See Gl. 4.4 (p. 17), 16, postscript (p. 81), 28.2-3 (pp. 121-22), 33.3 and postscript (pp. 136-37). A more complete presentation would need to examine Schleiermacher's distinctions (1) between empirical and speculative knowing and (2) between the subjective and the objective consciousness. But the essential point is clear enough without any further attempt to look into the epistemological and psychological principles that underlie it.

31. Quoted from his wife's reminiscences in *The Life of Schleiermacher as Unfolded in His Autobiography and Letters,* trans. Frederica Rowan, 2 vols. (London: Smith, Elder, 1860), 2:337. Admittedly, he was under the sedative effects of opium when he said it, but the sentiment was not out of keeping with the principles and practice of his life.

32. Gl. 19, postscript (pp. 92-93), 27.1-4 (pp. 112-17).

33. *Inst.,* 1.14.1 (1:160). Calvin's demand that theology should be immediately conducive to piety, and not just about piety, is reflected in his description of speculation as "frigid" (see, e.g., *Inst.,* 1.2.2 [1:41], where the English translation has "idle" for *frigidis*).

34. Ibid., 1.14.4 (1:164). It will be noted that the rule is implicitly twofold: it both excludes some things and regulates the approach to what is included. *Pietas* is both a limit and a hermeneutic principle. Karl Friedrich Nösgen held that this principle of interpretation betrayed Calvin into reading the Bible according to his own subjective religiousness; and this, Nösgen held, was one respect in which Calvin was the precursor of Schleiermacher. See chapter 11, p. 194, above.

35. Schleiermacher not only points dogmatics toward practical theology as its goal, most explicitly in his *Kurze Darstellung des theologischen Studiums* (see p. 212 below), but also, in his own way, means to say that the philosophical route to God cannot "generate piety" (Gl. 33.3 [p. 136]). Calvin, for his part, occasionally echoes Luther's view that philosophy is unobjectionable *in suo loco* (especially in *Inst.,* Book 2, chap. 2); and he even seems to approach Schleiermacher's epistemological-psychological foundations when he locates speculation and piety respectively in the *cerebrum* and the *cor* (ibid., 1.5.9 [1:61-62]). But this is perhaps not much more than a curiosity, since Calvin intends a *knowledge* that takes root in the heart, not Schleiermacher's "subjective consciousness" or "feeling."

36. Calvin, *Inst.,* 1.2.2 (1:41), 1.5.10 (1:63); Schleiermacher, Gl. 169.1 (p. 735), proposition 54 (p. 211), 172.1 (p. 748). Calvin, it should be noted, is mainly interested in the divine attributes as *virtutes Dei,* and Schleiermacher is pointing in much the same direction in his view that "we can exhibit divine attributes only as modes of the divine causality" (Gl. 82, postscript [p. 341]). For both of them the attributes can only be predicated of God in a qualified sense. But Schleiermacher carries even further the principle that God "speaks sparingly of his essence" (*Inst.,* 1.13.1 [1:121]): he holds that the divine immensity and spirituality, which for Calvin were attributes of God in himself, properly refer to the divine causality (Gl. 53, postscript [p. 211], 55.1 [p. 219]).

37. *Inst.*, 1.17.2 (1:214), 3.23.2 (2:950). The Scholastic "absolute will" Calvin finds impious because it separates God's justice from his power.

38. This ought to have been plain enough from what Calvin actually says in the favorite chapters extracted from Books 1 and 3. He takes particular care to confine the doctrine of election within the limits of piety alone. For specific references and a fuller discussion, see chapter 8 above.

39. *An Ammon*, S. W. 1,5:377.

40. Schleiermacher, Gl. 4.4 (pp. 16–18).

41. *Dogmengeschichte*, 4^2:561.

42. *Inst.*, 1.2.1 (1:40–41). Cf. Schleiermacher, Gl. 4.3–4 (pp. 15–18).

43. *Inst.*, 2.6.4 (1:347); cf. 2.6.1 (1:341). These references are to the second part of the *Institutes*, on God the Redeemer; but it should be noted that an association of *pietas* with *paterna cura* appears already in 1.2.1 (1:41). It follows that piety is for Calvin an inward attitude rather than (as our usage sometimes hints) an outward display. Like Luther's Christian *iustitia*, Calvin's *pietas* is something hidden. Ceremonies were appointed to make it manifest, but they are not certain proofs of its existence; and God's injunction is that we make trial of our love for him by love for our brother (Comm. Gal. 5:14, C. O. 50:251). See Lucien Joseph Richard, *The Spirituality of John Calvin* (Atlanta: John Knox Press, 1974), p. 120. Richard points out that in Erasmus the pejorative term, which stands in contrast to inward *pietas*, is *devotio* (ibid., p. 89).

44. Warfield identifies Book 1, chap. 10, as "the opening of [Calvin's] discussion of the doctrine of God" ("Calvin's Doctrine of God," p. 412), and his attempted reconstruction of Calvin's implicit definition of God is documented overwhelmingly from Book 1 (ibid., 416–19).

45. Ibid., p. 425; see also p. 423. In his interpretation of *Inst.*, 1.2.1 (1:43 in Battles's translation) Warfield does not, like Battles, make love for God *loco patris* the reason why the pious mind adores God *loco domini* (Warfield, "Calvin's Doctrine of God," p. 424). But his elevation of the divine fatherhood is emphatic. Just a few years after Warfield's essay first appeared, Nösgen arrived at exactly the opposite conclusions about what is central in Calvin's doctrine of God (not love but omnipotence) and concept of piety (not love but fear). Nösgen, "Calvins Lehre von Gott," esp. pp. 696–97. Nösgen's travesty of the theology of Calvin was already dated at the time of its publication. But perhaps Warfield should not, without qualification, have cited the Lutheran Köstlin in his support, since even Köstlin—rightly, in my opinion—saw the love of God in Calvin's theology as limited by the doctrine of election ("Calvin's *Institutio*," pp. 425–26). Luther no doubt gets himself into difficulties with his assertion that God is pure love *(eitel liebe)*, but Calvin has his own difficulties because the desire for logical consistency holds him back from making the assertion unequivocally at all. See chap. 8, n. 84, above.

46. "Briefly, he alone is truly a believer who, convinced by a firm conviction that God is a kindly and well-disposed Father toward him, promises himself all things on the basis of his generosity; who, relying upon the promises of divine benevolence toward him, lays hold on an undoubted expectation of salvation" (Inst., 3.2.16 [1:562]). Battles points out that in Calvin the classical sense of

pietas as "filial obedience" is carried over (*Piety of John Calvin*, p. 15). It is clear that this filial obedience is a possibility for fallen man only by redemption. But the interesting question remains: In what respect, if at all, does the revelation of God in redemption enlarge the content of "piety" or add to the knowledge of God the Creator, seeing that "paternal care" (n. 43 above) already belongs to the initial definition of "piety"? Picking up Warfield's language, Dowey "precipitates" as the two-in-one attribute that answers to the revelation of God the Redeemer "gratuitous mercy" ("gratuitous favor," "gratuitous goodness"), for which the New Testament's word is *agape (Knowledge of God*, pp. 205–20). Does even this, one may ask, go beyond the actual content of, so to say, prelapsarian Adamic piety? The distinction between the two "knowledges" is more clearly maintained by Schleiermacher than by Calvin, whose image of the Creator already bears proleptically the features of the Redeemer. On Calvin, see Paul Wernle, *Der evangelische Glaube nach den Hauptschriften der Reformatoren*, vol. 3: *Calvin* (Tübingen: J. C. B. Mohr [Paul Siebeck], 1919), pp. 394–96; Otto Ritschl, *Dogmengeschichte des Protestantismus*, 3:162–63.

47. Schleiermacher, *Predigten in Bezug auf die Feier der Uebergabe der Augsburgischen Confession* (1831), K. S. 3:135.

48. Gl. 166.2 (p. 729). By God's "love" Schleiermacher understands the disposition in God that corresponds with the desire of a person for union with an other (ibid., 165.1 [pp. 726–27]).

49. Ibid., 167.2 (p. 732).

50. Faith is inward assurance of Christ's redeeming power. It is brought about by the Word, but the Word viewed less as the declaration of a divine promise than as the portrayal of Christ—and so the instrument of his continuing activity, influence, and presence (Gl. 14.1 [pp. 68–69], 105.1 [p. 467], 108.1 [p. 483], 108.5 [pp. 490–92]). Faith is simply surrender of oneself to Christ's influence, and it could not exist at all unless he called it forth: he offers himself as the bread of life, and to believe is to partake of him, to accept living fellowship with him (*Predigten in Bezug auf die Feier der Uebergabe der Augsburgischen Confession*, K. S. 3:47, 56). That this way, too, of relating Word and faith answers to one side of Calvin's thinking in his chapter on faith, needs no detailed proof. See further chapter 6 above.

51. Schleiermacher, Gl. 170.2 (p. 739).

52. In these two paragraphs I have condensed Schleiermacher's argument in Gl. 170 (pp. 738–42); but I have not, for the present purposes, taken account of the union of human and divine that Schleiermacher postulates in the "common spirit of the church." On the twofold appeal to Scripture and facts of experience, see the postscript (p. 741).

53. Ibid., 172.1 (p. 748).

54. Ibid., 172.3 (pp. 749–50).

55. See Antonio Rotondò, *Calvin and the Italian Anti-Trinitarians*, trans. John and Anne Tedeschi, Reformation Essays and Studies, no. 2 (St. Louis: Foundation for Reformation Research, 1968), pp. 11–12, 17–19. Calvin does sometimes note differences between Servetus and the Antitrinitarians: see, e.g., *Inst.*, 1.13.23 (1:149). But it was the kinship that impressed him.

56. My chief debts on this theme are to Warfield, Koopmans, and Nijenhuis: Benjamin B. Warfield, "Calvin's Doctrine of the Trinity," *Princeton Theological Review* 7 (1909):553-652; Jan Koopmans, *Das altkirchliche Dogma in der Reformation,* trans. from the Dutch (1938) by H. Quistorp, Beiträge zur evangelischen Theologie, vol. 22 (Munich: Chr. Kaiser Verlag, 1955); W. Nijenhuis, "Calvin's Attitude towards the Symbols of the Early Church during the Conflict with Caroli," *Ecclesia Reformata: Studies on the Reformation,* Kerkhistorische Bijdragen, no. 3 (Leiden: E. J. Brill, 1972), pp. 73-96 (first published in Dutch in the *Nederlands Theologisch Tijdschrift* 15 [1960-61]:24-47). On the basis of these three studies, at least four points may be made. (1) At the psychological level, Calvin was wounded in his self-esteem as a teacher and believed his ministry was threatened. (2) He had historical doubts about the creeds: he did not believe that the so-called Nicene Creed could be the formulary promulgated at the Council of Nicaea, and he found no evidence that the Athanasian Creed was ever authorized by a duly constituted church. (3) He was alarmed by a tyranny of words that seemed to attach more virtue to the guarding of old formulas than to agreement on their substance. (4) He had theological reservations about the formula *Deus de Deo,* which seems to jeopardize the aseity of the Son.

57. *Adversus P. Caroli calumnias* (1545), C. O. 7:312-13. Cf. *Inst.,* 1.13.13 (1:138).

58. *Inst.,* 1.13.19 (1:144); 1.13.18 (1:142), 1.15.4 (1:190); 1.13.29 (1:159). Calvin tolerantly permits any reader who has the time and the inclination to read Augustine's *De Trinitate,* Books 10 and 14, and *De civitate Dei,* Book 11 (Comm. Gen. 1:26, C. O. 23:25-26); but it does not seem to have occurred to him that for Augustine these works were exercises of piety, not merely diversions. Schleiermacher shared both Calvin's anxiety that eternal generation may imply subordination and his suspicion that it may not mean anything at all (Gl. 171.2 [p. 743]; cf. 171.5 [p. 747], on the notion of the Father's exclusive *auto-theotes* in Origen).

59. *Inst.,* 1.13.29 (1:159).

60. *Inst.,* 1.13.1 (1:121), 13.20 (1:144), 13.17 (1:141-42).

61. *Catechismus* (1538), C. O. 5:337. Cf. the French *Catechisme* (1537), C. O. 22:52 (O. S. 1:396); translated as *Instruction in Faith* (1537), trans. Paul T. Fuhrmann (Philadelphia: Westminster Press, 1949), p. 46. In the *Institutes* Calvin says that the name "God" is empty unless we grasp the three persons (*Inst.,* 1.13.2 [1:122]).

62. *Ad quaestiones Blandratae responsum* (1557 or 1558), C. O. 9:331, trans. Joseph Tylenda, "The Warning That Went Unheeded: John Calvin on Giorgio Biandrata," *Calvin Theological Journal* 12 (1977):24-62; see p. 61.

63. *Inst.,* 1.13.3-5 (1:123-28). Koopmans rightly speaks of the *prohibitive Funktion* Calvin assigns to the technical trinitarian terms (*Das altkirchliche Dogma,* p. 55). For Schleiermacher's critique of the inherited christological and trinitarian vocabulary, see Gl. 96 (pp. 391-98), 171 (pp. 742-47).

64. *Inst.,* 1.13.21 (1:146); *Ad quaestiones Blandratae responsum,* C. O. 9:331 (Tylenda, p. 61). In substance, Calvin is not far removed from Schleier-

macher's views on the formal use of philosophical concepts (Gl. 16, postscript [pp. 81-83]).

65. Rotondò, *Anti-Trinitarians*, p. 28.

66. Erasmus to Lorenzo Campeggio, 6 December 1520, E. E. 1167.421 (4: 410). This is why the identification of Erasmus as the precursor of an undogmatic Christianity, though constantly reaffirmed, never quite convinces. From the extensive and fascinating literature on Erasmus and dogma one may refer to the well-documented essays by McConica and de Vogel: J. K. McConica, "Erasmus and the Grammar of Consent," in *Scrinium Erasmianum: Mélanges historiques publiés sous le patronage de l'Université de Louvain à l'occasion du cinquième centenaire de la naissance d'Érasme*, ed. J. Coppens, 2 vols. (Leiden: E. J. Brill, 1969), 2:77-99; C. J. de Vogel, "Erasmus and His Attitude towards Church Dogma," ibid., pp. 101-32.

67. Karl Zickendraht, *Der Streit zwischen Erasmus und Luther über die Willensfreiheit* (Leipzig: J. C. Hinrichs, 1909), pp. 63-65.

68. Gl. 96.3 (p. 396), 172.2 (p. 748).

69. See Warfield's remarks on F. C. Baur and I. A. Dorner ("Calvin's Doctrine of the Trinity," pp. 557-59, 583 n. 48). Warfield is critical of Baur's and Dorner's historical claims about the Reformation and dogma; but he himself swings too far in the opposite direction, claiming that in Calvin's insistence on the *autotheotes* of the Son the Nicene *homoousios* at last comes into its own (ibid., p. 652).

70. *Inst.*, 1.13.5 (1:126-27), 13.19 (1:143-44). Cf. *Ad quaestiones Blandratae responsum*, C. O. 9:332 (Tylenda, p. 62).

71. Gl. 172.2 (p. 749).

Chapter Thirteen

1. Marta Troeltsch, in her foreword to Ernst Troeltsch's lectures on dogmatics, posthumously published at the request of "friends and students" (Gl., p. vi). Since chapter 13 is mainly an appraisal of this single work, references to Troeltsch's *Glaubenslehre* are given in the text, as far as possible, by page only. Unfortunately, there is no English translation.

2. See Heinrich Schmid, *The Doctrinal Theology of the Evangelical Lutheran Church*, trans. Charles A. Hay and Henry E. Jacobs, 3d ed. (1899; reprint ed., Minneapolis, Minn.: Augsburg Publishing House [1961]), introduction and part 1, chap. 1, esp. pp. 27-28. Cf. the parallel discussion in Heinrich Heppe, *Reformed Dogmatics Set Out and Illustrated from the Sources*, rev. ed., ed. Ernst Bizer, trans. G. T. Thomson (London: George Allen and Unwin, 1950), chaps. 1-4.

3. *Kurze Darstellung des theologischen Studiums zum Behuf einleitender Vorlesungen*, 3d critical ed., ed. Heinrich Scholz (1910; reprint ed., Darmstadt: Wissenschaftliche Buchgesellschaft [1961]), secs. 26-28 (the concept of "historical theology"; cf. sec. 188), 81-85 (its three divisions), 94-97 and 195 (its two aspects; cf. secs. 90 and 166-67). Section 33 of the first edition (cited by

Scholz in a footnote on p. 11) makes the essential point in these words: "Die christliche Kirche als das zu Regierende ist ein Werdendes, in welchem die jedesmalige Gegenwart begriffen werden muss als Produkt der Vergangenheit und als Keim der Zukunft." The second edition of the *Kurze Darstellung* (1830) has been translated by Terrence N. Tice as *Brief Outline on the Study of Theology* (Richmond, Va.: John Knox Press, 1966).

4. Schleiermacher, Gl. 19 and 27.

5. Ibid., 2.2 (pp. 4–5) and 11.5 (p. 59). Schleiermacher speaks here of "apologetics," which the *Kurze Darstellung* identifies as one "side" of philosophical theology. See *Kurze Darstellung*, secs. 39–40 (the task of philosophical theology; cf. sec. 21), 252–56 (the relation of philosophical and historical theology; cf. secs. 29, 35, 37, and 65).

6. Ferdinand Christian Baur, *Die christliche Gnosis oder die christliche Religions-Philosophie in ihrer geschichtlichen Entwicklung* (Tübingen: C. F. Osiander, 1835), pp. 637–56 (including, in an extended note on pp. 646–52, references to the earlier exchange between Schleiermacher and Baur); David Friedrich Strauss, *Der Christus des Glaubens und der Jesus der Geschichte: Eine Kritik des Schleiermacher'schen Lebens Jesu* (1865; reprint ed., Texte zur Kirchen- und Theologiegeschichte, no. 14, Gütersloh: Gerd Mohn, 1971), which refers also to Strauss's earlier criticisms of Schleiermacher in the popular version of his own life of Jesus (1864); Wilhelm Dilthey, *Leben Schleiermachers,* vol. 1, 2d ed. enlarged, ed. Hermann Mulert, (Berlin: Walter de Gruyter, 1922), pp. 765–98 (on Schleiermacher's *Die Weihnachtsfeier),* vol. 2: *Schleiermachers System als Philosophie und Theologie,* ed. Martin Redeker (2 part-vols., Berlin: Walter de Gruyter [published simultaneously by Vandenhoeck and Ruprecht, Göttingen, as Dilthey's *Gesammelte Schriften,* vol. 14], 1966), pp. 473–507 (on the significance of Christ, esp. in the *Glaubenslehre).*

7. See, e.g., Schleiermacher, Gl. 89, 93, 98; *Kurze Darstellung,* sec. 108.

8. Posthumously edited for Schleiermacher's *Sämmtliche Werke* by K. A. Rütenik: *Das Leben Jesu: Vorlesungen an der Universität zu Berlin im Jahr 1832 gehalten,* S. W. 1, 6 (Berlin: Georg Reimer, 1864). Publication of these lectures was the occasion for Strauss's detailed critique in his *Christus des Glaubens.*

9. See esp. Schleiermacher, Gl. 93.2 (p. 378); cf. 7.3, 8.4, 11.5, 86.1, 89.3.

10. Against what he considered the incurably apologetic motives of theology, he stood for history *nach Möglichkeit ohne Tendenz:* Overbeck, *Über die Christlichkeit unserer heutigen Theologie,* 2d ed. (1903; reprint ed., Darmstadt: Wissenschaftliche Buchgesellschaft, 1963), p. 181; cf. pp. 3–4, where Overbeck acknowledges the influence of F. C. Baur. But he considered it equally an error of "our present-day theology" that by *historical* interpretation it sought access to Christianity as a *religion* (ibid., p. 36).

11. "Rückblick auf ein halbes Jahrhundert der theologischen Wissenschaft" (1908), G. S. 2:226; cf. Troeltsch, Gl. 3 (p. 56). There is now an English translation of "Rückblick" in *Ernst Troeltsch: Writings on Theology and Religion,* trans. Robert Morgan and Michael Pye (Atlanta: John Knox Press, 1977), pp. 53–81.

12. It is, of course, the third objection—that Schleiermacher's Jesus was *kein eigentlich geschichtliches Faktum* (Gl. 6 [p. 86])—which links Troeltsch most closely with the criticisms of Baur, Strauss, and Dilthey. Cf. "Weiterentwickelung der christlichen Religion," R. G. G. 5:1882. We shall find reason to doubt Troeltsch's claim that his own *Glaubenslehre*, by contrast, "will show not the slightest inclination to monism" (Gl. 11 [p. 130]; cf. 4 [pp. 68–69], 5 [p. 77]).

13. "The Dogmatics of the 'Religionsgeschichtliche Schule,' " *American Journal of Theology* 17 (1913): 1–21 (German in G. S. 2:500–524); esp. p. 17, n. 1 (G. S. 2:515, n. 39) and pp. 8–9 (G. S. 2:507–8). The former remark is not quite identical in the German version, which, however, gives a reference (without page number) to a similar statement in "Rückblick." The reference is doubtlessly to G. S. 2:225–26, where Troeltsch adds that of Schleiermacher's actual teachings scarcely one stone is left standing on another. Cf. also Troeltsch's important piece, "Schleiermacher und die Kirche," in *Schleiermacher der Philosoph des Glaubens*, essays by Ernst Troeltsch and others, Moderne Philosophie, no. 6 (Berlin-Schöneberg: Buchverlag der "Hilfe," 1910), p. 34.

14. In a *Bewusstseinstheologie* the divine object may be had only indirectly, through the veil *(Schleier!)* of subjective experience. But this is a real "having" since the subjectivity is thought of as "God-filled" (Gl. 11 [p. 132]). See also Gl. 1 (p. 14: "Wie Schleiermacher, so bauen auch wir auf dem gegenwärtigen Bewusstsein der Gemeinden") and the methodological remarks on the doctrines of God (Gl. 11.2) and redemption (Gl. 28 [p. 356]). A *Bewusstseinstheologie* is distinguished from a *Theologie der Tatsachen*, which supposes it possible to assert objective theological facts (cf. "Heilstatsachen," R. G. G. 2:2066–67), and its method is said to be "historical-psychological" instead of the old "dogmatic" method ("Prinzip, religiöses," R. G. G. 4:1843).

15. "Dogmatics," pp. 6, 15 (G. S. 2:505–6, 514); "Geschichte und Metaphysik," *Zeitschrift für Theologie und Kirche* 8 (1898): 27–29; "Rückblick," pp. 221–26. For the shift from natural theology to history of religions as theology's frame of reference, see also Gl. 1.1, 11.3, 11 (p. 135); "Logos und Mythos in Theologie und Religionsphilosophie" (1913), G. S. 2:805–6.

16. German *prinzipielle Theologie* (Gl. 1.1). Cf. "Dogmatics," p. 5, where the phrase "theology in the distinctive sense of the word" mistranslates *prinzipelltheologische* (G. S. 2:504).

17. "Dogmatics," pp. 6–7, 10–15 (G. S. 2:505–6, 508–14).

18. Ibid., pp. 13–14 (pp. 512–13). Cf. "Prinzip, religiöses," col. 1846; "Über historische und dogmatische Methode in der Theologie" (1898), G. S. 2:729–53. See further n. 67 below.

19. "Schleiermacher und die Kirche," p. 27; "Dogmatics," p. 15 (G. S. 2:514).

20. "Dogmatics," pp. 16–18 (G. S. 2:514–17). Cf. Schleiermacher, *Kurze Darstellung*, sec. 28.

21. The phrase *die Krone des theologischen Studiums* comes from the first edition (see Scholz, p. 10, n. 2). Of great importance for assessing Troeltsch's interpretation at this point are Schleiermacher's balancing of "ecclesial" and

"scientific" interest and his location of historical theology on the scale: see, e.g., Schleiermacher, Gl. 17; *Kurze Darstellung*, secs. 9-13, 66, 193.

22. Scholz, e.g., in his introduction to the *Kurze Darstellung* (p. xxviii).

23. "Dogmatics," p. 18 (G. S. 2:516-17). Cf. "Glaube, IV: Glaube und Geschichte" (R. G. G. 2:1447-1456), where Troeltsch speaks of the "poetic liveliness and freedom without which *Glaubenslehren* are unthinkable" (col. 1456).

24. The exception was Richard Rothe: see Scholz, pp. xxii–xxiii.

25. Troeltsch traces this development in "Rückblick."

26. "Prinzip," col. 1846. The particular *historisch-psychologische Wirklichkeit* intended in this passage is the "essence" or "principle" of Christianity, which only a "deed" can transform into a *geltende Wahrheit*. See further sec. III below.

27. "Dogmatics," p. 14-15 (G. S. 2:513). (Note Troeltsch's cautiousness here in using the term "metaphysical," which belongs more properly to philosophical than to religious discourse.) The historical-religious propositions have a mediating function, and in this sense Troeltsch can call the historical elements in faith "foundations of revelation and knowledge for present faith" ("Glaube und Geschichte," col. 1456).

28. See Troeltsch's remark concerning the *Reden* in "Adolf v. Harnack und Ferd. Christ. v. Baur," *Festgabe von Fachgenossen und Freunden A. von Harnack zum siebzigsten Geburtstag dargebracht* (Tübingen: J. C. B. Mohr [Paul Siebeck], 1921), pp. 284-85. There is a translation in Wilhelm Pauck, *Harnack and Troeltsch: Two Historical Theologians* (New York: Oxford University Press, 1968), pp. 97-115; see p. 102.

29. "Dogmatik," R. G. G. 2:109; cf. "Dogmatics," p. 17 (G. S. 2:516). Although he does not use *historische Theologie* in Schleiermacher's sense, Troeltsch does speak of a *Theologie des Historimus* ("Geschichte und Metaphysik," p. 69; see also "Adolf von Harnack," p. 287) and of a *religionsgeschichtliche Theologie* ("Über historische und dogmatische Methode," p. 738). It should be noted that Troeltsch considers it a "travesty" if some theologians after Schleiermacher turned his mediating theology into a "churchly-biblicistic dogmatics" ("Dogmatics," p. 7 [G. S. 2:506]), even though he himself frequently spoke of the "ecclesiasticizing" *(Verkirchlichung)* that marked the work of the later Schleiermacher (see, e.g., "Rückblick," p. 225, n. 10). "Dogmatics" (in the old sense) exists today, he thinks, only in the narrowest theological circles (*Die Bedeutung der Geschichtlichkeit Jesu für den Glauben* [Tübingen: J. C. B. Mohr (Paul Siebeck), 1911], p. 21), notably in America (Gl. 1 [p. 7]). Perhaps the reason why the old term persists nonetheless is not merely custom but the inflexibility of the new term, which lacks German cognates as well as a convenient English equivalent ("doctrine of faith"?): see "Dogmatics," p. 17 [G. S. 2:516], where the translator may have missed the sense of the German *gewisse sprachliche Vorteile.*

30. Karl Barth, "Evangelical Theology in the Nineteenth Century," *God, Grace and Gospel,* trans. James Strathearn McNab, Scottish Journal of Theology Occasional Papers, no. 8 (Edinburgh and London: Oliver and Boyd, 1959), pp.

57-58; "The Humanity of God," ibid., p. 34. In the *Church Dogmatics,* vol. 4: *The Doctrine of Reconciliation,* pt. 1, trans. G. W. Bromiley (New York: Charles Scribner's Sons, 1956), pp. 386-87, Barth remarks that some of those who left the foundering ship took the route to Catholicism: e.g., Gertrud von le Fort immediately after she had seen Troeltsch's *Glaubenslehre* through the press!

31. Friedrich Gogarten, "Historicism," in *The Beginnings of Dialectic Theology,* vol. 1, trans. Keith R. Crim and Louis de Grazia, ed. James M. Robinson (Richmond, Va.: John Knox Press, 1968), p. 349; Hermann Diem, *Dogmatics,* trans. Harold Knight (Edinburgh and London: Oliver and Boyd, 1959), pp. 4-9; Gotthold Müller, "Die Selbstauflösung der Dogmatik bei Ernst Troeltsch," *Theologische Zeitschrift* 22 (1966): 334-46. Cf. also Thomas W. Ogletree, *Christian Faith and History: A Critical Comparison of Ernst Troeltsch and Karl Barth* (New York and Nashville: Abingdon Press, 1965), p. 60.

32. Walter Bodenstein, *Neige des Historismus: Ernst Troeltschs Entwicklungsgang* (Gütersloh: Gerd Mohn, 1959), p. 17. Cf. p. 207: Troeltsch was a "wrecked theologian."

33. Benjamin A. Reist, *Toward a Theology of Involvement: The Thought of Ernst Troeltsch* (Philadelphia: Westminster Press, 1966), esp. chap. 6.

34. See, e.g., Wilhelm F. Kasch, *Die Sozialphilosophie von Ernst Troeltsch,* Beiträge zur historischen Theologie, no. 34 (Tübingen: J. C. B. Mohr [Paul Siebeck], 1963), esp. chap. 8 and pp. 85, 250. Dyson has similarly called for an approach to Troeltsch suited to a post-neo-orthodox scene, but he has assigned only a very minor place in Troeltsch's career to the dogmatic writings and accordingly did not make use of them in his dissertation. A. O. Dyson, "History in the Philosophy and Theology of Ernst Troeltsch" (diss., University of Oxford, 1968), pp. 7-10, 289-90.

35. Besides the literature already cited, see, on the question of *Tatsachenwahrheiten,* Ignacio Escribano Alberca, *Die Gewinnung theologischer Normen aus der Geschichte der Religion bei Ernst Troeltsch: Eine methodologische Studie,* Münchener Theologische Studien, 2, 21 (Munich: Max Hueber, 1961), pp. 89, 121, 126, 188ff.; esp. p. 190.

36. This is the source to which Bodenstein, in the final analysis, traces the shortcomings of Troeltsch (*Neige des Historismus,* p. 56; cf. pp. 59, 99-100, 133), and he finds that the failure is connected with the deficient religious experience of this "all too modern man" (ibid., p. 135).

37. *Theology of Involvement,* pp. 191-192, 202.

38. *Deutsche Literaturzeitung* 47 [n.s. 3] (1926): 2131, 2133. It must be admitted that Marta Troeltsch's foreword invited precisely such an interpretation of the *Glaubenslehre* as "ein menschliches Dokument, in dem der Schwerpunkt auf dem spontanen und lebendigen Bekenntnis liegt" (Gl., p. v).

39. *Theology of Involvement,* pp. 155-56; cf. p. 251, n. 103.

40. So, for instance, Bodenstein's objections to Troeltsch's conception of God (*Neige des Historismus,* pp. 66-68; cf. pp. 32-33) take no account of the two-sideness of the *Gottesbegriff* presented in Gl. 18 (pp. 266-78). Similarly, the notion of a *Tatsachenwahrheit,* supposedly lacking in Troeltsch's thought, seems to be expressly affirmed in Gl. 6 (p. 93); but Escribano Alberca neglects

both the *Glaubenslehre* and the other most pertinent discussion, *Die Bedeutung der Geschichtlichkeit Jesu.*

41. See the introductory remarks to the *Glaubenslehre* by Marta Troeltsch and Gertrud von le Fort (pp. vi, ix). Even after the point where the pressures of time caused the lectures to be broken off (Gertrud von le Fort indicates that it was in the chapter on the soul, but this seems to be a slip for chap. 4, on redemption), the *Glaubenslehre* is completed by materials from other lectures (chap. 4) or by drafts made earlier for undelivered lectures (chaps. 5 and 6). See pp. ix–x and 351 as well as the chapters concerned. The most thorough investigation of Troeltsch's *Glaubenslehre* known to me is a University of Chicago dissertation, which shows that Gertrud von le Fort was Troeltsch's helper rather than his assistant (in any official sense) and that the lectures on which the published version was based were in fact delivered in 1912–13, not 1911–12. Walter E. Wyman, Jr., "The Concept of *Glaubenslehre*: Ernst Troeltsch and the Theological Heritage of Schleiermacher" (diss., University of Chicago, 1980).

42. E.g., the six objections of the "modern world," listed by Troeltsch himself, against connecting faith and history ("Glaube und Geschichte," cols. 1450–52).

43. See chapter 14 and the Conclusion.

44. *Pace* Dyson, "History in Troeltsch," p. 290.

45. "Dogmatics," pp. 13, 19 (G. S. 2:511, 517–523). Note that the positive advantages of the new theology, which in the German (G. S. 2:519–523) follow the answers to objections, do not appear in the English.

46. Commenting on Schleiermacher's theological method, Troeltsch observes that the treasure of inherited ideas must be saturated with the inner unity of the religious sentiment *(Gesinnung)* which fills the present moment ("Schleiermacher und die Kirche," p. 27). In the *Kurze Darstellung,* Schleiermacher speaks more narrowly of the prevailing *philosophy* as the coefficient (along with the utterances of primitive Christianity) in the articulation of the religious consciousness: see secs. 166–67, 177–82 (with the parallels in the first edition).

47. "Dogmatik," cols. 108–9; note the phrase "substantial [and not merely formal] transformations of the religious and ethical sensibility [*Empfindens*]." In the *Glaubenslehre* Troeltsch distinguishes three (or perhaps four) theological norms: beside Bible and tradition he places "modern life," but all of these are "synthesized" only in personal experience, which is thus the "decisive source and authority" (Gl. 2.5).

48. See, e.g., "Erlösung, II: Dogmatisch," R. G. G. 2:484; "Theodizee, II: Systematisch," R. G. G. 5:1188–89.

49. It also means rethinking the doctrine of God (Gl., pt. 2, chap. 1) and speculating on the probability that the universe must have other goals than the redemption of man (Gl. 12 [pp. 179–80], 17.3).

50. On the contrast between Pauline and Hellenistic ideas of salvation, see Wilhelm Bousset, *Kyrios Christos: Geschichte des Christusglaubens von den Anfängen des Christentums bis Irenaeus,* 3d ed., unaltered reprint of the 2d ed., Forschungen zur Religion und Literatur des alten und neuen Testaments, no. 21 [n.s. no. 4] (Göttingen: Vandenhoeck and Ruprecht, 1926), p. 140.

51. With the discussion of the particularity of divine love in Gl. 14.3 cf. the arts.

on "Theodizee" (R. G. G. 5:1186–92) and "Prädestination, III: Dogmatisch," (R. G. G. 4:1706–12).

52. Besides the relevant passages in the *Glaubenslehre,* see the encyclopaedia article "Eschatologie, IV: Dogmatisch," R. G. G. 2:622–32; cf. "Erlösung," cols. 482–83.

53. "Dogmatics," pp. 6–7 (G. S. 2:505–6).

54. The Buddhist doctrine of reincarnation, though hard to conceive, is found attractive by Troeltsch because, like the Roman Catholic doctrine of purgatory, it holds out the hope of further growth and purification (Gl. 14.3 [a], 14 (p. 231], 35). Occasionally, there are also hints of a qualitative eternity—present in every historical moment, but mythically represented as lying in the future (Gl. 23.3, 23 [p. 325]).

55. "Eschatologie," col. 630.

56. Ibid., cols. 627, 628, 630.

57. Troeltsch makes explicit use of the Neoplatonic theme of emanation and return, though it cannot denote a merely natural process (Gl. 28 [p. 364], 35). But even the surrender of the self, in his eschatology, retains its roots in the personal variety of mysticism: the self does not sink down into a lifeless cosmos, but into God and along with others (Gl. 28 [pp. 362–63]). Although the final moment is inconceivable, high points of religious experience afford a foretaste: "The mysticism of love, which lets the self-will sink into the Universal Will, is the final word" (Gl. 35).

58. *The Sufficiency of Christianity* (London: James Clarke [1923]), p. 228.

59. "Weiterentwickelung," col. 1885.

60. Cf. "Dogmatics," pp. 11–13, 20–21 (G. S. 2:510–12, 518–19).

61. Karl Barth to Eduard Thurneysen, 1 January 1916, in *Antwort: Karl Barth zum siebzigsten Geburtstag* (Zollikon-Zurich: Evangelischer Verlag, 1956), p. 845. He has always conceived of criticism, Barth explains, as a means of liberation from tradition, not as constitutive of a new, liberal tradition (ibid., p. 846).

62. "Glaube und Geschichte," cols. 1452–55.

63. Hence one of the four "needs" for a dogmatics is simply to order and reduce the luxuriant growth of *Glaubensvorstellungen* (Gl. 3.9, 3 [p. 55]). The other needs are for drawing out the logical unity of the religious concepts, establishing their relationship with nonreligious knowledge, and formulating them suitably for practical use.

64. "Prinzip," col. 1844; cf. "Weiterentwickelung," cols. 1881–83.

65. The personality and proclamation of Jesus are the *eigentlich klassische Quelle,* and the Bible has decisive normative rank because it offers the picture of Jesus and the means for understanding it (Gl. 2.2). These affirmations must therefore qualify Troeltsch's repeated claim that the Christian revelation is to be found in "the totality of Christianity's historical manifestation" ("Dogmatik," col. 108; cf. Gl. 3.2–3 and the article "Offenbarung, III: Dogmatisch," R. G. G. 4: 918–22, esp. col. 921.) However, two further points must be noted if the place of Scripture in Troeltsch's *Bewusstseinstheologie* is to be correctly stated. (1) The Bible "receives its due," not directly, as though it were a formal dogmatic norm, but indirectly: because it influences the present-day Christian life

that furnishes the immediate data of dogmatics (Gl. 1.3). (2) The essence or principle of Christianity, derived only in part from the biblical sources, itself serves as the foundation of the third, most proper task of dogmatics; hence it tends, in practice, to occupy the place held in the old dogmatics by scriptural authority. See Gl. 1.2; "Dogmatics," pp. 12, 20, (G. S. 2:511, 519); "Prinzip," col. 1846.

66. Troeltsch adds, though without argument, that "for Schleiermacher, too, *Glaubenslehre* meant a decision."

67. And it contributes materially to the constructive task—*pace* Seeberg, who (in his review, col. 2130) voiced the suspicion that Troeltsch's fondness for historical surveys betrayed a deficiency of systematic talent. The constitutive role of *Dogmengeschichte* in Troeltsch's *Glaubenslehre* makes his dogmatics even more markedly a "historical theology" than Schleiermacher's and brings him somewhat closer to the method of F. C. Baur.

68. "Glaube und Geschichte," col. 1456.

69. "Offenbarung," cols. 921-22. The inescapability of individual decision is reaffirmed with respect to specific dogmatic issues: e.g., the particularity of grace (Gl. 14 [pp. 228, 231]) and the choice of one religion rather than another (Gl. 12 [p. 159]).

70. See further "Prinzip," cols. 1842-44 (where Troeltsch uses the terms "intuition," "divination," "depth and refinement of perception"); "Dogmatics," pp. 17-19 (G. S. 2:516-17); "Logos und Mythos," pp. 820-21. The locus classicus, of course, is the essay, "Was heisst 'Wesen des Christentums'?" (1903 [G. S. 2:386-451]), in which Troeltsch argues that the task of *Wesensbestimmung*, though it rests upon history, must pass beyond the historical task as normally conceived (p. 398). The question is not what the essence *was* (even in the teaching of Jesus), but what it *is* for us (p. 420)—indeed, what it *is to be* (pp. 424, 429).

71. The metaphor is suggested by one of Troeltsch's own phrases ("Was heisst 'Wesen des Christentums'?" p. 433).

72. "Dogmatik," col. 109.

73. "Offenbarung," col. 922. In response to the charge of subjectivism, Troeltsch could, on occasion, provide what the *Glaubenslehre* appears to lack: a strong plea for the dual corporate context of dogmatics in both academy and church. See especially "Was heisst 'Wesen des Christentums'?" pp. 436-39.

74. "Glaube und Geschichte," col. 1452.

75. "Kirche, III: Dogmatisch," R. G. G. 3:1153. But this does not prevent Troeltsch from discarding the term "church" because of its institutional and supernaturalist overtones (ibid., col. 1155).

76. "Offenbarung," cols. 918-19. "Romantic" is a word of many meanings. The limited sense I intend should be clear. The debate over the "new romanticism" of Stefan George and his circle focused on other issues: see, e.g., Friedrich Gogarten, "Against Romantic Theology: A Chapter on Faith," in *The Beginnings of Dialectic Theology*, pp. 317-27.

77. See *Schleiermachers Sendschreiben über seine Glaubenslehre an Lücke*, ed. Hermann Mulert, Studien zur Geschichte des neueren Protestantismus, Quellenheft no. 2 (Giessen: Alfred Töpelmann [J. Ricker], 1908), pp. 47-51.

78. Review of Troeltsch's *Glaubenslehre*, cols. 2130-31; cf. col. 2128.

79. Part I of the *Glaubenslehre* is, accordingly, not historiography, but "religiously interpreted history" (Gl. 5 [pp. 78-79]; cf. Gl. 6.5, 28.3-4).

80. Troeltsch affirms this notion both as a general principle (Gl. 3.7-8, 3 [pp. 52-54]) and with respect to particular Christian symbols, such as creation (Gl. 15 [p. 242]) and the last things (Gl. 13.3 [d], 21 [p. 299]).

81. Schleiermacher's theory of religious language, which Troeltsch characterized as "agnostic," treats the inherited Christian symbols as pictorial and pliable expressions of "incommensurable experience" ("Rückblick," pp. 200-201, 207-8).

82. It is in this passage (Gl. 11 [p. 132]) that Troeltsch speaks of subjective experience as "God-filled" (see n. 14 above).

83. See also "Geschichte und Metaphysik," p. 28; "Glaube, III: Dogmatisch," R. G. G. 2:1441-45.

84. Quoted by Agnes von Zahn-Harnack, *Adolf von Harnack* (Berlin-Tempelhof: Hans Bott, 1936), pp. 39-40.

85. *Kurze Darstellung*, the title to pt. 2.

86. G. S., vol. 3: *Der Historismus und seine Probleme*, Bk. 1: *Das logische Problem der Geschichtsphilosophie* (1922; reprint ed., Aalen: Scientia Verlag, 1961), p. ix.

87. Besides the classic discussion in Troeltsch's *Die Absolutheit des Christentums und die Religionsgeschichte* (Tübingen: J. C. B. Mohr [Paul Siebeck], 1902; 2d ed., 1912), see also, from the Heidelberg period, "Dogmatics," pp. 9-11, 21 (G. S. 2:508-9, 519); "Rückblick," pp. 224-25; *Die Bedeutung der Geschichtlichkeit Jesu*, pp. 47-51. In addition, Troeltsch constantly returns to the problem of absoluteness in the R. G. G. articles: "Kirche," col. 1155; "Offenbarung," cols. 920-21; "Theodizee," col. 1191; "Weiterentwickelung," col. 1885; etc. Although the superiority of Christianity is the express presupposition for Christian theology and for the existence of theological faculties ("Rückblick," p. 225), and although Troeltsch holds on to the notion of Christianity as "high point" and even "point of convergence" of mankind's religions, the "absoluteness" means no more than best *for us* and *for now*. One can see why Barth, already before Troeltsch's last thoughts on the question, could represent him as holding only a "temporary social significance" for the church pending the next ice age ("Unsettled Questions for Theology Today" [1920], *Theology and Church: Shorter Writings 1920-1928*, trans. Louise Pettibone Smith [London: S. C. M. Press, 1962], pp. 60-61). For an English translation of *Die Absolutheit*, 3d ed., see Troeltsch, *The Absoluteness of Christianity*, trans. David Reid (Richmond, Va.: John Knox Press, 1971).

88. "Glaube und Geschichte," cols. 1454-55.

Chapter Fourteen

1. Arthur Drews, *Die Christusmythe* (Jena: E. Diedrichs, 1909). There is an English translation from the 3d German ed. by C. Delisle Burns: *The Christ*

Myth (London: T. Fisher Unwin [1910]), from which all my citations will be taken.

2. *The Christ Myth*, pp. 23, 25.

3. Ibid., p. 19. For another summary of the thesis, see ibid., pp. 285-36.

4. Ibid., p. 293.

5. *Das Leben Jesu, kritisch bearbeitet*, 2 vols. (Tübingen: C. F. Osiander, 1835-36); *Der Christus des Glaubens und der Jesus der Geschichte* (Berlin: F. Duncker, 1865).

6. *Kritik der Evangelien und Geschichte ihres Ursprungs*, 4 vols. (Berlin: Gustav Hempel, 1850-51). Bruno Bauer's theory concerning the real origins of Christianity was developed in *Christus und die Cäsaren: Der Ursprung des Christentums aus dem römischen Griechentum* (Berlin: Eugen Grosser, 1877).

7. Martin Kaehler, *Der sogenannte historische Jesus und der geschichtliche, biblische Christus* (Leipzig: A. Deichert, 1892).

8. Johannes Weiss, *Die Predigt Jesu vom Reiche Gottes* (Göttingen: Vandenhoeck and Ruprecht, 1892). In Troeltsch's opinion, Ritschlianism had been reactionary in its neglect of Strauss, and he understood the rise of the *religionsgeschichtliche Schule* out of Ritschlianism as the exact counterpart to Strauss's polemic against Schleiermacher. See *Die Bedeutung der Geschichtlichkeit Jesu für den Glauben* (Tübingen: J. C. B. Mohr [Paul Siebeck], 1911), p. 20. Troeltsch and Weiss were both associated with the *religionsgeschichtliche Schule*.

9. See Shirley Jackson Case, *The Historicity of Jesus* (Chicago: University of Chicago Press, 1912), pp. 39 (n.2), 54-56.

10. See Benjamin B. Warfield, "Christless Christianity," *Harvard Theological Review* 5 (1912): 425-26.

11. Reference will be made particularly to the following: Wilhelm Bousset, "Die Bedeutung der Person Jesu für den Glauben: Historische und rationale Grundlagen des Glaubens," in *Fünfter Weltkongress für Freies Christentum und Religiösen Fortschritt, Berlin 5. bis 10. August 1910: Protokoll der Verhandlungen*, ed. Max Fischer and Michael Schiele (Berlin-Schöneberg: Protestantischer Schriftenvertrieb G.m.b.H., 1911), pp. 291-305; Wilhelm Herrmann, *Die mit der Theologie verknüpfte Not der evangelischen Kirche und ihre Überwindung*, Religionsgeschichtliche Volksbücher für die deutsche christliche Gegenwart, series 4, vol. 21 (Tübingen: J. C. B. Mohr [Paul Siebeck], 1913); Friedrich Loofs, *What Is the Truth about Jesus Christ? Problems of Christology* (Edinburgh: T. and T. Clark, 1913); Johannes Weiss, *Jesus von Nazareth: Mythus oder Geschichte? Eine Auseinandersetzung mit Kalthoff, Drews, Jensen* (Tübingen: J. C. B. Mohr [Paul Siebeck], 1910); Georg Wobbermin, *Geschichte und Historie in der Religionswissenschaft . . .* , supplement to *Zeitschrift für Theologie und Kirche*, 1911 (Tübingen: J. C. B. Mohr [Paul Siebeck], 1911). For Troeltsch, see n. 8 above.

12. See, e.g., Benjamin W. Bacon's article, "The Mythical Collapse of Historical Christianity," *Hibbert Journal* 9 (1911): 731-53, which was partly a response to earlier articles in the same journal.

13. Shirley Jackson Case offered a review of the debate, "The Historicity of Jesus: An Estimate of the Negative Argument," *American Journal of Theology*

15 (1911): 20–42, which was subsequently incorporated into his book, *The Historicity of Jesus* (see n. 9, above), with very extensive references to the burgeoning literature. Of several other pertinent articles in *The American Journal of Theology*, reference will be made only to the following: Douglas C. Macintosh, "Is Belief in the Historicity of Jesus Indispensable to Christian Faith?" (15 [1911]: 362–72), and William Adams Brown, "The Place of Christ in Modern Theology" (16 [1912]: 31–52).

14. *Jesus von Nazareth*, p. 4.

15. *The Christ Myth*, p. 22.

16. Ibid., p. 13.

17. See, in particular, the concluding section of *The Christ Myth*, pp. 292–300.

18. *The Christ Myth*, p. 12.

19. *Adonis, Attis, Osiris* [*The Golden Bough*, 3d ed., pt. IV], 3d ed., 2 vols. (London: Macmillan, 1922), 1:311, n. 2.

20. *The Christ Myth*, p. 18.

21. "The Place of Christ," p. 32.

22. Bacon, "The Mythical Collapse," pp. 751–52.

23. Bousset, "Die Bedeutung der Person Jesu," pp. 295, 298. Wobbermin (*Geschichte und Historie*, p. 55) regards "one-sided historicism" as a vain effort to avoid metaphysics.

24. Bacon, "The Mythical Collapse," p. 752. Cf. Brown, "The Place of Christ," p. 39, and (for an earlier instance of the same move) Adolf Harnack, *Christianity and History*, Eng. trans. by Thomas Bailey Saunders, 2d ed. (London: Adam and Charles Black, 1900), pp. 52–68.

25. "History may open the door, but it cannot compel us to enter in," as William Adams Brown put it ("The Place of Christ," p. 43).

26. "Die Bedeutung der Person Jesu," p. 295. Bousset also points out that what is essential in the Gospels was itself a question variously answered (ibid., pp. 295–97).

27. *The Christ Myth*, pp. 288, 290–91.

28. Ibid., p. 15.

29. *The Truth about Jesus*, chaps. 3–5, passim. See, e.g., pp. 129, 138, and 218. "Conservative," of course, is a purely relative term. Loofs might fairly be characterized as a "conservative Ritschlian" or "right-wing liberal" (cf. n. 92, below), whereas Warfield was strictly orthodox.

30. "Christless Christianity," p. 424.

31. Ibid., pp. 453, 455.

32. Ibid., pp. 424–25, 436. Naturally, Warfield judged reason a more slender reed on which to rest one's faith than history, since, although Calvin himself located the seat of religion in the aboriginal disposition of man's rational nature, what warrants the assumption that reason impaired by sin is still sufficient? From the fact of sin Warfield then infers the necessity for a historical expiation (ibid., pp. 446–48).

33. Ibid., pp. 441–43.

34. "Belief in the Historicity of Jesus," pp. 366–68, 371–72.

35. *American Journal of Theology* 16 (1912): 108.

36. "Die Bedeutung der Person Jesu," pp. 298–304.

37. Harnack, *Christianity and History*, p. 21. For Harnack himself, it was precisely to history that we "owe what we are" (ibid., p. 24).

38. "Die Bedeutung der Person Jesu," pp. 304–5.

39. For Troeltsch's notion of a historicist theology, see chap. 13 above.

40. The main source for his standpoint on this problem is *Die Bedeutung der Geschichtlichkeit Jesu* (n. 8 above), but parallel discussions occur in other works of the same period in his career, especially in his *Glaubenslehre*, secs. 6, 8, and 28, and in his encyclopedia article "Glaube und Geschichte," R.G.G. 2:1447–56. I have retained my own translations of *Die Bedeutung der Geschichtlichkeit Jesu*, although there is now a complete English version of it in *Ernst Troeltsch: Writings on Theology and Religion*, trans. and ed. Robert Morgan and Michael Pye (Atlanta, Ga.: John Knox Press, 1977), pp. 182–207. The *Glaubenslehre* and the article on faith and history remain untranslated. A useful portrayal of the intellectual setting of Troeltsch's christological ideas will be found in George Rupp, *Culture Protestantism: German Liberal Theology at the Turn of the Twentieth Century*, American Academy of Religion Studies in Religion Series, no. 15 (Missoula, Mont.: Scholars Press, 1977).

41. *Die Bedeutung der Geschichtlichkeit Jesu*, pp. 1–4. Troeltsch does not mention Drews by name in this essay, but he does discuss him elsewhere, most fully in his article "Aus der religiösen Bewegung der Gegenwart" (1910), reprinted in G.S. 2:22–4; see pp. 36–43.

42. *Die Bedeutung der Geschichtlichkeit Jesu*, pp. 5, 17–19. Warfield (see n. 32 above) wrote a very unsympathetic review of this essay by Troeltsch in *Princeton Theological Review* 10 (1912): 647–54.

43. *Die Bedeutung der Geschichtlichkeit Jesu*, pp. 5–10, 18–19. In this "modern" view the connection is "accidental and purely historical-factual," albeit "pedagogical and hard to dispense with as a symbol" (ibid., pp. 18–19, 30).

44. Ibid., pp. 10–13. Cf. p. 19, where the *Mischformen* are grouped together as the *Vermittelungstypus*.

45. Ibid., p. 14. Cf. p. 30.

46. Ibid., pp. 14–16, 21–23. In an interesting response on behalf of the mediating theology, Wilhelm Fresenius insisted that theology simply presents the *Selbstzeugnis* of faith, and this entails no denial that others may find other routes to God: "Die Bedeutung der Geschichtlichkeit Jesu für den Glauben," *Zeitschrift für Theologie und Kirche* 22 (1912): 250. Cf. Brown, "The Place of Christ," p. 37.

47. *Die Bedeutung der Geschichtlichkeit Jesu*, pp. 23–25. The parasitical character of religious individualism is a constant theme in Troeltsch. See further "Glaube und Geschichte," R.G.G. 2:1448; "Kirche," R.G.G. 3: 1153–54.

48. *Die Bedeutung der Geschichtlichkeit Jesu*, p. 24.

49. Ibid., pp. 27–30. Against the Christ-myth theory, Troeltsch thus holds that the *Christuskult* arose from an internal response on the part of Jesus' followers and that the Hellenistic mythology only clothed a historical phenomenon. Cf. Gl. 8.2 and 8 (p. 112).

50. The purpose of *Die Bedeutung der Geschichtlichkeit Jesu* is precisely to bring about a better grasp of the meaning of Jesus' historicity for faith. See esp. p. 47.

51. Ibid., pp. 31, 34, 47, etc.

52. Ibid., pp. 31–33.

53. Troeltsch does not mention Bousset. His example of a "symbolist" is Samuel Lublinski (ibid., p. 31). Such a viewpoint he considers to be essentially that of an outsider (pp. 31–32), in which case it could hardly be distinguished from religious individualism. But Bousset, at least, by no means lacked a sense for religious community, neither did he make the hunger for symbols merely aesthetic. Obviously, there is need for differentiation even within the symbolist-rationalist type, just as there is need for greater care than Troeltsch here displays in the use of the word "mythical."

54. Ibid., p. 33.

55. Ibid., pp. 33–40. The shift from the needs of the individual believer to the needs of the total community is in recognition of the possibility that some individuals can ignore the historical questions, whereas the community as a whole cannot.

56. Ibid., p. 34.

57. Cf. ibid., p. 37.

58. In the *Glaubenslehre* (8.4), Troeltsch adopts the traditional *munus triplex*, though it cannot be denied that the notion of "prophetic personality" remains regulative.

59. Cf. Thomas W. Ogletree, *Christian Faith and History: A Critical Comparison of Ernst Troeltsch and Karl Barth* (Nashville, Tenn.: Abingdon Press, 1965), p. 72.

60. *Die Bedeutung der Geschichtlichkeit Jesu*, pp. 40–42.

61. Ibid., pp. 30, 42.

62. Ibid., pp. 47–51. The absolutist language of Schleiermacher is undeniable, but it is occasionally qualified by just the kind of point that Fresenius (see n. 46 above) urged in defense against Troeltsch. So, for instance, with sec. 93 of Schleiermacher's *Der christliche Glaube* (Gl.) one should compare sec. 11.5.

63. The "historicizing and psychologizing of our entire view of man and his earthly existence" (*Die Bedeutung der Geschichtlichkeit Jesu*, p. 35) is, for Troeltsch, fundamentally the same as the "social-psychological point of view" (ibid., p. 30). Cf. the phrase "historical-psychological" viewpoint, used (e.g.) in Gl. 8.4. Troeltsch held that what Schleiermacher achieved in his own *Glaubenslehre* was a new kind of dogmatics grounded in a "sociology of the religious consciousness": see "Schleiermacher und die Kirche," in *Schleiermacher der Philosoph des Glaubens*, essays by Troeltsch and others, Moderne Philosophie, no. 6 (Berlin–Schöneberg: Buchverlag der "Hilfe," 1910), p. 27.

64. The presupposition and consequence of the *Vermittelungstypus*, according to Troeltsch, were already out of harmony with Schleiermacher's own general view, especially in his ethics—"his greatest and most characteristic intellectual creation" (*Die Bedeutung der Geschichtlichkeit Jesu*, p. 13). Further on, Troeltsch asserts that there is a disharmony between the "Second Adam" motif and Schleiermacher's "otherwise developmental thinking" (ibid., p. 45).

65. At the time of the *Reden*, according to Troeltsch, Schleiermacher's sermons already were stressing the "significance of the historical," and even in the *Reden* themselves, where the historical was generally less evident, the first traces of a sociological interpretation *(Begründung)* are to be found (ibid., pp. 45–46). Troeltsch's language indicates that he has in mind the fourth, not the fifth, address.

66. Ibid., pp. 35–36, 39–40.

67. Ibid., pp. 31–32, 39.

68. "Glaube und Geschichte," R.G.G. 2:1448.

69. Gl. 8.1.

70. Note especially the phrase "die Wurzelung in geschichtlicher Tatsächlichkeit" (*Die Bedeutung der Geschichtlichkeit Jesu*, p. 31).

71. If one were to ask concerning the content, and not only the logical status, of the Christian symbol, it would need to be argued that it is a "historical" symbol also as symbol *of* historicity, in the sense that it is *about* historical existence. It is not a vegetation myth, but a matter of ethical decision.

72. *Die Bedeutung der Geschichtlichkeit Jesu*, p. 7.

73. Ibid., pp. 49–50.

74. Gl. 28.2. Troeltsch goes on to assert that present experience, in turn, is stimulated by the picture of Christ. Cf. also ibid., 24.3. Elsewhere, he affirms the dual character of Christ's person as both "starting point" and "guarantee" of faith: see, e.g., "Glaube und Geschichte," R.G.G. 2:1448–49.

75. Gl. 8 (p. 115). "Es gehört zu ihm auch das, was aus ihm geworden ist, der Geist, der unendlich vieles hervorgebracht hat, was vordem nicht war" (ibid., 1 [pp. 11–12]). Similarly, his words are known only through the "stream of life which springs out of them" (ibid., 6 [p. 86]). Again, faith may "think into" the personality of Jesus the further gains of history, and only that which can be continually transformed anew into the present is properly "historical" ("Glaube und Geschichte," R.G.G. 2:1454).

76. Gl. 28.2–4.

77. Ibid., 2.3; cf. 24.5.

78. In *Die Bedeutung der Geschichtlichkeit Jesu*, too, the personality of Jesus is presented, not as an isolated phenomenon, but as embedded in a larger historical whole (pp. 38–40, 43, 50). Similarly, the faith of the primitive church is said to have freed the "Spirit of Christ" from the "historical manifestation of Christ" and to have viewed it as *ein entwicklungsfähiges Prinzip* (ibid., p. 44).

79. Ibid., p. 40.

80. Ibid., p. 44. Other religious personalities, too, may become symbols of Christian faith, but the "Christian-ness" of the Christian principle will always be guaranteed by reference to the personality of Jesus (ibid., pp. 39–40).

81. Ibid., pp. 42–44.

82. Ibid., p. 39: "... die Ausdeutung des Christusbildes aus der ganzen vorausgehenden und folgenden Geschichte." In a religious tradition are united the strong impression of favored individuals and the accumulated resources of entire generations ("Offenbarung," R.G.G. 4:920–22). In Troeltsch's usage,

"tradition" is "continuing revelation" (see, e.g., Gl. 3.2–3 and chap. 13, sec. III, above).

83. Gl. 6.2, 6.4, 6.5. As so often, however, Troeltsch maintains in this passage that the life of the community is inseparably bound up with the representation of its "historical foundations." Cf. "Glaube und Geschichte," R.G.G. 2:1448, 1456.

84. Gl. 27.1. Cf. Gl. 6 (p. 92), where Troeltsch speaks of the past as present in that it attains historicity in us.

85. "Erlösung," R.G.G. 2:487 (my emphasis). Cf. "Kirche," R.G.G. 3:1153. Rupp is critical of my interpretation of Troeltsch, especially in this third section of my essay (see his *Culture-Protestantism*, pp. 31–32). But since he also expresses agreement with me ("as Gerrish himself observes"), the exact point of the criticism is none too clear. It appears to be about my use of the words "drastic," "decisive," and "correspondence," and I am not inclined to retract them. When Troeltsch asserts that an unfavorable answer to the question of the historicity or even the knowability of Jesus would spell the beginning of the end of the symbol of Christ, I can only judge—without the exaggeration Rupp imputes to me—that his stand in the Christ-myth debate is *drastic*, and that he makes the question of origins *decisive*. In interpreting the question of origins as, for Troeltsch, the question of *correspondence* between the symbol and Jesus as he actually was, I intended no more and no less than is logically entailed by his own adverbial formulation, that "a real man *so* lived, struggled, believed, and overcame" (my emphasis). Rupp's concluding quotation from Troeltsch's "Aus der religiösen Bewegung der Gegenwart" (1910; G.S. 2:40–41) only heightens the difficulties in Troeltsch's position. If it is neither possible nor necessary to separate what Jesus actually was and what the faith of millennia has projected onto him, what does that say about the knowability of Jesus?

86. Cf. Troeltsch's own reference to a *begriffliche Verbindung* in *Die Bedeutung der Geschichtlichkeit Jesu*, p. 30. The connection there, however, is between the Christian idea and the centrality of Christ in cult and doctrine. Troeltsch turns later to the connection of the picture of Christ with the fact of Jesus.

87. *Pace* Hermann Diem, *Dogmatics*, trans. Harold Knight (Edinburgh and London: Oliver and Boyd, 1959), pp. 8–9.

88. In the *Glaubenslehre* (Gl. 6.4), he states expressly what is implicit in *Die Bedeutung der Geschichtlichkeit Jesu:* that the connection of faith and history is *lediglich psychologisch*.

89. *The Christ Myth*, pp. 15, 297.

90. Troeltsch claims that an absolute or inner necessity for the historicity of Jesus exists only for orthodoxy (*Die Bedeutung der Geschichtlichkeit Jesu*, p. 19). He does seem, however, to move beyond a purely psychological need for facts about Jesus when he speaks of faith as interpreting facts which only historiography can establish. This distinction of roles he regards as something entailed by *historische Denkweise* (ibid., p. 33). It is strict historical science that must—and does—provide the nucleus of facts for faith to interpret (ibid., p. 51). But does not this logical distinction between the role of faith and the role of

historical science also imply a logical dependence in that faith propositions cannot occur without historical propositions? In that case, if the facts in question are about the historical Jesus, it is not quite true that, for Troeltsch himself, the connection of faith and the historical Jesus is purely psychological. On the contrary, he moves another step closer to orthodoxy, even though he abides by the principle that the past may not be made into the object of faith (Gl. 6 [p. 92]; cf. 6 [p. 93] and 8 [p. 113]).

91. In Troeltsch's view, orthodoxy in fact risked nothing, for its "facts" were established by authority, not historiography (*Die Bedeutung der Geschichtlichkeit Jesu*, p. 19).

92. Troeltsch included Herrmann among his advocates of the *Vermittelungstypus*. But Herrmann may be said to occupy a position somewhat "on the left" of liberalism in the sense that he was less tied than some to the grounding of theology in historically verifiable features of Jesus' ministry. The same holds for Wobbermin and Fresenius. In the United States, a somewhat similar route was envisaged by William Adams Brown, but only as a kind of last refuge should his preferred, more Troeltschian standpoint have to be surrendered: if confidence in the historicity of Jesus *were* lost, the Gospel picture would nonetheless remain as itself a "fact" and a "symbol"—indeed, as a *sacramental* sign. See "The Place of Christ," pp. 38 (n.6), 40, 44, 49 (n.16).

93. *Die mit der Theologie verknüpfte Not*, p. 26. The doubts of historical science concerning Jesus' historicity could only be a salutary reminder to faith of where it really stands (ibid., pp. 28-31).

94. *Geschichte und Historie*, pp. 74-75. As the title of his essay indicates, Wobbermin's argument turns around the distinction, which he admits to be linguistically arbitrary (pp. 3-4), between *Geschichte* (the actual connection of men as spiritual-moral beings in their development) and *Historie* (the scientific investigation of *Geschichte*). It is interesting that, although he defines his views in relation to those of Kaehler and Herrmann, he makes acknowledgments to Harnack and Kaftan and finds in Ritschl the actual stimulus for the question of Jesus' historicity (pp. 34 [n.2], 47).

95. "Die Bedeutung der Geschichtlichkeit Jesu," p. 258.

96. Ibid., pp. 249-50. Fresenius can as well say that faith establishes the fact (*pace* Troeltsch) as that the fact creates faith (ibid., pp. 261, 263, 265).

97. Besides the .passages already cited from *Die Bedeutung der Geschichtlichkeit Jesu*, see p. 33, where Troeltsch insists that the fundamentals of Jesus' preaching and personality can only be established as *geschichtliche Wirklichkeit* by historical-critical means. Cf. Gl. 8 (pp. 106-7) and "Rückblick auf ein halbes Jahrhundert der theologischen Wissenschaft" (1908), G.S. 2:219ff. "Rückblick" is translated into English in Morgan and Pye, pp. 53-81. In Troeltsch's judgment, Martin Kaehler only drew out the implications of Ritschl's position ("Rückblick," G.S. 2:213; Morgan and Pye, p. 70).

98. Hermann, *Die mit der Theologie verknüpfte Not*, p. 26; Wobbermin, *Geschichte und Historie*, p. 83; Kaehler, *Der sogenannte historische Jesus*, pp. 32, 46. Cf. Herrmann's earlier study, *The Communion of the Christian with God Described on the Basis of Luther's Statements*, Eng. trans. by J. Sandys

Stanton, 2d ed., revised by R. W. Stewart (New York: G. P. Putnam's Sons, 1906), pp. 226–27.

99. *The Leviathan*, ed. Michael Oakeshott (Oxford: Basil Blackwell [1946]), p. 243.

100. *Geschichte und Historie*, pp. 63–71; against Bousset's alternatives of *Beweisen* and *Aufweisen*. Fresenius makes much the same point in opposition to Troeltsch and defines the third option as taking something for valid because *geschichtlich wirksam*: "Die Bedeutung der Geschichtlichkeit Jesu," pp. 257–58. Of course, there is also the orthodox option of resting faith's claims on authority.

101. "Das Historische kann unmöglich als etwas Fundamentales gelten, denn es ist nichts Primäres, sondern etwas durchaus Sekundäres" (*Geschichte und Historie*, p. 51).

102. Ibid., p. 5.

Chapter Fifteen

1. Calvin to John Laski, August 1556, C.O. 16:263 (no. 2520).

2. The expression "the two Reformation churches" shows signs of its Continental origin. Since 1970 the World Alliance of Reformed Churches has included the Congregationalists as well as the Presbyterians and the churches of Continental Reformed origin.

3. Cited by Eberhard Busch, *Karl Barth: His Life from Letters and Autobiographical Texts*, trans. John Bowden (Philadelphia: Fortress Press, 1976), p. 365.

4. Heinrich Meyer, "Das Ergebnis des Abendmahlsgesprächs in der Sicht eines lutherischen Theologen," *Zur Lehre vom heiligen Abendmahl: Bericht über das Abendmahlsgespräch der evangelischen Kirche in Deutschland 1947–1957 und Erläuterungen seines Ergebnisses*, ed. G. Niemeier (Munich: Chr. Kaiser Verlag, 1961), p. 36.

5. Ibid., pp. 5–6.

6. The text of the 1971 draft of the Leuenberg Agreement and the revised text of 1973 will be found in Marc Lienhard, *Lutherisch-reformierte Kirchengemeinschaft heute: Der Leuenberger Konkordienentwurf im Kontext der bisherigen lutherisch-reformierten Dialoge*, Ökumenische Perspecktiven, no. 2, 2d ed. (Frankfurt am Main: Otto Lembeck and Josef Knecht, 1973), pp. 123–32 and supplement (pp. i–x). An English translation of the draft appeared in *Dialog* 11 (1972): 48–52.

7. Paul C. Empie and James I. McCord, eds., *Marburg Revisited: A Reexamination of Lutheran and Reformed Traditions* (Minneapolis, Minn.: Augsburg Publishing House, 1966), preface.

8. Ibid., p. 191.

9. J. S. Whale, *Christian Reunion: Historic Divisions Reconsidered* (London: Lutterworth Press, 1971), p. 75.

10. An American Lutheran, Carl E. Braaten, remarks: "There was always

something anomalous about a church that insisted on a *consensus of doctrine* as a precondition of fellowship, but did nothing to realize it when the consensus arrived." Braaten, "Churches of the Reformation, Unite!" *Dialog* 11 (1972), p. 11; his emphasis.

11. Trans. in *Dialog* 11 (1972), p. 49.

12. Even the question of confessionalism (i.e., of subscription to binding creeds) is a party, rather than a confessional (i.e., denominational), issue, to which I return in sec. III below. There was indeed, at the time of the Reformation, a difference between the Lutherans and the Reformed inasmuch as the Reformed churches produced neither a single preeminent confession (like Augsburg) nor a single collection of authorized creeds (like the *Book of Concord*). There *may* even be tokens of a different confessional spirit in the fact that, while the Augsburg Confession ends with a pledge to satisfy the gainsayer with still more Scripture, the Scots Confession (1560) begins by begging the gainsayer who finds something in the confession contrary to God's Word "that it wald pleis him of his gentilnes, and for Christiane cheriteis saike, to admonische us of the same in wrytt." But the bitter debates over the Westminster Confession (1647) in the Presbyterian churches make it plain that the strictest confessionalism is by no means a uniquely Lutheran phenomenon. And it simply is not true, though one often hears it said, that Reformed willingness to produce new creeds must entail a disowning of the old; witness the fact that the new confession of the United Presbyterian Church in the U.S.A. (1967) did not supersede the earlier Reformed confessions but was added to them, much as the Augsburg Confession was added to the ancient Ecumenical Creeds. I have discussed Reformed confessionalism in a number of other places, most recently (though not most fully) in my *Tradition and the Modern World: Reformed Theology in the Nineteenth Century* (Chicago: The University of Chicago Press, 1978); see esp. pp. 185–86 and the further references on p. 233, n. 14. It seems clear to me that Barth's simple antithesis between Reformed adoption of confessions "for the time being" and Lutheran endorsement of the Augsburg Confession "for all posterity *(ad omnem posteritatem)*" would have to be qualified in the light of Reformed experience in Britain and America. Karl Barth, "The Desirability and Possibility of a Universal Reformed Creed" (1925), *Theology and Church: Shorter Writings 1920-1928*, trans. Louise Pettibone Smith (London: S.C.M. Press, 1962), esp. pp. 114–15.

13. See the remarks in the Leuenberg Agreement about "differences of doctrine which do not cause separation": *Dialog* 11 (1972), p. 52.

14. The main events surrounding the presentation of the Lutheran confession are outlined in Philip Schaff, *Bibliotheca Symbolica Ecclesiae Universalis: The Creeds of Christendom, with a History and Critical Notes*, 3 vols., 6th ed., ed. David S. Schaff (New York and London: Harper and Brothers [1931]), 1:225–30, 366–68 (on Zwingli's confession), and 526–29 (on the Tetrapolitan Confession). Although Philip of Hesse was persuaded to add his signature to the Lutheran confession before its presentation to the emperor, Lutheran policy at Augsburg followed Melanchthon's at Marburg: unity with Rome was presumed to be a higher goal than unity with other evangelicals. Cf. Roland H. Bainton,

Here I Stand: A Life of Martin Luther (Nashville, Tenn.: Abingdon Press, 1950), p. 320. Only when this policy had failed, did the Lutherans turn back to their Marburg partners in debate.

15. See chapter 2, n. 69, above.

16. See W. Nijenhuis, "Calvin and the Augsburg Confession" (1960–61), Eng. trans. in Nijenhuis, *Ecclesia Reformata: Studies on the Reformation*, Kerkhistorische Bijdragen. no. 3 (Leiden: E. J. Brill, 1972), pp. 97–114, esp. pp. 104–5.

17. Ernst Bizer, *Studien zur Geschichte des Abendmahlsstreits im 16. Jahrhundert* (1940; reprint ed., Darmstadt: Wissenschaftliche Buchgesellschaft, 1962), pp. 244–47.

18. Calvin to Andrew Zebedee, 19 May 1539, C.O. 10^2:346 (no. 171).

19. Calvin to William Farel, 26 February 1540, C.O. 11:24. (no. 211).

20. See, for instance, Calvin's *Defensio sanae et orthodoxae doctrinae de sacramentis* (1555), C.O. 9:19. Cf. *Secunda defensio piae et orthodoxae de sacramentis fidei contra Ioachimi Westphali calumnias* (1556), C.O. 9:91.

21. Nijenhuis, "Calvin and the Augsburg Confession," p. 109. Cf. the remarks made by Nijenhuis in another essay in the same volume: "Calvin's Attitude towards the Symbols of the Early Church during the Conflict with Caroli" (1960–61), *Ecclesia Reformata*, pp. 90–91. For the phrase *cui ... subscripsi* in Calvin's letter to Martin Schalling, 25 March 1557, see C.O. 16:430.

22. Nijenhuis writes: "Yet even without accepting this sentence [in the letter to Schalling] as evidence, we may assume that Calvin ... signed this confession on the occasion of the colloquia" ("Calvin and the Augsburg Confession," pp. 109–10).

23. Quoted in Garnier to Heinrich Bullinger, 10 December 1554, C.O. 15:336 (no. 2058).

24. Nijenhuis, "Calvin and the Augsburg Confession," p. 112–13. Hence, even without claiming that Calvin literally signed the Augsburg Confession in its unaltered form, Nijenhuis asserts that "for two important years the Reformer lived and worked as a supporter of the C.A. Invariata and as such he was sent as a delegate to Worms" (ibid., p. 113).

25. Wilhelm H. Neuser, "Calvins Beitrag zu den Religionsgesprächen von Hagenau, Worms und Regensburg (1540–41)," *Studien zur Geschichte und Theologie der Reformation: Festschrift für Ernst Bizer*, ed. Luise Abramoswki and J. F. Gerhard Goeters (Neukirchen-Vluyn: Neukirchener Verlag, 1969), pp. 213–37, esp. pp. 218–19. The Concord states: "Nach dem aber [sie] diese alle bekennen, das sie inn allen Artikeln der Confession und Apologia der Euangelisschen fursten, gemess und gleich halten und leren wollen, wolten wir gern und begeren auffs hochst, das eine Concordia auffgericht wurde." Bizer, *Geschichte des Abendmahlsstreits*, pp. 118–19.

26. The difference between the two versions—at least from Calvin's viewpoint—must not be exaggerated. To begin with, in his usage the verb *exhibere* (used in the Variata) meant not just "to show" but "to proffer" (sc. the body and blood of Christ), as is abundantly clear from the terms he uses as equivalent both in Latin and in French. Secondly, article 10 of the Invariata makes no mention of

the ubiquity of Christ's body or of a *manducatio impiorum*. Calvin believed there were other ways to preserve the legitimate intent of these two Lutheran notions: he held that by the action of the Holy Spirit the body of Christ is given to all the communicants, whether they believe it or not, but is received only by faith. See *Inst.*, 4.17.33 (2:1407); cf. ibid., 3.2.34 (1:582), where an analogous statement is made concerning the Word. The fact is that Calvin could readily have subscribed to article 10 of the Invariata at any stage of his career—even in its German version. More puzzling is his endorsement of the Wittenberg Concord, which does teach a reception of the body by the unworthy (see Bizer, *Geschichte des Abendmahlsstreits*, p. 118; for Calvin's acceptance of the Concord, cf. ibid., pp. 244–46); but it will be remembered that the subtle shift from a *manducatio impiorum* to a *manducatio indignorum* was widely regarded as a deliberate compromise. See further chapter 7 above.

27. *The Book of Concord: The Confessions of the Evangelical Lutheran Church*, ed. Theodore G. Tappert (Philadelphia: Fortress Press, 1959), p. 504. In actual fact, the original manuscripts submitted to the emperor have not survived. It is interesting that "churches reformed according to the Word of God" (ibid., p. 501) here means the Lutherans, not the Reformed.

28. Ibid., p. 463.

29. See, for instance, C.O. 9:70, 9:91, 16:430, 18:130.

30. See further Gerrish, ed., *The Faith of Christendom: A Source Book of Creeds and Confessions* (Cleveland, Ohio: The World Publishing Company, 1963), pp. 34–35.

31. See chapter 2 above, p. 31.

32. Cf. Schaff, *Creeds of Christendom*, pp. 471–73.

33. I owe this information to personal conversations with Weber at Göttingen in 1962.

34. Schaff, *Creeds of Christendom*, pp. 354–55. The Reformed had political motives for professing agreement with the Augsburg Confession, just as the Lutherans had political motives for claiming that the confession itself was in agreement with the Catholic Faith. In each case recognition—or toleration—depended upon it.

35. Calvin to Gaspard de Coligny, 24 September 1561, C.O. 18:733 (no. 3530).

36. Calvin to Theodore Beza, 10 September 1561, C.O. 18:683–84 (no. 3513).

37. Calvin to Eberhard von Erbach, 30 September 1561, C.O. 18:752 (no. 3538).

38. For information on the Augustana tercentennial I have relied mainly on Gustav Adolf Benrath, *Schleiermachers Bekenntnispredigten von 1830, ihrer Entstehung und ihrem Inhalt nach untersucht und dargestellt* (Königsberg i. Pr.: Hartung, 1917).

39. Not everyone would accept this way of putting it. Barth, for instance, disapproved of the "union" because it was *not*, in his opinion, born from a common confession but from a lack of understanding. His remarks were made against the background of the German church conflict of his own day: "Conflict in the Church today," he writes, "is not centred on the Lord's Supper but

on the first commandment and it is on this question that we have to 'confess' today." Barth, *The German Church Conflict*, Eng. trans., Ecumenical Studies in History, no. 1 (Richmond, Va.: John Knox Press, 1965), p. 27.

40. K.S. 3:11-154. Schleiermacher's important foreword to the sermons will be found in K.S. 2:261-78, immediately after his open letter to von Cölln and Schulz (ibid., pp. 225-53). On Schleiermacher's attitude to the Reformation confessions, see further chapter 11 above.

41. Schleiermacher, K.S. 2:229-30.

42. Benrath, *Schleiermachers Bekenntnispredigten*, p. 38.

43. See, e.g., Schleiermacher, K.S. 3:27-29, 108.

44. Ibid., pp. 13-24, esp. p. 20. In a note on the first sermon (ibid., p. 348, n. 1), Hirsch mentions that Schleiermacher's great rival, G. W. F. Hegel, took a similar line in *his* festival address.

45. Ibid., pp. 25-35, esp. pp. 25-26 and p. 33.

46. Ibid., p. 37.

47. Ibid.

48. Ibid., p. 108.

49. See Schleiermacher's foreword to the sermons: K.S. 2:278. Cf. Benrath, *Schleiermachers Bekenntnispredigten*, p. 14.

50. K.S. 3:108-22.

51. Ibid., pp. 123-35, esp. pp. 123 and 127. For a discussion of this sermon, see Hans Walter Schütte, "Die Ausscheidung der Lehre vom Zorn Gottes in der Theologie Schleiermachers und Ritschls," *Neue Zeitschrift für systematische Theologie und Religionsphilosophie* 10 (1968): 387-97.

52. I have noted its occurrence only in the German version of articles 2, 3, and 23.

53. K.S. 3:135; cf. p. 123. Perhaps Schleiermacher singled out this particular theme because it was hinted at in the gospel for the day (Matt. 22:1-14, the Parable of the Marriage Feast) and afforded him the opportunity to protest against a style of preaching that had become fashionable in the pietistic revival.

54. See n. 12 above. The fact that Schleiermacher was publicly identified as Reformed will very likely strike us these days as something quite extraneous to the debate over the Augsburg Confession. In other respects, however, as I have argued elsewhere, his Reformed origins need to be taken more seriously than they have been. Gerrish, *Tradition and the Modern World*, esp. chap. 1 and chap. 4, pp. 112-19.

55. For Protestants, the problem of change (and consequent division) may have been muted by the historical accident that neo-orthodoxy rose to prominence just in the years when the ecumenical movement was being consolidated, so that Protestantism looked more theologically uniform than it appears to be today.

56. K.S. 3:34.

57. Paul Tillich's brilliant depiction of the shifting anxieties of Western man in his *Courage To Be* (London: Nisbet, 1952) is well known. Less familiar are Ernst Troeltsch's profound reflections—much earlier in our century—on the same theme of changing religious sensibility. See Chapter 13 above, pp. 217-19.

58. See, for instance, the discussion in Albrecht Peters, "Rechtfertigung–heute," *Luther: Zeitschrift der Luthergesellschaft* 39 (1968): 49–59.

59. On the use of confessional documents, see the references given in nn. 12 and 30 above. As for the notion of God's "wrath," it has become, like the notion of the *deus absconditus*, one of the classical means of thematizing the negative side of Christian experience, and as such it may be possible to reappropriate it. Schütte, for instance, suggests that "wrath" might be translatable into the language of *Gottesferne* ("Lehre vom Zorn Gottes," p. 397). See also chapter 8 above, pp. 141–49.

60. Martin Luther, *Vorrede auf die Epistel S. Pauli an die Römer*, W.A.D.B. 7.10.9; L.W. 35:370.

61. Albrecht Ritschl, Prolegomena to *The History of Pietism*, trans. Philip Hefner, *Albrecht Ritschl: Three Essays* (Philadelphia: Fortress Press, 1972), p. 117.

62. Luther, *Acht Sermon D.M. Luthers* (1522), W.A. 10^3.18.14–19.3.

63. Calvin, *Discours d'adieu aux ministres*, C.O. 9:891–92.

64. Abraham Kuyper, *Calvinism* (reprint ed., Grand Rapids, Mich.: William B. Eerdmans, 1943). The persistence of this trait throughout the historical metamorphoses of the Reformed tradition is striking; in our own century it has been reaffirmed, for instance, in Karl Barth's talk about the church's responsibility to mold the state into the likeness of the Kingdom of God. Barth, "The Christian Community and the Civil Community," Eng. trans., *Community, State, and Church: Three Essays* (Garden City, New York: Doubleday, 1960), p. 171.

65. It must also be conceded that the contrast has sometimes been drawn, on the Reformed side, in a spirit of rash self-congratulation. That the impact of Calvinism on culture is not necessarily an unambiguous good ought to be plain enough from the history of the Reformed church in South Africa; quietism is not the only rock on which Christian social ethics may be shipwrecked.

66. Studies of the economic and political significance of Calvinism are so numerous that the various rival theses can be lined up in anthologies; see, for example, Robert W. Green, ed., *Protestantism and Capitalism: The Weber Thesis and Its Critics* (Boston: D. C. Heath, 1959), and Robert M. Kingdon and Robert D. Linder, eds., *Calvin and Calvinism: Sources of Democracy?* (Lexington, Mass.: D. C. Heath, 1970). I have referred to the much more limited secondary literature on Calvinism and science in chapter 10 above.

67. Ernst Troeltsch, *The Social Teaching of the Christian Churches*, trans. Olive Wyon, 2 vols. (1931; reprint ed., Chicago: University of Chicago Press, 1981), 2:540; cf. p. 576. Troeltsch, like Ritschl, saw Calvinism as Lutheranism modified by the Anabaptist ideal; see, e.g., ibid., p. 593, where the link between the two is identified as Martin Bucer.

68. Ritschl, *Three Essays*, pp. 109 and 114.

69. William H. Lazareth, "Luther's 'Two Kingdom Ethic' Reconsidered," *Marburg Revisited*, pp. 165–76, esp. p. 176. Paul Althaus, by contrast, interpreted Luther as opposed to any idea of "christianizing" *institutions*, the lordship of Christ being maintained in the world through the activitity of Christian *persons*.

Althaus, "Luthers Lehre von den beiden Reichen im Feuer der Kritik," *Luther-Jahrbuch: Jahrbuch der Luther-Gesellschaft* 24 (1957): 40–68, esp. pp. 47, 50, and 68.

70. Cf. art. 27. The *Apology* on art. 16 expressly mentions the monks: *Book of Concord*, p. 223.

71. Tappert's translation (*Book of Concord*, p. 223), based on the Latin *(non mutare civilem statum)*, has "does not change the civil government." The German version uses the substantive *Weltregiment*. See *Die Bekenntnisschriften der evangelisch-lutherischen Kirche*, 4th ed. (Göttingen: Vandenhoeck and Ruprecht, 1959), p. 309. I have avoided the common English translation of *weltliches Regiment* as "civil government" where that might seem to equate the earthly kingdom with the state (which is more properly the referent of the terms *Polizei* and *Obrigkeit*). As article 16 makes clear, *weltliches Regiment* (the Latin is *De rebus civilibus*) embraces, among other things, business activity and family life as well as "politics." Cf. arts. 23 and 27.

72. *Book of Concord*, p. 222.

73. The Latin here reads *politica administratio* for the German *weltlich Regiment (Bekenntnisschriften*, p. 122).

74. Althaus, *Der Geist der lutherischen Ethik im Augsburgischen Bekenntnis* (Munich: Chr. Kaiser, 1930), pp. 44–45. He recalls this statement in the article already referred to (n. 69 above), where he also cites a similar judgment from Helmut Gollwitzer's *Die christliche Gemeinde in der politischen Welt* (1954). Althaus, "Luthers Lehre von den beiden Reichen," p. 50, n. 28.

75. Althaus, "Luthers Lehre von den beiden Reichen," pp. 67–68. On the misuse of Luther's doctrine, he refers to a similar judgment made by Franz Lau (ibid., p. 61, n. 61). Althaus grants that over the years the Lutheran clergy did in actual fact become unduly submissive civil servants (ibid., p. 62).

76. Barth, "Ein Brief nach Frankreich" [Barth to Pastor Westphal, December 1939], *Eine Schweizer Stimme 1938–1945* (Zollikon-Zurich: Evangelischer Verlag, 1945), pp. 108–17, esp. p. 113, and the related "Brief an Pfarrer Kooyman (Holland)" [28 February 1940], ibid., pp. 118–22, esp. p. 122.

77. "Brief an Pfarrer Kooyman," p. 122.

78. *The German Church Conflict*, p. 75.

79. Busch, *Karl Barth*, p. 311. The four points historically at issue between Lutherans and Reformed were stated in the Saxon Visitation Articles of 1592, published in German the following year as a part of the campaign to stamp out crypto-Calvinism; they concern the Eucharist, the person of Christ, baptism, and predestination (text in Schaff, *Creeds of Christendom*, 1:347–49). Three of the four reappear in the Leuenberg Agreement, which does not speak of baptism as a divisive issue. But the Agreement goes on to mention doctrinal differences that have not historically been taken as grounds for separation; the list includes the themes of law and gospel, church and society, the two kingdoms, and the sovereignty of Christ, all of which, like the old divisive issues, will readily be seen to constitute a distinctive "family" of dogmatic themes. Some of the doctrinal differences have been taken up in discussions since Leuenberg; see esp. Marc Lienhard, ed., *Zeugnis und Dienst reformatorischer Kirchen im Europa der*

Gegenwart: Texte der Konferenz von Sigtuna (10. bis 16. Juni 1976), Ökumenische Perspektiven, no. 8 (Frankfurt am Main: Otto Lembeck and Josef Knecht,
1977).

80. *Von weltlicher Oberkeit, wie weit man ihr Gehorsam schuldig sei* (1523),
W.A. 11.245-81; L.W. 45:75-129. In his dedicatory preface to Duke John the
Steadfast, Luther expressly states his desire to instruct the princes in such wise
that they will remain Christians and *Christ will remain Lord* (W.A. 11.246.6;
L.W. 45:83).

81. It should also be pointed out that Barth did not always follow through
consistently the logic of the "sanctuary" metaphor *(sakraler Raum)*; he admitted
that moral principles he himself derived from the gospel have sometimes been
justified by others on the basis of natural law. Barth, *Community, State, and
Church*, p. 180.

82. I have particularly in mind the notion of sin that runs through Luther's
Römerbriefvorlesung (1515-16), W.A. 56; L.W. 25.

83. Lazareth, "Luther's 'Two Kingdom Ethics'," p. 167.

84. I know of only two substantial essays on the subject: Joachim Rogge,
"Kritik Calvins an Luthers Zwei-Reiche-Lehre?" *Theologie in Geschichte und
Kunst: Walter Elliger zum 65. Geburtstag*, ed. Siegfried Herrmann and Oskar
Söhngen (Witten: Luther-Verlag, 1968), pp. 152-68; and Joachim Staedtke,
"Die Lehre von der Königsherrschaft Christi und den zwei Reichen bei Calvin,"
Kerygma and Dogma 18 (1972): 202-14.

85. In the *Institutes*, the most striking statement of the two kingdoms doctrine
occurs in Calvin's discussion of Christian freedom (book 3, chap. 19). But it
receives two further applications in book 4: in the chapters on the power of the
church (see esp. chaps. 10 and 11) and civil government (chap. 20). And the
regnum Christi has already made its appearance in book 2, chapter 15, where
Calvin presents his influential doctrine of the *munus triplex*. For additional
references, see the subject index in *Calvin: Institutes of the Christian Religion*,
ed. John T. McNeill and trans. Ford Lewis Battles, 2 vols., Library of Christian
Classics, vols. 20-21 (Philadelphia: The Westminster Press, 1960). A close
scholarly analysis of these passages (and of parallel ones in others of Calvin's
writings) is greatly to be desired.

86. *Inst.*, 3.19.15 (1:847), trans. Battles.

87. Not to present Barth's position in a misleading way, it should be added
that he knew Calvin could not go unscathed by criticism of the two kingdoms
doctrine; see, e.g., Barth, *Rechtfertigung und Recht*, Theologische Studien,
no. 1, 2d ed., (Zollikon-Zurich: Evangelischer Verlag, 1944), pp. 4-7. But why,
in that case, speak as though the separation of the kingdoms were a peculiarly
Lutheran problem? On the other side, I do not wish to suggest that talk of different rulers and different laws is peculiarly Calvinist; see, for comparison,
Luther's remarks in *Von weltlicher Oberkeit*, W.A. 11:262.3ff.; L.W. 45:105.

88. *Inst.*, 4.20.2, 3, and 9 (2:1487-88, 1495).

89. The notion that there is a strong christocratic tendency in Reformed
theology is not simply a by-product of "Barthianism"; it is already alluded to
by Troeltsch in his *Social Teaching*, 2:886, n. 327, where he refers to Choisy's
work on the Christian state. But, once again, it is far from clear that we have to

do with a peculiarly "Calvinist" idea (see n. 80 above). Psalm 2 has been the subject of a long tradition of Christian exegesis!

90. Josef Bohatec, *Calvins Lehre von Staat und Kirche mit besonderer Berücksichtigung des Organismusgedankens* (Breslau: M. and H. Marcus, 1937), p. 619. Bohatec's judicious interpretation shows how Calvin viewed church and state as mutually dependent *(aufeinander angewiesen)* in a manner that preserves their natural autonomy *(urtümliche Selbständigkeit)* and excludes alike a Zwinglian state-church and a theocratic (i.e., church-dominated) state (ibid., p. 625; cf. p. 614).

91. *Inst.*, 4.11.3–5 (2:1215–17). (Calvin does not himself use the term "caesaropapism" in this passage.) The duty of the government to maintain pure religion and worship in the state plainly did not, in Calvin's own mind, collapse the distinction between the two "powers." As Bohatec points out, he frowned not only upon the reform of the church in England under Henry VIII (which made the king supreme head of the church), but also upon the interference of some of the German princes in ecclesiastical affairs. Closer to home, in Geneva, it was certainly against Calvin's will, Bohatec asserts, that one of the syndics customarily appeared at the meetings of the consistory bearing his emblem of office. Bohatec, *Calvins Lehre von Staat und Kirche*, pp. 615–18.

92. Staedtke, "Calvins Genf und die Entstehung politischer Freiheit," *Staat und Kirche im Wandel der Jahrhunderte*, ed. Walther Peter Fuchs (Stuttgart: W. Kohlhammer, 1966), p. 104. Rogge, who cites this judgment of Staedtke's, similarly finds in Luther's and Calvin's statements on the two kingdoms only distinctions within a general agreement, not two divergent tendencies ("Kritik Calvins an Luthers Zwei-Reiche-Lehre?" p. 167).

93. "Die Lehre von der Königsherrschaft Christi," p. 213.

Conclusion

1. Ernst Troeltsch, *The Absoluteness of Christianity and the History of Religions,* trans. from the 3d German ed. [1929] by David Reid (Richmond, Va.: John Knox Press, 1971), p. 85.

2. *The Spiritual Exercises of St. Ignatius,* trans. Louis J. Puhl (Westminster, Md.: Newman Press, 1951), pp. 157, 160. On the intention of these rules see Joseph deGuibert, *The Jesuits, Their Spiritual Doctrine and Practice: A Historical Study,* trans. William J. Young and ed. George E. Ganss (Chicago: Institute of Jesuit Sources, 1964), p. 171.

3. See chap. 5, p. 91, above.

4. *Of the Laws of Ecclesiastical Polity,* V, vii, 3; Everyman Library edition (London: J. M. Dent [1907]), 2:29.

5. *Vision and Authority, or the Throne of St. Peter,* 2d ed. (London: Hodder and Stoughton, 1928), p. 90.

6. Karl Mannheim, *Essays on the Sociology of Knowledge,* ed. Paul Kecskemeti (London: Routledge and Kegan Paul, 1952), pp. 102, 105.

7. Warfield, *The Inspiration and Authority of the Bible,* ed. Samuel G. Craig (reprint ed., London: Marshall, Morgan and Scott, 1951), p. 156.

8. At a Reformation convocation at Yale Divinity School (30–31 October 1980), I enlarged on these remarks in a lecture entitled, "Protestantism and Progress: The Chief Article Then and Now." Publication is anticipated in the October 1983 number of *The Journal of Religion*.

9. Pope Paul VI, *On the Holy Eucharist: Mysterium Fidei* (Washington, D.C.: National Catholic Welfare Conference, 1965), p. 6 (=para. 24).

10. I tried to state these reasons in the first chapter of my *Tradition and the Modern World: Reformed Theology in the Nineteenth Century* (Chicago: University of Chicago Press, 1978), where I have also given a fuller discussion of the concept of tradition. It may not be superfluous to add that by a "progressive" interpretation of Protestant thought I mean to allow for change, not for uninterrupted improvement, although I do think that the two major shifts I have referred to were both advances. As I have indicated above (p. 373, n. 71, and p. 222), neither Schleiermacher nor Troeltsch held the naive doctrine of inevitable progress that is commonly attributed to liberal Protestantism.

Bibliographical Postscript

For reasons stated in the preface, no concluding bibliography is given. A comprehensive list of publications—one that would cover the whole range of my topics—would in any case be inordinately long (or inordinately selective); and if divided by subject, it would be very unevenly balanced. But further bibliographical resources are available for each of the four thinkers who have figured most prominently in the preceding chapters, and some of the more useful ones may be mentioned.

Luther research is a well-organized field: literature surveys appear with some regularity, and continuing lists are published annually. Of the surveys two may be mentioned, which between them carry the story back to the end of World War II. In the third number of *Lutheran World* 13 (1966) a team of authors provides surveys of Luther research in several countries since 1945 (pp. 257–316). Jack Bigane and Kenneth Hagen cover the next ten years in their *Annotated Bibliography of Luther Studies, 1967–1976*, Sixteenth Century Bibliography, no. 9 (St. Louis, Mo.: Center for Reformation Research, 1977). A very extensive continuing bibliography appears in the *Lutherjahrbuch: Organ der internationalen Lutherforschung* (published in Göttingen by Vandenhoeck and Ruprecht). It is not unusual for the list to break into four figures—over 1,000 titles in a single year that have something to do with Luther. More selective—but more useful, because annotated—is the annual section on Luther in the team-produced Literature Review of the *Archive for Reformation Research*, published by Gerd Mohn of Gütersloh for the German Verein für Reformationsgeschichte and the American Society for Reformation Research.

The Literature Review in the *Archive* also has an annual section on Calvin. Another, very comprehensive continuing bibliography on Calvin is included in the *Calvin Theological Journal*, published by Calvin Theological Seminary in Grand Rapids, Michigan. A supplement to the old bibliography in the *Corpus Reformatorum* (C. O. 58:513–86) will be found in Wilhelm Niesel, *Calvin-Bibliographie 1901–1959* (Munich: Chr. Kaiser Verlag, 1961), which has in turn been supplemented by D. Kempff, *A Bibliography of Calviniana, 1959–1974*, Studies in Medieval and Reformation Thought, vol. 15 (Leiden: E. J. Brill, 1975).

John T. McNeill's bibliographical essay, "Thirty Years of Calvin Study," *Church History* 17 (1948):207–40, was revised and extended to 1968 (which makes it "Fifty Years of Calvin Study") for inclusion in the reissue of Williston Walker, *John Calvin: The Organiser of Reformed Protestantism* (1906; reprint ed., New York: Schocken Books, 1969).

Bibliographies of post-Reformation figures are not nearly as industriously organized. However, there is one very comprehensive bibliography for Schleiermacher (with 1,928 entries): Terrence N. Tice, *Schleiermacher Bibliography: With Brief Introductions, Annotations, and Index*, Princeton Pamphlets, no. 12 (Princeton, N.J.: Princeton Theological Seminary, 1966). The lack of any supplements is of course a problem, especially since the bicentennial of Schleiermacher's birth in 1968 occasioned a flurry of new writing. Titles appearing in English since Tice are noted in my bibliographical essay in *Religious Thought in the Nineteenth Century*, edited by Ninian Smart (Cambridge: Cambridge University Press, forthcoming).

The literature on Troeltsch is scantier, but a steady interest in him has been maintained since, say, the publication of Bodenstein's work (1959). This can be verified from the most useful Troeltsch bibliography currently available: by Jacob Klapwijk, in *Ernst Troeltsch and the Future of Theology*, edited by John Powell Clayton (Cambridge: Cambridge University Press, 1976). It aims at completeness, except that the first section, "Recent Editions of Troeltsch's Works," is intended only to supplement the chronological list of Troeltsch's works by Hans Baron in G. S. 4.

Index